The Labor
Relations
Process

The Labor Relations Process

William H. Holley, Jr.
Auburn University

Kenneth M. Jennings
University of North Florida

The Dryden Press
Hinsdale, Illinois

Acquisitions Editor: Anita Constant
Developmental Editor: Nedah Abbott
Project Editor: Jane Perkins
Art Director: Stephen Rapley
Production Manager: Peter Coveney

Text and cover design by James Buddenbaum

Copy editing by Flora Foss
Indexing by Sheila Ary
Photo research by Jo-Anne Naples
Permissions by Mili Ve McNiece

Library of Congress Catalog Card Number: 79–51065
ISBN: 0–03–046556–7

Printed in the United States of America
1   144   987654

Cover photos by Owen Franken, Stock, Boston; and by Robert McKendrick.
Photos, page ii: left, reproduced from the collection of the Library of
Congress; right, by Burk Uzzle, Magnum. Photos, page iii: left,
courtesy of Wide World Photos; right, by Bohdan Hrynewych, Stock, Boston.
Part 1 photo, page 3, by Burk Uzzle, Magnum. Part 2 photo, page 167,
from Business Week, by Jeff Bates. Part 3 photo, page 303, by Bohdan
Hrynewych, Stock, Boston. Part 4 photo, page 429, by Paul Fusco,
Magnum. Cases photo, page 567, by Owen Franken, Stock, Boston.

This book is dedicated to Ali and Bret, who kept the pencils sharpened, and to Betty and Jackie, who gave them a reason for moving.

The Dryden Press Management Series

William F. Glueck
Consulting Editor

Altman and Hodgetts
Readings in Organizational Behavior

Bedeian
Organizations: Theory and Analysis

Byars and Rue
Personnel Management:
Concepts and Applications

Duncan
Essentials of Management,
2nd Edition

Gaither
Production and Operations Management:
A Problem-Solving and Decision-Making
Approach

Gatza, Milutinovich and Boseman
Decision Making in Administration: Text,
Critical Incidents and Cases

Gellerman
Management of Human Relations

Gellerman
Management of Human Resources

Gellerman
Managers and Subordinates

Glueck
Management, 2nd Edition

Glueck
Management Essentials

Glueck and Jauch
The Managerial Experience: Cases, Exercises
and Readings, 2nd Edition

Grad, Glans, Holstein, Meyers, Schmidt
Management Systems, 2nd Edition

Greenlaw
Readings to Accompany Modern Personnel
Management

Greenlaw and Biggs
Modern Personnel Management

Hand and Hollingsworth
Practical Readings in Small Business
Management

Harbaugh, Byars, and Rue
Readings and Cases in Personnel Management

Higgins
Organizational Policy and Strategic
Management: Text and Cases

Hodgetts
The Business Enterprise: Social Challenge,
Social Response

Hodgetts
Management: Theory, Process, and Practice,
2nd Edition

Hodgetts
Modern Human Relations

Hodgetts and Altman
Organizational Behavior

Holley and Jennings
The Labor Relations Process

Hollingsworth and Hand
A Guide to Small Business Management: Text
and Cases

Karmel
Point and Counterpoint in Organizational
Behavior

Lindauer
Communicating in Business, 2nd Edition

McFarlan, Nolan, and Norton
Information Systems Administration

Mayerson
Shoptalk: Foundations of Managerial
Communication

Miner
The Challenge of Managing

Miner
Theories in Organizational Behavior

Naumes and Paine
Cases for Organizational Strategy and Policy,
2nd Edition

Paine and Naumes
Organizational Strategy and Policy, 2nd Edition

Paine and Naumes
Organizational Strategy and Policy: Text, Cases,
and Incidents

Robinson
International Business Management, 2nd
Edition

Viola
Organizations in a Changing Society:
Administration and Human Values

Editor's Foreword

Among the new titles in the Management Series, **The Labor Relations Process** is outstanding. I believe that it will quickly become the most widely used text in its field.

A major emphasis of this book is emerging labor-management relationships; in addition, thorough treatment is given to the labor arbitration process and employee discipline. Students and instructors will also find full discussions of current issues such as unions and minorities, union response to quality of work life, and employer efforts to maintain non-union status—to name but a few.

The Labor Relations Process combines a lively and readable style with an innovative treatment of current topics and a research-oriented approach. The result is stimulating and complete coverage of the area of labor-management relationships. This book is clearly a valuable addition to the Dryden Press Management Series. I believe students will enjoy reading the book as much as professors will enjoy teaching from it.

William F. Glueck

Preface

The Labor Relations Process hopes to accomplish at least three objectives. First, it will provide the reader with an understanding and appreciation of the fundamental principles and concepts of labor relations. Some readers will approach this subject with limited related experience, their attitudes toward labor unions and management having been shaped by their families, associates, and sketchy news coverage of labor-management issues. Yet almost every individual who works or will work for a private or public organization will be either directly or indirectly affected by labor-management relationships. For example, individuals in production positions must administer the agreements; those in finance and accounting departments must calculate the cost of the agreements; sales management personnel must anticipate the effect of a strike on product availability and subsequent price change; and nonunion employees must consider how negotiated agreements will affect their wages and fringe benefits. Thus, this book will provide valuable insights into a topic which contributes to the reader's career development regardless of his or her professional field of interest.

A second objective of this book is to create a continuing interest in the subject matter. In colleges and universities, labor relations courses are often taken as electives. It is hoped that the completion of *The Labor Relations Process* will create in students a lasting interest in the subject. For example, we hope that in the future the reader will take special interest in such occurrences as Walter Cronkite's assessment of various labor issues, union leaders' testimony before Congress, answers to correspondents on Meet the Press, and so on.

Finally, this book is intended to encourage the reader to pursue a career in labor relations. As readers progress through its contents, it will become clear to them that participation in union-management relations will demand all of the behavioral science and managerial skills and theories obtained in academic and management development courses. Not only must one know *and be able to interpret accurately legal implications and decisions, but many related issues such as productivity bargaining and unions and minorities have long-term, significant societal implications. Thus, we firmly believe that a career in labor relations is challenging, stimulating, and rewarding, and we hope that **The Labor Relations Process** will influence its readers to share our opinion.*

In approaching its topic, our book combines theoretical and practical insights on the assumption that each is insufficient without the contributions of the other. This combination is in part accomplished through numerous practitioner and academic quotations inserted throughout the book. These quotations have been carefully screened and selected for their general applicability. They are an integral portion of the book, providing the inexperienced reader with representative industrial relations insights and the experienced scholar with a provocative means for comparison. Additionally, each section of the book has been subjected to critical academic and practitioner review. From reviewers' suggestions and comments a more balanced academic-practitioner perspective has been provided. We are grateful for the reviewers' time, insights, and efforts; their names are indicated in our acknowledgments.

This book differs from other labor relations books in several respects. First, its contents relate entirely to the model of the labor relations process which is discussed in Chapter 1. The next twelve chapters explain the various aspects of this process, while the final four chapters enable the reader to apply the labor relations process to different situations, such as those in the public sector, foreign countries, and selected occupations in professional sports, health care, and agriculture.

Second, the book was written with both the beginning student and the professional scholar in mind. For the beginning student, the text has been written in such a way as to explain principles and concepts without confusing them. For the professional scholar, the content is well documented from the best sources that we could find at the time of writing. The rather extensive reference section included at the end of each chapter credits the many contributors for their research in the field of labor relations. More importantly, it is hoped that most readers will regard the references as useful stimuli and starting points for continuing research on the subject.

Finally, this book offers pertinent material which is not found in other books written before 1978, when data on important subjects such as labor law reform issues, President Carter's wage-price guidelines, and the Civil Service Reform Act were not available. We have also included in our book other materials which have inexplicably been omitted in other texts. Rather than devoting a great deal of attention to the history of the labor movement, we decided to discuss historical insights as they apply to our chapter topics—for example, the history of public employee bargaining, arbitration, and so on.

Any errors of omission and commission are the responsibility of the authors. We have attempted to obtain the most appropriate materials that were available to us. We encourage readers to call any omissions to our attention, and we actively encourage readers to initiate a dialogue with us so that we can improve on this edition in the next one.

Many individuals have enhanced the quality of this book. We are most grateful to the following professors who have read the entire book and have made valuable suggestions: Milton Derber, University of Illinois; James Dworkin, Purdue University; William Glueck, University of Georgia; David A. Gray, University of Texas at Arlington; William Maloney, Ohio State University; Roy Moore, Southern Mississippi University; David Shulenberger, University of Kansas; and William Werther, Arizona State University.

Similar appreciation is extended to many individuals who have read portions of this book and have contributed their expertise in specialized areas: Gwynne Berry, NASA Headquarters, Washington, D.C.; Marc Grossman, United Farm Workers; Alexander Hadden, Of-

fice of the Commissioner of Baseball; Dan C. Heldman, National Right to Work Legal Defense Foundation Inc.; Eileen Hoffman, Federal Mediation and Conciliation Service, New York office; Wayne Howard, the University of Pennsylvania; Truly Kincey, Auburn University; Terry Leap, Louisiana State University; Marvin Miller, Major League Baseball Players Association; Ed Perron, NASA Headquarters, Washington, D.C.; Stephen Shapiro, University of North Florida; William Simkin, former director of the Federal Mediation and Conciliation Service; Ron Smith, Union Carbide Corporation; Hans Stadtlander, Morton Salt Company; and Albert Zack, AFL–CIO.

We are grateful to A. Dale Allen, Asa Gardiner, Matt Jewett, Jerald Robinson, and Alex Simon for furnishing an excellent selection of unpublished arbitration cases.

Special thanks is extended to those who helped along the way: Achilles Armenakis, Art Bedeian, Ernie Brown, Jack Davis, Hubert Feild, Bob Ford, William Giles, Langston Hawley, Frank McLaughlin, Don Mosley, Tom Noble, Jay Smith, and Rudy White. We also wish to thank those individuals who have either directly or indirectly aided in the preparation of the contents or in the production of the book: Theresa Briscoe, Linda Doane, Denise Ganson, Janet King, Janice Martin, Marsha Newman, Peggy A. St. John, Pat Watson, and Bessie E. Yellen.

Finally, we would like to thank the Dryden staff and others for their fine work on the book. We are especially grateful to Nedah Abbott, Anita Constant, Peter Coveney, Rita Madsen, Jane Perkins, Stephen Rapley, Adrian Russert, Mary Weiss, and Alan Wendt at Dryden; and to Flora Foss, Sheila Ary, Beverly Peavler, Maggie Jarpey, Jo-Anne Naples, and Mili McNiece, at Naples Editing Services.

William H. Holley, Jr.
Auburn University

Kenneth M. Jennings
University of North Florida

Contents

The Labor
Relations
Process

Part 1 introduces the labor relations process which will be discussed throughout the book, placing it in historical and legal perspectives. It also examines how employees become unionized and the relationships between the various organizational components of labor.

Part 1

Recognition of the Rights and Responsibilities of Unions and Management

Chapter 1

Labor-Management Relationships in Perspective

"The American system of industrial relations is characteristic of our free society."

Sumner H. Slichter, James J. Healy, and E. Robert Livernash

Currently, there are approximately 21 million union members and 160,000 collective bargaining agreements in the United States. These statistics are significant for several reasons. They demonstrate the magnitude of labor relations activities in the United States, indicating that these activities are neither rare nor insignificant. They also suggest the difficulty of making generalizations regarding labor relations. In essence, it is nearly impossible to speak of the typical labor agreement, union member, collective bargaining behavior, or union-management relationship.

On the other hand, the magnitude of labor relations activities necessitates the development of a framework which will focus on certain related dimensions and allow investigation of similarities and differences in the labor relations process. The labor relations process *is one in which management and the exclusive bargaining agent for the employees (the union) jointly decide upon and enforce terms and conditions of employment (work rules). This framework is needed in order for the practitioner and academician to consistently examine the outcomes of the labor-management relationship. This chapter provides an overview of the labor relations process and introduces those elements which are discussed throughout the remainder of the book.*

Elements in the Labor Relations Process

Exhibit 1–1 illustrates many elements which are commonly found in the labor relations process. These elements can be applied to the labor relations activities at a single manufacturing facility, at a small number of facilities, at all of the facilities owned by a single company, or in an entire industry. The exhibit cites three major categories: the focal point of labor relations—work rules; the participants in the process—union and management organizations, employees, and the government; and constraints or influences affecting the parties in their negotiation and administration of the work rules.

The Focal Point of Labor Relations — Work Rules

Any academic discipline needs a focal point so that research, investigation, and commentary can generate applicable insights. Unfortunately, labor relations have lacked any academic focal point for some time. While academicians and practitioners have realized that labor relations involve union and management officials, few of these participants' activities fall exclusively in the labor relations category. Industrial sociologists have examined employee alienation, psychologists have investigated causes of job satisfaction, economists have studied wage determination, and political scientists have assessed the structural relationships of the internal union organization and its members and leaders. In short, labor relations have lacked a consensually defined focal point, one that would place the various piecemeal investigations and observations into a proper analytical framework.

This situation was changed in 1958 with the publication of John Dunlop's *Industrial Relations Systems.* Dunlop suggested that the center of attention in labor relations should be the work rules negotiated between management and union officials. It is important to understand the influences determining whether the rule exists and, if so, its particular content.[1] *Work rules* can be placed in two general categories: (1) rules governing compensation in all its forms—overtime payments, vacations, holidays, shift premiums, and so on, and (2) rules specifying the employees' and employers' job rights and obligations, such as performance standards, promotion qualifications and procedures, job specifications, and layoff procedures. Additional examples of work rules are furnished in Exhibit 1–2.

Some work rules, such as the first one in Exhibit 1–2, are common to many occupations or industries. Others may be unique to a particular job classification, such as those for Playboy Bunnies, baseball players, and cemetery employees. Work rules likewise may vary according to their vague or specific nature; for example, consider the "democracy in public college education" provision cited in Exhibit 1–2. This rule at first appears rather insignificant; yet unions and management could easily become heatedly involved over the meaning and intent of the word *democracy*. For example, a professor who supported an unpopular political cause might contend that his or her employment discharge violated the "democratic ideal" cited in the labor agreement.

Exhibit 1–1 Elements in the Labor Relations Process

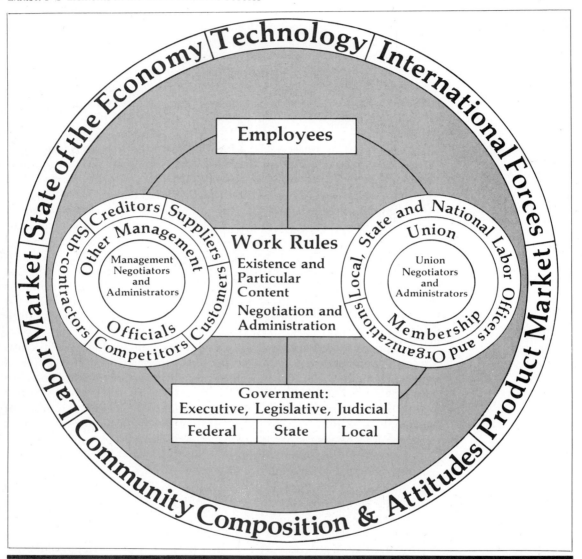

Source: Slightly modified from material supplied by Milton Derber of the University of Illinois.

An analysis of work rules regardless of their clarity or scope helps us understand the complex output of the labor relations process. The formal labor agreement in this sense represents a compilation of jointly negotiated work rules. However, as discussed in Chapter 8, labor relations activities are not limited to the mere existence and content of the work rule; it is also appropriate to examine how the particular rule is administered between union and management officials.

Exhibit 1–2 Examples of Work Rules	Work Rule	Job or Industry Classification
	After consultation with the Shop Committee, the Corporation shall make reasonable rules in each plant regarding smoking. Any protest against the reasonableness of the rules may be treated as a grievance.	**Auto Assembly**
	Discharge and Suspension for Lack of Bunny Image. (1) The parties acknowledge the great importance of Bunny Image and its maintenance to PCI, to the Clubs and to Bunnies, due in part to the established recognition of Bunnies as unique and distinctive Playboy employees. . . . The parties acknowledge the difficulty of defining "Bunny Image" and agree that determination of Bunny Image for purposes of discharge or suspension may include, but is not limited to, the physical appearance of a Bunny and the impression she conveys to customers and others.	**Entertainment— Nightclubs**
	An employee reporting for work on his regularly-scheduled shift, unless he is notified by the Company not to report at least sixteen (16) hours prior to the scheduled starting time, shall be given work which is available, but in the event he is not permitted to start work, or works less than one hour, he shall be given four hours' pay. In the event that an employee works more than one hour of his regular shift before being sent home because of lack of work, he will receive eight (8) hours' pay. This provision shall not apply in the event that an employee refused available work which he is physically able to perform or in the event that catastrophes, failures of utilities or acts of a public enemy interfere with work being provided.	**Steel Industry**
	Single Rooms on the Road. A Player may elect prior to the commencement of the championship season to have single rooms in the Club's hotels on all road trips. The cost of such rooms shall be paid by the Player except that the Club shall pay a portion of the cost equal to 50% of the Club's usual rate for a double room at the hotels involved.	**Professional Baseball**
	Democracy in Public College Education. The Board and the Union recognize and agree that while democratic principles should prevail in every American school system, urban colleges in a city as diverse in population as is Chicago must be exemplary in their expression and practice of the democratic ideal.	**Clerical and Technical Employees at a College**
	Gravedigging: In all cases where a grave is dug straight down, a second man shall be assigned to assist the digger after a depth of five feet is reached.	**Cemeteries**

Sources: Various collective bargaining agreements in the United States.

Reviewing work rules also offers insights into the dynamic nature of the labor relations process, since the participants' desires and abilities to effect these desires change over time. For example, the contemporary work rules for airline stewardesses would most certainly differ from the following three work requirements formulated in the 1930s: (a) swat flies in the cabin after takeoff, (b) prevent passengers from throwing lighted cigar butts out the windows, and (c) carry a railroad timetable in case of plane trouble.[2] Similarly, some union and management officials attempt to change work rules which they feel are outdated. One example which demonstrates changing times is the case of a police union in Milwaukee attempting to alter management's rule prohibiting unmarried couples from living together.[3]

Work rules are not formulated in a vacuum. Instead, they are negotiated and administered by the participants in the labor relations process, who are in turn subjected to many related influences and constraints.

The Participants in the Labor Relations Process

Several *union and management officials* negotiate and administer the work rules; however, these individuals do not always represent a consensus attitude within their respective organizations. It is difficult to speak of *the* management or *the* union position on a particular labor relations issue. There are often many different interest groups generating possible internal conflict within each organization. For example, there are other management officials, like the production manager, the comptroller, and others; and the union membership is composed of groups whose interests may differ—old and young, craft and unskilled, males and females.

As will be further discussed in Chapter 8, management's first-line supervisors typically hear and attempt to resolve employees' grievances on the production floor. In some cases, they are surprised to learn that higher level management officials have overturned their decision on a grievance and have taken an opposite position. Alert union leaders may use dissension among top management officials to influence labor relations activities and the company's position toward unions. Of course, labor unions are not immune to differing attitudes and factions within their own memberships. For example, recent labor settlements negotiated and approved by Arnold Miller, president of the United Mine Workers Union, were rejected by the membership.[4]

The second circle surrounding both management and union negotiators (see Exhibit 1–1) demonstrates the pressures and potential influences on the respective managements and unions. Management must be conscious of its competitors, who may challenge the company's product in quality, price, and/or service; at the same time, it must provide a return to the owners (stockholders) by operating in such a way as to retain its customers, pay its creditors, and maintain its supply of raw materials and parts. Unions at each level must operate within the policies and rules of their local and national unions as well as those of the AFL-CIO if the national union chooses to affiliate with this federation. Moreover, since union officers are elected, they must continue to provide those services and benefits that members believe are important. Thus, both union and management negotiators have pressures, policies, and rules that guide their behavior.

Employees are included as a separate category since they can have loyalties to both management and union organizations.[5] This situation is found in both the private and public sectors; for example, public employees such as firefighters, police, and teachers may feel torn between the critical or professional nature of their jobs and the strategic advantages of a strike. Since their desires may shape the existence and content of particular work rules, employees can be considered the third participant in the labor relations process.

In many instances, the employees' racial or ethnic backgrounds may shape their particular work rule preferences. For example, if most of the employees at a facility are black, then there will probably be pressure for a holiday commemorating Martin Luther King's death or birthday. A unique example involves the Navajo Indians working at an Arizona coal mine, who asked that their union's health and retirement fund be used to pay fees charged by Navajo medicine men. While these miners relied on regular physicians to treat most physical injuries, they relied on medicine men to ease aches, pains, and emotional problems.[6]

In other cases, the age of the employees might affect the content of the work rules. If the average age of employees at a facility were fifty, there would probably be more emphasis on pension plan improvements, whereas a younger work force might stress maternity benefits or higher hourly wages.

Union and management negotiators and the employees must take into account a fourth participant—the *government*, with its executive (or administrative) regulations and decisions, legislative (or statutory) actions, and judicial decisions. If the union, management, and employees at a particular facility wish to negotiate a compulsory retirement age of sixty, it will be inconsistent with the statutory limit of age seventy found in the 1978 amendments to the Age Discrimination in Employment Act. To cite another example, coal miners have long believed that if females worked in the mines, bad luck would result. However, union and management officials would be violating the Equal Employment Opportunity Act if they negotiated a provision prohibiting female employees from working in the mines. Perhaps more widespread is the controversy over negotiated seniority provisions which are used for administrative decisions, such as promotions and layoffs, and affirmative action programs monitored by the government. This issue will be discussed in more detail in Chapters 10 and 12.

Finally, governmental actions which do not directly pertain to labor relations may also have an impact on work rules. For example, the

An employee's feelings of loyalty for both management and union can lead to emotional conflict. Here a policewoman, ordered to arrest picketing fellow police officers, found herself unable to carry out the order.

government is currently considering ending its regulation of the trucking industry in the hope that competition among trucking firms will be increased, thereby reducing inflationary pressures. This governmental policy could increase management pressure to obtain concessions from the unions in the labor agreements so that they might more effectively deal with competition resulting from deregulation.[7]

Influences Affecting the Participants' Negotiation and Administration of the Work Rules

Thus far we have suggested that the desires and composition of the labor relations participants can affect the development of work rules. However, these participants are in turn influenced by several variables or constraints (see the outer circle of Exhibit 1–1) in their labor relations activities. These influences may relate to the particular firm, the local community, or society in general. The following is not intended to be an exhaustive discussion of these influences but to furnish a few illustrations of how they can affect the existence and content of work rules.

Technology Perhaps the most immediate and persistent influence on the work rules is the technology of the particular workplace. *Technology* is defined to include the equipment used in the operation, the pace and scheduling of work, and characteristics of the work environment and tasks to be performed.[8] Consider, for example, the major equipment found at a steel mill—namely, blast furnaces, which require very high temperatures for operation. These furnaces cannot be simply turned on and off like a household oven. Often several days are required for either reaching these high temperatures or for cooling the furnaces for necessary repairs. This equipment characteristic in turn has several implications for the facility's work rules. In essence, steel mills must be operated twenty-four hours a day, seven days a week—a situation prompting related work rules such as wage premiums for working the night shift, weekends, and holidays.

The pace and scheduling of the workday could also affect the work rules of certain occupations. For example, bus companies optimizing their productivity and revenue would concentrate on rush hour traffic (6:00–9:00 A.M., 3:00–7:00 P.M.), when buses would stand a pretty good chance of being filled with passengers. Problems remain in scheduling work because it is possible that many bus drivers would have a daily work schedule of three hours on, three hours off, one hour on, two hours off, four hours on. Because of the nature of the work, most labor agreements in related industries have provisions pertaining to the permissible number, length, and possible compensation of intervals (times off) between daily work assignments.

Professional sports are not free of potential scheduling problems. Management could conceivably schedule a night game in New York City for one day and then have the baseball team fly to Los Angeles, where it would play two games (a doubleheader) the following day. Of course, many of the baseball players would object to the schedule, an attitude which precipitated the following current labor agreement provision: "(4) (a) A game will not be scheduled to start after 6 P.M. if either Club is scheduled to play a day doubleheader the next day."[9]

Finally, the work environment and tasks to be performed can also influence work rules; for example, particular safety equipment is required on certain jobs in the manufacturing and construction industries. A more specific example relates to actors performing at dinner theatres. The lights in dinner theatres are usually turned off between the acts of a play. Actors retire to their dressing rooms during the intermission, while the stage crew changes the stage scenery for the next act. The actors then return to the stage via aisles which are commonly surrounded by dinner tables before the lights are turned back on for the new act. Those who have attended a dinner theatre might wonder how the actor safely walks to the stage in virtual darkness. This concern has apparently been shared by union officials because the Actors' Equity Association labor agreement governing employment in dinner theatres includes a detailed provision requiring proper spacing and placement of guide-lights.[10]

International Forces The international influence on the labor relations process was most vividly reflected in the United States' involvement in World War I and World War II. The impact of these wars on domestic labor relations activities will be described in more detail in Chapter 2. However, it should be noted that President Franklin Roosevelt, realizing that U.S. production output could not be jeopardized during World War II, established a War Labor Board, which in turn encouraged union and management officials to negotiate provisions in their labor agreement for the administration of work rules.

The 1973 Arab oil embargo resulted in the lowering of the maximum speed limit to 55 miles per hour, a reduction which has been continued due to unpredictable events in Mideast countries and in the interest of energy conservation. This limit aroused truck drivers, who are typically paid by the mile for their services. They receive less pay for the same number of hours if they abide by the legal and lower speed limits. While the authors were unable to uncover a contract provision resulting from this event, there is little doubt of the related union concerns, especially when coupled with recent wage-price guidelines.

A more widespread impact of the oil embargo on labor relations occurred in 1973 and again in 1979, when the possibility of gas rationing was seriously considered by the government. In fact, the projected drop in sales of large, low gas mileage cars resulted in the layoffs of 289,000 automotive employees in 1973.[11]

Product Market The *product market* is where the company either sells its product or purchases key elements for its manufacture. Considering the first element, management would be more vulnerable if a strike occurred at a time major customer sales were anticipated. Consider, for example, when a brewery anticipates a peak market demand for its product. Clearly, management at the brewery would not prefer a labor agreement expiring, and possibly leading to a strike, during the summer months. Indeed, one major brewery has been successful in changing the contract expiration date from June 1 to March 1.

The second dimension of the product market is illustrated by the United Auto Workers Union's (UAW's) deep concern that many of the parts for automobiles are being manufactured in foreign countries. If this practice continues, it is likely that a provision in the labor agreement will eventually be negotiated to restrict the number of automobile parts manufactured in foreign countries. [12]

Community Composition and Attitudes The influence of community composition and attitudes can be examined from two perspectives: (a) influential individuals and/or organizations within the community and (b) cultural values and traditions which are reflected in the community's population. Similarly, the geographical scope of the community can be subject to varying definitions; it can represent the local municipality or a broader geographical region. This variable can even be extended to include societal differences in labor relations patterns (Chapter 16). Consider, for example, the goals of a prominent Japanese union leader outlined in Exhibit 1–3. While the following discussion considers domestic applications of the community influence, it is safe to say that no U.S. union leader would approach the goals outlined in Exhibit 1–3 with

Exhibit 1–3 Japanese Union Leader's Standard of Living Goals for the 1980s	Bachelorhood: **A typical factory hand in his early 20s "will live in a small private apartment of one six-mat room and one three-mat room [a mat is 18 square feet]," says Nakamura. "He will work a five-day week, own a refrigerator, color TV, skis and a car and take three domestic trips and a week's vacation abroad every year. He will go to the movies ten times a year and attend five sporting events."** Young Marrieds: **After his wedding, at around the age of 25, the typical worker will move into slightly larger quarters—a "2 dk" apartment (two rooms plus a dining room–kitchen) in a company-subsidized housing project. He will buy a sewing machine for his wife and, for the first time, acquire a telephone.** Growing Family: **"At 36," Nakamura continues, "the worker buys his own 88-square-meter [947 square feet] house. By then, he has two children. He also has an air conditioner, a piano and golf equipment, and the rooms are carpeted."** The Provider: **In middle age, the model employee provides his children with the best possible education. "By the time he is 50, his son has graduated from a private university," says Nakamura. "His daughter has completed junior college."** The Senior Citizen: **At 60, the mandatory retirement age, Nakamura's typical union member trudges off, safe and secure, into his sunset years of contentment.**

Source: "Five Ages of Man," *Newsweek*, May 24, 1976, pp. 42–43. Copyright 1976 by Newsweek, Inc. All rights reserved. Reprinted by permission.

management representatives, especially if he or she wanted to be reelected.

The very existence of a labor union can be largely determined by community influences. A company selecting a location for a new production facility often has to contend with a group of influential community citizens. In many cases, these groups, with or without the support of the community's population, have thwarted the efforts of some predominantly unionized, high-wage companies to locate in the area.[13] Attitudes of community citizens and/or potential employees can also strongly influence the possibility of a facility becoming unionized. One assessment of white workers in the South suggests that these employees have had the following cultural beliefs: independence, reliance on individual accomplishment, and general distrust of "outsiders." These beliefs can make it difficult for any union organizer who attempts to persuade the employees at a southern industrial facility to join a particular union.[14]

If a facility becomes unionized, community attitudes can shape the subsequent work rules desired by management or union officials. In many cases, this influence occurs when union and management officials reach an impasse over a particular issue. Chapter 7 describes various strategies used by management and labor to resolve a negotiations impasse. One related tactic involves soliciting support from community residents. For example, teachers desiring limitations on the maximum number of students allowed in a classroom might stress to the affected community that increased class size would lower educational quality. Educational administrators, on the other hand, would probably indicate to the community that a teachers' strike over this issue would place educational funding in jeopardy.

The mass media often serve as both generator and conduit of community opinion. Unfortunately, few empirical studies have investigated the effects of the mass media on labor relations participants and work rules in the United States.[15] The news media are profit-making businesses, and at least one prominent union official contends that this orientation biases the reporting of labor relations activities:

The media tend to cover collective bargaining as if it were a pier six brawl. The intricate moves and tradeoffs that really make up bargaining aren't as newsy as impassioned rhetoric or a picket line confrontation.

Reporters are given little training in covering collective bargaining. They are told to look for the "news"—the fist fight, the walkout, the heated exchange—and, as a result, frequently miss the "story," which is the settlement. . . .

Every union proposal is a "demand," every management proposal is an "offer."[16]

Labor Market The skills and wage levels of employees in the local labor market can affect negotiated work rules. Management is often concerned with the skill levels of employees in the particular community. For example, a firm needing skilled employees from a relatively unskilled labor market would probably wish to negotiate work rules regarding apprenticeship programs. Management under these circumstances would also consider negotiating a probationary period which would give them a relatively free hand in determining whether an employee remains on the payroll during the first ninety days of employment.[17] Within this probationary period, management could terminate an unskilled or nonproductive employee, and the union could not protest the action through the grievance procedure.

Both management and union representatives are also interested in the compensation rates for comparably skilled employees in the labor market. At a minimum, the wages paid by other companies in the local area affect negotiated wage rates. In some cases, particularly in the construction trades, some unions have had to reduce their wages to fight off nonunion competition.[18]

State of the Economy In a sense, the state of the economy can reflect all of the preceding influences discussed in this section, particularly if viewed in micro as well as macro terms. The rate of inflation, in either local or national areas, will often affect work rules—notably, union insistence that a labor agreement include provisions which will increase the wages if there are increases in the cost of living (see Chapter 13). Similarly, an increase in interest rates could retard home and industrial construction projects. Under these circumstances, work rules might be negotiated to insure that construction workers are not laid off and/or that they receive some compensation for the reduced work load.

The unemployment rate, another key economic indicator of the state of the economy, affects the possible existence and content of work rules which provide job protection. Chapter 6 discusses the various ways in which the unemployment rate can affect the bargaining power of union and management officials.

Steps in the Labor Relations Process

The labor relations process is comprised of three phases:

1. *Recognition of the legitimate rights and responsibilities of union and management representatives.* This phase includes the legal right of employees to join unions (see Chapter 3), union organizing drives (see Chapter 4), the rights and obligations of management and union officials, and the reasons employees join unions (discussed later in this chapter).
2. *Negotiation of the labor agreement, including appropriate strategies and tactics and impasse resolution techniques.* Strikes and mediation are examples of the latter (discussed in Chapter 7). This phase is usually the most publicized by the media, even though phases 1 and 3 are equally essential.

3. *Administration of the negotiated labor agreement—applying and enforcing the terms of the agreement on a daily basis.* This phase of the process (discussed in detail in Chapters 8 and 9) accounts for the most time and energy spent by union and management officials and usually involves a larger number of these officials than the preceding phases.

Clearly, the sequence of the labor relations process is cumulative. Seldom do formal negotiations occur if the parties have not first recognized each other's legitimate rights and responsibilities. Similarly, the first two phases are necessary for the existence of the third phase—administration of the labor agreement. Of course, not all labor-management relationships have focused on these three phases. Indeed, employees and their representative unions at some public and private sector facilities are still striving to accomplish the first phase of the process.

A most important aspect of the labor relations process is the quality of the relationship between management and the union officials. In a general sense, there are probably as many different relationships as there are union and management officials negotiating and administrating labor agreements. Yet these relationships often fall into one or more of the following categories: sympathetic, codified, and power.[19]

Sympathetic relations occur when union and management representatives show sympathetic regard for each other's positions and are guided by such appreciation. This relationship often involves personal sentiments, understandings, and concern for the other party's position.

Codified relations occur when the parties accord each other privileges, prestige, and authority in terms of defining codes—applicable labor laws and the provisions of the negotiated labor agreement. Both parties falling into this relationship category go strictly by the book in dealing with each other; there is little room for modifying or improvising these relationships on the basis of personal experiences and concerns involving the other party.

Power relations are often marked by an opposition of interests, with each party attempting to achieve his or her goals at the expense of the other: "Since action is neither held to an application of a code nor guided by a consideration for the other's welfare, a premium is placed on the successful pursuit of *one's own goal,* thus inevitably introducing egotism and possibilities of ruthlessness that have always made power action morally suspect."[20]

It is possible that the interacting union and management officials develop relationships that fall into all of the previously mentioned categories, depending upon the particular issue involved. For example, union and management officials will likely exhibit sympathetic or problem-solving relationships in dealing with an alcoholic employee, for this employee could harm other employees as well as lower industrial efficiency. The extent to which the union-management relationship shifts from sympathetic to power depends on several factors, such as differing goals and value systems, perceived legitimacy for the other side, past relationships and experiences with each other, and the participants' personalities.[21]

Thus far we have discussed the elements and phases of the labor relations process. However, this discussion has not yet approached the underlying reasons for unions and why employees may feel the need of joining a union. The next section will examine the various reasons employees join unions instead of remaining in a nonunion environment.

Why Employees Join Unions

Work and Job Conditions

As suggested by one contemporary song, "Workin' Man Blues," the conditions of the workplace and the job can either alienate employees or lead them to believe that they will lose their jobs:

I keep my nose on the grindstone,
work hard everyday.
I might get a little tight on the weekend,
after I draw my pay.
I'll go back workin',
come Monday morning I'm right back with the crew.
And I drink a little beer that evening,
   Sing a little bit of these workin' man blues.

Sometimes I think about leaving,
do a little bumming around.
I want to throw my bills out the window,
catch a train to another town.
I'll go back workin',
gotta buy my kids a brand new pair of shoes.
I drink a little beer in a tavern
   Cry a little bit of these workin' man blues.

© 1969 Blue Book Music.

Hence, the alienation and job scarcity consciousness theories of why employees join unions will be briefly discussed. Since employees do not tend to join unions for only one or two reasons, related work rules prompting employees to join unions will also be discussed in this section.

Alienation Karl Marx maintained that employees might seek collective action to relieve their feelings of alienation about work conditions. According to Marx, the extensive use of machinery in manufacturing operations under capitalist ownership and control results in the employee being alienated from the work. In essence, the employee becomes an "appendage of the machine," with little skill and knowledge required in his or her performance.[22] The depersonalized nature of work allows no consideration of the individual's needs or concerns. Instead, the employee is completely dominated by the production process and derives neither meaning nor satisfaction from the work. The employee's work performance does not satisfy any work-related need (such as the needs for creativity, self-expression, self-fulfillment, and pride in accomplishment). Work is viewed as being merely a means to satisfy needs external to the work environment (food, shelter, and clothing, for example).[23]

Marx felt that employees would become aware of their common plight and that their resulting class consciousness would prompt them to overthrow the capitalistic system. Another possible result of class consciousness neither publicized nor encouraged by Marx was employees joining a union to alleviate their alienated condition.

To be sure, there is some evidence that U.S. workers are alienated today. For example, several of the employee interviews in Studs Terkel's best seller, *Working*, reflect working conditions and employee concerns similar to those described by Marx.[24] However, two related factors appear to disprove the theory that employees join unions because of their class-conscious attempts to remedy their sense of alienation in work experiences.

First, clear-cut working class or class consciousness compelling employees to join a union or to engage in other collective activities to improve their working situation does not appear to exist in United States history. The presence of geographical, occupational, and social mobility in the United States results in loosely defined social groupings which make membership identification difficult.[25] Consider, for example, the term *middle class* as it is used in the United States. The term is so loosely defined and subject to so many differing interpretations as to make it an impossible predictor of collective action.

A second problem in identifying alienation as the stimulus causing employees to join unions occurs when we assume that the working class (however poorly defined) is more alienated than other employees, who are usually reluctant to join a union. One of the more publicized related studies, *Where Have All the Robots Gone?*, indicates that fewer than 25 percent of the employees have negative attitudes toward their work. Further, negative attitudes toward work do not vary a great deal between blue-collar and white-collar employees, the latter often being reluctant to join unions.[26] Two observers of the labor movement believe that many employees might either repress or deny their alienation, pursuing instead the more immediate gratifications generated by "the spectacles of the market place" (new cars, attendance at professional sports events, and so on).[27]

As discussed more fully in Chapter 12, there are few if any U.S. unions actively involved in bargaining for more "meaningful" work. However, unions can and do address a possible aspect of employee alienation, namely the employees' desire to speak their minds without fear of management reprisal. Two authors commenting on this aspect suggested in

Dissatisfaction with job factors such as low wages has long been a force motivating employees to organize and seek more favorable work rules—in this century, most typically through joining a union.

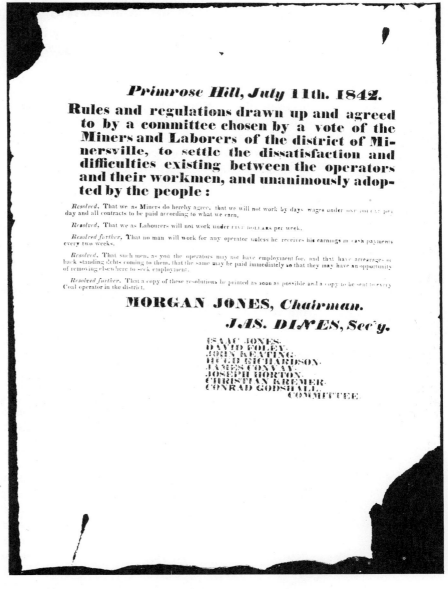

Primrose Hill, July 11th. 1842.

Rules and regulations drawn up and agreed to by a committee chosen by a vote of the Miners and Laborers of the district of Minersville, to settle the dissatisfaction and difficulties existing between the operators and their workmen, and unanimously adopted by the people :

Resolved, That we as Miners do hereby agree, that we will not work by days wages under one dollar per day and all contracts to be paid according to what we earn.

Resolved, That we as Labourers will not work under five dollars per week.

Resolved further, That no man will work for any operator unless he receives his earnings in cash payments every two weeks.

Resolved, That such men, as you the operators may not have employment for, and that have arrearages or back standing debts coming to them, that the same may be paid immediately so that they may have an opportunity of removing elsewhere to seek employment.

Resolved further, That a copy of these resolutions be printed as soon as possible and a copy to be sent to every Coal operator in the district.

MORGAN JONES, *Chairman.*

JAS. DINES, *Sec'y.*

ISAAC JONES.
DAVID FOLEY.
JOHN KEATING.
HUGH RICHARDSON.
JAMES CONWAY.
JOSEPH HORTON.
CHRISTIAN KREMER.
CONRAD GODSHALL.
COMMITTEE.

an article written over thirty years ago that "intertwined with the motives for union membership is the almost universal desire to tell the boss to 'go to hell.'"[28] A union typically indicates to its potential members that the employees' rights to voice their opinions regarding a managerial action are protected by negotiated grievance procedures and disciplinary policies (see Chapters 8 and 11).

Finally, employees might be dissatisfied with aspects of their jobs while not being alienated from their work. Some research has shown that employees might join unions if they (a) are dissatisfied with physical characteristics of the workplace, low wages, or lack of benefits and (b) believe that a union will help them achieve the job-related conditions important to them.[29]

Scarcity Consciousness — The Need for Job Security Perhaps a more accurate observation of the union movement was made by Selig Perlman, who suggested that employees are attracted to unions on the assumption that unions will protect their jobs. Perlman suggested that Marx was wrong in thinking the employee will become increasingly concerned with political ideologies. According to Perlman, employees are neither particularly alienated nor class conscious. Instead, many employees, particularly manual workers, strongly believe they are living in a country of limited opportunity. Perlman replaces Marx's class consciousness with *scarcity consciousness*—the employees' collective belief that jobs are difficult to obtain and retain. Thus, employees turn to unions to solve these perceived difficulties. The union then

---

asserts its collective ownership over the whole amount of opportunity, and, having determined who are entitled to claim a share in that opportunity, undertakes to parcel it out fairly, directly or indirectly, among its recognized members, permitting them to avail themselves of such opportunities, job or market, only on the basis of a "common rule." Free competition becomes a sin against one's fellows, anti-social, like a self indulgent consumption of the stores of a beleaguered city, and obviously detrimental to the individual as well. A collective disposal of opportunity, including the power to keep out undesirables, and a "common rule" in making bargains are as natural to the manual group as "laissez-faire" is to the business man.[30]

Unions therefore are attractive to the many employees concerned about job security today, regardless of their skill or occupational level.[31] Consider, for example, the work-related concerns of a college basketball coach. Depending upon the university's size and performance of the basketball team, the coach can receive a multiyear contract with a particular university. The wages and outside interests (for example, television shows) generated by this contract could result in a salary in excess of $100,000 a year. Yet a notably successful basketball coach, Al McGuire, when asked about the major job-related problem facing coaches, responded:

Security, mainly. Your life depends on a 19-year-old, freckle-faced player. Your unity and your whole season can be blown if the cheerleader gets pregnant. Look, I know the fears coaches have. I know how it is when you've lost five or six in a row and the flower of your youth is gone and you're worrying about what you can do next. I know what it's like when the student body is booing and the papers are writing bad things.[32]

Few employees are currently immune from the possibility of a layoff; therefore, employees might join a union in the hope of increasing their job security. The union can in turn strengthen the employees' job security in several ways.

Make-work rules which prescribe certain procedures for performing a job, thereby insuring that a certain number of employees will be assigned work, can be negotiated. These rules are discussed in more detail in Chapter 12; however, an example is the requirement that no more than two floral sprays can be carried with a casket in the funeral hearse. This rule insures in many cases that a second employee will be needed to drive a flower car.

Apprenticeship programs are usually an attempt to insure that qualified people are available for certain skilled jobs. However, these programs can also insure that jobs will be reserved for those individuals who complete the apprenticeship program. For example, a Hollywood property craftsmen union has an apprenticeship program requiring at least two years of prop-making work experience and 1,500 hours of studio training in such techniques as rain making and cobweb construction. This program helps to insure a quality work force, but it also insures that a union member who has completed the program will not be displaced by the son or daughter of a motion picture producer desiring a job during summer vacation from college.

Negotiated seniority and layoff provisions (discussed in Chapter 12) usually do not prevent management from reducing the number of employees at a particular facility. However, most related provisions indicate that those having more job seniority (work years) at a particular facility will be the last to be laid off. Should some of these employees be laid off, they would eventually be called back to work in the order of their seniority; that is, those employees having the most seniority would be called back to work first.

Lobbying for legislation protecting employees' job rights has been a viable alternative used by unions throughout the years. Here, unions attempt to strengthen job security by pressing for restrictions against cheap labor— foreign citizens, child labor, prison labor—quotas or restrictions against imported products, and adjustment assistance to employees who are displaced as a result of foreign competition.[33]

Related Work Rules Prompting Union Membership In many cases, employees may be required to join a union in order to keep their jobs. One study found that 74 percent of the investigated labor agreements contained a *modified union shop* or *union shop* provision which required certain or all employees to be union members if they wished to keep their jobs.[34] Thus, union membership can be a requirement for continued employment, the employees' personal desires notwithstanding. On the other hand, it cannot be assumed that many of these employees would drop their union membership if there were no union security contract provision.[35] The union security issue remains one of the more controversial and emotional in labor relations activities. Several pros and cons of this issue are discussed in Chapter 10.

Employees' Social Backgrounds and Desires

Employees' social backgrounds and desires are not completely independent from the preceding category in indicating why employees join unions. For example, workers' social backgrounds and desires might strengthen their perceptions of working conditions and affect subsequent decisions about joining a union. Yet the reasons discussed in this section can in most cases be attributed to the potential union member irrespective of the particular working conditions faced by that individual.

Employees' previous experiences with a union can strongly affect their decision to join one. Indeed, many might be influenced by parental attitudes and experiences regarding unions. One active union member stated, "I attended union meetings with my father before I was ever inside a church."[36]

From their social backgrounds employees also bring qualitative assessments of their exposures to union organizations and activities. For example, one union member commented, "My dad was a great union man and that's where I got it—if it wasn't union, it wasn't no good."[37] However, these endorsements can go both ways. Favorable parental comments regarding unions may be offset for some employees by the opposite opinion of a spouse or work associate.

One recent empirical study of over 1,200 employees during union organizing campaigns has partially supported the offsetting nature of personal experiences and the opinions of employees' relatives. For example, the employees' decisions to vote for a union were not significantly correlated with members of their families being union members. Similarly, prior union membership was not significantly associated with a vote for the union in the campaign, suggesting that many members who had been union members elsewhere were not entirely satisfied with union representation. Additional analysis indicated that employees' sex, race, and job seniority did not explain very well their preference for unions.[38] In short, it appears that employees' social backgrounds do not explain group voting behavior; that is, what influences an individual might not be characteristic of the group. This lack of explanation is probably due to a combination of complex, potentially offsetting relationships among all the variables found in employees' social backgrounds.

Unions as well as all formal organizations potentially satisfy the members' needs by providing "a means of developing, enhancing, or confirming a sense of identity and maintaining self-esteem."[39] Thus, unions can appeal to two interrelated social needs of members, the need for affiliation or belonging and the need for status.

The need for affiliation or identifying with others is brought into focus during a union organizing drive when the potential member sees other employees expressing their positive support for a union. The terms *peer pressure* and *bandwagon effect* have been used to describe the influences of other employees on the potential member. It is important to note, however, that the need for affiliation can be a double-edged sword regarding union membership; an employee conforming to the prevailing pattern of his or her work associates could be either pro- or anti-union.

The possible benefit of social affiliation offered by the union is strengthened or weakened by the degree of prestige or self-esteem it offers its members. Some employees join a union for the same reason they would join any social organization, namely, to enjoy the responsibility and status associated with being a member of that organization. This feature can be particularly attractive to employees whose jobs are basically interchangeable and carry very few elements of prestige or room for advancement.

Employees who become union officers can often attain prestige or self-esteem in their dealings with management officials:

As a shop steward or union officer or member of the grievance committee, a worker can become "a fellow your buddies look to." Such positions give him the opportunity to win other workers' approval by being "a fellow who stands up to the boss" with impunity. The role of "a fellow who stands up to the boss" is made more significant because the definition of the boss has been enlarged to include not merely the foreman but "the head office in Pittsburgh." He can win prestige as "a guy that gets results" in such matters as the distribution of work, assignment to jobs, seniority policy, and protection from discrimination.[40]

Chapter 8 discusses the notion that union officers and management officials are equals in their day-to-day administration of the labor agreement. However, as the preceding quotation suggests, the union steward can often emphatically disagree with a management official six levels above the steward on the organization chart. This ability to challenge without fear of reprisal is not usually afforded nonunion employees or even management officials when they deal with their organizational superiors.

As discussed earlier in this section, the perceived lack of prestige associated with unions in certain occupations might discourage employees from becoming union members. In some occupations, notably teaching, the union movement progressed slowly at first because employees regarded unions as being unprofessional. Many employees in other occupations (for example, office employees and retail clerks[41]) have tended to identify their career potential more with management and have therefore been reluctant to join unions.

Union Organizing and the White-Collar Employee

Unique aspects of the white-collar employee classification add new dimensions to thinking about why employees join unions and offer some promising challenges to organized labor as well. Shifts in labor force distributions toward more service industries and white-collar occupations have spurred an interest in white-collar unions. These labor force trends have become increasingly important to the union movement. Organized labor realizes that its political goals regarding social welfare, tax reform, and economic planning can be achieved only if it has an adequate membership base, and it must gain white-collar union members to offset losses in blue-collar union membership.[42]

Presently, the United States has a smaller proportion of white-collar union members than other industrialized countries,[43] and it appears that white-collar unionization has lost its momentum[44] except among health care and government employees. This situation is due in part to differences between white-collar and blue-collar employees. White-collar employees usually have more education, closer identification with management, and greater interest in changes in job design.[45] Labor organizers have traditionally had some difficulty in convincing white-collar employees that a union organization could effectively deal with these characteristics.

However, there are some grounds for union optimism in organizing white-collar employees, particularly when these employees are concerned with traditional issues such as wages, working conditions, and job security[46] as well as with emerging issues such as disenchantment with merit-based promotion systems,[47] limited opportunity for advancement, lack of career progression programs, shift work, and routine and uninteresting jobs. Indeed, two-thirds of the executives polled by the Conference Board believed that white-collar unions were on the upswing, and some even believed that by 1990 most white-collar employees would be union members.[48] The accuracy of these predictions depends on a number of variables:

☐ The extent of union organizing efforts.

☐ Reactions of white-collar employees to the continuing depersonalization and routinization of their jobs.

☐ Gains in negotiated wages and fringe benefits of blue-collar relative to white-collar employees.

☐ The extent to which white-collar employees view unions as a means of bettering their conditions of employment.[49]

Managers, a subgroup of white-collar employees, show many similarities to their white-collar counterparts, but one important difference is that they supervise other individuals, who may be unionized employees. Little is known about managers' interest in labor unions and collective bargaining.[50] However, some evidence suggests that managers, especially at the lower echelons, are dissatisfied with their employment situations.[51] Some of the perceived difficulties are poor job security, lack of involvement in corporate decisions, increased responsibility without commensurate authority, and disproportionate blue-collar wage gains.[52]

One study reveals that managers are becoming more and more frustrated and discontented with corporate life, and nearly one-half of the middle managers favor changing the U.S. labor laws to require employers to recognize and bargain with manager unions. Although unions have shown little interest in organizing managers, about 75 percent of the personnel executives involved in this study endorsed a proposal for informal meetings with manager groups, and one-third of the manager respondents believed that they would consider joining a managers' union.[53]

Managerial interest in negotiating with higher management officials presently is subject to legal and practical complications. While there is no law which prohibits top management from negotiating with a union of managers, there is no law that requires top management to recognize and bargain with any such union. Further, supervisors or managers are not protected by current labor legislation (the National Labor Relations Act discussed in Chapter 3) and therefore might be discharged for union activities.[54] Thus, managers' situations are similar to blue-collar employees' before 1935 in that they would probably be forced to strike or picket to obtain recognition. The success of their organizational efforts would depend on their ability to effectively curtail production or gain the sympathetic support of other unions at the facility by honoring their picket lines. Since neither is likely, prospects of managerial unions are remote.[55]

Another white-collar subgroup is the professional, whose work is primarily nonroutine and intellectual in nature. Like other white-collar employees, professionals often find themselves denied participation or even a voice in the decision-making processes, no matter how knowledgeable they are. Similarly, some of the characteristics of the professional's job—spontaneity, exuberance, dignity, freedom to perform, identification with the product—have diminished over time.[56] In response to the changing nature of their employment situation, a number of professional groups have reconciled their professional standards with unions and have become heavily organized. Musicians, actors and actresses, newspaper reporters, airline pilots, teachers and professors, bank employees, engineers, scientists, and physicians and dentists are among the professional groups which have affiliated with unions in varying degrees.[57]

Because engineers and scientists are relatively well-paid and tend to have managerial aspirations, they have generally shunned unions but have still looked to their professional societies to represent them in areas common to their professional interests. Many of them well remember the massive layoffs, lost pensions, and compressed salaries of the 1960s in the aerospace and defense industries.[58] Should such events recur, new or renewed interest among the engineers and scientists will probably emerge. Like other professional employees, they have remained concerned over such issues as sharing the credit for accomplishments or discoveries while bearing the blame for inputs into critical decisions. These issues will remain speculative topics for union and management officials and students of industrial relations for some time.[59]

Summary

The labor relations process occurs when management and the exclusive bargaining agent for the employees (the union) jointly decide upon and enforce terms of the labor agreement. Work rules constitute the focal point of the labor relations process and pertain either to compensation in all its forms or to the employees' and employers' job rights and obligations.

At first glance, it might appear that union and management officials are the only participants in the labor relations process. Complexities arise with the realization that it is difficult to speak of *the* management or *the* union position on a particular labor relations issue. Instead, union and management officials are members of their respective organizations subject to internal conflicts and external pressures. Employees represent a third participant category in the labor relations process since they can have loyalties to both union and management officials. Various sociodemographic characteristics of the employee group (race, age, and sex) can exert a strong influence on the existence and content of work rules. A fourth participant category is the government, with its executive decisions, legislative action, and judicial decisions. The participants in the labor relations process are influenced in their rule-making efforts by several variables or constraints, such as technology, international forces, the product market, community composition and attitudes, the labor market, and the state of the economy.

The labor relations process consists of three sequential phases: (1) recognition of the legitimate rights and responsibilities of union and management representatives, (2) negotiation of the labor agreement, and (3) applying and enforcing the terms of the agreement on a daily basis. A most important aspect of the process is the quality of the relationship between union and management officials. These relationships can fall into one or more of the following categories: sympathetic, codified, and power.

Additional insights into the labor relations process are found by considering why employees join unions instead of remaining in a nonunion environment. The work environment can prompt the employee to join a union by contributing to feelings of alienation or scarcity consciousness, or related work rules may require union membership. Employees' preferences for unions can also be influenced by their social backgrounds and desires and their general occupational level. White-collar employees have increasingly turned to unions to solve their problems, despite their traditional tendency to identify with management more than blue-collar workers.

Discussion Questions

1. Exhibit 1–1 establishes the focal point of the labor relations process and many variables which affect the process. Select an academic discipline such as political science, economics, or sociology, and indicate three specific ways the discipline could add insights into the labor relations process.

2. Discuss the different dimensions of technology, indicating how this variable might contribute to two unique and specific work rules for unionized employees at a grocery store. Also indicate with examples how one other external constraint or influence (see the outer circle of Exhibit 1–1) could affect the work rules at a grocery store.

3. Explain how a management official and a union official can have both sympathetic and power relationships with each other.

4. Compare and contrast the alienation and scarcity consciousness theories of why employees join unions. Which, if either, of these theories would be more appropriate in explaining why professional baseball players would join a union?

5. To what extent are white-collar employees similar to blue-collar employees in their desires to join a union? To what extent are they different?

References

[1] John Dunlop, *Industrial Relations Systems* (New York: Henry Holt, 1958), pp. 13–16.

[2] "Labor Letter," *Wall Street Journal*, November 22, 1977, p. 1.

[3] "Cohabitation Costs Cops Their Jobs," *New Times*, October 16, 1978, p. 16.

[4] Robert Sam Anson, "Hearts and Mines: Arnold Miller's Perilous Ascent," *New Times*, April 3, 1978, pp. 18–19. For a case study of internal union differences, see a transcript of "Inside the Union," *CBS Reports*, March 6, 1979. The union member-leader relationship is discussed in more detail in Chapter 5.

[5] For an early study of employee dual loyalty, see Theodore V. Purcell, *Blue Collar Man: Patterns of Dual Allegiance in Industry* (Cambridge: Harvard University Press, 1960).

[6] "Labor Letter," *Wall Street Journal*, March 22, 1977, p. 1.

[7] "How Deregulation Hurts the Teamsters," *Business Week*, November 27, 1978, p. 71. For a consideration of how deregulation has affected collective bargaining in the airline industry, see William M. Carley, "Squaring Off: United Airlines Strike Reflects Industry Drive to Curb Labor Costs," *Wall Street Journal*, May 11, 1979, pp. 1, 25.

[8] For an additional discussion of technological dimensions and impacts on the negotiated work rules see Dunlop, *Industrial Relations Systems*, pp. 33–61.

[9]*Basic Agreement (1976–1979) between the American League of Professional Baseball Clubs, and the National League of Professional Baseball Clubs, and Major League Baseball Players Association*, p. 4.

[10]*Actors' Equity Association Agreement and Rules Governing Employment in Dinner Theatres (1973–1974)*, p. 24.

[11]For a more detailed account of this event, see John R. Emshwiller, "Layoff Lament: For the Auto Workers, Extended Joblessness Is Becoming a Reality," *Wall Street Journal*, October 29, 1974, pp. 1, 30.

[12]John R. Emshwiller, "Looking Homeward: Auto Workers Decry Rise in Foreign Output of Parts for U.S. Cars," *Wall Street Journal*, March 19, 1976, pp. 1, 23.

[13]Douglas Sease, "Yankee Go Home," *Wall Street Journal*, February 10, 1978, pp. 1, 29. See also "Labor Letter," *Wall Street Journal*, August 16, 1977, p. 1.

[14]John Filiatreau, "The White Worker in the South," *Dissent*, Winter 1972, pp. 78–82.

[15]For two related studies pertaining to mass media and the industrial relations process in England, see David Morley, "Industrial Conflict and the Mass Media," *Sociological Review*, May 1976, pp. 245–268; and Paul Hartmann, "Industrial Relations in the News Media," *Industrial Relations Journal* 6 (Winter 1975–1976), pp. 4–18.

[16]Lane Kirkland, "Labor and the Press," *American Federationist* 82 (December 1975), p. 3. See also Albert J. Zack, "The Press Bias on Labor," *American Federationist* 84 (October 1977), pp. 1–7.

[17]Clark Kerr, "The Collective Bargaining Environment," in Clinton S. Golden and Virginia D. Parker, eds., *Causes of Industrial Peace under Collective Bargaining* (New York: Harper & Bros., 1955), pp. 10–22.

[18]See, for example, "Labor Letter," *Wall Street Journal*, September 13, 1977, p. 1; and "Labor's Next Wage Push," *Business Week*, March 27, 1978, pp. 41–42.

[19]Herbert Blumer, "Social Structure and Power Conflict," in Arthur Kornhauser, Robert Dubin, and Arthur M. Ross, eds., *Industrial Conflict* (New York: McGraw-Hill, 1954), pp. 232–239.

[20]Ibid., p. 235.

[21]Leon C. Megginson and C. Ray Gullett, "A Predictive Model of Union-Management Conflict," *Personnel Journal*, June 1970, pp. 495–503. For an early examination of divergent industrial relations patterns see Benjamin M. Selekman, "Varieties of Labor Relations," *Harvard Business Review* 27 (March 1949), pp. 175–199.

[22]Karl Marx and Friedrich Engels, "Manifesto of the Communist Party," in H. Beer, ed., *The Communist Manifesto* (New York: Appleton-Century-Crofts, 1955), p. 16.

[23]Karl Marx, "Estranged Labor," in Robert C. Tucker, ed., *The Marx-Engels Reader* (New York: W. W. Norton, 1972), p. 60.

[24]Studs Terkel, *Working* (New York: Random House, 1972). See also Bennett Kremen, "No Pride in This Dust," *Dissent*, Winter 1972, pp. 21–28; and Rick King, "In the Sanding Booth at Ford," *Washington Monthly* 7 (January 1976), pp. 36–44.

[25]Kenneth E. Boulding, *The Organizational Revolution* (Chicago: Quadrangle Books, 1968), pp. 166–167.

[26]Harold L. Sheppard and Neal Q. Herrick, *Where Have All the Robots Gone? Worker Dissatisfaction in the '70s* (New York: Free Press, 1972), p. 193.

[27]Daniel Bell, *Work and Its Discontents* (New York: League for Industrial Democracy, 1970), p. 33; and Stanley Aronowitz, *False Promises: The Shaping of American Working Class Consciousness* (New York: McGraw-Hill, 1973), pp. 409–410.

[28]Clinton S. Golden and Harold Ruttenberg, "Motives for Union Membership," in E. Wight Bakke, Clark Kerr, and Charles W. Anrod, eds., *Unions, Management, and the Public* (New York: Harcourt, Brace, 1948), p. 49.

[29]M. D. Dunnette and W. K. Kirchner, *Psychology Applied to Industry* (New York: Appleton-Century-Crofts, 1965), pp. 199–200; and Henry S. Farber and Daniel H. Saks, "Why Workers Want Unions: The Role of Relative Wages and Job Characteristics" (working paper, Cambridge, Mass.: M.I.T., 1978), pp. 27–28. See also W. Clay Hamner and Frank J. Smith, "Work Attitudes as Predictors of Unionization Activity," *Journal of Applied Psychology* 63 (1978), p. 415; William J. Bigoness, "Correlates of Faculty Attitudes toward Collective Bargaining," *Journal of Applied Psychology* 63 (1978), pp. 228–233; Chester A. Schreisheim, "Job Satisfaction, Attitudes toward Unions, and Voting in a Union Representation Election," *Journal of Applied Psychology* 63 (1978), pp. 548–552; J. G. Getman, S. B. Goldberg, and J. B. Herman, *Union Representation Elections: Law and Reality* (New York: Russel Sage Foundation, 1976); Edward L. Harrison, "Employee Satisfaction and Voting Behavior in Union Representation Elections," in Dennis F. Ray and Thad B. Green, eds., *Toward Renewal of Management Thought and Practice* (State College, Miss.: Southern Management Association, Mississippi State University, 1978), p. 169.

[30]Selig Perlman, *A Theory of the Labor Movement* (1928; reprinted New York: Augustus M. Kelley, 1968), p. 242.

[31]For an assessment of contemporary scarcity consciousness as it applies to employees in the automobile industry, see John R. Emshwiller, "Change in Attitudes: Recalled Auto Worker Finds His Outlook on Life Is Different," *Wall Street Journal*, February 3, 1977, pp. 1, 22.

[32]Larry Keith, "A Conversation with Chairman Al," *Sports Illustrated,* November 28, 1977, p. 36.

[33]See, for example, Bureau of National Affairs, "4,000 More in Steel Given Adjustment Aid," *Daily Labor Report* (Washington, D.C.: Bureau of National Affairs, December 29, 1977), p. 3; and "Labor's New Push for Protection," *Business Week,* December 26, 1977, pp. 31, 32.

[34]Bureau of National Affairs, *Basic Patterns in Union Contracts,* 8th ed. (Washington, D.C.: Bureau of National Affairs, 1975), p. 96.

[35]Martin Estey, *The Unions: Structure, Development, and Management,* 2d ed. (New York: Harcourt Brace Jovanovich, 1976), p. 84.

[36]Joel Seidman, Jack London, and Bernard Karsh, "Why Workers Join Unions," *Annals of the American Academy of Political and Social Science 274* (March 1951), pp. 775–784.

[37]Ibid.

[38]Getman, Goldberg, and Herman, *Union Representation Elections,* pp. 66–68.

[39]Edgar H. Schein, *Organizational Psychology,* 2d ed. (Englewood Cliffs, N.J.: Prentice-Hall, 1965), p. 70.

[40]E. Wight Bakke, "Why Workers Join Unions," *Personnel* 22 (July 1947), p. 3.

[41]Albert A. Blum, "The Office Employee," in Albert A. Blum et al., *White-Collar Workers* (New York: Random House, 1971), p. 17; and Martin Estey, "The Retail Clerks," in Blum et al., *White-Collar Workers,* p. 46.

[42]Everett M. Kassalow, "White-Collar Unions and the Work Humanization Movement," *Monthly Labor Review* 100 (May 1977), pp. 9–13.

[43]In 1974, for example, only 13 percent of the white-collar workers in the United States were union members, as compared with 24 percent in Germany, 38 percent in Great Britain, 41 percent in Australia, 58 percent in Norway, and 70 percent in Sweden. D. W. Rawson, "A Note on Manual and Nonmanual Union Membership in Australia," *Journal of Industrial Relations,* December 1974, pp. 394–397.

[44]Bureau of National Affairs, *Labor Relations Reporter: News and Background Information* 98 LRR 57 (Washington, D.C.: Bureau of National Affairs, May 15, 1978). Included as white-collar employees are office and clerical employees, technical employees, draftsmen, engineering assistants, semiprofessionals, salespersons (not retail), newspaper and editorial employees, radio and television station employees, insurance claim adjusters, and telephone operators.

[45]Claude Edwards, *Some Reflections on White-Collar Collective Bargaining* (Kingston, Canada: Queens University, 1977), pp. 1–2; and Kassalow, "White-Collar Unions," pp. 11–13.

[46]Edward R. Curtin, *White-Collar Unions* (New York: National Industrial Conference Board, 1970), pp. 71–72.

[47]Edwards, "Some Reflections," p. 3.

[48]Curtin, *White-Collar Unions,* pp. 71–72.

[49]Edward R. Curtin, "The Facts about White-Collar Unionization," *Conference Board Record* 6 (June 1969), pp. 11–13.

[50]Heinz Hartman, "Managerial Employees—New Participants in Industrial Relations," *British Journal of Industrial Relations* 12 (1974), pp. 268–269.

[51]"The Unhappy Foreman at Wheeling-Pittsburg," *Business Week,* May 22, 1978, p. 32.

[52]Alfred T. DeMaria, "Is This the Decade Managers Unionize?" *MBA* 6 (1972), p. 13.

[53]Alfred T. DeMaria, Dale Tarnowieski, and Richard Gurman, *Manager Unions* (New York: American Management Association, 1972), pp. 1–2.

[54]E. V. Wahn, "Collective Bargaining Rights of Managerial Employees in the United States and Canada," *Labor Law Journal* 27 (June 1976), pp. 343–344.

[55]DeMaria, "Is This the Decade?" pp. 13–16.

[56]Jack Golodner, "Professionals Go Unions," *American Federationist* 80 (October 1973), pp. 6–8.

[57]Dennis Chamot, "Scientists and Unions: The New Reality," *American Federationist* 81 (September 1974), pp. 8–12; Charles J. Coleman and Jane A. Rose, "Bank Unionization: States and Prospects," *Monthly Labor Review* 98 (October 1975), pp. 38–41.

[58]Eileen Hoffman, *Unionization of Professional Societies* (New York: Conference Board, 1976), p. i.

[59]Frances Bairston and Leonard Sayles, "Bargaining over Work Standards by Professional Unions," in Gerald Somers, ed., *Collective Bargaining and Productivity* (Madison, Wis.: Industrial Relations Research Association, 1975), pp. 110–118.

Chapter 2

Evolution of Labor-Management Relationships

"**The history of the trade union movement has shown that when organized workers were a very, very tiny percentage of the work force, they still accomplished and did things that were important for the entire work force.**"

George Meany

Labor has played a most prominent role throughout American history. Yet organized labor—*employees joining a somewhat formal, continuing organization for collective bargaining purposes—is a relatively new phenomenon, beginning after the Civil War. Consequently, little attention will be given to the period preceding the Civil War, and this chapter will focus mainly on three time periods: 1869 to World War I (1917-1918), World War I to World War II (1941-1945), and World War II to the present.*

The history of organized labor in the United States is viewed through two interrelated dimensions. Relationships between labor and management are discussed to determine how various strategies and outcomes have been influenced over time. And significant labor organizations which have attempted to influence labor-management relationships in the United States are examined.

The philosophy of the current major organization of unions, the American Federation of Labor–Congress of Industrial Organizations (AFL-CIO), has been influenced by four major labor organizations: the Knights of Labor (KOL), the Industrial Workers of the World (IWW), the American Federation of Labor (AFL) under the leadership of Samuel Gompers, and the Congress of Industrial Organizations (CIO). These organizations' philosophies and strategies have provided important lessons, both negative and positive, to the AFL-CIO. The reader can compare the relative effectiveness and differences of the labor organizations discussed in this chapter along the following criteria for success:

☐ The structural and financial stability of the union organization.

☐ The extent to which the union organization created an abrupt rupture in existing labor-management relationships or the established political system. Of particular importance is the extent to which each labor organization accepted the wage system, in which employees work for management and are paid for their services.

☐ Supportive or disruptive features of the broader social environment (such as legislation, media, and public opinion).

☐ The identification of the union organization's leaders with union members and the extent to which the union's goals appeal to membership interests.

This chapter emphasizes some of the more representative episodes and generalizations of labor history, which help to explain the roots of current labor-management relationships and which can be applied to other historical observations discussed throughout the book.

Organized Labor before 1869

The first signs of spontaneous industrial organization in America were employee *guilds* based on the English pattern—joint associations of employers and craftspeople who were either independent or directly employed. In 1648, the Boston coopers and shoemakers formed a joint employer-employee guild in order to enforce manufacturing standards, thereby hoping to reserve or protect jobs, to check competition from the newly arrived immigrants, however competent they might be.

In addition to the guilds, there were also in the incorporated cities of New York and Philadelphia a number of *licensed trades*—occupations regarded as essential to the public welfare, whose members were licensed and regulated by the city corporations. These trades, like the guilds, represented employer-employee concerns over the possibilities of outside competition, which they felt would result in inferior goods.[1]

Thus, unions as we know them today were nonexistent before 1800; their historical counterparts, guilds and trades, pressed for concerns which typically benefited employees and employers alike. The first exception occurred in 1768 in Philadelphia when printers struck to maintain their existing wages. The strike was settled in the employees' favor, and the "union" went out of existence shortly after achieving its goal.[2] Employee-oriented strikes or job actions were largely unknown in the period 1800–1818 since only two industries (shoemaking and printing) had the semblance of collective bargaining. The Philadelphia cordwainers' (shoemakers') strike in 1806 (discussed in Chapter 3) was an exception. For the most part, there were only a few scattered strikes, usually over wages, and no general labor philosophy or movement existed in the United States.

In 1820, employers, attempting to counter the effects of an economic depression and domestic as well as foreign competition, sought cheaper sources of labor. For example, the use of prisoners as a labor source was fairly common by 1825. The employers' actions were met by several employee strikes, although there was no attempt to extend the strikes beyond the immediate employees involved. Attempts to organize local employees into a more permanent, broader-based organization resulted in a very loose structure, one which had no administrative or disciplinary controls over the actions of local members.[3]

While this historical time period appears to offer few insights into an understanding of contemporary unions, at least two general events which occurred between 1850 and 1869 had a significant impact on the growth of organized labor. The Civil War refined and encouraged mass production techniques, which, in turn, reduced the previous necessity for skilled craftspeople. Mass production meant a concentration of a new and large source of semiskilled and unskilled employees under one factory roof—a situation which held attractions for organized labor.

A second factor was the use of employer *scapegoating*—blaming violent incidents on outside, possibly foreign, "labor agitators." For example, much media attention was given to the Molly Maguires, Irish immigrants who engaged in violence against the railroad and coal mining operators beginning in the 1860s. The rising threat of organized labor's opposition to employer activities was met by the media, which attributed many atrocious deeds—including assassinations—to the Molly Maguires. There is no written evidence (such as letters or minutes of meetings) which proves that the Molly Maguires actually existed as an organization, much less that they were allied with organized labor. However, the point was clear; attempts by employees to engage in collective bargaining during this time were identified with violent, anti-American values and actions.[4]

Thus, the early history of organized labor in the United States taught employers two lessons:

1. Employees appeared to become increasingly concerned with working conditions as technology allowed products formerly made by craftspersons to be mass produced.
2. Employers learned that they might have to rely on outside forces such as the government and the media to quell employee unrest.

Both of these factors are further discussed in the subsequent sections on labor history.

1869 to World War I

The period 1869 to World War I saw the formation of three national labor organizations: the Knights of Labor (Knights or KOL), the American Federation of Labor (AFL) under Samuel Gompers, and the Industrial Workers of the World (IWW). Each of these organizations will be discussed in terms of its orientations and goals, organizational structure, and strategies and tactics. Reasons suggested for the demise of the KOL and the IWW and other items discussed apply to the criteria for labor organization's success listed on page 31. Three prominent labor episodes of this period are also discussed: the drive for an eight-hour work day (including the Haymarket Riot of 1886), the Homestead strike (1892), and the Pullman strike (1894).

The Knights of Labor

Goals and Organization of the Knights The Knights of Labor was founded by Uriah S. Stephens as a secret society in 1869. Secrecy was maintained until 1882 so that the members would not be discharged by their employers for participating in a labor organization.

There are two major reasons for discussing the Knights. It represented a union national in scope, larger than any previous union in American history. In the early 1880s, it had a steady growth, reaching over 100,000 members in 1885. Between 1885 and 1886, the organization's membership increased sharply to 700,000. The Knights had achieved more power, prestige, and notoriety than any other previous labor organization.[5] The KOL's goals and strategies also deserve consideration since both contributed to its demise as an effective organization. In short, the Knights served as an important negative lesson to the American Federation of Labor and more contemporary labor organizations in establishing and achieving their objectives.

The Knights strongly objected to the method of industrial organization and operation which began during the Civil War. This view led them to establish two major interrelated goals:

1. Change the existing labor-management relationships so that the depersonalized and specialized aspects of mass production can be avoided.
2. Attain moral betterment for employees and society.

The KOL's goals can best be grasped through the views of Terence V. Powderly, its leader and chief spokesman from 1879 to 1883. Mr. Powderly felt that mass production reduced the employees' feelings of pride and personal accomplishment.[6] In previous times, employees could be satisfied with their craftsmanship, a sense of skilled accomplishment in fashioning quality products from beginning to end. Mass production created several specialized employee classifications, each contributing to the completed product. Powderly placed this situation in perspective by considering the shoemaker situation:

The man who was called a shoemaker thirty years ago made shoes; the man who claims to be a shoemaker today makes only part of a shoe. What was once a trade in itself is a multiplicity of trades. Once there were shoemakers, now we have Beaters, Binders, Bottomers, Buffers, Burnishers, Channellers, Crimpers, Cutters, Dressers, Edge Setters . . . and several other workers at the shoe trade, and they all consider themselves shoemakers.[7]

Powderly also believed that bankers and owners of gold were the villains of the industrial society. He felt that these individuals influenced Congress to pass legislation beneficial to their financial interests during the Civil War:

They diminished the volume of currency; reduced the price of labor and property; they demanded gold bonds for their almost worthless paper, and changed the terms of contracts to give themselves gold instead of currency. Everything that entered into consumption in the poor man's home was heavily taxed in order to pay for gold. Monopolies were born and nourished, and the Congress of the United States gave them millions of acres of the nation's lands.[8]

The Knights believed that changing the existing industrial and societal system would help accomplish their second goal, moral betterment and increased dignity for their members. Powderly claimed that members must place their concerns on a "higher" ground than material working conditions, as these physical effects were but stepping stones to "a higher cause, of a nobler nature . . . the more exalted and divine nature of man, his high and noble capabilities for good."[9] The leadership of the KOL was continually concerned that its members would devote too much attention to improving working conditions, a situation which would cheapen their goal of moral betterment—to make every man his own master.[10]

The moralistic overtones of the Knights guided their membership policies, organization structure, and strategies and tactics. Since moral betterment affected all members of society, the Knights encouraged people of all callings to join their organization except professional gamblers, stockbrokers, lawyers, bankers, and those who lived in whole or in part by the sale or manufacture of intoxicating liquors.[11] Employers were also encouraged to join the KOL, the rationale being that they along with employees were being duped by financiers and once educated to this fact would join hands with the employees in improving society.

The Knights had three organizational units: local assemblies, district assemblies, and an executive board.

☐ *Local assemblies,* the basic unit in the KOL, were comprised of at least ten members and were of two types: *trade* assemblies (membership limited to employees in a particular craft) and *mixed* assemblies (members of several trades and even employers). The local assembly had two functions: to educate its members on KOL's principles and to serve as the members' bargaining agent. In 1886, the Knights claimed 1,100 local assemblies.

☐ *District assemblies* were geographical units comprised of five or more local assemblies. Each district assembly elected delegates to the annual KOL convention or General Assembly, which was the KOL's supreme authority and which elected the General Executive Board.[12] The General Assembly also legislated policy and resolved all disputes brought before it.

☐ The *General Executive Board* consisted of the national officers, including the highest position in the Knights, the Grand Master Workman. The General Executive Board had a great deal of power and served important trouble-shooting functions in attempting to restrain strikes or conclude job actions already begun.

In summary, the Knights had two major organizational characteristics: organizational units based on vague geographical limits instead of employee classifications and centralized authority resting at the top level (General Executive Board). As will be seen later in this section, the structure of the KOL differed dramatically from that of the AFL.

Strategies to Accomplish the Knights' Goals The Knights used at least four strategies to accomplish their goals. *Political action* was viewed as

Leading Management
Figures

George W. Pullman

John D. Rockefeller

Andrew Carnegie

Jay Gould

Pullman (Source: Reproduced from the collection of the Library of Congress.) Rockefeller (Source: Courtesy of the Bettmann Archive.) Carnegie (Source: Courtesy of the Bettmann Archive.) Gould (Source: Courtesy of the Bettmann Archive.)

John L. Lewis

Terence V. Powderly

Eugene V. Debs

Samuel Gompers

Lewis (Source: Courtesy of the AFL-CIO.) Powderly (Source: Reproduced from the collection of the Library of Congress.) Debs (Source: Reproduced from the collection of the Library of Congress.) Gompers (Source: Reproduced from the collection of the Library of Congress.)

important, particularly since the Knights felt that previous legislation had led society down the wrong road. The Knights believed that politicians were motivated by self-interest and therefore required careful watching. However, the Knights approached this strategy through the existing political system; there was no effort to form an independent political party. The KOL did actively lobby against importation of foreign labor and for appropriations to public school systems.

A second strategy was the *encouragement of producer and consumer cooperatives.* Unlike the Socialists, the Knights did not want the cooperatives to be owned by the state. Instead, current employees would save enough from their wages to either purchase the operation or establish a new cooperative. Since factories would be owned by the employees, conflict between labor and capital would cease.[13] Cooperatives would also enable the employees to become their own masters; they would have a voice in decision making, including the determination of a fair distribution of profits.

The Knights' leadership believed cooperatives would affect the established wage-profits system most directly; yet they made little attempt to establish a cooperative or to financially aid approximately a hundred cooperatives established at the local or district level during the mid-1880s. Most of the cooperatives failed because of "inefficient managers, squabbles among shareholders, lack of capital, and injudicious borrowing of money at high rates of interest."[14]

The KOL pursued a third strategy when it *actively avoided the use of strikes* to obtain its goals. The Knights' leadership often actively discouraged strikes and, in some cases, demoralized strikers with their statements.[15] Some leaders viewed strikes as a last resort, feeling they would distract members from the major goal of moral betterment and lessen the common interests of employers and employees. Indeed, the General Executive Board set up a complicated procedure that local assemblies had to follow before they could obtain strike funds.[16] Powderly believed that no employees should be able to enter a strike which would result in other employees losing their jobs; therefore, procedure was needed to insure that every employee possibly affected by a strike would have a voice in the strike decision.[17] Yet the red tape involved in obtaining strike funds caused a great amount of dissension between the KOL leaders and members. Local assemblies that conducted strikes were left on their own financially, and the members bitterly resented the lack of support from the board.[18] It became common for the local assembly to conduct strikes without support from the Executive Board—in 1886, there were at least 538 local assemblies participating in either a strike or boycott of an uncooperative employer's products.

The Knights' leadership preferred a fourth strategy to the strike; namely, *education* of the members and citizens as to the evils of the existing industrial system as well as the Knights' goals for societal improvement. Usually the leaders would meet with members of local assemblies in private sessions to inform them of the organization's goals and objectives. The emphasis on education instead of job action efforts (strikes and boycotts) will be further discussed in the next section.

Reasons for the Knights' Failure and Demise Despite tremendous growth, the KOL experienced a sudden demise. One reason for its growth must be the successful strike taken by the local assemblies against Jay Gould's railroads in 1885, in which the Knights showed the public that an aggressive, well-disciplined group could take on one of the most powerful financiers and win. Yet this explanation might be overstated, particularly since neither the Knights nor the newspapers publicized the events. Another reason for the KOL's growth is its identification with the eight-hour work day, an issue which was important to the nation's work force.[19]

Perhaps more important to the subsequent development of labor organizations are the reasons for the Knights' failure and demise.

Faulty assumptions in the KOL's orientation. The Knights were reform oriented, interested in changing existing aspects of the society. With the advantages of hindsight, it becomes clear that the KOL erred in assuming that technological advancement could be halted and possibly reversed. The KOL also overestimated the extent to which employers and employees shared common interests. While there are some common grounds, each group is motivated by self-interest. Employers are concerned about increased efficiency and profitability of the operation, while employees are concerned about job security and improvement of working conditions.

The organization's third faulty assumption was that all categories of employees would have identical interests. The KOL was ahead of its time in its attempt to organize unskilled employees—an effort eventually and successfully accomplished by the Congress of Industrial Organizations (CIO) in the late 1930s. However, as further discussed in Chapter 10, employees do not all have the same interests, particularly if they have different skills and work classifications. The *one big union* approach (enrolling nearly anyone who expressed an interest in the Knights) was further complicated by many immigrant members whose differences in race, language, and religion presented barriers.[20]

A lack of protective or supportive legislation governing the rights of employees to join unions and engage in collective bargaining. This point will be further discussed in the next chapter. Suffice it to say that the Knights as well as other labor organizations before 1935 did not have the full force of the law on their side.

Inability of the KOL's leadership (particularly Powderly) to identify with members' goals. The Knights insisted upon adopting a middle-class program for the American labor force, which they refused to contemplate in industrial, working-class terms. Many of the members showed little, if any, interest in the Knights after they joined. Almost all local assembly meetings required the members to dress up after a day's work to engage in intellectual discourse. In essence, the members had nothing to do except "ceremonialize, play politics, and study."[21] Mr. Powderly stressed reform rather than identification with the membership. He did not devote full efforts to the labor movement or to understanding members' needs. Much of his detached attitude was due to his somewhat egotistical assessment of his position in the union. He once replied to lower-level KOL officials who requested his meeting with KOL members:

I will talk at no picnics. . . . When I speak on the labor question I want the individual attention of my hearers and I want that attention for at least two hours and in that two hours I can only epitomize. At a picnic where . . . the girls as well as the boys swill beer I cannot talk at all.[22]

The preference for intellectual deliberation over immediate, gut-level response is perhaps best viewed through Powderly's approach to the eight-hour day movement.

The Eight-Hour Day Movement and the Haymarket Riot

One of the more important reforms desired by many employees in the late 1800s was reducing the prevalent ten-hour work day to eight hours. Samuel Gompers, who was a Knights member and an official of other labor organizations (Federation of Organized Trades and Cigar Makers' Union), pressed Powderly to support a nationwide general strike (May 1, 1886) for the eight-hour work day. Powderly was receptive to the eight-hour day, as it would give employees more leisure time to pursue intellectual activities. However, he did not join with Gompers since he did not believe the length of the work day was the major problem: "To talk of reducing the hours of labor without reducing the power of machinery is a waste of energy."[23]

Supporters of the eight-hour day believed that this practice, if instituted, would result in more people working, thereby reducing the unemployment problem. On May 3, 1886, some workers striking over this issue in Chicago became involved in a skirmish with the police, with at least four strikers being killed. A leader of this dispute published an inflammatory circular urging "Revenge!" and "Workingmen to Arms!" The circular also indicated that a mass rally would be held the next day at Haymarket Square in Chicago. The stage was set for an event which virtually eliminated the effectiveness of the KOL.

On May 4, 1886, approximately three thousand people attended the scheduled meeting, a meeting that began peacefully, for the police who monitored the meeting were ordered by their chief to return to the station.

A mass rally by strikers supporting the eight-hour day movement began peacefully but ended in violence and death in Chicago's Haymarket Square.

Source: Reproduced from the collection of the Library of Congress.

However, Police Captain Bonfield, whom the governor of Illinois later charged as being responsible for the incident, subsequently ordered the police back to the meeting. During a speech a bomb was thrown into the gathering of police, killing seven and wounding sixty. What happened next is uncertain. The *Chicago Tribune* reported that "anarchists and rioters poured in a shower of bullets before the first action of the police was taken."[24] Yet another report in the same article stated the police opened fire on the crowd immediately after the bomb exploded. Regardless of the order of events, the police did shoot into the crowd, killing several and wounding two hundred.

Eight individuals allegedly responsible for the incident were arrested. Four of the eight were hanged, one committed suicide in prison, and three were eventually pardoned by the governor of Illinois after serving some of their sentence. Their trial was at best shoddy; for example, the hand-picked jury included a relative of one of the bombing victims.[25] The trial never did establish who threw the bomb; however, the accused were judged guilty by the *Chicago Tribune* before the trial took place. More specifically, the paper stressed that the "mob" was led by "two wiry whiskered foreigners,"[26] who were "Nihilistic Agitators."[27]

The Knights were not directly labeled in the immediate press accounts of the strike or in the subsequent series of unsuccessful strikes over the eight-hour day which involved nearly 340,000 employees. However, the strikes contributed to the organization's demise for at least two paradoxical reasons. A substantial body of public opinion labeled the Knights as being involved in the strikes. Yet many of the Knights' members criticized the leadership for not participating enough in the related events during and after Haymarket.[28] Indeed, Powderly strongly discouraged strikes over the eight-hour day, believing instead that members should write essays on the subject. Thus, the Haymarket Riot dramatically reflected the split between the KOL and the newly-formed American Federation of Labor, under Gompers, an organization which was to flourish and endure.

The Emergence of the American Federation of Labor

Origin and Goals of the AFL The AFL, an outgrowth of the Federation of Organized Trades and Labor Unions of the United States and Canada, was formed in 1886 after some of its member unions (most notably the Cigar Makers) were expelled from the Knights.[29] As previously mentioned, Samuel Gompers, a major founder of the AFL, was a member of the Knights but became disenchanted with the leadership's long-range social reform philosophy. Gompers was also upset about KOL activities involving the cigar makers—most notably, KOL's raiding of its members and supplying strikebreakers when the cigar makers struck firms.

He met with the Knights in December 1886 to discuss these problems, but the meeting did not resolve the situation. Indeed, Gompers became incensed when a pamphlet was circulated among KOL representatives. The pamphlet attacked Gompers personally by indicating "the General Executive Board has never had the pleasure of seeing Mr. Gompers sober."[30] Also, in retrospect, KOL leaders blundered when they concentrated on influencing craft employees, a move which resulted in bitter reactions from the trade unions. The Knights would have been better off (and still consistent with their goals) if they had devoted more attention to the unskilled employees where the trades did not have any argument.[31]

It is impossible to discuss the AFL apart from Gompers, since "in the early years, the A. F. of L. existed only in the person of Gompers and in the annual conventions."[32] With the exception of 1895, Gompers was president of the AFL from its founding in 1886 until his death in 1924. Therefore, much of the discussion of the goals, strategies, and organization of the AFL will be from the perspective of Gompers, a point of view that relates strongly to the current thinking of organized labor; there has been relatively little change in orientation, strategies, and organization since the time of Gompers.

Gompers placed little emphasis on intellectual betterment, and he scorned other union leaders' pretensions to show labor union members the course of action they should pursue.[33] He criticized the KOL as representing "a hodge-podge with no basis for solidarity with the exception of a comparatively few trade assemblies."[34] Gompers believed that the goals and organization of the AFL should flow directly and naturally from the members' needs, not from the pronouncements of top leaders who try to structure the movement on their artificial view of what ought to be:

History here and elsewhere likewise discloses the indisputable fact that whenever revolutionary policies were pursued, wherever passion supplanted reason and good judgment, wherever progressive measures were displaced by destructive methods, invariably destitution, suffering, ruin and chaos followed in their wake; better things to come were delayed and the hope of a brighter day was dimmed, if not destroyed.[35]

The AFL was strongly suspicious of any rival system which did not accept the existing industrial system, capitalism, although this attitude was somewhat blurred in the first ten years of its operation. Gompers had been a socialist in his early years and was initially sympathetic to socialism's cause. For example, he wrote in 1889 that the continuing class conflict "cannot cease until the laborers shall be the capitalists, i.e., the capitalists shall be the laborers. In other words they shall be one and the same."[36]

However, any enthusiasm Gompers may have had for socialistic principles dampened over the years and culminated in a bitter hatred.[37] In 1913, he stated before a congressional committee:

Without egotism and I hope very little of vanity, I will say I came to the conclusion many years ago that it is our duty to live our lives as workers in the society in which we live, and not to work for the downfall or destruction, or the overthrow of that society, but for its fuller development and evolution.[38]

Gompers viewed the socialist philosophy as economically unsound, socially wrong, and practically impossible to apply in terms of industrial realities. He maintained that the "truth" or essence of labor unions should be measured in terms of their economic accomplishments.

Thus, the AFL's major if not sole goal was to *improve the material conditions of members through the existing capitalistic system.* This goal was attacked by the critics of the AFL as representing pure and simple unionism. Gompers embraced this intended insult; indeed, he seemed to devote most of his attention to insuring that the AFL's "pure and simple" approach to collective bargaining successfully differentiated itself from other labor organizations.

There were two major objectives of *pure and simple unionism.* The primary objective was economic betterment of the organization's members:

Economic betterment—today, tomorrow, in home and shop, was the foundation upon which trade unions have been built. Economic power

is the base upon which may be developed power in other fields. It is the foundation of organized society. Whoever or whatever controls economic power directs and shapes development for the group or the nation.[39]

Gompers also stressed a second objective of pure and simple unionism—the enhancement of the capitalistic system, which can benefit both groups. Workers can obtain more only if capitalism continues to flourish. Without capitalism neither employees nor employers receive revenues. The AFL therefore believed labor and management had a certain community of interests.

Trade unionism became closely interwoven with the institutional pattern of capitalism. Unions obtained popularity and strength by bending capitalism to the short run interests of the workers.[40]

Unlike Powderly, Gompers did not interpret the community of interests to represent complete employer-employee agreement on all issues. He realized that major differences of opinion would occur over the distribution of revenues and that employees would probably have to pressure employers in order to receive their fair share.

Strategies and Organization of the AFL This realization prompted the AFL to rely on one of its three major tactics—the *strike.* Unlike the Knights, Gompers believed the strike was a viable collective bargaining alternative:

A workman must convince his employer that he is entitled to an advance in wages. . . .

Why should the wage-earner work for less than living wages, which he would have to do if he could not strike? The worker is expected to continue to work at whatever wages his employer is willing to give in order to save the public from inconvenience.[41]

The second strategy of the AFL was *involvement in the political arena.* Early evidence of the AFL's political emphasis was its desire for the government to restrict the importation of Chinese settlers.[42] Until 1906, however, the AFL's leaders refused to become directly involved with political campaigns, although members were urged to campaign and contribute funds. Also, there were AFL delegates to the Republican and Democratic conventions in 1908 and 1912.[43]

Lobbying efforts of the AFL intensified when the organization's headquarters was moved to Washington, D.C., in 1897. Gompers became an aggressive lobbyist and attached himself to the political party in power.

His first real political connections were with the Republicans, although he supported Democratic candidates from 1908 to 1920.[44] From the AFL's inception until World War I there was no real attempt to create keen political awareness among the membership or to increase its political strength by joining with other self-interest groups.[45] Gompers preferred that any political efforts be spent on lobbying for change through existing political parties, not on establishing an independent third party. In essence, he did not want trade union activity playing second fiddle to the political efforts which would be necessary in establishing a third political party. His preferred alternative was to reward politicians who favored organized labor's concerns and punish the political enemies of organized labor. This alternative was approached by either mobilizing votes for the current "friends" or withholding political support from the existing "enemies." Gompers was also concerned that if a third political party were established, it would fall into the socialists' control.[46]

The third AFL tactic was *to secure increased status for organized labor and collective bargaining*. Gompers devoted much attention to the National Civic Foundation, formed in 1899 to promote industrial peace through collective bargaining. This organization, comprised of prominent labor, management, and political officials, attempted to guide public opinion toward the positive aspects of collective bargaining. However, at least one observer of industrial relations has questioned the success of this tactic, believing that "its rhetoric surpassed its performance."[47]

The AFL's organizational structure was based on two related principles: *exclusive jurisdiction* and *decentralized authority*. The AFL avoided the concept of "one big union" organization—which proved to be ineffective for the KOL—and insisted on the principle of exclusive jurisdiction. This principle rested on the twofold observation that (a) each craft or trade had unique working conditions and job interests and (b) combining members of different trades into one organization would jeopardize those interests and cause unnecessary dissension. The AFL thus believed in one union representing a particular craft; for example, separate unions would represent the carpenters, painters, and cigar makers.

Gompers also strongly believed the AFL was a voluntary organization held together by the mutual self-interests of members. Unlike Powderly, who believed that centralized authority was necessary to achieve the Knights' objectives, Gompers viewed the central AFL as a "rope of sand," dependent entirely on the acceptance of its members. Thus, the real authority rested with various national unions and their member locals. As will be further discussed in Chapter 5, these principles continue to influence contemporary union organizations.

The organizational activity as well as the organizational structure of the AFL must be considered. Gompers was a most active union organizer; he claimed to have helped in organizing twenty-eight unions representing different crafts, such as painters, paper makers, firefighters, and post office clerks.[48] Much of this effort was due to Gompers' view of himself as "one of the boys"—he took pride in his ability to socialize with the members on their own terms.

In spite of Gompers' efforts, the AFL's early growth was not spectacular. Its original membership of 150,000 had increased to only 250,000 six years later. The initial slow growth was due to the counterattack of industry (discussed in the section on World War I to World War II), the generally repressive attitude of the government and the courts, and the difficulties raised by the depression of 1893. Yet Gompers could view these modest membership gains as a tribute to the AFL's powers of "stability and permanency."[49]

From its formation until World War I, the AFL was directly or indirectly involved in three prominent events: the Homestead and Pullman incidents and the formation and demise of the Industrial Workers of the World (IWW).

The Homestead Incident

The Carnegie Steel Works, located in Homestead, Pennsylvania, was ironically the scene of one of the more violent episodes in labor history. The founder of these operations, Andrew Carnegie, was a renowned philanthropist who gave every indication of being receptive to organized labor. In one article, written before the Homestead incident, he stated that a strike or a lockout was a "ridiculous affair" since it only represented a test of strength instead of determining what was "fair and just."[50] Carnegie also believed that labor-management problems would occur in large firms run by salaried managers instead of owners, because the former group had no permanent interest in the desires of the workingmen.[51]

Carnegie's remarks proved prophetic in the Homestead incident of July 6, 1892. Although many have labeled the incident a strike, one labor historian has noted that no strike vote was ever taken by the membership,[52] and the employer prohibited the employees from working. During negotiation between the mill and the Amalgamated Association of Iron, Steel, and Tin Workers (an affiliate of the AFL), a fifteen-foot-high solid board fence, topped with barbed wire, was constructed around the building. Andrew Carnegie was vacationing in Scotland during negotiations and had delegated these duties to a management official named Henry Clay Frick. The union labeled the structure around the steel mill "Fort Frick." Members were also undoubtedly aware that Frick was negotiating with Pinkerton detectives while labor-management negotiations were being conducted. Frick intended to use Pinkerton detectives inside the facility to protect the company's property and as strikebreakers.

On June 30, 1892, the company made its last offer, which represented a substantial reduction of previous wages,[53] and locked out its four thousand employees. Workmen then began an around the clock surveil-

Part 1/Recognition of the Rights and Responsibilities of Unions and Management

The bloody confrontation between Pinkerton agents and employees of the Carnegie Steel Works in Homestead, Pennsylvania, in 1892 was one of the most violent in labor history and actually set back the cause of unions in the steel industry.

Source: Courtesy of the AFL-CIO.

lance of the plant. One newspaper account indicated, "The line of pickets covers the river, roads, and railways so tightly that no stranger can enter the town without being known to the strikers."[54] On the morning of July 5, three hundred Pinkertons gathered at Ashtabula, Ohio, and proceeded by rail to Youngstown, Ohio. They then traveled up the Monongahela River by barge. On July 6, word had reached the townspeople that the Pinkertons would be entering the plant from the river. Six thousand people lined the river banks at 2:00 A.M., and employees prepared two small cannons, one on each side of the river, to be used on the Pinkertons.[55]

The Pinkertons attempted to land by the company's beach at 5:00 A.M.;

shots were exchanged, and three Pinkertons were killed. Shooting by both sides continued for twelve hours, with an additional seven townspeople being killed and fifty wounded. The Pinkertons surrendered to the townspeople and were forced to run a bloody gauntlet before being locked up for their protection. The townspeople had taken the weapons from the Pinkertons, a situation which resulted in 8,700 National Guard militiamen being sent to secure the town. There were few further incidents, particularly since union leaders believed the troops would discourage further attempts by Pinkertons or strikebreakers.[56] The incident ended for all purposes some five months later (November 20, 1892) when the Amalgamated lifted its prohibition against returning to work.

Homestead has been labeled the Waterloo of unions in the steel industry. National membership in the Amalgamated dropped from 24,000 in 1892 to 8,000 in 1894. On the local level, only 800 of the original Homestead employees were reinstated. Carnegie's mills showed a dramatic increase in profits when the union was eliminated,[57] a message that must have encouraged other employers to take an anti-union stance.

While Homestead represented a victory for management, the AFL and organized labor did benefit to some extent from the situation. First, Gompers demonstrated to existing and potential union members his very real concern about the Homestead situation.[58] The funds contributed by the AFL to help defray the workers' legal expenses also demonstrated that the AFL was interested in helping its member unions in a material sense.[59] Finally, the Homestead situation received more sympathetic newspaper accounts than those describing the Haymarket Riot. The press did charge Carnegie with provoking the situation. For example, the *Chicago Tribune* criticized the company's use of Pinkertons strongly and contended that Carnegie's company as well as any large industrial organization "has duties and obligations toward society which it must not forget, and not the least of them is to do all in its power, and make all of the concessions it can, to preserve civil and industrial peace."[60] At a minimum, the press could not continually criticize the involved union or employees in this incident, especially since no individual was found guilty of participating in the incident.

The Pullman Strike

Strikes were not uncommon in the railroad industry; for example, the Great Upheaval of 1877 involved independent railroad employee associations protesting wage cuts. It was a bitter and violent confrontation in which more than a hundred employees were killed and several hundred were badly wounded.[61]

Yet the Pullman strike of 1894 assumes significance because of the principal personalities involved (Eugene Debs and George Pullman) and an organization (the American Railway Union or ARU) which had the potential to challenge the AFL for union members. It also approached being the only revolutionary strike in the United States; it became a nationwide strike in one industry and came near to involving all industries. [62]

As a result of the 1893 depression, the Pullman Company laid off 3,000 of its 5,800 employees and cut wages 25 to 40 percent. Both actions were important since they occurred in the milieu of George Pullman's company town. This town represented a social, paternalistic experiment by the owner of the Pullman Palace Car Company. The company owned all of the houses, buildings, and services in the town; employees were not allowed to own their own homes. [63] Pullman did not correspondingly reduce rents and charges for other services; thus the wage cuts resulted in some employees having a net two-week pay of $1 to $6 during the winter of 1893–94.

This situation generated much hostility among employees, many of whom were members of the American Railway Union (ARU), formed in 1893. The ARU was completely independent from the AFL; indeed, it competed for members with the AFL-affiliated railway brotherhoods. The ARU accepted any white employee, regardless of specific job classification, so that railroad employees could present a unified front to the railroad companies. [64] It was attractive to many employees because employers previously had been able to create dissension among the different craft unions by playing one off against the other in wage negotiations.

The ARU's local unions had sole authority to call a strike, and the Pullman strike began on May 11, 1894. Debs, the union leader, informed the strikers that the strike should represent a protest against philosophical issues instead of mere material betterment: "The paternalism of Pullman is the same as the interest of a slave holder in his human chattels. You are striking to avert slavery and degradation."[65]

At first the strikers followed Debs' orders not to damage railroad property. The ARU instead adopted a strategy of not operating any train which included a Pullman sleeping car—the common practice was to cut these cars from the train and move them to the side tracks. If any employee was discharged for this action, then the entire crew would quit, leaving the train immobilized. This tactic, employed in twenty-seven states and territories, was intended to make railroad carriers put pressure on Pullman to agree with ARU's bargaining position.

However, the railroad employers rallied behind Pullman and countered the union's strategy by hiring strikebreakers. They also decided to include federal mail on nearly every train and were able to obtain an injunction on July 2 (subsequently upheld by the Supreme Court) to prevent any employee from interfering with the delivery of the mail. Employees could no longer engage in their strike strategy of rendering the trains inoperative. Some sixteen thousand troops, dispatched by President Cleveland to enforce the injunction, either delivered the mail and operated the trains or protected strikebreakers so that food and other perishable items could be delivered throughout the country.

The strike then took a particularly ugly turn; employees burned at least seven hundred railroad cars in Chicago on July 7, 1894. Interestingly, management was also criticized for this incident, at the least for failing to take minimum security measures such as guarding or locking the railroad cars. At a maximum, some management officials may have provoked the incident to receive additional support from the government. This second possibility is suggested because all of the burnt cars were old (the more expensive Pullman cars were not on the property), and very few of the cars were loaded with any product.[66]

The resulting negative public opinion and increased action by the federal troops forced Debs to seek Gompers' cooperation. Debs wanted Gompers to call a national strike to enforce Debs' last offer, which was simply management's reinstatement of the striking employees. Gompers refused to support Debs, contending that he did not have authority to call a general strike. Gompers also believed that the proposed settlement would, in effect, admit to the public that the ARU had failed to win material benefits for its members. Much of Gompers' reluctance was due to his view of Debs as being "a leader of irregular movements and lost causes."[67] However, Gompers' inaction might have also been due to his desire to eliminate a potential rival to the AFL and bolster his reputation in the business community.

Debs was eventually convicted and sentenced under the Sherman Antitrust Act of 1890; and the ARU, which had grown to 150,000 members in one year, quickly faded from existence. Organized labor did learn an important lesson from this strike; namely, it would be difficult to alter the existing system against the wishes of a persistent, if not exceptionally stubborn, owner (Pullman),[68] the federal government (troops, injunctions, legislation), the AFL (which supported this system), and negative public opinion (fueled by exaggerated and dramatic newspaper articles).[69]

The Rise and Fall of the IWW

The Industrial Workers of the World (IWW) was formed as an alternative to the AFL on June 27, 1905. "Big Bill" Haywood, initial organizer of the IWW, originated the organization's goals in calling the convention of 209 delegates to order with the following remarks:

Fellow Workers . . . We are here to confederate the workers of this country into a working class movement that shall have for its purpose the emancipation of the working class from the slave bondage of Capitalism. . . . The aims and objects of this organization should be to put the working class in possession of the economic power, the means of life, in control of the machinery of production and distribution without regard to capitalist masters.[70]

The initial goal of the IWW was to overthrow the existing capitalistic system by any means, since it felt that employers and employees had nothing in common. The IWW and the Knights agreed on one point: the existing wage and profit system had to be changed. The Knights, however, stressed that employees and employers had common interests and that change must be peaceful and gradual. The IWW, on the other hand, had no reservations about using any method which would result in the *quick destruction of capitalism.*

The IWW also wanted to remove any societal aspect or group which supported capitalism. This approach placed the IWW into direct opposition with the AFL. The IWW regarded the AFL as an "extension of the capitalist class"[71] since it advocated "pure and simple unionism," which was dependent on capitalism. Haywood believed that Gompers had sold out the ARU when he had not supported Debs in the Pullman strike, and he viewed Gompers as an arrogant, power-hungry leader.[72] Thus, the IWW appeared to have two general enemies: capitalism and the AFL, which did not recognize a working class movement or hourly employees as being a class-conscious group apart from the rest of society. An analysis of the IWW reveals that establishing goals can be an easier task than accomplishing them.

The IWW never did establish an effective organization; in fact, its leaders never made up their minds about precisely what kind of organizational structure it should adopt.[73] Most of the IWW officials agreed with Haywood's objective of organizing "every man that earns his livelihood either by his brain or his muscle."[74] But major differences arose over how to organize one big union into an effective organization. Organizational differences were also increased by two factions which stressed different strategies and goals—conservatives and radicals.[75]

The conservative faction stressed the "pure and simple unionism" of the AFL and believed that the IWW should work from within—placing members in the AFL's unions who would gradually teach the AFL members that capitalism is a questionable philosophy to follow. The radical faction adhered more directly to Haywood's philosophy and the IWW constitution's tenet that improving working conditions through collective bargaining would simply make the members "better paid slaves" while misapplying energy needed to work for the quick revolutionary overthrow of capitalism.[76]

In addition to organizational differences, there were at least four reasons for the demise of the IWW which served as negative lessons for contemporary organized labor.

1. **Lack of permanent membership and financial base.** A large proportion of the IWW consisted of itinerants—individuals who were either unemployed or traveled from job to job, particularly in the agriculture, mining, and lumber industries. The transitory nature of IWW members contributed to an unstable financial base. Many IWW leaders

thought the members' dues should not be mandatory; instead, they should be paid out of a voluntary "inner conviction."[77] Apparently, many members did not share this "inner conviction"; for example, in 1907 only 10,000 members out of the total 31,000 members paid any dues. The lack of revenues resulted in meager strike funds, and by 1909 the organization was deeply in debt.

2. **Inability of the IWW to appeal to members' interests.** The IWW did not consider the short-run material interests of its members. Its major emphasis on long-term philosophical goals and its concern with propaganda as a means to achieve these goals failed to demonstrate tangible signs of success on a continuous basis.[78] The average trade unionist, in or outside the IWW, had no desire to help the underdog. Indeed, it was all he could do to look out for himself.[79]

3. **Identification of the IWW with sabotage and violence.** The relationship between the IWW and sabotage and violence was ambiguous. The IWW in 1914 became the only labor organization to ever officially endorse sabotage at its convention.[80] Yet no local, state, or federal authority could ever establish legal proof of any IWW-instigated violence.[81] The IWW often stated that sabotage does not equal destruction of equipment. For example, employees could "sabotage" the company by "malicious obedience" (following the work rules to the letter, thereby creating a slowdown) and by informing customers that the company's product was of inferior quality. However, at least one article in the IWW's paper, the *Industrial Worker*, indicated how emery dust and ground up glass could cause the destruction of machinery.

   Evidence suggests that the IWW's leadership denounced any type of physical violence.[82] Yet there are also some accounts of incidents where IWW members and leaders pledged a "life for a life" or "an eye for an eye."[83] At a minimum, it appears that the IWW did not actively discourage its link with violence, a situation which is amplified in the following reason for the IWW's demise.

4. **Alienation of the news media and government officials.** The newspapers enhanced the IWW's reputation for violence by labeling members as "desperate villains who set fire to wheat fields, drove spikes into sawmill-bound logs, derailed trains, destroyed industrial machinery, and killed policemen."[84] Part of this negative image was enhanced by leaders of IWW factions who would damn each other in the press. The IWW also engaged in several "free speech fights" or soap box speeches in local communities. In many of these speeches, the IWW would shout antisocial comments such as "there is no God."[85]

   The press, never enthusiastic about unions in general, reserved a special hatred for the IWW. One editorial against the IWW stated:

They would be much better dead, for they are absolutely useless in the human economy; they are the waste material of creation and

should be drained off into the sewer of oblivion there to rot in cold obstruction like any other excretement.[86]

The IWW also remained alienated from the government. It did not actively use the existing political system because many of its transient members could not meet voter registration requirements. It also incurred the wrath of the federal government when it refused to support involvement in World War I, proclaiming instead that the war represented a capitalistic plot. The government responded to the IWW's antiwar stance by arresting over a hundred leaders and sentencing most of them to prison terms ranging from five to twenty years. In effect, the IWW went out of existence in 1918, even though the organization remains today with a handful of members.

The onset of World War I found the AFL on questionably firm ground. It had been the first nationally organized labor movement to withstand a severe economic depression, a hostile press, reluctant or hostile employers, and three rival labor organizations (KOL, ARU, and IWW). Yet the AFL had internal pressures from at least three sources: (a) socialists and other related political groups which advocated independent political action and the organization of unskilled, industrial employees;[87] (b) pacifist members who wanted the AFL to remain neutral or take a stand against the war;[88] and (c) member unions which became involved in jurisdictional problems caused by increased specialization and technological change (for example, the plumber was no longer responsible for the complete installation of the water and heating system for a building). Perhaps the most lingering concern of the AFL was that the largest proportion of the organizable labor force, the unskilled, industrial employees, remained essentially outside the ranks of organized labor.[89] This concern and its eventual resolution are discussed more in the following section.

World War I to World War II

The period from World War I to World War II witnessed several important phenomena:

1. The inability of unions, particularly the AFL, to make substantial membership gains in the 1920s.
2. The development of employer strategies to retard union growth.
3. Increased union concern over organizing the unskilled, industrial employees, which led to a bitter rivalry between the AFL and CIO (Congress of Industrial Organizations).

Some union organizing drives in various industries will be cited briefly to give a further indication of the problems and prospects facing organized labor in this period.

Union Organizing after World War I: Problems and Prospects

The AFL overcame its initial reluctance toward participating in World War I and eventually pledged its cooperation when the United States became directly involved in the war. The government, aware of the necessity of uninterrupted production during wartime, responded by attempting to meet labor's concerns. Governmental agreements with the AFL provided for the enforcement of trade union standards in all government contracts; labor representatives were appointed to all government agencies, including the War Labor Board; and Gompers was made a member of the Advisory Commission of the National Council of Defense.[90] In short, organized labor was elevated to a more prominent status than had heretofore been seen in our society. Accordingly, the AFL had a sizable growth in membership during this period (an increase from 2,370,000 members in 1917 to 3,260,000 members in 1919). Legislative interests were also met; a long-time AFL goal of severely restricting immigrants, a strongly competitive labor source, was accomplished.[91]

The rather sharp increase in the cost of living that followed World War I, coupled with the newly recognized status of labor, resulted in an unprecedented number of strikes. For example, the Seattle General Strike occurred in 1919, along with other strikes by actors, New York waterfront employees, and coal miners. The most widespread strike occurred in 1919 in the steel industry, where some 367,000 employees walked off the job in seventy major cities.

The strike actually resulted in a setback to organized labor in the steel industry. Many possible factors contributed to the setback; some were notably similar to those found in the Homestead and Pullman incidents, while others reflected a typical situation unions faced in the 1920s and early 1930s. Of crucial importance were internal union difficulties: an organizing campaign conducted by twenty-four unions instead of one common industrial union, improvised leadership rather than a consistent union approach to the issue, and poor financial resources. U.S. Steel was also successful in withstanding the strike by using strikebreakers and maintaining strong ties with other companies and social institutions, like the press and the pulpit. Thus the strike was terminated without a labor agreement, and it would take another fifteen years before organized labor would make inroads into the steel industry.[92]

To be sure, the steel industry did not reflect all industrial reactions to collective bargaining. However, it does appear that many unions were comparatively powerless to organize employers, such as U.S. Steel, which firmly believed unions were not in the firm's best interests. For example, another 1919 strike almost paralyzed the coal industry when no miners returned to work until President Wilson persuaded them to accept a temporary 14 percent wage increase and submit all other issues to a newly appointed Bituminous Coal Commission. In 1920, the commission awarded increases ranging from 20 to 30 percent; yet this was the last victory for mine workers for several years.[93]

In spite of increased status and militancy, something went wrong for organized labor in the 1920s—the "Golden Twenties" for the majority in the U.S., it was a dreary decade for labor.[94] Between 1920 and 1924, total union membership declined from 5,110,000 to 3,600,000; membership in AFL unions dropped from 4,078,000 to 2,866,000. By 1930, total union membership dropped to 3,400,000, and AFL membership dropped to 2,700,000.[95] This decline was due to at least two major factors: (a) aggressive counteractions by employers; and (b) organized labor's inability to overcome anti-union sentiment among potential union members.[96]

Counteractions by employers. Concerned with the increased status given labor during the war, employers actively engaged in efforts to roll back gains in union membership. Many tactics, which fall into two general categories—*aggressive opposition toward labor unions* and *formation of an acceptable alternative to unions*—were devised in the 1920s and continued in the 1930s to thwart union growth.

Employers actively opposed unions through the open shop movement, which is discussed in more detail in Chapters 4 and 10. The alleged purpose of this movement was to insure that employees had the freedom to determine whether they would choose to join a union. Rationale for this movement was found in its companion name, the American Plan—employers felt that employees should adhere to the traditional American value of "rugged individualism" instead of the "foreign," "subversive," and "corrupt" principles of labor unions.[97]

Many employers equated *open shop*—the right to join or not to join unions—with no unionized employees. Several steps were taken to insure that no employee would be able to join a union. For example, some employers would hire industrial spies to determine which employees had pro-union sentiments.[98] These employees would then be discharged and possibly *blacklisted*—their names given to other employers, who would refuse to hire them. Employer violence against participants in union organizing drives was also a potential strategy to counter unions during this period.[99]

A variation of the open shop or American Plan occurred in the 1930s, with the development of the Mohawk Valley Formula. This approach was used when a union attempted to organize or strike a facility in the community. The Mohawk Valley Formula would then be implemented with the following steps:

Form a citizens' committee in the community, label the union leaders as outside agitators, stir up violence or the fear of violence, have a "state of emergency" declared, organize a back-to-work movement, and finally have the back-to-work employees march into the plant protected by armed police.[100]

Employers also countered unions with a second approach, providing an alternative model to unionism. The 1920s saw widespread employer *paternalism,* which assumed that the employer had a superior wisdom and knew what was best for the employees.[101] Examples of paternalistic practices included free lunches, baseball fields, vacations, pensions, and employee counseling.[102] Employers felt that employees receiving these benefits would be indebted to the employer and realize that unions would be unnecessary since they could not bargain for what the employees already had.

Another substitute model for unions involved the establishment of *Employee Representation Plans* (ERPs), or company unions. There were an estimated 403,675 members in company unions in 1919, and they reached a peak enrollment in 1928 of 1,547,766.[103] On the surface, ERPs appeared identical to unions—selected employee representatives would discuss working conditions with management representatives. Yet ERPs differed from unions in several important respects. One major difference pertained to the autonomy of the two groups. Unions realized that there were differences of opinion between themselves and management and that hard bargaining might be needed to resolve these differences in a desired fashion. Autonomy was particularly weak in ERPs when the employer was able to influence the election of the employee members and could veto any decision made by the joint labor-management committee. Unlike unions, ERPs were usually limited to a single facility, and employees under ERPs could neither press for work rules which would remove unfair competition from other facilities nor push for legislation at the local, state, or federal level.[104]

Labor's inability to overcome anti-union sentiment. The lack of organizing gains during the 1920s also has to be attributed to the anti-union sentiment of potential union members and the activities and attitudes of organized labor. Part of this problem may have been due to the relatively good economic conditions that prevailed:

While job insecurity may have deterred some employees from joining unions in the face of employer opposition, many of them apparently felt that unions were no longer as necessary as they had formerly believed them to be. What profit strikes or other agitation for collective bargaining when the pay envelope was automatically growing fatter and a more abundant life seemed to be assured with our rapid approach to the final triumph over poverty?[105]

Many potential members also believed that much of organized labor was corrupt and subject to control by the socialists and communists. Racketeering had become a feature of some local union-employer relationships. For example, in one incident a union official signed a two-paragraph agreement with three employers which guaranteed no wage increase for three years and required all employees to join the union or be discharged. None of the employees had ever solicited the union, nor did they ever see a union official during the life of the contract. This "sweetheart" arrangement or contract was often coupled with financial kickbacks to the union official, meaning the employer paid the union official a portion of the wage savings.[106]

Some labor unions had also been accused of harboring communists and other political radicals. Many prominent union leaders would occasionally accept help from almost any group that would devote time and effort in organizing employees, believing that they could control these political elements once the local union had been established.[107] However, they overestimated their controlling ability in some instances. One former president of the Steelworkers Union recalled how communists could dominate local union meetings by using the *V technique*, where the leader would find a seat in the center of the auditorium about the second or third row.

A few rows back, two of his associates would locate about ten seats apart, and this same pattern would be followed all the way to the rear of the hall. When the chief spokesman opened debate, his line would then be parroted all the way through the V behind him, giving an illusion of widespread strength. They would also wait until other union members, tired and bored, had gone home before trying to push through their own proposals.[108]

Thus labor, particularly the AFL, devoted much of its attention during the 1920s to overcoming its negative public image.[109] These efforts detracted from active organizing efforts, particularly since Gompers had lost much of his former physical enthusiasm for this activity. In 1924, Gompers died, and his successor, William Green, did not revive any major organizing activities. The lackluster performance of the AFL during the 1920s set the stage for a most dramatic split and eventual redirection of organized labor—the formation of the Congress of Industrial Organizations (CIO).

Rise of the CIO and Industrial Unionism

There was major disagreement within the AFL over what to do with regard to organizing the large ranks of unskilled and semiskilled employees. Tremendous technological shifts occurring during and after World War I reduced the demand for highly skilled employees; hence an increasing percentage of the labor force consisted of production workers. In 1926, for example, 85 percent of the hourly employees at Ford Motor Company required less than two weeks of training.[110] Craft employees no longer dominated the industrial scene; if the AFL wanted to significantly increase its membership, it would need to organize the industrial employees.

Many of the AFL unions did not want to bring industrial employees into their organizations. Some AFL leaders believed these employees were inferior to craft employees and possessed less bargaining power, while others thought the inclusion of these employees would confuse and distort the AFL's organization. William Green himself could not (or would not) view industrial employees as being compatible with the AFL's organizational principle of exclusive jurisdiction.[111]

Some leaders thought that a separate union would be needed for each company's or industry's products—if General Electric had fifty different products, then fifty different AFL unions (each having exclusive jurisdiction over its members' interests) would be needed for effective collective bargaining.[112] Other leaders believed that industrial unionism would at least weaken the AFL's concept of organized labor. The president of one AFL union urged his members to stamp out "the awful serpent of industrial trade unionism that would destroy this International and weaken the entire structure of the Labor Movement."[113]

The issue came to a head in 1935 under the direction of John L. Lewis, president of the AFL's United Mine Workers Union. The AFL rejected the concept of industrial unionism through three separate votes at its 1935 convention.[114] On November 9, 1935, the Committee for Industrial Organizations (CIO) was formed. Its purpose was allegedly "educational and advisory"; in reality, it was intended to promote organizing the unorganized, particularly those in the mass production industries.[115]

In January 1936, AFL leaders were shocked to find that the Committee for Industrial Organizations had been formed in the AFL—they had thought the industrial unionism issue had been buried once and for all at the 1935 convention. The CIO not only discussed the industrial union concept but also requested the immediate granting of industrial union charters to a number of industries such as the rubber workers and the auto workers. The CIO further insisted that an organizing campaign be started at once in the steel industry.[116]

The AFL was confronted with the most serious challenge in its history, and its leaders were confused as to the appropriate remedy. In retrospect, it appears that Green made a serious blunder when he simply ordered the CIO to dissolve or get out of the AFL. There was no evidence to suggest that influential members of the CIO, with the possible exception of John L. Lewis, wanted to leave the AFL organization.[117] Personalities intensified the issue. John L. Lewis, a powerful man in voice and action, sought and obtained power and publicity in his union activities.[118] Lewis managed to provoke AFL leaders into a confrontation while at the same time whipping his United Mine Workers members into a "lather of rage" against the AFL.[119]

The rupture over the industrial unionism issue resulted in seven unions with almost a million members forming a rival and completely independent labor organization, the Congress of Industrial Organizations (CIO).[120] One observer of this split noted that, "when the A.F. of L. suspended the CIO in August, 1936, it kicked out not only one-third of its membership, but most of its brains and all of its militancy."[121]

The organization of the CIO coincided with a significant upsurge in union membership. By November 1937, the CIO had organized 75 percent of the steel industry, 70 percent of the automobile industry, 65 percent of the rubber industry, and about one-third of the maritime and textile industries.[122] The AFL also saw rapid growth in membership during the late 1930s and the 1940s. It organized the mass production employees into local labor unions and national councils assigned to various craft unions. The steady growth of the AFL during the late 1930s was also aided by employers' preference to deal with the more conservative organization instead of taking their chances with the new and unpredictable CIO.[123]

Why did union membership increase dramatically in the 1930s and 1940s? This question is particularly important since the CIO, like the unsuccessful Knights and IWW before it, organized employees of different crafts into one union for each industry. There appear to be at least five reasons for the growth in unionism during this period.

Strong CIO leadership. The aggressive and effective CIO leaders (John L. Lewis, Sidney Hillman, David Dubinsky, among others) infused new life into a movement previously content with resting on its laurels. Most of the CIO union leaders had extensive organizing experience and prided themselves on keeping in touch with their membership.[124] Yet caution has to be taken in attributing too much to individual accomplishments, as the upsurge of the CIO and other union memberships was also due to tireless efforts of many union organizers who typed up circulars, contacted prospective members, and provided routine services which insured union election victories. In fact, one biographer of John L. Lewis indicated his lack of involvement in the many organizing chores; instead, he preferred "arriving only in time for the triumphant finale."[125]

Realistic goals. The CIO shared only a superficial similarity with the KOL in grouping employees with different job interests, believing that organizing along industrial lines would still consider the common interests of employees. More importantly, the CIO dramatically differed from the Knights and the IWW in its goals—short-run gains instead of long-range reform—which paralleled the AFL's "pure and simple" unionism approach, including support of the established economic order, as illustrated in a 1937 response of John L. Lewis:

I think most people have come to realize, that we cannot progress industrially without real cooperation between workers and management, and that this can only be brought about by equality in strength and bargaining power of labor and management. Labor is sincere in its desire to help. It looks forward to an industrial procedure which will increase productive efficiency and lower prices to the consumer.[126]

The effective use of sit-down strikes. The CIO also developed a most successful tactic which aided in employer recognition of its unions—the *sit-down strike,* in which employees stayed inside the plant instead of picketing outside. This technique was very successful since employers were reluctant to physically remove the employees from the plant for fear that their equipment could be damaged in the confrontation.

The tactic was initially applied by the IWW at a General Electric facility in 1906, but the most famous of these strikes occurred in December 1936 at a General Motors facility in Flint, Michigan. At one time, 26,000 General Motors employees had belonged to a union; in early 1936, there were only 122 union members, many of whom were management spies.[127] A local grass roots organization was secretly established to build up the union at Flint. The sit-down strike was locally planned; Lewis and the CIO preferred to organize the steel industry before attempting major organizing drives in the automobile industry. The CIO, however, did lend its active support once the strike was under way.[128]

The sit-down strike at Flint lasted forty-four days and received widespread community support, while hindering GM's efforts to reverse its negative profit situation of previous years.[129] The end of the strike resulted in employer recognition of the union, a fact which was noticed by many other employees. Between September 1936 and June 1937 some 500,000 employees in the rubber, glass, and textile industries put the technique to use. Although effective, the sit-down strike was short-lived, because public opinion eventually frowned on this tactic, and a subsequent decision by the Supreme Court declared such strikes illegal.

Passage of the Wagner Act. Another (and perhaps the most significant) reason for the increased number of union members was the passage of the Wagner Act in 1935 (discussed in more detail in Chapter 3). The federal government indicated through this law that collective bargaining was in the national interest. More important were the provisions establishing the National Labor Relations Board to administer union representation elections, define employer unfair labor practices, and enforce the legal rights of employees to join unions.

Changes in employees' attitudes. Many employees' previously negative attitudes toward organized labor changed dramatically. They had experienced the Great Depression of the 1930s and realized that job security could not be solely achieved through hard work and loyalty to the employer. These employees now viewed unions as a mechanism which could promote job security as well as other material benefits.

Thus by the onset of World War II, organized labor had reversed its membership decline of the 1920s, rising to almost 9 million members in 1940. Yet the rivalry between the CIO and the AFL was intense and violent as AFL and CIO organizers often physically clashed over the right

Part 1/Recognition of the Rights and Responsibilities of Unions and Management

to represent factory employees. James Hoffa, a former president of the International Brotherhood of Teamsters (then an AFL union), recalled violent organizing drives of 1941 between the CIO and his union:

Through it all the members wore two pins, putting on a Teamster button when we were around and switching to a CIO button when those guys showed up. They were waiting to see which union was going to win the battle. You couldn't really blame them. They were scared out of their britches because they didn't want to get caught in the bloody middle.[130]

The CIO-AFL rivalry existed in almost every industry[131] and extended to the local level, where it was common for an employer to have both AFL and CIO unions representing the same employees. Even employers with the best intentions could not build an effective labor-management relationship in this environment.

World War II to the Present

Organized labor was concerned about the events leading up to World War II. The AFL's pre–World War II sentiment was in part shaped by the suppression of organized labor as well as Jewish people in Germany. In 1933, the AFL's Executive Council urged that the federation join with other domestic groups in a boycott of German goods and services. Yet the AFL opposed any actions by the U.S. government which might increase the possibilities of involvement in the war, such as a blockade of German ships.[132]

By 1941, labor increased its cooperation with the wartime efforts. For example, shortly after the bombing of Pearl Harbor, John L. Lewis commented, "When the nation is attacked, every American must rally to its defense. All other considerations become insignificant."[133] An example of joint union-management cooperation was the participation of both on War Production Board subcommittees. Such panels weighed employee suggestions which saved 31 million man hours and $44 million during World War II.[134]

The cooperative spirit was not total, particularly from the standpoint of strikes taken during wartime. In February 1943, organized labor complained to President Roosevelt that the cost of living during wartime had increased far beyond wage increases permitted by the government under the 1942 "Little Steel Formula."[135] The United Mine Workers conducted a series of strikes to obtain wage increases of $2 a day in 1943. These actions resulted in President Roosevelt seizing the mines, but eventually a compromise wage settlement was obtained.

The public viewed these and other strikes with anger and alarm, considering them violations of the no-strike pledge announced by organized labor in 1941. Negative public sentiment increased when labor strikes continued and, after 1942, increased every year of the war. However, the number of employee days lost to strikes was estimated to be the equivalent of no more than one day per year per worker for the four war years.[136] Yet the mere act of participating in a strike was viewed by some as unpatriotic.

Labor's collective bargaining concerns shifted at the end of the war to the issues of full employment and further wage increases in order to sustain national purchasing power and thereby create an expanding market for industrial goods. Labor, remembering World War I's reconversion period, was also concerned about employer policies aimed at restricting union growth and wage gains.

Unions backed their postwar concerns with strikes. "During no period in the history of the United States did the scope and intensity of labor-management conflicts match those recorded in the year following VJ Day, August 14, 1945."[137] In this one-year period, over 4,600 strikes, involving 5 million workers and resulting in almost 120 million man-days of idleness, affected almost every major industry. They were basically nonviolent, representing instead economic tests of strength and endurance. Generally, both labor and management wanted to be free to resolve their differences at the bargaining table without the government interference and wage restrictions which were present during World War II. These concerns increased when President Truman called a joint labor-management conference in 1945. However, continued strike activity was no doubt responsible for the legislation of the 1947 Taft-Hartley amendments to the National Labor Relations (Wagner) Act (discussed in more detail in Chapter 3).

Developments in Organized Labor since World War II

Three major developments have occurred in organized labor since World War II: increased concern over new collective bargaining issues, organizing drives aimed at public and white-collar employees, and the merger of the AFL and the CIO.

Increased Concern over New Collective Bargaining Issues The return to peacetime after World War II and, particularly, the Korean War saw increased efforts to extend the provisions of the labor agreement to include all aspects of the collective bargaining relationship. In the late 1950s and early 1960s, the relative scarcity of jobs coincided with the need for price stability to ease the deficit in international payments.

Unions directed their collective bargaining efforts toward guaranteeing members job security in the face of possible technological advances and wages which would compensate for inflation. Organized labor's response toward technological change (discussed in more detail in Chapter 12) brought notable results during this period, including the Automation Fund Agreement between Armour and Company and the Packinghouse Workers and Meat Cutters unions (1959), the Mechanization and Modernization Agreement in the Pacific Coast longshore industry (1960), and the Long-Range Sharing Plan negotiated between Kaiser Steel and the United Steelworkers (1962).

The trend in multiyear labor agreements after World War II put pressure on union leaders to safeguard wage increases against the possibilities of inflation. In 1948, General Motors and the United Auto Workers negotiated a long-term agreement with a cost-of-living provision which adjusted wages for inflationary changes during the life of the contract. This contract provision spread to other labor-management negotiations. In 1952, almost 3 million workers (approximately 20 percent of the employees covered by labor agreements) had cost-of-living provisions in their contracts. [138]

Organization of White-Collar and Public Employees The second major development in organized labor occurring since World War II involves the organization of different types of employees. More specifically, white-collar employees (discussed in Chapter 1) and public employees (discussed in Chapters 14 and 15) have received increased attention from union organizers.

Merger of the AFL-CIO Perhaps the most dramatic postwar development in organized labor was the merger of the AFL and the CIO. The intense rivalry between the AFL and the CIO did not end with the return to peacetime after World War II. However, the presence of three influences during the 1950s resulted in the eventual merger of these organizations in 1955. [139]

First was the change in the presidents of the AFL and the CIO. On October 25, 1940, in a radio speech broadcast to an estimated 25 to 30 million people, John L. Lewis claimed that President Roosevelt could only be elected for a third term with the help of organized labor. He also stated that a vote for Roosevelt would represent a vote of no confidence for Lewis's administration of the CIO—Lewis would retire as president of the CIO if Roosevelt won a third term. [140]

After Roosevelt's election victory, Lewis resigned, and Phillip Murray assumed the post. Murray continued the verbal feud against the AFL and its president, William Green. However, in November 1952, both Green and Murray died. Their successors (Walter Reuther of the CIO and George Meany of the AFL) had no particular fondness for each other; indeed, their relationship became rather hostile in 1966–1967. [141] Yet Meany and Reuther, unlike Green and Murray, had not previously gone on record against each other. Therefore, a merger could occur without either president losing face.

Another influence contributing to the AFL-CIO merger was the recognized ineffectiveness of union raiding. The two labor organizations investigated employee representation elections in which the AFL tried to organize CIO employees and vice versa. During a two-year period (1951–

1952), 1,245 such elections involved some 366,740 employees, with only 62,000 employees changing union affiliation. This figure overestimates the number affected, because it does not consider the offsetting nature of elections. An AFL union could organize a CIO factory of 1,000 employees only to have a CIO union organize an AFL factory of 1,000 employees—the net change would be zero. In fact, the extensive raiding during 1951 and 1952 resulted in a net gain for the AFL of only 8,000 members or only 2 percent of the total number of employees involved.[142]

Both the AFL and the CIO finally realized that organized labor would benefit if the energies devoted to raiding each other were spent on organizing nonunion employees. Thus many of the AFL and the CIO unions signed a "no raiding agreement" in 1954. Instead of concentrating on disruptive differences emphasized in raiding activities, the two major federations could now look at similar goals which might be more easily attained by a merger.

One similar goal was the desire of both organizations to reward their political friends and punish their political enemies. In many instances, the independent organizations failed to achieve this goal. For example, they were unable to defeat Senator Taft (one of the authors of the Taft-Hartley Act who was perceived as being antilabor) and failed to elect Adlai Stevenson (supporter of organized labor) over Dwight D. Eisenhower. Both organizations felt that a merger might increase their effectiveness in the political arena.

The AFL-CIO merger on December 12, 1955 involved 15,550,000 members, making the new organization the largest trade union center in the world. The president of the AFL-CIO, George Meany, believed this merger would lead to more employees becoming unionized and to a greater political influence for labor within the American two-party system.[143] In an interview some twenty-two years later, Mr. Meany indicated that the AFL-CIO merger was "the accomplishment I take the most pride in, and it is the one that has meant the most to the labor movement and its future."[144]

The merger resulted in the continued reduction of union raiding. It also reduced the influence of union locals within the national unions—they could no longer threaten to affiliate with another national union in the rival organization.[145] However, as will be further discussed in the next section, the AFL-CIO merger has not resulted in a tremendous increase in union membership or political influence. It did reduce the former divisiveness within organized labor, but it cannot be concluded that the merger was a significant impetus for growth and change.

Aspects of Organized Labor Unchanged since World War II

Organized labor as it existed at the end of World War II compared to its present state appears to have more similarities than differences. The following six similarities are interrelated generalizations that apply to many labor organizations, although there are possible exceptions when individual unions are considered. A brief discussion of these similarities will suggest the problems and prospects of labor as well as the extent, if any, to which the following negative assessment is applicable today:

> The American trade union movement is on the downgrade, its spirits low, its operations static, its horizons narrow, its public image dismal, and its forces engaged in precisely the kind of family feuding that preceded the splitting of the old AFL in the days of William Green.[146]

1. Organized labor remains a minority, yet influential, movement in our society.[147] Since World War II, the proportion of unionized employees in the civilian work force has never exceeded 28 percent. In 1974, there were 21,643,000 union members representing almost 22 percent of the civilian work force. Yet organized labor's influence on economic and political issues in society can on occasion be pronounced. Clearly, a settlement negotiated between a major corporation and a labor union can have spillover effects on the wage policies of other corporations, union and nonunion.

Also, politicians at least on a superficial basis regard organized labor as an influential force. For example, no president of the United States has made a practice of inviting nonunion employees and/or strikebreakers to the White House for the traditional Labor Day Speech. The vast majority of this audience consists of union leaders or members. Similarly, no political leader in the United States aspiring to the presidency proclaims himself to be anti-union.[148]

2. Organized labor has had limited effectiveness in the political community. At first glance, this generalization appears inconsistent with the one previously discussed. However, there is a difference between having influence and effectively using that influence in rewarding political friends and punishing political enemies. Organized labor has contributed much in time and money in various political campaigns. However, it has seldom, if ever, been able to deliver a large proportion of its members' votes toward any one candidate.

Since World War II, the relationship between organized labor and the Democratic and Republican political parties has been confusing[149] and not always effective.[150] A detailed assessment of organized labor's political effectiveness cannot be accomplished in this book. To give somewhat recent examples, in 1972, the Committee on Political Education (COPE), the political action arm of the AFL-CIO, raised $2.8 million for congressional candidates, with slightly more than half of labor-backed candidates achieving election victory. In 1976, organized labor's political preferences fared better, and labor's political backing helped President Carter win key political victories in New York and Ohio.[151]

Yet completely effective political action depends on the ability of the

Democratic and Republican parties to represent a consensual group and appeal to the divergent interests of union members. We have seen, particularly in recent times, that there is no such thing as *the* Democratic or *the* Republican party. Indeed, the terms appear to be labels without substance, umbrella organizations housing politicians with extremely divergent political, social, and economic viewpoints. Labor realizes that a blanket endorsement of one party would mean accepting some politicians with contrary views. However, it is not easy to insure that members will split their ballots, voting for organized labor's candidates instead of one party.

Labor's political strength is won by persuading its members that their self-interest is at stake and that they should act to defend it.[152] Even if union members share similar social goals, such as ending pollution and preventing crime, they may differ as to the desired union involvement in attaining the goals.[153] Also, keep in mind that union members have preferences that extend beyond the work situation.[154] It would be difficult to predict how a union member who was strongly against abortions would vote for a prolabor political candidate in favor of abortions on request. Additional problems in mobilizing political support are found in the third similarity.

3. There is difficulty in achieving consensus among unions and among members. Understandably, agreement among the diverse national unions within the AFL-CIO federation and members within national and local unions is rare. This problem occurs in any large organization, particularly one which grants a large amount of autonomy to its members. The AFL-CIO is always subject to national unions withdrawing from its organization. The federation also realizes that many national unions can get along quite well without its support. For example, the 1957 expulsion of the Teamsters from the federation did not hinder the Teamsters' ability to increase its membership, grow in influence, and engage in collective bargaining. Likewise, the United Auto Workers, who chose to leave the AFL-CIO, continue to prosper.

Lack of consensus is also found at the local union level, especially when younger employees become members. Most labor unions have had a long tradition of struggle and sacrifice; their leaders have risked physical hardships in order to insure that the employer merely recognized their union. However, in many cases tradition has been forgotten, and many of the younger members are now asking the leaders, "What have you done for me lately?"

Many union leaders have difficulty in understanding the younger union members. For example, an estimated 40 percent of the United Auto Worker membership is under thirty years of age. President Douglas Fraser once indicated that younger members "have different values than people of my generation." Walter Reuther also admitted having some difficulty with the younger members. One journalist familiar with Reuther commented, "Walter didn't like liquor so you can imagine what he thought of pot."[155]

4. Organized labor has continually pursued short-range material goals instead of long-range reform. The Knights of Labor appeared to teach organized labor a permanent lesson—goals should relate to members' needs instead of being abstract attempts to change the existing societal system. The period since World War II has witnessed tremendous economic growth and technological change; therefore, union leaders believe these issues deserve more attention than other societal concerns.[156]

Labor's priorities have been often challenged by members of the academic and intellectual community, who claim that labor should use its strength to press for progressive social change and legislation. Some hostility exists between organized labor and members of the intellectual community. Many intellectuals believe that the labor movement is "facing dynamic new challenges with old leaders and old ideas."[157] Many union leaders reply that intellectuals, in their work and in their surroundings, are out of touch with the everyday struggles faced by union members. Union leaders have also contended that the ivory tower views of academicians have been blurred by their stereotypic view of union members' behaviors and hopes and that academicians need to "get their hands dirty" on the line so they will make a more accurate assessment of unionism.[158]

5. Collective bargaining tactics and issues remain largely unchanged since World War II. Although there has been greater emphasis in *pattern bargaining* (in which a collective bargaining settlement of one company or industry influences subsequent collective bargaining tactics at other locations) since World War II, the basic tactics (strikes, inventory buildups, etc.) remain the same. However, one major exception, the Experimental Negotiating Agreement in the steel industry, and other cooperative efforts are discussed in Chapter 7.

6. Organized labor has had to contend with negative public attitudes. No longer viewed as the underdog in U.S. society, labor has in fact become a phenomenon of some public concern. Some are concerned about what they consider excessive wage demands won by labor unions. The public reads many newspaper accounts of affluent union members. For example, one article in the *Wall Street Journal* describes the details of the "country club" social life of Appalachia's coal miners, who earned between $25,000 and $35,000 in 1978.[159]

Labor has been somewhat effective in shaking leftist elements from its organization[160] and has taken strong positions against communist nations. Also, George Meany, then president of the AFL-CIO, and most organized labor leaders have given enthusiastic support in U.S. war efforts, including the Vietnam War—support for which labor was often criticized.

On the other hand, the media have consistently presented incidents of corruption in some labor unions[161] and highlighted certain practices where union members seem to receive payment for not working. These restrictive or make-work practices have been publicized in the railroad and construction industries, although elements of them extend to other areas, such as the supermarket industry.[162]

Perhaps the most important definition of an organization's success comes from its leaders and members. There is no substantial evidence to suggest that organized labor is extremely concerned about expanding its membership or its influence in the political arena (the Labor Law Reform Bill discussed in Chapter 3 representing a possible exception) or advancing long-range social reform issues. Similarly, there is no reason to believe that there is substantial negative public opinion which will affect its major goal, namely, collective bargaining with management about union members' working concerns.

Organized labor may, however, have a serious future challenge in achieving consensus within its membership. This challenge will be particularly significant if various membership factions, such as younger employees, challenge traditional old-line union leaders with new goals and priorities.

Summary

In obtaining a contemporary perspective of organized labor, one must be aware of the evolution of labor-management relationships as well as various labor organizations which have attempted to influence those relationships. Current labor organizations have learned important lessons from their historical counterparts. Criteria for success were suggested as a means of comparing the effectiveness of various labor organizations and were discussed in this chapter. Organized labor did not exert much of an influence before 1869, although employees became increasingly concerned with working and market conditions associated with mass production. The bulk of the chapter is concerned with the active years of organized labor, occurring in the following time periods: 1869 to World War I, World War I to World War II, and World War II to the present.

Three major labor organizations developed in the period from 1869 to World War I: the Knights of Labor (KOL), the American Federation of Labor (AFL) under Gompers, and the Industrial Workers of the World (IWW). These organizations' major goals, strategies, and organizational characteristics were discussed, and, in the cases of the KOL and the IWW, reasons for their demise were given. Also discussed were the Haymarket Riot and the Homestead and Pullman strikes.

The period immediately following World War I saw limited growth in union membership. Many of the factors contributing to this situation were discussed, including several strategies used by employers to counter union organizing campaigns. Internal differences occurred within the AFL regarding the potential advantages of organizing the heretofore nonunion unskilled and semiskilled employees working in our nation's factories. This disagreement led to the formation of a rival union organization, the Congress of Industrial Organizations (CIO), whose major objective was to organize industrial employees. The CIO was effective in achieving substantial membership gains in the late 1930s and 1940s.

Three major developments have occurred in organized labor since World War II. There has been increased concern over new collective bargaining issues; organizing drives have been aimed at public and white-collar employees; and the AFL and the CIO have merged. Although several influences prompted the AFL-CIO merger, the impact of this event on contemporary union-management relationships is difficult to assess. As suggested by the concluding section, there appear to be more similarities than differences when the state of organized labor at the end of World War II is compared to its present state. Organized labor remains a minority, yet influential, movement in our society. It has continued to have a minimal effectiveness in the political community, possibly because of negative public opinion and the difficulty of mobilizing younger union members. Finally, the strategies and tactics of collective bargaining are basically unchanged since World War II.

Discussion Questions

1. "Strive for the better day" was stated by Gompers (AFL); however, the remark could have just as easily been stated by Powderly (KOL) or Haywood (IWW)—but with entirely different meaning. Explain.
2. Considering the criteria for labor organization success mentioned on page 31, why did the AFL survive and the IWW fade into obscurity?
3. Briefly explain how the Haymarket, Homestead, and Pullman incidents helped as well as hurt the AFL.
4. Discuss the various employer tactics used to thwart union growth in the 1920s and 1930s.
5. Why was the CIO successful in organizing members in the late 1930s when it had the same "one big union" approach which proved most unsuccessful for the KOL in the 1880s?
6. What were several reasons behind the merger of the AFL and the CIO? To what extent will these or other reasons continue this merger into the near future, say, the next ten years?

7. Discuss two similarities of organized labor as it existed at the end of World War II and as it does in the present. Speculate as to how these similarities might be modified in the near future.

References

[1]Henry Pelling, *American Labor* (Chicago: University of Chicago Press, 1960), pp. 12–13.

[2]David J. Saposs, "Colonial and Federal Beginnings," in John R. Commons et al., eds., *History of Labour in the United States* (1918; reprint ed. New York: Augustus M. Kelly Publishers, 1966), vol. I, p. 111.

[3]Edward B. Mittelman, "Trade Unionism 1833–1839," in Commons et al., eds., *History of Labour*, p. 430.

[4]See, for example, Anthony Bimba, *The Molly Maguires* (New York: International Publishers, 1970), p. 14; and Charles A. McCarthy, *The Great Molly Maguire Hoax* (Wyoming, Pa.: Cro-woods, 1969). For a detailed examination of the Molly Maguires see Wayne G. Broehl, Jr., *The Molly Maguires* (Cambridge, Mass.: Harvard University Press, 1964).

[5]William C. Birdsall, "The Problems of Structure in the Knights of Labor," *Industrial and Labor Relations Review* 6 (July 1953), p. 546.

[6]For a discussion of how the expansion of the markets affected unionization among the shoemakers see John R. Commons, *Labor and Administration* (New York: Macmillan, 1913), pp. 210–264.

[7]T. V. Powderly, *Thirty Years of Labor: 1859–1889* (Columbus, Ohio: Excelsior Publishing House, 1889), p. 21.

[8]Ibid., pp. 58–59.

[9]Ibid., p. 163.

[10]Philip Taft, *Organized Labor in American History* (New York: Harper & Row, 1964), p. 90.

[11]Gerald N. Grob, *Workers and Utopia* (Evanston, Ill.: Northwestern University Press, 1961), p. 35. Powderly was most concerned about the evils of drinking; for example, he spent almost fifty pages of his autobiography, *Thirty Years of Labor*, discussing this issue.

[12]Birdsall, "The Problems of Structure," p. 533.

[13]Melton Alonza McLaurin, *The Knights of Labor in the South* (Westport, Conn.: Greenwood Press, 1978), p. 39.

[14]Joseph G. Rayback, *A History of American Labor* (New York: Macmillan, 1968), p. 174.

[15]Joseph R. Buchanan, *The Story of a Labor Agitator* (1903; reprint ed. Westport, Conn.: Greenwood Press, 1970), pp. 318–323.

[16]For details of these procedures see Taft, *Organized Labor*, p. 91.

[17]Powderly, *Thirty Years of Labor*, pp. 152–157.

[18]It should be noted that local assemblies were somewhat responsible for this situation, as they contributed only $600 to the General Assembly's strike funds in 1885–1886 (McLaurin, *The Knights of Labor*, p. 54). For more details of KOL's strike activities see Norman J. Ware, *The Labor Movement in the United States: 1860–1895* (1929; reprint ed. Gloucester, Mass.: Peter Smith, 1959), pp. 117–154. It should be further noted that the Knights made more effective use of boycotts than any previous union. However, as was true with strikes, the boycott was instigated by the local assemblies and forced on the Knights' national leaders (Grob, *Workers and Utopia*, p. 61).

[19]Donald L. Kemmerer and Edward D. Wickersham, "Reasons for the Growth of the Knights of Labor in 1885–1886," *Industrial and Labor Relations Review* 3 (January 1950), pp. 213–220.

[20]Foster Rhea Dulles, *Labor in America: A History*, 3d ed. (New York: Thomas Y. Crowell, 1966), p. 127.

[21]Ware, *The Labor Movement*, p. 96.

[22]Dulles, *Labor in America*, p. 135.

[23]Powderly, *Thirty Years of Labor*, p. 514. It should also be noted that Powderly believed Gompers misled employees by advocating the eight-hour day without telling them that their wages would be proportionately reduced. Most workers thought they would receive ten hours payment for eight hours of work.

[24]"A Hellish Deed!" *Chicago Tribune*, May 5, 1886, p. 1.

[25]For additional details of the rigged nature of the trial see Samuel Yellen, *American Labor Struggles* (1936; reprint ed. New York: Arno Press, 1969), pp. 60–65.

[26]"A Hellish Deed!"

[27]"Their Records," *Chicago Tribune*, May 5, 1886, p. 1.

[28]Sidney Lens, *The Labor Wars: From the Molly Maguires to the Sitdowns* (Garden City, N.Y.: Doubleday, 1973), p. 67.

[29]It should be noted that the origination of the AFL was changed to 1881 in 1889 to include activities under the Federation of Organized Trades. At least one historian has claimed that the revised date is regrettable since the parent organization (Federation of Organized Trades) had little similarity to the AFL in terms of effective organization and broad-based support (Ware, *The Labor Movement*, p. 251).

[30]Samuel Gompers, *Seventy Years of Life and Labor* (New York: E. P. Dutton, 1925), p. 266.

[31]Ware, *The Labor Movement*, pp. 70–71.

[32]Norman J. Ware, *Labor in Modern Industrial Society* (1935; reprint ed. New York: Russell & Russell, 1968), p. 262.

[33]Dulles, *Labor in America*, p. 155.

[34]Gompers, *Seventy Years of Life and Labor*, p. 245.

[35]Samuel Gompers, *Labor and the Employer* (1920; reprint ed. New York: Arno Press, 1971), pp. 33–34.

[36]Stuart Bruce Kaufman, *Samuel Gompers and the Origins of the American Federation of Labor: 1848–1896* (Westport, Conn.: Greenwood Press, 1973), p. 173.

[37]For details of this relationship see Gompers, *Seventy Years of Life and Labor*, pp. 381–427.

[38]Louis Reed, *The Labor Philosophy of Samuel Gompers* (1930; reprint ed. Port Washington, N.Y.: Kennikat Press, 1966), p. 20. See also an editorial by Gompers in the *American Federationist*, June 1924, p. 481.

[39]Gompers, *Seventy Years of Life and Labor*, pp. 286–287, 381–427.

[40]Max M. Kempelman, "Labor in Politics," in George M. Brooks et al., eds., *Interpreting the Labor Movement* (Ann Arbor, Mich.: Industrial Relations Research Association, 1967), p. 41.

[41]Gompers, *Labor and the Employer*, p. 202.

[42]Philip Taft, *The AF of L in the Time of Gompers* (1957; reprint ed. New York: Octagon Books, 1970), p. 302.

[43]Ibid., pp. 296–297.

[44]Ware, *Labor in American Industrial Society*, pp. 268–270.

[45]Marc Karson, *American Labor Unions and Politics: 1900–1918* (Carbondale, Ill.: Southern Illinois University Press, 1958), p. 29.

[46]Reed, *The Labor Philosophy of Samuel Gompers*, pp. 106–110.

[47]Milton Derber, *The American Idea of Industrial Democracy: 1865–1965* (Urbana: University of Illinois Press, 1970), p. 117.

[48]Gompers, *Seventy Years of Life and Labor*, p. 342. For additional details regarding early AFL organizing see Taft, *AF of L in the Time of Gompers*, pp. 95–122.

[49]Dulles, *Labor in America*, pp. 163–164.

[50]Andrew Carnegie, "An Employer's View of the Labor Question," in *Labor: Its Rights and Wrongs* (1886; reprint ed. Westport, Conn.: Hyperion Press, 1975), p. 91.

[51]Ibid., p. 95.

[52]Yellen, *American Labor Struggles*, p. 81.

[53]For details of the wage package see Ibid., pp. 77–80.

[54]"Surrounded by Pickets," *New York Times*, July 4, 1892, p. 1.

[55]"Mob Law at Homestead," *New York Times*, July 7, 1892, p. 1.

[56]"Leader O'Donnell Is Glad," *New York Times*, July 12, 1892, p. 2; "Bayonet Rule in Force," *New York Times*, July 13, 1892, p. 1.

[57]Lens, *The Labor Wars*, p. 77.

[58]"A Talk with Gompers," *New York Times*, July 7, 1892, p. 2; and "Provoked by Carnegie," *New York Times*, July 7, 1892, pp. 2, 5.

[59]Taft, *AF of L in the Time of Gompers*, p. 136.

[60]"Arbitrate the Homestead Strike," *Chicago Tribune*, July 8, 1892, p. 4. See also "The Origin of the Trouble," *New York Times*, July 8, 1892, p. 2.

[61]Yellen, *American Labor Struggles*, p. 3.

[62]Lens, *The Labor Wars*, p. 81.

[63]For additional details about the town see Almont Lindsay, *The Pullman Strike* (Chicago: University of Chicago Press, 1967), pp. 38–60.

[64]For more details regarding ARU's organization see Philip S. Foner, *History of the Labor Movement in the United States*, vol. II (New York: International Publishers, 1955), p. 256.

[65]Lindsay, *The Pullman Strike*, p. 124.

[66]Ibid., p. 215.

[67]Gompers, *Seventy Years of Life and Labor*, p. 403.

[68]William H. Carwardine, *The Pullman Strike*, 4th ed. (1894; reprint ed. New York: Arno Press, 1969), p. 29.

[69]See, for example, Foner, *History of the Labor Movement*, vol. II, p. 269. For a further discussion of the use of federal troops in the railroad industry during this period, see Jerry M. Cooper, "The Army as Strikebreaker: The Railroad Strikes of 1877 and 1894," *Labor History* 18 (Spring 1977), pp. 179–196.

[70]*Proceedings of the First Convention of the Industrial Workers of the World* (New York: Labor News Company, 1905), p. 1.

[71]Ibid., p. 143.

[72]Bill Haywood, *Bill Haywood's Book: The Autobiography of William D. Haywood* (New York: International Publishers, 1929), p. 73.

[73]Melvyn Dubofsky, *We Shall Be All: A History of the Industrial Workers of the World* (Chicago: Quadrangle Books, 1969), p. 481.

[74]Haywood, *Bill Haywood's Book*, p. 181.

[75]Lens, *The Labor Wars*, pp. 154–155.

[76]For additional details pertaining to these factions see Dubofsky, *We Shall Be All*, pp. 105–119; and Joseph Robert Conlin, *Bread and Roses Too* (Westport, Conn.: Greenwood Publishing, 1969), pp. 97–117.

[77]Dubofsky, *We Shall Be All*, p. 137.

[78]David J. Saposs, *Left-Wing Unionism* (1926; reprint ed. New York: Russell & Russell, 1967), p. 148.

[79]Louis Adamic, *Dynamite: The Story of Class Violence in America* (1934; reprint ed. Gloucester, Mass.: Peter Smith, 1963), p. 174.

[80]Foner, *History of the Labor Movement*, vol. III, p. 161.

[81]Dubofsky, *We Shall Be All*, p. 163.

[82]Conlin, *Bread and Roses Too*, pp. 97–117. See also Fred Thompson, *The IWW: Its First Fifty Years* (Chicago: Industrial Workers of the World, 1955), pp. 80–87.

[83]Adamic, *Dynamite*, pp. 163–164.

[84]Conlin, *Bread and Roses Too*, p. 96.

[85]Foner, *History of the Labor Movement*, vol. III, p. 465.

[86]Conlin, *Bread and Roses Too*, p. 68.

[87]Taft, *AF of L in the Time of Gompers*, p. 253.

[88]For additional details see Frank L. Grubbs, Jr., *The Struggle for Labor Loyalty: Gompers, the AFL, and the Pacifists, 1917–1920* (Durham, N.C.: Duke University Press, 1968).

[89]James O. Morris, *Conflict within the AFL: A Study of Craft versus Industrial Unionism, 1901–1938* (1958; reprint ed. Westport, Conn.: Greenwood Press, 1974), pp. 9–10.

[90]Dulles, *Labor in America*, pp. 225–226.

[91]Rayback, *A History of American Labor*, p. 275.

[92]Taft, *Organized Labor*, pp. 355–358; and Francis Fox Piven and Richard A. Cloward, *Poor People's Movements* (New York: Pantheon Books, 1977), p. 104. For details of this strike see Lens, *The Labor Wars*, pp. 196–219.

[93]Rayback, *A History of American Labor*, p. 307.

[94]Lens, *The Labor Wars*, p. 222.

[95]Ibid., pp. 296, 312.

[96]Derber, *The American Idea*, p. 246. For an application of these reasons to a specific industrial situation during this time period see Stephen L. Shapiro, "The Growth of the Cotton Textile Industry in South Carolina: 1919–1930" (Ph.D. diss., University of South Carolina, 1971), pp. 168–171.

[97]Dulles, *Labor in America*, p. 246.

[98]For additional details regarding this tactic see Clinch Calkins, *Spy Overhead: The Story of Industrial Espionage* (1937; reprint ed. New York: Arno Press, 1971).

[99]It should be noted that violence was limited neither to this time period nor to the employer. One of the more publicized episodes of employer violence was the Ludlow Massacre of 1914. The mining camps in Colorado were involved in a strike for union recognition when, on April 20, militiamen opened fire on a tent colony, killing two strikers and one boy. They then set fire to the tents, killing two women and eleven children. For more details of this event see Leon Stein, ed., *Massacre at Ludlow: Four Reports* (reprint ed.; New York: Arno Press, 1971). Perhaps one of the more vivid examples of union violence occurred in Herrin, Illinois (1922), where miners tortured and killed at least twenty-six management officials and strikebreakers. For details of this episode see Saul Alinsky, *John L. Lewis: An Unauthorized Biography* (New York: Vintage Books, 1970), pp. 43–50.

[100]Richard C. Wilcock, "Industrial Management's Policies toward Unionism," in Milton Derber and Edwin Young, eds., *Labor and the New Deal* (Madison: University of Wisconsin Press, 1957), p. 293.

[101]Ware, *Labor in Modern Industrial Society*, p. 405.

[102]For a case study of paternalism see "Welfare Work in Company Towns," *Monthly Labor Review* 25 (August 1927), pp. 314–321.

[103]Morris, *Conflict within the AFL*, pp. 40–41. For more details on ERPs see Ware, *Labor in Modern Industrial Society*, pp. 414–435. For a contemporary assessment of the problems and prospects facing the single-firm, independent union see Arthur B. Shostak, *America's Forgotten Labor Organization* (Princeton: Industrial Relations Section, Department of Economics, Princeton University, 1962).

[104]Derber, *The American Idea*, pp. 220–221.

[105]Dulles, *Labor in America*, p. 245.

[106]This example was drawn from a more detailed account of racketeering during this period found in Sidney Lens, *Left, Right, and Center: Conflicting Forces in American Labor* (Hinsdale, Ill.: Henry Regnery, 1949), pp. 86–108.

[107]David M. Oshinsky, *Senator Joseph McCarthy and the American Labor Movement* (Columbia: University of Missouri Press, 1976), p. 89. See also Melvyn Dubofsky and Warren Van Tine, *John L. Lewis: A Biography* (New York: Quadrangle/New York Times Book Company, 1977), p. 288.

[108]David J. McDonald, *Union Man* (New York: E. P. Dutton, 1969), p. 185.

[109]James O. Morris, "The AFL in the 1920s: A Strategy of Defense," *Industrial and Labor Relations Review* 11 (July 1958), pp. 572–590.

[110]Bruce Minton and John Stuart, *Men Who Lead Labor* (New York: Modern Age Books, 1937), pp. 14–15.

[111]Ibid., p. 8.

[112]Morris, *Conflict within the AFL*, p. 177.

[113]Ibid., p. 216.

[114]For additional details pertaining to the background of this historic convention see Herbert Harris, *Labor's Civil War* (1940; reprint ed. New York: Greenwood Press, 1969), pp. 22–60.

[115]Lens, *The Labor Wars*, p. 284.

[116]Alinsky, *John L. Lewis*, p. 82.

[117]Philip Taft, *The AFL from the Death of Gompers to the Merger* (1959; reprint ed. New York: Octagon Books, 1970), p. 155.

[118]Cecil Carnes, *John L. Lewis: Leader of Labor* (New York: Robert Speller Publishing, 1936), p. 299.

[119]David Dubinsky and A. H. Raskin, *David Dubinsky: A Life with Labor* (New York: Simon and Schuster, 1977), p. 226.

[120]The seven unions were: The United Mine Workers; The Amalgamated Clothing Workers; The International Ladies Garment Workers Union; United Hatters; Cap and Millinery Workers; Oil Field, Gas Well and Refinery Workers; and The International Union of Mine, Mill, and Smelter Workers.

[121]Benjamin Stolberg, *The Story of the CIO* (1938; reprint ed. New York: Arno Press, 1971), p. 28.

[122]Ibid.

[123]Milton Derber, "Growth and Expansion," in Derber and Young, *Labor and the New Deal*, p. 13.

[124]See, for example, John Hutchinson, "John L. Lewis: To the Presidency of the UMWA," *Labor History* 19 (Spring 1978), pp. 185–203.

[125]James Arthur Wechsler, *Labor Baron: A Portrait of John L. Lewis* (New York: William Morrow, 1944), p. 71.

[126]S. J. Woolf, "John L. Lewis and His Plan," in Melvyn Dubofsky, ed., *American Labor since the New Deal* (Chicago: Quadrangle Books, 1971), pp. 110–111.

[127]Lens, *The Labor Wars*, p. 295.

[128]Irving Howe and B. J. Widick, *The UAW and Walter Reuther* (1949; reprint ed. New York: De Capo Press, 1973), p. 55.

[129]Sidney Fine, *Sit-Down: The General Motors Strike of 1936–1937* (Ann Arbor: The University of Michigan Press, 1969), pp. 156–177.

[130]James R. Hoffa and Oscar Fraley, *Hoffa: The Real Story* (New York: Stein and Day Publishers, 1975), p. 65.

[131]For a detailed account of the AFL-CIO rivalries in several industries see Walter Galenson, *The CIO Challenge to the AFL* (Cambridge, Mass.: Harvard University Press, 1960).

[132]Joseph C. Goulden, *Meany* (New York: Atheneum, 1972), p. 117.

[133]Rayback, *A History of American Labor*, pp. 373–374.

[134]Richard B. Morris, ed., *The U.S. Department of Labor Bicentennial History of the American Worker* (Washington, D.C.: U.S. Government Printing Office, 1976), p. 236.

[135]For details of this formula and the extent that cost of living estimates exceeded this formula see Taft, *Organized Labor in American History*, pp. 549–553 and 557–559.

[136]Dulles, *Labor in America: A History*, p. 334.

[137]Arthur F. McClure, *The Truman Administration and the Problems of Postwar Labor 1945–1948* (Cranburry, N.J.: Associated University Presses, 1969), p. 45.

[138]Robert M. MacDonald, "Collective Bargaining in the Postwar Period," *Industrial and Labor Relations Review* 20 (July 1967), p. 568.

[139]For a more detailed discussion of the historical attempts at the merger of the AFL and CIO organizations see Joel Seidman, "Efforts toward Merger 1935–1955," *Industrial and Labor Relations Review* 9 (April 1956), pp. 353–370.

[140]For a transcript of Lewis' speech see the *New York Times*, October 26, 1940, p. 12.

[141]Frank Cormier and William J. Eaton, *Reuther* (Englewood Cliffs, N.J.: Prentice-Hall, 1970), p. 417.

[142]"Document: AFL-CIO No-Raiding Agreement," *Industrial and Labor Relations Review* 8 (October 1954), p. 103.

[143]George Meany, "Merger and the National Welfare," *Industrial and Labor Relations Review* 9 (April 1956), p. 349.

[144]"George Meany Speaks Out on Inflation, Jobs, Carter," *U.S. News & World Report*, September 12, 1977, p. 86.

[145]Richard A. Lester, *As Unions Mature* (Princeton, N.J.: Princeton University Press, 1958), p. 25.

[146]Robert Bendiner, "What's Wrong in the House of Labor?" *Reporter*, October 12, 1961, p. 41, cited in B. J. Widick, *Labor Today: The Triumphs and Failures of Unionism in the United States* (Boston: Houghton Mifflin, 1964), p. 9.

[147]Some of the similarities discussed in this section draw from the discussion of Taft, *Organized Labor*, pp. 707–709.

[148]Widick, *Labor Today*, p. 117.

[149]Max M. Kampelman, "Labor in Politics," in George W. Brooks et al., eds., *Interpreting the Labor Movement* (Ann Arbor, Mich.: Industrial Relations Research Association, 1967), p. 188.

[150]Dick Bruner, "Labor Should Get Out of Politics," in Charles M. Rehmus and Doris B. McLaughlin, eds., *Labor and American Politics: A Book of Readings* (Ann Arbor: University of Michigan Press, 1967), p. 430. For an assessment of organized labor's limited effectiveness in the political arena since the 1930s see Piven and Cloward, *Poor People's Movements*, pp. 161–172.

[151]Charles W. Dunn, *American Democracy Debated* (Morristown, N.Y.: General Learning Press, 1978), pp. 210–211.

[152]Patricia Cayo Sexton and Brendan Sexton, *Blue Collars and Hard-Hats: The Working Class and the Future of American Politics* (New York: Random House, 1971), p. 307.

[153]See, for example, a study reported in Sar A. Levitan, ed., *Blue Collar Workers: A Symposium on Middle America* (New York: McGraw-Hill, 1971), pp. 165–171.

[154]Donald E. Stokes, "Voting Research and the Labor Vote," in Rehmus and McLaughlin, eds., *Labor and American Politics*, pp. 387–389.

[155]William Serrin, *The Company and the Union* (New York: Alfred A. Knopf, 1973), p. 13.

[156]For a more thorough union perspective of labor's role in social reform see Jack T. Conway, "Ideological Obsolescence in Collective Bargaining," in Walter Fogel and Archie Kleingartner, eds., *Contemporary Labor Issues* (Belmont, Calif.: Wadsworth Publishing Company, 1970), pp. 202–212.

[157]A. H. Raskin, "The Fat Cats of Labor," in David Boroff, ed., *The State of the Nation* (Englewood Cliffs, N.J.: Prentice-Hall, 1965), p. 50. For a further related discussion see Harold L. Wilensky, *Intellectuals in Labor Unions* (Glencoe, Ill.: The Free Press, 1956).

[158]Brendan Sexton, "The Working Class Experience," *American Economic Review* 62 (May 1972), p. 152.

[159]George Getschow, "Digging for Dollars: Coal Miners Are Living 'Good Life' as Wages Soar with Oil Prices," *Wall Street Journal*, November 10, 1978, pp. 1, 40.

[160]For a discussion of these elements see Bernard Karsh and Phillips L. Garman, "The Impact of the Political Left," in Derber and Young, eds., *Labor and the New Deal*, pp. 77–119.

[161]For a fuller discussion of this issue see John Hutchinson, *The Imperfect Union: A History of Corruption in American Trade Unions* (New York: E. P. Dutton, 1972).

[162]Herbert R. Northrup, Gordon R. Stockholm, and Paul A. Abodeely, *Restrictive Labor Practices in the Supermarket Industry* (Philadelphia: University of Pennsylvania Press, 1967), pp. 67–119.

Chapter 3

Legal Influences

"[The] labor of a human being is not a commodity or article of commerce. Nothing contained in the antitrust laws shall be construed to forbid the existence and operation of labor [unions]."

Clayton Act of 1914

Labor relations law serves as the foundation for most of our labor relations activities. This chapter is placed early in the book so that a proper foundation can be established for such subjects as organizing unions, negotiating labor agreements, and assuring employee rights. Further, it is essential today not only to know the law but to understand and appreciate the interrelationships between the law and the labor relations processes.

This chapter logically follows the historical development of unions in the United States because labor relations law and union development go hand in hand. Law as it pertains to labor is traced from the first court case involving union activities through the development of common law and the use of antitrust legislation that inhibited the growth of unions to the laws that pertain to most private firms, the Norris–La Guardia, Wagner, Taft-Hartley, and Landrum-Griffin Acts. Since these acts cover the major portion of U.S. industries and businesses, a substantial amount of space is devoted to their content. The Railway Labor Act, which principally covers railroads and airlines, is also explained and assessed. A final section briefly considers several other laws which can affect the labor relations process.

Bases of Labor Relations Law

Labor relations law in the United States has as its bases the U.S. Constitution, statutory law, judicial decisions and interpretations, and administrative decisions by agencies of the executive branch. Likewise, at the state and local government levels, law is developed and established by analogous documents and actions.

Several provisions of the U.S. Constitution have been interpreted as applying to labor relations activities. For example, Article I, Section 8, which authorizes Congress to regulate commerce, has been used to determine the constitutionality of several statutory enactments. The First Amendment, which assures the rights of peaceful assembly and free speech, usually has been interpreted as allowing employees to form and join unions and has provided the justification for union picketing (to communicate information to possible union members and union supporters). The Fifth and Fourteenth Amendments contain due process provisions, and the Fourteenth Amendment provides equal protection under law. These amendments have been used for employment protection in discharge decisions, refusal to hire cases, and discrimination cases regarding equal employment opportunity where either state or federal employees are involved.

Statutory law can be created and amended by legislative enactment at the federal, state, or local levels of government. Congress has enacted numerous labor relations laws in the interest of employees and employers, public welfare, and interstate commerce. Three major ones—the Norris–La Guardia Act, the National Labor Relations Act, as amended, and the Railway Labor Act—are discussed at length later in the chapter. State legislatures may pass laws and local municipalities pass ordinances to fill voids in the federal laws or to cover issues not covered by federal laws, such as the right of public employees to engage in collective bargaining.

The judicial branch of government, with its accompanying court system at the federal, state, and local levels, functions to determine a law's constitutionality and conformity to legal standards, to assess the accuracy of interpretations by administrative agencies, and to issue injunctions that restrict or require certain activities. In addition, the courts must decide issues which law or statutory guidance do not and make rulings under the general guides of "equity." Such decisions and rulings constitute case, or common, law, which has developed over the years, setting precedents and providing guidance for future decisions.

The executive branch, the administrator of the laws through various governmental agencies, makes rules (often called Executive Orders) and decisions within the framework of the statutes or laws. These decisions are legal and binding although they are subject to appeal to the courts. As long as the decisions are within the authority of the administrative agency and are accurate interpretations of its delegated authority, they have the same effect as law.

Some of the more important administrative agencies mentioned throughout the book include:

☐ **National Labor Relations Board (NLRB):** Administers the National Labor Relations Act as amended by the Taft-Hartley and Landrum-Griffin acts, conducts union representation elections, and adjudicates unfair labor practice complaints.

☐ **Federal Mediation and Conciliation Service (FMCS):** Provides mediation services to unions and management in collective bargaining and assists these parties in selecting arbitrators in grievance administration.

☐ **U.S. Department of Labor (DOL):** Performs many labor-related services, such as research and data-collecting functions; administers wage laws, supervises offices under the Occupational Safety and Health Administration, and enforces federal contract compliance under equal employment opportunity requirements. In addition, its secretary serves as the President's cabinet member responsible for labor relations matters.

☐ **National Mediation Board:** Handles union representation issues under the Railway Labor Act, provides mediation services to parties in negotiations, assists in disputes over contract interpretation, and in cases involving emergency disputes proposes arbitration and certifies the dispute to the President as an emergency.

☐ **National Railroad Adjustment Board:** Hears and attempts to resolve railroad labor disputes growing out of grievances and interpretation or application of the labor agreements.

☐ **State and Local Administrative Agencies:** Numerous agencies at the state and local levels of government are responsible for the enforcement and administration of state laws and local ordinances involving labor relations topics.

Early Legal Interpretations Involving Labor-Management Relationships (1806–1931)

As the previous chapter demonstrated, in earlier times labor unions in the United States had to struggle for their existence. With the absence of legislative direction, the judiciary system not only controlled the relationships between labor unions and employers but also played a key role in limiting the organization of unions for many years, especially from the 1800s to the 1930s.

Criminal Conspiracy

The first labor relations case in the United States occurred in 1806, when a group of journeymen shoemakers in Philadelphia were indicted, convicted, and fined $8 each for forming an illegal criminal conspiracy. The shoemakers had joined a combination of workmen in an attempt to raise their wages, refusing to work with nonmembers or at a wage rate less than they demanded. Twelve jurors found the shoemakers guilty of forming an illegal coalition for the purpose of raising their own wages while injuring those who did not join the coalition.[1]

The application of the criminal conspiracy doctrine to attempts by employees to organize unions aroused much public protest, not only from employees but also from factory owners who feared the closing of their factories if the workers' feelings grew too strong. These feelings were undoubtedly considered when the Supreme Judicial Court of Massachusetts *(Commonwealth v. Hunt)* set aside the conviction for criminal conspiracy of seven members of the Journeymen Bootmakers Society who refused to work in shops where nonmembers were employed at less than their scheduled rate of $2 per pair of boots. While not rejecting the criminal conspiracy doctrine, Justice Shaw cut the heart from it by insisting that the purpose of the concerted activity must be considered, not just the fact that the activity occurred. His decision stated that an association of workers could be established for "useful and honorable purposes" as well as for purposes of "oppression and injustice"; however, the means of achieving these purposes could also be legal or illegal. Therefore, to determine its legality, an investigation must be made of the objectives of the particular labor union involved and of the means used to achieve its objectives.[2]

Civil Conspiracy

The *Commonwealth v. Hunt* decision virtually ended the use of the criminal conspiracy doctrine in labor relations. However, the courts developed the civil conspiracy doctrine, which holds that a group involved in concerted activities can inflict harm on other parties even though it is pursuing a valid objective in its own interest.[3] In the *Vegelahn v. Guntner* case, a Massachusetts court issued an injunction against a union that was picketing for higher wages and shorter hours. While the court agreed that the purposes were legitimate, it concluded that the picketing and a refusal to work would lead to more serious trouble, and injunctive relief was warranted.[4]

Breach of Contract

Breach of contract, a common law rule, was used by employers in restricting union membership and union organizing activities. For example, an employer would require its employees to sign a *yellow-dog contract*—an agreement stating that they would neither join nor assist in organizing a union. Since this contract would be a condition of continued employment, any violation would allow the company to discharge the employee. In addition, if any union organizers attempted to solicit union members among those who had signed yellow-dog contracts, they would be interfering with a legal contractual relationship between the employer and its employees. Thus, the employer could go to court and secure an injunction against the union organizers and any union-related activities. Union organizers who violated the court order then could be charged with contempt of court and possibly fined and imprisoned.[5]

Application of Antitrust Legislation to Labor Unions

In the late 1800s, an attempt was made to guard against increasing business monopolies, concentration of ownership, and business combinations that eliminated competition. One such attempt was the passage of the Sherman Antitrust Act of 1890, whose coverage neither specified nor excluded labor unions. Section I states that "every contract, combination in the form of trust or otherwise, or conspiracy, in restraint of trade or commerce among the several states . . . is hereby declared to be illegal."[6] Such wording made it debatable whether Congress had intended labor unions to be covered.

The answer was not given until 1908 in the landmark decision, *Loewe v. Lawlor* (better known as the Danbury Hatters case). The United Hatters of America, having organized seventy of eighty-two firms in the industry, wanted to organize Loewe and Company, a nonunion employer. They sought to have their union recognized and to have only union members employed (a closed shop). When the company refused, the union struck, strikers were replaced, and operations were continued. Recognizing the strike failure, the United Hatters organized a nationwide boycott assisted by the American Federation of Labor and directed toward all retailers, wholesalers, and customers. The boycott was successful, costing the company $85,000 during the year. Thereupon the employer went to court and eventually appealed to the Supreme Court. The high court ruled that unions were covered under the Sherman Act, that the union owed the company $252,000 (treble damages), and that the membership was responsible for payment.[7]

Once the *Loewe* decision was publicized, organized labor concluded that it must seek changes in the act. An aggressive campaign led to the enactment of the Clayton Act of 1914. Included among its provisions were:

[The] labor of a human being is not a commodity or article of commerce. Nothing contained in the antitrust laws shall be construed to forbid the existence and operation of labor [unions] . . . nor shall such organizations . . . be held or construed to be illegal combinations or conspiracies in restraint of trade. . . .

No restraining order or injunction shall be granted . . . in any case between an employer and employees . . . growing out of a dispute concerning terms or conditions of employment, unless necessary to prevent irreparable injury to property. . . .

No such restraining order . . . shall prohibit any person or persons . . . from ceasing to perform work . . . recommending, advising, or persuading others by peaceful means so to do, . . . peacefully persuading any person to work or abstain from working, . . . peacefully assembling in a lawful manner, and for lawful purposes.[8]

When Samuel Gompers, president of the AFL, read the provisions of the act, he proclaimed it U.S. labor's Magna Charta. Gompers' joy, however, was short-lived; a series of Supreme Court decisions in the 1920s left no doubt that the Clayton Act was not labor's Magna Charta. In fact, the Clayton Act probably hurt union growth and development more than it helped, because under the act employers could seek injunctions on their own, whereas before, only the U.S. district attorneys could.

The first major case occurred in 1921 and involved the printing press industry. The union had been successful in organizing all of the four major manufacturers of printing presses except Duplex Printing Press. While the three unionized companies operated under an eight-hour day and union wage scale, Duplex continued a ten-hour day and paid below the union scale. Failing to unionize Duplex, the union organized a strike, which was also unsuccessful. Because Duplex was operating at a lower cost than the other companies and posed an economic threat to them, the unions formed a boycott, refusing to install or handle Duplex products and warning users against operating Duplex equipment. The company sued for an injunction under the Clayton Act, and the Supreme Court ruled that unions were not exempt from antitrust legislation when they departed from normal and legitimate union activities. Therefore, the Clayton Act restricted injunctions only when a boycott involved an employer and its own employees. Since many of the boycott activities were conducted by sympathetic union members, not employees of Duplex, the use of the injunction was legal.[9]

Another Supreme Court decision in the same year defined "peaceful picketing" as a single representative at each plant entrance announcing that a strike is occurring and trying to peacefully persuade employees and others to support the strike.[10] With only one person on the picket line, the unions would obviously be unable to demonstrate their strength and unity in the strike.

With injunctions easier to obtain, a series of devastating Supreme Court decisions, absence of favorable labor legislation, use of anti-union tactics such as "goon squads," blackmail, and blacklisting, and the U.S. economy beginning a period of economic prosperity in the 1920s, the labor movement entered a comparatively static period. This was a time of regrouping, self-analysis, and establishment of new strategies.

The Norris–La Guardia Act

In the early 1930s, with the beginning of the country's most severe economic depression, political pressure on Congress mounted, and there was general dissatisfaction with judicial restrictions in labor relations. In 1932 Congress passed the Norris–La Guardia Act (also called the Federal Anti-Injunction Act). Marking a change in philosophy in labor relations, the act allowed employees "full freedom of association, self-organization, and designation of representatives of (their) own choosing, negotiation of terms and conditions of . . . employment" and "freedom from employer interference, restraint, or coercion." Further, it recognized employees' right to freedom from employer interference in their efforts of "self-organization and other concerted activities for the purpose of collective bargaining or other mutual aid or protection."[11]

The act restricted the role of the federal courts in labor disputes. Foremost was the restriction of issuance of any injunction, temporary or permanent, in any case involving or growing out of a labor dispute,[12] except where the employer, in open court and under cross-examination, could prove the following:

1. Unlawful acts had been threatened or committed.
2. Substantial and irreparable injury to the employer's property would follow.
3. Greater injury would be inflicted upon the employer by denial of an injunction than upon the union by granting injunction.
4. Employer had no adequate remedy at law.
5. Public officers were unable or unwilling to furnish adequate protection.
6. The employer had made every effort to settle the dispute through collective bargaining (including mediation, voluntary arbitration, and so on) before going to court.

If and when an injunction was issued, it would stop only specific acts; thereby the general, all-encompassing injunctions that had become customary were prohibited. In addition, individuals held in contempt of court (usually labor leaders who violated a court injunction) would be allowed a trial by jury.

The Norris–La Guardia Act also declared that the yellow-dog contract was unenforceable in federal courts.[13] However, many companies continued the practice of discharging employees for union activities. This provision did allow union organizers more freedom in contacting employees about joining unions with less fear of a breach of contract violation, a tactic that had been used successfully against them.

With no administrative agency under the Norris–La Guardia Act, it was impossible to enforce the act's new policy on behalf of interested employees or unions. Yet two judicial decisions under the act indicated more positive interpretations for organized labor. In both cases, the companies were denied injunctions because of the existence of a labor dispute.[14] A dramatic demonstration of the court's change in viewpoint on labor disputes occurred when the Supreme Court ruled that labor disputes were not covered under the Sherman Act, even though a union had seized a plant, declared a sit-down strike, remained in possession of the plant for nearly a month, and caused over $200,000 worth of damage to the company.[15]

Another case involved the Supreme Court's refusal to issue an injunction against a union that became involved in a private work dispute. Two

Part 1/Recognition of the Rights and Responsibilities of Unions and Management

unions claimed the right to erect and dismantle machinery at an Anheuser Busch Plant in St. Louis and later struck and led a nationwide boycott of Anheuser Busch beer against the producer, who was essentially an innocent bystander in the labor dispute. Furthermore, the union action arising from a labor dispute was not subject to damage suits or criminal proceedings.[16]

Historical Development of the National Labor Relations Act and Its Amendments

In addition to the Norris–La Guardia Act, 1932 witnessed a new president, Franklin Roosevelt, who was backed strongly by labor unions, and a new Congress receptive to labor legislation as a means of ending a long depression. One of the first acts of this new administration was to encourage Congress to pass the National Industrial Recovery Act—a law designed to stabilize economic activity by allowing businesses to form associations drawing up codes of fair competition to standardize marketing, pricing, financial, and other practices. Upon approval of the codes by the National Recovery Administration, firms could display the "Blue Eagle" symbol that supposedly signified compliance and identified firms from which customers should purchase their goods and services. Section 7 of the act required the codes to guarantee employees the right to unionize without employer interference, and a National Labor Board was later established to help settle disputes and to determine violations under Section 7.

Because the act did not require employers to deal with unions and the National Labor Board could not enforce its orders effectively, most employers chose to recognize and develop their own company unions. Prompted by the board's failure, increasing employer resistance, and growing strike activity, in 1934 Congress issued a joint resolution calling for the president to establish a National Labor Relations Board to investigate violations under Section 7 and to hold elections to determine whether the employees would choose a union to represent them.[17] This board, created like its predecessor by executive order of the president, had trouble enforcing its orders and determining employee organizational units for conducting elections. Then, in 1935, the Supreme Court ruled the codes of fair competition unconstitutional, invalidating the National Labor Relations Board.

Senator Robert Wagner, chairman of the National Labor Relations Board and an active participant in labor law matters, in 1935 steered through Congress a separate labor relations law—the Wagner Act or National Labor Relations Act (NLRA). Standing on its own, it guaranteed certain employee rights, detailed specific employer unfair labor practices, and created the National Labor Relations Board to enforce its provisions. The board would adjudicate unfair labor practices and conduct representation elections (specific provisions are covered later in the chapter).

For the next two years, significant employer resistance to the act mounted because most employers believed it would be ruled unconstitutional like the National Industrial Recovery Act.[18] However, in 1937 the Supreme Court decided five labor relations cases—the most publicized, *NLRB v. Jones & Laughlin Steel Corp.* [301 U.S. 1(1937)]—and declared the Wagner Act constitutional.

With Supreme Court recognition of the Wagner Act and the improvement of economic conditions in the United States, unions experienced tremendous growth and power.[19] In fact, for the next ten years, union activities caused many to believe that the labor relations pendulum had swung too far toward unions. Examples that precipitated much public antagonism were strikes over representation rights between CIO and AFL unions, numerous boycotts that hurt innocent bystanders, numerous walkouts over bargaining issues, refusal to negotiate in good faith with employers, and coercion of applicants to become members of unions before qualifying for employment.

As a reaction to organized labor's actions, in 1947 Congress amended the National Labor Relations Act by enacting the Taft-Hartley Act, or Labor Management Relations Act. Calling it a "slave labor act," labor groups immediately mounted a successful campaign to have President Truman veto the bill; however, Congress easily overrode Truman's veto. Regaining much balance in labor relations legislation, the act reorganized the NLRB and included union unfair labor practices covering such topics as union security, bargaining requirements, boycotts by unions not involved in the dispute, and strikes over work assignments.

With the Taft-Hartley Act, unions lost their favorable legal position. Their memberships as a percentage of the labor force began to stabilize, then to decline steadily. (Reasons for the decline are explained in Chapters 2 and 5.)

In the late 1950s, a special senate committee headed by John McClellan vigorously pursued the abuses of power and corruption of union leaders, particularly those of the Teamsters and specifically of Dave Beck and James Hoffa.[20] Exposing shocking examples of corruption and abuses to the U.S. public, Congress reacted in 1959 by passing the Landrum-Griffin Act, also called the Labor-Management Reporting and Disclosure Act. Its first six titles pertain mostly to union internal affairs and government (covered in Chapter 5), and Title VII further amends the Taft-Hartley Act.

Since that time, several serious attempts have been made to further amend the NLRA.

1. In 1965 organized labor mounted a major campaign to amend Section 14 (b), a provision which allows states to outlaw various forms of union security, such as union shops, in their states (see Chapter 10 for details).

2. Another effort, initially backed by the Nixon administration, was designed to place all transportation under the NLRA. Under its provisions, the president would have alternative courses of action available

to stop national emergency strikes in the transportation industry. But when Frank Fitzsimmons, president of the Teamsters, publicly announced his support for Nixon as president in 1972, the administration let its efforts for new legislation quietly die.

3. In 1975 Congress passed the so-called "common situs" picketing bill, which would allow construction unions to picket an entire worksite even though the labor dispute involved only one union. President Ford had agreed with Labor Secretary John Dunlop and labor leaders that he would sign the bill; but under heavy pressure from business, he vetoed it—whereupon, John Dunlop resigned as secretary of labor.

4. Several successful legislative attempts have pertained to the health care industry (see Chapter 17) and inclusion of the postal service under the NLRA (see Chapter 15).

5. In 1978 an embittered battle for labor law reform was launched. The bill was designed to require representation elections within a month from the date the NLRB received the petition for an election. Also, it called for compensation for employees whose employer refused to bargain in good faith in initial negotiations and included double back pay for employees who were unfairly discharged by employers for union activities. Further, it authorized the withdrawal of federal government contracts from employers who continued to commit flagrant unfair labor practices. Strongly backed by the Carter administration and passed in the House by a strong majority, the bill met its death by a successful Senate filibuster when those who favored the law failed to secure enough voting strength to end the filibuster. Passage of the labor law reform remains a high legislative priority with the AFL-CIO;[21] however, in early 1979, the AFL-CIO announced that it would be a dormant issue until 1981.

The National Labor Relations Act: The Wagner Act of 1935 as Amended by the Taft-Hartley Act in 1947 and the Landrum-Griffin Act in 1959

The National Labor Relations Act is discussed primarily from a current perspective. Little attention is given to indicating the origin of each specific provision so that unnecessary confusion can be avoided.

Statement of Public Policy

The United States was in the midst of its most severe economic depression when the Wagner Act was passed, establishing a new national labor relations policy and giving some indication of the changing role of the federal government in national economics. It recognized that employer denials of the employees' right to organize and employer refusal to accept collective bargaining had previously led to strikes and industrial conflicts. It also acknowledged that inequality of bargaining power between employees and employers affected the flow of commerce and aggravated recurring economic depressions by depressing wages and purchasing power and thereby prevented the stability of wages and working conditions. Further, it recognized that protection by law of the right of employees to organize and bargain collectively would promote the flow of commerce, restore equality of bargaining power, and encourage friendly adjustment of industrial disputes.

The Congress declared that the purpose of the new U.S. labor relations policy was

to eliminate the causes of certain substantial obstructions to the free flow of commerce and to mitigate and eliminate these obstructions when they have occurred by encouraging the practice and procedure of collective bargaining and by protecting the exercise by workers of full freedom of association, self-organization, and designation of representatives of their own choosing, for the purpose of negotiating the terms and conditions of their employment or other neutral aid or protection.[22]

After twelve years of experience under the Wagner Act, Congress further defined national labor relations policy with the Taft-Hartley amendments. These acknowledged that industrial strife could be minimized if employees and labor unions as well as employers recognized one another's rights and declared that no party had the right to engage in activities or practices that jeopardized the national health or safety.

Rights of Employees

Under Section 7 of the NLRA, employees were assured certain rights: to form and organize their own labor organizations, to become members of labor unions or to refuse to join, to bargain collectively through representatives of their own choosing, and to engage in other concerted activities for the purpose of collective bargaining or other forms of mutual aid or protection, such as strikes, picketing, and boycotts.

However, these rights are not unlimited; they have been frequently restricted. For instance, employees cannot refrain from paying union membership dues and fees if there is a contract provision requiring such payment as a condition of continued employment. (These union-shop agreements are discussed in Chapter 10.) The right to strike can be limited by a strike's objective, its timing, and the conduct of the strikers. For example, if a strike's purpose is to achieve a contract provision forcing the employment of only union members, its purpose is illegal; therefore the strike is illegal. If a strike occurs when there is a no-strike provision in the contract, the timing of the strike is inappropriate, and all striking employees can be discharged.

Even where a strike is timely and has a legitimate objective, the strikers do not have the right to threaten or engage in acts of violence. For example, neither sit-down strikes nor refusals to leave the plant are protected strike activities. Strikers have also exceeded their rights when persons are physically blocked from entering a struck plant or threats of violence are made against workers not on strike. Picketing and boycott

Labor law has attempted to balance the interests and concerns of both unions and management.

activities are likewise limited. (Limitations on picketing are covered under unfair labor practices in this chapter, and boycott and other picketing restrictions are explained in Chapter 7.)

Collective Bargaining and Representation of Employees

The act specifies important elements of collective bargaining. (Because representational procedures and elections are nearly always prerequisites to collective bargaining, they are explained in detail in the following chapter.) Collective bargaining requires both the employer and the representative of the employees to meet at reasonable times and confer in good faith with respect to wages, hours, and other terms and conditions of employment. While the act does not compel either party to agree to a proposal from the other party or to make a concession, it does require the negotiation of an agreement "in good faith". If an agreement is reached, it must be reduced to writing and executed in good faith.

Other procedural requirements cover those times when either party may desire to change an existing contract. First, the party requesting a change, usually the union, must notify the other party in writing sixty days before the expiration date of the existing agreement of a desire to change it. Upon receipt of the request, the other party, usually management, must offer to meet and negotiate a new contract. Within thirty days after notifying the other party, the initiating party must notify the Federal Mediation and Conciliation Service of the existence of a dispute if no agreement has been reached on the proposed changes. Both parties are required to continue to negotiate without a strike or lockout until sixty days after the first notice or until the contract expires, whichever is later.

Only when the contract expires and other procedural obligations have been fulfilled is the union allowed to strike.

Unfair Labor Practices

While unfair labor practices of employers were included in Section 8 (a) of the Wagner Act of 1935 to protect employees from employer abuse, unfair labor practices of labor organizations were added in 1947 and 1959 for employer, employee, and union member protection.

Unfair Labor Practices: Employer First, the employer is forbidden to interfere with, restrain, or coerce employees in the exercise of the rights presented above. Violations include employer threats to fire workers if they join a union, threats to close the plant if the union is organized—especially when other plants owned by the employer are located in the same area—or questioning employees about their union activities. If such violation does occur, the employee or the union may file an unfair labor charge with the NLRB, which then initiates its enforcement procedure (covered later in the chapter). Employees are also protected in pursuing their joint working condition concerns even if they do not belong to a labor organization.

The board had been excessively restrictive in its rulings on employer expressions about unionism, regarding many employer speeches to employees as unlawful interference with union activities. However, in 1947 restrictions were eased. Employers were given the right to explain their labor policies, present the advantages and disadvantages of unions, and communicate orally and in writing their arguments and opinions as long as they contained "no threats of reprisal or force or no promise of benefits."[23] (Application and interpretation of this provision as it pertains to union election campaigns will be covered in Chapter 4.)

Attempting to dominate, interfering with the formation of, and financing and supporting a labor union are all prohibited employer activities. For instance, the existence of a *company union*, one which receives financial help from the company, is illegal. Nor are companies allowed to pressure employees into joining a particular union, to take an active part in organizing a union, to promote one union over a rival union during a representation election campaign, or to otherwise engage in "sweetheart" arrangements with union officials.

Employer discrimination against employees in terms of hiring, tenure of employment, or terms and conditions of employment for the purpose of encouraging or discouraging union membership constitutes other unfair labor practices. However, if the labor agreement requires union membership as a condition of employment and the employee does not pay the required union initiation fees and membership dues in accordance with the agreement, the employee may be discharged (see Chapter 10).

Another unfair labor practice pertains to discharge of or discrimination against an employee because he or she had filed charges or given testimony in an NLRB investigation, hearing, or court case under the act. If employees are refused reinstatement, demoted, or laid off because they have filed charges with the NLRB or testified at NLRB hearings, their employers have committed unfair labor practices.

A final employer unfair labor practice covers an employer's refusal to bargain in good faith about wages, hours, and terms and conditions of employment with the representative chosen by the employees. Employer obligations include the duty to supply information, to refrain from unilateral action, and to negotiate with employees after purchasing a unionized plant. (For a more thorough discussion see Chapter 6.) Refusing to meet the union for purposes of negotiation, refusing to provide cost data concerning an insurance plan, announcing a wage increase without consulting the union, and subcontracting work normally performed by bargaining unit employees without notifying the union that represents the affected employees and without giving the union an opportunity to bargain over the change in the conditions of employment are prohibited practices.

Unfair Labor Practices: Labor Union Unfair labor practices committed by unions were included in both major amendments in 1947 (Section 8 [b]) and 1959. The first forbids a union or its agents to restrain or coerce employees in the exercise of their rights guaranteed under the act. Examples include mass picketing that prevents entrance to the plant by nonstriking employees, threats to employees for not supporting the union, refusal to process a grievance because the employee has criticized the union officers, and refusal to refer an employee to a job based on such considerations as race or lack of union activities.

A second union unfair labor practice pertains to actions that cause an employer to discriminate against an employee with regard to wages, hours, and conditions of employment or for the purpose of encouraging or discouraging union membership. (For example, the company may be forced to assign better jobs to union members. Or, when two unions compete to represent the same workers, the company may side with the less aggressive union by assigning better jobs to its members.) Such prohibited practices include causing an employer to discharge employees who circulate a petition challenging a union practice or who make speeches against a contract proposal.

A third provision imposes on unions the same duty as employers to bargain in good faith. Refusing to negotiate with the employer's attorney, refusing to process a grievance because of race, sex, or union activities, and striking a company to compel it to leave a multi-employer bargaining unit are some activities illegal under the amended act.

The fourth unfair labor practice includes four prohibited activities. The union may not force, threaten, require, or induce

□ An employer or self-employed person into joining a union or entering into a *hot-cargo agreement* (signed agreement stating that union members will not be required to handle "hot cargo"—goods made by nonunion labor and workers at a struck plant except in the garment industry).

□ Any person into using, selling, handling, and transporting goods of a producer, processor, or manufacturer that is not directly involved in a labor dispute (secondary boycott—covered in more detail in Chapter 7).

□ Any employer to recognize or bargain with a particular labor organization if another labor organization has already been certified by the NLRB.

□ Any employer to assign certain work to employees in a particular labor union, trade, or craft rather than another. (A special procedure for handling such disputes over work assignments was made available and is covered in Chapter 12.)

Unions are prohibited from charging excessive or discriminatory membership fees. Any alleged discrepancy would be investigated by the NLRB in accordance with the practices and customs of other unions in the particular industry and wages paid to the affected employees. For example, if a union raises its initiation fee from $75.00 to $250.00, an amount equal to four weeks' pay, when other unions charge only $12.50, the practice would be declared illegal. Also prohibited is charging black or female employees higher fees so as to discourage their membership. Labor unions are also forbidden to cause or attempt to cause an employer to pay for services that are not performed or not to be performed; this practice, known as *featherbedding*, is discussed further in Chapter 12.

Enforcement of the Act

National Labor Relations Board Because the rights of employees provided by the act are not self-enforcing, the NLRB was established to administer and enforce it. The NLRB includes a five-member board and its staff; the General Counsel and its staff; and fifty regional and field offices located in major cities. While the General Counsel has final authority to investigate and issue complaints and general supervisory responsibilities over the regional and field offices, the board establishes policy and serves as the judge in final appeals within the NLRB structure. In other words, the General Counsel's role is like that of a prosecutor, and the board's more like that of a judge.

The agency has two major functions: (a) supervising and conducting representation elections (covered in Chapter 4) and (b) adjudicating employer and union unfair labor practices. Contrary to some beliefs, the NLRB processes are set in motion only when requested in writing and filed with the proper NLRB office. Such requests are called petitions in the case of elections and charges in the case of unfair labor practices.

While the NLRB has authority to enforce the act in all cases involving interstate commerce, it has exercised its discretion and established jurisdictional standards for those cases it will accept and it believes have a substantial effect on commerce. (See the appendix to the chapter, NLRB's Jurisdiction Standards.) For example, a gas station, hotel, retail store, or apartment complex must gross $500,000 in annual volume before the NLRB will accept its petition or charge, whereas gross annual receipts of private colleges and universities must reach $1 million.

NLRB Procedure Regarding Unfair Labor Practices The procedure for an unfair labor practice complaint (see Exhibit 3–1) starts when an employee, employer, labor union, or individual files a charge with an NLRB office. Then the party that is charged is notified that an investigation of the alleged violation will be conducted. In many cases, the parties themselves may agree to a resolution before the investigation, and no further steps are needed. However, if no settlement is reached, an unfair labor practice hearing is conducted before an administrative law judge, who makes findings and recommendations to the board based on the record of the hearing. All parties are authorized to appeal the administrative law judge's decision directly to the board. The board considers the information provided and data collected, and if it believes an unfair labor practice has occurred, an order to cease and desist such practices and to take appropriate affirmative action is issued.

Cease and desist orders simply direct the violators to stop whatever activities were deemed unfair labor practices. The board exercises some discretion in determining *appropriate affirmative action,* and typical orders to employers include:

☐ Disestablish an employer-dominated company union.

☐ Offer employees immediate and full reinstatement to their former positions, and pay them back their wages plus interest.

☐ Upon request, bargain collectively with the exclusive bargaining representative of the employees.

Orders to unions include:

☐ Refund excessive or illegally collected dues plus interest.

☐ Upon request, bargain collectively in good faith with the prescribed employer.

The Role of the Judiciary The courts under the enforcement provisions of the act serve two major purposes: (a) provide injunctive relief where appropriate and (b) review appealed decisions and orders of the NLRB.

Exhibit 3–1 Basic Procedures in Cases Involving Charges of Unfair Labor Practices

Charge

Filed with NLRB Regional Director; alleges unfair labor practice by respondent.

Injunction

Regional Director <u>must</u> ask District Court for temporary restraining order in unlawful boycott and strike cases.

Investigation

Regional Director determines whether formal action should be taken.

Withdrawal–refusal to issue complaint–settlement

Charge may be withdrawn before or after complaint is issued. Regional Director may refuse to issue a complaint; his refusal (dismissal of charge) may be appealed to General Counsel. Settlement of case may occur at this point or at later stages (informal agreement subject to approval of Regional Director; formal settlement agreement executed simultaneously with or after issuance of complaint, subject to approval of Board).

Injunction

Regional Director <u>may</u> ask District Court for temporary restraining order after complaint is issued in <u>all</u> cases of an unfair labor practice.

Complaint and answer

Regional Director issues complaint and notice of hearing. Respondent files answer in 10 days.

Hearing and report

Administrative Law Judge conducts hearing and files report recommending either (1) order to cease and desist from unfair labor practice or (2) dismissal of complaint.

Dismissal by Administrative Law Judge

Administrative Law Judge may grant motion to dismiss complaint. If so, appeal may be taken to <u>NLRB</u>.

Dismissal

NLRB finds respondent not guilty of unfair labor practice and dismisses case.

Cease and desist

NLRB finds respondent guilty of unfair labor practice and orders him to cease and desist.

Other disposition

NLRB sends case back to Regional Director for further action.

Court review

Dismissal order may be appealed to the Circuit Court of Appeals and from there to the U.S. Supreme Court.

Court enforcement and review

Circuit Court of Appeals enforces NLRB order or reviews appeal by aggrieved party. U.S. Supreme Court reviews appeals from CCA.

Source: Management & Audit Branch, Division of Administration, NLRB, revised November 1975.

As part of the enforcement procedure, the act authorizes the NLRB to petition for an injunction in connection with unfair labor practices where either an employer or a union fails to comply with a board order. It also provides that any person aggrieved by a board order may appeal directly to an appropriate court of appeals for a review. Upon reviewing the order, the court of appeals may enforce the order, return it for reconsideration, alter it, or set it aside. The final appeal, of course, is to the U.S. Supreme Court, which may be asked to review a decision, especially where several courts of appeal have differed in their interpretations of the law.

Assessment of the Administration of the NLRB

Overall, the administration of the NLRB, the General Counsel, and the regional offices must be labeled an administrative success. Under delegated authority from the board and supervision of the General Counsel, the regional offices have handled a large number of elections efficiently and economically and have performed their prosecuting functions promptly.[24] In fiscal 1978, the forty-third year of the NLRB, 53,261 cases were filed, of which 39,652 were unfair labor practices (a 5 percent increase over 1977). More than $13.5 million was recovered for 5,533 workers who suffered monetary losses as a result of unfair labor practices, and 8,240 representation elections among 420,000 employee voters were conducted. Since 1935, over 30 million ballots have been cast in over 300,000 representation elections.[25]

Another measure of the success of the NLRB has been its record with the courts. Even though the Supreme Court (as well as the NLRB) has been accused by some of having a pro-union bias, the bottom line for determining the NLRB's compliance with its constitutional powers is the frequency with which its decisions have been upheld or overturned. In this regard, the results are fairly clear; the NLRB has a most supportive record with the high court. In fact, since 1957, 73.9 percent of the NLRB cases that have been appealed to the Supreme Court have been upheld,[26] and in the 1977–78 term, all four NLRB decisions were upheld.[27]

While the board has continually faced new problems, such as union officers' failure to carry out the duty of representing their members fairly, deferral to arbitration of certain statutory rights, and preplanned and repetitive violations of the act, the subject that has caused the most criticism has been the inadequacy of the board's remedial powers. At present, it has no constitutional penal powers; it cannot award damages; it cannot impose severe penalties even when the violations are flagrant and repetitive. For individuals who have been discriminatorily discharged and deprived of employment for improper reasons, reinstatement with back pay plus interest rarely covers the real costs that accompany the period of unemployment.[28]

The board's record of obtaining reinstatement for unfairly discharged employees has not been impressive either. For example, two studies conducted in different NLRB regions (New England[29] and Texas[30]) revealed distressing results of the NLRB orders for reinstatement. In both studies, not only were less than a majority placed back on the job, but a surprisingly high percentage of those reinstated left their jobs after reinstatement.

Nonpartisan analysts have agreed that the board's remedies for serious unfair labor practices regarding refusal to bargain in good faith in the initial contract have been woefully deficient. Several attempts have been made to broaden the NLRB's authority, but none have succeeded thus far.[31] For example, when the NLRB attempted to assert itself by imposing a checkoff provision on an employer who had not bargained in good faith[32] and requiring the company to compensate its employees for monetary losses incurred as a result of the company's unlawful refusal to bargain with the certified union, the courts overruled the NLRB, stating that it had gone beyond its statutory authority.[33]

Even though these data demonstrate pessimistic findings, it is highly debatable whether stricter, harsher, and costlier remedies would reduce the number of unfair labor practice charges filed. Although several unions, former NLRB members, and at least one circuit court of appeals have endorsed financial reparations to employees in specific refusal to bargain cases, the intent of the act is not to reduce the intake of cases but to promote fair collective bargaining whereby management officials and union representatives are free to jointly determine their particular working conditions.[34]

Some have suggested that the board should press more vigorously to fully realize its present enforcement authority in the courts; however, this would require more resources for the NLRB since they have a considerable backlog of work. While orders of the NLRB are not self-enforcing, the board applies to the appropriate court of appeals for enforcement of its order. If the NLRB order is enforced by the court, it becomes a lawful decree of that court, requiring compliance and backed with civil contempt sanctions. If court-enforced orders are violated, the violator can be held in contempt of court and can be subject to more serious penalties.[35]

Railway Labor Act

Forerunners

Once considered the model labor relations law and hailed as highly successful,[36] the Railway Labor Act has been subjected in recent times to severe criticism. Like other labor laws, the Railway Labor Act did not develop overnight; rather it resulted from years of union activity and attempts at passing laws accommodating railroad labor relations.

Unionization started in the domestic railroads in 1863, when the Brotherhood of Locomotive Engineers organized.[37] While the early efforts in the legislative arena by labor unions were devoted to social legislation and state labor laws,[38] unions were instrumental in passing the Arbitration Act of 1888. Recommended by President Cleveland, this act stemmed from strikes and strife involving the Gould Railway System in the Southwest and the Chicago, Burlington, and Quincy Railroad.[39] It provided for voluntary arbitration and presidential investigation of labor disputes. Although the voluntary arbitration provision was never utilized, the presidential investigative powers were invoked during the Pullman strike in 1894. In this case, the U.S. attorney general, once an attorney for the Chicago, Burlington, and Quincy Railroad, obtained a sweeping injunction against the strike, and federal troops were called in. However, by the time the presidential commission could make its report, the strike had been broken. Still, its recommendations did lead to the next congressional enactment.

Since the Arbitration Act was proven inadequate, Congress enacted the Erdman Act in 1898. Retaining the arbitration provisions of its forerunner, the Erdman Act permitted any party to a labor dispute to petition the commissioner of labor and the chairman of the Interstate Commerce Commission to serve as mediators. If mediation efforts were unsuccessful, the two mediators were empowered to urge the parties to accept arbitration. The law was unique in prohibiting employer discrimination against any employees because of their union membership and establishing a prison sentence for violators (declared unconstitutional in 1908).[40]

While provisions of the Erdman Act were not used until 1906, between 1906 and 1913 sixty-one cases were settled under its provisions, mostly by mediation. In recognition of the importance of mediation, the act was amended in 1913 by the Newlands Act, which established a permanent Board of Mediation and Conciliation. This board had jurisdiction over negotiation disputes as well as authority to interpret agreements. During the next few years, the board was used frequently and with apparent success.[41]

During World War I the federal government took over the railroads, placing them under the Railroad Administration. Unions prospered and grew in strength in this period since it was illegal to discriminate against union members; national labor agreements were signed; boards of adjustments were created to settle grievances. At the conclusion of the war, railroads returned to private ownership, but Congress decided to maintain some of its wartime controls. It passed the Transportation Act of 1920, which created a U.S. Railroad Labor Board for mediation and arbitration and an adjustment board for settling grievances.

With unions determined to retain any gains made during the wartime era and railroads equally determined to erode them, numerous disputes (about 13,000) were filed during the five years the law was in effect. Repudiated by unions and ignored by the railroad companies, it became completely ineffective when the Supreme Court rejected the board's application for enforcement of one of its decisions to have a railroad carrier cease dealing with a company-dominated union.[42]

The Passage of the Railway Labor Act

After a number of attempts to amend the Transportation Act, a new law, the Railway Labor Act,[43] drafted jointly by a committee of railroad executives and union representatives, was passed in 1926. The Railway Labor Act relied almost entirely on collective bargaining for settling labor disputes, but it established mandatory mediation by the Board of Mediation if bargaining failed and recommended arbitration if mediation failed. To assist in dispute resolution, the president was granted authority to appoint an emergency board composed of neutrals to investigate railroad labor disputes and recommend procedures and terms for agreement. This approach was designed to arouse public opinion, which would pressure the parties to arrive at terms of agreement on their own.[44] (More detailed discussion of dispute resolution under the Railway Labor Act can be found in Chapter 7.)

Although the Railway Labor Act has been amended several times,[45] its purposes remain largely the same:

☐ To avoid interruptions of commerce.

☐ To forbid any limitation on employee's right to organize and join labor unions.

☐ To provide complete independence for both parties in carrying out purposes of the act.

☐ To provide prompt and orderly settlement of disputes over pay, rules, and working conditions.

☐ To provide prompt and orderly settlement of disputes over grievances and contract interpretation.[46]

Major tests for the Railway Labor Act came in 1930 and 1937. The first test involved the Brotherhood of Railway Clerks, which presented the Texas and New Orleans Railway with a set of proposed wage increases. In response, the railroad company discharged identified union members and created its own company union. The Brotherhood sought an injunction to restrain the company from interfering with employee rights granted under the act, and the company responded by declaring that the act should be held unconstitutional in accordance with the First and Fifth Amendments.[47] In 1930 the Supreme Court declared that the Railway Labor Act was constitutional and that the company had no right to interfere with the employee rights to select their bargaining representative.[48]

The 1937 test came after the Virginia Railway Company had refused to deal with System Federation Number 40, a labor union certified by the mediation board, and continued to deal only with the previously organized company union. The Supreme Court ruled that the purpose of the act was "aimed at securing settlement of labor disputes by inducing collective bargaining with the true representative of the employees and by preventing such bargaining with any who do not represent them."[49] Thus, these two Supreme Court decisions not only upheld the constitutionality of the Railway Labor Act but declared that employers must negotiate with the appropriately certified union and could not interfere with the employees' rights to organize and join unions.

Amendments

As indicated above, the Railroad Labor Act has been amended several times to correct deficiencies or omissions. The first major amendment, occurring in 1934, provided assistance to unions by barring employers from attempting to influence employees in selecting their bargaining representatives. Further, employers were directed to bargain collectively with certified labor representatives, and company-dominated unions and yellow-dog contracts were forbidden.

The 1934 amendment established the National Railroad Adjustment Board, a bipartisan group of eighteen union and eighteen management representatives, to assist in resolving grievances and interpreting provisions of the labor agreements. Where the board could not agree to a settlement, the amendment provided that the grievance be settled by an arbitrator selected by the parties. A three-member National Mediation Board replaced the Board of Mediation, and it was empowered to conduct representation elections in addition to its role in resolving conflicts over negotiating *new* labor agreements. Two years later, the act was amended again, and coverage was extended to a new and developing industry—air transportation—although the airlines were allowed to continue and maintain their local system boards for grievance resolution.[50]

Administrative Agencies

Two very important administrative agencies under the Railway Labor Act are (a) the National Mediation Board (NMB) and (b) the National Railroad Adjustment Board (NRAB).

The National Mediation Board. The National Mediation Board, composed of three presidential appointees with terms of three years, is responsible for representation elections and mediation activities. Representative elections are conducted by the NMB to determine whether the majority of employees want to be represented by a union, and if so, the election will identify the particular union. Its mediation activities involve the reconciliation of differences in negotiating *new* agreements with reference to wages, hours, and working conditions and differences over interpretation of provisions in the agreement. When mediation fails, the mediation board must recommend voluntary arbitration in hopes that an agreement can be reached.

The National Railroad Adjustment Board. The National Railroad Adjustment Board, comprised of an equal number of company and union representatives, was created in 1934 to hear disputes growing out of grievances and to interpret provisions in the labor agreements concerning pay, hours, and working conditions.[51] If the NRAB is unable to obtain agreement, the disputes are referred to arbitration.

Assessment of the Railway Labor Act

Any assessment of the Railway Labor Act must be kept in proper perspective. There are over 7,000 labor agreements in the railroad and airline industries, and about 1,000 railroad and 200 airline agreements (mostly local) are involved in negotiations during any given year.[52] Further, any measure of its effectiveness must be made with reference to the act's objectives—to promote free collective bargaining and protect the public from interrupted flows of commerce.[53]

Regarding negotiations, mediation has been the most important method of intervention under the act; however, very few nationwide railroad wage cases have been settled by mediation since 1936. Its greatest success has been in minor controversies after the major issues have been resolved. This does not mean that mediation is unimportant—minor disputes left unresolved could easily lead to major strikes in future negotiations.

One problem continually facing the NMB is that the parties involved often do not genuinely attempt to settle the issues on their own. Perhaps the mere presence of a special agency established solely to serve at no additional cost and assist in resolving disputes encourages its overuse. On the other hand, disputants have been accused of using it as a means of preparing for the emergency board intervention instead of actually negotiating with the other party.

Between 1926 and 1934, the act was highly effective: only two minor strikes occurred; only ten emergency boards were needed. And from 1934 until 1941 only one dispute was presented to an emergency board. During this time the Railway Labor Act was proclaimed the "model law," but then the case results began to change. By 1970, 176 cases (almost 5 per year) were taken to emergency boards. Not only were emergency boards quite common, but the procedures severely inhibited collective bargaining, and recommendations of the boards at critical times were handled with political expediency.[54]

With increasing support from the federal government to support the railway industry, decline in employment, changing technology, and less than optimistic projections for the railroad carriers, the period from 1971 to 1976 brought faint evidence that the administration of the Railway Labor Act and union-management relationships under the act had improved. Only nine emergency boards were appointed during this time (well below the long-term average). The low number is deceptive and prematurely optimistic, however, because Congress became heavily involved in resolving labor disputes in the railroad industry by enacting ad hoc legislation.[55]

The Railway Labor Act has been frequently criticized because the parties that seek its help fail to use voluntary arbitration. Under the act, the NMB must request that the parties arbitrate their disputes if mediation should fail. However, because either may refuse this request without penalty, a number of major disputes have been referred to the emergency boards rather than voluntarily arbitrated.[56]

Actual data, however, may alleviate these criticisms. Parties in conflict have actually accepted voluntary interest arbitration 350 times between 1935 and 1975, involving 60 different labor unions, 152 railroad companies, and 26 airlines. (Pan American World Airways alone has been involved in 30 such arbitration cases.) Thus, while not widely publicized, voluntary interest arbitration has played a far more important role in maintaining industrial peace between rail and air carriers and the unions representing employees than is generally realized. While its importance should not be overstated, neither should the extent of its use go unrecognized.[57]

The operations of the NRAB and other special boards have not been very successful. Since 1934, over 70,000 cases have been filed with the board.[58] By the end of 1975, there were over 21,000 grievances pending before it, special adjustment boards, and public law boards. Many of these possessed little merit, and most neutral observers have concluded that the problem with such a high number of grievances cannot be alleviated until both parties are forced to pay for their own arbitration costs—the practice in all other industries.[59] While these procedures cost the unions and companies only the salaries and fees of their own representatives, taxpayers' support of the NRAB and its referees amounts to around $800,000 per year.[60]

Promising Developments

Several events and developments that have occurred recently provide the basis for some optimism:

1. The most recent national railroad agreements have included a fixed term, a no-strike clause, and common expiration dates. These changes have moved collective bargaining closer to the pattern common in other industries and in effect have reduced the opportunities for conflict.
2. Recent negotiations have also been characterized by union-management cooperation, which has resulted in fewer conflicts and outside interventions.
3. Emergency board procedures have been drastically improved, and excessive ritualism and legalism so prevalent in the 1960s have been reduced.
4. Encouraging progress has been made on some long-standing manning and work-rule issues such as the fireman on diesel trains, combined road and yard service, and interdivisional runs.
5. New leadership has had a positive influence on both management and

unions, and neutrals and government officials have provided capable assistance in the bargaining and dispute resolution processes.

Critical issues remain to be resolved: work rules in some agreements that are more restrictive than others, intercraft wage structure problems, crew size, and others.[61] But there is still reason to be optimistic if the 1971–1976 trend can be sustained. As one authority has said:

No labor law can ensure peaceful and constructive labor relations. Although specific Amendments to the Railway Labor Act may be desirable—notably, in connection with representational questions—we should be careful about casting into oblivion a law that both parties, on balance, seemingly want to retain.[62]

Other Laws That Affect Labor Relations

Other statutes and executive orders, more narrow in scope, influence labor relations either directly or indirectly. The following section only highlights their major provisions; however, practitioners find that detailed knowledge of them is essential to most business operations.

Wage Legislation

The *Fair Labor Standards Act*, as amended, establishes a minimum wage, maximum hours, overtime pay, and child labor standards for covered firms. Since nearly all unionized firms already pay more than the minimum wage, this requirement does not have a great impact on labor relations. However, the requirements for time-and-a-half pay for hours over forty per week and child labor provisions are relevant.[63]

The *Equal Pay Act*, which was actually a 1963 amendment to the Fair Labor Standards Act, prohibits employers from discriminating on the basis of sex in the payment of wages for equal work. Pay differentials may exist, but they must be justified on the basis of skill, effort, responsibility, working conditions, seniority, merit, quantity or quality of production, or some factor other than sex.[64]

The *Davis-Bacon Act* requires recipients of federal government contracts of more than $2,000 for construction, alteration, or repair of public buildings or public works to pay wages determined by the Secretary of Labor as prevailing for similar construction work in the locality in which the work is to be performed.[65]

The *Walsh-Healy Public Contract Act* requires holders of federal government contracts exceeding $10,000 to pay their employees the prevailing wage rate for similar work in their industry. In addition, workers must be paid at least one and one-half times their basic rate of pay for all hours greater than eight per day or forty per week, whichever number of overtime hours is greater.

The *Work Hours Act of 1962* provides a uniform eight-hour day, forty-hour week, and overtime pay of one and one-half times regular rate for work performed under certain federal government contracts.[66]

Wage-Price Guidelines and Controls

On occasion, the federal government has believed it necessary to intervene on the side of the public to stabilize wage-price relationships. Between 1940 and 1974, wage-price stabilization programs were adopted five times: during World War II (1942–1945), during the postwar reconversion period (1945–1946), during the Korean War (1951–1952), during the Kennedy-Johnson administration (1962–1966), and during the Nixon period (1971–1974).[67]

With authority from the Economic Stabilization Act of 1970, President Carter launched a voluntary anti-inflation program in April 1978, but after an inflation rate of 10 percent per year was announced in October 1978, he decided to introduce Phase II of this program. Presenting it to the public on nationwide television, he disclosed the features discussed below.

Wage guidelines. Workers were asked to settle for wage-and-benefits increases averaging 7 percent over the years 1978 to 1981, with no more than 8 percent in the first year. With exemptions to employees earning less than $4 per hour and those under signed contracts, this wage guideline would be applied to groups of workers, not individuals. As an incentive for increased production, it would allow increases above the 7 percent guideline in cases where changes in work rules and practices showed demonstrable productivity increases. In October 1979, President Carter established a fifteen-member Pay Advisory Committee with equal representation from business, labor, and the public. This committee, headed by John Dunlop, will review the wage guidelines and make recommendations to redress wage inequities.

Price guidelines. Firms were expected to limit their overall price increases to one-half of one percent below the average annual price increase of 1976–1977. If a firm could not meet this standard, it must demonstrate its inability by presenting data of before-tax profit margins of no higher than the best two of the last three years. Moreover, if wage rate increases were less than one-half a percentage point less than the 1976–1977 base period, price reduction greater than the guideline would be expected.

Monitoring. The Council on Wage and Price Stability would be expanded to closely monitor adherence to the wage and price standards, especially by the top 400 firms with sales over $500 million and all major collective bargaining settlements. Further, the council would have authority to obtain, if necessary, information on prices, profits, and wages and then to point out publicly those not complying with the standards.

Government purchases. After January 1979, the federal government, a major purchaser of goods and services, would begin requiring firms awarded contracts in excess of $5 million to certify that they were adhering to the wage-price guidelines.

(The president's right to withhold federal government contracts from companies violating the wage-price guidelines was challenged by the AFL-CIO, nine of its affiliated international unions, and twenty-four Republican member of Congress. Although the challenge was successful in a federal district court in the District of Columbia, an appeals court reversed the lower court's decision. On further appeal in early July 1979, the Supreme Court let stand the appellate court's ruling, thereby upholding the president's right to withhold government contracts.)

Freeze on federal hiring. A ceiling would be placed on federal hiring, and only one-half of all federal government employees who retire or quit would be replaced, in effect reducing the number of employees by 20,000.

Penalties for violators. Violators would first be warned, then publicly denounced for failure to comply. Continued violation would mean exclusion from bidding on federal government contracts and, possibly, unfavorable regulatory and antitrust action and looser protection against foreign imports. These measures would be based on the assumption that any wage or price increase above the standard indicates inflationary conditions caused by shortages, excessive market power, or artificial shelter from competition.

Real wage insurance. President Carter announced that he would recommend to Congress a program for workers who were members of groups meeting the pay standard. Those groups would receive a tax rebate if the rate of inflation in a given year exceeded 7 percent. Such tax rebate would equal the difference between the actual rate of inflation and 7 percent multiplied by an individual's pay. But if the inflation rate were less than 7 percent, the tax rebate would not be applied.[68] Such a plan is similar to Arthur Okun's suggestion made during President Ford's WIN (Whip Inflation Now) conference in 1974.[69]

Initial reaction to the Carter program was quite mixed. The U.S. dollar regained some of its lost strength, indicating a favorable reaction on the international money market. Business leaders diplomatically pledged their support. Some union leaders, for example, Fitzsimmons of the Teamsters, initially indicated a willingness to cooperate,[70] while George Meany, president of the ALF-CIO, rebuffed the Carter program and called for mandatory wage-and-price controls covering every source of income.[71]

During 1979, the wage guidelines have been the basis of conflict in union and management negotiations and have even led to strikes—for example, the Teamsters' strike, the Machinists' strike against United Airlines, the Rubber Workers' strike against Uniroyal, and numerous minor strikes.[72] Other difficulties have also emerged in the administration of the Carter wage-price guideline program. They include Congress's reluctance to legislate the real wage insurance program, negotiated settlements that exceed the 7 percent wage guideline, the court ruling mentioned earlier—and later overturned—challenging President Carter's right to withhold government contracts, numerous complaints about excessive price increases by business firms,[73] and difficulties in handling wage inequities of employees of nonunion employers.[74]

Employment Discrimination Laws and Executive Orders

The *Equal Employment Opportunity Act of 1972*, which amended Title VII of the Civil Rights Act of 1964, prohibits any form of employment discrimination by companies, labor unions, and employment agencies on the basis of race, color, religion, sex, or national origin. Creating the Equal Employment Opportunity Commission, the act provides an enforcement procedure that includes investigations, attempts at conciliation, and suits filed on behalf of the complainant.

The *Age Discrimination in Employment Act of 1967*, as amended in 1978, prohibits employment discrimination against those who are between the ages of forty and seventy, forbids forced retirement based on age before age seventy, permits compulsory retirement for executives who are entitled to pensions of $27,000 per year or more, and authorizes jury trials in covered cases.[75]

Executive Order 11246, as amended by Executive Order 11375, prohibits employment discrimination in the federal government and by federal government contractors and subcontractors receiving $10,000 or more. Those having contracts of $50,000 or more are required to establish affirmative action plans that prescribe specific goals and procedures for increasing the percentage of minority employees. Firms that fail to comply could lose part or all of their contracts.[76]

The *Vocational Rehabilitation Act of 1973* (Section 503) requires holders of federal government contracts in excess of $2,500 to take affirmative action to employ and advance in employment qualified physically and mentally handicapped individuals. Further, if any handicapped individual believes that any federal contractor has failed to comply with the act or refuses to do so, such individual may file a complaint with the Department of Labor, which will investigate the complaint and take such action as the facts and circumstances warrant. In addition, Section 504 extends coverage to organizations receiving federal financial assistance and is enforced by the Department of Health, Education, and Welfare.[77]

Other Labor Relations—Related Laws

The *Military Selective Service Act of 1967* requires employers to restore veterans (those whose total military service time does not exceed four years) to the positions they held before entering the armed services or to similar positions of like seniority, status, and pay.

Also, the *Vietnam Era Veteran Readjustment Assistance Act* requires employers with government contracts of $10,000 or more to take affirmative action to employ and advance disabled veterans and qualified veterans of the Vietnam War.[78]

The *Social Security Act of 1935*, as amended, established two national systems of social security for protection against loss of income due to unemployment, old age, disability, and death: (1) retirement, survivors and disability insurance, and health insurance for persons over 65, and (2) unemployment insurance, which operates under a state-administered, federal-state plan whose operating costs are paid by the federal government.[79]

Other rather important laws include the Employee Retirement and Income Security Act of 1974 (covered in Chapter 13), the Occupational Safety and Health Act (covered in Chapter 12), and the various state laws and local ordinances which pertain to wages and hours, public sector labor relations, and equal employment opportunity.

Summary

This chapter has included the major provisions of federal labor relations laws in the United States. The knowledge and understanding of these legal influences are imperative for the full appreciation of the remaining chapters in this book, because nearly all issues in labor relations are either directly or indirectly influenced by labor relations law.

While many think of law in terms of statutes passed by the U.S. Congress or various state legislatures, labor relations and other types of law proceed not only from statutes but also from the U.S. Constitution, judicial decisions, and administrative decisions of government agencies. Similar laws and decisions develop at the state and local government levels.

Developing the legal influences historically, this chapter began with the early struggles of labor unions to exist as they faced unsympathetic judiciary and lack of any permissive legislation. Several hurdles included the criminal conspiracy and civil conspiracy doctrines as well as the breach of contract rulings. Then the Sherman Act, passed primarily to control business monopolies, was applied to labor unions also. With support of labor, the Sherman Act was amended by the Clayton Act; however, this act also proved unfavorable to unions.

While the 1920s did bring passage of the Railway Labor Act, little legislative action occurred in other sectors. However, the 1930s, with the country's most severe economic depression, brought about major changes. The enactment of the Norris–La Guardia Act changed the public policy toward labor relations. Not only did it recognize employees' rights to various freedoms, such as freedom of association and self-organization, it also restricted the role of the federal courts in labor disputes.

Recognizing several deficiencies in the Norris–La Guardia Act, Congress passed the National Labor Relations Act in 1935. This act dealt with employer unfair labor practices, established an administrative agency—the NLRB—and guaranteed a number of employee rights, such as the right to form and join unions and to participate in concerted actions. Then, in 1947 and again in 1959, Congress amended the National Labor Relations Act, with passage of the Taft-Hartley and the Landrum-Griffin Acts, respectively. The 1947 amendments added union unfair labor practices and restrictions on union security clauses, and the 1959 act added regulations of government and internal operations of unions and amended strike, picketing, and boycott activities.

Starting in 1863, union activity in the railroad industry played a key role in the legislative arena. The Arbitration Act of 1888 resulted primarily from labor unions' efforts. Other statutes—the Erdman Act of 1898, the Newlands Act of 1913, and the Transportation Act of 1920, forerunners to the Railway Labor Act—provided the foundation for railroad and airline labor law as it stands today. The Railway Labor Act, whose major purpose is to provide for stable and effective labor relations without major interruptions in commerce, established procedures for resolving labor disputes and created the National Mediation Board and National Railroad Adjustment Board to facilitate efforts in accomplishing the act's purposes. While the assessment may seem less than optimistic, several recent developments that give some evidence of success have been recognized: acceptance by the parties, recent no-strike clauses, improved employer-union cooperation on important issues, new leadership in both unions and management, and improved emergency board procedures.

The final section related to wage, wage-price stabilization, equal employment opportunity, and other laws that affect labor relations. While some of these laws affect labor relations more than others, each is important to those organizations and/or unions which it covers.

| Discussion Questions | 1. How have the major labor relations laws helped or hindered the development of unions? |

Discussion Questions

1. How have the major labor relations laws helped or hindered the development of unions?

2. How were yellow-dog contracts used against union organizers? How were they used to slow union growth?

3. Why did the 1914 Clayton Act, called by AFL president Samuel Gompers U.S. Labor's Magna Charta, prove to be less than a benefit to unions?

4. What was missing in the Norris–La Guardia Act (regarding adminis-

tration of the law) that was present in the National Labor Relations Act? Why was its absence important?

5. Although the National Labor Relations Act gives employees certain rights, these rights are not unlimited. Discuss.

6. The NLRB has been criticized for its lack of success in the actual reinstatement and continued employment of discharged employees under the NLRA. What could be changed in the NLRA or its administration that would improve the record on reinstatement?

7. The Railway Labor Act, once called the "model labor law," has been criticized by many. What are the reasons underlying this criticism? Why has the act lost its favorable status?

8. Why is it essential that there be a separate labor relations law for the railway and airline industries?

References

[1]J. R. Commons and E. A. Gilmore, *A Documentary History of American Industrial Society* (Cleveland, Ohio: A. H. Clark, 1910), p.68.

[2]*Commonweath v. Hunt*, 45 Mass. 4 (1842).

[3]E. E. Herman and G. S. Skinner, *Labor Law* (New York: Random House, 1972), p. 21.

[4]*Vegelahn v. Guntner*, 44 N.E. 1077 (1896). See Herbert L. Sherman, Jr., and William P. Murphy, *Unionization and Collective Bargaining*, 3d ed. (Washington, D.C.: Bureau of National Affairs, 1975), p. 3.

[5]*Hitchman Coal & Coke Company v. Mitchell*, 245 U.S. 229 (1917).

[6]26 Stat. 209 (1890).

[7]*Loewe v. Lawlor*, 208 U.S. 274 (1908).

[8]38 Stat. 731 (1914).

[9]*Duplex Printing Press Co. v. Deering*, 254 U.S. 443 (1921).

[10]*Truax v. Corrigan*, 257 U.S. 312 (1921).

[11]47 Stat. 70 (1932).

[12]A labor dispute was defined as "any controversy concerning terms or conditions of employment, or concerning the association or representation of persons in negotiating, fixing, maintaining, changing, or seeking to arrange terms or conditions of employment regardless of whether or not the disputants stand in the proximate relation of employer and employee." 47 Stat. 70 (1932).

[13]Ibid.

[14]*Lauf v. E. G. Shinner & Co.*, 303 U.S. 315 (1938); *New Negro Alliance v. Sanitary Grocery Co.*, 303 U.S. 552 (1938).

[15]*Apex Hosiery Co. v. Leader*, 310 U.S. 467 (1940).

[16]*United States v. Hutcheson*, 312 U.S. 219 (1941).

[17]Alvin L. Goldman, *The Supreme Court and Labor-Management Relations Law* (Lexington, Mass.: D. C. Heath, 1976), pp. 26–28; and Sherman and Murphy, *Unionization and Collective Bargaining*, pp. 7–9.

[18]Goldman, *The Supreme Court*, pp. 28–31.

[19]Sherman and Murphy, *Unionization and Collective Bargaining*, p. 9.

[20]Goldman, *The Supreme Court*, pp. 31–39.

[21]"The Continuing Priority of Labor Law Reform," *American Federationist* 85 (November 1978), p. 8.

[22]This section was taken from the Wagner Act, 49 Stat. 449 (1935); Labor Management Relations Act, 61 Stat. 136 (1947); Landrum-Griffin Act, 73 Stat. 519 (1959); Office of General Counsel, National Labor Relations Board, *A Guide to Basic Law and Procedures under the National Labor Relations Act* (Washington, D.C.: Government Printing Office, 1976), unless otherwise noted.

[23]Cindy M. Hudson and William B. Werther, Jr., "Section 8(c) and Free Speech," *Labor Law Journal* 28 (September 1977), pp. 608–614.

[24]Edward B. Miller, *An Administrative Appraisal of the NLRB* (Philadelphia: Industrial Research Unit, University of Pennsylvania, 1977), p. 130.

[25]National Labor Relations Board, *43rd Annual Report of the NLRB, 1978* (Washington, D.C.: Government Printing Office, 1979), pp. 1–2.

[26]Roger Handberg, Jr., "The Supreme Court and the NLRB," *Labor Law Journal* 26 (November 1975), pp. 737–739.

[27]Gregory J. Mounts, "Labor and the Supreme Court: Significant Decisions of 1977–78," *Monthly Labor Review* 102 (January 1979), p. 51.

[28]John H. Fanning, "We Are Forty—Where Do We Go?" *Labor Law Journal* 27 (January 1976), pp. 5–6.

[29]Les Aspin, "Legal Remedies under the NLRA," in G. G. Somers, ed., *Proceedings of the Annual Meeting of the Industrial Relations Research Association* (Madison, Wis.: Industrial Relations Research Association, 1970), pp. 265–267. A study in the 1960s revealed that in seventy-one New England companies where 194 workers were unfairly discharged, only 85 were actually placed back on the job, and 23 others placed on preferential hiring lists. The reasons given by employees for not going back to their jobs were fear of company retaliation (39 cases) and possessing a better job (28 cases). Surprisingly, of the 85 who were actually reinstated, 60 had left their companies within two years.

[30]Elvis C. Stephens and Warren Chaney, "A Study of the Reinstatement Remedy under the National Labor Relations Act," *Labor Law Journal* 25 (January 1974), pp. 31–46. This study was conducted in 1971–72 and involved 86 companies and 43 unions. In these cases 217 discriminatees were ordered reinstated; 129, or 59 percent, refused reinstatement, most (114 of the 129) due to fear of company backlash. Only 88 accepted reinstatement, but only 57 were reinstated immediately; 31 were placed on a preferential list, and only 13 of these were eventually hired. Overall, only 70 were actually reinstated, and more damaging, six months after reinstatement, 60 were no longer employed by their companies. Most (66.7 percent) had left their jobs claiming unfair employer treatment.

[31]Frank W. McCulloch and Tim Bornstein, *The National Labor Relations Board* (New York: Praeger Publishers, 1974), p. 180.

[32]*H. K. Porter Co. v. NLRB*, 73 LRRM 2561 (1970).

[33]*Auto Workers v. NLRB*, 76 LRRM 2573 (1971); *Ex-Cell-O Corp. v. NLRB*, 77 LRRM 2547 (1971).

[34]Bernard Samoff, "The Case of the Burgeoning Load of the NLRB," *Labor Law Journal* 22 (October 1971), pp. 264–265.

[35]Douglas S. McDowell and Kenneth Huhn, *NLRB Remedies for Unfair Labor Practices* (Philadelphia: Industrial Research Unit, University of Pennsylvania, 1976), pp. 245–246.

[36]Sherman and Murphy, *Unionization and Collective Bargaining*, p. 6.

[37]R. J. Sampson and M. R. Farris, *Domestic Transportation*, 2d ed. (Boston: Houghton Mifflin, 1970), p. 344.

[38]Maryland passed a law in 1878; in the next ten years New Jersey, Pennsylvania, Ohio, Iowa, Kansas, New York, and Massachusetts followed suit.

[39]Charles M. Rehmus, "Evolution of Legislation Affecting Collective Bargaining in the Railroad and Airline Industries," in Charles M. Rehmus, ed., *The Railway Labor Act at Fifty*, (Washington, D.C.: Government Printing Office, 1977), p. 4.

[40]Rehmus, "Collective Bargaining," pp. 5–6. *Adair v. U.S.*, 208 U.S. 161 (1908) was the case deciding the provision's unconstitutionality.

[41]Ibid., p. 6.

[42]Ibid., p. 7.

[43]44 Stat. 577 (1926).

[44]Rehmus, "Collective Bargaining," p. 9.

[45]1934, 1936, 1940, 1951, 1964, 1966, and 1970.

[46]44 Stat. 577 (1926), as amended.

[47]Rehmus, "Collective Bargaining," p. 11.

[48]*Texas & New Orleans R.R. v. Brotherhood of Railway and Steamship Clerks*, 281 U.S. 548 (1930).

[49]*Virginia Ry. v. System Federation No. 40*, 300 U.S. 515 (1937).

[50]Rehmus, "Collective Bargaining," pp. 14–15. The remaining amendments were comparatively minor: the 1940 amendment clarified the coverage of rail operations in coal mines; 1951, the closed shop was prohibited, but the union shop was allowed; 1964, the terms of office for members of the National Mediation Board were classified; 1966, special adjustment boards were authorized to hear and resolve grievances on local properties; 1970, membership on the National Railroad Adjustment Board was reduced to 34—half management-appointed and half union-appointed.

[51]45 U.S.C. Sections 154–158.

[52]Charles M. Rehmus, "The First Fifty Years—And Then," in Rehmus, ed., *Railway Labor Act at Fifty*, p. 246.

[53]Beatrice M. Burgoon, "Mediation under the Railway Labor Act," in Rehmus, ed., *Railway Labor Act at Fifty*, p. 23.

[54]Herbert R. Northrup, "The Railway Labor Act: A Critical Reappraisal," *Industrial and Labor Relations Review* 25 (October 1971), p. 7.

[55]Donald E. Cullen, "Emergency Boards under the Railway Labor Act," in Rehmus, ed., *Railway Labor Act at Fifty*, pp. 175–176.

[56]Northrup, "A Critical Reappraisal," p. 8.

[57]Rehmus, "First Fifty Years," pp. 250–251.

[58]Northrup, "A Critical Reappraisal," pp. 17–22.

[59]Rehmus, "First Fifty Years," pp. 248–249.

[60]Northrup, "A Critical Reappraisal," pp. 17–22.

[61]Cullen, "Emergency Boards," pp. 176–183. Also see "The Railroads Lose Their Bargaining Unity," *Business Week*, April 10, 1978, pp. 31–32.

[62]Mark L. Kahn, "Labor-Management Relations in the Airline Industry," in Rehmus, ed., *Railway Labor Act at Fifty*, p. 128.

[63]Employment Standards Administration, Department of Labor, *Federal Labor Laws and Programs* (Washington, D.C.: Government Printing Office, 1971), pp. 79–100.

[64]John E. Burns and Catherine G. Burns, "An Analysis of the Equal Pay Act," *Labor Law Journal* 24 (February 1973), pp. 92–95; Donald Elisburg, "Equal Pay in the U.S.: The Developments and Implementation of the Equal Pay Act of 1973," *Labor Law Journal* 24 (April 1978), pp. 195–208.

[65]Jerry E. Pohlman, "Hard-Core Unemployment, Public Housing Construction, and the Bacon-Davis Act," *Labor Law Journal* 22 (April 1971), pp. 195–203; and Donald Elisburg, "Wage Protection under the Davis-Bacon Act," *Labor Law Journal* 28 (June 1977), pp. 323–328.

[66]Employment Standards Administration, *Federal Labor Laws and Programs*, p. 94.

[67]Milton Derber, "The Wage Stabilization Program in Historical Perspective," *Proceedings of the 1972 Annual Spring Meeting of the IRRA* (Madison, Wis.: Industrial Relations Research Association, 1972), p. 453.

[68]Fact sheet on President Carter's anti-inflation program released by the White House, October 24, 1978, reprinted in the *Atlanta Constitution*, October 25, 1978; "Inflation: The Big Fight Opens," *Time*, October 30, 1978, pp. 120–121; Richard J. Levine and Urban C. Lehner, "Wage-Price Program Includes Possible Tax Rebate for Workers Who Meet a 7 Percent Annual Pay Standard," *Wall Street Journal*, October 25, 1978, p. 3.

[69]"Trade, Wage Insurance, and Alfred Kahn," *Business Week*, November 13, 1978, p. 18.

[70]"Business, Labor Reviews of Carter's Anti-Inflation Proposals Are Mixed," *Wall Street Journal*, October 26, 1978, p. 3.

[71]Mandatory Wage, Price Controls Urged by AFL-CIO; Voluntary Plan Assailed," *Wall Street Journal*, November 1, 1978, p. 3.

[72]"Labor Walks Out on the 7%," *Business Week*, May 28, 1979, pp. 46–47.

[73]"Planning the New Guidelines," *Business Week*, June 18, 1979, pp. 46–47.

[74]"Nonunion Anger against 7%," *Business Week*, June 11, 1979, pp. 84–88.

[75]Bureau of National Affairs, *1978 Age Discrimination Act Amendments* (Washington, D.C.: BNA Books, 1978), pp. 3–12.

[76]Equal Employment Opportunity Commission, *Laws and Rules You Should Know* (Washington, D.C.: Government Printing Office, 1975), pp. 78–90. There is also an executive order on age discrimination.

[77]Public Law, 93–112, 1973.

[78]Rudolph Oswald and J. Douglas Smith, "Veterans' Reemployment Rights: Their Effect on Collective Bargaining Agreements," *Labor Law Journal* 22 (September 1971), pp. 547–548.

[79]Employment Standards Administration, *Federal Labor Laws and Programs*, p. 138.

Appendix to Chapter 3

The NLRB's Jurisdictional Standards

The board's standards in effect on July 1, 1976, were as follows:

1. **Nonretail business.** Direct sales of goods to consumers in other states, or indirect sales through others (called outflow), of at least $50,000 a year; or direct purchases of goods from suppliers in other states, or indirect purchases through others (called inflow), of at least $50,000 a year.

2. **Office buildings.** Total annual revenue of $100,000, of which $25,000 or more is derived from organizations which meet any of the stan-

dards except the indirect outflow and indirect inflow standards established for nonretail enterprises.

3. **Retail enterprises.** At least $500,000 total annual volume of business.

4. **Public utilities.** At least $250,000 total annual volume of business, or $50,000 direct or indirect outflow or inflow.

5. **Newspapers.** At least $200,000 total annual volume of business.

6. **Radio, telegraph, television, and telephone enterprises.** At least $100,000 total annual volume of business.

7. **Hotels, motels, and residential apartment houses.** At least $500,000 total annual volume of business.

8. **Privately operated health care institutions.** At least $250,000 total annual volume of business for hospitals; at least $100,000 for nursing homes, visiting nurses associations, and related facilities; at least $250,000 for all other types of private health care institutions defined in the 1974 amendments to the act. The statutory definition includes: "any hospital, convalescent hospital, health maintenance organization, health clinic, nursing home, extended care facility, or other institution devoted to the care of the sick, infirm, or aged person." Public hospitals are excluded from NLRB jurisdiction by Section 2(2) of the act.

9. **Transportation enterprises, links and channels of interstate commerce.** At least $50,000 total annual income from furnishing interstate passenger and freight transportation services; also performing services valued at $50,000 or more for businesses which meet any of the jurisdictional standards except the indirect outflow and indirect inflow standards established for nonretail enterprises.

10. **Transit systems.** At least $250,000 total annual volume of business.

11. **Taxicab companies.** At least $500,000 total annual volume of business.

12. **Associations.** These are regarded as a single employer in that the annual business of all association members is totaled to determine whether any of the standards apply.

13. **Enterprises in the territories and the District of Columbia.** The jurisdictional standards apply in the territories; all businesses in the District of Columbia come under NLRB jurisdiction.

14. **National defense.** Jurisdiction is asserted over all enterprises affecting commerce when their operations have a substantial impact on national defense, whether or not the enterprises satisfy any other standard.

15. **Private universities and colleges.** At least $1 million gross annual revenue from all sources (excluding contributions not available for operating expenses because of limitations imposed by the grantor).

16. **Symphony orchestras.** At least $1 million gross annual revenue from all sources (excluding contributions not available for operating expenses because of limitations imposed by the grantor).

17. **Day care centers.** At least $250,000 total annual volume of business.

18. **Law firms.** At least $250,000 total annual volume of business.

Through enactment of the 1970 Postal Reorganization Act, jurisdiction of the NLRB was extended to the United States Postal Service, effective July 1, 1971.

In addition to the above-listed standards, the board asserts jurisdiction over gambling casinos in Nevada and Puerto Rico, where these enterprises are legally operated, when their total annual revenue from gambling is at least $500,000.

Ordinarily if an enterprise does the total annual volume of business listed in the standard, it will necessarily be engaged in activities that affect commerce. The board must find, however, based on evidence, that the enterprise does in fact affect commerce.

The board has established the policy that where an employer whose operations affect commerce refuses to supply information concerning total annual business, the board may dispense with this requirement and exercise jurisdiction.

Finally, Section 14(c)(1) authorizes the board discretion to decline to exercise jurisdiction over any class or category of employers where a labor dispute involving such employers is not sufficiently substantial to warrant the exercise of jurisdiction, provided that it cannot refuse to exercise jurisdiction over any labor dispute over which it would have asserted jurisdiction under the standards it had in effect on August 1, 1959. In accordance with this provision the board has determined that it will not exercise jurisdiction over racetracks; owners, breeders, and trainers of racehorses; and real estate brokers.

In addition to the foregoing limitations, the act states that the term *employee* shall include any employee *except* the following:

Agricultural laborers.
Domestic servants.
Any individual employed by a parent or spouse.
Independent contractors.
Supervisors.
Individuals employed by an employer subject to the Railway Labor Act.
Government employees, including those employed by the U.S. Government, any government corporation or federal reserve bank, or any state or political subdivision such as a city, town, or school district.

Supervisors are excluded from the definition of employee and, therefore, not covered by the act.

Chapter 4

How Unions Are Organized

Unions are here to stay. . . . Some among even the best of employers might occasionally fall into short-sighted or careless employee practices if it were not for the presence or distant threat of unions.

Lemuel Boulware, <u>Statesman in Industrial Relations</u>, 1964.

The previous chapters have shown that the United States has a wide variety of unions. They may range from a single independent local union of less than ten members which groups members for the purpose of negotiating employment conditions with a single employer to a large international union representing over 2 million members and negotiating with over a thousand different employers. Unions may differ in organization structure, activities, types of industries represented, membership skills, bargaining strategies, centralization of authority, affiliation with the AFL-CIO, and so on.

Because it would be impossible to explain the multitude of features of the numerous unions, this chapter focuses on some of the most essential elements of unionization: (1) How employees are organized into unions, with explanation of the NLRB procedure, the determination of an appropriate bargaining unit, the election campaign, and the election, and (2) employer activities designed to maintain nonunion status or prevent union formation.

How Employees Are Organized into Unions

While academic research has focused on many aspects of unionization, employees themselves are concerned with relatively few questions. Employees mainly consider whether forming and joining a union will increase their wages and benefits, promotional opportunities, and job security. In an expectancy theory framework, can the employees expect to satisfy their job-related goals and needs by forming or joining a union? Will the union provide the means for achieving these goals?[1] If employees perceive that a union will help them attain their goals, they will likely vote for it in an election and support its activities afterwards. If they are not convinced, they will not vote for the union and, if subsequently required to join it, will not support its activities.

Contemporary union organizers, like their counterparts in management, must understand the psychology of the workplace, the workers' needs and goals, and the labor relations climate in which employees work. To be successful, they must be able to diagnose each of these elements at particular sites and at particular time periods. Because conditions change and employee needs may change, the diagnosis must be timely and accurate. As indicated in Chapter 1, employees join unions for a variety of reasons—alienation, job security, dissatisfaction with wages, benefits, physical environment of the workplace, and so on. However, recognition of the reasons does not make unionization campaigns a reality or guarantee their success. The union organizers must be able to (a) sort out these complex factors for the employees on a group or individual basis and (b) operationalize in the employees' language how the union can fulfill their needs in the specific work environment.

Many union organizers are becoming more sophisticated and knowledgeable about employee interests, job expectations, and work-related concerns. As an example, Exhibit 4–1 lists a number of work-related concerns and problems determined by the 1977 national survey of the Survey Research Center of the University of Michigan.[2] To the right of each is a possible course of action the union could take to satisfy the concern or alleviate the problem. The union organizer would bring to the employees' attention outcomes which could result from such activities by the union on their behalf.

Although the items listed pertain to national data, experienced and professional union organizers would be able to relate them to employee concerns at a particular facility, explaining what the union could do to help employees resolve job-related problems and achieve individual goals. Companies, knowing full well that the unions' strategies and activities are becoming more sophisticated, likewise expend considerable effort in explaining that the employees can achieve goals and resolve problems through the company alone, without any need for a union. (The company effort to remain nonunion will be explained later in the chapter.)

Union organizers and management both must be aware that job-related needs, interests, concerns, and goals may differ among individual em-

Exhibit 4-1 Union's Strategy and Courses of Action to Achieve Employee Goals and Resolve Job-Related Problems	Examples of Work-Related Problems and Employee Concerns	What the Union Could Negotiate with the Company
	Desire for improvement of present fringe benefits	Negotiate better benefits for bargaining unit employees
	Desire for additional fringe benefits	Negotiate new benefits, such as dental insurance and legal aid, which would not be provided on the company's initiative
	Earns less than deserved compared to others doing similar work	Emphasize comparable wages (local, regional, national, industry); provide data from other unions, Department of Labor, and wage surveys
	Exposed to one or more safety and health hazards	Highlight the role of union safety committees and the responsibilities of the company and rights of the union under OSHA
	Difficult to get work days and hours changed	Negotiate work schedule procedures with rules and policies which are administered fairly and in accordance with the contract
	Inconvenient or excessive hours	Negotiate hours and days of work with advance notice to employees when they work at inconvenient times, call-in pay, overtime, flexitime systems, and so on
	Difficult to get duties changed	With job content declared as a *mandatory* negotiable issue, the union could present alternative job descriptions, combine tasks, and so on
	Inadequate time for leisure activities	Attempt to obtain shorter hours and workweek, more holidays, and longer vacations for time worked
	Skills underutilized in present job	Negotiate promotion policies and procedures; institute a job bidding plan
	Unpleasant work environment	Negotiate working conditions and transfer opportunities; institute safety and health committee

Source for work-related problems: Graham L. Staines and Robert P. Quinn, "American Workers Evaluate the Quality of Their Jobs," *Monthly Labor Review* 102 (January 1979), pp. 3–12. Survey data courtesy of the Center for Political Studies, University of Michigan.

ployees, employees of different employers, occupational groups, and so on. For example, teachers at a particular school may be primarily interested in job security; professional white-collar employees may be most concerned about starting salaries of inexperienced employees and promotion opportunities; older factory employees may be more concerned about pensions and retirement policies, and young workers more concerned about wages.

While the union and company must be aware of these differences, the fact generally remains that all employees have some identifiable needs which can be either gratified or frustrated on the job. The main question the union organizer (and the management personnel who may be trying to remain nonunion) must ask is: Can the union and its activities facilitate the gratification of employee needs or alleviate employee frustration? The answers to this question on an individual and group employee basis go far in determining whether employees will choose to elect a union as their bargaining representative.

Alternative Methods for Establishing Unions

In most cases, a union attains exclusive bargaining agent status through the secret ballot representation election.[3] However, the NLRB has discretionary authority to use alternative methods. For example, in its *Gissel* decision the Supreme Court upheld the NLRB conclusion that a union may be certified as the exclusive bargaining agent if a majority of employees sign union authorization cards (see Exhibit 4–2) stating that they want the union to represent them for collective bargaining purposes. While the Court concluded that secret-ballot elections were superior, it ruled that the NLRB could order employers to bargain with the union under the following conditions:[4]

1. Evidence reveals that a fair, impartial election would have been *impossible* at the time that the election was held.
2. Authorization cards were clear and unambiguous.
3. Employee signatures were obtained without threat or coercion.
4. A majority of employees in the bargaining unit had signed the cards.[5]

In essence, the NLRB and the courts concluded that holding another election where the employer had made a fair and impartial election impossible would not be a realistic remedy because a rerun election would favor the party that had committed unfair labor practices, interfering with the first election.[6]

In a few cases the union may request employer recognition and then offer to prove that a majority of employees want to join the union. The union may offer to submit signed authorization cards to an impartial third party (arbitrator, mediator, or clergyman) who will check the signatures on the cards against payroll or W-4 signatures. If the employer agrees to this process, the majority status can be affirmed and union recognition be extended.[7] (Employers may choose this approach if they agree with conclusions of a research report based on 146 NLRB elections showing that the cost per employee in a representation election was $126.60.)[8]

Generally, there is strong opposition to granting union recognition without an election. There have been strong allegations that employees were pressured or forced into signing cards. Examples of extreme cases include the refusal of union organizers to leave employees' houses until the cards are signed, obtaining signatures after drinking parties, and

Exhibit 4–2
Examples of Union
Authorization Cards

United Food & Commercial Workers International Union

Affiliated with AFL-CIO-CLC

AUTHORIZATION FOR REPRESENTATION

I hereby authorize the United Food & Commercial Workers International Union, AFL-CIO-CLC, or its chartered Local Union(s) to represent me for the purpose of collective bargaining.

_____   _____
(Print Name)   (Date)

_____   _____
(Signature)   (Home Phone)

_____ _____ _____ _____
(Home Address)   (City)   (State)   (Zip)

_____ _____
(Employer's Name)   (Address)

_____ _____ _____
(Hire Date)   (Type Work Performed)   (Department)

Day Shift _____   Night Shift _____   Full Time _____   Part-Time _____

_____ _____
(Hourly Rate)   (Day Off)

Would you participate in an organizing committee?   Yes _____   No _____

27 ⬦ 27   PRINTED IN U.S.A.

U.R.W.

FOR BETTER   **WORKING CONDITIONS**   **JOB SECURITY**

Date _____

I, THE UNDERSIGNED EMPLOYEE OF

Print Company Name _____

designate and authorize the United Rubber, Cork, Linoleum and Plastic Workers of America, AFL-CIO, to act as my collective bargaining representative with my employer.

                                              (Job)

Print Your Name _____   Dept. No. _____

Print Address _____
                            (City — State — Zip)

Phone _____ Shift Worked: Day ☐   Afternoon ☐   Midnight ☐

Starting Rate Per Hour _____ Top or Present Rate _____ Job Worked _____

Signature X _____
                  (must be signed, not printed)

Source: Courtesy of the United Food & Commercial Workers International Union and the United Rubber Workers.

threatening injury to or perpetrating violence against employees who refuse to sign. These extremes reveal obvious violations of employees' rights, but in the overwhelming majority of cases, the employee who signs the card desires union representation.[9]

Opposition to union recognition without elections is also based on another valid reason as revealed in a 1977 research study of 1,174 elections covering 77,000 employees. This study showed that signed authorization cards were relatively poor predictors of union success in elections—even in cases where over 75 percent of the employees had signed the cards. [10]

Initiation of Organizing Campaigns

Representation Election Procedure

Campaign initiation. Union organizing campaigns usually start at the plant level; either the workers themselves ask the union to help or union organizers identify a company or plant with problems and get in touch with the workers by handbill or personal contact. In a few cases, major efforts by the international union and AFL-CIO are launched, such as the efforts to organize the Southern textile firms. The vital first step is the establishment of two-way communication between the employees and the union.

Next comes the educational process in which the union points out employees' problems, compares wages at their facility to wages at unionized facilities, and explains the role of the union in helping to satisfy their job-related needs. In other words, the union will attempt to convince the workers to join the union, then to sign union authorization cards [11] (see Exhibit 4–2), and to support the forthcoming organizing campaign by wearing union buttons, attending meetings, and signing up others. [12] While various means are available to gain support, research indicates that one-to-one contact, peer contact and persuasion, and high quality, professionally designed written communication are most effective. [13] Other efforts used by unions include television and radio advertising, "hotline" telephone numbers, group meetings, and hand billing.

Companies often learn of union organizing attempts from supervisors or rank and file employees and through actual observation before they receive official notification (by letter or telegram) from the union demanding recognition. Some companies react vigorously, while others do little to acknowledge any union's attempt to organize the employees. Some employers tell their employees about their opposition and urge them not to sign union authorization cards. Because the cards may specifically state that the signee favors union representation, any employee signature assists the union in establishing itself in the company. Other employers publish no-solicitation rules [14] that apply to all nonemployees and are specifically designed to curtail unionization efforts. If posted, these rules must have been in effect prior to the organizing campaign. [15]

Filing a petition for the election. Prior to 1935, in order to obtain recognition the union had to show its strength and employee interest in representation by such actions as strikes. The Wagner Act and the NLRB changed this situation by developing procedures and guidelines for peacefully determining the majority interest of employees through elections or some other comparable demonstration. The procedure is initiated when the potential bargaining representative for the employees files a petition for an election.

The NLRB is authorized to conduct an election only when such a petition has been filed by an employee, group of employees, any individual or labor organization, or an employer. Usually the petition is filed after a union has requested union recognition from the employer and the request is denied. If filed by an employee or on behalf of employees, the petition must be supported by evidence (usually by authorization cards) that a substantial interest in union representation (30 percent of the bargaining unit) exists. Further, it must show that the employer has declined a request by the union to recognize it as the employee representative.[16]

After receiving a petition, the NLRB will promptly notify the company and request a listing of employees. Companies are not required to submit a list but usually comply with the request as an act of good faith. Next, the NLRB will arrange a conference with the company and union to discuss the possibility of a consent election. Here, both sides may agree to the appropriate bargaining unit, voter eligibility, ballot, and time and place for the election, and a consent election will be held. If either party refuses to agree on any of these items, a formal hearing to settle these matters will be requested and conducted.[17]

Election investigation and hearing. If the union and management officials do not agree to a consent election, the NLRB must investigate the petition, hold a hearing if necessary, and then direct an election if it finds that there is a question of employee representation. This investigation will secure answers to the following questions:

1. Does the board have jurisdiction? (See Chapter 3.)
2. What is the appropriate bargaining unit?
3. Does substantial interest in representation (30 percent) exist among employees in the unit?
4. Are there any barriers to an election in the form of existing unions, prior elections, or present labor agreements?[18]

Appropriate bargaining unit. The appropriate bargaining unit is a grouping of jobs or positions in which two or more employees share common employment interests and conditions and which may reasonably be grouped together for collective bargaining purposes. Determination of the appropriate bargaining unit is left to the discretion of the NLRB, which decides in each representation case how employee rights can best be protected under the act. The board's discretion has, however, been limited in several ways:

☐ Professional employees cannot be included in a unit composed of both professional and nonprofessional employees, unless a majority of the professional employees vote to be included in a mixed unit.

☐ A proposed craft unit would not be ruled inappropriate simply because a different unit has been previously approved by the board unless a majority of employees in the proposed craft unit vote against being represented separately.

☐ Plant guards may not be included in any bargaining unit which has nonguard employees in the unit.

☐ Excluded are agricultural laborers, public employees (except postal employees), independent contractors, supervisors, and managers, although some of these may be covered in separate state statutes. [19]

The NLRB's determination of bargaining unit strongly influences whether the union will win the election, whether one union will prevail in an interunion contest, whether craft employees will have their own union or be included in a plant-wide unit, or whether the union will include key employees who could give direction and leadership for the bargaining unit employees. The composition of the bargaining unit is important to the employer as well as to the public. Should a plant have several small bargaining units, the employer may face different unions in negotiations several times throughout the year, which could cause continuous instability in labor relations. Separate units concerned with similar jobs may cause disputes over rights to jobs, leading to strikes or slowdowns. Should a small bargaining unit be merged with a nationwide bargaining unit, any confrontation that resulted in a strike could cause a nationwide shutdown and complications for customers in need of the companies' products. [20]

The bargaining unit itself may cover employees in one plant, in two or more facilities of the same employer, or in some industries (coal mining, construction, and trucking) of several different employers. The NLRB considers a number of relevant factors in determining the composition of the appropriate bargaining unit:

☐ Interests of employees and employer.

☐ Community of interest, such as wages, working conditions, training, and skill.

☐ History of collective bargaining either at the location in question or another facility owned by the company.

☐ Transfers of employees among various facilities.

☐ Geography and physical proximity of the workplaces.

☐ Employer's administrative or territorial divisions.

☐ Degree of separation (or distinctiveness) of work or integration (or interrelatedness) of work. [21]

Where the relevant factors do not give a clear indication for the composition of the appropriate bargaining unit, an election (commonly called a *Globe election*, from the original NLRB case) may be held to determine employee interests. For example, one group of electricians in a steel plant might wish to be represented by the International Brotherhood of Electrical Workers (IBEW) instead of the United Steelworkers of America (USWA). The USWA wants to include all electricians in a bargaining unit composed of all production and maintenance workers in the plant. Under such circumstances, the electricians' vote will determine whether they will be members of the Steelworkers, a separate electricians' union (IBEW), or no union.[22]

Barriers to the elections. There are several rules that make a petition for a representation election untimely. The first is a legal requirement which prohibits any NLRB representation election where one has been held in the last twelve months and where a petition for election covers a group of employees who are already covered by an existing contract and already members of a legally certified union.[23]

The second barrier to elections is an administrative determination that was made in the interest of stable and effective labor relations. The NLRB rule, called the *contract bar doctrine*, specifies that a valid, signed agreement for a fixed period of three years or less will bar any representation election for the life of the agreement (a longer contract is still limited to three years). Thus, the contract bar doctrine could extend the twelve-month statutory limitation on elections to three years. To do otherwise would be unfair to union and management officials who have negotiated a multiyear labor agreement in good faith.[24]

Eligibility of voters. Before an election is conducted, voter eligibility must be determined. Usually, those employees on the payroll just before the date of the election are eligible. While the employee must be employed in the unit on the date of the election, exceptions are made to allow employees who are on sick leave, on vacation, temporarily laid off, or on temporary leave, such as military duty, to vote in the election. In addition, the NLRB will occasionally consider irregularity of employment, such as in the construction, food processing, and longshoring industries. Also, strikers who have been replaced by permanent employees are allowed to vote in any election within twelve months after the strike begins. This policy insures that management does not provoke a strike and hire replacements who could vote out the union.[25]

"Names and addresses" rule. Within seven days after the regional director of the NLRB has approved a consent election or after an election has been directed, the employer must file a list of names and addresses of all eligible voters with the regional director. This information is then made available to the union. Refusal to comply could be identified as a bad faith act on the part of the employer and cause the election to be set aside or the NLRB to seek the names and addresses by subpoena.[26] The purpose of this disclosure rule is to give the unions the right of access to employees that management already possesses.[27]

The election. The representation election, acclaimed as "one of the great innovations of American labor law,"[28] is conducted by NLRB officials within forty-five days of the petition filing in 80 percent of the cases. NLRB data show 90 percent of the eligible employees actually vote in the elections, a participation rate far above that in local, state, and federal elections.[29] The high voter turnout in union representation elections might be due to the convenient voting procedure (usually carried out on company property) and the belief of many employees that their vote more directly affects their lives (at least their working conditions) than political elections at the local, state, and national levels. Finally, both union and management realize that an employee could express union preference to a union representative and an opposite preference to the management representative to avoid a confrontation during the election campaign. Neither side is sure of employee voting preferences when faced with a secret ballot; therefore, union and management officials actively work to get out the vote.

Using a ballot with the appropriate company and union designations (see Exhibit 4–3), a secret-ballot election is usually conducted under NLRB supervision during working hours at the employer's location. However, the NLRB has discretionary authority to conduct it by mail ballot if a regular election is not fair and reasonable. For example, if it is physically impractical for eligible voters to cast their ballots at a centralized location for such reasons as widely scattered work, adverse weather conditions, or excessive travel required, the regional director of the NLRB may conduct the election by mail balloting.[30]

The NLRB must determine whether the majority of the employees in an appropriate bargaining unit want to be represented for collective bargaining purposes. It defines *majority* as the simple majority rule generally accepted in democratic elections, which means that those choosing not to vote in the election have decided to assent to the wishes of the majority who did vote. Therefore, a majority of the employees who vote (50 percent plus one of those voting) in the election must favor representation before a union will be certified by the NLRB.[31]

If two or more choices are placed on the ballot, a runoff election may be necessary between the choices receiving the two highest numbers of votes in the initial election. If the majority votes "no union," no representation election can be held for twelve months. If a union receives the majority of the votes, the NLRB will certify it as the exclusive bargaining agent of the employees in the bargaining unit.

After the votes have been counted, either party has five days to file objections alleging misconduct or to challenge the ballots of voters whom

Exhibit 4–3
Example of a Secret
Ballot for a Union
Representation
Election

```
┌─────────────────────────────────────────────────────────┐
│              UNITED STATES OF AMERICA                     │
│          National Labor Relations Board                   │
│          OFFICIAL SECRET BALLOT                           │
│              FOR CERTAIN EMPLOYEES OF                     │
├─────────────────────────────────────────────────────────┤
│  Do you wish to be represented for purposes of            │
│  collective bargaining by ·                               │
│                                                           │
│                                                           │
├─────────────────────────────────────────────────────────┤
│        MARK AN "X" IN THE SQUARE OF YOUR CHOICE           │
│                                                           │
│         YES                           NO                  │
│         ☐                             ☐                   │
│                                                           │
└─────────────────────────────────────────────────────────┘
      DO NOT SIGN THIS BALLOT. Fold and drop in ballot box.
      If you spoil this ballot return it to the Board Agent for a new one.
```

Source: National Labor Relations Board.

one party believes should not have voted in the election.[32] This part of the representation process receives considerable criticism because the delay in assessing the ballot challenges and objections concerning misconduct seems excessive. Although only 15 percent of the elections require post-election proceedings, the time can be considerable,[33] and if decisions are appealed to the courts, it could take years before the final outcome is determined.

Duties of the exclusive bargaining agent and employer. The bargaining representative chosen by the majority of the employees in the appropriate unit has the duty to represent equally and fairly *all* employees in the unit regardless of their union membership. The employer has a comparable obligation, that is, to bargain in good faith with the exclusive bargaining agent and to refuse to bargain with another union seeking to represent the employees. Further, any negotiated labor agreement covers all employees in the bargaining unit, regardless of their union membership status.[34]

Decertification Procedure

Whenever employees believe that the union is not representing the interest of the majority, a *decertification procedure* is available. In recent years, decertification elections have been on the increase; researchers have identified a variety of reasons for this:

□ Fairer treatment of employees by the employer.

□ Poor job by unions (especially smaller unions) in providing services to members.

□ Inability of unions to negotiate an effective first contract after winning bargaining rights. [35]

□ Striking employees having skills that can be readily replaced, [36] so that when a strike occurs, the employer hires replacements.

Any employee, group of employees, or employee representative may file a petition for a decertification election twelve months after the union has been certified or upon expiration of the labor agreement, not to exceed three years. While employers cannot petition for a decertification election, they can question the union's majority status and petition the NLRB for a representation election. [37]

Although employers must be careful of their role in the decertification process, they have exhibited growing interest in it. [38] For example, a one-day management conference offered for $275 per person is designed to teach management representatives about the entire process of decertification. [39] With the number of petitions for decertification increasing from 624 in 1967 to 1,794 in 1977 and the number of elections growing from 234 to over 800 during this period, many employers have concluded that they should become more involved, especially since they are becoming aware that they do not necessarily have to play a passive role in the decertification process. [40]

When management chooses to become involved in the decertification campaign, it usually relies on four major tactics:

1. Meetings with employees, either one-to-one, in small groups, or with the entire unit.
2. Use of legal or expert assistance for advice in the campaign.
3. Letter campaigns to employees at their homes.
4. Improvement of the employment climate at the workplace by developing more effective performance appraisal, personnel development programs, and improved communication.

While management must consider the economic costs of a campaign, it must also consider the implications of both possible election outcomes and legal issues involved in its participation. For example, if management campaigns vigorously for decertification but the union wins, what type of labor-management relationships will result? If the results are close, will the relationships be unstable in the future? Should the union lose, will a more militant union seek representation after a year? These factors and others should play an important role in determining the specific strategy of the employer.[41]

Any members of a company's management staff, from first-line supervisors upward, must be wary of committing unfair labor practices. In fact, the NLRB views very carefully any aid provided employees by employers in any decertification effort. However, the employer may provide aid in some areas:

☐ Answer employee inquiries on how to decertify unions by referring the employees to the NLRB.

☐ Respond to specific employee questions about the decertification process in a manner which conveys no coercion or other unfair labor practices.

☐ Furnish an employee or any representative of a group of employees with a current list of employee names and addresses.[42]

Yet the employer must be aware of related unlawful activities, such as:

☐ Obtaining NLRB forms for employees who may be interested in union decertification.

☐ Providing services such as typing, assistance in phrasing the petition for decertification, and use of company stationery to employees who are interested in launching a decertification campaign.

☐ Initiating discussions on how or whether to decertify the union.

☐ Allowing supervisors or any other persons identified with management to promote the decertification process.[43]

The employees, like the employer, must be aware of possible consequences of their activities attempting to decertify the union. Decertification advocates must be prepared for pressure from union officials, ostracism from fellow employees who may be pleased with the union and involved in its activities, and expulsion from the union. The NLRB has upheld the union's right to discipline union members who actively participate in the campaign to decertify the union, as long as the disciplinary action does not affect the employees' employment status.[44]

Conduct of the Representation Election Campaign All elections are conducted according to NLRB standards, which are designed to assure that employees in the bargaining unit can indicate freely whether they want to be represented for collective bargaining purposes. However, election campaigns differ substantially, and the strategies of individual unions and employers vary widely. For example, handbills similar to those in Exhibit 4–4 are frequently used in addition to speeches, informal talks, interviews, and films. Thus, the election campaign, one of the most interesting and controversial activities in labor relations, has led to a body of doctrines and rules, some of which have been volatile in recent years.

Exhibit 4–4
Examples of
Handbills Distributed
during
Representation
Election Campaigns

VOTE **NO**
OR <u>YOUR</u> GOOSE
MAY BE COOKED

IF you have signed a card, you can now .... VOTE NO

IF you want STEADY WORK and don't want STRIKES .... VOTE NO

IF you *don't* want DUES, FINES and ASSESSMENTS .... VOTE NO

IF you *don't* want UNION DOMINATION .... VOTE NO

IF you *don't* want CONSTANT UNCERTAINTY .... VOTE NO

IF you *don't* want to PAY for what you ALREADY HAVE .... VOTE NO

BE SURE TO VOTE

**This Will Be a Secret Ballot — No One Can
Ever Know How You Voted**

DO NOT SIGN THE BALLOT — only mark it with an X in the NO

Remember: — FAILURE TO VOTE is the SAME as a Yes Vote for
the Union, Since They Need Only a Majority of the Votes Cast.

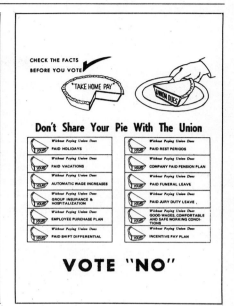

CHECK THE FACTS
BEFORE YOU VOTE

"TAKE HOME PAY"   UNION DUES

Don't Share Your Pie With The Union

Without Paying Union Dues PAID HOLIDAYS	*Without Paying Union Dues* PAID REST PERIODS
Without Paying Union Dues PAID VACATIONS	*Without Paying Union Dues* COMPANY PAID PENSION PLAN
Without Paying Union Dues AUTOMATIC WAGE INCREASES	*Without Paying Union Dues* PAID FUNERAL LEAVE
Without Paying Union Dues GROUP INSURANCE & HOSPITALIZATION	*Without Paying Union Dues* PAID JURY DUTY LEAVE
Without Paying Union Dues EMPLOYEE PURCHASE PLAN	*Without Paying Union Dues* GOOD WAGES, COMFORTABLE AND SAFE WORKING CONDITIONS
Without Paying Union Dues PAID SHIFT DIFFERENTIAL	*Without Paying Union Dues* INCENTIVE PAY PLAN

VOTE "NO"

LOOK   OUT   BELOW

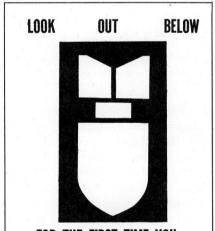

**FOR THE <u>FIRST</u> <u>TIME</u> YOU
WORKERS ARE GOING TO GET
SOME ATTENTION FROM THE <u>BOSS</u>**

— **BEWARE** —
THE COMPANY HAS HIRED A HIGHLY PAID UNION BUSTING
PROPAGANDA FIRM TO TRY TO SCARE YOU AND KEEP
YOU FROM VOTING FOR THE UNION

— **BEWARE** —
YOU WILL BE HEARING
FALSE RUMORS THEY HAVE ALREADY STARTED.

FALSE - The Union will cut out all four hour workers;

TRUE - The Union is here to help workers, not cut out jobs.
We dare this company to <u>even try</u> to cut out a 4 hour
job because of the Union.

— **BEWARE** —
WATCH FOR <u>MISLEADING</u> <u>PICTURES</u>
WATCH FOR DOUBLE TALK IN <u>NEWSPAPERS</u>
WATCH FOR PHONY RADIO BROADCAST
WATCH FOR LETTERS FROM THE BOSS
DON'T BE MISLED BY SUCH TACTICS!!!!!

see inside some samples ———→

Campaign doctrines and the NLRB. The *totality of conduct doctrine*, while confusing and controversial, guides the NLRB interpretations of unfair labor practice behavior. This doctrine essentially means that isolated incidents, such as campaign speeches, must be considered as a whole within the scope of the general circumstances of the campaign and with the possibility that other specific violations have occurred.[45] The best description of *totality of conduct* may have come from Judge Learned Hand, who wrote:

> Words are not pebbles . . . ; they have only a communal existence; and not only does the meaning of each interpenetrate the other, but the aggregate take their purpose from the setting in which they are used, of which the relation between the speaker and the hearer is perhaps the most important part.[46]

One of the more enduring doctrines has been the *laboratory conditions doctrine* established in the *General Shoe* decision in 1948. In this case, the NLRB clearly specified that its function was

> to provide a laboratory in which an experiment may be conducted, under conditions as nearly ideal as possible, to determine the uninhibited desires of the employees. It is our duty to establish these conditions; it is our duty to determine whether they have been fulfilled. . . . [If] the standard drops too low [and] the requisite conditions are not present, . . . the experiment must be conducted over again.[47]

In 1962 the NLRB established further campaign standards concerning preelection campaigns and held that it would overturn an election whenever an unfair labor practice occurred during a critical phase of the campaign. It concluded that conduct that interferes with the employees' exercise of "a free and untrammeled choice" in an election is cause to set aside the outcome of an election.[48] In the same year, the NLRB, in setting aside an election, established guidelines that stood for fifteen years and were used to determine whether employer or union speeches constituted sufficient interference with employee rights to a fair election.[49] Subjects covered in these guidelines included:

1. Misrepresentation of material facts or other similar company trickery.
2. Presentation of information by a person known by employees to have special knowledge about the information presented.
3. Presentation of information so close to the election that the other party or parties have no opportunity to make an effective reply.
4. A reasonable probability that the misrepresentation may have a significant effect upon the election.
5. Lack of qualification to evaluate the statements.[50]

The NLRB has emphasized that "absolute precision of statement and complete honesty are not always attainable in an election campaign, nor are they expected by the employees." It has also recognized that both union and management have the right to conduct "free and vigorous" campaigns and that "exaggeration, inaccuracies, half-truths, and name-calling, though not condoned, [would] not be grounds for setting aside elections."[51] Thus, the NLRB has concentrated on misrepresentations that are *substantial* departures from the truth.[52]

Captive Audience—"Twenty-four Hour Rule." One approach, usually taken by management, includes presenting "captive audience" speeches, which are delivered to employees during working time. Whereas the NLRB earlier required the company to offer the union equal time during working hours, its rule has been altered significantly. For example, now neither the union nor management may make a captive audience speech within twenty-four hours of the election; however, the employer may deny any union request to reply to a company speech on the company premises during working hours as long as the union has another means by which to effectively communicate with the employees.[53] But if the union has no acceptable means of communicating with the employees, as in the lumber and logging industry where employees live on company property, and if the employer's unfair labor practices have created a serious election campaign imbalance, the NLRB and the courts may grant the union access to plant bulletin boards, parking lots, and entrances so that it may communicate with the employees.[54]

Polling or questioning employees. Polling employees or asking questions about their interests in unions was considered unlawful interference with employee rights in earlier days. This rigid position on employer inquiry has become more flexible. The present NLRB rule states that activities regarding polling of employees by an employer will not be an unlawful interference if each of the following safeguards is taken:

☐ The purpose of the inquiry is to determine the accuracy of the union's claim that it represents a majority of the employees and this purpose is clearly communicated to the employees.

☐ The employees are polled by secret ballot and assurances are given against any employer reprisal.

☐ The employer has not otherwise committed any unfair labor practices.[55]

Distribution of union literature on company property. The NLRB and the courts have long held that except in special circumstances employees may not be prohibited from distributing union organizing materials in nonworking areas on their own time[56] *unless* the employer can show that such activity would disrupt production, employee work, and plant discipline. For example, employees of restaurants and retail establishments cannot distribute union materials in customer areas, and employees of health-care institutions cannot distribute materials in areas designated strictly for patients.[57] However, distributing materials in such places as hospital cafeterias predominantly patronized by hospital employees cannot be prohibited.[58] In addition, the employer cannot prohibit distribution of union material if the basis for the prohibition is that part of its content includes political issues, such as right-to-work laws and minimum wages.[59]

Showing of films during election campaigns. Films presented to discourage workers from joining unions have taken on new dimensions, especially since the 1950s, by production of the movie *And Women Must Weep* by the National Right to Work Committee. This movie portrays union violence, strikes, vandalism, phone threats, a house bombing, and even the shooting of a baby of a dissident union member. Frequent use of the film by employers prompted the International Association of Machinists to produce a rebuttal film, entitled *Anatomy of a Lie,* which projects no evidence of a connection between the shootings and other misconduct and the union's activities. On-site interviews with persons involved in the strike are shown to reveal an exact opposite view of the employer film, and the president of the union is filmed stating that nearly 99 percent of the union members voted to strike. The NLRB's position regarding the showing of these films has varied; its current position is that their showing does not constitute an unfair labor practice and alone is not sufficient cause to have the results of an election set aside.[60]

The Nonunion Firm

Employer Attempts to Maintain Nonunion Status

The fact that less than one-fourth of the nonagricultural labor force are union members is in part due to employers' actions aimed at maintaining a union-free work environment. Employers have attempted to maintain nonunion status through many methods, ranging from effective personnel programs to the use (or misuse) of related legal procedures. Obvious and substantial interest by nonunion employers is evident in a multitude of programs, such as *How to Maintain Nonunion Status,*[61] *Winning Union Organizing Campaigns,*[62] and related publications.[63]

These efforts have elicited strong union reactions, as evidenced by recent caustic articles in the AFL-CIO publication, *American Federationist:* "Peddling the 'Union Free' Guarantee"[64] and "The Consultants Who Coach the Violators."[65] Yet, some believe that it is only the unenlightened employers who should be classified as "union busters"; the "smart" nonunion employers are attempting to operate without a union because they believe it is a "sound business decision."[66]

It is impossible to state one single motive for employer actions. Some employers are openly anti-union and would seriously consider almost any method that would keep their organizations free from unions. Other employers sincerely believe that their effective personnel programs and policies render unions unnecessary. Regardless of the motive, many nonunion employers believe that "management that gets a union deserves it. . . . No labor union has ever captured a group of employees without the full cooperation and encouragement of managers who create the need for unionization."[67]

Today, some major corporations (IBM, Texas Instruments, Eastman Kodak, Delta Airlines) remain largely or totally nonunion, and a multitude of small companies carry nonunion status. Some of these companies clearly state their position on unions. For example, Texas Instruments' position is stated in the company handbook which is given to all employees. It states:

TI believes a union would be detrimental to TI and to TIers because it would reduce the operational flexibility and efficiency that have contributed greatly to both TI's success and the growth goals of individual TIers. Most TIers apparently agree, since historically they have not felt the need for a union in their quest for job security, job satisfaction and good economic benefits. As a result, TI is one of the largest non-union companies in the U.S. TI hopes that TIers will continue to feel the same way and, in turn, expects to continue its pledge to make company and employee goals as compatible as possible.

TI has instituted many personnel programs, such as Success Sharing, including a profit sharing plan, a pension plan and an employee stock option purchase plan, that are designed to relate your personal goals for financial security to TI's own goals for growth, productivity and profitability.[68]

In addition, it has a brochure entitled "TI and Unionism" which is also distributed to employees.

Other companies likewise have their position on unionism published for employee consideration. Excerpts similar to that below are frequently included:

Our company does not believe it necessary for our employees to organize unions in order to deal directly with management. In addition, it is not necessary now nor do we believe it ever will be necessary to join a union in order to work at our company.

We believe our employees would rather deal with management directly, rather than through a union. We also believe that our employees value their freedom to handle their own affairs and to speak on their own behalf, rather than being dictated to and controlled by an outside union which knows nothing about their jobs and is interested more in the union dues than their job interests. We believe that where there are unions there is trouble, strife, and discord; therefore, we intend to oppose unionism by every proper means.

> As President of _____ and one who is vitally interested in your welfare, I want you to know that you have the right to reject the union and to refuse to sign these union cards. Union organizers will tell you that these cards will be kept confidential, but they must be shown to the National Labor Relations Board if the union pursues an election. I am calling this to your attention because I don't want you to be tricked into signing a card which may be used against your interest.[69]

While these statements clearly indicate that the employer would rather not deal with the union, they are within the rights of the employers to express their opinion on unionism.

Some nonunion companies concentrate on developing a sound personnel program instead. Subscribers to this approach would agree to the following:

> The primary objective of a sound personnel program is to contribute to the success and profitability of the business. Lower unit labor costs through greater employee productivity, improved product quality, and reduced absenteeism and turnover, are but some of the benefits. Employees benefit too. Working in a healthy, profitable enterprise, they enjoy steady, secure work and regular improvements in wages, fringe benefits and working conditions. A company's non-union status is a by-product of this program.[70]

Companies subscribing to this approach offer their employees benefits and opportunities comparable to those that unionized companies provide their employees as a result of labor negotiations. These include:

- ☐ Wages, benefits, and so on equal to or better than union firms'.
- ☐ Grievance procedure.
- ☐ Posting job openings so that eligible employees can apply.
- ☐ Improved supervision by better selection, training, and evaluation.
- ☐ Effective communication.
- ☐ Downward communication by bulletin boards, company newspapers, and handbooks.
- ☐ Upward communication by group meetings, complaint boxes, attitude surveys, open-door policies, and counseling.
- ☐ Restructuring the organization—providing the climate to keep the organization alive and vibrant by reducing the levels of supervision, forcing delegation, building work teams, enlarging and enriching jobs, and experimenting with methods of training.[71]

Other, more extreme tactics used by some companies to avoid unionization are:

□ Developing a spy network (tattle-tales) to identify union supporters.

□ Refusing to hire former employees of unionized companies (but giving the applicant a reason other than prior union affiliation for employment denial).

□ Establishing a case for discharge (including documentation) of known union advocates.

□ Seeking to determine prospective employees' attitudes toward unions from interviews, references, and so on, then refusing to hire them (again giving another reason) if they are pro-union.

□ Giving psychological tests (job interest questionnaires) to determine the likelihood that an applicant will be interested in a union.

□ Locating new plants in areas where union membership is low and expanding the company's nonunion plants.[72]

Some employers facing union organizing campaigns have committed unfair labor practices deliberately, with the expectation of economic returns to them. A recent research study demonstrated that "under realistic conditions it is economically feasible for employers to secure economic gains by violating the National Labor Relations Act."[73] Even more disappointing was the conclusion that

---

in the past, the compliance system [of the National Labor Relations Act] has been inadequate to the extent that some employers have found it profitable to commit unfair labor practices in order to forestall unionization. Those employers obeying the law because "it's the law" have faced a greater probability of incurring costs of unionization and may have been at a competitive disadvantage to employers who violated the law. Such inequities do not encourage compliance with the law and provide evidence of the need for labor law reform.[74]

The unfortunate reasons behind these activities are simply that the risks of this approach are relatively low. Violations are not criminal; no one is imprisoned or fined for violating the National Labor Relations Act. Social costs are not high because most of the public is unaware of the employers who flagrantly violate the law. Too, the potential gains for these employers include not only the possibility of forestalling unionization but also of employees losing interest in unions after a long period of judicial appeals.[75]

Examples of Attempts to Avoid Unionization

Two of the most publicized examples involve J. P. Stevens and the Darlington Manufacturing Company, which the unions have accused of committing premeditated unfair labor practices. The first case involves J. P. Stevens, a textile firm employing 44,000 in eighty-five plants. Only 3,000 employees are members of any union. J. P. Stevens' management continues to maintain that its employees do not want a union to represent them, and the union continues to claim the opposite and to point out that Stevens' commission of unfair labor practices has kept unions out. The union calls attention to the fact that the NLRB has found Stevens guilty of violating the National Labor Relations Act in fifteen separate legal cases since 1965. These NLRB decisions were upheld eight times by the federal appeals court and three times by the Supreme Court. In these cases, more than $1.3 million in back pay has been awarded 289 workers whose rights were violated,[76] and an enormous amount of legal fees have been paid.

Although the union's campaign continues to use traditional organizing tactics like card-signing, handbilling, consumer boycott, and support of AFL-CIO and other unions, it has also introduced some innovative approaches:

☐ Securing support of national church organizations and student groups on seventy-five university and college campuses.[77]

☐ Forcing resignation of J. P. Stevens officials who are members of the boards of directors of other companies.[78]

☐ Pressuring TV hostess Dinah Shore, a member of several labor unions, to stop advertising for J. P. Stevens.[79]

☐ Attending stockholder meetings and sponsoring proposals to stop Stevens' anti-union campaigns.[80]

In the meanwhile, chairman of the board for J. P. Stevens insists, "We are a law-abiding firm."[81] Further, the company "makes no apologies for its determination to keep the union out of its plants."[82]

Another example of a drawn-out organizing effort involves the Darlington Manufacturing Company. In 1956, the employees voted 256 to 248 to be represented by the Textile Workers Union of America (TWUA). There were charges of unfair labor practices by both sides. The union alleged that the company had threatened to close the plant to chill the union drive; the company contended that such a decision was a legitimate right of management. Using the proper legal appeals, the case finally went to the Supreme Court, which ruled on behalf of the union and employees and upheld the NLRB's decision. The Court sent the case back to the NLRB to carry out its order to cease and desist committing unfair labor practices and to take affirmative action by reinstating employees to their jobs with back pay. The board did not modify its previous ruling, the company appealed again, and enforcement was ordered again in 1968. Thereafter, the TWUA sought to locate those who were entitled to back pay and reinstatement. Not surprisingly, it found scores unaccounted for; some had died, and some had changed their names. Even as late as 1974, almost twenty years after the initial election, the company was still questioning and challenging the back pay computations.[83]

Employee committees. Another tactic is the use of employee committees. Although the NLRA has outlawed company unions and unlawful assistance to unions affiliated with national organizations, some companies have organized and supported employee committees for the purpose of discussion and resolving grievances.[84] Even though these committees differ from traditional unions in their discussions with employers because they do not negotiate labor agreements, they could subsequently come under the provisions of the National Labor Relations Act if their discussions over wages and employment conditions are interpreted as negotiations by the NLRB. Further, the employer could be directed to recognize and bargain with committee members as a labor union.[85]

Double-breasted construction companies. In the construction industry, where an estimated one-third of the nonresidential work is performed by nonunion construction firms and the percentage has been growing in the last few years, nonunion firms have been successful. They have been able to pay less per hour than the union scale, to employ people at different wage scales, and to save on fringe benefits, while having a flexible and strike-free work environment.[86] Some firms have become involved in the *double-breasted* or *dual shop movement.* In these cases, the unionized contractor creates a nonunion subsidiary or an affiliated company to compete more effectively against nonunion contractors, especially for smaller projects. While the building and construction trade unions strongly contend that these firms are in reality only one firm and should recognize the union, the employers maintain their separate corporate identity.[87] A determination of their legal separateness for labor relations purposes involves investigations of the following by the NLRB and court: commonality of management and supervision, commonality of personnel and labor relations policies, commonality of ownership and financial control, and interrelationship of operations.[88]

New Union Strategies Countering Employers' Efforts to Maintain Nonunion Status

In response to nonunion employers' strategies in maintaining the nonunion status, unions have been forced to return to the drawing board to design new strategies. One example is the use of telephone taped speech in which an employee may call a well publicized number and receive the "union message" for the day or week during an organizing campaign.[89] These messages range from benefits for joining unions and anticompany messages to personal testimony of a popular, well-known plant employee.

Another much publicized union strategy is the exercise of financial clout. As owners of significant amounts of stocks and investments and as holders of large bank accounts, unions have pressured banks and insurance firms by threatening to withdraw funds unless they cease dealing with certain anti-union firms. In a related effort, unions have realized that their pension fund assets have climbed to a staggering $501.5 billion, most of which is solely administered by employers. Unions now are claiming that the members actually own their funds, want a voice in the way the funds are invested in anti-union firms, and plan to make the subject a negotiable issue in the future.[90]

The United Auto Workers has pressured General Motors to abandon its so-called southern strategy and to enter an agreement concerning the union's attempt to organize twelve new plants located in the South. Their agreement requires that preferential consideration be given UAW members who are currently employed if they seek jobs in the new plants. While only about 2 percent of GM's 475,000 production workers would end up working in southern plants, those transferred would help the UAW organize their workers.[91]

The Rubber Workers, in its 1979 labor agreements, was able to negotiate a *neutrality pact* with the major rubber companies (except Goodyear) under which the companies would take a neutral position when the union attempted to organize nonunion rubber manufacturers.

Summary

This chapter discussed how unions are organized and how employers try to avoid unionization. Starting with the employees' perceived needs and job-related concerns, the role of unions in fulfilling these needs and concerns was discussed.

Unionization efforts progress from first contacts with employees to the signing of authorization cards, petition for election, hearings, determination of the appropriate bargaining unit, and the eventual representation election. Within this framework numerous rules, regulations, and legal requirements govern the union certification process. In addition, the duties of the union—the exclusive bargaining agent—to represent the bargaining unit employees are explained. If employees do not believe that the union is representing the majority interest, decertification procedures are available.

Noting that less than one-fourth of the nonagricultural labor force is unionized, the next section highlights a number of ways employers attempt to maintain nonunion status—some focusing on positive personnel practices and programs, but others involving tactics which could be considered unfair labor practices. The cases of two companies (J. P. Stevens and Darlington Manufacturing Company), the use of employee committees, and the presence of nonunion employers in the construction industry—all examples well publicized by organized labor—were used as illustrations. In response to companies' efforts to remain nonunion, new union strategies such as the use of union financial clout and neutrality pacts have been devised and implemented.

Discussion Questions

1. By referring to the reasons why employees become members of unions given in Chapter 1, assess the *means* used by union organizers to meet these needs.

2. Select an organization with which you are familiar, and determine the number of possible bargaining units which would be appropriate for collective bargaining in its structure.

3. Explain the contract bar doctrine. How would it influence the negotiation of the first labor agreement?

4. Discuss the shifting position of the NLRB regarding representation election campaigning. Appraise each position.

5. Prescribe a "do" and "don't" list for supervisors involved in unionization campaigns so they will not commit any unfair labor practices.

6. Why do you believe employers are becoming more interested in decertification elections?

7. Explain the following statement: "It is not the union that organizes the workers; it is management."

8. What new strategies have unions used to counter employer efforts to maintain nonunion status? Appraise the effectiveness of these strategies.

References

[1]Victor H. Vroom, *Work and Motivation* (New York: Wiley, 1964), p. 30.

[2]Graham L. Staines and Robert P. Quinn, "American Workers Evaluate the Quality of Their Jobs," *Monthly Labor Review* 102 (January 1979), pp. 3–12.

[3]National Labor Relations Board, *A Guide to Basic Law and Procedures under the National Labor Relations Act* (Washington, D.C.: Government Printing Office, 1976), pp. 10–11.

[4]Robert E. Williams, Peter A. Janus, and Kenneth C. Huhn, *NLRB Regulation of Election Conduct* (Philadelphia: Industrial Research Unit, University of Pennsylvania Press, 1974), pp. 371–372.

[5]NLRB v. Gissel Packing Co., 395 U.S. 575 (1969).

[6]Herbert L. Sherman, Jr., and William P. Murphy, *Unionization and Collective Bargaining*, 3d ed. (Washington, D.C.: Bureau of National Affairs, 1975), pp. 69–70.

[7]Stephen I. Schlossberg and Frederick E. Sherman, *Organizing and the Law* (Washington, D.C.: Bureau of National Affairs, 1971), pp. 97–99.

[8]Woodruff Imberman, "How Expensive Is an NLRB Election?" *MSU Business Topics* 23 (Summer 1975), pp. 13–18.

[9]Robert Lewis, "The Law and Strategy of Dealing with Union Organizing Campaigns," *Labor Law Journal* 25 (January 1974), p. 45.

[10]Marcus H. Sandver, "The Validity of Union Authorization Cards as a Predictor of Success in NLRB Certification Elections," *Labor Law Journal* 28 (November 1977), pp. 698–701.

[11]An authorization card signifies that the employee desires to be represented by the union in collective bargaining. The employee thereby authorizes the union to represent him with his employer. The signed card may be used later by the union as proof of majority representation, as support to demand recognition, and as evidence that there is "substantial interest" among the bargaining unit to support a petition to the NLRB for representation election. Schlossberg and Sherman, *Organizing and the Law*, p. 50.

[12]Ibid., pp. 41–42.

[13]David B. Stephens and Paul R. Timm, "A Comparison of Campaign Techniques in Contested Faculty Elections: An Analysis of the Florida Experience," *Journal of Collective Negotiations in the Public Sector* 7 (1978), pp. 167–177.

[14]This rule must be applied equally to all forms of solicitation, such as politicians seeking votes and charitable organizations seeking contributions.

[15]Lewis, "Law and Strategy," pp. 42–48.

[16]National Labor Relations Board, *Guide to Basic Law*, pp. 11–16.

[17]Lewis, "Law and Strategy," pp. 45–47.

[18]National Labor Relations Board, *Guide to Basic Law*, p. 11.

[19]Ibid., pp. 9–11.

[20]Schlossberg and Sherman, *Organizing and the Law*, p. 60.

[21]John E. Abodeely, *The NLRB and the Appropriate Bargaining Unit* (Philadelphia: Industrial Research Unit, University of Pennsylvania, 1971), pp. 7–86.

[22]Sherman and Murphy, *Unionization and Collective Bargaining*, pp. 60–61.

[23]National Labor Relations Board, *Guide to Basic Law*, pp. 13–14. There are exceptions, such as when the agreement is not in writing, has not been signed, or has not been ratified.

[24]Ibid.

[25]Ibid. However, permanent replacements are also eligible to vote in the same election.

[26]*Excelsior Underwear, Inc.*, 156 NLRB 1236 (1966).

[27]Sherman and Murphy, *Unionization and Collective Bargaining*, p. 39.

[28]William P. Murphy, "Reforming the National Labor Relations Act," in Barbara D. Dennis, ed., *Proceedings of the Thirtieth Annual Meeting: Industrial Relations Research Association* (Madison, Wis.: Industrial Relations Research Association, 1978), p. 157.

[29]Ibid., pp. 158–159.

[30]Williams, Janus, and Huhn, *NLRB Regulation*, pp. 371–372.

[31]Ibid., pp. 391–395.

[32]National Labor Relations Board, *Guide to Basic Law*, p. 17.

[33]Murphy, "Reforming the National Labor Relations Act," p. 161. For example, if the regional director proceeds to an investigation, the median time is 41 days; if a hearing is held, the time extends to 58 days; if the issue goes to the board, another 87 days are required.

[34]National Labor Relations Board, *Guide to Basic Law*, p. 8.

[35]James B. Dworkin and Marian Extejt, "Why Workers Decertify Their Unions: A Preliminary Investigation," paper to be presented at the Annual Meeting of the Academy of Management, August 1979.

[36]I. Chafetz and C. R. P. Fraser, "Union Decertification: An Exploratory Analysis," *Industrial Relations* 18 (Winter 1979), p. 68.

[37]Kenneth C. McGuiness, *Silverberg's How to Take a Case before the National Labor Relations Board*, 3d ed. (Washington, D.C.: Bureau of National Affairs, 1967), p. 179.

[38]Ibid., p. 10; and Woodruff Imberman, "How to Win a Decertification Election," *Management Review* 66 (September 1977), pp. 26–28, 37–39.

[39]Executive Enterprises, *The Process of Decertification*.

[40]William E. Fullmer, "When Employees Want to Oust Their Union," *Harvard Business Review* 56 (March–April 1978), pp. 163–170. Also see William T. Downey, "The *Mar-Jac* Rule Governing the Certification Year," *Labor Law Journal* 29 (September 1978), pp. 608–614.

[41]Fullmer, "When Employees Want to Oust Their Union," pp. 167–169.

[42]William A. Krupman and Gregory I. Rasin, "Decertification: Removing the Shroud," *Labor Law Journal* 30 (April 1979), pp. 234–235.

[43]Ibid., p. 236.

[44]*Tawas Tube Production, Inc.*, 151 NLRB 9 (1965).

[45]Sherman and Murphy, *Unionization and Collective Bargaining*, pp. 39–40.

[46]*NLRB v. Federbush Co.*, 121 F.2d 957 (1941).

[47]*General Shoe Corp.*, 77 NLRB 124 (1948).

[48]*Dal-Tex Optical Co.*, 137 NLRB 1782 (1962).

[49]*Hollywood Ceramics*, 140 NLRB 221 (1962).

[50]Cindy M. Hudson and William B. Werther, Jr., "Section 8 (c) and Free Speech," *Labor Law Journal* 28 (September 1977), p. 611.

[51]*Hollywood Ceramics*, 140 NLRB 221 (1962).

[52]"NLRB Member Truesdale on *General Knit* Decision," *News and Background Information*, 99 LRR 307 (1978). It should be noted that the NLRB reversed the *Hollywood Ceramics* position in a 1977 decision (*Shopping Kart Food Market, Inc.*, 228 NLRB 190), indicating that it would not probe into the truth or falsity of the parties' campaign statements. However, in late 1978, the NLRB (with a new member) returned to the *Hollywood Ceramics* principles—illustrating the point that NLRB policy is not set in concrete. Instead, it represents the personalities and desires of board members.

[53]Hudson and Werther, "Section 8 (c)," pp. 612–613. Also see *Peerless Plywood Co.*, 107 NLRB 427 (1953); and *Livingston Shirt Co.*, 107 NLRB 400 (1953).

[54]Max Zimny, "Access of Union Organizers to Private Property," *Labor Law Journal* 25 (October 1974), p. 624.

[55]Hudson and Werther, "Section 8 (c)," p. 613. Also see *Blue Flash Express, Inc.*, 109 NLRB 591 (1954); and *Struknes Construction, Inc.*, 165 NLRB 1062 (1967).

[56]*Republican Aviation Corp. v. NLRB*, 324 U.S. 793 (1945).

[57]"Justices Twice Back Right to Distribute Union Literature on Company Property," *Wall Street Journal*, June 23, 1978, p. 6.

[58]*Beth Israel v. NLRB*, 46 U.S.L.W. 4765 (June 22, 1978).

[59]*Eastex, Inc. v. NLRB*, 46 U.S.L.W. 4783 (June 22, 1978).

[60]Joseph A. Pichler and H. Gordon Fitch, "And Women Must Weep: The NLRB as Film Critic," *Industrial and Labor Relations Review* 28 (April 1975), pp. 395–410.

[61]"Fair Plant, 'Easy Task,' Keeps Union Door Shut," *Kansas City Star*, July 21, 1977. The price in 1978 was $450 per person for a two-day program.

[62]Executive Enterprises, New York, N.Y.; $275 per person for a one-day program.

[63]Scott Myers, *Managing without Unions* (Reading, Mass.: Addison-Wesley Publishing, 1976); Louis Jackson and Robert Lewis, *Winning NLRB Elections* (New York: Practising Law Institute, 1972); and I. Herbert Rothenberg and Steven B. Silverman, *Labor Unions, How to: Avert Them, Beat Them, Out-Negotiate Them, Live with Them, Unload Them* (Elkins Park, Pa.: Management Relations, 1973).

[64]Charles McDonald and Dick Wilson, "Peddling the 'Union-Free' Guarantee," *American Federationist* 85 (April 1979), pp. 12–19.

[65] Phillis Payne, "The Consultants Who Coach the Violators," *American Federationist* 84 (September 1977), pp. 22–29.

[66]Peter J. Pestillo, "Learning to Live without the Union," in Barbara D. Dennis, ed., *Proceedings of the Thirty-first Annual Meeting: Industrial Relations Research Association* (Madison, Wis.: Industrial Relations Research Association, 1979), pp. 233–239.

[67]Charles L. Hughes, *Making Unions Unnecessary* (New York: Executive Enterprises Publications, 1976), p. 1.

[68]*TI and You . . . the TIer's Handbook* (Dallas: Texas Instruments Incorporated, 1978), p. iv.

[69]Paraphrased from a company which shall remain anonymous.

[70]Jackson and Lewis, *Winning NLRB Elections*, p. 3.

[71]V. Clayton Sherman, "What the Nonunion Company Can Learn from the Unionized Company," *Industrial Relations Guide* (Englewood Cliffs, N.J.: Prentice-Hall, 1970), pp. 42, 145–42, 148; and Peter J. Pestillo, "Learning to Live without the Union," pp. 233–239.

[72]Techniques told to authors by employers and union organizers.

[73]Charles R. Greer and Stanley A. Martin, "Calculative Strategy Decisions during Organization Campaigns," *Sloan Management Review* 19 (Winter 1978), p. 73.

[74]Ibid.

[75]Ibid., pp. 61–74.

[76]Kenneth A. Kovach, "J. P. Stevens and the Struggle for Union Organization," *Labor Law Journal* 29 (May 1978), pp. 300–308. Also see J. Gary DiNunno, "J. P. Stevens: Anatomy of an Outlaw," *American Federationist* 83 (April 1976), pp. 1–8.

[77]Noreen McGrath, "Boycott of Textile Company Supported at 75 Colleges," *Chronicle of Higher Education*, November 6, 1978, p. 10.

[78]"Two Stevens, New York Life Directors Resign in Another Textile Union Victory," *Wall Street Journal*, September 13, 1978, p. 6.

[79]Lloyd Shearer, "Dinah's Problem," *Parade*, November 5, 1978. Bob Hope, a member of four unions, refused to cross a union picket line at a Marriott Hotel where 1,500 guests were waiting for a special appearance.

[80]"Gathering Momentum against J. P. Stevens," *Business Week*, March 20, 1978, pp. 147–148.

[81]Ibid., p. 147.

[82]Ibid., p. 148.

[83]Phillip Sparks, "The *Darlington* Case: Justice Delayed Is Justice Denied," *Labor Law Journal* 26 (December 1975), pp. 759–766. Also see Sherman Dallas and Beverly K. Schaffer, "Whatever Happened to the *Darlington* Case?" *Labor Law Journal* 24 (January 1973), pp. 3–11.

[84]Sherman and Murphy, *Unionization and Collective Bargaining*, p. 47.

[85]*NLRB v. Cabot Carbon Co.*, 360 U.S. 203 (1959). The union challenged a General Foods job enrichment program that divided employees into work groups for the purpose of working job assignments, scheduling overtime, and discussing job-related concerns with a consultant (with management representatives in attendance on occasion). While the NLRB ruled that no union existed, it could raise interesting issues in the future. *General Foods Corporation and American Federation of Grain Millers, AFL-CIO and Its Local 70*, 231 NLRB 122 (1977).

[86]"Open-Shop Construction Picks Up Momentum," *Business Week*, December 12, 1977, p. 108.

[87]Tim Bornstein, "The Emerging Law of the 'Double-Breasted' Operation in the Construction Industry," *Labor Law Journal* 28 (February 1977), pp. 77–79.

[88]Joseph F. Canterbury, Jr., "Dual Shops in the Construction Industry," in Bernard J. King and Donald W. Savelson, eds., *Construction Industry Labor Relations 1977* (New York: Practising Law Institute, 1977), pp. 459–462.

[89]Used by the International Brotherhood of Electrical Workers in a campaign to organize clerical workers of Alabama Power Company, Birmingham, Alabama, fall 1978.

[90]"Embattled Unions Strike Back at Management," *Business Week*, December 4, 1978, pp. 54–55; "More Unions Brandish Money as a Weapon," *Business Week*, February 26, 1979, pp. 47–48; and R. W. Merry, "A Big Bertha for Bank Unions," *Wall Street Journal*, April 3, 1979, p. 5.

[91]Leon Bornstein et al., "Developments in Industrial Relations," *Monthly Labor Review* 101 (November 1978), pp. 45–46; and "Why GM Abandoned Its 'Southern Strategy,' " *Business Week*, October 16, 1978, p. 50.

Part 1/Recognition of the Rights and Responsibilities of Unions and Management

Chapter 5

Union Organizations

Unions' external relations express their reason for being and their uniqueness as organizations. . . . Internal relations are concerned in large measure with creating the organizational conditions which maximize their effective power vis-à-vis the enterprise.

Arnold S. Tannebaum, "Unions," in Handbook of Organizations, 1965.

Having explored how unions are organized and how nonunion employers attempt to maintain their nonunion status, it is now appropriate to turn to the manner in which the various organizational levels of unions operate. This chapter presents an explanation of the craft and industrial union characteristics, the functions of local union officers, and local union government and operations. The national or international union (the terms are considered interchangeable in the chapter), which is composed of the local unions within a craft or industry, is explained in a similar framework. Not to be overlooked are the various intermediate levels of union organizations which provide specific functions for their affiliated unions. A fourth level for many union organizations is the federation, or the AFL-CIO, whose organization structure, functions, and officer responsibilities are also discussed. The chapter concludes with a section on the status of union membership and growth in the United States, and reasons for the slowing growth are explained.

Organizational Levels of Unions

The Local Union

Although there are generally four levels of unions—local, national (or international), intermediate, and the federation of unions—the local union is the main point of contact for the individual employee. The typical union member often identifies more closely with the local union than with the other union levels. He or she attends and sees local officers at the local meetings and workplace. When the union member has a grievance, the local union officers are the first to assist. When a strike occurs, the local union officers are the ones who make continuous contact with the strikers on the picket line. Although the national union may negotiate the master labor agreement under which the local union member works and the AFL-CIO may deal with the president and Congress on vital issues facing the nation, the local union serves as the vital link between the individual union member and the national union which in turn might link with the AFL-CIO.

Organizationally, the local union is a branch of the national union. It receives its charter from the national union, and it operates under the national union's constitution, bylaws, and rules. The constitution of the national union prescribes the number and types of officers, their duties and responsibilities, and the limits of their authority. Although union constitutions vary in length and content, they often mandate certain financial reports and require that a certain number of meetings be held, that the local labor agreement conform to the master labor agreement negotiated by the national union if there is industrywide bargaining, and that approval to call a strike be obtained by the local union. With the trend toward greater centralization of authority by the national union, the local union over the years has lost much of its operational flexibility.

Local Craft versus Industrial Unions The operation of the local union in large part depends on the nature and type of workers and membership. Although there is not a clear-cut division between them, unions can be divided generally into two groups: craft and industrial.

Differing union organizations. Craft unions are composed of members who have been organized in accordance with their craft or skill, for example, bricklayers, electricians, carpenters, ironworkers, etc. Industrial unions have been organized on an industry basis, for example, the Steelworkers, Autoworkers, Rubber Workers, Mine Workers, Textile Workers, and so on. This, of course, does not mean that there are no skilled workers in the steel, auto, rubber, or textile industries; but it does mean the electricians and bricklayers in a steel plant or a coal mine operation would likely be members of the Steelworkers and United Mine Workers, respectively.

Differing scope of the labor agreement. The craft and industrial unions differ in other ways that have an effect on their operations at the local, regional, and national levels. First, the craft unions, which frequently represent the building trades, usually negotiate short labor agreements (supplemented by detailed agreements on special topics, such as apprenticeship programs and safety) which cover a geographic region, and each has considerable independence from the national union compared to industrial unions. Because of the nature of their work, craft union members may work on several different job sites for several different employers in a given year, still working under the same labor agreement. The labor agreement covers the various construction companies in the area and a number of the building trades unions for the particular geographic area.

The industrial union, on the other hand, may be covered by a national labor agreement negotiated between the company and the national union, which covers all of the company's unionized plants. For example, a General Motors plant in Los Angeles is covered by the master agreement—well over 100 pages long, it explains in detail the wage plan, transfers, pensions, layoffs, etc.—and a local agreement is negotiated to cover matters of concern to the specific local plant and its employees.

Differing skills. Types of skills help demonstrate another difference in local union operations. The craft members are highly skilled artisans who have completed formal training, usually in a formal apprenticeship program. Many industrial employees, on the other hand, do not require much prior job training. Therefore, the craft union members often feel that they have higher status than their industrial counterparts. The training programs available for the industrial union members are usually offered by the company, whereas the training received by members of craft unions is jointly controlled and operated by the unions. So craft unions select those who will be offered the apprenticeship training, while companies alone select the trainees in the plants. Such an arrangement has allowed the craft unions to limit the numbers in the craft, sometimes only to their families and friends. In addition, the administration of these apprenticeship programs may adversely affect minority group members, a situation discussed in Chapters 10 and 12.

Differing job characteristics. The nature of work also creates a unique opportunity for craft unions to operate under conditions that approximate a closed shop. Since many of the work assignments last only a short period, the craft members return to the union hiring hall for their next assignment after their part of a project is completed. Upon receiving the assignment, the union members could report to another job site and work, possibly for another company. Usually, these arrangements are worked out in advance by the business agent of the craft union and the companies who agree to operate under the existing labor agreement. In other words, the union hiring hall serves as a clearinghouse or placement office for the construction companies as well as the union members. Since the hiring hall must be operated in a nondiscriminatory manner, nonunion workers may also use it. In comparison, the typical member of the industrial union is hired by the company and will work for the same employer—usually at the same facility—until employment is terminated.

Differing leadership roles. The last difference pertains to the roles of the business agent and shop stewards of the craft union and the local union officials of the industrial unions. The *business agent*, the full-time administrator of the local craft union, provides many of the same services as the local union president of a large industrial union. They are both considered the key administrative officials of their respective local unions, and they lead the local union negotiations and play a key role in grievance administration. However, the business agent has additional duties, such as administering the union hiring hall, serving as the chief "watchdog" over the agreement, and appointing an employee on each job site to serve as the shop steward. The *shop steward*, who may be the first person on the job or a senior employee, will handle employee grievances, represent the business agent on the job, and contact the business agent if anything goes wrong.

In local industrial unions, the president may or may not be full-time. If the job is full-time, the salary comes from union dues. If the job is part-time, the president is compensated from the union treasury only for the time that is lost off the job (at the regular rate of pay). The presidential duties include participating in local negotiations, maintaining the local lodge, assisting in grievance administration, and assuring that management abides by the agreement. On many occasions, a staff member of the national union (usually the international union representative) assists local officers in negotiations and in administering the labor agreement and makes sure that the local's activities conform to the national constitutions and directives. The shop steward, the elected representative in each department in the plant or facility, represents the members at local union meetings, handles grievances at the shop level, and collects dues, if necessary.[1]

Government and Operation of the Local Union The government of the local union is affected by its periodic meetings and by the constitution of its national union.

Participation in meetings. Although attendance at the union meeting often varies between 5 and 10 percent, it reaches a high level when the union members themselves perceive a potential payoff for participation (for example, representing their department or interest groups such as older members, and so on),[2] or when the union is confronted with important business or a crisis, such as during negotiations or when a strike seems certain. Unions and their members have been criticized for their lack of attendance, but formal attendance cannot be taken as the real measure of membership participation. Much membership participation takes place on an informal basis at the plant level between employees, among friends during lunch, or between shop steward and members during rest breaks. The influence of these informal channels over union policies and actions should not be underestimated.[3]

Research into union member participation has helped identify certain characteristics of active union members. They usually have jobs higher in pay, skill, seniority, and job status. As far as personal characteristics are concerned, they are more likely to be older, male, and married and tend to be well integrated in social life, for example, to belong to organizations, fraternal groups, sports teams, or veterans' organizations outside the plant. Finally, they have a higher degree of job satisfaction, a favorable feeling toward the union as well as the company (discussed in Chapter 1 as *dual loyalty*),[4] and higher order needs, such as growth, accomplishment, and decision making.[5]

The union leaders and their followers almost always attend local union meetings, as do departmental representatives, "hard core" members, pressure groups, social groups, and aspirants to union leadership positions. Locals have tried a number of techniques to increase attendance of regular members, such as providing beer and sandwiches, showing movies, fining members who miss a specified number of meetings or refusing to let them seek an elected office, and providing door prizes. While some gimmicks may increase the attendance in the short run, many members still feel the meetings are "long, boring, and frustrating affairs."[6]

Local meetings are held at a time that meets the approval of the majority. While they often start late and last too long, the average length is about two hours. The content inspires little attendance because much of the time is devoted to reading reports from the treasurer, project leaders, and committee chairpersons. Opportunities are provided for members to discuss these reports, but this procedure itself takes time, especially when a grievance involving someone in attendance is presented or when a controversial issue is raised before the meeting as a whole. Parliamentary procedure is used, at times to excess by quasi-parliamentary experts who may want to tie up the meeting. Although the meeting may stray from the ideal, generally the business of the local is accomplished.[7]

Functions of the meeting. While the local union meeting may seem boring and nonrepresentative, it serves several vital functions in the local union government. First, the meeting is the union's single most important governmental activity; and all authority at the local level is derived from it. Second, the meeting provides an opportunity for members to communicate with leaders, express gripes directly, and call attention to their concerns. Likewise, it is an opportunity for leaders to give information to members, show off results, seek union support, and give directions to the membership. Last, the meeting is the supreme legislative body; this is where decisions are made on such items as disposition of grievances and approval of expenses and constitutional changes, election of officers, and ratification of the contract.[8]

The National (International) Union[9]

The national or international union in the United States occupies the "kingpin" position in organized labor "because of its influence in collective bargaining—the core function of American unions."[10] Size alone (See Table 5–1) indicates the magnitude of the influence of national unions—millions of members work under labor agreements that are directly or indirectly the result of national union actions. The local union operates under its constitution and directives, and the federation (AFL-CIO) derives its influence, prestige, and power from the affiliated national unions.

The national union operates under a *constitution* adopted in a convention by representatives from locals. These constitutions have evolved over time through three stages: first, the locals were initially careful to restrict the power of the national union; second, as national unions became more active in collective bargaining, political action, and so on, the locals became subordinate bodies; and third and presently, the constitution includes provisions that not only authorize the major national union functions but also protect individual rights and rights of locals in relation to the national union.[11]

The Convention The supreme governing body of the national union is its *convention*, which is usually held annually or biennially.[12] It serves the national union in many ways: as the constitutional assembly, the legislature of the national union, the supreme court for judicial decisions, and the means for nominating officers (and the election in many cases). The convention provides the time and place for national officers to report to the members their accomplishments and disclose their failures. It provides the agenda for policy formulation, program planning, and rule

Table 5–1 National Unions	Unions	Membership
	Teamsters[a]	1,953,000
	Auto Workers[a]	1,499,000
	National Education Association[a]	1,696,000
	Steelworkers	1,286,000
	United Food and Commercial Workers	1,236,000
	Electricians (IBEW)	1,012,000
	Machinists	921,000
	Carpenters	769,000

[a]Not affiliated with the AFL-CIO.

Source: Preliminary data from U.S. Department of Labor, Bureau of Labor Statistics, *Directory of National Unions and Employee Associations, 1978* (Washington, D.C.: Government Printing Office, in press).

making. It represents the time in which the voice of the membership holds leaders accountable for their actions. However, not all activities are official; the convention provides a reward for drudgery work at the local, an opportunity for politicking and public relations, and a time and place for the members to "let their hair down."

The convention makes use of the *delegate system* in which the number of delegates allowed depends on the number of members in the local. Since even the smallest union is allowed one delegate, the number of delegates is not in direct proportion to the size of the local, although larger locals usually have more delegates. The convention conducts its business similarly to Congress and various state legislatures in that much committee work (including the possible holding of hearings) is performed prior to debate and vote on the convention floor. However, much work takes place in the bars and smoke-filled rooms.[13]

Although many subjects may go before the convention, several continue to emerge year after year:

☐ Internal government: dues, financial matters, authority of the president, executive board, and locals.

☐ Collective bargaining: problems with current agreements, membership requests for future negotiations, establishing bargaining priorities, determination of strategy for next negotiations.

☐ Resolutions in support of or against domestic and international public policies: labor law reform, wage-price guidelines, international balance of payments, loss of jobs to foreign countries.[14]

Leadership and Administration Between conventions, the national union is led by its executive board, whose members are elected by the membership. In some cases, executive board members are elected on a regional basis, and they are responsible for regional intermediate organizations that maintain contact between the locals in the region and the national. The relationship between the executive board and the national union president is usually specified in the constitution. For example, some national union presidents primarily carry out the policies of the executive board; others direct the affairs of the national union, subject to the approval of the board. However, the largest group of presidents have virtually unrestricted authority to appoint their staff, regulate locals, and direct the activities of the national union. The rationale for allowing such great authority to be vested in the chief executive is that the union frequently finds itself in struggles with employers or other situations where it must act decisively and quickly. Thus, a strong executive is needed and a single spokesman for the union is required. However, the concentration of power creates opportunities for misuse of power, and an internal system of checks and balances must be devised to assure democracy and adequate representation. Experiences that brought on the passage of Titles I to VI of the Landrum-Griffin Act have shown that internal control often does not work effectively, and governmental regulation is essential.

Even with the legislation, unions have a difficult time dealing with member apathy. For example, only 33 percent of 275,000 members of the International Union of Electrical Workers (IUE) voted in the last election of national union officers, and only 193 of the 600 local unions were represented at the national union convention. In response to this apathy and lack of participation, the delegates to the convention voted to have the officer elections conducted at the convention rather than by direct vote of the rank-and-file, further removing the individual member from a role of active participation in union decisions. [15]

One slight sign of an improved democracy and active participation by members has been the increased turnover rates of national union presidents. The period of 1973–1975 witnessed fifty changes in national union leaders, up from thirty-six during the 1971–1973 period. This higher turnover rate is misleading, however, because only three of these cases resulted from an election defeat; eighteen were caused by death of the incumbent and fifteen by retirement. Further, high turnover continues to occur more frequently in the smaller unions and at the local levels than at the national level. [16]

The operational departments of nationals may vary in kind and number, but the typical national union will have at least the following departments: (1) executive and administration; (2) financial and auditing; (3) organizing and servicing; and (4) technical staff, which includes research, education, economics, law, publications, and public relations.

The executive and administrative group includes the president, vice-president(s), secretary-treasurer, and their assistants. This group will be chiefly responsible for the activities of the overall union. In some cases the vice-president may concentrate on organizing or collective bargaining, whereas the secretary-treasurer naturally will focus on financial matters.

The organizing and service functions are usually handled by international union representatives employed by the national but assigned to a regional office to assist the locals in that geographic area. In addition, if there are unorganized workers in the area, this representative usually devotes some efforts to organizing these workers. The technical staff departments may be one-person shops that provide expert assistance to locals on a broad range of subjects, such as selecting arbitrators, carrying out economic research, and writing news releases. [17]

Services to and Control of Locals As indicated earlier, the locals are constitutionally subordinated to the national union, but the degree of subordination varies with the union. The national provides services to the local union in several ways while at the same time controlling local union leaders. For example, where a national product market exists, the national labor agreement with one firm establishes the pattern by negotiating a master agreement (corporate-wide agreements are negotiated in the steel, auto, rubber, aircraft, and electrical appliance industries). For example, in 1979 the United Rubber Workers negotiated first with Uniroyal before negotiating with Goodyear, Goodrich, and Firestone. The master agreement establishes the pattern for all relevant agreements negotiated by the same national with other companies in the same industry. Following the negotiations of the master agreement between the national and the company, the local union will negotiate a local agreement with the plant officials, covering local rules, policies, and benefits. Deviations are possible, but they must be okayed by the national union.

The national union assists locals in collective bargaining, grievance administration, strike activities, and internal financial administration. These services also provide an opportunity for national union staff members to assure that the local unions are conforming to national policies.

The international union representative, in addition to organizing new unions, also helps the local unions in grievance administration and labor arbitration. The national supports the local in strike situations, but the local must get approval in order to qualify for strike benefits. The national union provides counseling and consultation for internal financial administration (bookkeeping, dues collection, purchases, financing union lodges, and so on), but trusteeship (receivership) procedures are available whereby the national union can set aside the local for abuses such as malfeasance, corruption, and misuse of funds in favor of a trustee under national direction.[18]

Dues, Fees, and Distribution of Funds Although all union members pay dues or fees to their national unions, the amount and form vary considerably. Such fees are the chief source of revenue for unions, and some national unions receive less than $6 per member monthly while others receive more than $16. Some unions set a single rate, but most allow the local some flexibility in making the final determination. Frequently, dues are collected via a dues checkoff system (discussed in more detail in Chapter 10). The member agrees to a payroll deduction of union dues, which are collected by the employer and paid directly to the union.

Initiation fees in most cases are less than $40 per member; however, several specialized unions with small membership, such as Director's Guild, Football Players, Mineworkers, and Ironworkers, charge over $100, and the Radio Association charges $2,000. Some of these high dues may be misleading because the payments often include premiums for insurance, pension payments, and other benefits.

The local unions forward a portion of the monthly dues for each member to the national union. Table 5–2 presents the results of a study of 169 national unions in which about one-third of the unions representing nearly 50 percent of the members require the local to pay between $2.00 and $3.99 per month per member to the national union.

The nationals use these funds for various purposes beneficial to the membership. While the largest percentage of funds goes to the general

Table 5–2 Portion of Monthly Dues Forwarded to National Unions	169 National Unions (21,426,000 Members)		
	Amount of Dues	Number of Unions	Membership (in Thousands)
	Less than $1.00	11	474
	$1.00 to 1.99	26	2,077
	$2.00 to 3.99	55	10,689
	$4.00 to 5.99	32	3,237
	$6.00 and above	27	1,757
	Undetermined	18	3,192

Source: Charles W. Hickman, "Labor Organizations' Fees and Dues," *Monthly Labor Review* 100 (May 1977), p. 22.

fund, which covers administrative and operational costs and salary expenses, allocations are made to other accounts such as a strike fund, a convention fund, union publications, educational activities, and a retirement members fund. [19]

Use of union dues and fees for political purposes and non–collective bargaining activities has come under fire in the last few years. Union members who disagree with the manner in which their unions contribute or use their funds have challenged their respective unions. Recent court decisions have caused several unions, such as the Machinists, Auto Workers, and American Federation of State, County, and Municipal Employees, to adopt dues rebate plans. These plans allow a rebate of a portion of member dues spent on political activities if the member requests it in advance (usually annually).

A district court judge in California has ruled that if a union uses dues and fees of protesting employees for non–collective bargaining activities and purposes, it breaches its fiduciary duty of fair representation."[20] In addition, the judge listed twelve activities, including political ones, that were considered non–collective bargaining activities. [21] If this decision is allowed to stand, it may alter significantly the role of unions in the political arena. While unions can continue to solicit volunteer contributions through such units as the AFL-CIO Committee on Political Education (COPE), the Auto Workers' Community Action Program (CAP), and the Mine Workers' Coal Miners' Political Action Committee (COMPAC), collections may be more difficult.

Mergers of National Unions Encouraged by the AFL-CIO merger but mostly spurred by rising costs, the need for stronger bargaining positions, expensive jurisdictional disputes, decline of some U.S. industries, [22] avoidance of external controls, and the need for self-preservation, [23] mergers of national unions have occurred at a quickening pace (fifty-seven since 1956; twenty-one in the last seven years). [24] In recent years, important union mergers have occurred in the paper industry, railroad industry, the postal service, and state government employees. In 1979, the Retail Clerks and Meat Cutters and Butchers agreed to merge, giving the new United Food and Commercial Workers over 1.2 million members.[25]

Typically, mergers have not succeeded immediately in welding together functions, organization units, and staff members. They have required time, patience, and good will of all parties, as officers and staff members who have different personalities and modes of operation have been meshed. The local unions must be accommodated as well as the employers and the collective bargaining relationships. Mergers have been particularly difficult when one of the unions feels a loss of its autonomy and when the merger occurs between unions whose prior dealings have been characterized by intense rivalry. Often members' pride is hurt, and fear surfaces when they find out that their union may be submerged by another.

In a more positive vein, the resulting larger unions have more clout with industrial giants and can negotiate more as equals. The greater size generates resources to provide better training in collective bargaining, grievance administration, and steward leadership; to offer greater strike benefits; to lobby more effectively for legislation; and to maintain a staff to combat unfair labor practices. Moreover, successful mergers reduce the risks to smaller unions from technological change, economic recessions, declines in membership, unemployment, and financial strains.[26] The potential advantages of a merger coupled with the risks of not merging suggest that mergers of national unions will be continued in the future.[27]

Intermediate Organizational Units

Within the union structure between national headquarters and the locals lie the intermediate organizational units—regional or district offices, trade conferences, conference boards, and joint councils. These units usually operate under the guidance of their various national unions, but their activities are important to the union members and employers in their areas.

The *regional* or *district offices* house the regional or district officers, the staff, and the international union representatives for the geographic area served. For example, Michigan has a number of Auto Workers' district offices; the Steel Workers have district offices in Pittsburgh, Birmingham, and elsewhere. The offices are established to better serve locals from their respective national unions.

Trade conferences are set up within national unions to represent a variety of industrial groups. For example, the Teamsters' Union has established eleven trade conferences for such groups as freight, laundry, airlines, and moving and storage. These groups meet to discuss various mutual problems and topics of interest.

Conference boards are organized within national unions in accordance with the company affiliation to discuss issues that pertain to the union and the particular company. For instance, each of the national unions within the steel, auto, rubber, and electric industries has established conference boards which meet to discuss negotiations and related problems. Delegates are chosen from the local unions to represent the interests of their constituents at meetings, to plan the next negotiations, and then to relay these plans to the local union members.

Joint councils involve groupings of local unions which have common goals, employers, and interests. Examples are the building trades councils established in most metropolitan areas in the United States. They negotiate with the association of construction employers in the area, coordinate their activities, and assist in resolving jurisdictional disputes between unions.

The American Federation of Labor and Congress of Industrial Organizations (AFL-CIO)

The American Federation of Labor and Congress of Industrial Organizations (AFL-CIO), while not including all U.S. labor unions, is composed of 105 national and international unions that have more than 60,000 local unions and 13,600,000 members. In addition, there are a number of directly affiliated local unions having 57,000 members.[28] Members represent a wide diversity of occupations, such as actors, construction workers, barbers and hairdressers, steelworkers, bus drivers, railroad workers, telephone operators, newspaper reporters, sales clerks, garment workers, engineers, school teachers, and police.[29] These AFL-CIO affiliates maintain day-to-day relationships with several hundred thousand employers and administer more than 160,000 labor agreements. Most (98 percent) of these agreements are negotiated without strikes or other forms of conflict and serve as the basis of employment conditions under which many work.

Established in 1955 when the American Federation of Labor and the Congress of Industrial Organizations merged, the AFL-CIO recognized the principle that both craft and industrial unions are an appropriate, equal, and necessary part of U.S. organized labor. The federation accepts the principle of *autonomy*—each affiliated union conducts its own affairs; has its own headquarters, offices, and staff; decides its own economic policies; sets its own dues; carries out its own contract negotiations; and provides its own services to members.

No national union is required to affiliate with the AFL-CIO. About sixty unions, including two of the largest—Teamsters and United Auto Workers—remain outside the AFL-CIO. (The Teamsters were asked to leave, and the UAW left over differences with the AFL-CIO leadership.) Member unions are free to withdraw at any time; however, their voluntary participation plays an essential role that advances the interest of every union. National unions continue their membership because they believe that a federation of unions serves purposes their own individual unions cannot serve as well.

Examples of the AFL-CIO services include:

The 1955 merger of the American Federation of Labor and the Congress of Industrial Organizations created an association of both craft and industrial unions that now provides services to more than 13 million members.

Source: Courtesy of AFL-CIO and Merkle Press.

☐ Speaking for organized labor before Congress and other branches of government.

☐ Representing U.S. labor in world affairs, keeping in direct contact with labor unions throughout the free world.

☐ Coordinating activities such as community services, political education, lobbying, and voter registration with greater effectiveness.

☐ Helping to coordinate efforts to organize nonunion workers throughout the United States.

Another vital service enhances the integrity and prestige of AFL-CIO unions—they must operate under established ethical practice codes covering union democracy and financial integrity. The federation also assists in keeping down conflicts that cause work interruptions by mediating and resolving disputes between national unions, such as organizing disputes and conflicts over work assignments.[30]

Organization Structure The AFL-CIO organization structure, shown in Exhibit 5–1, illustrates the importance of the *convention*. Meeting every two years and at times of particular need, delegates decide on policies, programs, and direction for AFL-CIO activities. Each national union (international) is authorized to send delegates to the convention. The number of delegates is determined by the size of the union but is not in direct proportion to the size of the union, so that each union will be represented at the convention. In addition, other affiliated organizations, such as state labor councils, are represented by one delegate each.

Between conventions, the governing body is the Executive Council, comprised of the president (currently Lane Kirkland*), secretary-trea-

*George Meany had been president of the AFL-CIO from 1955 until his retirement in November 1979.

Exhibit 5–1
Structural
Organization of the
American Federation
of Labor and
Congress of
Industrial
Organizations

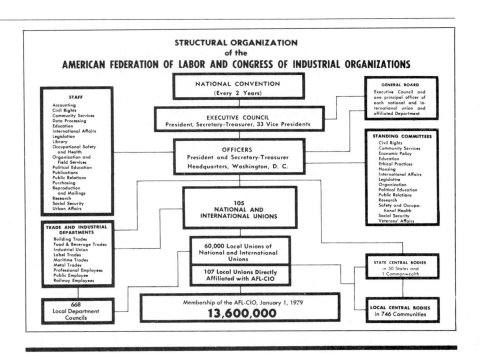

Source: *American Federationist,* the official monthly magazine of the AFL-CIO.

surer (currently Thomas Donahue), and thirty-three vice-presidents elected by majority vote at the convention. The Executive Council meets at least three times a year and handles operational duties involving legislative matters, union corruption, charters of new internationals, and judicial appeals from member unions.

Between meetings of the Executive Council, the president, who is the chief executive officer, has authority to supervise the affairs of the federation and to direct its staff, and the secretary-treasurer handles all financial matters. To assist in his administration, the president has appointed fifteen *standing committees* on various subjects and with the assistance of the AFL-CIO staff provides related services to member unions. The staff, located at headquarters in Washington, D.C., corresponds closely to these standing committees in order to better serve the member unions. (See Exhibit 5–1 for a listing of standing committees and staff divisions.) The *General Board,* composed of the Executive Council and one officer from each member union, is available to act on matters referred to it from the Executive Council.

The AFL-CIO has established fifty *state central bodies* (plus one in Puerto Rico) to advance the statewide interests of labor through political, lobbying, and organizing activities, which involve attempts to elect friends of labor, to have favorable legislation passed, and to organize nonunion workers, respectively. Each local union of AFL-CIO–affiliated unions in a particular state may join the state organization and participate in and support its activities. In addition, 746 *local central bodies* have been formed by local unions of the national affiliates to deal with civic and community problems and other matters of local concern.

To accommodate and serve the interests and needs of various trade and industrial unions, the AFL-CIO has established eight *trade and industrial departments.* The Industrial Union Department represents the interests of industrial unions, mostly members of the former CIO. Another department, the Union Label Department, promotes the purchases and sales of union-made goods and services. The remaining departments represent the interests of such union groups as the building trades, food and beverage trades, maritime employees, metal trades, public employees, and railway employees. In addition, throughout the United States where there is sufficient interest and support, 668 *local department councils* have been organized.[31]

The AFL-CIO's operations are financed through regular member dues, called *per capita taxes,* which are paid by affiliated unions on behalf of their members. Currently, the per capita tax is $.13 per month or $1.56 per year for each member. Thus, the AFL-CIO's operating budget is over $18 million, of which $17.5 million covers regular operating expenses. A major portion of the budget goes to the salaries of the staff. For example, AFL-CIO President George Meany's salary was $90,000 in 1977, and Secretary-Treasurer Lane Kirkland's was $60,000. (These seem high until compared to the highest paid U.S. executives'. For example, the annual total compensation for David Mahoney, chairman, Norton Simon, was $2.03 million; Archie McCardell, president, International Harvester, was paid $1.907 million; Henry J. Gray, chairman, United Technologies, was paid $1.683 million.)[32] The detailed financial report of the AFL-CIO is submitted to the delegates at each convention.

Other AFL-CIO activities are educational and informational, presenting the federation's stance on a variety of issues. For example, the AFL-CIO publishes a monthly magazine—the *American Federationist*—which includes articles of concern to organized labor, a weekly *AFL-CIO News* that keeps members up-to-date on current events that pertain to them, and various reports on problems and policies of organized labor. The AFL-CIO maintains the George Meany Center for Labor Studies, offering short courses in union leadership development, and a Speaker's Bureau to provide labor speakers for high school and college classes, and makes available educational films to interested groups for a nominal fee.[33]

In the political arena, the AFL-CIO receives much attention. The representative of organized labor, it serves as the focal point of political activities. Not only does it lobby aggressively for favorable legislation, but it publishes the voting records of each senator and representative at both federal and state levels. It attempts to influence appointments, such as Supreme Court Judge, Secretary of Labor, and National Labor Relations Board members, which are important to organized labor.[34] Its policy of "Reward Your Friends, Punish Your Enemies" has not changed much since Samuel Gompers' days. The AFL-CIO's Committee on Political Education (COPE) has a network in each state and in most large communities. COPE seeks voluntary contributions to provide funds for its activities, which include voter registration, "get-out-the-vote" campaigns, preparation of leaflets and posters, and research on behalf of its candidates.[35] Although the Federal Election Campaign Act of 1971, amended in 1974, has restricted financial contributions to federal candidates, the AFL-CIO, COPE, and state and local bodies can still amass amazing support to help their candidates for office, especially when the candidate is clearly the choice of organized labor.[36]

While organized labor has played a major role in U.S. politics, it is not a subdivision of a national political party. However, over the years it has been more closely aligned with the Democratic Party, both philosophically and politically. It has become perhaps the single most important political force that has supported government programs to help the socially and economically disadvantaged. It has supported consumer and environmental protection and safety and health legislation which has benefited union members as well as others.

Organized labor has accumulated much power and influence through its own established network and has also been instrumental in organizing other politically active groups with socially oriented objectives, such as minorities and senior citizens. However, organized labor's overall political strength and actual effectiveness should not be exaggerated. In some states and municipalities, union membership is so negligible that its influence is inconsequential. In others, where union membership is high, its influence is significant, and political candidates must actively solicit its support.[37]

Union Corruption and the Landrum-Griffin Act

Corruption, racketeering, and embezzlement have been discovered in some local and national unions. Union abuses of power were exposed by the McClellan hearings of the late 1950s.[38] Enormous amounts of Teamster pension funds have been allegedly misused.[39] The slaying of Joseph Yablonski, who ran and was defeated in the Mine Workers' presidential election by Tony Boyle, was an example of violence of the most serious kind. (Months later, Boyle was sentenced for contracting for this murder.) Then, in late 1978, Paperworker president Joseph Tonelli pled guilty to charges of embezzling $360,000.[40]

The AFL-CIO established the Ethical Practices Committee in its efforts to control corrupt practices and racketeering of its member unions, and its Executive Council was given the authority to suspend any affiliated union with corrupt practices.[41] Then, in 1959, the U.S. Congress showed its concern with union abuse and the potential misuse of union power by amending the National Labor Relations Act through passage of the Landrum-Griffin Act (the Labor-Management Reporting and Disclosure Act). Title VII of the act pertains to amendments to the NLRA, but the remainder covers union operations and government.

☐ Title I guarantees union members equal participation in internal union affairs; the right of free speech and assembly; reasonable and uniform dues, fees, and assessments; freedom to sue the union and its officers; and fair and equitable treatment in discipline cases.

☐ Title II requires disclosure by union officers and employees (and employers and their agents) about financial dealings, trusteeships, and any private arrangements made with any employees.

☐ Title III regulates union trusteeships, including rules for their establishment and maintenance, and the protection of the rights of members of unions under trusteeship.

☐ Title IV regulates the conduct of union elections. These provisions are designed to insure fairness and participation in the election and to challenge the results should any illegality be found.

☐ Title V sets forth fiduciary responsibilities of union officers and representatives, disqualifies criminals and former Communists from holding union offices, and requires certain union officers to be bonded to assure the faithful discharge of their duties and responsibilities.[42]

Now, over twenty years after the Landrum-Griffin Act was passed, its impact is still debated. Research indicates that the act has had a minimal impact on national union constitutions, but it has contributed to making union members far more aware of their individual rights concerning appeals, freedom of speech, and participation in union affairs, and of their legally protected guarantee of these rights. In addition, union members have become more aware of the procedures required for the conduct of elections, and more members are watchful to assure that election regulations are followed. Not to be underestimated is the fact the secretary of labor may be called in to investigate election irregularities; in fact, the act authorizes the secretary to investigate the election without individual charges from union members. Thus, it has created a new atmosphere and psychology among the union establishment and has certainly caused union officers to take greater care in their own administrations. [43]

Status of Union Membership

Union membership in the United States declined by about 3 percent from 1974 to 1976—the first drop since the 1960–1962 reporting period. In actual members, the total dropped from 20.2 million to about 19.6 million. Table 5–3 shows the fluctuation in membership since the 1960s, indicating an upward trend over time. However, the table also reveals that membership in unions has declined as a percentage of the total labor

Table 5–3
National Union and Employee Association Membership, Totals and Proportion of Labor Force and Nonagricultural Employment, 1958–1978

Year Unions and Associations	Union Membership (in Thousands)	Total Labor Force		Nonagricultural Employees	
		Number (in Thousands)	Percent Members	Number (in Thousands)	Percent Members
1968	20,721	82,272	25.2	67,951	30.5
1970	21,248	85,903	24.7	70,880	30.0
1972	21,657	88,991	24.3	73,675	29.4
1974	22,809	93,240	24.5	78,265	29.1
1976	22,662	96,917	23.4	79,382	28.3
1978	22,798	102,537	22.2	85,763	26.6
Unions					
1960	17,049	72,142	23.6	54,234	31.4
1962	16,586	73,442	22.6	55,596	29.8
1964	16,841	75,830	22.2	58,331	28.9
1966	17,940	78,893	22.7	63,955	28.1
1968	18,916	82,272	23.0	67,951	27.8
1970	19,381	85,903	22.6	70,920	27.3
1972	19,435	88,991	21.8	73,714	26.4
1974	20,199	93,240	21.7	78,413	25.8
1976	19,634	96,917	20.3	79,382	24.7
1978	20,238	102,537	19.7	85,762	23.6

Source: U.S. Department of Labor, Bureau of Labor Statistics, *News* (Washington, D.C.: Government Printing Office, September 3, 1979).

force.[44] In 1978, union membership represented only 23.6 percent of the labor force and 26.6 percent of the employees in the nonagricultural establishments.[45]

These percentages seem low, but they average those in industries that are heavily unionized, such as transportation, manufacturing, mining, and contract construction, and others that are less unionized, such as banks, agriculture, and insurance. Table 5–4 demonstrates the broad percentage categories of thirty-five industries by the degree of unionization. In addition, the degree of unionization is not equal geographically—the North and Northeast are heavily organized and the South and Southwest less so than the average (see Table 5–5).

A number of researchers have attempted to identify the reasons for the decline in union membership as a percent of the labor force or, more descriptively, "union stagnation." While there seems to be no single reason for this lack of growth,[46] a number of explanations have been given. The reasons below may overlap to some extent; each attempts to explain the causes for lack of union growth:

1. Structural changes in employment are occurring, with the heavily unionized industries (such as manufacturing, railroads, and mining) either declining or growing at a lesser rate than less unionized industries (such as services, finance, and trades).[47]
2. Shifts in the product and labor markets have affected organized firms; for example, some firms have folded, plants have closed, plants have

---

Table 5–4 Industry Classification by Degree of Unionization

75 percent and over	25 percent to 50 percent
Ordnance	Printing, publishing
Transportation	Leather
Transportation equipment	Rubber
Contract construction	Furniture
	Machinery
50 percent to 75 percent	Lumber
Electrical machinery	Chemicals
Food and kindred products	Electric, gas utilities
Primary metals	
Mining	**Less than 25 percent**
Telephone and telegraph	Nonmanufacturing
Paper	Instruments
Petroleum	Textile mill products
Tobacco manufacturers	State government
Apparel	Local government
Fabricated metals	Service
Manufacturing	Trade
Stone, clay, & glass production	Agriculture, fisheries
Federal government	Finance

Source: U.S. Department of Labor, Bureau of Labor Statistics, *Directory of National Unions and Employee Associations, 1975* (Washington, D.C.: Government Printing Office, 1977), pp. 70–71.

Table 5–5 Distribution of Membership of National Unions and Employee Associations by State	State	Percent Nonagricultural Employee Union Members	Rank	State	Percent Nonagricultural Employee Union Members	Rank
	Alabama*	23.9	26	Montana	31.1	17
	Alaska	37.2	7	Nebraska*	17.8	38
	Arizona*	21.1	32	Nevada*	31.4	16
	Arkansas*	18.1	37	New Hampshire	19.0	36
	California	33.3	12	New Jersey	32.3	13
	Colorado	23.0	29	New Mexico	17.6	40
	Connecticut	30.3	19	New York	45.4	1
	Delaware	23.5	27	North Carolina*	9.8	50
	Florida	14.7	46	North Dakota*	19.7	35
	Georgia*	15.8	44	Ohio	36.4	9
	Hawaii	38.7	6	Oklahoma	16.8	42
	Idaho	20.6	34	Oregon	32.2	14
	Illinois	37.1	8	Pennsylvania	40.9	4
	Indiana	36.2	10	Rhode Island	30.3	18
	Iowa*	25.1	24	South Carolina*	10.3	49
	Kansas*	17.5	41	South Dakota*	15.1	45
	Kentucky	28.9	20	Tennessee*	20.9	33
	Louisiana	17.7	39	Texas*	14.2	47
	Maine	22.8	30	Utah*	21.5	31
	Maryland–D.C.	25.5	23	Vermont	23.2	28
	Massachusetts	26.6	22	Virginia*	16.1	43
	Michigan	42.4	2	Washington	40.6	5
	Minnesota	28.3	21	West Virginia	41.9	3
	Mississippi*	13.3	48	Wisconsin	32.1	15
	Missouri	33.4	11	Wyoming*	24.3	25

*Right-to-work state (see Chapter 10).

Source: U.S. Department of Labor, Bureau of Labor Statistics, *Directory of National Unions and Employee Associations, 1975* (Washington, D.C.: Government Printing Office, 1977), pp. 75–76.

moved to less organized sections of the U.S. (the West and South), and organized companies have lost business to nonunion firms.

3. Interindustry shifts in employment to newer, high-technology industries, such as computers, technical equipment, and scientific instruments, also affect union growth, for the employees in these industries have always been difficult to organize.

4. The occupational mix is changing toward more professional, technical, and service (white-collar) employees—also traditionally difficult to organize.

5. More organizations are learning how to operate their businesses on a nonunion basis through enlightened management, double breasting (see Chapter 4), anti-union campaigns, and so on. In other words, management has become more sophisticated in understanding the reasons workers organize unions and more aggressive within the legal framework in presenting its viewpoint to the employees.

6. Changing demographics in the work force have helped to slow union growth; women, the better educated, and the younger employees who are new entrants have traditionally been more difficult to organize.
7. Surprisingly, the rapid expansion in legal job rights through the Equal Employment Opportunity Act, Occupational Safety and Health Act, Employee Retirement and Income Security Act, and other legislation has helped make union organizing more difficult. The legal rights give employees a free ride in areas for which the union once was the primary protector and provider, and the increasing costs of these programs to the employers have caused them to stiffen their resistance to unions, to be more cost conscious, and to increase their level of managerial sophistication in personnel practices. [48]
8. Union officials place much blame on deficiencies in the labor relations laws. Preelection time delays, contested elections, lengthy appeals, and stalled negotiations are possible under the National Labor Relations Act. They claim that companies are allowed to frustrate the objectives of the NLRA and negate the results of free employee choices through secret-ballot elections. [49]

Other reasons given for union stagnation have been: (a) faulty unionization strategies where unions have focused too heavily on well-entrenched markets and have neglected the high-growth, low–union density markets; (b) the declining image workers and the public have of organized labor due to the advanced age of most labor leaders and the absence of young, aggressive, and imaginative leaders; (c) recent political setbacks, such as the failure of Congress to amend the NLRA by passing the Labor Law Reform Bill, even after President Carter supported the bill, and (d) lower priority in time, effort, and funds going into union organizing with higher priority going to maintaining and servicing the present unions. [50]

Questions for Unions in the 1980s

With these declines, organized labor is faced with significant challenges and important questions:

1. Can organized labor develop new techniques that appeal to the needs of workers in the less unionized sectors (such as health-care, white-collar, textile, service, finance, and agriculture workers) and in the South, West, and Southwest? [51]
2. Will union leaders be able to renew the direction of organized labor and regain lost prestige and influence? (A 1978 Harris poll gave labor leaders a 15 percent confidence rating, tying them with Congress for next to last place.) [52]
3. Will organized labor be able to appeal to groups of employees now entering the labor market in large numbers for the first time, such as women and young people? Can it accommodate their interests regarding such issues as flexible hours, seniority lists, pension benefits,

Part 1/Recognition of the Rights and Responsibilities of Unions and Management

desire for challenging work, and more leisure time? Can it deal with the new breed of workers—the overqualified placed in blue-collar jobs, workers who don't trust management or the union?[53]

4. Can it continue to mobilize what some people consider the best political machine in the country to elect public officials?[54] (Organized labor backed President Carter and helped elect the majority in both the House and the Senate, but thus far it cannot identify itself with too many success stories.)

5. Can organized labor combat and deal with employers who have hired expert labor relations consultants and attorneys to keep unions out of companies[55] or who have designed personnel programs that create a work climate not conducive to unionization?

6. Will unions be able to take advantage of the predicted labor market glut of highly educated persons within the age range of 25 to 44 (which will reach 50 percent of the labor force by 1990)?[56] Much depends on the employer's reaction to this labor market glut and the way white-collar employees are treated in terms of employer practices (such as promotions, job security, career opportunities, and wage increases). Will the unions be able to react positively to employer practices unacceptable to employees?

Summary

Once organized, unions usually become part of a larger unit of organized labor. A local union becomes part of a national union, and most national unions affiliate with a federation of unions called the AFL-CIO. Because these unions vary so widely in structure, interest, and function, an attempt was made to identify the general purposes, activities, and operational matters which are pertinent to most. Much of the discussion related to the governance of the various levels of unions as set up in the local union meetings and the conventions of the national unions and the AFL-CIO. Other topics of importance to union government and operations include duties and responsibilities of union officers, union finances, and political and lobbying activities.

With the exposure of union corruption and abuses of power by the McClellan committee in 1958–1959, Congress reacted by passing the Landrum-Griffin Act (or the Labor-Management Reporting and Disclosure Act) to guarantee union members certain rights of participation in union affairs, to regulate union elections and trusteeships, and to assure financial and reporting compliance.

Growth patterns of union membership have shown an overall decline in recent years, and a long-term trend of a lower percentage of union membership as a percentage of the labor force has been noted. Experts who have studied the issue of union stagnation attribute it to a variety of causes, for example, a lessened growth rate in industries which are heavily unionized and interindustry shifts in employment to newer, high-technology industries whose employees are difficult to unionize. Organized labor's ability to overcome its present decline will depend upon its ability to adapt its techniques to needs of the changing work force and of employees currently not being reached, to regain lost prestige and influence with the public, and to effect political moves advantageous to unions.

Discussion Questions

1. Select a craft union and an industrial union and point out the differing characteristics of these two types of unions.

2. Compare the government of the local union to student governments and municipal governments, with special attention to participation by members.

3. Explain why and how national union presidents have been able to accumulate so much authority and power.

4. Differentiate among the business agent of a local union, a shop steward, and an international union representative. How do their roles differ?

5. Since the AFL-CIO does not negotiate labor agreements on behalf of national unions, how can it claim to be the "spokesman for organized labor" in the United States?

6. Considering the reasons given to explain union stagnation, what are your predictions for union growth in the 1980s? Why?

References

[1] Allan Nash, *The Union Steward: Duties, Rights and Status* (Ithaca, N.Y.: New York State School of Industrial and Labor Relations, 1977), pp. 20–22.

[2] John C. Anderson, "Local Union Participation: A Re-examination," *Industrial Relations* 18 (Winter 1979), p. 30.

[3] Arnold S. Tannenbaum, "Unions," in James G. March, ed., *Handbook of Organizations* (Chicago: Rand McNally, 1965), p. 745–748.

[4] Ibid., pp. 745–747.

[5] William Glick, Phillip Mirvis, and Diane Harder, "Union Satisfaction and Participation," *Industrial Relations* 16 (Spring 1977), p. 145.

[6] Leonard R. Sayles and George Strauss, *The Local Union*, rev. ed. (New York: Harcourt, Brace & World, 1967), pp. 96–100.

[7] Ibid., pp. 93–96.

[8] Ibid., pp. 100–105.

[9] National and international unions are nearly synonymous; the small difference is that internationals may have locals outside the United States. Thus, in this book, the terms will be used interchangeably.

[10] Jack Barbash, *American Unions* (New York: Random House, 1967), p. 69.

[11] Ibid., pp. 71–72.

[12] The Landrum-Griffin Act requires a convention at least every five years, and some unions, such as the Teamsters, take the limit of five years.

[13] George Strauss, "Union Government in the U.S.: Research Past and Future," *Industrial Relations* 16 (Winter 1977), p. 234.

[14] Barbash, *American Unions*, pp. 76–80.

[15] John Hoerr, "Union Democracy and Apathy Don't Mix," *Business Week*, October 2, 1979, p. 28.

[16] U.S. Department of Labor, Bureau of Labor Statistics, *Directory of National Unions and Employee Associations, 1975* (Washington, D.C.: Government Printing Office, 1977), p. 55.

[17]Barbash, *American Unions*, pp. 81–88.

[18]Ibid., pp. 89–93.

[19]Charles W. Hickman, "Labor Organizations' Fees and Dues," *Monthly Labor Review* 100 (May 1977), pp. 19–24.

[20]Nels E. Nelson, "Union Dues and Political Spending," *Labor Law Journal* 28 (February 1977), pp. 109–119.

[21]Examples include recreation, social and entertainment activities, organization and recruitment of new members, convention attendance, general news publications, support of pending legislation, and contributions to charity. Ibid., pp. 117–118.

[22]Charles J. Janus, "Union Mergers in the 1970s: A Look at the Reasons and Results," *Monthly Labor Review* 101 (October 1978), p. 13.

[23]John Freeman and Jack Brittain, "Union Mergers Process and Industrial Environment," *Industrial Relations* 16 (Spring 1977), pp. 173–174.

[24]Janus, "Union Mergers," p. 13.

[25]"The Big New Retailing Union Eyes the Services," *Business Week*, March 5, 1979, pp. 73–74.

[26]Janus, "Union Mergers," pp. 13–15.

[27]Ibid., p. 22.

[28]*This Is the AFL-CIO* (Washington, D.C.: American Federation of Labor and Congress of Industrial Organizations, 1977), p. 1.

[29]Ibid.

[30]Ibid., pp. 1–3.

[31]U.S. Department of Labor, Bureau of Labor Statistics, *Directory of National Unions and Employee Associations, 1975* (Washington, D.C.: Government Printing Office, 1977), pp. 1-4.

[32]"Annual Survey of Executive Compensation," *Business Week*, May 14, 1979, p. 79.

[33]*This Is the AFL-CIO*, pp. 8–10.

[34]Marvin Caplan, "What Washington Labor Lobbyists Do," in Charles M. Rehmus, Doris McLauglin, and Frederick H. Nesbitt, eds., *Labor and American Politics*, rev. ed. (Ann Arbor: University of Michigan Press, 1978), pp. 225–229.

[35]*This Is the AFL-CIO*, pp. 10–12.

[36]Edwin M. Epstein, "Labor and Federal Elections: The New Legal Framework," *Industrial Relations* 15 (Summer 1976), pp. 257–274. Also see Philip Taft, "Internal Union Structure and Functions," in Gerald G. Somers, ed., *The Next Twenty-five Years of Industrial Relations* (Madison, Wis.: Industrial Relations Research Association, 1973), pp. 1–9.

[37]J. David Greenstone, *Labor in American Politics* (Chicago: University of Chicago Press, 1977), pp. xiii–xxix.

[38]Sherman and Murphy, *Unionization and Collective Bargaining*, p. 12.

[39]"Dissidents in the Teamsters Are Gaining Clout," *Business Week*, November 13, 1978, pp. 136–139.

[40]"Paperworkers' Chief Enters a Guilty Plea to Embezzling Charge," *Wall Street Journal*, October 23, 1978, p. 16.

[41]Woodrow Ginsburg, "Review of Literature on Union Growth, Government, and Structure: 1955–1969," *A Review of Industrial Relations Research*, vol. 1 (Madison, Wis.: Industrial Relations Research Association, 1970), pp. 232–233.

[42]Sherman and Murphy, *Unionization and Collective Bargaining*, p. 12.

[43]Ginsburg, "Review of Literature on Union Growth," p. 244–250.

[44]Union and association membership as a percentage of the total labor force declined by more than one percentage point between 1974 and 1976, continuing a trend that had begun in the early 1950s but had been temporarily halted in 1974.

[45]BNA Editorial Staff, *Labor Relations Yearbook, 1977* (Washington, D.C.: Bureau of National Affairs, 1978), pp. 247–248.

[46]Albert A. Blum, "Why Unions Grow," *Labor History* 9 (Winter 1968), pp. 39–41.

[47]Leo Troy, "Trade Union Growth in a Changing Economy," *Monthly Labor Review* 92 (September 1969), pp. 3–5.

[48]Myron Roomkin and Hervey A. Juris, "Unions in the Traditional Sectors: The Mid-Life Passage of the Labor Movement," in Barbara D. Dennis, ed., *Proceedings of the Thirty-first Annual Meeting: Industrial Relations Research Association* (Madison, Wis.: Industrial Relations Research Association, 1979), pp. 213–222.

[49]Richard Prosten, "The Longest Season: Union Organizing in the Last Decade, a/k/a How Come One Team Has to Play with Its Shoelaces Tied Together?" in Dennis, *Proceedings of the Thirty-first Annual Meeting: Industrial Relations Research Association*, pp. 240–249.

[50]James B. Dworkin and Marian Extejt, "Why Workers Decertify Their Unions: A Preliminary Investigation," paper presented at the Annual Meeting of the Academy of Management, August 1979; and Ronald Berenbeim, "The Declining Market for Unionization," *Conference Board Information Bulletin*, no. 44, August 1978, pp. 2–11.

[51]Alan Kistler, "Trends in Union Growth," in J. L. Stern and B. D. Dennis, eds., *Proceedings of the 1977 Annual Spring Meeting; Industrial Relations Research Association* (Madison, Wis.: Industrial Relations Research Association, 1977), pp. 541–544.

[52]"Labor Comes to a Crossroads," *Time*, September 4, 1978, p. 38.

[53]"Labor's Big Swing from Surplus to Shortage," *Business Week*, February 20, 1978, pp. 75–78.

[54]"Are Unions Losing Their Clout?" *U.S. News & World Report*, October 4, 1976, pp. 29–32.

[55]Kistler, "Trends in Union Growth," p. 540.

[56]Roomkin and Juris, "Unions in the Traditional Sectors," pp. 220–222.

Part 2 pertains to key activities in the labor relations process: the negotiation and administration of the work rules. These topics are approached from the vantage point of legal and quasi legal (labor agreement) proscriptions on related behavior as well as with an eye to the practical realities forged out of the relationships between union and management officials.

Part 2

Negotiation and
Administration of the
Labor Agreement

Chapter 6

Negotiating the Labor Agreement

"How much of the collective bargaining process has any real meaning? How much of it is empty ritual?"

Albert A. Blum

Collective bargaining, interchangeably called negotiations, is a common feature of everyday life. Newspapers and other media vividly document international negotiations (such as Egypt and Israel's and the Vietnamese peace negotiations) as well as dramatic confrontations between government officials and terrorist organizations. Negotiations are also a central feature of our interpersonal activities—we continually make deals or exchange favors with our friends and work associates. While this chapter covers collective bargaining between union and management officials over conditions of employment, many aspects of negotiations have broader applications to other bargaining activities in our society.

This chapter first places collective bargaining in perspective, indicating several characteristics of labor-management negotiations. The various activities of union and management representatives are also discussed in the light of applicable legal influences.

Collective Bargaining in Perspective

Negotiations Defined

The "Bargaining Range": Focal Point of Collective Bargaining Union and management officials both enter collective bargaining with their own ideas of an acceptable settlement, although both parties know the other will not agree entirely with their position. Therefore, both parties usually enter negotiations with a variety of acceptable positions, which gives them some room for maneuvering.[1]

These positions are given priorities and grouped into two *bargaining ranges,* one for management, the other for the union. (See Exhibit 6–1 for an illustration.) The bargaining ranges represent a multitude of priorities for union and management officials. Exhibit 6–1 contains only a few issues for illustrative purposes; however, it is common for the parties to negotiate a hundred or more bargaining issues. (See Exhibit 6–2 for a general list of issues which may appear in a collective bargaining agreement and be included in the bargaining range.)

Both management and union representatives have upper and lower limits on their respective ranges. Management's upper limit is usually determined by its objectives (profitability, growth, and so on). A settlement above this perceived upper limit would be incompatible with the company's objectives.[2] For example, management would close, move its operations, or bring new employees into its existing facility rather than agree to a settlement that would make operating unprofitable. On the other hand, management would not like to be known as the cheapest employer in the area, nor would it want to be unable to recruit, retain, and reward its employees. These concerns help place a lower limit on management's bargaining range—a point management feels is necessary to maintain current employee morale and output.

The union's upper settlement limit is usually shaped by two factors: (a)

Exhibit 6–1   Bargaining Ranges for Union and Management Negotiators

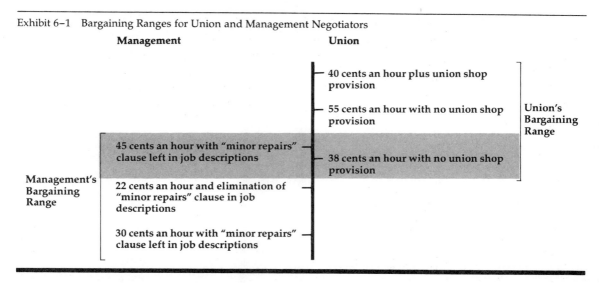

employment levels and (b) ability to promote and sustain a strike over an unrealistic settlement proposal. The union realizes that there can be a tradeoff between a high economic settlement and total number of jobs at a facility—employers might offset their newly negotiated labor costs by laying off some employees.[3] To some extent, the union's upper limit is governed by its desire to maintain the existing labor force or dues-paying membership.

The union also realizes that its members might want to strike over an unrealistic, pie in the sky proposal presented by the union. Some individuals believe that unions do not have upper limits on their bargaining range, that union leaders will press for outrageous proposals on the rationale that "it does not hurt to ask," and "nothing ventured, nothing gained." These unrealistic proposals can backfire on the union leaders if they raise membership desires for an appropriate settlement. Assume, for example, that the union anticipates the employer's upper limit represents a total settlement cost of 75 cents an hour per employee. The union could hold firm to its upper limit of $1.50 an hour per employee; however, it would incur tremendous risks. First, it would be difficult to motivate employees to go out on strike, particularly if they were satisfied with the 75 cent package. Even if it succeeded in calling a strike, the union would have difficulty convincing employees to return to work on terms similar to management's prestrike offer. Union leaders who raised members' expectations would be placed in the awkward position of having to convince their members that the strike had not been in vain.

On the other hand, the union realizes that there is a lower limit and that a settlement below this limit would result in membership dissatisfaction. Because union leaders are strongly influenced by their desires to assure the survival of the union and their continued roles as union officers,[4] they would never accept a settlement below their minimum, except in extreme cases. If members accepted such a settlement, they could subsequently express their dissatisfaction in one or more of the following ways: (a) voting in new union officers; (b) withdrawing their membership from the union; (c) reducing their support for the current officers through wildcat strikes or the formation of uncontrollable factions;[5] or (d) voting out the existing union. To avoid such consequences, union negotiators rarely accept below their minimum (lower limit).

The bargaining ranges, while bounded by upper and lower limits, represent a multitude of priorities for union and management officials. The assigning of priorities to these issues and their possible combinations produces bargaining ranges of an almost infinite number of possibilities. Bargaining ranges are also subject to change over time, usually becoming finalized as the contract expiration date approaches. During the course of negotiations, management and union officials may receive additional information causing them to alter their own upper and lower limits.

This section has focused on only one characteristic of negotiations: each party's attempt to obtain a settlement within its bargaining range. Addi-

Representatives of the union (United Rubber Workers) and management (B. F. Goodrich) negotiate to resolve their conflicting interests within a mutually acceptable bargaining range.

Source: Jeff Bates for *Business Week*.

tional characteristics of collective bargaining emerge from a look at the differences between negotiations and games.

Negotiations versus Games Some consider the terms negotiations and games identical. For example, one approach to collective bargaining, *game theory*, at least implicitly makes this assumption; and much of the public regards a good negotiator as a good poker player. To be sure, some similarities exist. Both activities represent a conflict of interest between two or more parties, skill is involved, and the parties attempt to achieve their respective goals. Yet, several profound differences between games (such as poker, baseball, or chess) and labor-management negotiations do exist.

First, games have a known set of values for the parties involved; therefore, each competitor can measure its own and its opponent's progress. In labor-management negotiations, however, "the negotiator has little or no control over the complex variables, and the innumerable strategies that the opponent may bring into the struggle."[6] Returning to Exhibit 6–1, it is difficult, if not impossible, to determine the value that the union gives to a union shop clause that requires union membership after thirty days of employment. In fact, a key task of labor negotiators is to determine their opponent's bargaining range without revealing their own upper and lower limits. Hence, opponents' values on various proposals usually remain vague or are not revealed to the other party.[7]

Games also feature rather rigid rules of conduct; for example, a baseball team is only allowed three outs an inning. In negotiations, both parties still have a great deal of discretion in developing and using strategies and tactics. Strategies of competitors in games are limited by rules, while the opponent's strategy in labor negotiations can become very unpredictable.

The third major difference between games and negotiations is that a game has a definite ending, usually with an absolute winner and loser. The objective in negotiations is to achieve agreement, not victory.[8] Labor-management negotiation is a continuous process with no real termination point and no absolute winner; indeed, union and management are free to define "victory" in their own terms.[9] For example, if management decided to go for a total victory, the union would likely opt for a strike which could hurt both sides.[10] If the union returned from the strike as a clearly defined loser, it would have the duration of the labor agreement to win back concessions through daily labor agreement administration and the grievance procedure (discussed in Chapters 8 and 9). Successful negotiations occur when both parties believe they have gained something, even though a "gain" for management might mean maintaining the status quo on certain issues. Thus, two major aspects permeate collective bargaining, including the formulation of the bargaining range:

First, each side needs the other. The union needs jobs for its members at acceptable wages and conditions; the employer needs an efficient work effort at a minimum cost. Second, each side is capable of withholding for a time something the other side needs. The union withholds labor by striking or imposing other sanctions; the employer can say no to union demands and/or actually withhold employment.[11]

Labor-management negotiation, or *collective bargaining,* is therefore a process whereby union and management officials attempt to resolve conflicting interests over various working conditions in a manner which will sustain and possibly enrich their continuing relationship.

Characteristics of Labor-Management Negotiations

Collective Bargaining's Subprocesses The preceding definition of collective bargaining includes a wide variety of activities occurring between union and management organizations. These activities can be grouped into four possibly distinct and independent subprocesses.[12]

Distributive bargaining occurs over some issues when one party's goals conflict with those of the other party. Certain issues, particularly wages, heighten conflict of interest in that one party tends to gain at the other party's expense. Each negotiator tries to obtain and modify the opponent's position and values assigned to these issues. This process is illustrated later in the chapter under our discussion of the bargaining power model.

Integrative bargaining occurs when both parties attempt to resolve a common problem or concern to their mutual benefit. Many of the administrative issues discussed in Chapter 11 are resolved by integrative or problem-solving bargaining. An illustrative issue is alcoholism among bargaining unit employees. Management is concerned about the alcoholic employee's higher absentee rate and poorer work performance. The union fears that this employee could pose a safety hazard to other employees. Therefore, both union and management officials attempt to resolve this issue in a mutually beneficial manner. [13]

Attitudinal structuring involves activities aimed at attaining a desired relationship between the parties, "in particular such attitudes as friendliness-hostility, trust, respect, and the motivational orientation of competitiveness-cooperativeness."[14] This subprocess does not pertain to particular issues; instead, each party attempts to change the opponent's attitudes and the relationships which affect the negotiation process and subsequent administration of the labor agreement.

Intra-organizational bargaining refers to activities employed by management and union negotiators to achieve consensus within their respective organizations. However, bargaining teams are seldom unified; in fact, union and management negotiators often have more difficulty with members of their respective negotiating teams than with each other. [15]

Management's chief negotiator sometimes takes a back seat to other management officials, particularly lawyers, at the bargaining table. When a settlement is reached, it is also subject to second guessing by other officials, who contend that management negotiators could have obtained a better deal with a tougher negotiation philosophy. [16] The union is not exempt from internal disputes either, particularly since its chief negotiator is seldom given a free hand in selecting the negotiating committee. In many cases, at least one member of the union's negotiating team is a political rival of the union's chief negotiator. More prevalent are factions which attempt to obtain various bargaining demands regardless of the chief negotiator's preferences.

Management and union negotiators spend much time in resolving differences within their respective organizations. One observer of labor-management negotiations has maintained that

a large share of collective bargaining is not conflict but a process by which the main terms of the agreement, already understood by the negotiators, are made acceptable not to those in charge of the bargaining but to those who will have to live with its results![17]

Contract negotiations usually feature all of the aforementioned subprocesses; yet collective bargaining activities are subject to variations in style and structure.

The Style of Labor-Management Negotiations It is impossible to describe a "typical" labor-management negotiation since there are over 165,000 labor agreements in the United States.[18] The particular negotiation style is influenced by the familiarity of the parties and the extent to which the bargaining relationships have been established and are viewed by the parties as being mutually acceptable.

Assuming these variables exist in most negotiations, the style of labor-management negotiations is governed by the negotiators' attempts to obtain concessions (distributive bargaining) or jointly solve a problem (integrative bargaining) in a manner satisfactory to their respective constituents (intra-organizational bargaining) and ongoing labor-management relationships (attitudinal structuring). Both chief negotiators realize their counterpart is an influential if not determining force in the eventual settlement. In many cases, they realize that they will have to live with each other long after the contract has been signed. Finally, each knows that the other has to deal with conflicting goals of other members on the negotiating team.

Most negotiations are conducted in an atmosphere of respect and honesty.[19] Respect is an interpersonal variable seldom researched by academicians. It is not synonymous with friendship—one can dislike and respect an individual at the same time. Management and labor negotiators seldom socialize with each other; however, they can respect each other for their technical competence and experience. They also can respect the negotiators' personal qualities, such as the ability to go out on a limb in standing up for what is right, admitting when they are wrong, and perhaps most important, *credibility*, or keeping their word when they have taken a concrete position.

Closely related to respect is honesty. It permits each party to rely on the statements of the other. There is, however, a thin line between dishonesty and withholding the truth—union and management officials are not going to volunteer items which could damage their respective bargaining positions.[20] Successful negotiators are skilled in asking the correct questions and interpreting omissions from the other party's remarks.

As suggested earlier in the section, many union and management negotiators realize that their interactions are constrained by other members on their respective bargaining teams. Each chief negotiator realizes that the other has to look good before his or her negotiating team; consequently, they seldom issue unnecessary ultimatums or force the other party to take an unyielding position over many issues. In short, both negotiators often give the other party a chance to save face by giving several options or alternatives in the bargaining sessions.

Face saving is in some cases enhanced by rituals and role playing. For example, management officials in the automobile industry used to let Walter Reuther, president of the United Auto Workers, take center stage before the media during the opening sessions of their labor-management negotiations.[21] One author has emphasized some ritualistic elements of collective bargaining, such as the elaborate charts and tables which are ignored after serious negotiations begin. This author also suggests that irrelevant material or propaganda parade as facts, or, as contended by one union research director, "a fact is as welcome at a collective bargaining table as a skunk at a cocktail party."[22] Similarly, one management negotiator has suggested that his union counterpart approaches him at the start of negotiations and whispers, "We'll get together privately and talk about what we are really going to do to make a deal as soon as this show is over."[23]

While negotiations may involve some posturing and ritualistic elements, a far more prominent feature is communication between the chief management and union negotiators. In many cases, they have to convey their preferences and positions to each other while at the same time giving their fellow bargaining team members a slightly different impression. For instance, consider the following situation. The chief union negotiator discusses the company's latest negotiation proposal with the union members, who, in turn, feel that he or she should go back to the table and press management for a more favorable settlement. Believing that the company's proposal was reasonable, the union negotiator must communicate this preference to management and at the same time convince the bargaining committee she fought for their rights. Confronted with this difficult situation, the union negotiator might open the next bargaining session by forcefully stressing to management: "'The membership disagreed' with the company's economic proposal. 'The present contract will not extend beyond 12:00 tonight.'"

At first glance, the union negotiator's statement seems strong and unyielding. However, a skilled management negotiator would analyze it through three questions:

1. How *final* is the statement?
2. How *specific* is the statement?
3. What are the *consequences* associated with this statement?

At second glance, the statement appears neither final nor specific. In fact, management could interpret it to mean the union negotiator is relatively satisfied with the proposal, particularly if no specific recommendations for improvement follow. Finally, the union negotiator, by stating "the present contract will not extend," does not give a clear indication that a strike will occur if the offer is not changed.

Since maintaining communications between parties during negotiations is essential to the bargaining process, negotiating several issues (a *package*) at the same time is preferable to the item-by-item, or "yes-no," approach. The item-by-item negotiations technique does not allow the parties to communicate their preferences realistically and at the same time maintain flexibility in their decision making.

In using the *package approach*, each party combines several bargaining issues for discussion purposes. For example, the union might propose dropping issues 2 (union shop), 7 (birthday off), and 9 (voluntary overtime) from its bargaining list if management would agree to issues 3 (eliminating subcontracting) and 10 (optional retirement after thirty years). Management might then present the following counterproposal: agree to issues 3 and 10 if the union drops issues 2, 7, 9, and 11 (free dental care). This process would be repeated until the parties eventually resolved the issues in dispute.

The advantage of this approach is that both parties indicate which issues they will concede (for the union, issues 2, 7, and 9; for management, issues 3 and 10); and, if agreement is not reached, these issues are still considered negotiable. Moreover, both parties keep track of these proposals because they offer insights into their opponent's bargaining preferences.

Collective Bargaining Structure: Units Influencing Content and Scope

Four employee units are either directly or indirectly involved in most labor-management negotiations: the unit of direct impact, informal work groups, the appropriate bargaining unit, and the negotiation unit.[25] Each of these units will be discussed separately, although they are in many cases interrelated.

The unit of direct impact. The *unit of direct impact* is a settlement negotiated by other parties which influences the current labor-management negotiations. Although not present at the bargaining table, this unit can shape the goals and outcome of the current negotiations. For example, a labor settlement between management and the police might be used in subsequent negotiations between management and the fire fighters. The unit of direct impact can also be a facility or industry whose situation is regarded by the union and management as comparable to the current negotiations situation. For instance, the 1976 strike in the rubber industry was in large part due to the absence of a cost-of-living wage adjustment in the previous (1973) settlement. Many union members and leaders regarded the "Big Three" automobile manufacturers as their unit of direct impact. Comparisons with the cost-of-living adjustments received by the United Auto Workers union during this time period (1973–1976) strongly prompted the United Rubber Workers to strike for cost-of-living adjustments in the 1976 negotiations.

Informal work groups. Every organization has several *informal work groups* (for example, the night shift crew or the company baseball or bowling team) which, in turn, have unique bargaining preferences. In some cases, the informal work group's interests are directly represented by a member of the union bargaining committee. But most of these groups do not have direct representation at the bargaining table; instead they exert influence on union officers at union meetings and informal discussions away from the bargaining table.

The appropriate bargaining unit. The *appropriate bargaining unit* (ABU) discussed in Chapters 3 and 4 is determined by the National Labor Relations Board and is superimposed over several informal work groups at a particular organization. Union and management officials must bargain over working conditions applicable to the ABU; however, they can combine two or more ABUs in their formal negotiations. This alternative is further discussed in our consideration of the negotiation unit which is formally represented by union officials at the bargaining table.

The negotiation unit. The *negotiation unit* can be the same as the ABU. This would typically be the case where the employer owns only one facility and the NLRB has determined that the employees at that facility should be included in one appropriate bargaining unit. However, in some cases, the negotiation unit represents a combination of several ABUs, a situation commonly referred to as *centralized bargaining*—union officials representing more than one bargaining unit interact with their management counterparts during formal negotiations. There are two major types of centralized bargaining:

1. **Single employer–multiplant bargaining.** For illustrative purposes, assume one company has three separate facilities, each having a separate ABU. The employer and union representatives at these three facilities might combine into one negotiating unit for collective bargaining purposes.

2. **Multi-employer bargaining.** More than one employer and the corresponding union or unions form one negotiation unit at the bargaining table. This type of centralized bargaining is common in the trucking, construction, longshore, and newspaper industries.

Union and management officials have some flexibility in determining their negotiation unit for collective bargaining purposes. In many cases, it is shaped by several considerations: product interdependence, market factors, the particular bargaining issue, and legal guidelines.

Assume, for example, a company has three manufacturing facilities, each having a separate ABU. Further, products at these facilities are independent of each other—each facility can produce a completed product without parts or products from other facilities. Examples of product independence would be three steel mills, each completing a similar product, or three facilities having unrelated products (say Facility A produces baseball gloves, Facility B produces cereal, and Facility C produces marbles). The parties must determine whether they want to negotiate separately with these three facilities (and corresponding ABUs), which would probably result in three separate contract expiration dates.

The other option would be centralized bargaining—combining the three facilities into one negotiation unit—which would probably result in a common contract expiration date. In this situation, management would prefer the first option, particularly in the steel mill example. If one facility is out on strike, management could transfer some of the orders from that facility to the other two facilities where the contracts have not expired. The union prefers centralized bargaining in this situation, realizing that a strike could effectively shut down the company's entire operations, thereby increasing union bargaining strength.

If the products at the facilities in our example are interdependent (Facility A's product is needed for Facility B, which is in turn completed with products at Facility C), then management would probably prefer centralized bargaining—a common expiration date and one possible strike at all facilities—instead of three different contract expiration dates and possible separate strikes at each of the facilities. The second alternative could in effect shut down manufacturing operations three times compared to one shutdown under centralized bargaining.

Market factors also influence the degree of centralization of the bargaining unit. In a highly competitive market, a multi-employer (centralized) negotiation unit would be desirable to employers who fear that their firms would be placed at a competitive disadvantage if other employers subsequently negotiated lower wage rates. Combining with other employers into a multi-employer negotiation unit alleviates this fear while minimizing another problem—the loss of customers to competitors during a strike.

Unions are also concerned about market problems in some industries (construction, coal, trucking, ladies' garment, longshore, and so on) and attempt to extend the negotiation unit to include the entire geographical area in which the product is competitively produced. This is to prevent a few employers from separately negotiating lower wages, which would allow production at lower costs, thereby attracting customers from the other firms and resulting in employee layoffs. In essence, the unions are attempting to standardize wages, hours, and other terms of employment in order to exclude them as a competitive factor and force the employers to compete on the basis of other factors, such as product design, service, marketing, and so on.

Multi-employer bargaining offers some additional advantages and disadvantages. Both labor and management can pool their respective negotiation expenses by hiring a few experts to negotiate an agreement covering several firms. Yet a corresponding disadvantage of centralized bargaining is that the hired negotiators usually do not have extensive knowledge of each other's attitudes and strategies. Centralized bargaining tends to become more formal and to emphasize only major issues, leaving "minor" issues to be worked out at the individual locations after the contract has been signed. Finally, multi-employer bargaining does not always eliminate dissension among the member employers, as strongly evidenced in the 1977 Longshoremen's negotiations with the multi-employer Council of North Atlantic Shipping Associations. A bargaining association is usually as strong as its weakest member—an employer might pull out of the association if it feels it can get a better deal negotiating separately with the union.

The nature of the particular issue can also affect the particular bargaining structure. Certain issues (pensions, cost-of-living clauses, voluntary overtime, and so on) can have common applicability to all of the employer's facilities, while others are unique to an individual facility. Some industries, notably automobile and steel, have a two-tiered bargaining structure—some issues are negotiated on a multi-plant basis while, at the same time, local issues are being negotiated at the individual appropriate bargaining units.

Finally, certain legal guidelines can influence the particular negotiation unit's composition. Currently, the union can have representatives from other unions (desiring a centralized negotiation unit) at the bargaining table as negotiating team members. If the employer only desires to negotiate with the single union, then that union cannot delegate its authority to accept or reject the employer's settlement to the representatives of the other unions sitting at the bargaining table. "Moreover, the courts have ruled out as unlawful a 'lock-in' agreement between unions, which deprives individual unions of the right to sign a contract until all other unions have agreed to sign."[26]

Thus far the discussion has approached collective bargaining's characteristics from the standpoint of the practitioners. A brief discussion of how the various academic disciplines approach collective bargaining is necessary for a fuller appreciation of the negotiations process.

Theoretical and Empirical Approaches to Collective Bargaining Many researchers have attempted to generate and test hypotheses relating to bargaining behavior. One book devoted to analyzing these research efforts lists over a thousand related studies in its bibliography.[27] While an in-depth discussion of these research efforts is beyond the scope of this chapter, this section briefly describes the types of research into collective bargaining and suggests possible limitations of related research investigations.

Empirical approaches to collective bargaining tend to fall into three general classifications: (a) psychological, (b) economic, and (c) game-theoretic.[28] The personality or *psychological* approach focuses on the decision makers rather than the entire bargaining process. The major emphasis is on the negotiators' personalities and their perceived use of various interpersonal strategies to modify each other's attitudes.[29]

Economic investigations of the collective bargaining process[30] analyze unions as one would analyze a business firm and tend to view employees and employers as economic agents trying to maximize wages and profits, respectively. When employees organize, the union becomes the economic agent, which attempts to maximize the wage bill for its members.

As suggested earlier, the union's efforts are constrained by a desire to maintain union membership, a constraint which discourages pushing wages so high that employment is significantly reduced. Economic approaches also focus on productivity as the principal determinant of collective bargaining settlements, particularly in the case of wages.

Somewhat related to the preceding bargaining approach is *game theory*, which focuses on strategic interaction between two or more parties in interdependent decision making. A classic example of this approach, "the prisoner's dilemma," was first popularly described by Luce and Raiffa in 1957[31] (see Exhibit 6–3).

Limitations of empirical approaches. Each approach offers insights into collective bargaining's realities. There are, however, at least two general concerns facing related research efforts: (a) their focal points and (b) methodological constructs of labor-management negotiations. Most psychological approaches to negotiations focus on the fixed elements of collective bargaining—union and management negotiators—and their ability to modify the various values in the bargaining range. Yet this approach tends to overlook other essential elements of decision making—namely, the form and content of bargaining issues. To use a rather crude analogy, "the driver, marksman and cook are important ingredients in their respective processes, but they are secondary or ancillary to matters of mechanics, ballistics, and recipes."[32]

The economic and game-theory approaches also have focal limitations because they assume away many of the interesting elements that make collective bargaining work in an understandable fashion.[33] These approaches tend to focus on those variables which can be easily measured and quantified, and stress mathematical simplicity and elegance[34] rather than the vague yet ever present political and ethical values attached to the many collective bargaining issues.

The bargaining range is usually viewed by these approaches as being quantifiable in precise terms—the higher the point is on the range, the more expensive the settlement is in dollars and cents. Returning to Exhibit 6–1, we can see this is not always the case. For example, the top of the union's bargaining range is less expensive in dollars to management than the position which is second from the top. This occurs when the union wishes a relatively noneconomic yet important item, a union shop clause which can preserve and strengthen the union as an institution. Similarly, Exhibit 6–1 indicates that management's perceived lowest offer on its bargaining range (30 cents an hour) costs more in terms of dollars than its next lowest offer, which includes elimination of "minor repairs" from the employees' job descriptions. To be sure, this clause is financially important to management; it allows the use of production employees on certain maintenance jobs instead of necessitating a wait for maintenance employees who might have to be paid overtime to complete these jobs.

Exhibit 6-3
Description and
Discussion of
the Prisoner's
Dilemma Game

Two suspects are taken into custody and separated. The district attorney is certain that they are guilty of a specific crime, but he does not have adequate evidence to convict them at a trial. He points out to each prisoner that each has two alternatives: to confess to the crime the police are sure they have done, or not to confess. If they both do not confess, then the district attorney states he will book them on some very minor trumped-up charge such as petty larceny and illegal possession of a weapon, and they will both receive minor punishment; if they both confess they will be prosecuted, but he will recommend less than the most severe sentence; but if one confesses and the other does not, then the confessor will receive lenient treatment for turning state's evidence whereas the latter will get "the book" slapped at him. In terms of years in a penitentiary, the strategic problem might reduce to:

		Prisoner 2	
		Not confess	Confess
Prisoner 1	Not confess	1 year each	10 years for 1 and 3 months for 2
	Confess	3 months for 1 and 10 years for 2	8 years each

Consider the situation confronting Prisoner 1, which is identical, of course, to that facing Prisoner 2. Assuming he wishes to minimize his stay in prison (3 months), Prisoner 1 should confess and hope that Prisoner 2 chooses not to confess. If, however, Prisoner 2 reasons the same way, and also chooses to confess, each will end up with an 8-year term, whereas, by both not confessing, each could have received only a 1-year sentence. A "not confess" decision in this situation may be seen as a cooperative choice, since it results in a minimal sentence for the other prisoner (either 3 months or 1 year) and may result in the most favorable joint outcome for the two prisoners—1 year each. A "confess" choice, on the other hand, may be seen as competitive, inasmuch as it results in a maximal sentence for the other prisoner (8 or 10 years) and may result in exploitation (if the other prisoner chooses not to confess).

It is precisely because the Prisoner's Dilemma represents a mixed-motive situation, in which there is incentive both to cooperate and to compete, and because these motives are contrasted so elegantly, that this paradigm has become the object of such overwhelming interest to bargaining researchers.

Sources: Exhibit text through diagram excerpted by permission from R. D. Luce and H. Raiffa, *Games and Decisions: Introduction and Critical Survey* (New York: Wiley, 1957), p. 97. Exhibit text following diagram from Jeffrey Z. Rubin and Bert B. Brown, *The Social Psychology of Bargaining and Negotiations* (New York: Academic Press, 1975), pp. 20–21. © 1975 Academic Press. Used by permission.

Yet the costs associated with minor repairs and union security clauses are not subject to precise measurements as is true with more economic issues in the bargaining range, like wages.

Union and management officials also assign ethical importance to various items, which can distort their economic measurement. For instance, if an influential union committeeman, who has recently broken his leg, believes that full insurance coverage for broken legs is ethically just, he probably would agree to a related change in insurance coverage even if it meant a lower wage settlement for the union membership.

In short, the bargaining ranges for union and management include many issues which cannot be precisely measured in dollars and cents. Further, both parties are politically motivated in their negotiations,[35] assigning imprecise yet very significant values to certain items which either preserve their discretion and organizational strength or reward certain influential participants on their respective negotiating teams. Many economists believe that nonmonetary items can be quantified in terms of the trade-offs for dollarized issues—the dollar equivalent that management and union officials will assign to relatively noneconomic issues such as the union shop. This consideration represents a fundamental requirement for research into collective bargaining. Unfortunately, few research investigations have attempted to operationalize this concern.

Many empirical investigations into collective bargaining are also subject to methodological limitations. Consider, for example, the following instructions given to respondents in a related and prominent study.

You will be paired at random with another person. You will not see this person or speak with him at any time. You will never know the identity of your opponent nor will he be aware of yours.[36]

Most related research is hampered by union and management negotiators' reluctance to divulge their attitudes and "secrets of negotiating success."[37] Much research depends on laboratory experiments under controlled conditions for hypothesis formulation; yet the respondents in these studies (college students) usually do not have to live with the negotiated settlement or the other party long after the settlement has been reached. As stated earlier in the chapter, the negotiations process is continuous, involving interpersonal relationships, tactical expertise, accountability to other individuals, and knowledge of the other party's expectations based on past successes and failures.

Most research efforts have furnished valuable insights into collective bargaining behaviors and outcomes, but additional research should feature at least two considerations.

1. Bargaining issues, strategies, and eventual outcomes have many facets which need the insights offered by several social sciences (economics, political science, sociology, and psychology).
2. Empirical and theoretical researchers should realize that collective bargaining has had limited published input from labor relations practitioners; therefore, more is needed from union and management practitioners who actually negotiate agreements before they speculate on their collective bargaining behaviors.[38]

**Union-
Management
Activities in
Negotiations**

**Preparing for
Negotiations**

Union and management often begin preparing for the next negotiations the day after the current contract has been signed;[39] and preparation does not stop with the first negotiation meeting. Indeed, many of the activities discussed below continue throughout collective bargaining.

Selection of the Negotiation Team Several considerations face the chief negotiators in the selection of their respective negotiating teams. Personal attributes are a major factor in the selection process. Both chief negotiators desire members who can keep their emotions and opinions in check. An indiscreet negotiation team member can unintentionally reveal confidential settlement points and strategies to the other team. While the chief negotiator is the principal figure in negotiations, there are some occasions when the two teams divide into joint labor-management sub-committees to resolve particular proposals and contract language. Hence, interpersonal skills are essential requisites for team members.

The individual's experience and background are also considered in the selection process. Management wants at least one line manager who supervises bargaining unit employees on its team to either interpret or answer related negotiation issues. Unions also prefer to select team members from a variety of operating departments to insure membership representation and the discussion of working concerns which might be uniquely related to a particular department.

Finally, political considerations are also involved in the selection of negotiation team members. In many cases, the union negotiating team is elected by the members, and the union's chief negotiator has little input into the selection process. If discretion is allowed, the chief negotiator will at least think twice before appointing a political rival or member of an opposing faction to the negotiation team. On the other hand, management is very reluctant to select an individual having a higher organizational rank than the chief negotiator on the bargaining team. For tactical purposes, management's chief negotiator prefers a way out when confronted with a union's request. Often, this individual will inform the union that "I have to see my boss on this issue." This ploy is eliminated when the negotiator's boss is there at the bargaining table.

Anticipating, Formulating, and Costing Proposals Management relies on several sources in anticipating what the union will seek in collective bargaining. A review of recent contract settlements negotiated by the company's competitors and other firms located in the same geographical area may suggest issues desired by the union. The company and union may have negotiated settlements at other facilities which might also be used as a starting point in the current negotiations. Some management officials obtain bargaining insights by reviewing the proceedings of the national union's convention.[40]

A review of the local bargaining situation at the facility is essential in

Part 2/The Collective Bargaining Process

anticipating union bargaining issues. Much attention is given to the previous negotiation, particularly to those issues that the union actively sought and reluctantly dropped. Compromise settlements on previous issues also generate valuable clues since compromise does not mean permanent resolution of the issue.

An analysis of previous grievances at the facility can also illustrate certain trouble spots. General Motors, for example, uses a computerized analysis of number, type, and resolution status of grievances in their negotiations preparation. However, caution has to be taken not to over-emphasize these grievances. As mentioned in Chapter 8, unions often step up grievance activity just before negotiations to dramatize wide-spread concern over certain bargaining issues—a concern perhaps more tactical than real.

A key managerial activity in proposal formulation is a close analysis of the labor agreement to determine desirable changes in contract language. Management will attempt to change the contract language in order to reduce labor costs and give itself more discretion in operations. Assume, for example, that the current provision restricts supervisors entirely from performing any bargaining unit work. Since this provision makes no exceptions, management would probably seek to change this language to allow supervisors to perform bargaining unit work under at least three conditions: (a) when training new employees, (b) in emergency situations (usually interpreted to mean when employees' lives or production equipment are jeopardized), and (c) when experimental production efforts are involved.

Both management and the union are concerned about the legal implications of current contractual language, particularly in terms of recent decisions by the National Labor Relations Board and the courts.[41] Management and union officials would also like to nullify the impact of adverse arbitration decisions. This can be accomplished by inserting contract language contradictory to the arbitrator's decision into the subsequent labor agreement.

Both parties would also be interested in knowing if various administrators of the labor agreement (union stewards and first-line supervisors) have difficulties in implementing certain labor agreement provisions on the shop floor. Efforts will also be made to research data from government reports and various labor relations services (Bureau of National Affairs, Commerce Clearing House, and Prentice-Hall). Data from these and other sources give both parties substantial information with which to prepare for negotiations.

Unions often have an added consideration in proposal formulation—their members' expectations. The union generally encourages its members to present issues they feel are important in the upcoming negotiations. Some of these issues are contradictory; others are irrelevant to the union leaders' bargaining goals. One of management's goals during negotiations is to determine whether the goals stressed by union negotiators are sincere concerns or merely artificial recitals of union members' superfluous suggestions.

Management's overriding concern in negotiation preparations is the eventual cost of the union's proposals. Costing proposals can become a very involved process. Unfortunately, there has been little published research into costing practices. One notable exception has suggested that many management officials do not use sophisticated costing practices in labor-management negotiations, because management negotiators fail to take into account:

☐ The precise financial impact of the labor agreement on corporate profits.

☐ The opportunity costs of new contract provisions in terms of lost production (for example, the effect of a proposed ten-minute cleanup time provision).

☐ Expertise and figures from financial managers, who usually do not sit in on formal negotiations and do not consult with industrial relations managers on a periodic basis.[42]

Yet, management negotiators include at least some costing considerations in their labor negotiations efforts. Two such methods are preparation of employee background data and the calculation of the cost of a cent-per-hour wage increase. Management usually obtains statistical summaries of employees cross-tabulated by several variables (age, sex, marital status, seniority, job classifications). These summaries provide immediate information necessary to cost out a variety of union negotiation proposals such as vacations, funeral pay, and pensions.

A most significant calculation pertains to the cost of a cent-per-hour wage increase. Since wages are inevitably discussed in negotiations, a cost figure is needed to formulate management's bargaining range and to determine whether a union's wage proposal is excessive. An illustrative calculation of a cent-per-hour wage increase for a bargaining unit of 1,000 employees is presented below:

$20,800	Straight time pay (1,000 employees × 40 hours a week × 52 weeks × $.01)
900	Premium pay related to wages (1,000 employees × estimated 60 hours per year overtime, holiday, and call-out premium worked × $.015)
5,200	Benefits directly affected by the wage increase (profit sharing, pensions, life insurance, employer contributions to social security, and so on) estimated for illustrative purposes at 25 percent of the straight time wage rate
$26,900	Cost of a cent-per-hour wage increase

The wage total calculated above does not take into account opportunity costs or the spillover effect on wages of nonunion company employees, who will probably receive the negotiated wage increase as a minimum in their subsequent salary increases. Additionally, many cost categories, such as overtime and holidays worked, have to be estimated from past payroll records and future production and manning requirements.

Some proposals are not easily costed. Assume, for example, a current contract provision provides a Sunday work premium of 75 cents an hour if the employees have no absences during their regularly scheduled work week. The union proposes that employees working on Sunday receive this premium regardless of their attendance record during the week. Management can examine past payroll records to estimate the added cost of this proposal, a difficult task if there are thousands of employees involved and an uncertain indicator of extra absences that might occur if this proposal is accepted.

Other proposals are almost impossible to cost out because no records have been kept and there is no way to obtain accurate data, as in the case of a union's proposal to include deaths of employees' first cousins for the three-day paid funeral leave provision. Management should maintain accurate and separate cost categories on benefits paid during the previous year. For strategic puposes, the union prefers to stress proposals which cannot be costed out, thereby weakening management's related statistical objections during negotiations. Preparations are necessary so that each party can effectively use its various collective bargaining strategies and tactics.

Strategies and Tactics for Determining the Eventual Settlement — The Bargaining Power Model

Each party in negotiations has to actively persuade the other to accept its bargaining position. In essence, there are three bargaining positions: "yes," "maybe—keep on talking," or "no." Naturally, each party would prefer the other to take the first or at least the second alternative. Yet there has to be an overall framework which governs the various strategies and tactics in the negotiations process. For example, Exhibit 6–4 presents two possible situations involving union and management bargaining ranges.

It would appear at first glance that the first situation is more conducive to settlement than the second. Although the first situation has a common acceptance zone, there is no reason to think the parties will automatically reach agreement, particularly if union and management negotiators incorrectly assess each other's bargaining ranges (Points A and B on the respective ranges).

More importantly, neither situation portrayed in Exhibit 6–4 indicates where the eventual settlement will be reached. Both parties arrange their stategies and tactics in a manner that will enhance their *bargaining power* and eventual settlement. In other words, the settlement will be determined by the relative bargaining power of each party.

One of the better known bargaining power models was suggested by Chamberlain and Kuhn,[43] a model further expressed in two equations presented in Exhibit 6–5. These equations can apply to individual issues

Exhibit 6–4   Bargaining Range Alternatives in Labor-Management Negotiations

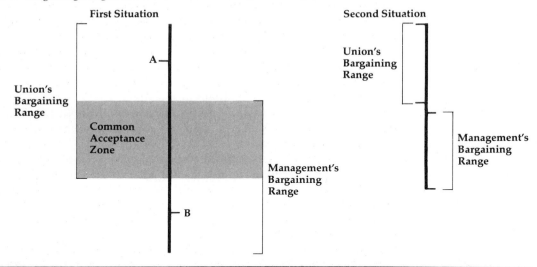

or to the eventual package settlement. Their model furnishes insights into the eventual settlement point as well as providing a framework for examining bargaining strategies and tactics.

There are at least two major assumptions of the bargaining power model:

1. Union and management negotiators are rational individuals.
2. If it costs more for a party to disagree than to agree with the other, then the party will agree to the other's position.

Therefore, each side can increase its bargaining power by reducing the cost to the other of agreement or increasing the cost to the other of disagreement.

This strategic framework can be illustrated with a union bargaining proposal for ten minutes cleanup time before the end of the work shift. Management would probably refuse this item unless the union presented arguments relating to the bargaining power model. First, the union could reduce management's cost of agreeing with the cleanup time proposal by eliminating some of its original bargaining proposals—if management agrees to cleanup time, the union will drop four bargaining items. The union negotiator might also reduce management's agreement costs with an argument along the following lines:

There are currently many different cleanup practices at our facility. Some departments do not have cleanup time while other departments let their employees stop work a half hour early for cleaning up. If you calculated the total cleanup time in the plant, it would probably

Exhibit 6–5 Bargaining Power Equations for Union and Management	Union's Bargaining Power =	$\dfrac{\text{Management's Cost of Disagreeing}}{\text{Management's Cost of Agreeing}}$

$$\text{Management's Bargaining Power} = \frac{\text{Union's Cost of Disagreeing with Management}}{\text{Union's Cost of Agreeing with Management}}$$

Source: Equations are modified slightly from Allan M. Cartter and F. Ray Marshall, *Labor Economics*, rev. ed. (Homewood, Ill.: Richard D. Irwin, 1972), p. 283. © 1972 by Richard D. Irwin, Inc. Used by permission.

amount to fifteen minutes per employee. Worse yet, you cannot currently discipline employees who are abusing cleanup time since there are so many different practices in the plant. This contract provision would enable management to wipe the past practice slate clean. Management could instruct the supervisors to rigidly enforce this provision, which could actually save the company money.

In case management does not accept the above argument, the union could follow the second strategic approach—increasing management's cost of disagreeing with the union. The ultimate related argument would be to threaten a strike unless the cleanup time provision was granted. This threat might carry some weight, particularly if management knew there was widespread dissatisfaction over this issue. However, chances are that management would view this as an idle threat and would not believe its disagreement cost had increased.

There is a related threat, however, which could raise management's cost of disagreeing with the union over this issue. The union could make related arguments regarding safety hazards at the facility and suggest two alternatives: management can allow cleanup time before the end of the shift or the union can lodge a safety complaint with the Occupational Safety and Health Administration (OSHA). Management negotiators would prefer the first alternative over the second since they know that it would not cost the union anything to file the complaint, and an OSHA investigation might uncover other safety problems whose correction would be more expensive.

Several variables can affect the bargaining power equations in Exhibit 6–4 (discussed in detail in Chapter 7 as strike decision criteria); however, two variables will be briefly discussed here to illustrate the bargaining power model's function. Unemployment can affect both equations. High unemployment increases the union's cost of disagreeing with management since potential strikers would find it difficult to find employment at other firms. And it reduces management's disagreement costs since high unemployment tends to make it easier for management to find strike replacements.

The timing of negotiations has a significant impact on the bargaining power model. The backlog of customer orders to be filled after the contract expiration date adds a major dimension. One facet of negotiations timing illustrating the effect on bargaining power concerns the time at which profit-sharing checks are mailed. If the company mails them to employees one day before the labor agreement expires, management's bargaining power is reduced. Then union members have added money to spend, and their costs of disagreeing with management are reduced.

In some situations, it is difficult to determine the other party's disagreement costs associated with the timing of negotiations. In at least one situation, a management negotiator appears to have been taken by the union in timing of negotiations. This management official was approached by the union's negotiator, who stated that if the contract expiration date was pushed ahead, the union would work for wages under the old agreement until the new contract expiration date arrived. The official carefully considered the union's request and agreed, after determining that the new contract expiration date would not increase the union's bargaining power.

However, much to the management negotiator's chagrin, the new contract expiration date coincided with the opening day of hunting season. Thus, management's bargaining power and the union's disagreement costs were dramatically reduced, particularly since the employees at the facility were avid hunters. With the new contract expiration date, the union leaders could give the membership two alternatives: (a) accept the company's offer and forget about the hunting season, or (b) strike and go hunting without angering their spouses since employees could use their subsequent vacation time for family outings. It would not take an exceptionally skilled orator to persuade the union members to accept the second option.

The bargaining power model has at least two limitations:

1. *Cost* is a term covering many imprecise considerations. For example, it is difficult to compare political cost units such as possible defeat of the incumbent union officials with economic units associated with a wage increase. Imprecision is increased when each party assigns probabilities to the other's actions—management has to estimate both the cost of a strike and the probability that the union will actually call a strike.

2. The bargaining power model can be subject to sudden, dramatic change. Consider, for example, management receiving a sudden influx of rush orders from a major customer near the contract expiration date. Management's disagreement costs could be sharply increased, particularly if the major customer indicates it will take unfinished orders to a competitor.

However, the limitations of the bargaining power model do not eliminate its usefulness. Union and management officials do assign costs, however crudely, and direct their strategies toward increasing the other party's disagreement costs relative to agreement costs. The particular strategies used in collective bargaining are further influenced by legal considerations.

Legal Influences Affecting Collective Bargaining

The preceding sections have reviewed collective bargaining from the perspectives of the union and management organizations and their respective members. However, as stated in Chapter 1, the government influences collective bargaining through decisions made by the National Labor Relations Board (NLRB) and the courts. This ever present third party influence leads negotiators to consider the following two questions:

1. What constitutes good faith bargaining?
2. What are the legal consequences associated with violation of a collective bargaining obligation?

The Legal Requirements Concerning Good Faith Bargaining

The National Labor Relations Act requires that the parties negotiate in *good faith*—that they demonstrate a sincere and honest intent to consummate a labor agreement and exhibit reasonableness in their bargaining position, tactics, and activities.[44] However, *good faith* represents a state of mind difficult to define precisely.

The NLRB and the courts deal with this concept in their interpretation of the following provisions of the Labor Management Relations Act:

8(a)(5) It shall be an unfair labor practice for an employer . . . to refuse to bargain collectively with representatives of his employees, subject to the provisions of Section 9(a).

8(b)(3) It shall be an unfair labor practice for a labor organization or its agents . . . to refuse to bargain collectively with an employer, provided it is the representative of his employees subject to Section 9(a).

8(d) [Collective bargaining entails] the performance of the mutual obligation of the employer and the representative of the employees to meet at reasonable times and confer in good faith with respect to wages, hours, and other terms and conditions of employment, or the negotiation of an agreement, . . . incorporating any agreement reached if requested by either party, but such obligation does not compel either party to agree to a proposal or require the making of a concession.

The good faith bargaining obligation is imposed equally on union and management; either will be guilty of an unfair labor practice if it fails to live up to its bargaining obligation. However, this obligation does not specifically require that a party must agree to the other's proposal or make a concession to the other party.[45] Violations of good faith bargaining can come from four sources: the nature of the bargaining issues, specific bargaining actions (called per se violations), totality of conduct, and successor employer bargaining obligations.

The Nature of the Bargaining Issues Over the years, the NLRB and the courts have categorized bargaining issues as illegal, mandatory, or voluntary. *Illegal* subjects are not bargainable, and the parties cannot insert them into the labor contract even if they are in agreement over the issue. Examples of illegal subjects include a closed shop, a "whites only" employment clause, mandatory retirement at sixty-two, and compensation arrangements which violate the provisions of the Fair Labor Standards Act (for example, not paying bargaining unit employees overtime for work in excess of forty hours per week).

Mandatory subjects are related to wages, hours, and other conditions of employment. Examples of mandatory subjects are wage systems, bonus plans, pensions, profit sharing, vacations, holidays, plant rules, grievance procedures, and management rights.[46] These subjects must be bargained, and the party advancing these subjects may insist on their inclusion to a point of impasse. However, failure to reach agreement does not automatically constitute a bargaining violation.

Union and management officials can also negotiate *voluntary* (also called permissive or nonmandatory) subjects like industry promotion plans, strike insurance, interest arbitration clause, and benefits for retired employees. Unlike mandatory issues, these do not require either party to bargain. In fact, insisting on their bargaining and inclusion in the labor agreement would be an unfair labor practice.

Specific Bargaining Actions In some cases a specific, single action by an employer constitutes an unfair labor practice in bargaining. Examples of per se violations for union and management are presented below.[47]

Management commits a per se violation whenever it:

☐ refuses to meet with the union to negotiate its proposals,

☐ insists to a point of impasse on a provision requiring that a secret ballot election be held before a strike can be called,

☐ refuses to supply cost and other data relating to a group insurance plan, or

☐ announces a wage increase without consulting the union.

A union commits a per se violation when it:

☐ insists on a closed shop or discriminatory hiring,

☐ refuses to meet with a legal representative of the employer about negotiations, or

☐ refuses to negotiate a management proposal involving a mandatory subject.

Totality of Conduct In some situations, the NLRB and the courts have determined that one activity alone does not constitute a bargaining violation; however, a combination of activities, *totality of conduct*, might reflect a violation of the duty to bargain. A prominent and controversial example of this legal consideration involved General Electric's bargaining approach, *Boulwarism*, named after the vice-president of General Electric, Lemuel Boulware.

General Electric contended that it simply approached bargaining in a manner similar to its product marketing—by finding out what the employee desired, and, on the basis of employee survey results, formulating a bargaining proposal. G.E. contended that this approach was not capricious, but "fair and firm," as management's bargaining position was based on a careful examination of the "facts" and was capable of being altered if the union presented new and significant information at the bargaining table. Some contended that this approach represented a sincere bargaining effort, one that was not aimed at destroying the union, but rather at eliminating a time-consuming and unnecessary ritual from collective bargaining (for instance, initial unrealistic offers which both parties know will not be accepted).[48]

However, General Electric's totality of conduct was found violative of good faith bargaining, primarily because it went directly to the employees rather than working through the employees' exclusive bargaining agent (the union). The NLRB found several bargaining activities which contributed to General Electric's "take it or leave it" bargaining approach. These activities included: refusals to supply cost information on an insurance program, vague response to the union's detailed proposals, prepared lecture series instead of counter offers, and a "stiff and unbending patriarchal posture" even after it was apparent that the union would have to concede to the employer's terms.[49]

Other factors involving employer or union conduct have provided indicators of good and bad faith bargaining. The following factors, while they probably would not individually constitute bad faith bargaining, might be considered so if many of them were committed together.[50]

☐ **Surface bargaining:** The party is willing to meet at length and confer but merely goes through the motions of bargaining. It includes making proposals which cannot be accepted, taking an inflexible attitude on major issues, and offering no alternative proposals.

☐ **Concessions:** Although the LMRA does not require the making of concessions, the term *good faith* certainly suggests a willingness to compromise and make a reasonable effort to settle differences.

☐ **Proposals and demands:** Advancing proposals which open the doors for future discussions indicates good faith, whereas proposals that foreclose future negotiations and are patently unreasonable are reflectors of bad faith.

☐ **Dilatory tactics:** Refusal to meet, unreasonable procrastination in executing the agreement, delay in scheduling meetings, willful avoidance of meetings, evasive tactics, delay in providing data for bargaining, and similar tactics are evidence of bad faith.

☐ **Imposing conditions:** Attempts to specify conditions on bargaining or the administration of the agreement will be scrutinized closely to determine whether such conditions are onerous or unreasonable (for example, insisting that all grievances be resolved before collective bargaining can start). In addition, the requirement of agreement on a specific item as a prerequisite to negotiating other issues reflects bad faith bargaining.

☐ **Unilateral changes in conditions:** Such actions as changing the compensation or fringe benefits plan unilaterally during bargaining is a strong indicator of bad faith bargaining. Unilateral changes per se may not be illegal, but justification must be reasonable and accurate.

☐ **Bypassing the representative:** Since the collective bargaining agreement supersedes the individual employee contract, the employer must not refuse to negotiate over mandatory issues. The duty to bargain is essentially equivalent to the duty to recognize the exclusive bargaining representative of the employees. Attempts to bypass this representative are evidence of bad faith.

☐ **Commission of unfair labor practices:** Committing unfair labor practices (such as threatening to close the plant, promoting withdrawal from the union, reducing working hours, and engaging in discriminatory layoffs) during negotiations is indicative of conduct inconsistent with good faith bargaining.

In addition, the NLRB and court rulings have been consistent in deciding that unions should have sufficient information to understand and intelligently discuss the issues raised in collective bargaining. Without such information, the union would be unable to properly perform its collective bargaining and contract administration duties. This information is, however, subject to the following prerequisites:

1. The union must make a good faith demand or request for the information.
2. The information sought must be relevant to the bargaining relationship.
3. When the employer alleges that it is financially unable to meet a union wage demand, financial information relevant to the negotiations must be supplied to the union.
4. The information must be supplied to the union promptly and in a form reasonably useful for negotiation purposes.[51]

Successor Employer Bargaining Obligations When a new employer takes over a plant which has an exclusive bargaining representative, the bargaining unit may remain intact unless sufficient change occurs whereby majority status is lost. The test of *successor employer bargaining obligations* depends on a number of factors: the degree of change brought about by new ownership, whether the company's operations or products change, whether most employees remain, and whether the plant remains in the same location.[52]

The employer violates its legal obligation to bargain in good faith if after purchasing another business it continues operations intact and with predecessor employees and refuses to bargain after notifying the employees that previous benefits will not be continued.[53] The union has a similar obligation because it cannot force the successor employer to bargain if the successor willingly adopts the contract already negotiated between the union and the predecessor employer.[54]

The *Burns International Detective Agency Inc.* case is a prominent illustration of the successor employer's obligation to bargain. Burns, the employer, bid successfully on a contract to provide guard services at an aircraft manufacturer's installations but refused to honor the contract between the predecessor employer and the certified bargaining units and further refused to bargain with the same union. The Supreme Court held the successor employer violated good faith bargaining since Burns hired a majority of its work force from the former employees of the predecessor, continued the former operations substantially intact, knew in advance that the union was the certified bargaining representative with a contract, and provided essentially the same working conditions and services. Burns had to honor the contract and negotiate with the union.[55]

Other decisions have provided further insights into the application of the successor employer bargaining obligation. In one case, the employer violated its bargaining obligation when it took over a franchise, retained all the employees, and made unilateral changes in the wages and employment conditions.[56] In another case, the successor employer did not violate its bargaining obligation when it hired a majority of the predecessor's employees and established unilateral wages and employment conditions but agreed to later negotiations.[57] A subsequent decision indicated that the successor employer, who hired substantially all of the predecessor's employees, could legally establish the initial wages and employment conditions but must be willing to negotiate further over these issues.[58]

Legal Remedies Associated with Violations of Good Faith Bargaining

In 1976, 30.1 percent (7,848 of 26,105) of NLRB cases alleging employer violations involved employer refusal to bargain in good faith, and 7.8 percent (900 of 11,533) of NLRB cases alleging union violations involved similar union activities.[59] Although there are many cases to be handled, the NLRB is limited in its remedial powers. As one NLRB member illustrates this situation: "The Board under the act is constituted as the midwife of the bargaining relationship. It oversees the birth of that relationship and attempts to prevent any miscarriage."[60]

Once a violation is found, the board orders the violator to cease and desist bad faith bargaining and to take affirmative action. These actions include bargaining upon request, posting notices pledging to bargain in good faith, and notifying offices of the NLRB of steps being taken to comply with the order.[61]

Union officials have contended that the lack of significant remedies makes correction of good faith bargaining violations a farce. Since NLRB decisions can be appealed to the courts, it might take three or more years for a final determination. If the final decision finds the company guilty, affected employees are not entitled to any make-whole remedies applied to the affected employees.[62]

Attempts to expand the NLRB's remedial power have failed. In the *H. K. Porter* case, the NLRB granted the union a contract clause which allowed checkoff of union dues after the employer repeatedly refused to bargain in good faith on the checkoff issue. The Supreme Court concluded that the bargaining obligation "does not compel either party to agree to a proposal or require the making of a concession," and "it is the job of Congress, not the Board or the courts, to decide when and if it is necessary to allow governmental review of proposals for collective bargaining agreements and compulsory submissions to one side's demands."[63] In addition, the NLRB cannot currently order an employer to compensate employees for monetary losses incurred as a result of an employer refusal to bargain until it has obtained a court test of the validity of certification.[64]

Summary

This chapter has examined characteristics of and influences on the collective bargaining process. While collective bargaining shares some similarities with games, some important differences illustrate the complex nature of collective bargaining activities. Games usually feature an absolute winner and loser; successful negotiations occur when both parties believe they have gained something. Unlike players, the negotiators have no fixed rules or values assigned to the bargaining objectives they have given priorities and arranged in their bargaining ranges. Each negotiator attempts to determine the other party's bargaining range without revealing his or her own.

Negotiators are also involved in other subprocesses of collective bargaining, such as distributive and integrative bargaining, attitudinal structuring, and intra-organizational bargaining. The good negotiator must command the respect and honesty of the other negotiator, maneuver the individuals on the negotiating team, and be an attentive listener in assessing the other negotiator's remarks and package proposals.

Collective bargaining is usually influenced by other factors besides the management and union bargaining teams. Indeed, several units are involved in collective bargaining (unit of direct impact, informal work groups, the appropriate bargaining unit, and the negotiation unit). Negotiators must decide whether combining appropriate bargaining units into one negotiation unit (centralized bargaining) serves a strategic advantage given related legal constraints.

Many academic disciplines and related research investigations have generated insights into collective bargaining. Bargaining factors that are difficult to quantify and the reluctance of negotiators to reveal their attitudes and activities have limited the applicability of research. Still, a multidiscipline approach derived from collective bargaining experiences would generate appropriate insights for academicians and practitioners.

Collective bargaining activities include preparing for negotiations (selecting the negotiation team and formulating as well as costing proposals) and persuading the other party to accept these proposals. The second activity is affected by the bargaining power model, based on the theory that each party attempts to convince the other that it would cost more to disagree than agree with its proposals.

Legal considerations affect collective bargaining as well as other aspects of the labor-management relationship. Particularly significant is the requirement to bargain in good faith. Legal concerns and remedies reveal further complexities which must be anticipated and understood by the negotiators.

Discussion Questions

1. "Good labor-management negotiators are usually good poker players." Discuss the extent to which this statement is true (a) from the perspective of successful interpersonal skills and qualities of negotiators and (b) in terms of similarities and differences between negotiations and games.

2. What are some situations in which management or the union would prefer centralized bargaining? In what instances might both prefer centralized bargaining? Discussion should take into account specific legal considerations affecting centralized bargaining.

3. Our discussion of bargaining power only touched on two variables: timing of negotiations and the unemployment situation. Relate three other variables (from either Exhibit 1–1 or your own experience) to the bargaining power model, indicating how they could affect the equations.

4. Assume that you are a management negotiator and the union presents the following negotiation proposal: Any overtime assignment will be guaranteed a minimum of two hours at time and one-half the base hourly rate for the classification. Previously, employees working overtime received time and one-half payment for the hours they worked but no two-hour guarantee. Indicate in some detail how you would cost out this proposal. Also discuss some arguments the union might

use to make it easier to accept this proposal (to reduce your agreement costs).

5. Good and bad faith regulations might be easier to define than implement. Discuss problems management and unions believe they face in attempting to bargain in good faith. (Boulwarism and legal remedies, for example, are considered problems by management and unions, respectively.) What recommendations would you suggest for improving these situations?

6. Assume you are establishing a research project to investigate an aspect of collective bargaining. Indicate (a) a rather specific, narrow topic for investigation, (b) hypotheses or key questions you would examine, (c) and how you would operationalize or measure the key variables. Also discuss some limitations of your research effort as well as the particular academic discipline(s) influencing your project.

References

[1]Carl M. Stevens, *Strategy and Collective Bargaining Negotiations* (New York: McGraw-Hill, 1963), p. 34.

[2]Richard E. Walton and Robert B. McKersie, *A Behavioral Theory of Labor Negotiations* (New York: McGraw-Hill, 1965), pp. 19, 23.

[3]We maintain that union leaders can be influenced by the possibility of employment reductions associated with a high economic settlement. Yet we also agree with Arthur Ross's observation that this relationship is nearly "unpredictable" before negotiations and "undecipherable" after negotiations. Arthur M. Ross, *Trade Union Wage Policy*.

[4]Wallace N. Atherton, *Theory of Union Bargaining Goals* (Princeton, N.J.: Princeton University Press, 1973), p. 4.

[5]Jeffrey Z. Rubin and Bert Brown, *The Social Psychology of Bargaining and Negotiation* (New York: Harcourt Brace Jovanovich, 1975), p. 50.

[6]Gerard I. Nierenberg, *Fundamentals of Negotiating* (New York: Hawthorn Books, 1973), p. 20.

[7]For an empirical study involving negotiators' uncertainties over opponents' issues see W. M. Balke, K. Hammond, and G. Meyer, "An Alternative Approach to Labor-Management Relations," *Administrative Science Quarterly* 18 (September 1973), pp. 311–327.

[8]Nierenberg, *Fundamentals*, pp. 21, 24.

[9]Hjalmar Rosen and R. A. H. Rosen, "The Union Bargaining Agent Looks at Collective Bargaining," *Personnel* 33 (May 1957), p. 541; David L. Cole, "Focus on Bargaining: The Evolving Techniques," *American Federationist* 81 (May 1974), p. 15.

[10]Otomar J. Bartos, *Process and Outcome of Negotiations* (New York: Columbia University Press, 1974), p. 15.

[11]Jack Barbash, "Price and Power in Collective Bargaining," *Journal of Economic Issues* 11 (December 1977), p. 847.

[12]Walton and McKersie, *A Behavioral Theory*, pp. 4–6. For an empirical study of union and management negotiators which lends some support to the independent nature of these processes see Richard B. Peterson and Lane Tracy, "Testing a Behavioral Theory Model of Labor Negotiations," *Industrial Relations* 16 (February 1977), pp. 35–50.

[13]For a discussion of various union-management efforts in this area see Gordon H. Cole, "Alcoholism: Tragedy on the Job," *American Federationist* 83 (May 1976), pp. 1–4.

[14]Walton and McKersie, *A Behavioral Theory*, p. 5.

[15]David L. Cole, *The Quest for Industrial Peace* (New York: McGraw-Hill, 1963), pp. 9–13.

[16]George J. Berkwitt, "Industrial Relations Is Nowhere," *Dun's Review* 99 (February 1972), pp. 58–60.

[17]Albert A. Blum, "Collective Bargaining: Ritual or Reality?" *Harvard Business Review* 39 (November–December 1961), p. 65.

[18]For a rich, detailed account of the variety of collective bargaining relationships see Frederick H. Harbison and John R. Coleman, *Goals and Strategy for Collective Bargaining* (New York: Harper & Bros., 1951), pp. 4–6.

[19]Paul Diesing, "Bargaining Strategy and Union-Management Relationships," *Journal of Conflict Resolution* 5 (December 1961), p. 369.

[20]Rosen and Rosen, "The Union Bargaining Agent," p. 540.

[21]William Serrin, *The Company and the Union* (New York: Knopf, 1973), p. 179.

[22]Blum, "Collective Bargaining." See also the discussion of ritualistic elements (such as "snow job") in Frank L. Acuff and Maurice F. Villere, "Games Negotiators Play," *Business Horizons* 19 (February 1976), pp. 70–76.

[23]Meyer S. Ryder, Charles M. Rehmus, and Sanford Cohen, *Management Preparation for Collective Bargaining* (Homewood, Ill.: Dow Jones-Irwin, 1966), p. 61.

[24]Walton and McKersie, *A Behavioral Theory,* p. 96.

[25]Much of this discussion on bargaining structure draws from Arnold Weber, "Stability and Change in the Structure of Collective Bargaining," in Lloyd Ulman, ed., *Challenges to Collective Bargaining* (Englewood Cliffs, N. J.: Prentice-Hall, 1967), pp. 13–36. See also Herbert R. Northrup, "Reflections on Bargaining Structure Change," in Gerald G. Somers, ed., *Industrial Relations Research Association: Proceedings of the Twenty-sixth Annual Winter Meeting* (Madison, Wis.: Industrial Relations Research Association, 1974), pp. 137–144.

[26]Abraham Cohen, "Coordinated Bargaining Structures of Collective Bargaining," *Labor Law Journal* 26 (June 1975), p. 385. For a detailed review of the literature pertaining to centralized bargaining, including its history as well as related union-management attitudes, see the preceding article as well as the same author's "Union Rationale and Objectives of Coordinated Bargaining," *Labor Law Journal* 27 (February 1976), pp. 75–82; George H. Hildebrand, "Cloudy Future for Coalition Bargaining," *Harvard Business Review* 46 (November–December 1968), pp. 114–128; Herbert J. Lahne, "Coalition Bargaining and the Future of Union Structure," *Labor Law Journal* 18 (June 1967), pp. 356–359; William N. Chernish, *Coalition Bargaining: A Study of Union Tactics and Public Policy* (Philadelphia: University of Pennsylvania Press, 1969); and Kenneth O. Alexander, "Union Structure and Bargaining Structure," *Labor Law Journal* 24 (March 1973), pp. 164–172.

[27]Rubin and Brown, *The Social Psychology of Bargaining.* See also Milton Derber, *Research in Labor Problems in the United States* (New York: Random House, 1967), pp. 301–341.

[28]I. William Zartman, "Negotiation as a Joint Decision-Making Process," *Journal of Conflict Resolution* 21 (December 1977), pp. 623–625.

[29]For an example of this approach, see Bertram I. Spector, "Negotiation as a Psychological Process," *Journal of Conflict Resolution* 21 (December 1977), pp. 607–618.

[30]See, for example, Oran R. Young, *Bargaining: Formal Theories of Negotiation* (Urbana: University of Illinois Press, 1975), pp. 131–242; John G. Cross, *The Economics of Bargaining* (New York: Basic Books, 1969); and Allan M. Cartter and F. Ray Marshall, *Labor Economics* (Homewood, Ill.: Richard D. Irwin, 1972), pp. 242–243.

[31]R. D. Luce and H. Raiffa, *Games and Decisions: Introduction and Critical Survey* (New York: Wiley, 1957).

[32]Zartman, "Negotiations as a Joint Decision-Making Process," p. 624.

[33]Ibid.

[34]Bartos, *Process and Outcome,* p. 4.

[35]For a discussion of political considerations affecting the union's negotiation goals see Clark Kerr, "Economic Analysis and the Study of Industrial Relations," in Campbell R. McConnell, ed., *Perspectives on Wage Determination* (New York: McGraw-Hill, 1970), pp. 81–84.

[36]Lawrence Fouraker and Sidney Siegel, *Bargaining Behavior* (New York: McGraw-Hill, 1963), p. 31.

[37]For exceptions to this approach see Peterson and Tracy, "Testing a Behavioral Theory Model"; and Arnold Weber, "Union Decision Making in Collective Bargaining" (M. A. thesis, University of Illinois, 1951).

[38]For examples of empirical studies furnishing political science and sociological insights into industrial relations behavior see Jack W. Skeels, "Measures of U.S. Strike Activity," *Industrial and Labor Relations Review* 24 (July 1971), pp. 515–525; and Robert N. Stern, "Toward an Empirical Merger: Sociological and Economic Conceptions of Strike Activity," in James L. Stern and Barbara D. Dennis, eds., *Industrial Relations Research Association: Proceedings of the Twenty-eighth Annual Winter Meeting* (Madison, Wis.: Industrial Relations Research Association, 1976), pp. 56–63.

[39]Ryder, Rehmus, and Cohen, *Management Preparation,* p. 9.

[40]Bruce Morse, *How to Negotiate the Labor Agreement* (Detroit: Trends Publishing, 1974), p. 19.

[41]Ryder, Rehmus, and Cohen, *Management Preparation,* p. 64.

[42]Michael H. Granof, *How to Cost Your Labor Contract* (Washington, D.C.: Bureau of National Affairs, 1973), pp. 5, 19. For another costing approach see W. D. Heisel and Gordon S. Skinner, *Costing Union Demands* (Chicago: International Personnel Management Association, 1976).

[43]Neil W. Chamberlain and James W. Kuhn, *Collective Bargaining,* 2d. ed. (New York: McGraw-Hill, 1965), pp. 162–190.

[44]Archibald Cox, "The Duty to Bargain in Good Faith," *Harvard Law Review* 71 (1958), p. 1418.

[45]National Labor Relations Board, *A Guide to Basic Law and Procedures under the National Labor Relations Act* (Washington, D.C.: Government Printing Office, 1976), p. 7.

[46]Bureau of National Affairs, *Labor Relations Expediter*, pp. LRX87–LRX99. It should be noted that the NLRB's right to categorize collective bargaining subjects as mandatory, voluntary, and illegal was upheld by the Supreme Court. *NLRB v. Wooster Division of Borg-Warner Corporation*, 356 U.S. 342 (1958).

[47]National Labor Relations Board, *Guide to Basic Law*, pp. 28, 36.

[48]For management's position in General Electric's bargaining see Virgil B. Day, "Bad Faith Bargaining?" in Walter Fogel and Archie Kleingartner, eds., *Contemporary Labor Issues* (Belmont, Calif.: Wadsworth Publishing, 1968), pp. 388–392; and Lemuel R. Boulware, *The Truth about Boulwarism* (Washington, D.C.: Bureau of National Affairs, 1969).

[49]NLRB v. General Electric, 72 LRRM 2530 (1969); *General Electric v. NLRB*, 397 U.S. 965 (1970).

[50]Charles J. Morris, *The Developing Labor Law* (Washington, D.C.: Bureau of National Affairs, 1971), pp. 286–309. See also the 1973, 1974, and 1976 supplements to this volume for an updated legal consideration of these activities.

[51]Ibid., pp. 309–316.

[52]Bureau of National Affairs, *Labor Relations Expediter*, LRX102.

[53]*Overnite Transportation Company v. NLRB*, 64 LRRM 2307 (1967).

[54]*Kota Division of Dura Corp.*, 182 NLRB 51 (1970).

[55]*Burns International Detective Agency Inc.*, 80 LRRM 2225 (1972).

[56]*Howard Johnson Co.*, 80 LRRM 1769 (1972).

[57]*Emerald Maintenance, Inc.*, 80 LRRM 2801 (1972).

[58]*Wayne Convalescent Center, Inc.*, 81 LRRM 2129 (1972).

[59]National Labor Relations Board, *42nd Annual Report* (Washington, D.C.: Government Printing Office, 1977), p. 269.

[60]Peter D. Walther, "The Board's Place at the Bargaining Table," *Labor Law Journal* 28 (March 1977), p. 131.

[61]B. M. Schieber, "Honesty in Bargaining," *American Federationist* 82 (April 1975), p. 20.

[62]For a more detailed discussion of these remedial problems see Elliot Bredhoff, "The Scope of 'Good Faith Bargaining' and Adequacy of Remedies," in Somers, *Industrial Relations Research Association: Proceedings of the Twenty-sixth Annual Winter Meeting*, pp. 109–118.

[63]*H. K. Porter*, 73 LRRM 2561 (1970).

[64]*Ex-Cello Corp.*, 74 LRRM 1740 (1970).

Chapter 7

Resolving the Collective Bargaining Impasse

"She grew tired of
   chasing
   rainbows, . . .
But I guess she was
   right
'cause I'm at the end,
I've found the pot,
but there's no gold
   inside."

Mickey Newbury*

How often have you seen headlines declaring "97 Percent of Labor Agreements in 1975 Negotiated Peacefully without Strike" or "99 Percent of Employees' Time Did Not Involve Strikes in 1975"? Rarely? Probably never! More than likely you have read: "Coal Miners' Strike to Cause Massive Layoffs in United States" or "Strikes Involving 6 Million Employees Averaged over 27 Days in 1974."

Media coverage of labor-management activities often overemphasizes labor conflicts, even though a very high percentage of unions do not strike to obtain a negotiated agreement. In fact, an overwhelming majority of the relationships between the union and management are peaceful, with only minor, resolvable conflicts.

This chapter discusses the ratification of the negotiated labor agreement and explains the impasse resolution procedures involving third parties, such as mediation, varieties of contract arbitration, and fact-finding. It also examines impasse resolution procedures involving only union and management representatives and looks at strikes and pickets in terms of their administrative and legal considerations. A concluding section briefly illustrates the potential of various union-management cooperative efforts aimed at avoiding negotiation impasses.

Contract Ratification

Negotiators, after resolving their differences and agreeing on tentative contract language, submit the proposed agreement to the union members for ratification; this usually requires a favorable majority vote.[1] Although a vote by the members is not legally necessary, some affirmation via referendum or delegated authority is normally used in the ratification process. For example, the United Auto Workers and United Mine Workers have a direct referendum; whereas the Steelworkers have delegated authority for ratification to a bargaining committee. In recent years, union members have shown increasing interest in greater participation, and more ratification elections have been held.

The ratification process determines whether members can live with the proposed agreement, even though they may not be completely satisfied with all of its provisions. Acceptance by the membership gives management some assurance that the employees will comply with the letter and spirit of the agreement. A vote to accept, therefore, is considered a commitment or willingness to be bound by the agreement.[2] When and if union members find the agreement unacceptable, they may vote to reject it, as they have in about 11 percent of the cases between 1968 and 1977.[3]

Reasons for Rejection of Tentative Agreements

The rejection of tentative agreements is an often debated subject. There has been disagreement over the reasons behind and the significance of contract rejections. One study of 1,973 related cases attempted to determine the reasons for tentative contract rejections by the membership. The most frequent reason given for rejection was that employees felt that they were shortchanged in comparison to other agreements in their vicinity. The data (fact, hearsay, rumors, misleading data, and so on) governing this reason are not important. What is significant is that members will reject contracts if they feel the provisions would make them "second-class citizens." Internal union politics was given as the second most frequent reason mentioned for contract rejection. Sometimes union leaders are elected by slight majorities; their rivals will campaign against any labor agreement negotiated regardless of its purported benefits.

Other factors contributing to contract rejections relate to other types of internal union problems, such as feelings of inequity and lack of upward communication within the union itself. For example, in industrial unions, skilled workers usually represent a minority of the membership, having little bargaining strength. These members might vote to reject the contract when they compare their wage rates to those of highly-paid skilled tradesmen in the building and construction industry.

Other groups (women, racial minorities, younger workers, and so on) continue to claim intraplant inequities. Although equal employment opportunity laws have been passed, wage differentials continue to exist for racial minorities and women. Moreover, young employees with low seniority view pensions and layoffs, which are usually based on seniority or retirement age, differently from the older employees, causing additional internal friction. Unless any of these subgroups feels that the agreement reflects its own personal needs, it assuredly will vote to reject the entire agreement.[4]

Another study, examining 1970–1971 data from the Federal Mediation and Conciliation Service (FMCS), found that the primary cause of rejection is union members' economic concerns—rejection percentages generally corresponded to a downturn in economic activity. In over half of the cases studied, high employee expectations coupled with reasons for union members to question the employer's wage offer led to rejection of the tentative contract. To confirm their conclusions, the researchers followed up on the agreements that were ultimately accepted and found that 65 percent included an increase in the wage package above that of the tentative settlement.[5]

A third study of about a thousand contract rejections concluded that the definition of contract rejection in previous studies had been too broad, overestimating the number of contract rejections and overemphasizing their problematic nature. These researchers found considerably lower rejection rates after redefining the term *contract rejection*. For example, less than 2 percent of the tentative agreements were rejected when all members of the bargaining committee recommended acceptance, and less than 3 percent were rejected when a majority of the bargaining committee recommended acceptance. Therefore, their conclusion was that contract rejection should be defined as the membership's rejection of the union bargaining committee's contract acceptance recommendation, not management's final contract proposal.[6]

Although scholars will continue to debate the definition of contract rejection and argue about whether a problem really exists, analysis of particular cases raises several interesting and somewhat contradictory possibilities:

1. Union negotiators may involve contract rejection as part of their bargaining strategy. For instance, rejection of a tentative agreement may indicate to management that the members want a more favorable package. When the bargaining committee presents the proposed agreement for a vote without any endorsement, it can return to the bargaining table after a contract rejection with renewed confidence and commitment from the membership.
2. Contract rejection may crystallize and possibly resolve some serious underlying problems of communication within the union, upward and downward. For example, members may not understand the terms of the agreement and their implications; the leaders may have misjudged the needs and wishes of the membership.
3. Contract rejection may serve as one of the indicators of weakness in the union leadership. Rarely do union members give their leaders full authority to negotiate a contract without a ratification vote.

4. Factionalism within a union—young versus old, black versus white, male versus female, craft versus production workers, personality differences, political differences, and so on—certainly cannot be overlooked as an internal problem in unions which can result in contract rejection.[7]

Impasse Resolution Procedures Involving a Third Party Neutral

Usually both parties attempt to resolve impasses, which can occur either before or after the contract's expiration date. In some cases, union and management officials need third parties either to facilitate the negotiation process or to resolve the bargaining difference with finality. There are four impasse resolution procedures involving third parties: mediation, interest or contract arbitration, mediation-arbitration (med-arb), and fact-finding.

Mediation

Many union-management impasses are resolved with help from third-party mediators, obtained either from the Federal Mediation and Conciliation Service (FMCS) or from state agencies. Mediators perform a number of functions: they assist in scheduling meetings, keeping the parties talking, carrying messages back and forth, and making suggestions. Unlike the arbitrator, the mediator has no authority to make binding decisions and must rely on persuasion and recommendations; the negotiators make the final decisions.[8] The mediator is the "invited guest" who can be asked to leave. However, acceptance of mediators is an indicator of the effort of one or both of the parties to bargain in good faith.

The FMCS was involved in 23,450 cases in 1977,[9] and the trend toward using mediation in dispute settlement continues upward. Added to this number should be the activities of separate mediation agencies in some eighteen states and Puerto Rico that assist parties in their own jurisdictions.

The mediation process is much more an art than a science. There is no general theory of mediation; rather it has been described as a process that "has been helpful in a haphazard way largely because of the talents of certain individuals who themselves would find it difficult to say why they had been successful."[10] Because there are no set rules, different mediators are able to obtain equally good results by different methods; therefore, mediation does not permit much generalization.

One analytical approach to the process focuses on personal qualities of the mediator—quickness of mind, evenness of temper, sense of humor, and knowledge and understanding of the industry. William E. Simkin, former director of the FMCS, developed a list of sixteen qualities sought in a mediator—all of which would be difficult to find in any one individual. Among the appropriate qualities are the patience of Job, the wit of the

Irish, the broken-field dodging abilities of a halfback, the physical endurance of the marathon runner, the hide of a rhinoceros, and the wisdom of Solomon.[11]

Carl Stevens' study of mediation focusing on the mediator's functions and tactics has identified several causal factors that lead to negotiated settlements—the bottom-line criterion of successful mediation.[12] Timing of the mediator's involvement was identified as one of the most important considerations. The mediator should enter before the parties become too fixed in their positions but not so early as to upset the power balance between the parties, causing them to harden their bargaining positions.

In some instances, the mere entrance of the mediator may be sufficient for dispute settlement. For example, assume that one of the chief negotiators leaves an active negotiation in a temper tantrum, vowing never again to return to the bargaining table. Upon subsequent reflection, the negotiator realizes a mistake was made but feels that calling the opposing negotiator would be embarrassing and perhaps indicate weakness. A common tactic used in such situations would be to call the mediator, who could schedule another meeting. Thus, mediation in this sense represents a very potent face-saving device.

A successful mediator clarifies perceptions of the bargaining climate and possible costs of impasse. For instance, if the parties disagree on data about cost of living, comparative wage rates, and productivity, the mediator could assist in reaching agreement on the statistical data. When negotiators tend to underestimate the costs of a strike or lockout or to overestimate the cost of an agreement, the mediator may be able to provide insights enabling them to evaluate their positions more realistically.

Helping each party to understand the tactics or intentions of the other can also aid the bargaining process. If management bluffs about its willingness to accept a strike or to allow an ongoing strike to continue indefinitely, the mediator may attempt to diagnose management's true intentions and then advise the union. On the other hand, if the union threatens a strike to obtain an excessive bargaining demand, the mediator could attempt to diagnose what the union is "really trying to say" and so inform the company negotiator. The mediator, in determining the true intentions of one party, may advise the other, who may realistically believe the mediator, but not the other party. By holding private caucuses with each, the mediator is privy to much confidential information. While no mediator would reveal this information to the other party, he or she can determine the magnitude of the real differences and encourage the parties that a settlement may be near if they continue bargaining.

The mediator often facilitates the bargaining process by proposing alternate solutions to the parties. There can be little effective bargaining without an overlap of at least some of the issues. Therefore, the mediator must create and propose alternate solutions, compromised settlements, and definitions of the respective bargaining positions.

In addition to mediating activities, mediators must be conscious of the perceptions of the parties and his or her own position. Not only must the mediator be uninvolved in any actions or tactics of deception and coercion, but he or she must also retain the qualities of neutrality, objectivity, and professionalism.

Interest (or Contract) Arbitration

Interest or contract arbitration involves the selection of a neutral or panel to hear the bargaining positions of the parties and make a final and binding decision on what should be included in the negotiated agreement. This process differs from grievance or rights arbitration (see Chapter 9), which is concerned with interpreting the language of the existing labor agreement. Less used in the private sector than grievance arbitration, interest arbitration makes up in relevance what it lacks in numbers because each decision is significant. In those industries using interest arbitration, it has been voluntarily implemented, except in the railroad industry, where Congress has on occasion compelled the parties to arbitrate.

Interest arbitration dates back to arbitration of labor disputes in coal mining, street railways, and newspaper, book, and job printing at the turn of the century. Later, it was used in men's clothing, hosiery, and railroad industries. More recently, the steel and airline industries have agreed to use it in resolving contract terms (see Chapter 3 for airline experience), but a number of industries, such as automobiles, chemical, petroleum, rubber, and textiles, still have had little or no experience with interest arbitration.

While interest arbitration involves a multitude of issues, few cases fail to involve wages. In fact, Bernstein estimated that between 1945 and 1950 25 percent of the interest arbitration cases involved wage disputes. Yet the actual number of arbitration cases must be kept in perspective—it has been estimated that only a fraction of 1 percent of all general wage changes negotiated between 1945 and 1967 were decided via arbitration.[13]

Although interest arbitration is not common in the private sector, many parties consider it an alternative procedure for impasse resolution. They realize that strikes are costly to both union and management personnel and also strain relationships. But with the trend toward longer contracts and away from wage reopener clauses, the opportunities for contract arbitration are reduced, and the risks of arbitration are increased. In other words, longer contracts require fewer negotiation times but extend the length of time that the parties may have to live with the arbitrator's decision.

A second difficulty with interest arbitration is the growing problem of "legalese" surrounding contract terms,[14] as illustrated by the following negotiated labor provision:

Section 8: In making promotion decisions of employees in Plant One to fill vacancies that occur or expect to occur, by reasons of a permanent vacancy

or the creation of a new job, a notice of the vacancy will be posted in Plant One, and any employee at work in said Plant who deems himself capable of performing the job and is qualified or can qualify under Section 5, Article III, may make application for the job during the seventy-two (72) hour posted period by signing the application form which will be prepared and also signed by the Superintendent of Plant One, wherein the posted job opening exists; provided that the applicant has not been awarded a posted job for which he made application during the preceding two months, and further provided the applicant is assigned on another job with the same or a lower rate of pay than the rate of pay of the posted vacancy at the time he makes application.[15]

A serious problem arises when arbitrators attempt to interpret the meaning of such clauses in a manner equitable to management and the union.

Based on experiences with interest arbitration, management and unions have varied opinions of the process. Both parties prefer the arbitrator's decision when it reflects their own final position, demonstrates a clear and impartial understanding of the issues, and avoids a strike. On the other hand, both parties have concerns about this process—for example, the delay in scheduling an arbitrator, the extra cost involved, and preparations for arbitration detracting from serious collective bargaining efforts. In addition, management becomes particularly concerned if the arbitrator fails to take into account the economic effect of the decision or if the award is above the norm for the industry.[16]

Mediation-Arbitration (med-arb) Med-arb occurs when the parties agree in advance that contract language, whether reached by mediation or arbitration, will be final and binding. Usually no decisions on the contract language will be sent back to the parties—either the board of directors or the union membership—for ratification. Once the parties agree to med-arb, those issues that cannot be resolved by mediation will be resolved by arbitration. The neutral will wear the mediator's hat at first, but if no agreement is reached by a predetermined date, he or she will become the arbitrator and decide the remaining unresolved issues. Under this procedure, most issues will be resolved by the parties because, in addition to the traditional pressures, there will be the pressure of knowing that the mediator-arbitrator will make a final and binding decision, if the parties do not.

An example of med-arb in the private sector involved a San Francisco printing company that published two local newspapers and had bought new automated equipment called scanners. The scanners required numerous changes in the work and the collective bargaining agreement over such issues as loss of jobs, seniority, and newly assigned work. These issues were important to both parties and perhaps would have been too complicated for a traditional arbitration hearing. Such wide differences could have resulted in a strike; however, the flexibility of the med-arb procedure resulted in a successful resolution of the issues.[17] Med-arb was also used in the 1978 postal negotiations, in which Professor James Healy of Harvard University served as mediator-arbitrator (see Chapter 15).

Final Offer Selection Arbitration *Final offer selection (FOS) arbitration* is a type of interest arbitration which gives the arbitrator the authority to select one of the proposals made by the parties. Procedurally, union and management present their separate final proposals to the arbitrator, who selects only one proposal, making no change in any of the provisions. Since the parties know in advance that the arbitrator cannot make a compromise decision, they will try to present to the arbitrator an acceptable proposal. Theoretically, if both parties attempt to present acceptable proposals, they will possibly settle their differences without third-party intervention.

This strategy differs from conventional interest arbitration, where arbitrators may compromise or "split the difference" in the proposals—causing the union to inflate its proposals and management to lower its offer. As a result, conventional interest arbitration has been labeled as having a "chilling effect" on collective bargaining because it artificially widens the gap between the parties during negotiations.

FOS arbitration has been used much more frequently in the public sector (a more thorough analysis can be found in Chapter 14), and it has received much notoriety in arbitration of baseball salaries. It was also given attention in the early 1970s when the Nixon administration included FOS arbitration as an option under its proposed change to the Railway Labor Act. After the administration dropped its support for the proposal during the 1972 presidential campaign, little else was heard about the plan.

Although FOS arbitration has rather obvious theoretical appeal, it can have some shortcomings, particularly if standards for arbitration decisions are not supplied. More importantly, the labor negotiations usually involve several issues, making FOS arbitration a very complex process. If the parties do not change or compromise their initial positions on some or all of these issues, the offers will not converge. The arbitrator must then select one of the extreme proposals, possibly heightening union-management tensions during the life of the contract and causing future difficulties in negotiating subsequent contracts.[18]

Another criticism of FOS arbitration is that it tends to lead to an intertemporal compromise; that is, in the long run arbitrators appear to have given awards to both management and unions in equal proportions, thus balancing the winners and losers over time. Preliminary analysis of data from FOS arbitration in baseball and three public sector jurisdictions has found "rather meager support for the intertemporal compromise criticism."[19]

Advocates of FOS arbitration have been pleased with its results. Rehmus believes that it certainly does not harm collective bargaining, that in fact it supports the process and may even obviate its own use.[20] Peter Seitz, an arbitrator for baseball salary disputes, assessed the process as follows:

The procedures used have had extraordinary success in encouraging the bargaining parties to submit realistic figures to each other and to eliminate the "out of this world" haggling of the past—clubs that were niggardly or tight-fisted in their offers ran the risks of having an arbitrator select the more reasonable player's figures; players who grossly overrated their value to the clubs ran the risk of ending up with the clubs' offers. This, I believe, led to moderation in positions and a salutory respect for the realities.[21]

Fact-Finding

Somewhere between the extremes of mediation and interest arbitration lies *fact-finding*. This is a semijudicial process in which the major focus is placed on gathering the facts and using some of the principles of mediation and arbitration. The fact finder's purpose is to assess the facts presented and gathered and to organize and display them publicly in the hopes that the parties will feel an obligation to settle their differences.

Fact-finding began after World War II, immediately after the National War Labor Board was disbanded in 1945. In fact, during a nine-month period between November 1945 and August 1946, twelve fact-finding boards were appointed. Involved were such companies as General Motors, U.S. Steel, Greyhound, and Western Union; other industries included oil, meat packing, sugar, western longshoremen, and nonferrous metals. Since 1947, when the Taft-Hartley Act was passed, fact-finding boards have been used predominantly in major disputes. During eight years of the Kennedy-Johnson administration, twenty boards were appointed.

Fact-finding can be classified into four categories:[22]

1. *Fact-finding without recommendations after a stalemate develops.* The notion here is that the facts alone, if identified, will help settle the dispute. Publicizing the facts would bring pressure on the negotiators from their constituencies. The fact-finding report, if published, also may enable editorial writers and columnists to alter or emphasize their preconceived assessments of the disputes. Although fact finders may not make recommendations, they may place blame on one of the parties. In a New York newspaper strike-lockout dispute, the union was blamed, but as in most other private disputes, the report did not facilitate a settlement.

2. *Fact-finding without recommendations in preparation for negotiations.* This approach involves the appointment of an impartial person or agency

well in advance of negotiations to develop factual background and data for future use of the bargaining teams. Although rarely used, it was implemented by the West Coast longshore industry to develop preliminary data to negotiate the Mechanization and Modernization Agreement and by impartial members and staff of the Armour Automation Committee, who wanted to prepare for problems in the meat-packing industry.

3. *Fact-finding without recommendations on the issues but with procedural or directional recommendations.* An example of this fact-finding category occurred after a six-month strike in a nonferrous metal industry dispute, when a board was created to investigate the bargaining climate and structure and possible causes for labor disputes. Although the board's recommendations for revising the bargaining structure were not accepted, its work provided the basis for future settlements.

4. *Fact-finding with recommendations.* Neutrals in this category are appointed to make specific recommendations on disputed issues after finding the facts. The procedural aspects are superficially similar to arbitration: hearings are conducted; both parties must be present for conferral with the neutral; and after gathering facts, the neutral writes the report. The major difference is that the recommendations are not binding. Both parties must study the report before deciding to reject or accept the recommendations. Acceptance cannot be overemphasized because fact finders' recommendations produce no settlement if either party rejects them. With so many features involved in the process, it should not be surprising that the approach sometimes fails.

Mediation, arbitration, and fact-finding all involve a third party, who either assists or directs union and management officials in resolving a negotiation impasse. As is discussed in the following section, management and union officials might prefer not to use a third party in this situation, but to rely instead on economic tests of strength.

The Strike and Related Activities between Union and Management

Work stoppages include both strikes and lockouts that cause a business to stop production, distribution, and sales of its goods or any organization to cease its operations. Generally, a *strike* is a temporary stoppage of work by a group of employees for the purpose of expressing a grievance or enforcing a demand. The *lockout* is an act by an employer of withholding or denying employment during a labor dispute in order to enforce terms of employment on a group of employees.[23]

Within this general framework there are a number of different types of strikes, usually labeled in accordance with their cause, purpose, nature, or accompanying activities:

- **Economic strikes** are worker stoppages to gain economic goals such as higher wages, improved pensions, and vacations.
- **Wildcat strikes** are strikes that violate provisions of the labor agreement, or in some cases are those conducted without approval from higher union officials.
- **Unfair labor practice strikes** are worker stoppages that occur in relation to an unfair labor practice. Examples include strikes to achieve a closed shop and strikes in reaction to employer discrimination.
- **Sympathy strikes** are worker stoppages by employees who have no dispute with their own employer but are striking out of sympathy and support for another union.
- **Sit-down strikes** occur when employees report for work in their usual manner but do not work. Instead they occupy their work place and allow no work to be done.
- **Slow-down strikes** take place when employees continue to work, but work at a slower pace to express a grievance or to achieve a contract demand.
- **Jurisdictional strikes** occur under two conditions: (a) when two unions conflict over work assignments (for example, plumbers strike when laborers are directed to unload a truck full of plumbing materials), and (b) when employees interested in one union strike and picket an employer even though another union is already the exclusive bargaining representative for the appropriate bargaining unit.

Usually accompanying the strike, especially the economic strike, are pickets and boycott. *Picketing* refers to the outside patrolling of the employer's premises, usually using placards and handbills to achieve a specific objective. For example, *recognitional picketing* is used to gain recognition of the union as the employees' bargaining representative. *Informational picketing* occurs when the union attempts to inform the public that a labor dispute exists between the workers and their organization. *Consumer picketing* attempts to persuade customers to refuse to purchase products from the employer with whom the union has a labor dispute. Often the employees and their supporters also *boycott* the employer, or refuse to purchase products made by the employer with whom they have the dispute.

Table 7–1 shows that work stoppages in the 1970s continued at a comparable pace in terms of duration, workers involved, and days idled per worker to those of 1940 through 1970. Even though 1972–1973 data brought forward some optimism about the possible decline in work stoppages, these data proved to be low because of the influence of wage-price controls. Table 7–2 attempts to display the major issues involved in work stoppages, but experience has cautioned against arbitrary labeling. Work stoppages are not caused by one factor alone, but usually

Table 7–1
Work Stoppages in the United States, 1930–1978

Years	Number	Duration (Mean Number of Days)	Workers Involved		Days Idled	
			Number (Thousands)	Percent of Total Employed	Percent of Working Time	Per Worker
1930–1939 (Average)	2,015	21.2	911	4.1	NA[a]	17.4
1940–1949 (Average)	3,893	16.5	2,311	5.4	.31	12.2
1950–1959 (Average)	4,248	19.9	2,198	4.3	.50	17.4
1960–1969 (Average)	4,104	23.5	1,809	2.8	.22	19.9
1970	5,716	25.0	3,305	4.7	.37	20.1
1971	5,138	27.0	3,280	4.5	.26	14.5
1972	5,010	24.0	1,714	2.3	.15	15.8
1973	5,353	24.0	2,251	2.9	.14	12.4
1974	6,074	27.1	2,778	3.5	.24	17.3
1975	5,031	26.8	1,746	2.2	.16	17.9
1976	5,648	28.0	2,420	3.0	.19	15.6
1977	5,506	29.3	2,040	2.4	.17	17.6
1978	4,300	NA	1,600	NA	NA	NA
1979 (Jan.–Feb.)	627	NA	206	NA	NA	NA

[a]NA = not available.
Source: U.S. Department of Labor, Bureau of Labor Statistics, *Work Stoppages, 1977 and First Nine Months of 1978* (Washington, D.C.: Government Printing Office, 1979), p. 3; U.S. Department of Labor, Bureau of Labor Statistics, *Monthly Labor Review* 102 (May 1979), p. 103.

Table 7–2
Work Stoppages According to Major Issues, 1977

Major Issue	Total
All stoppages	5,506
General wage	3,135
Supplemental benefits	78
Wage adjustments	141
Hours of work	15
Other contract matters	276
Union organization and security	252
Job security	211
Plant administration	1,002
Other working conditions	137
Interunion or intraunion matters	246
Not reported	13

Source: U.S. Department of Labor, Bureau of Labor Statistics, *Work Stoppages, 1977 and First Nine Months of 1978* (Washington, D.C.: Government Printing Office, 1979), p. 7.

Striking employees may picket the struck firm to inform the public of the dispute and to gain recognition for their goal or union.

Source: © 1979 by Rick Grosse, San Francisco, California.

by many factors. Even so, there can be little argument that the main issue is wages, followed by plant administrative issues.

Criteria Involved in Union-Management Strike Decisions

When negotiators have failed to reach an agreement by the time the previous labor agreement expires, both union members and officers and management officials have to seriously consider whether a strike is in their best interests. In most cases union members return to work after the negotiators agree temporarily to a tentative settlement but postpone a final decision on whether to strike until the ratification vote is taken. In some cases, as with the United Mine Workers, union members will not work without an agreement fully ratified by the membership. In other cases, such as the 1979 rubber negotiations, the contract may be extended for a short time if negotiators believe they are close to agreement.

Regardless of the approach used, each union must consider a number of factors before the members will vote to approve and commit themselves to a strike. Likewise, management must analyze its own situation to determine whether to take a strike. In addition, each party attempts to assess the position of the other party in order to determine the relative strength of each factor considered. For example, if management can operate at nearly 100 percent capacity during a strike, this would certainly be a positive factor for management and a negative one for the union.

Although the factors that unions consider in their determination to strike are fairly easy to identify, the relative importance will vary with the particular circumstances of each case. For example, union members may know in advance how much income they will lose each day of a strike but be unable to predict its length. More difficult to weigh is the balance between income lost due to the strike and the expected income increase gained as a result of the strike. Thus, the union members must take into account imprecise data in their strike decision. These data can be grouped into four broad categories: cost considerations; goodwill, public image, and government intervention; strategic purposes of the strike; and previous strike experience.

Cost Considerations While employees consider their lost wages and other accompanying costs of a strike, management looks at its own figures to compute how much a strike will cost. These include fixed costs like rent, interest on loans, payments for equipment, and salaries. Also, customers may be lost, unless there is significant customer loyalty, and the costs of stockpiling and building inventories and preparing for the strike can cost millions of dollars. Or, when the employer prepares by stockpiling and building inventories and no strike occurs, then the employer has other complicated problems—whether to continue full operation, who to lay off, and how to temporarily or permanently retrench—all long-run cost factors.[24]

Operating the plant during a strike with management personnel and nonstriking employees must be considered. But such operation is more difficult than anticipated in some cases because it is occasionally accompanied by violence on the picket line, resulting in injury to persons and property—overturned cars, broken windows, and in some cases shooting and sabotage. These activities often lead to the use of local police to maintain order, the seeking of injunctions, and other efforts that further strain the labor-management relationship. Thus management's decision to operate during a strike involves many uncertainties.

Employer costs may also depend on the durability or perishability of the product or the substitutability of goods or services offered by the company. A strike for a short period at a large automaker having a large stockpile of autos would be only a small inconvenience; in fact, it could even save the automaker money if inventories were excessive. However, a farmworker strike of two weeks during harvest season could cause enormous damage, and the cost to the farmer would be prohibitive. A strike by a local bus service that transports only a small percentage of the commuters might be inconsequential, especially if these commuters will be able to find alternative means of getting to work. But if the bus service transports a large percentage of commuters, serious and time-consuming traffic problems could develop, leading to poor public relations for the employer and the union.

While many of the effects and costs of a strike rest with the immediate employer and the union, strikes against employers producing basic materials that are used by other industries extend the effects and the costs of the strike to other employers and union members.[25] The 1959 steel strike was felt throughout the country; the 1977–1978 coal strike certainly had an impact on companies that used coal as an energy source for their power. In the future, with more and more interdependence in the industrial sector, few strikes can occur that will not have an impact on operations and employees in other industries.

Strike Benefits and Public Aid for Strikers The strike benefits received by many union members, usually less than $50 per week, often determine whether union members will vote to strike as well as how long they will strike. Although the amount that each union member receives during a strike is minimal, the total amount of annual strike payments can be large. For example, in 1972 alone, $61.6 million was disbursed by fifty unions, $24.2 million by the United Auto Workers alone. In the same year, nearly 14.9 million workers, representing over 70 percent of all union members, were covered by national union strike benefit plans.[26]

Unions use several approaches in the design of their strike benefit plans and the manner in which the benefits are disbursed. Some unions earmark a certain proportion of their total per capita receipts, some levy temporary assessments as needed, and others have no separate funds but pay from the union treasury. The United Rubber Workers once used a special assessment of $5 per member to replenish its strike funds, and the Chemical Workers activates its crisis strike plan when the balance in the strike fund falls below $50,000. Most unions pay strike benefits when funds are available and the strike has been sanctioned by the national union leadership, but there are often additional stipulations: that the member be in good standing, complete a waiting period, and establish a need for the payments.[27] In some cases the AFL-CIO establishes a contribution fund for striking employees, as was the case in the 1977 Coors Brewery strike.

When the strike is settled, the strike benefits usually end (although the United Rubber Workers extends payments for an additional two weeks). In other cases, the benefits stop or the payments are reduced before the strike is over. Some unions set a minimum for their strike fund balance, and payments cease when the minimum is reached. Other unions will either terminate or reduce the benefits for individual members who work for other employers or cannot perform their strike duties.[28]

One controversial source of funds for strikers is public aid. Related striker assistance programs include food stamps, aid to families with dependent children (AFDC), medical assistance, general assistance, and unemployment insurance.[29] Some of these programs are federal and, under certain conditions, all employees qualify; others are administered only within an individual state and only residents qualify.

Public support programs for strikers date back to the New Deal era of the 1930s. Recently, public support has been given strikers during the 1976 Rubber Workers and Auto Workers strikes and the coal strike of 1977–1978. These payments remain subject to political and philosophical controversy regarding costs of public support, the desirable structure and length of welfare payments, and the relative bargaining power of the parties.[30]

Advocates of public aid and assistance for strikers make several arguments for their availability:[31]

☐ Strikers are taxpayers who pay their taxes when they work. When they don't work, they should receive aid.

☐ Tax dollars are used to feed hungry people in other countries and prisoners in this country. Strikers who are needy should receive the same consideration.

☐ Even though some persons may be against public aid for strikers, they should not be against public aid for the wives and children—those who are directly affected.

☐ If providing public aid to strikers is subsidizing a strike against a company, letting new contracts or failing to cancel existing contracts while a strike is in effect subsidizes the company's positions against the union.

☐ Eligibility for public support is based on need as determined by law, not on whether a person is on strike.

Opponents to public support to strikers argue that:

☐ Legislatures never intended to provide public aid to strikers, particularly since strikers have refused bona fide employment by refusing to go back to work.

☐ Giving public aid to strikers violates a traditional policy of governmental neutrality in labor-management relations.[32]

☐ If strikers' attitude—"others are entitled to it, so I am"— spread to the general public, it would cause a general attitude modification toward work, reducing workers' incentive, increasing the rolls of public aid recipients, increasing welfare costs and wasting government funds.[33]

☐ Collective bargaining as a process depends on a viable strike mechanism to insure a proper balancing of the costs of disagreement and the costs of agreement at the negotiations table. Therefore, availability of public support for strikers increases the propensity of unions to strike and causes the strike to be longer, costlier, or both.

☐ There is no reason to think public assistance would make strikers less bitter or violent in their strike activities.[34]

Strike Insurance — Mutual Aid Pacts (MAPs) Employers can mitigate strike costs by establishing strike insurance and *mutual aid pacts* (MAPs). These arrangements include "an agreement by which competing employers contract that, if one of them is struck, the others will indemnify it by some predetermined amount of money to help withstand the impact of the strike."[35] Although a number of industries—for example, newspaper publishing, rubber, air and rail transportation, Hawaiian sugar cane, and California fruits and vegetables—have had experience with these agreements, only a few industries have characteristics that are conducive to strike insurance and mutual aid pacts: homogeneity, time-sensitive product, high fixed production costs, multiple unions, and labor atmosphere with high incidence of strife.[36]

The most publicized MAP was formed in 1958 when several airlines entered an agreement to provide cash payment to any struck airline from other members of the pact. These payments were designed to approximate the additional profits to the nonstruck airlines that resulted from increased income due to the strike and to approximate 50 percent of the company's operating expenses during the first two weeks, 45 percent during the third week, 40 percent during the fourth, and 35 percent thereafter. Each member company's contributions would equal 1 percent of its operating revenue from the previous year.[37]

Several studies have found mixed effects of the MAP on the process of collective bargaining. One study concluded that MAPs increase the length of strikes by lowering the airline companies' costs of disagreement.[38] Another study drew similar conclusions but also found that airline strikes have become more frequent, union demands have not moderated, and costs and benefits have actually escalated.[39] Others have argued that the airline pact itself has not caused strikes; rather, strikes have occurred as the result of other bargaining and economic factors.[40] While the effects have been mixed, one is certain: MAPs have caused unions to counteract employers' actions by reinforcing strike benefit programs, securing other union support and assistance, and seeking help from the AFL-CIO. Further, the Airline Deregulation Act of 1978 made some modifications of the industry's MAP[41]; these modifications kept United Airlines from receiving MAP support during the 1979 Machinists' strike.

Goodwill, Public Image, and Government Intervention Goodwill, public image, and possible government intervention are factors that influence the decision to strike or to take a strike. *Goodwill,* especially important in small plants, pertains mostly to internal relationships. For instance, neither management nor the union wants antagonistic attitudes to develop that linger after the strike. Neither wants plant relations to deteriorate or trust between the parties to decline. Therefore, careful attention must be given to goodwill throughout the process. *Public image* involves mostly the attitudes and opinions of people external to the particular strike. Union and company officials certainly do not want their activities labeled irresponsible or heedless of the public interest.[42] Possible government intervention for vital industries must be considered, especially if management or the union believes government intervention will weaken its respective bargaining position.

Strategic Considerations of a Strike While the main purpose of the strike is to secure a contract, it serves other purposes. For example, it may be part of an overall union strategy to help resolve internal problems. It may have a cathartic effect on the union members, removing accumulated tensions and releasing frustrations resulting from monotonous jobs. In fact, strikes under these conditions might improve productivity when the strikers return to work. A strike might also help to unify union members—rallying the diverse prestrike membership factions to work toward a common goal.

In some cases, the union calls a strike just to show management it can unify the membership over a collective bargaining issue. Over a period of time, the threat of a strike loses its effectiveness. If such threats are not carried out, management views the union leader as "the boy who cried wolf." Therefore, union leaders are sometimes forced to carry out a bluff or threat in order to substantiate future threats.

Union leaders might also believe that their members would be more

A proposed agreement between union and management is submitted to union members for ratification. These International Association of Machinists and Aerospace Workers members, employed by Boeing, will resume their strike if they reject the proposal.

Source: Courtesy of Wide World Photos.

willing to accept a slightly modified final offer if they have not received wages during a brief strike. In this sense, strikes are used to "roll the steam" out of employees and their initially unrealistic expectations.[43]

Unions also have to consider the effects of a strike on their institutional security. During the strike, some union members might accept jobs elsewhere and decide not to return after the strike. Sometimes employers hire permanent replacements for union strikers, and the negotiations are never consummated. Possibly rival unions are waiting on the sideline for the legally recognized union to falter.[44] With these considerations, the union must be aware that a concerted decision to strike may be a risk to its own survival.

Previous Strike Experiences An assessment of previous strike experiences unique to the particular situation must be considered by unions and management. Strikes can range from very peaceful conflicts of short duration to outrageous, unlawful conflicts of months, even years. They have no uniform sequence, although strikers are usually most enthusiastic during the early days of the strike. Indeed, the first few days on a picket line often draw a large proportion of union members in an almost carnival-like atmosphere. After several months, it may be difficult to recruit members to walk the picket line.

Frustrations, antagonisms, and anxieties usually increase as the strike continues, with increased membership pressure being placed on union leaders to resolve the impasse.[45] The relative peacefulness of a strike is influenced by the attitudes of community citizens, particularly merchants and creditors, toward the dispute. The striker's spouse is perhaps the most influential individual in shaping the striker's behavior and attitudes. It is of course much easier for a striker to sustain a long strike if her or his spouse lends moral and, in some cases, financial support to the cause. On the other hand, tensions created by the strike can create permanent divisions among family members, friends, and other groups in the community as the strike endures and as individuals are asked for their support.[46]

Tensions can be heightened if the company continues to operate the business with either supervisory personnel or strike replacements. Bernard Karsh has described several possible striker responses to this situation in his detailed account of one industrial strike:[47]

☐ Mill supervisors hung in effigy on lampposts around the mill.

☐ Bedroom sized mirrors brought to the picket line to reflect the sunrays on the nonstriking workers to annoy them while they tried to work.

☐ Setting up circular saw blades mounted on wooden horses for strikers to pound with automobile axles as hammers (the noise is deafening).

☐ Setting fire to fifty-gallon oil drums filled with old tar and tar paper, then placing them in an alley directly in front of a loading dock and shipping entrance so that the odor from the flames would be drawn into the mill every time the door opened.

☐ Throwing rocks through windows, tacks in driveways, and egg shells filled with colored paint on cars.

Preparing for a Strike

Both parties must prepare for a possible strike before the contract expiration date, whether a strike is called or a settlement is reached. Union leaders must be certain of the extent to which members will actively participate during a strike and present a unified front against the employer. Division within the ranks causes much difficulty and dilutes the union's bargaining strength.

As the strike date approaches, union officers must schedule pickets, assure appropriate support for those on the line, and properly prepare the pickets for various situations, such as what to do when strike replacements cross the picket line. The union also has to determine qualified recipients of strike benefits as well as to inform the members of appropriate procedures for obtaining food stamps and other forms of public aid. Finally, communication channels (telephone hot lines) must be established to inform members of the negotiations' progress.

Management often spends much time in its strike preparations, particularly if it is essential that the employer continue to operate during a strike, as public utilities must do. Many organizations have emergency strike manuals that provide specific and detailed plans in the event of a strike. The manual typically has two major components: (a) specific job assignments for nonstriking employees, professional personnel, and managers and (b) checklists of appropriate strike activities, such as notifying customers and suppliers, contacting law enforcement officials, and providing food and housing for those staying on the job.[48] Management might also seek professional assistance from employer colleagues, such as members of the American Society for Personnel Administration, which has published a *Strike Preparation Manual.*[49]

Although union and management officials carefully consider the advantages and disadvantages of strikes, lockouts, and pickets, they are not entirely free to implement these activities as they please. Various legal considerations can raise additional problems and prospects.

Legality of Strikes and Related Activities

The Right to Strike The right to strike has long been subject to philosophical debate. Opponents of the right to strike usually cite examples of violence and civil disobedience which have occurred in strike activities. In the history of the United States, many violent strikes have resulted in significant damage to property and loss of lives—the Chicago Haymarket bombings, the dynamiting of the *Los Angeles Times* building in 1910, the mass killings at the Ludlow, Colorado, coal mines in 1914, and the massacre during a coal miner strike in Williamson County, Illinois, in

1922. Although violence has subsided over the years, it has not been completely eliminated, as evidenced by the Kohler strike[50] in the late fifties and the coal miner strike in Harlan County, Kentucky, in the seventies.

Strike opponents also contend that strikers infringe on some of the employers' property rights. One critic of strikes has noted the strike

is not even merely the simultaneous and collective act of a large group of workers in "withholding their labor." The strikers have not simply given up their jobs. On the contrary, they not only contend that they are still employees of the company at the jobs at which they are refusing to work, but that they are the only legitimate employees.

They claim an *ownership* of such jobs. They mean to prevent the struck company from offering—and anybody else from taking—the jobs that they have themselves abandoned. They also physically prevent existing employees from continuing their work.[51]

Yet advocates of the strike suggest that employee strikers are simply asserting rights common to managers and other individuals:

If a corporate manager can decide to limit production so as not to over-supply the market or a farmer or independent craftsman decide not to work because working conditions are burdensome, why should workers not be allowed to stop or slow production in order to obtain a greater return for their efforts, or in order to improve conditions under which they work?[52]

In this sense, strikes are basic to the industrial relations system—inseparable from collective bargaining because they cannot be severed without hurting both.[53] Strikes are usually not entered into lightly; they are not simple expressions of ill will or irrationality. Indeed, both parties realize that the strike can hurt as well as help their respective positions.[54]

The potential or actual occurrence of strikes is an inherent aspect of labor-management relationships where the parties seek to obtain their preferences over their opponent's disagreement.[55] Unions that *always* agree with management over the years cease to be unions; similarly, management will reduce its effectiveness if it *always* agrees with the union. Therefore, conflict is apparent, possibly inherent, in collective bargaining, and strikes are sometimes viewed as a necessary alternative for expressing this conflict.

Legal guidelines have been formulated which attempt to minimize the controversy over the right to strike by balancing employee and employer rights during a strike. The *Commonwealth v. Hunt* decision (1842)—discussed in Chapter 3—was the first judicial act that recognized employees' right to participate in concerted activities for their own economic welfare.

The National Labor Relations Act guarantees certain rights to employees, among them the right to join and form unions, to bargain collectively, and to "engage in other concerted activities for the purpose of collective bargaining or other mutual aid or protection." Section 13 also states: "Nothing in this Act, except as specifically provided for herein, shall be construed so as to interfere with or impede or diminish in any way the right to strike or to affect the limitations or qualifications on that right."

However, this right is not absolute; there are restrictions on national emergency strikes, secondary strikes, jurisdictional strikes, unfair labor practice strikes, and recognitional strikes. Yet current legislation implicitly assumes that most strikes occur only after months of intensive negotiations under the rules established by the NLRB as interpreted by the courts. While both parties are required by law to negotiate in good faith, they do not always reach agreement and strikes do occur, but usually only after authorization from the national office and a strike vote by the membership.[56]

Many legal questions concerning strikes, pickets, and boycotts involving the employees' immediate, or *primary*, employer have been resolved over the years by statute or judicial decisions. Other activities concerning employers not directly involved in the labor dispute (*secondary* employers) are usually subject to much more complex legal interpretation. While secondary activities often have narrow applications, their significance is especially pertinent to those unions and employers that frequently face these issues.

Strikes and Related Activities Involving the Primary Employer When the union and management fail to reach an agreement upon the expiration of their labor agreement, the union normally calls a strike accompanied by picket lines and a boycott of the product. If only the immediate employer and the union are involved, the strike, picket, and boycott are considered primary. The overwhelming majority of strikes, pickets, and boycotts that occur in the United States in any given year are of this type. For example, the 1979 United Rubber Workers' strike involved primary strikers; employees of Uniroyal walked off their jobs when negotiations broke off and the contract had expired. Picket lines were set up at every plant for the purpose of gaining support for the strike. At the same time, the United Rubber Workers refused to purchase tires and other products made by Uniroyal and sought support from friends, family members, other union members, and other sources. A similar situation existed in the 1979 Machinists' strike on United Airlines. During such economic strikes, the primary employer can legally hire permanent replacements. Employees therefore risk more than lost wages when they strike; they also run the risk of forfeiting their jobs if the employer replaces them during the strike.

However, practical considerations can prevent the employer from exercising the legal right to replace strikers with other personnel. It is not easy to replace all of the striking employees, particularly if the firm requires a large number of replacements. This problem is compounded when the operations are somewhat complicated, since many employees will have to be trained in a short period of time. Finally, extreme tensions can occur between strikers and strike replacements at the picket line, possibly resulting in violence and community disorder.

Additional activities involving the primary employer include lockouts and wildcat strikes. The right of single employers to lock out employees is the analogue of employees' right to strike. *Lockouts* can be used legally by employers after an impasse has been reached over a mandatory bargaining issue. They have also been approved by the NLRB to prevent seizure of a plant by a sit-down, to forestall repetitive disruption in plant operations by "quickie strikes," to avoid spoilage of perishable materials, and to avert the immobilization of automobiles brought in for repairs.[57]

Yet the right to lock out employees is qualified, particularly since the NLRB maintains that the employer already has the power to counterbalance the strike by permanently replacing the strikers, stockpiling, subcontracting, maintaining operations with nonstrikers, and unilaterally instituting working conditions once the contract has expired.[58] However, this power is limited by the fact that primary economic strikers are authorized to vote in any representation or decertification elections for twelve months, and if the employer commits an unfair labor practice by discharging employees who later strike, the strikers may be reinstated with full back pay.

The NLRB and courts have been more lenient in situations in which the union attempts to "whipsaw" by striking individual employers in a multi-employer bargaining association to force a more favorable agreement. In the Teamsters' strike of 1979, nonstruck members of the association temporarily locked out their employees in reaction to the Teamsters' strike against only a selected number of trucking companies. The association legally claimed that "a strike against one is a strike against all." Failure to cease operations by all companies would imperil the employers' common interest in bargaining on a group basis and significantly dilute their bargaining strength.

Because unions often strike members of a multi-employer association one at a time, hoping to put pressure on the struck firm while the others operate, the NLRB and the courts have allowed temporary lockouts to preserve the association's unity. In addition, nonstruck firms in a multi-employer bargaining association have been allowed to hire temporary replacements to preserve the bargaining unit structure and to maintain operations. Because the struck firm can hire permanent replacements in order to continue operations, the courts have reasoned that it would be unfair to require that the nonstruck firms be shut down completely while the struck firm operates.[59]

Wildcat strikes include work stoppages that involve the primary employer-employee relationship and that are neither sanctioned nor stimulated by the union, although union officials might be aware of them. They can vary in terms of length and number of affected departments in the facility. They may also take the form of heavy absenteeism for several days, especially under no-strike pledges and contracts.[60] These stoppages might be caused by membership dissension and factionalism[61] or may have the union leader's tacit support in order to gain a particular management concession.

Since most labor agreements provide for arbitration as the final step in the grievance procedure and such agreements to arbitrate are usually accompanied by a no-strike clause, a wildcat strike represents a violation of the labor agreement. Employers can respond to wildcat strikes in several ways: (a) requesting informally and formally that strikers return to work, (b) contending that employees have voided their labor agreement, (c) disciplining or discharging the strikers, and (d) bringing suit against the union for damages suffered.[62] Two Supreme Court decisions discussed in Chapter 9 (*Boy's Market* and *Buffalo Forge*) suggest that employees can be legally enjoined from continuing a wildcat strike under certain conditions.

Strikes and Related Activities Involving Secondary Employers Secondary parties are those who are not directly bound by the terms of the labor agreement in dispute. They are not at the bargaining table; therefore, they are not responsible for the negotiations impasse. However, they are often indirectly brought into negotiations when the union attempts to persuade them to influence the primary employer to agree with the union's proposals.

Consumer boycotts and picketing, common situs picketing, the ally doctrine, and hot cargo agreements are secondary activities discussed below to illustrate the point that it is not always easy to distinguish between a primary and secondary party to a negotiations impasse.

Consumer boycotts and picketing. *Consumer boycotts and picketing* include handbilling, carrying placards, and urging customers to refuse to purchase products from a particular retail or wholesale business. For example, the striking employees of a clothing manufacturer might legally boycott and picket a retail clothing store owned by the manufacturer, say, the factory outlet for irregulars or seconds. But if these employees travel considerable distance to picket a retail clothing store that sells many items—one of which is bought from the manufacturer—the legal issue becomes more complex.[63] Consumer picketing in front of a retail clothing store in another city (a secondary employer) violates the NLRA *if* the picketers attempt to convince customers to refuse to shop at the store. But if the picketers make an appeal to the customers to refuse to buy only the struck product (clothing items produced by the manufacturer or the primary employer), the picket is legal.

A leading case, *Tree Fruits*, involved a strike against some fruit packing firms that were members of a multi-employer bargaining association and that sold Washington State apples to Safeway, a retail grocery chain.[64] As part of the boycott effort, the union picketed and handbilled forty-six Safeway stores, appealing to the customers to refrain from buying Washington State apples. The union carefully avoided making appeals to employees at the stores, closely instructed the individuals on the picket line, and made certain there was not a general appeal to request that potential customers not patronize the store. As a result, the picketing was peaceful, the employees continued to work, no obstructions occurred, and the courts upheld the legality of the picketing activities.[65]

Although the precedent set by the *Tree Fruits* case does allow opportunities for the union to perform legal consumer picketing, there are limitations. A union cannot picket a bank using services of a janitorial firm with which the union has a labor dispute, and unions cannot picket a retail store making a broad appeal to "look for the union label." Nor can employees of a bakery that sells bread to a restaurant legally picket a restaurant, requesting that potential diners go elsewhere,[66] especially since the bread loses brand identity when served in the restaurant. Finally, employees of a cabinet manufacturer cannot picket a furniture store selling the manufacturer's cabinets if they make a general appeal to the public not to patronize the store.[67]

Common situs and reserve gate picketing. *Common situs picketing* involves both the primary and secondary employers who share the same physical work premises, as is the case at construction sites and shipping docks. The problem arises when the union that is picketing the primary employer also adversely affects the work or business of the neutral employer located at the same site.

Common situs picketing is a complex and ambiguous issue because both the employer and the employees are given somewhat opposing legal rights. The union has the right to picket the primary employer with whom it has a labor dispute and to bring economic pressure on its immediate employer. Yet the neutral or secondary employer has a right to be free from economic pressure from unions with whom it has no bargaining relationships.[68]

Before 1951, unions argued that the employers who occupied the same work site (*common situs*) were so intertwined that a labor dispute with one employer was a labor dispute with all; therefore, unions alleged that there were no neutral employers on the site. The Supreme Court ruled on a case involving a general contractor on a construction project who subcontracted some electrical work to a nonunion subcontractor who paid less than the union scale.[69] When the nonunion employees arrived at work, the union set up pickets on the entire work site, and other union employees honored the picket line and refused to work. The union's strategy was to force the nonunion subcontractors off the job, and the general contractor complied with the union demands by terminating the contracts. Although the contractor complied, it took the case to the NLRB, and appealed eventually to the Supreme Court. The Court ruled that general contractors and subcontractors on a building site were separate business entities and should be treated as neutrals with respect to each other's labor controversies.[70]

Unions have been limited further in their flexibility in applying economic pressure via picketing at work sites from another case in which the company (General Electric) used independent contractors for constructing a new building, rearranging operations for a new product, and performing general repair work. In order to minimize contact between GE employees and employees of the contractor, a separate gate (*reserve gate*) was set aside for employees of the contractor. The union called a strike and picketed all gates, including the separate gate, and most of the employees of the contractor honored the picket line. The NLRB found that picketing at the separate gate was designed to enmesh employees of a neutral employer in the labor dispute and was therefore illegal. On appeal, the Supreme Court agreed to sustain the NLRB order unless the NLRB found through further investigation that the separate gate was established for the purpose of entry by employees who performed work that was necessary for the normal operations of the plant—work normally performed by GE employees.[71]

Ally doctrine. A secondary boycott, which involves three parties—the union, the primary employer, and the secondary employer—raises legal questions over the neutrality of the secondary employer. To determine neutrality the NLRB has developed the *ally doctrine:* If a secondary employer is closely associated with the primary employer and its labor dispute with the union, neutrality is lost, and the secondary employer should be treated as a primary party to the labor dispute. For example, a secondary employer would lose its neutrality by accepting a subcontract to do work that would normally be done by workers on strike.

This work performed by the employees of the secondary employer can be classified as *struck work,* which includes "work, which but for the strike would be performed by the employees of the primary employer."[72] Another situation occurs in cases where the business relationship of the primary and secondary employer is so intertwined as to almost create a co-employer relationship.[73] Such close business relations can easily develop within conglomerated firms owning a large variety of manufacturing processes or businesses. The courts have held that when the primary and the secondary employer are so closely related, picketing the secondary employer is permissible.[74]

Yet the courts have determined that single employers can be protected when distance between facilities is great and the operations are autonomous. For example, when union members having a labor dispute with the *Miami Herald* went to Detroit to picket the *Detroit Press* (both owned by Knight Newspapers), the board found the common ownership *alone* did not create an allied relationship.[75] In fact, more recently the board has concluded that separate divisions of the same corporation may also be able to claim protection from secondary picketing if the dispute exists at only one division.[76]

Hot-cargo argreements. Designed to promote union-made products and support union members on strike, *hot-cargo agreements* were negotiated in labor agreements to specify that employees may refuse to use or handle products of certain employers, such as nonunion companies and companies experiencing strikes. Before the enactment of the Landrum-Griffin Act in 1959, these clauses were not illegal and were considered loopholes in the provisions of the Labor Management Relations Act, which dealt with secondary boycotts. While they had the same effect as secondary boycotts, they adversely affected neutral employers. In 1959, they were made unfair labor practices,[77] although the 1959 amendments included a special provision for the apparel, clothing, and construction industries.[78]

Where labor disputes develop to the stage in which they are regarded as having an adverse effect on the U.S. national interest, they assume a special significance. Legal procedures discussed in the following section are available for these occasions.

Resolution Procedures for National Emergency Disputes Occasionally, strikes occur which have an adverse impact on national economic or defense interests; these are classified as *national emergency strikes*. A number of research studies have shown that the economic effects of such strikes often have less impact than a casual observer may believe. Furthermore, it has been extremely difficult to estimate all the effects of a particular strike, even after it is over. After years of debate, there is still no consensus on what constitutes an emergency strike or on the actual number of emergency strikes that have occurred in our nation's history.[79]

The federal government uses three methods in dealing with national emergency strikes: presidential actions including seizure, procedures under the Railway Labor Act, and procedures under the Labor Management Relations Act.

Presidential intervention and seizure. *Presidential seizures* or attempts at seizure have occurred seventy-one times under four presidents—Lincoln, Wilson, Franklin D. Roosevelt, and Truman—in the interests of maintaining production when actual strikes or threatened strikes caused national emergencies. They have been used mostly during wars (World War I, 3 times; World War II, 51 times; Korean War, 3 times), although declared war has not been an essential requisite. In more recent years, presidents have confined their intervention to exceptional cases, chosen carefully, given the possibility of a legislative or judicial resistance.

A more common presidential approach is the application of pressure and inducements on the parties to resolve the strike without compulsion.[80] Well-known "arm-twisting" maneuvers of then Vice-President

Nixon in the 1959 steel strike and of President Johnson on several occasions were well publicized. Direct involvement of one of President Carter's cabinet members (Secretary of Labor Ray Marshall) in the 1977–1978 coal mining negotiations was viewed by millions on television.

Procedures under the Railway Labor Act. The Railway Labor Act provides a procedure for resolving national emergency work stoppages in the railroads and airlines which includes the following steps:

1. The parties to a labor agreement give a 30-day notice of a desire to change the agreement.
2. The National Mediation Board (NMB) attempts to mediate the dispute.
3. If mediation fails, the NMB recommends voluntary interest arbitration.
4. If arbitration is rejected, the NMB gives notice that it has failed, and for 30 days the wage rates, working rules, working conditions, etc., remain the same.
5. If the dispute threatens to substantially interrupt interstate commerce in any section of the country and deprive it of an essential transportation service, the president is notified and an emergency board is appointed.
6. The emergency board investigates the disputes and reports, with recommendations, within 30 days. During this time, the status quo is maintained.[81]

Since the act's passage in 1926, its emergency provisions have been invoked nearly 190 times, an average rate of four times per year, and work stoppages have occurred at the end of the sixty-day period at a rate of one per year since 1947.[82] Before 1941, the parties never refused the recommendations of the emergency boards. However, since a 1963 congressional decision regarding firemen on diesels, it has become quite common for one of the parties to pursue its interest to the fullest extent by relying more on third-party intervention and ad hoc legislation than on its own negotiations.[83] Congress intervened eight more times, until in 1975 the Nixon administration stated that Congress would no longer be asked to intervene; then the parties started and have continued to reach settlements on their own.[84]

Procedures under the Labor Management Relations Act. The enactment of the Labor Management Relations Act in 1947 authorized the president to invoke its national emergency provisions, Sections 206 to 210, in labor disputes of the national emergency magnitude. These provisions provide a step-by-step procedure to halt the strike for eighty days and provide the parties assistance in resolving their disputes.

Exhibit 7–1 displays the steps in the national emergency procedure of the Labor Management Relations Act. It includes the requirements specified for all parties: the sixty-day notice to the other party that a

Exhibit 7-1 National Emergency Procedure under LMRA

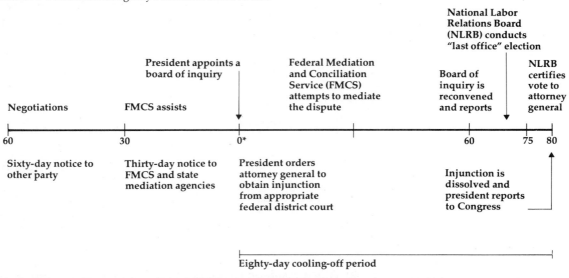

*0 day: Date on which contract expires—may or may not be first day of planned strike; date of injunction if president invokes the LMRA procedures.

Source: Diagram created by Dr. Roy Moore, Chairman,Management Department, University of Southern Mississippi, Hattiesburg, Mississippi.

change in the present agreement is desired and the thirty-day notice to the Federal Mediation and Conciliation Service and state agencies that the negotiations are in process and a settlement has not been reached.

The first step for the president is the appointment of a board of inquiry when the strike or the threat of a strike is believed to be of sufficient severity to imperil the national health or safety. Because of the urgency of the matter, the board will investigate the issues in dispute, gather relevant facts, and make a report to the president in a very short time—usually in about one day.

When the report is received and studied by the president, he *may* direct the attorney general to secure an eighty-day injunction from an appropriate federal district court to prevent or end the strike. Once the injunction is issued, the board is reconvened and after the first sixty days of the injunction period will be asked to report to the president on the employer's last offer and any other relevant factors. During the interim period, the FMCS continues to assist the parties in reaching a settlement. After the board reports the final employer offer, the NLRB will conduct and certify a secret ballot election (between the sixtieth and eightieth days of the injunction period) to determine whether the employees will accept this offer. If they refuse, the attorney general must ask the federal district court to dissolve the injunction at the end of eighty days, and the union may legally strike. The last step involves a full and comprehensive report by the president to Congress, accompanied by any recommendations that he may have.

Some examples. Although the national emergency strike provisions have been invoked, on the average, just over once per year during the last thirty years, national emergency strikes have involved some of the more interesting personalities of the labor movement—for example, John L. Lewis and David McDonald. In the 1948 coal miners' strike, United Mine Workers President John L. Lewis was found guilty of both criminal and civil contempt of court and was fined $20,000; his union was fined $1,400,000 for criminal violations. Neither fine was ever paid.

The 1959 steel strike, lasting 119 days and involving 12 basic steel producers, also received considerable national attention because it affected other industries—auto, construction, and coal. The negotiations took place at very high levels and involved not only top company and union officials but also the president, vice-president, and secretary of labor.[85]

The 1977–1978 coal strike, coinciding with public concern over the energy crisis and high utility bills, probably received more day-to-day media coverage and national attention than any previous strike. Daily broadcasts and interviews with company and union officials educated millions about the processes of collective bargaining during crisis periods and informed many about national emergency strikes and the Taft-Hartley injunction. Interestingly, the Taft-Hartley Act was invoked and a temporary injunction was obtained. However, the district court judge lifted the injunction ten days later when the attorney general failed to prove that a national emergency existed, the strikers refused to return to work, and the federal government refused to enforce the temporary injunction.

During New York's paralyzing public transportation strike and other emergency strikes, President Johnson threatened to send Congress legislative proposals to deal with strikes that cause irreparable damage to the national interest.[86] President Nixon actually did send proposals to give the president a choice of procedures: allowing partial strikes in selected operations, submission of unresolved issues to final offer selection arbitration, and extension of the expiration date of the labor agreement. For political reasons, none of these proposals was ever vigorously pursued by Johnson or Nixon.

Throughout the years, every time there has been a major strike, critics have become vocal about the inefficacy of the procedures for dealing with national emergency strikes. One critic wrote:

When all the people have to suffer because of the willfulness and ineptitude of economic power blocs, the establishment of improved gov-

ernmental machinery for breaking deadlocks is an affirmation—not a denial—of democracy.

In general, the mechanics of bargaining require recasting to get rid of the explosive notion that the world stops on the date the contract runs out. The existence of an expiration deadline ("no contract, no work") has become the single most powerful element in the deification of force as the determinant of equity in industrial relations.[87]

Other critics have been more specific. For example, the strongest criticism has been directed toward the rigidity and predictability of the procedures. When each step is predicted, either party may include the issuance of the injunction as part of its bargaining strategy. Another area of criticism is the secret ballot election on the employer's last offer, which has often solidified the union position rather than facilitating the bargaining process toward settlement. Lastly, because the presidential boards of inquiry are prohibited from proposing settlements, their effectiveness in securing the necessary public support and pressure to move the parties toward settlement is limited.[88]

Cooperation between Union and Management to Reduce Conflicts

Preceding sections of this chapter have emphasized conflict in impasse resolution. However, there is a growing support for greater union-management cooperation during the existing agreement and the negotiations for the new agreement. Although there is still support for the belief that we cannot have free collective bargaining without reliance on the strike, management and labor have learned that many basic common interests outweigh the use of the strike.[89] This opinion is easier stated than implemented. For example, management and union officials in the rubber industry agreed after the 1976 strike to establish a three-member panel of distinguished labor relations experts to recommend better ways to resolve disputes. However, after the first six months, union and management officials had met only once.[90]

Labor-management cooperation, while greater than in the past, is still relatively low. Employers fear cooperative efforts might give unions increased prestige and reduce managerial prerogatives. Other employers question the value of the individual worker's contributions toward cooperative efforts.[91] Some union officials are also reluctant to participate in cooperative efforts if they believe these efforts' sole goal is to increase productivity, which can ultimately reduce the size of the work force. Other union leaders believe that these projects might result in a "happier" work force, thereby adversely affecting membership allegiance.[92]

A major influence in delaying cooperative efforts is the absence of signals upward from the rank-and-file for involvement in these projects. In fact, unions continue to focus their efforts and interests in collective bargaining on the traditional issues—wages, job security, economic supplements, and so on[93]—and overall there has been limited interest in union-management motivational programs via collective bargaining.[94] However, union-management cooperative efforts will be enhanced if:

1. Both parties share a common interest in such areas as improvements in productivity, job security, survival of older, high-cost plants, international competition, and possible loss of sales and jobs.
2. There are highly educated employees who want a chance to participate.
3. Employees show an interest in the quality of work life.[95]

While these conditions may be present in most settings, the fact remains that only 3.6 percent of 1,570 labor agreements studied by the Bureau of Labor Statistics in 1976 included labor-management study committees that examined such sensitive issues as subcontracting, seniority, and wage incentives and made appropriate recommendations to the negotiators. On the other hand, there were more joint committees which periodically met separately from negotiations to improve safety conditions (these existed in 31.2 percent of the 1,570 agreements).[96]

Some successful examples of labor-management cooperation to improve the quality of work life and productivity have been noted (see Chapter 12). Three examples which are more directly related to minimizing negotiation impasses are the Jamestown, New York, community effort, the Relations by Objectives program established by the FMCS, and the Experimental Negotiating Agreement.

The Jamestown Plan

Jamestown, New York, a town of 40,000, once facing a loss of jobs and plants due to poor labor relations climate, was on the road to economic disaster. In 1972, the mayor decided to meet separately with union and management officials, then they all agreed to meet together and listen to a presentation from an official from the FMCS. The outcome was the Labor-Management Committee of Jamestown, composed of fifteen union and fifteen management representatives. Although its beginning was marked by controversy and hostility, four goals were established: (a) improve labor relations, (b) develop manpower, (c) assist industrial development programs, and (d) achieve productivity gains in existing industries.[97] After three years of existence, the turnaround was remarkable: strikes and grievances were reduced; several plants were saved from liquidation, in some cases with the help of the joint cooperative projects; employment and training increased; and because of a favorable labor relations climate, a 1,500-person plant decided to locate in Jamestown. The success of the project inspired officials of nearby Buffalo to establish a joint committee patterned after Jamestown's.[98]

Relations by Objectives

In 1975 the FMCS introduced a new program—Relations by Objectives (RBO). This program was designed for labor-management situations in which the relationships have been extremely poor. For example, the first twenty-one programs involved labor management situations that accounted for 2.5 million workdays lost due to strikes.[99] The goal of RBO has been to help employers and unions minimize conflicts by analyzing particular problem areas, deciding what union and management would like to see in an ideal relationship, and discussing ways in which the parties can implement their goals.

A typical program includes the following:

☐ Labor and management groups are divided into four teams, each with labor and management members and one mediator. Their assignment is to determine what they expect from the RBO program.

☐ After reviewing a film on poor attitudes on the shop floor that adversely affect contract negotiations, each team is asked to: (1) analyze the attitudes of supervision and various union stewards, (2) list the problems shown in the film, and (3) recommend ways to change the labor-management relationship.

☐ The total group is then reassembled to report each team's assignments and discuss the local situation.

☐ The mediators draw up four statements that the groups complete:
1. According to the company, the union should . . .
2. According to the company, the company should . . .
3. According to the union, the company should . . .
4. According to the union, the union should . . .

☐ Objectives are consolidated and then assigned to each team, which is to suggest ways to accomplish the objectives.

☐ Union and management teams meet separately to review proposals and formulate specific steps for achieving objectives.

☐ Both parties then meet to work out an agreement on their action steps, assign responsibility for follow-up, and establish a timetable for events.[100]

Although RBO is still rather new, its effectiveness has been assessed in at least two incidents: United Parcel Service and the Teamsters in New York City and Georgia Pacific Corporation and five unions (Paperworkers, Machinists, Carpenters, Firemen and Oilers, and International Brotherhood of Electrical Workers) in Woodland, Maine.

In New York, the Teamsters were involved in a thirteen-week strike in 1974. Since they had a history of wildcat strikes, RBO was suggested and then accepted. In September 1975, the program began in the same vein that had characterized earlier relationships, with exchange of sharp criticisms. Gradually, both parties got down to business, faced their problems, and mapped out corrective action steps. After one year, no wildcat strikes had occurred, relations had improved, grievances had declined, productivity was up, and a joint alcoholic treatment program had begun.[101]

The Georgia Pacific Corporation paper mill in Woodland, Maine, had been experiencing frequent wildcat strikes and grievances over minor annoyances. In the spring of 1974, 700 members of five different unions struck for three weeks. Strike-related violence became so extreme that Route 1, a major highway, was closed to protect motorists.[102] As a result, the mill management and the unions agreed to work with the FMCS in the RBO program. The meetings went on for three days with such intensity that some sessions lasted up to eighteen hours. Preliminary analysis shows a 70 to 80 percent reduction in grievances, a virtual halt to "harassment type" grievances, and the beginning of a cooperative FMCS training program on problem solving which involves 120 supervisors and stewards. In addition, a wage problem that had defied solution during the strike was resolved in one day just one month after the RBO program.[103]

Experimental Negotiating Agreement (ENA)

An *Experimental Negotiating Agreement* (ENA) was negotiated by the United Steelworkers and ten basic steel companies on March 29, 1973, as an experiment in collective bargaining. It formulated a structure for arbitrating unsolved issues by a specific date prior to expiration of the labor agreement, which eliminated the possibility of a national steel strike in 1974.[104] While the union did agree to abandon the strike weapon on a national scale, it agreed only under certain preconditions:[105]

1. A 3 percent annual wage increase plus continuation of the cost-of-living clause.
2. A bonus of $150 for each employee, available from company savings due to strike avoidance.
3. Allowing local unions to strike over local plant issues and excluding certain fundamental issues, such as union shop and checkoff, from arbitration.

Some union members feared that use of arbitration would bring too much outside influence on the negotiations. I. W. Abel, president of USW at the time of signing, attempted to allay those fears by recalling the union's recent history, which has included third-party intervention in steel disputes:

☐ 1949: Presidential fact-finding board.

☐ 1959: Intervention by Vice-President Nixon and Secretary of Labor Mitchell during the 119-day strike.

☐ 1965: President Johnson inviting both sides to Washington and sending Air Force One to assure their arrival, then putting "both sides under virtual house arrest in the Executive Office Building next to the White House, [making sure that] meals were not too appetizing or nourishing [and engaging] in some arm twisting that only he could do."[106]

☐ 1968: Use of an arbitration panel to determine incentive pay coverage.

In these cases, the Steelworkers had no choice in selecting the third party; under ENA, it would have equal authority. Abel concluded:

There's no doubt that we've done our share of waging war with the basic steel industry over the years. Those of us still around have the scars to prove it. Sometimes the fighting amounted to little skirmishes, but at other times the future of the union and the industry was on the line. But after our shoot-outs and bargaining hassles, down through the years, conditions began to change, and problems of mutual concern began to emerge.[107]

This cooperative spirit may not have extended to the rank-and-file membership; in fact, it may have resulted primarily from political expediency. Abel had started an effort toward a joint no-strike agreement in 1967, but at the time the executive board would not give up the right to strike unless a membership poll approved it. By 1973, Abel was a respected and proven union president who had negotiated three agreements, had been reelected without challenge, and had the support of most national and district officers. Because the union constitution would require his retirement in 1977, the time was politically right for him to act innovatively without having to worry about another union election. Out of the relationship of mutual respect between Abel and the steel industry's chief negotiator, the Experimental Negotiating Agreement (ENA) was born.[108]

One analyst believes that the cooperative relationship in the steel industry is basically a defensive response by the parties to protect their own economic interests and not an emerging attitude of mutual trust. For years the parties have been hurt by strikes and threats of strikes; their actions have led to cyclical stockpiling of steel by consumers and significant penetration of foreign producers into domestic steel markets. Uncertain of U.S. production and high-cost inventories, customers have sought foreign sources, causing loss of steelworkers' jobs. In addition, union and company officials have continually been pressured by the federal government to resolve their differences without strikes. While there appears to be economic justification for ENA, an assessment of this program on union-management attitudes must be made after more related experiences have taken place.

Summary

This chapter focused on the efforts of labor unions, management, and third parties to resolve negotiation impasses. A discussion of contract ratification and membership rejection was highlighted. Earlier research has led to the conclusion that contract rejection is relatively high; however, more recent research finds a lower rate when contract rejection is redefined as rejection of the bargaining committee's recommended labor agreement.

Third-party procedures to assist the parties in resolving negotiation impasses were presented. These range from mediation—where the third party attempts to facilitate resolution by keeping the parties bargaining, acting as a go-between, and offering alternatives—to arbitration, a quasi-judicial procedure in which the bargaining positions are presented to the arbitrator, who makes a final and binding decision. Within this range are the med-arb procedure (which attempts mediation first and then arbitration if mediation fails) and fact-finding (in which the parties present their positions to the fact-finder, other facts are collected, and a report which includes a recommended resolution of the impasse is written and presented).

Not all bargaining issues are resolved through negotiations; strikes, boycotts, pickets, and related activities do occur. However, both parties have to seriously consider their positions and the consequences of their actions before taking any actions. Each hurts the costs, profits, and production of the companies and the income and public image of the union. While both parties may prepare for employee job actions, a high percentage of strikes, boycotts, and pickets have taken their toll in terms of costs to both parties.

The right to concerted actions by employees is an intricate part of the labor relations process and is guaranteed by law. On the other hand, possession of a right to strike does not mean that it should be exercised frequently. The data show that strikes occur very infrequently, but those that do occur can be damaging economically and are well publicized by the media.

Most strikes and related activities involve primary employers, but often secondary employers (not directly involved in the employer-employee relationship) are affected. A complex body of law and judicial decisions covers such activities as consumer boycotts and picketing; common situs and reserved gate picketing; employer-ally relationships; and hot-cargo agreements.

Strikes and related activities that have an adverse effect on the national interest may be declared national emergency strikes. In this regard, resolution procedures are available in the Railway Labor Act and the Labor Management Relations Act to facilitate their resolutions. While such impasses occur infrequently, they are significant when they do occur.

Efforts by unions and management to organize and develop cooperative efforts to reduce the possibility of conflicts are still a relatively infrequent occurrence. However, several unions and companies have spent much time and money and put forth much effort to minimize conflicts.

1. What are the chief reasons for rejection of tentative agreements by union members?
2. What problems may be caused as a result of contract rejection?
3. Define the major types of third-party interventions. How do they differ, and how do they appear similar?
4. What specific qualities should a mediator possess? Why do these qualities facilitate impasse resolution?
5. Why is interest arbitration used so infrequently in the private sector?
6. Think of a strike that has occurred recently and itemize the costs to the employer as well as to the employees on strike.
7. What are your political and philosophical views of public aid to strikers?
8. Discuss the following statement: "Strikes are an intricate and essential element of the collective bargaining process."
9. Define and discuss the various types of secondary activities of unions that may occur during impasses.
10. Explain the alternatives which could be made available for resolving national emergency strikes.
11. List the issues in which both management and the union can cooperate to their mutual advantage. Do you know of other cooperative efforts by union and management to reduce conflict between them? List the strong and weak points of these efforts.

References

[1] Clyde W. Summers, "Ratification of Agreements," in J. T. Dunlop and N. W. Chamberlain, eds., *Frontiers of Collective Bargaining* (New York: Harper & Row, 1967), pp. 82–83.

[2] Ibid., p. 83.

[3] Federal Mediation and Conciliation Service, *Thirtieth Annual Report* (Washington, D.C.: Government Printing Office, 1977), p. 26. The rejection rate ranged from 9.6 percent in 1973 to 12.4 percent in 1974. During this period, 9,061 of 82,253 cases (or 11.0 percent) closed by the FMCS were rejected by the membership in ratification elections.

[4] William E. Simkin, "Refusal to Ratify Contracts," *Industrial and Labor Relations Review* 21 (July 1968), pp. 528–529.

[5] Charles Odewahn and Joseph Krislov, "Contract Rejections: Testing the Explanatory Hypothesis," *Industrial Relations* 12 (October 1973), pp. 289–296.

[6] D. R. Burke and Lester Rubin, "Is Contract Rejection a Major Collective Bargaining Problem?" *Industrial and Labor Relations Review* 26 (January 1973), pp. 832–833.

[7] Summers, "Ratification of Agreements," pp. 88–98.

[8] William E. Simkin, *Mediation and the Dynamics of Collective Bargaining* (Washington, D.C.: Bureau of National Affairs, 1971), pp. 25–28.

[9] Federal Mediation and Conciliation Service, *Thirtieth Annual Report*, p. 21.

[10] Carl Stevens, "Mediation and the Role of the Neutral," in Dunlop and Chamberlain, *Frontiers of Collective Bargaining*, p. 271.

[11] Simkin, *Mediation*, p. 53.

[12] The rest of this section on causal factors of successful mediation is from Stevens, "Mediation and the Role of the Neutral," pp. 280–284.

[13] Jack Stieber, "Voluntary Arbitration of Contract Terms," in G. G. Somers and B. D. Dennis, eds., *Arbitration and the Expanding Role of Neutrals* (Washington, D.C.: Bureau of National Affairs, 1970), pp. 71–76. Also see Irving Bernstein, *Arbitration of Wages* (Los Angeles: University of California Press, 1954), p. 4; and R. U. Miller, "Arbitration of New Contract Wage Disputes: Some Recent Trends," *Industrial and Labor Relations Review* 20 (January 1967), pp. 250–264.

[14] Stieber, "Voluntary Arbitration," pp. 77–80.

[15]Adapted from sources which will remain unidentified.

[16]Stieber, "Voluntary Arbitration," pp. 92–94.

[17]Sam Kagel, "Combining Mediation and Arbitration," *Monthly Labor Review* 96 (September 1973), pp. 62–63.

[18]David E. Fuller, "The Impetus to Contract Arbitration in the Private Area," *Twenty-fourth Annual NYU Conference on Labor* (New York: Matthew Bender, 1972), pp. 95–98.

[19]Peter Feuille and James B. Dworkin, "Final Offer Arbitration and Intertemporal Compromise, or It's My Turn to Win," in B. D. Dennis, ed., *Proceedings of the Thirty-first Annual Meeting: Industrial Relations Research Association* (Madison, Wis.: Industrial Relations Research Association, 1979), pp. 87–95.

[20]Charles Rehmus, "Inducement of Final-Offer Arbitration," *Labor Relations Yearbook, 1974* (Washington, D.C.: Bureau of National Affairs, 1975), pp. 181–182.

[21]Peter Seitz, "Footnotes to Baseball Salary Arbitration," *Arbitration Journal* 29 (June 1974), pp. 102–103.

[22]Simkin, *Mediation*, pp. 237–242.

[23]U.S. Department of Labor, Bureau of Labor Statistics, *Analysis of Work Stoppages, 1975* (Washington, D.C.: Government Printing Office, 1977), p. 78.

[24]Albert Rees, *The Economics of Trade Unions* (Chicago: University of Chicago Press, 1962), pp. 34–37.

[25]Ibid., pp. 277–279.

[26]Sheldon M. Kline, "Strike Benefits of National Unions," *Monthly Labor Review* 98 (March 1975), p. 17.

[27]Ibid., pp. 21–22.

[28]Ibid., p. 22.

[29]The Supreme Court upheld New York's law authorizing the payment of unemployment compensation after eight weeks. *New York Telephone Co. et al. v. New York State Department of Labor et al.*, Supreme Court of the United States, No. 77–961, Slip opinion, March 21, 1979.

[30]Armand J. Thiebolt and Ronald M. Cowin, *Welfare and Strikes: The Use of Public Funds to Support Strikers* (Philadelphia: Industrial Research Unit, University of Pennsylvania, 1972), p. 3.

[31] G. C. Pati and L. G. Hill, "Economic Strikes, Public Aid, and Industrial Relations," *Labor Law Journal* 23 (January 1972), p. 32.

[32]Marc E. Thomas, "Strikers' Eligibility for Public Assistance: The Standard Based on Need," *Journal of Urban Law* 52 (August 1974), pp. 115–154.

[33]Pati and Hill, "Economic Strikes," p. 37.

[34] Thiebolt and Cowin, *Welfare and Strikes,* pp. 217–219.

[35]John S. Hirsch, Jr., "Strike Insurance and Collective Bargaining," *Industrial and Labor Relations Review* 22 (April 1969), p. 399.

[36]Ibid., p. 400.

[37]Marvin J. Levine and L. W. Helly, "The Airlines Mutual Aid Pact: A Deterrent to Collective Bargaining," *Labor Law Journal* 28 (January 1977), pp. 44–55.

[38]Ibid.

[39]S. H. Unterberger and E. C. Koziara, "Airline Strike Insurance: A Study in Escalation," *Industrial and Labor Relations Review* 29 (October 1975), p. 45.

[40]Hirsch, "Strike Insurance and Collective Bargaining," pp. 411–413; and Herbert R. Northrup, "Airline Strike Insurance: A Study in Escalation: Comment," *Industrial and Labor Relations Review* 30 (April 1977), p. 372.

[41]The act further specified requirements for acceptable MAPs:
1. No air carrier may receive payment which exceeds 60 percent of its operating expenses during the impasse.
2. Payments may not be payable for more than eight weeks during any strikes, and payments may not be made for losses incurred during the first thirty days of any labor strike.
3. Any party to a MAP will agree to submit the issues causing the strike to binding arbitration under the Railway Labor Act if striking employees request such binding arbitration.

[42]R. E. Walton and R. B. McKersie, *A Behavioral Theory of Labor Negotiations* (New York: McGraw-Hill, 1965), pp. 31–32.

[43]William Serrin, *The Company and the Union* (New York: Knopf, 1973), p. 4.

[44]Walton and McKersie, *Behavioral Theory*, pp. 31–32.

[45]George Getschow, "Strike Woes Pile Up for Leader of Local That Started It All," *Wall Street Journal*, August 8, 1977, pp. 1, 17.

[46]John R. Emshwiller, "Strike Is Traumatic for a Quiet Village in Michigan Woods," *Wall Street Journal*, July 30, 1977, pp. 1, 24.

[47]Bernard Karsh, *Diary of a Strike* (Urbana: University of Illinois Press, 1958), pp. 70–73.

[48]L. L. Helmer, "Facing Up to a Strike," in E. Marting, ed., *Understanding Collective Bargaining* (New York: American Management Association, 1958), p. 323.

[49]American Society for Personnel Administration, *Strike Preparation Manual* (Berea, Ohio: American Society for Personnel Administration, 1974). Also see L. C. Scott, "Running a Struck Plant: Some Do's and Don't's," *SAM Advanced Management Journal* 38 (October 1973), pp. 58–62; and John G. Hutchinson, *Management under Strike Conditions* (New York: Holt, Rinehart and Winston, 1966).

[50]E. W. Bakke, "Are Strikes War?" in E. W. Bakke, C. Kerr, and C. Arrod, eds., *Unions, Management, and the Public* (New York: Harcourt, Brace & World, 1967), p. 252.

[51]Henry Hazlitt, untitled, in Harold Hart, ed., *The Strike: For and Against* (New York: Hart Publishing, 1971), p. 64.

[52]Eugene McCarthy, untitled, in Hart, *The Strike*, p. 12.

[53]Theodore W. Kheel, "Is the Strike Outmoded?" *Monthly Labor Review* 96 (September 1973), pp. 35–37.

[54]For a discussion of strike costs see James Stern, "The Declining Utility of a Strike," *Industrial and Labor Relations Review* 18 (October 1964), pp. 60–72.

[55]Lloyd G. Reynolds, *Labor Economics and Labor Relations* (Englewood Cliffs, N.J.: Prentice-Hall, 1970), pp. 440–442.

[56]Kheel, "Is the Strike Outmoded?" pp. 35–37.

[57]*American Shipbuilding Co. v. NLRB*, 380 U.S. 300 (1965).

[58]Ibid.

[59]Walter E. Oberer and Kurt L. Hanslowe, *Labor Law* (St. Paul, Minn.: West Publishing, 1972), pp. 482–483. See *Buffalo Linen Supply Company*, 353 U.S. 85 (1956); and *Brown Food Store et al.*, 380 U.S. 278 (1965).

[60]K. C. Miller and W. H. Form, *Industrial Sociology*, 2d. ed. (New York: Harper & Row, 1964), pp. 385–388.

[61]Alvin W. Goldner, *Wildcat Strikes* (Yellow Springs, Ohio: Antioch Press, 1954), p. 95.

[62]Morrison Handsaker and Marjorie Handsaker, "Remedies and Penalties for Wildcat Strikes: How Arbitrators and Federal Courts Have Ruled," *Catholic University Law Review* 22 (Winter 1973), pp. 279–323. Summarized in *Industrial Relations Law Digest* 16 (July 1973), pp. 49–68.

[63]Ralph M. Dereshinsky, *The NLRB and Secondary Boycotts* (Philadelphia: Industrial Research Unit, University of Pennsylvania Press, 1972), p. 75.

[64]*Tree Fruits*, 377 U.S. 58 (1964).

[65]Allan Sloan, "Secondary Boycotts—Consumer Picketing," in Walter B. Connolly, Jr., ed., *Strikes, Stoppages, and Boycotts: 1978* (New York: Practising Law Institute, 1978), pp. 190–193.

[66]Ibid., pp. 194–196.

[67]National Labor Relations Board, *Forty-second Annual Report* (Washington, D.C.: Government Printing Office, 1977), p. 132.

[68]Dereshinsky, *NLRB and Secondary Boycotts*, p. 2.

[69]*NLRB v. Denver Building Trades Council*, 341 U.S. 675 (1951).

[70]Stephen J. Cabot and Robert J. Simmons, "The Future of Common Situs Picketing," *Labor Law Journal* 27 (December 1976), p. 775. A law allowing *common situs* picketing was passed by Congress but vetoed by President Ford. Another attempt was made in 1977 when President Carter said he would sign the bill; however, the House of Representatives refused to pass the law.

[71]Ibid.

[72]Dereshinsky, *NLRB and Secondary Boycotts*, pp. 50–59.

[73]Ibid.

[74]Robert J. Deeny, "Secondary Boycotts," in Connolly, *Strikes, Stoppages, and Boycotts, 1978*, p. 128.

[75]Ibid., pp. 134–135.

[76]Ibid.

[77]Dereshinsky, *NLRB and Secondary Boycotts*, pp. 96–97.

[78]Edward B. Robin, "Secondary Boycotts in the Construction Industry," in B. T. King and D. W. Savelson, eds., *Construction Industry Labor Relations, 1977* (New York: Practising Law Institute, 1977), pp. 101–103. This provision has been amended by a subsequent Supreme Court decision: *Connell Construction Co. v. Plumbers and Steamfitters Local Union No. 100*, 421 U.S. 616 (1975).

[79]Donald E. Cullen, *National Emergency Strikes* (Ithaca, N.Y.: NYSSILR, Cornell University, 1968), pp. 45–48.

[80]John L. Blackman, Jr., *Presidential Seizure in Labor Disputes* (Cambridge, Mass.: Harvard University Press, 1967), pp. 1–21.

[81]Charles J. Morris, "The Role of Interest Arbitration in a Collective Bargaining System," *Industrial Relations Law Journal* 1 (Fall 1976), pp. 515–516.

[82]U.S., Congress, House, House Document No. 91–266, *Congressional Record* 116, no. 30, 91st Cong., 2d. sess., March 2, 1970, p. H1385.

[83]Morris, "Role of Interest Arbitration," p. 516.

[84]Ibid., pp. 517–518.

[85]U.S. Department of Labor, Bureau of Labor Statistics, *National Emergency Disputes* (Washington, D.C.: Government Printing Office, 1969), pp. 1–31.

[86]A. H. Raskin, "Collision Course on the Labor Front," *Saturday Review*, February 25, 1967, p. 32.

[87]Ibid., pp. 32–35.

[88]Oberer and Hanslowe, *Labor Law*, pp. 901–902.

[89]David L. Cole, "The Search for Industrial Peace," *Monthly Labor Review* 96 (September 1973), p. 37.

[90]"No Give on Either Side in Rubber Talks," *Business Week*, March 26, 1977, p. 43.

[91]Sumner H. Slichter, James J. Healy, and E. Robert Livernash, *The Impact of Collective Bargaining on Management* (Washington, D.C.: Brookings Institution, 1960), p. 842.

[92]Ted Mills, "Human Resources: Why the Concern?" *Harvard Business Review* 53 (March–April 1975), pp. 127–129.

[93]Raymond Katzell et al., *Work Productivity and Job Satisfaction* (Chicago: Psychological Corporation, 1976), p. 95. Also see E. E. Lawler and J. A. Drexler, Jr., "Dynamics of Establishing Cooperative Quality-of-Work-Life Projects," *Monthly Labor Review* 101 (March 1978), pp. 25–27.

[94]A. A. Blum, M. L. Moore, and B. P. Fairly, "The Effect of Motivational Programs on Collective Bargaining," *Personnel Journal* 52 (July 1973), pp. 633–641.

[95]Edgar Weinberg, "Labor-Management Cooperation: A Report on Recent Initiatives," *Monthly Labor Review* 99 (April 1976), pp. 13–14.

[96]U.S. Department of Labor, Bureau of Labor Statistics, *Characteristics of Major Collective Bargaining Agreements, July 1, 1976*, Bulletin 2013 (Washington, D.C.: Government Printing Office, 1977), p. 21.

[97]National Commission on Productivity and Work Quality, *Recent Initiatives in Labor-Management Cooperation* (Washington, D.C.: Government Printing Office, 1976), pp. 17–18.

[98]Weinberg, "Labor-Management Cooperation," p. 15. Also see Brian Moore, National Commission on Productivity and Work Quality, *A Plant-Wide Productivity Plan in Action: Three Years of Experience with the Scanlon Plan* (Washington, D.C.: Government Printing Office, 1975), p. 20.

[99]Federal Mediation and Conciliation Service, *Twenty-ninth Annual Report*, pp. 42–43.

[100]George A. Weimer, "Defuse the Labor Bomb before It Explodes," *Iron Age*, March 7, 1977.

[101]Federal Mediation and Conciliation Service, *Twenty-ninth Annual Report*, pp. 43–44.

[102]"U.S. Mediators Try a New Role," *Business Week*, April 21, 1975, p. 108.

[103]National Commission on Productivity and Work Quality, *Recent Initiatives*, pp. 29–30.

[104]James A. Craft, "The ENA, Consent Decrees, and Cooperation in Steel Labor Relations: A Critical Appraisal," *Labor Law Journal* 27 (October 1976), p. 633.

[105]BNA Editorial Staff, *Labor Relations Yearbook: 1973* (Washington, D.C.: Bureau of National Affairs, 1973), p. 46.

[106]I. W. Abel, "Steel: Experiment in Bargaining," *American Federationist* 80 (July 1973), p. 5.

[107]Ibid., p. 2.

[108]Craft, "ENA," pp. 633–637.

Chapter 8

Contract Administration

"The right to present and have grievances redressed is fundamental in our society. It satisfies a vital need."

David L. Cole, The Quest for Industrial Peace, 1963.

The negotiation of the labor agreement is usually the most publicized and dramatic aspect of labor relations. Strike deadlines, negotiators in shirt sleeves working around the clock to avert a possible strike, and the economic settlement of the labor agreement receive attention from the news media. The day-to-day administration of the labor agreement, on the other hand, receives little if any recognition beyond that given by the involved parties. Yet contract administration is an important part of collective bargaining. Chapter 3 indicates that Section 8 (d) of the National Labor Relations Act defines collective bargaining in such a way that good faith bargaining extends from negotiating the agreement to resolving questions arising from the agreement (contract administration).

Contract administration extends beyond the negotiated labor agreement because grievance settlements over a period of time will establish interpretative principles or common laws that supplement or even modify the terms of the negotiated labor agreement. Administration of the negotiated contract gives dynamic meaning to its rather skeletal terms.

This chapter first defines grievances broadly, indicating the complexities which this definition encompasses, and discusses reasons employees file grievances. The grievance procedure is also examined in terms of its typical steps, the variety of relationships occurring among the grievance participants, and theoretical as well as practical concerns involved in contract administration. Finally, several reasons are given to show the importance of grievances, a fact further illustrated in Chapter 9.

Grievances: Definition and Sources

The core of contract administration consists of *employee grievances,* which can be defined as any employee's concern over a perceived violation of the labor agreement which is submitted to the grievance procedure for eventual resolution. Thus a grievance is distinguished from an employee's concern or complaint which is expressed, independent of labor agreement provisions, during the course of a typical work day.

Most grievances are reduced to writing, a factor which has several advantages:

1. Both union and management representatives need a written record of their daily problem resolutions. This record generates precedents which can guide future actions while also saving time in deciding subsequent related grievances.

2. Written grievances tend to reduce emotionalism present in many employee concerns. As the reader can recall from experience, an immediate verbal confrontation with someone by whom one feels he or she has been wronged allows the individual to blow off steam. However, the possible name-calling and obscenities at best blur real issues and facts and at worst irreparably harm the relationship between the parties. Consequently, writing the grievance can be viewed as necessary for its rational discussion.

3. Having the concern written out allows management representatives to focus on the employee's original grievance. As will be discussed further in the chapter, a grievance can proceed through several steps which involve many more individuals than the aggrieved employee. Union officials may alter an employee's initial concern into a broader philosophical issue. (For example, a complaint over the company's unilateral selection of candy bars for the vending machine could conceivably be magnified in subsequent steps to protest the company's arbitrary and capricious actions in other working conditions.) Management always has the option of returning to the concern(s) expressed in the original grievance.

4. Written grievances can benefit management in cases where the employee is apprehensive about signing a written protest. Even though most labor agreements permit a union officer to file a grievance on behalf of the grievant, requiring grievances to be written probably reduces the total number that management representatives must administer.

Our definition of a grievance is extremely broad and hinges on the employee's perception that he or she has a grievance. Assume, for example, that Employee A protests Employee B's "immoral" behavior. This protest could take the form of an oral complaint without reference to the grievance procedure, or the same employee could insist the complaint represents a violation of the terms of the labor agreement. The supervisor can attempt to convince the employee that the complaint is unrelated to the terms of the labor agreement, indicating that there is no provision pertaining to the exact behavior of any particular employee, especially off the job.

Yet what happens if the employee insists that the concern is a grievance and should be processed as such? Further, the employee cites a vague and probably unrelated contractual provision in the argument such as an article stressing the "company's obligation to maintain a work environment in as safe a condition as possible." After unsuccessfully discussing the issue with Employee A, the supervisor has two options: (a) to refuse to accept the employee's grievance or (b) to accept the employee's grievance and deny it in the written grievance answer on the basis that there is no contractual violation. Not wishing to risk a time-consuming unfair labor practice charge, the supervisor will probably take the second alternative.

The broad definition of a grievance realizes, then, that there is a difference between *accepting* an employee's grievance and *deciding the merits* of an employee's grievance. The broader definition safeguards against unfair labor practice charges and at the same time preserves management's right to deny the grievance in its written answer.

Reasons for Employee Grievances

In order to better understand the reasons behind employee grievances, the following hypothetical example is given. A first-line supervisor administers a labor agreement which has the following provisions pertaining to management's rights and the scheduling of work to be performed on a holiday:

Article III: Management Rights

Section 1. The company's right to hire, fire, and direct the working force, transfer or promote is unqualified as long as this right is not used in any conflict with any provision of this contract.

Article IX: Holiday Scheduling

Section 1. When less than a normal crew is required to work on a holiday, the following procedure will apply:

(a) The senior employee working in the classification desired will be given the opportunity to work.

(b) Employees assigned holiday work will be paid a minimum of eight hours at time and one-half the contract rate of pay.

(c) If an employee works out of classification on the holiday, the senior employee in the appropriate classification will also be paid a minimum of eight hours at time and one-half his or her contract rate of pay.

With these provisions in mind, consider the following chain of events. A crane operator is needed to work the July 4 holiday. The senior employee in this classification starts work on this shift; however, after he has worked one-half hour, the crane breaks down and can no longer be operated. Further, management believes the maintenance department will be able to repair the crane within three hours. It should be noted that all job classifications typically perform some minor housekeeping and cleanup work, such as dusting and picking up debris around the work station; however, there is also a janitor's classification in the labor agreement.

The first-line supervisor has three options. First, the employee can be sent home. However, according to Section 1 (b) of the labor agreement, management will have to pay that employee eight hours at one and one-half times the employee's hourly pay rate and the same amount to another employee who is called out to work once the crane is repaired. Consequently, option one is not attractive to management.

Option two would have the employee remain at work and in effect do nothing until the crane is repaired. Since management is already obligated to pay the employee for the entire shift, it does not cost any additional money to have the employee sit in the work shed until crane operations can be renewed. This, however, is not a pleasant option for the first-line supervisor, particularly if higher level management officials and other hourly employees see this individual being paid for not performing work.

Thus, option three, having the crane operator perform minor house-keeping chores until the crane is repaired, appears most beneficial to management. Yet there is a good possibility that this action would result in a grievance from the senior employee in the janitorial classification, asking payment for eight hours at time and a half since Section 1 (c) would apparently have been violated. The aggrieved employee could file this grievance for one or more of the following reasons.

1. *To protest a contractual violation.* When labor and management officials negotiate a labor agreement, they are mainly concerned with agreement over the major issues. The negotiators are not concerned with determining the precise meaning of every word in the labor agreement, particularly if there have been few or no previous problems arising from the contract language. Similarly, these officials cannot possibly anticipate all of the unique situations which could potentially distort or add to the negotiated terms of the labor agreement. Consequently, union and management negotiators often gloss over the "unimportant" provisions, leaving potential interpretational problems to those who must live with and administer the labor agreement on a daily basis.

In the crane operator example, local union officials could contend that the crane operator did "work out of classification"—a clear violation of Section 1 (c). Management, on the other hand, could contend that the needed holiday work was within the scope of a crane operator's job. Moreover, it had no intention of paying an employee an amount equal to twelve hours contract rate of pay simply to dust or straighten up the workplace. Another management contention could be that minor housekeeping chores are performed by all employees; therefore, the crane operator did not work out of classification on the day in question. Hence, Article III, Management Rights, would prevail in this situation. Thus, the interpretational differences over the terms of the labor agreement are magnified when the inevitable contractual gaps or areas in which the contract is silent surface (here, on appropriate procedures to follow when the equipment is temporarily out of order on holidays).

2. *To draw attention to a problem in the plant.* Some grievances do not protest violation of the labor agreement; instead, they stress that management has obligations beyond the scope of the labor agreement. Most grievances over alleged safety hazards fall into this category, as few labor agreements specify management's obligation in this area. The employee might realize that there is no contractual violation but still file the grievance to communicate concern to management over a safety issue. In our example, the grievance over holiday scheduling might have been filed, not over receiving payment for the senior janitor in the classification, but in order to give union officers the forum in which to stress the inadequate number of maintenance employees for equipment repair.

Unions quite often draw attention to a problem in the hopes of setting the stage for future labor agreement negotiations. As stated earlier in the chapter, the line distinguishing contract administration and contract negotiation is often thin. A common union tactic is to file several grievances over a particular issue to buttress and document its demands during negotiation of the subsequent labor agreement.

For example, labor unions adhering to the job protection philosophy discussed in Chapter 1 do not want supervisory personnel performing their members' work since these activities could reduce overtime opportunities or even result in employees being laid off. In the course of a work day, supervisors may perform several chores which could be classified as bargaining unit work. A union wishing to obtain a contractual restriction against supervisors performing bargaining unit work might encourage employees to file a grievance whenever the foreman engages in this practice no matter how minor that physical activity may be (for example, changing a light bulb). Armed with several grievances, in formal contract negotiations the union can dramatize its concerns that: (a) supervisors performing bargaining unit work is a widespread problem and (b) a contractual provision restricting foremen from performing bargaining unit work would save the company time and money by eliminating related grievances.

3. *To get something for nothing.* Some managers believe that a few employees file grievances to receive pay related to their skill in formulating and writing grievances instead of their work efforts. The janitor in our

crane operator example might not have been inclined to file a grievance at the time the work was denied. Indeed, he or she may have had previously scheduled holiday plans and refused to work if management had made the initial offer. However, assuming the janitor's classification paid $4 an hour, the janitor might have felt that time and one-half for eight hours ($48) worth the effort to file a grievance. This payment could be particularly attractive to an individual who did not have to alter holiday plans to obtain it.

Employees filing grievances for this reason find opportunities in the area of overtime administration. A common labor agreement provision requires management to equalize overtime opportunity among qualified bargaining unit employees desiring overtime. Additionally, management is often contractually required to pay the employee for the overtime worked by another employee if an administrative error was made. For example, assume the following list represents the names of employees in the electrician's classification who signed the daily overtime list, thereby volunteering to work overtime if the assignment occurs after the completion of their normal work shift.

Name of Employee	Number of Overtime Hours Worked and/or Refused since January 1
A. Jones	89 hours
T. Grant	76 hours
B. Simms	43 hours

The figure to the right of the employee's name represents the number of overtime hours worked by the employee to date and also includes any overtime assignments refused by the employee—if Jones refuses to work an eight-hour overtime assignment eventually worked by Grant, both employees are charged the eight hours for administrative purposes. If an overtime assignment for electricians is needed on the day in question, the supervisor checks the overtime list and determines that Simms is lowest in overtime hours. Consequently, the supervisor would give Simms the first opportunity to accept or refuse the overtime assignment.

Suppose, however, that Simms desires the overtime payment without actually having to work the overtime assignment. There are several rather dubious strategies Simms could use in this situation. Perhaps the best alternative would be to actively avoid (in some cases hide from) the supervisor. Confronted with an overtime emergency, the supervisor has to offer the assignment to Grant, the employee next lowest in overtime. The next day, Simms could file a grievance on the "administrative error" and be paid the equivalent of Grant's overtime assignment for no corresponding work effort. Needless to say, this reason for filing a grievance draws management's ire, particularly since some employees appear to make a contest out of acquiring grievance "freebies," or payment for time not worked.

4. *To make the grievant and union feel important.* In nonunion settings, the authority of managerial policies and actions often goes unchallenged. However, the grievance procedure permits, and in some cases encourages, an employee to protest an alleged wrong committed by management officials. Some employees bolster their perceived status in the organization by calling their organizational superiors on the carpet for an explanation of their actions. This motivation for filing a grievance is particularly likely in the case of a supervisor who flaunts authority unnecessarily, thereby creating tensions and grievances which protest the supervisor's personality as well as actions.

Similarly, some union officials wish to emphasize their importance and self-interests through grievance involvement. Those falling into this category use grievances and contract administration problems to advance to higher political office in the union or to bring themselves to management's attention for possible promotion in the management organization.

Grievances in these cases provide a forum where the union steward can demonstrate his or her verbal and intellectual capabilities to other management and union officials. Other union officials might wish to strengthen the union as an institution through the grievance procedure. Here, the union's (not the union official's) importance is stressed; the union is safeguarding its members from management's arbitrary and capricious actions. One union steward reflecting this reason has commented:

Every so often you'd hear a couple of guys really lambasting the foreman in the washroom—that's where you can really hear the gripes. But when I'd write up the grievance and take it to the fellows, they'd say it was too small. I'd say "the hell with you" and push it anyway.

Soon the company would be coming to me and saying, "Those guys don't have a grievance. They're perfectly satisfied." And I'd say, "The hell they don't. If you don't want to recognize it, I'll take it to the next step." I didn't care if the guys supported me, I went through with it.[1]

There are other, miscellaneous reasons employees file grievances. Motives are as varied and complex as the employees' personalities and life experiences.[2] For example, an argument with the employee's family, friends, or work associates might provoke a grievance. Other motives, such as poor employee/job match or a generally poor managerial climate, are perhaps more easily rectified by subsequent managerial action. Uncovering the motive behind a grievance may be helpful to management. However, it must be stressed that management must process the grievance even if it feels the employee's motives are illegitimate or improper.

The Grievance Procedure

Characteristics of the Grievance Procedure

The process for resolving employee grievances is specified in approximately 98 percent of existing labor agreements.[3] However, the procedures themselves are as varied as the labor agreements found in U.S. industry today. Some consist of only one step, whereas others contain as many as nine. While there is no one grievance procedure applicable to all labor-management relationships in the United States, the four-step procedure illustrated in Exhibit 8–1 and discussed below is fairly representative.

Exhibit 8–1   Example of a Typical Grievance Procedure

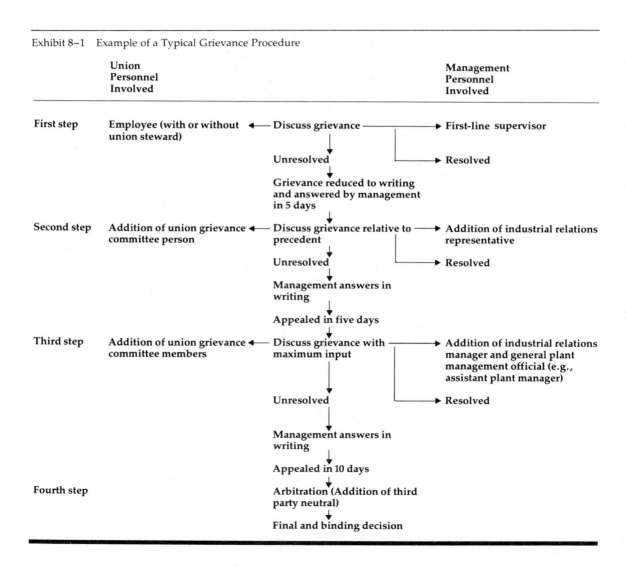

First step. This stage actually consists of two phases. First, the employee (with or without the union steward) discusses the concern with his or her first-line supervisor. If agreement is not reached, then a written grievance is filed by the grievant or the union steward acting on the grievant's behalf. The supervisor then answers the employee's grievance in writing.

The purpose of the discussion is to resolve the grievance as early and as informally as possible. However, in some cases, the oral discussion is *pro forma*—the employee initiates this step with a written grievance on the assumption that no amount of discussion will change his or her mind. As is true with the next two steps of the grievance procedure, if the employee accepts management's answer to the written grievance, then the grievance is considered resolved and subsequent steps are unnecessary.

Second step. In addition to the individuals in the first-step grievance meeting, the union grievance committeeperson and management's industrial relations representative are brought in to discuss the foreman's first-step grievance answer. Both of these individuals are aware of administrative precedent throughout the entire shop; their main role is to determine whether the grievance should be resolved at this stage on the basis of this precedent.

For example, say Employee A files a grievance protesting management's unilateral action in reducing wash-up time in her work area. The grievance committeeperson might be aware, however, that (a) the contract does not have a provision pertaining to wash-up time and (b) employees in other departments do not receive any time before the end of the shift to clean their hands. Therefore, he or she would probably encourage the grievant to accept the reduction in wash-up time rather than risk losing the privilege entirely in subsequent steps of the grievance procedure.

On another issue—for example, an employee working out of his or her normal work classification and demanding an upgrade in pay for the time worked—the industrial relations representative might reverse the foreman's first-step answer to avoid sending the grievance to the third step, where it might affect employees with similar work experiences in other departments. The second-step written grievance answer is furnished by the industrial relations representative, and any precedent resulting from this answer usually applies only to the particular work department instead of the entire facility.

Third step. The third-step meeting involves the same individuals as the second step but in addition includes the industrial relations manager and another management official (such as a general foreman, superintendent, or assistant plant manager) and members of the union's grievance committee (see Chapter 5). These individuals are added because the grievance answer at this level could affect the entire industrial operation, and both management and union representatives wish to obtain as much input as possible before making the decision.

These additional individuals serve other purposes, particularly from the union's standpoint. First, the third-step meeting can be used as a training or educational device for relatively new union officers. Since many labor agreements require paid time off for grievance meetings, a new union official can learn the often complex issues and strategies involved in grievance resolution at the company's expense. The union grievance committee can also serve tactical purposes and political functions because the sheer number of individuals on the committee can impress upon the grievant that the union is forcefully representing his or her interests.

Also, the committee can serve as a buck-passing device for the union steward or committeeperson who informs the grievant that he or she did all that was possible to win the grievance but was turned down by other members on the committee. Buck passing is not restricted to union personnel, since supervisors can claim to their managerial counterparts that they were not wrong, merely "sold out" by higher level management officials in subsequent steps of the procedure.

This step can also function as a therapeutic device for the grievant, who simply wishes to express concern to many levels of management officials. Perhaps the most important function of the third-step meeting is the inclusion of additional union and management officials who are not personally involved in the grievance outcome and can assess its merits with relative objectivity. The third-step grievance answer is usually written by the industrial relations manager because the decision probably will have plantwide implications and applications.

Fourth step—arbitration. The final step in the procedure, particularly in the private sector, involves the same individuals as step three and adds a selected third party neutral who hears the grievance and makes a final decision resolving the issue. The arbitration process of "rights" disputes over existing terms of the contract is of such significance and complexity that it warrants a more thorough discussion in a separate chapter (see Chapter 9); however, it should be mentioned that this process terminates the typical grievance procedure.

Even though they may vary in terms of steps, time limits for the processing of each step, and participants, grievance procedures represent a progression of the initial grievance to higher level management and union officials for consideration. Such procedures written in labor agreements have the drawback of being formal instead of tailored to an individual's personality and concerns. Yet this formality insures that any bargaining unit employee can have his or her grievance heard. While many procedures may appear inflexible, they merely serve as the arena for dynamic social relationships and interactions among management and union officials.

Grievance Participants and Their Relationships in the Grievance Procedure

The most frequent interaction in grievance resolution takes place between the first-line supervisor and the union steward. These relationships can be classified along dimensions presented in Chapter 1, as *codified*, *power*, or *sympathetic*.

Codified Relationships The rights and privileges of foremen and union stewards often stem from a defining code established through the labor agreements and various union and management publications. Union steward handbooks emphasize mutual rights and respect.

The Foreman is the key man in the company's collective bargaining set up just as you, the Steward, are the key man in the union set up. There is a small area of decision that the Foreman does make interpreting policy, and it is in this area that the union can gain by establishing a cooperative relationship.[4]

Generally, every effort should be made to settle a grievance as close to the source of the dispute as possible. The representatives of both groups have to live with any settlement reached. If they can arrive at one, rather than having it imposed on them from above, both parties will be better off. In addition, the further the grievance travels up the procedure the more difficult it becomes to settle, because it becomes a matter of pride or prestige. Therefore, both sides tend to back up their subordinates even when they feel they may have been wrong originally.

It is absolutely essential that the steward talk to the foreman after getting the worker's story. He can probably evaluate the complaint only after hearing both sides. The foreman may provide certain facts that were not available to the worker or the steward.[5]

Exhibit 8–2 stresses the union's obligation to state the grievance in an objective, rational manner, basing it on contractual violations instead of personality clashes.

Similarly, excerpts from American Management Association publications presented below emphasize the appropriate codes of conduct the foremen should follow when dealing with union stewards:

In labor management relations, there is no room for prejudice toward union representatives. The presence of the union organization in the plant effects a union-management marriage, and a corresponding obligation to observe the vows of recognition and good faith. In their grievance relationships, the foremen and the stewards are co-equals.[6]

Supervisors should be thoroughly informed about the rights and responsibilities of shop stewards under the contract and should take care to

---

Exhibit 8-2 Union Instructions Regarding Grievance Processing

(THE WRONG WAY)

FILL OUT IN TRIPLICATE

GRIEVANCE REPORT

USA Local Union No. ▮▮▮▮▮

Location ▮▮▮▮▮▮▮

Name ▮▮▮▮▮▮▮ Union Ledger No. ▮▮▮ Age ▮▮▮
Address ▮▮▮▮▮▮▮
Department ▮▮▮▮▮ Operation ▮▮▮▮ Check No ▮▮▮
Service

Nature of Grievance The foreman is against me. He always
has it in for me. Lots of times he
WHEN? gives me dirty jobs. Now he refuses
Be specific, to give me holiday pay when I ought to
give dates. get it. It's time he stopped discriminating against me.

SPELL IT OUT!
Is this another
WHY? *GET WHAT?* *grievance?*
What section or *Describe the* *What do these*
sections of the *adjustment* *statements*
contract are *sought.* *have to do with*
involved? *the Holiday*
Pay issue?

Form USA 122   PRINTED IN U.S.A.   **COPY FOR LOCAL UNION**

(THE RIGHT WAY)

FILL OUT IN TRIPLICATE

GRIEVANCE REPORT

USA Local Union No. ▮▮▮▮▮

Location ▮▮▮▮▮▮▮

Name ▮▮▮▮▮▮▮ Union Ledger No ▮▮▮ Age ▮▮▮
Address ▮▮▮▮▮▮▮
Department ▮▮▮▮▮ Operation ▮▮▮▮ Check No ▮▮▮
Service

Nature of Grievance I, the undersigned, a laborer in the Melt
Department, claim that the Company violated
Section 10 - Holidays, of the Basic Agreement
when it failed to pay me for the July 4th
unworked holiday even though I had satisfied
the eligibility requirements. I request that
the Company compensate me for 8 hours pay on
July 4th as provided in Section 10 - Holidays.

Form USA 122   PRINTED IN U.S.A.   **COPY FOR LOCAL UNION**

Source: Reprinted by permission from United Steelworkers of America, *The Grievanceman's Handbook* (n.p., n.d.), pp. 14, 15.

respect the steward's role. If the steward has the contractual right to investigate grievances, he should not be hampered in doing so, and if an employee requests a shop steward to assist in processing his grievance or to be present during disciplinary action, the supervisor should acquiesce promptly.[7]

Foremen and union stewards may be aware of the preceding normative philosophies and codes but often do not take them into account when interacting.[8] For example, the *AFL-CIO Manual for Shop Stewards* strongly urges union stewards to present their grievances directly to the first-line supervisor in the first step of the grievance procedure:

It is important to observe the steps in the grievance procedure even if the foreman has limited authority. Leapfrogging to a higher step may have undesirable effects. The lower level of management will resent this and will be more difficult to deal with the next time, or the company may seek to get the grievance thrown out because the proper steps were not followed.[9]

Yet some research has shown that many first-line supervisors believe union stewards violate this aspect of a codified relationship[10]—the supervisors maintain that they are often completely bypassed by the union steward in the grievance process.

Power Relationships Conflicting power relationships develop in situations where the foremen and union stewards pursue differing interests or goals. For example, both are encouraged by their respective superiors to be attentive to problems in the department. The foreman is encouraged to discover problems before they become grievances,[11] whereas the steward is encouraged to talk to the potential grievant before that employee talks to the foreman.

A steward has the responsibility of enforcing the contract in the best interests of all the workers. He should encourage workers who have grievances to come directly to him, not to the foreman. A worker who does not know the contract thoroughly may let the foreman talk him out of a just grievance. Or he may agree to a settlement that weakens the contract and limits the whole union.[12]

Another type of power relationship results from the union steward's knowing the labor agreement better than does his counterpart, the foreman. Union stewards can concentrate on particular provisions of the labor agreement and their application to the shop. The foreman, on the other hand, has major responsibilities for production scheduling, meeting departmental quality and quantity standards, participating in cost reduction programs, and so on, which reduce the amount of time available for grievance and labor agreement analyses.

The steward's relatively superior knowledge of the labor agreement provides the union with at least two strategic advantages over the foreman. First, stewards might be more able to turn a labor relations problem not covered by the labor agreement into a bona fide grievance. For example, guidance given to union stewards in a typical union steward's manual contends:

Almost every grievance is covered by some sections of the contract. An able grievanceman will know how to make the contract fit the case, as the contract should be more than just a piece of paper.[13]

Second, the union steward can directly put his or her labor agreement knowledge to advantageous use, given the chance to discuss the problem one-to-one with the foreman. One steward emphasizes the results of this practice: "Any steward who knows his stuff can talk rings around a foreman. If he says the foreman's wrong and talks enough, whether he's entirely accurate or not, he's apt to buffalo him."[14]

Intimidation is another power relationship strategy which can be employed by both the union steward and the foreman to obtain their respective objectives. In some situations the union steward anticipates that the foreman is vulnerable when he or she receives an excessive number of grievances—the foreman will be concerned with how management officials will react to this apparent inability to resolve labor relations problems. Of course, the grievances might not be valid, and other management officials might consequently consider the foreman to be defending the best interests of the company. But, as the following notation indicates, some management officials might hold the opposite opinion:

The good foreman doesn't have to have grievances. He has enough discretion to be able to settle most complaints—*if* he handles himself well. Many things—for example, pay for overtime work—he is able to adjust if the worker has been wronged. Other things, beyond his scope—for example, where company rules or policies are involved—can be settled if the foreman uses tact and diplomacy. There's no question that even when he can't begin action himself, he can settle the fellow's complaint.[15]

Consequently, a union steward can use the threat of additional grievances (bogus or real) to persuade the foreman to concede to the particular grievance in question or to alter the foreman's overall approach to industrial relations. The practice is explained by a union official:

A short time ago we had a lot of trouble with a certain foreman. . . . He was making them toe the line . . . no quitting early, work from whistle to whistle, no sitting down, no horseplay, this and that. I told the committeeman there, "You do the same thing. Every time he does any work, even if he picks up a box, write a grievance. . . . " The first thing you know grievances started mounting—finally had a pile like that.

Things got so bad . . . this foreman was removed from that department. He was moved to our department and it's his last chance. If he doesn't do good in this department, out he goes. So I went to the guy and told him, "It's your last chance here and you know it. You cooperate with us and we will cooperate with you. If you don't we'll put the screws on you and out you go." Things are working out pretty good so far.[16]

If the foreman believes that there is a strong possibility of his being returned to the bargaining unit, the steward's intimidation can be particulary effective.

I've been broken four or five times [returned to the bargaining unit], and that's a big scare right there for the simple reason that I've been previously warned regarding tussles with the union steward. [He said] "I'll remember this when you come back down to production." In other words, when we get out of salary and back down to production we have to be OK'd by the union in order to get back to our job again. So you're in the middle there and you don't know what you are going to do. I may be here a day, a month, a year, I don't know, and all of a sudden they don't need me any more, and I go back to production, and the union don't want me. That's not only with me, but a lot of supervisors are shaky on that point . . . we have no backing; whereas the workmen have the union to back them up, the foreman has nothing. You're either a good Joe or you're just out.[17]

Intimidation tactics are not always one-sided; a clever foreman can make industrial life very difficult for the union steward, probably without incurring an unfair labor practice charge. For example, many job classifications have a wide variety of work assignments, with some of these assignments being less desirable than others. A foreman could assign undesirable work assignments to the union steward, who would have little recourse as long as they were within his or her job classification. The foreman can also undermine the steward's formal position in the union by: (a) restricting the amount of freedom and time necessary for the steward to investigate the grievance and (b) refusing to resolve any grievance in the first step whenever the union steward is present with the grievant. It should be noted that these tactics are only successful if the union steward is inexperienced.

Regardless of the "success" of such actions, a grievance relationship governed by power and intimidation tactics distorts the primary purpose of contract administration—namely, rational decision making.

Sympathetic Relationships Sympathetic relations occur between individuals when each is aware of the other's situation and is guided by an understanding appreciation. An example of this appreciation comes from a union steward's comment:

You can't have industrial relations without giving and taking on both sides. You'll always win more cases by getting along with supervision than by being tough. You've got to swap and make trades. . . . Sometimes I have to talk like hell to explain some of the deals I make with them and sometimes I keep what I'm doing to myself if I see a chance to get something good later on. The thing some grievers never get through

---

their heads is that a lot of bosses are on the spot themselves. If you go a little easy on them when they're on the pan, by God—you make friends—they'll stand by you sometime when you're back of the eight ball. Sometimes when I have a rotten grievance, I'll take the case up to the soop [superintendent] and let him know I won't push it hard.[18]

In some extreme examples, union stewards have led (or offered to lead) wildcat strikes when their foremen did not receive a promotion to a higher position.[19]

Sympathetic relationships are aided when the foreman and the union steward realize that they both occupy marginal positions within their own organization. For example, many foremen do not have full authority to resolve grievances at the first step because other management officials, concerned with the precedential impacts of grievance decision, like to be continually informed of related supervisory activities. Foremen usually receive advice from an industrial relations representative on contract administration matters. However, the following remarks from an industrial relations representative indicate that there is a thin line between advice and direction.

We have to keep strings on the foreman. I see no way around it. He has neither the time nor the talent to be familiar with the contract or to understand the effects of his settlements on the whole plant. It is important that he doesn't give the plant away or put us in conflict with ourselves in grievance settlements.[20]

The industrial relations representative may work directly and informally with the supervisor involved in the grievance but nonetheless has the option of going to the supervisor's boss if the problem continues. As one labor relations representative puts it, "We go to his [foreman's] supervisor and lower the boom."[21] As suggested by the following supervisor's remarks, foremen might feel that members of the industrial relations department hinder their ability to manage:

How the hell do they (higher-echelon production management) expect me to get the job done! . . . They expect me to go along with their stupid orders when I can't even raise my voice without the permission of "high and mighty" personnel.[22]

Union stewards are also subjected to a variety of pressures in their contract administration activities. On the one hand, constituents expect their union steward to actively press every grievance, reasoning that the union's sole purpose is to represent its members. Consequently, it is difficult for the union steward to accept the foreman's first-step rejection of the grievance, even if he or she feels the foreman is correct. On the other hand, union officials receiving the grievance in subsequent steps of the grievance procedure tend to view the union steward as either ignorant of the labor agreement or gutless.

The preceding varieties of interpersonal relationships reveal how the *real* grievance procedure varies from that typically outlined in labor agreements.[23] Individual objectives, strategies, and personalities force the contractual procedure to be more flexible in practice. More importantly, as discussed in the following section, the process's numerous interacting relationships and human elements make it difficult to process grievances in accordance with theoretical industrial relations principles.

Effective Grievance Procedures: Theory versus Practice

The Clinical Approach Some students and practitioners of labor relations feel that a clinical rather than a legalistic approach to grievance resolution is most appropriate. The former approach attempts to uncover all of the causes of the employee's grievance, whereas the latter approach goes strictly by the labor agreement in determining whether a contractual violation has occurred. To be sure, the clinical approach can be regarded as more humane and fair. However, it has several limitations.

First, the labor agreement seldom considers issues of fairness and equity. For example, a provision found in most labor agreements allows management to require the junior employee (one having the least amount of seniority) in the work classification to work an overtime assignment if it is refused by the senior employees. But if the junior employee had previous plans for the evening of the overtime assignment, he or she might refuse to work. Refusal may mean suspension, say for two days, for failure to follow reasonable work orders. This same employee could then file a grievance protesting the suspension.

The clinical approach to grievance resolution would attempt to uncover any unique motivations for the employee's refusal and might even resolve the grievance in his or her favor. However, current managers, being justifiably concerned with precedent, would be reluctant to allow the employee's insubordination to go unnoticed, particularly since the employee acted in clear violation of the labor agreement.

The clinical approach also implies that management's grievance answer will be thorough and specifically tailored to the employee's unique grievance. Any employee who files a grievance after careful deliberation and personal soul searching expects more than the following three-word grievance answer: "No contract violation." However, management officials have long since learned that the time for a lengthy discussion is in the grievance meeting, not in the written grievance answer. The rationale for this belief is that a wordy grievance answer can often give the union ammunition not only for the specific grievance in question but for other grievances as well. Thus, while few individuals would argue with the principles and objectives of the clinical approach, its limitations have caused industrial grievance administration to become more legalistic.

Adherence to Procedures and Participants' Roles A second principle of effective contract administration requires that the grievance procedures and roles of participants be clearly defined and followed. Each party to a grievance should know the others' corresponding roles and responsibilities, and the time limits for grievance resolution should be clearly spelled out and honored. Practical obstacles to fulfilling this requirement occur when the labor agreement requires the first-line supervisor to treat the union steward as an organizational equal in the grievance process. It is difficult for a foreman, accustomed to giving daily work orders to the union steward, to turn around in a grievance meeting and consider the union steward as a peer. Some foremen can accept this situation; others, subscribing to one or more of the following beliefs, have problems:

This guy, Walker (union steward) here, doesn't realize that the gang is kidding him. They haven't got anything to kick about. All the stuff he is bringing up is old stuff. We've gone over it before with the other representatives. The other representative was sick of the job and gave it up. So the gang decided to elect this squirt because nobody else wanted the job. This fellow doesn't know anything about the department. He's only been there three months. He's only a kid and doesn't know what it's all about. I haven't got time to rehash this all over again. . . . He's not qualified to talk about anything that happens in my department, and I haven't got time to waste with him. He brings up all this stuff and nonsense just so he can be a big shot.[24]

This principle also suggests that first-line supervisors should have authority for resolving grievances at the first step of the procedure in order to give the employee a prompt, responsive answer.[25] In addition to promptness, supervisory resolution of grievances at the first step can help prevent the plantwide precedents that are established in the third step of the grievance meeting. However, other management officials, who prefer to be kept informed on employee grievances, instruct the supervisors to inform the industrial relations representative of the situation before taking any action. Being alert to this situation, the union steward will often bypass the supervisory middleman, taking the grievance directly to the industrial relations representative. Thus the advantages of supervisory resolution of grievances go untried.

Unfortunately, for various reasons, many first-line supervisors are quite willing to abdicate their supervisory authority in this area. Realistically, they see little direct reward (like pay increases) for effectively resolving grievances at the first step. Conversely, if a production problem occurs on the shop floor when the supervisor is in the office discussing an employee's grievance, he or she often faces a managerial reprimand.

Grievance procedures usually indicate the time limits in which an employee can file the grievance after discovering the alleged infraction and require a timely answer by management officials. In addition, appeal to each higher grievance step must be within prescribed time limits. For example, the employee may have fifteen days in which to file a grievance, and management may have to furnish its first-step grievance answer within five days after receiving it. Upon receiving management's first-step answer, the grievant might have five days to appeal to the second step. If it isn't sent to the second step within that contractually specified time period, the grievance is considered resolved.

Adhering to time limits benefits the union as well as management. The grievant desires a prompt resolution. (However, one related study found that the length of time elapsing between an employee's initial grievance and the arbitrator's decision averages 242 days.)[26] Similarly, grievances that are ignored or grievance procedures that contain no time limits could hurt management—the union could hold or delay grievances until it thought management was more vulnerable. However, time limits are difficult if not impossible to realize because the number of individuals who must be present at any one of the grievance steps poses extreme scheduling problems (for example, around vacations and different work shifts).

Individual, Objective Consideration of Each Grievance The third and final principle of effective grievance procedures requires that each grievance be considered on its individual merits. The grievant wishes to receive an answer uncolored by any political or tactical concerns, but the union must consider political influence and overall strategy in its determination of which grievances will be filed and pursued. Not all grievances are clear-cut issues; in fact, many involve rather confusing and somewhat opposing interpretations of the labor agreement. In these cases, management has two options—decide the grievance in the employee's favor or appeal the grievance to arbitration. The latter alternative is not always very attractive, particularly if management realizes there is little contractual guidance in the issue (as in the example on the holiday scheduling of a crane operator) and insufficient past practice or precedent to support the decision. There are many gray areas in contract administration which are open to interpretation. This uncertainty is compounded when the parties solicit a neutral party to resolve the issue in binding arbitration. Also, the arbitrator's decision might refute management's action in terms that further erode management's discretion in future matters. Unions also tend to use arbitration only as a last resort because several arbitration cases can drain the union's treasury.

In these instances, flexibility may be possible with the addition of an informal *third and one-half step* in the grievance procedure. This step is not found in the grievance procedure specified in the labor agreement. It occurs after management's "final" third-step decision but before the arbitrator hears the grievance. During the third and one-half step meetings, management and union representatives meet to discuss and trade grievances, dispatching several cases originally scheduled for arbitration. Usually the grievances involved in the negotiated package are settled without prejudice to either party's position in future related issues. This statement preserves management's discretion on these issues and the union's right to file future related grievances.

Opponents of this practice contend that valid employee grievances are bargained away for an expedient settlement. Grievance trading in the third and one-half step can also discourage first-line supervisors from actively trying to resolve grievances if they believe their efforts will be overturned in a mass grievance settlement. For example, the following remarks were made by a foreman who had sent an employee home for repeated tardiness. The employee filed a grievance with the foreman's supervisor, who sent the employee back to the job.

I went over to O'Brien's (the superintendent's office) to find out why he had overruled me. He handed me a line of salve about "having to do it." Said "it was a small item after all" and that he "might want a big favor from the union sometime in the future." He said, "We have to trade back and forth. Sometimes we give in; sometimes they give in. That's why we never have any big trouble!" Then he said he might have to reverse some of my decisions again sometime, but if he did, not to get sore about it, because he wouldn't mean no offense by it. Well damn that noise! If O'Brien wants to make me look like a fool every time I make a decision, why by God, he can make all the decisions. You know two can play that game. I can give the boys (workers) every damn thing he can give them. Then when they come up with a big one that I know damn well he can't give them, I'll tell 'em to take it up to him.[27]

As a result of management using the third and one-half step in the grievance procedure, unions might be encouraged to file more grievances in the belief that they can obtain more from a trade involving fifty fabricated grievances than they can from five legitimate ones. Furthermore, those settlements "without prejudice" can result in more grievances of the same sort since the issues are not considered jointly resolved by management or union officials.

Advocates state that this process merely represents another legitimate cooperative effort between labor and management officials in efficiently dealing with day-to-day administrative problems. These individuals indicate that the union's and management's organizational self-interests require considerations and possible use of the third and one-half step grievance trading session.

Significance of Employee Grievances

Employee grievances and the grievance procedure can have a substantial impact on union and management organizations. For example, the prevalence and resolution of employee grievances can be closely associated with potential union membership.

Employee representation plans by the score were defeated and absorbed by the CIO in the early days because the plan representatives could not get favorable settlements of grievances. The telephone workers' unions were built on grievances, without the aid of professional organizers. The grievance builds the union; over a period of time, practically every employee will be drawn into a grievance transaction affecting his job.[28]

As the preceding quotation suggests, grievance handling and resolution continues to remain a significant function of the union organization even after it has been established as the exclusive bargaining representative for a specified group of employees. Most, if not all, union members are interested in those policies and actions which directly affect their unique work situations; their assessment of the union's effectiveness will therefore be in part determined by their perception of union responsiveness toward any potential problems arising from these policies or actions. However, many specific problems of this nature cannot be resolved during formal collective bargaining negotiations, where time constraints and efficient decision making require discussions of problems pertaining to large numbers of employees. Union officials therefore demonstrate their intent to represent their constituents' particular job interests against conceivable arbitrary managerial actions through the use of the grievance procedure.

A union not demonstrating its interest in union members through a prompt and effective grievance procedure may find itself in trouble. Recently, the United Mine Workers union has been subject to much internal dissension, partly because of revised grievance procedures negotiated in 1974 to prevent unresolved grievances from turning into wildcat strikes. One of the problems with this newly negotiated procedure is that it has increased the length of time allowed to process a grievance. In fact, some UMW officials state it takes four to six months just to obtain a final grievance decision. This unusually long delay has caused many union members to become extremely dissatisfied with the union leadership.[29]

Management officials are also often concerned about the grievance procedure, but for different reasons. Management tends to view grievances from a production cost standpoint; they can intrude on the freedom to manage and mean loss of production time when hourly employees, production managers, and management staff representatives must devote attention to resolving grievances. If we assume that each of the grievance steps takes one-half hour at a minimum and seven employees are on the grievance committee, then it is possible for one grievance to consume eleven employee hours. This figure does not include preparation and research time, time required for any witnesses, and the additional time and expense associated with the arbitration hearing. Management realizes a tremendous annual expenditure when this figure is multiplied by the total number of grievances filed at a facility (in large facilities, often over 200 a year) and the wages of the various grievance participants. Management might place less emphasis on grievances' cost considerations if it wishes to weaken the union's treasury by processing grievances through the relatively expensive arbitration procedure discussed in the next chapter.

Management's grievance answer might also establish a precedent applicable to a larger number of employees, with a potential increased cost to the company. Also, grievances which employees believe unnecessarily delayed or handled unfairly might result in lost production output through resultant employee action such as work stoppages and industrial sabotage.

It is a mistake to *assume* uninterrupted continuance of employees' good will. Reserves of good will rapidly dissipate with the fog of misunderstanding and the lack of opportunity for presenting and adjusting real or fancied injustice.

In the absence of provisions for conference and full opportunity for airing grievances and frankly expressing views, it is a grievous mistake to assume that everything is "happy day" and that employees are satisfied with conditions. Without such contact it is impossible to grasp the changing views, problems, grievances and aspirations of our fellows or of those associated (employer and employee) in conducting an industry, bank, store, or any other business requiring capital and labor with management and supervision in between.[30]

The preceding excerpt, written over forty years ago, suggests grievances also furnish management with an upward channel of communication through which it can ascertain employee problems and find out what is happening on the shop floor. Unfortunately, in many cases management's examination of grievances is limited to a cursory review of grievance statistics.

To demonstrate what often happens: Assume that two foremen are in charge of two similar production departments, and Foreman A and Foreman B had two and thirty grievances, respectively, during the past year. But if top management is only aware of the respective number of grievances filed against the two supervisors and that more of Foreman B's time is spent in resolving grievances than Foreman A's, then top management might incorrectly conclude that Foreman B is an ineffective supervisor, incapable of commanding the employees' respect.

A closer examination of the grievances might reveal other explanations for this discrepancy. Perhaps Foreman B has the company "crybaby" in the department—an individual who, instead of working, either likes to hear himself talk or obtain free doughnuts and coffee in the air-conditioned quarters of the grievance meeting room. More importantly, Foreman A can easily reduce the number of grievances by giving his or her employees whatever they desire. Grievances are kept to a miminum; but Foreman A has "given the plant away to the union."

Management should be concerned with the absolute number of grievances, for this figure can be easily translated into operating costs. However, grievance statistics alone do not furnish essential insights into the merits of the grievances or supervisory effectiveness. In fact, management can negatively affect its profit figures by giving sole reliance to number of grievances instead of to the specific issue involved in the grievance.

Because grievance resolutions should be systematic and must be consistent among organizational units, grievance decisions should be communicated laterally to all foremen and managerial employees. All first-line supervisors should not only be aware of grievance activity in the organization but also be familiar with the criteria used in grievance decisions. This can be effectively accomplished through a "labor letter" sent by the industrial relations department on a regular basis. Here, the grievances along with managements' and unions' contentions can be briefly summarized and the final resolution of each grievance discussed, along with the corresponding reasoning for the decision. Hopefully, the labor letter educates supervisors regarding effective grievance resolution techniques and informs them of potential issues which might affect their departments in the near future.

Employee grievances will continue to represent a vital dimension of the labor-management relationship, giving meaning to the labor agreement while at the same time affecting the quality of plant labor relations. Often this process is more complicated and time consuming than formal labor negotiations. Consequently, contract administration deserves a significant amount of attention from practitioners and academicians if labor-management cooperation is to be either maintained or improved. The significance of employee grievances is further illustrated in the next chapter, which considers the terminal step in the grievance procedure—arbitration.

Summary

Employee grievances can be considered an extension of collective bargaining, particularly since grievance administration gives dynamic meaning to the negotiated terms of the labor agreement. Grievances are broadly defined as any employee's concern over a perceived violation of the labor agreement which is submitted to the grievance procedure for eventual resolution.

An employee might file a grievance for any of various reasons, such as to protest a contractual violation, to draw attention to a problem in the plant, to get something for nothing, or to feel more important. Regardless of motives for filing grievances, management must process them through the grievance procedure specified in the labor agreement.

Although no one grievance procedure applies to all labor-management relationships, a representative four-step grievance procedure was presented. Two of its important aspects are inclusion of higher level management and union personnel at each successive step and, particularly in the private sector, a final step involving binding arbitration by a third-party neutral.

The grievance procedure as actually carried out involves a variety of social relationships (codified, power, and sympathetic) enacted among the grievance participants in resolving the grievance according to appropriate contractual provisions. The variety of personalities and motives of the participants also makes it difficult to effect three rather lofty principles of grievance procedures: a clinical rather than a legalistic approach should be followed, the grievance participants' roles and grievance procedures should be clearly spelled out in the labor agreement, and each grievance should be decided on its own merit.

Employee grievances have different significance to the different parties involved. For example, unions can demonstrate their intent to represent their members' job interests by their approach to grievances. Management is concerned about grievances' cost as well as their impact on the freedom to manage. Grievances can also serve with some limitations as a source of upward communication and an indicator of the quality of labor-management relationships.

Discussion Questions

1. There is a thin line differentiating employee grievances and employee complaints. Discuss the problems involved in defining a grievance, indicating why a broad definition of employee grievances is both confusing and necessary.

2. Discuss two reasons grievances might be filed, furnishing examples of these reasons other than those found in the text.

3. Why does a grievance procedure have so many steps, since the employee is either right or wrong, and a one- or two-step procedure would save time and money? In your answer, discuss the various functions, opportunities, and problems each of the grievance steps can offer.

4. Formulate three rather specific ways the "real" grievance procedure

can differ from the grievance procedure established in the labor agreement.

5. Why is it difficult for union and management officials to resolve each grievance on its own merits?

6. Explain the various ways grievances are significant to management and union officials, indicating various similarities and differences between the two groups.

References

[1]Leonard R. Sayles and George Strauss, *The Local Union*, rev. ed. (New York: Harcourt, Brace & World, 1967), p. 50.

[2]W. W. Ronan et al., "Three Studies of Grievances," *Personnel Journal* 55 (January 1976), pp. 33–38.

[3]Bureau of National Affairs, *Basic Patterns in Union Contracts* (Washington, D.C.: Bureau of National Affairs, 1975), p. 32.

[4]United Automobile Workers, *Shop Steward Manual* (n.p., n.d.), pp. 10–11.

[5]*AFL-CIO Manual for Shop Stewards* (Washington, D.C.: AFL-CIO, March 1971), p. 36.

[6]Walter E. Baer, *Grievance Handling: 101 Guides for Supervisors* (New York: American Management Association, 1970), p. 53.

[7]William Karpinsky, "Front-Line Contract Administration," *Personnel* 33 (January 1957), p. 384.

[8]William F. Dowling, Jr., and Leonard R. Sayles, *How Managers Motivate: The Imperatives of Supervision* (New York: McGraw-Hill, 1971), p. 350.

[9]*AFL-CIO Manual for Shop Stewards* (n.p., n.d.), p. 37.

[10]John A. Patton, "The First Line Supervisor: Industry's Number One Problem," *Business Management* 40 (September 1971), p. 38. See also Ken Jennings, "Foremen's Views of Their Involvement with the Union Steward in the Grievance Process," *Labor Law Journal* 25 (September 1974), p. 541.

[11]Delbert C. Miller and William Form, *Industrial Sociology*, 2d. ed. (New York: Harper & Row, 1964), p. 401.

[12]International Chemical Workers' Union, *Handbook for Union Stewards* (n.p., n.d.), pp. 31–32.

[13]United Glass and Ceramic Workers of North America, *So You're A Grievanceman!* (n.p., n.d.), p. 15.

[14]James W. Kuhn, *Bargaining in Grievance Settlement* (New York: Columbia University Press, 1961), p. 29.

[15]Sayles and Strauss, *The Local Union*, p. 16.

[16]Miller and Form, *Industrial Sociology*, pp. 401–402.

[17]Robert Kahn et al., *Organizational Stress* (New York: Wiley, 1964), p. 61.

[18]Melville Dalton, "Unofficial Union-Management Relations," *American Sociological Review* 15 (October 1950), p. 613.

[19]Ibid.

[20]Kuhn, *Bargaining*, p. 19.

[21]Charles Myers and John Turnbull, "Line and Staff in Industrial Relations," in Joseph Litterer, ed., *Organizations: Structure and Behavior* (New York: Wiley, 1966), p. 313.

[22]Ross Stagner and Hjalmar Rosen, *Psychology of Union Management Relations* (Belmont, Calif.: Wadsworth, 1965), p. 62.

[23]Sayles and Strauss, *The Local Union*, p. 22.

[24]Paul Pigors, "The Old Line Foreman," in Austin Grimshaw and John Hennessey, Jr., eds., *Organizational Behavior* (New York: McGraw-Hill, 1960), p. 98.

[25]Robert McKersie and William M. Shropshire, Jr., "Avoiding Written Grievances: A Successful Program," *Journal of Business* 24 (April 1962), pp. 135–152. See also William B. Werther, Jr., "Reducing Grievances through Effective Contract Administration," *Labor Law Journal* 25 (April 1974), p. 212.

[26]Pearce Davis and Gopal C. Pati, "Elapsed Grievance Time: 1942–1972," *Arbitration Journal* 29 (March 1974), p. 21.

[27]Melville Dalton, "The Role of Supervision," in Arthur Kornhauser, Robert Dubin, and Arthur Ross, eds., *Industrial Conflict* (New York: McGraw-Hill, 1958), pp. 183–184.

[28]Joseph Kovner and Herbert Lahne, "Shop Society and the Union," *Industrial and Labor Relations Review* 7 (October 1953), p. 6. See also Joel Seidman et al., *The Worker Views His Union* (Chicago: University of Chicago Press, 1958), pp. 182–183.

29George Getschow, "Aggrieved over Grievances: Revised Complaint System Raises Tension in Coal Mines, Will Be Issue in 1977 Talks," *Wall Street Journal*, March 4, 1977, p. 30.

30H. A. Enochs, "Essentials of Labor Agreements," *Personnel Journal* 14 (January–February 1936), p. 247.

Chapter 9

Labor Arbitration: A System of Industrial Jurisprudence

"The decisions of the arbitrator must not only meet the theoretical tests of logic, but the pragmatic test of whether they will work out in the future day-to-day relationships in the plant."

John R. Abersold and Wayne E. Howard, Cases in Labor Relations, 1967.

The previous chapter illustrated how employee grievances affect labor-management relations. In some cases, grievances that are resolved by an arbitrator have an even greater influence on labor-management relationships since the arbitrator's decision often establishes a binding precedent for similar issues. The significance of labor arbitration is further illustrated by its heavy use—one recent study estimated that there were 30,000 arbitration hearings in 1977.[1]

This chapter will only consider grievance or "rights" arbitration (which interprets provisions of the existing contract); interest arbitration over terms of a new contract was discussed in Chapter 7. Arbitration is first discussed from a historical perspective; then elements of a typical arbitration proceeding and decision are described. Current jurisdictional issues involving the arbitrator and various government agencies are also discussed, and, finally, the process is appraised.

Development of Labor Arbitration

Arbitration was first used in 1865 but was fairly limited until World War II and the related operations of the War Labor Board. Yet the actual authority of arbitrators remained in doubt until four Supreme Court decisions in 1957 and 1960. Consequently, this section briefly describes the role of arbitration from 1865 to World War II, indicating how war conditions stimulated the use of the arbitration technique. Related Supreme Court decisions that gave legitimacy to the arbitration process are also emphasized.

1865 to World War II

Arbitration was initially concerned with negotiating working conditions, particularly with having employers recognize the legitimate existence of labor unions. In some situations the company would not accept the arbitrator's award; in others the company as well as the union representatives realized arbitration was an effective alternative to industrial warfare. Many industrial disputes during this period were resolved only through sheer tests of economic strength, and the results of these struggles often hurt both unions and managements. For instance, a union desiring resolution of a particular grievance was often required to mobilize the entire work force in a strike against the employer—a difficult task—before the company would conscientiously attempt to resolve the grievance.

To use a classroom analogy, assume a university professor on the first day of class singles out a particular student and informs the class that the student will receive an "F" for the final grade and that any student complaining about this grade will also receive an "F" for the course. Clearly, this is an arbitrary and capricious practice, and some students would feel compelled to protest the professor's action to the department chairman or the dean. However, many students, particularly those needing at least a "C" for the course to graduate at the end of the term, would refrain from protesting. It is likewise difficult to mobilize a large percentage of a union's members on behalf of a discharged employee, much less in support of a grievance involving payment for an alleged overtime infraction.

On the other hand, management realized it could be hurt if the union could effectively "pull the pin" over a particular grievance and shut down the plant. This uncertainty could be compounded if the union managed to walk out of the plant when management was particularly vulnerable (for example, had rush orders from a key customer).

Thus, in some situations, notably that of a clothing company, Hart Schaffner and Marx, in 1911, both labor and management representatives agreed to use arbitration as a reasonable alternative to costly strikes. A 1929 agreement in the hosiery industry appeared to accept the principle of arbitration. Under the terms of this agreement, the arbitrator was not given the power to change the terms of the existing agreement or decide the terms of a new agreement. The arbitrator could, however, interpret existing contract clauses and determine issues arising during the life of the contract that were not covered by existing terms.[2]

Factors limiting the growth of arbitration during this period were the relatively few unionized facilities and the vague language found in labor agreements, which gave little contractual guidance for the arbitrator's decision. Consequently, the early arbitration process combined elements of mediation and humanitarianism in an effort to reach a *consensus decision*, one that would be accepted by both parties to a grievance. The arbitrator under these circumstances had to draw on diplomatic and persuasive abilities to convince the parties the decision should be accepted.

World War II

Arbitration's popularity increased during World War II, when President Roosevelt's Executive Order 9017 provided for final resolution of disputes interrupting work that contributed to the war effort. Essential features of this order included a no-strike, no-lockout agreement and a War Labor Board comprised of four management representatives, four union representatives, and four representatives of the public—all presidential appointees. The board was to encourage labor agreements and, if necessary, resolve disputes over their terms.[3]

The advent of World War II encouraged the role of arbitration in several ways. First, there appeared to be at least a surface attempt to avoid labor-management disputes in recognition that wartime production was crucial to the nation's interests. For example, the president of the National Association of Manufacturers during this period stressed:

No industrial dispute of any kind must be allowed to interfere, even for a day or an hour, with the first job of this country and every citizen in it—namely, the speedy production of the vast amounts of war material called for by the nation's gigantic War Program. . . .

In the mutual give-and-take, management and labor alike must be prepared to "give until it hurts" in order that the flow of vital war material may continue unabated and in ever increasing volume.[4]

Labor's view was exemplified by a high ranking official of the American Federation of Labor, who also emphasized the spirit of sacrifice under the unusual wartime circumstances:

Labor well knows strong unions are more effective in collective bargaining than weak ones. When unions, therefore, agree not to use their collective power by means of a strike they have agreed to lay aside and not to use their defensive weapon from which constructive power is derived. Labor freely made this war sacrifice in order not to impede national defense of our free institutions which assume opportunities to all.[5]

Part 2/The Collective Bargaining Process

However, labor's and management's support for arbitration was qualified in practice and theory. For example, nearly 2,400 strikes and lockouts occurred in disputes subsequently certified to the National War Labor Board (NWLB), and nearly 900 strikes or lockouts occurred after the board's decisions. Management and union officials also expressed concern over the potential of dispute resolution through compulsory arbitration. Management wanted its previously held rights and prerogatives returned after the exceptional wartime circumstances ended, whereas labor officials cautioned against a fixed labor policy applying to all industries regardless of the varying working conditions. Mindful of these concerns, the NWLB urged labor and management officials to resolve their own disputes and encouraged the parties to carefully define the arbitrator's jurisdiction in the labor agreements. Thus, the board gave any negotiated restrictions full force when deciding cases and denied arbitration where it was reasonably clear that the arbitration clauses meant to exclude a subject from arbitral review. It further defined grievance arbitration as a judicial process, thereby limiting a decision solely to the evidence presented at the hearing.[6]

Results of the NWLB's activities further popularized and enriched the arbitration process, as the board resolved some 20,000 disputes during its tenure.[7] Additionally, these efforts served as a training ground for many arbitrators, who could apply their acquired skills to the arbitration process after the war effort.

The Postwar Years

Although the use of arbitration increased during World War II, the relationship among arbitrator, management, and union officials was far from resolved. Confusion about the enforceability of the arbitrator's award was magnified by the absence of any federal labor law and the presence of differing state statutes regarding arbitration. What would happen if one of the parties refused to abide by the arbitrator's decision? An initial answer came from Section 301 of the Taft-Hartley Act, which in effect said that suits for violation of a contract between an employer and a labor organization may be brought in any United States district court having jurisdiction over the parties.[8]

The Lincoln Mills Decision Greater clarity of the meaning of Section 301 was provided in the Supreme Court's 1957 decision on *Textile Workers Union of America v. Lincoln Mills of Alabama*. In this case, the labor agreement included a grievance procedure with arbitration as the final step in the process. The union had requested arbitration of several grievances and the employer refused; thereupon the union brought suit under Section 301 in the district court to compel arbitration. The court ruled in the union's favor, but the court of appeals reversed this decision on the basis that the lower court had no authority founded in either state or federal statute to grant relief. The Supreme Court subsequently determined that the intent of Section 301 was to insure that management and the union bargain in a responsible manner as set forth in the Taft-Hartley Act. The Court viewed the labor agreement as providing the employer with uninterrupted production during its existence. In other words, the union in effect guaranteed that it would abide by the terms of the labor agreement for its duration. Furthermore,

---

the agreement to arbitrate grievance disputes is the *quid pro quo* for an agreement not to strike. Viewed in this light, the legislation does more than confer jurisdiction in the federal courts over labor organizations. It expresses a federal policy that federal courts should enforce these agreements on behalf of or against labor organizations and that industrial peace can be best obtained only in that way.[9]

While *Lincoln Mills* resolved some of the questions over enforcing the arbitration provisions in the labor agreement, other questions regarding the arbitrator's role in this process remained. Either party could refuse to submit the grievance to arbitration if the labor agreement did not cover the issue in question. Some state statutes that made the agreement to arbitrate enforceable resulted in attempts to persuade the court to compel arbitration of the issue. Many courts then became involved in assessing the merits of a particular grievance and whether it should be arbitrated. These actions, of course, contradicted arbitral belief that arbitrators alone should rule on the merits of the grievance. Confusion resulted when labor and management representatives played the courts against the arbitrators in their attempts to obtain favorable decisions.

In 1960, the Supreme Court clarified and strengthened the arbitrator's role with three decisions commonly referred to as the "Trilogy." Because of their significant relationship to the arbitration process, these cases will be individually summarized.

United Steelworkers of America v. American Manufacturing Company

In this case, the union brought suit in district court to compel arbitration of a grievance involving an employee who was awarded 25 percent disability pay on a permanent basis. Two weeks after this determination the union filed a grievance charging the employee was eligible according to the seniority provisions of the labor agreement to return to the job. Management contended that the grievant was physically unable to perform the job and that this type of dispute was not arbitrable under their labor agreement. After reviewing the merits of the grievance, both the district court and court of appeals upheld management's action. However, the Supreme Court noted that there were no explicit restrictions placed on arbitration in the labor agreement; therefore, the grievance procedure should be given "full play" in the resolution of the dispute.

Accordingly, the Supreme Court reversed the lower courts' decisions with the following reasoning:

The function of the court is very limited when the parties have agreed to submit all questions of contract interpretation to the arbitrator. It is confined to ascertaining whether the party seeking arbitration is making a claim which on its face is governed by the contract. Whether the moving party is right or wrong is a question of contract interpretation for the arbitrator. . . .

The courts, therefore, have no business weighing the merits of the grievance, considering whether there is equity in a particular claim, or determining whether there is particular language in the written instrument which will support the claim. The agreement is to submit all grievances to arbitration, not merely those which the court will deem meritorious. The processing of even frivolous claims may have therapeutic values of which those who are not a part of the plant environment may be quite unaware.[10]

United Steelworkers of America v. Warrior and Gulf Navigation Company Here, the union grieved over employee layoffs which were in part due to management's contracting out work previously performed by bargaining unit employees. The collective bargaining agreement did state that "matters which are strictly a function of management shall not be subject to arbitration." Again, both the district court and court of appeals reviewed the merits of the grievance and decided against the union on the reasoning that contracting out was within management's discretion. However, the Supreme Court decision noted that the employment relationship generates a common law born out of the experiences of a particular industrial facility. The experiences and precedents shaping this common law also clarify the often vague terms and conditions expressed in the labor agreement. The reliance on common law suggests that the labor arbitrator is more effective than the courts in interpreting and resolving a dispute over the terms of an existing labor agreement.

The labor arbitrator's source of law is not confined to the express provisions of the contract, as the industrial common law—the practices of the industry and the shop—is equally a part of the collective bargaining agreement although not expressed in it. The labor arbitrator is usually chosen because of the parties' confidence in his knowledge of the common law of the shop and their trust in his personal judgment to bring to bear considerations which are not expressed in the contract as criteria for judgment. The parties expect that his judgment on a particular grievance will reflect not only what the contract says but, insofar as the collective bargaining agreement permits, such factors as the effect upon productivity of a particular result, its consequence to the morale of the shop, his judgment whether tensions will be heightened or diminished. . . . The ablest judge cannot be expected to bring the same experience and competence to bear upon the determination of a grievance, because he cannot be similarly informed.[11]

In assessing the exclusion from arbitration provisions, the Supreme Court interpreted "strictly a function of management" to mean that in which the contract expressly "gives management complete control and unfettered discretion." This issue would not have been arbitrable had there been an explicit statement excluding contracting out from the arbitration process. Since there was no related contractual language, the Supreme Court believed the arbitrator (not the lower courts) should resolve the contracting out issue.[12]

United Steelworkers of America v. Enterprise Wheel and Car Corporation The preceding two decisions underscored the arbitrator's role in interpreting the labor agreement, particularly in determining whether the grievance should be arbitrated. However, the role of the arbitrator in fashioning an appropriate grievance remedy remained unsettled. This decision concerned a grievance over management's dismissal of a group of employees who walked out of the plant to protest the discharge of another employee. Management refused to arbitrate the grievance; however, the district court, considering the union's suit under Section 301, ordered the case arbitrated. Eventually, the arbitrator determined that the employees should be reinstated to their jobs with back pay for all but ten days (to be considered as a disciplinary suspension). Management, noting that the labor agreement had expired before the arbitrator's decision was rendered, challenged the arbitrator's authority to fashion the reinstatement remedy. While the district court compelled compliance with the remedy, the court of appeals furnished advice as to what would constitute an appropriate remedy. Justice Douglas, in writing the Supreme Court's opinion, drew upon the previous decision and indicated the relatively superior knowledge arbitrators have in resolving industrial disputes:

A mere ambiguity in the opinion accompanying an award, which permits the inference that the arbitrator may have exceeded his authority, is not a reason for refusing to enforce the award. Arbitrators have no obligation to the court to give their reasons for an award. To require opinions free of ambiguity may lead arbitrators to play it safe by writing no supporting opinions. This would be undesirable for a well reasoned opinion tends to engender confidence in the integrity of the process and aids in clarifying the underlying agreement. Moreover, we see no reason to assume that this arbitrator has abused the trust the parties confided in him and has not stayed within the areas marked out for his consideration. It is not apparent that he went beyond the submission.[13]

In summary, the Supreme Court Trilogy greatly enhanced the authority and prestige of the arbitrator in interpreting the terms of the labor agreement and determining whether the issue is appropriate for arbitration. It also endorsed the arbitrator as most qualified to fashion an appropriate grievance remedy, with the qualification that the arbitrator has the express obligation to base the decision on the essence of the labor agreement. The courts remain available to a party contesting the arbitrator's jurisdiction, but doubts about the scope of the arbitration clause are usually resolved in favor of the arbitrator. To justify judicial intervention, the parties' intentions to exclude a matter from arbitration must be expressed in clear and unambiguous language in the labor agreement or a supplemental agreement.

Some Recent Court Decisions The Supreme Court has recently determined that the obligation to arbitrate a grievance cannot be nullified by the termination of a labor agreement. Management representatives in this case argued that arbitration is a feature of the contract which ceases to exist when a contract terminates; therefore, a grievance cannot be processed to arbitration if the labor agreement is no longer in effect. Consequently, management representatives felt that the issue of severance pay was not subject to arbitration since the labor agreement had expired and management had decided to permanently close its operations. However, the Supreme Court indicated that arbitration was still appropriate:

> While the termination of the collective-bargaining agreement works an obvious change in the relationship between employer and union, it would have little impact on many of the considerations behind their decision to resolve their contractual differences through arbitration. The contracting parties' confidence in the arbitration process and an arbitrator's presumed special competence in matters concerning bargaining agreements does not terminate with the contract. Nor would their interest in obtaining a prompt and inexpensive resolution of their disputes by an expert tribunal. Hence, there is little reason to construe this contract to mean that the parties intended their contractual duty to submit grievances and claims arising under the contract to terminate immediately on the termination of the contract; the alternative remedy of a lawsuit is the very remedy the arbitration clause was designed to avoid.[14]

Another issue resolved by the Supreme Court in recent years concerns how far the courts are willing to go in enforcing the role of the arbitrator. More specifically, what happens when one party is willing to arbitrate a grievance while the other party prefers to use the strike or lockout in order to resolve a dispute? As previously mentioned, a strike was a plausible alternative in resolving a grievance in the early years of arbitration. Also, the Trilogy did not specifically consider this alternative in its conclusions.

The award enforceability issue was brought before the courts in 1969 when a union protested a work assignment given to non–bargaining unit personnel. The union expressed its concern by striking even though the labor agreement contained a provision for arbitrating disputes over the terms of the agreement. In federal district court, management officials stressed that the union should use the contractually specified arbitration procedure and be enjoined from striking the employer. In its *Boy's Market* decision, the Supreme Court enforced injunctive relief in spite of the contrary philosophy of the Norris–La Guardia Act:

Indeed, the very purpose of arbitration procedures is to provide a mechanism for the expeditious settlements of industrial disputes without resort to strikes, lockouts, or other self-help measures. This basic purpose is obviously largely undercut if there is no immediate, effective remedy for those very tactics that arbitration is designed to obviate. . . .

The Norris–La Guardia Act was responsive to a situation totally different from that which exists today. In the early part of this century, the federal courts generally were regarded as allies of management in its attempt to prevent the organization and strengthening of labor unions; and in this industrial struggle the injunction became a potent weapon that was wielded against the activities of labor groups. . . .

Clearly employers will be weary of assuming obligations to arbitrate specifically enforceable against them when no similarly efficacious remedy is available to enforce the concomitant undertaking of the union to refrain from striking. On the other hand, the central purpose of the Norris–La Guardia Act to foster the growth and viability of labor organizations is hardly retarded—if anything, this goal is advanced by a remedial device that merely enforces the obligation that the union freely undertook under a specifically enforceable agreement to submit disputes to arbitration.[15]

The reasoning expressed in the *Boy's Market* decision has been narrowly applied; the decision was intended only for those situations which involve refusal to arbitrate according to grievance procedures established in the labor agreement. This distinction was emphasized in a subsequent Supreme Court decision[16] and in a district court finding regarding a 1977 strike over incentive pay plans by 14,000 iron-ore miners involving some United Steelworkers locals. The union members struck because they contended their hourly pay fell about 65 cents behind that of employees in steel-producing plants. The steel industry then sought an injunction against the strike, contending that the industry's Experimental Negotiating Agreement (ENA) provided for arbitration of unresolved negotiation issues. However, the federal district judge refused to issue an injunction because the incentive pay plan was not an issue covered by the ENA and was not subject to the grievance arbitration procedure of the local labor agreements.[17]

While the Supreme Court has encouraged and, in some cases, enforced the use of the arbitration process, additional consideration of the contemporary arbitrator's role is needed. The following section describes a typical arbitration proceeding as well as components and principles involved in an arbitrator's decision.

Elements of a Typical Arbitration Proceeding and Decision

Selection of Arbitrators

Before proceeding with arbitration, an initial decision has to be made regarding the number of "arbitrators" needed to resolve a grievance. In 1965, approximately 38 percent of the labor agreements specified a three-member board, with management and the union each nominating a member and these two individuals selecting the third member of the panel (the impartial arbitrator). Often this arrangement has been due to applicable state statutes (as in Georgia, South Carolina, and Texas).[18] Most decisions are made by the impartial arbitrator since the other two members of the panel are influenced by their respective management and union constituents. The most common method is to avoid the panel approach—the impartial arbitrator selected by management and union officials is solely responsible for the decision and obtains no help from other individuals in formulating the written opinion. In either case, the arbitrator's decision is final and binding unless, in extremely rare circumstances, both management and the union agree to disregard or set aside the arbitrator's award.

About 10 percent of the labor agreements in the United States provide for a *permanent arbitrator* or umpire to resolve all disputes during the life of the labor agreement.[19] Usually, this provision applies to large companies or industries, in which it is anticipated that a large number of grievances will be filed. Presumably, the permanent arbitrator can better allocate and schedule time to meet the grievance load of the union and employer, so that settlements can be reached more promptly. This type of selection arrangement also allows the permanent arbitrator to become more knowledgeable of the rather complex and unique terms of the parties' labor agreement and industrial operation. Assume, for example, that an arbitrator is hearing a grievance in the railroad industry for the first time. How long would it take for the arbitrator to accurately interpret the meaning of the following witness's testimony?

At 3 P.M. Mott Haven Yard was a busy place. A crew of gandy dancers tamped methodically on a frong near the switching lead. L.S. 3 was all made up and ready to be doubled over. She had forty-six hog racks on the head end and sixty-five empty reefers on the hind end. Her crew were all new men on the run. Mike Madigan, the hog-head, had just been set up. Bill Blanchard, the fire-boy, was a boomer who had recently hired out. Jack Lewis, the brains of the outfit, had been a no bill since he was fired out of the Snakes for violating Rule "G." Brady

Holms, the flagman, used to work the high iron in a monkey suit, and J. B. Wells was a "stu" brakeman, right off the street. Over on the hump lead, the yard rats were riding 'em in the clear and typing 'em down. The east side switcher was kicking loaded hoppers around, despite the violent washouts of the yardmixer who had discovered a hot box. Two Malleys were on the plug and three more were at the coal pocket. Our train, Number B.D. 5, was all ready to pull out.[20]

A permanent arbitrator saves time and expense since the parties do not have to repeatedly explain the unique meaning and implications of these terms in the arbitration hearing.

Greater consistency can be attained where one individual applies the same decision-making criteria to all of the arbitrated grievances. Consistent decisions aid union and management officials in the day-to-day administration of the labor agreement. They also should enable the parties to better predict the permanent arbitrator's subsequent decisions on similar issues, perhaps decreasing the number of frivolous grievances referred to arbitration as the parties become more certain of the arbitrator's reasoning. On the other hand, a retainer paid to the permanent arbitrator might encourage the parties to increase the grievance case load so that they can "get their money's worth."

Most labor agreements indicate that the arbitrator will be selected on an *ad hoc*, or case-by-case, basis. In 1973, approximately 80 percent of the labor agreements stated that union and management representatives could choose an arbitrator for a specific grievance, then select other arbitrators for subsequent grievances arising during the life of the labor agreement.[21] Particularly in the case of an established collective bargaining relationship, management and the union often reach an informal agreement regarding the appropriate arbitrator for a particular grievance. However, if they cannot agree, they usually obtain a list of arbitrators' names from either the Federal Mediation and Conciliation Service or the American Arbitration Association. In some cases, the parties request that these organizations select the particular arbitrator.

Clearly, for unions and companies having few grievances, ad hoc arbitrators are less expensive than permanent arbitrators. Regardless of the grievance load, ad hoc arbitration offers the advantage of flexibility. Permanent arbitrators usually are appointed by the parties for a specified period of time; neither side can discontinue the appointment alone if it views the permanent arbitrator's decisions with disfavor. There is no obligation to retain the ad hoc arbitrator in future grievances if one or both sides are displeased with the award.

Since some ad hoc arbitrators specialize in particular categories of grievances, such as job classification or wage incentives, they should be better informed than the permanent arbitrator on such issues. Permanent arbitrators may be more familiar with the parties, but may have seldom encountered a particular issue in their arbitration experience. Since both types of arbitrators have comparative advantages and disadvantages, management and union officials should carefully assess their particular situation before agreeing to either selection method.

Elements of the Arbitration Hearing

Prehearing briefs. *Prehearing briefs* highlighting the issues and positions of the parties can be filed by management and the union representative before the arbitrator arrives at the hearing. These optional briefs, which are infrequent, vary in length from a one-page letter to an extensively footnoted document. Some arbitrators see value in the prehearing brief, but others prefer to enter the hearing in a completely unbiased manner— the only information they would like to know in advance is the general subject matter of the grievance—whether it involves discipline, work assignment, or overtime payment.

The prehearing brief might backfire for the presenting party, who is subject to challenges on the assumed facts and inconsistencies that may surface in the witnesses' testimonies.

Facts presumed from preparatory interviews and investigations may wilt under examination at a hearing, permitting their exploitation by the other side. It is not unusual for a positive witness in the preparation stage to lose his certainty under questioning or for additional facts to become known at the hearing. These may prove embarrassing to initial arguments made either in a detailed opening statement or in a prehearing brief. Avoiding either would permit greater flexibility for handling the unanticipated in final argument.[22]

On the other hand, prehearing briefs can be viewed as keeping the parties honest—they must approach their contentions thoroughly and are forced to adhere to them during the arbitration proceedings.[23]

Perhaps more arbitrators would agree to the value of *prehearing stipulations*—joint union-management statements as to the issues involved and certain applicable grievance "facts." They save time in the arbitration hearing, for neither party feels obligated to repeat what the other has either previously said or agreed to in principle. Additionally, through the process of working together to stipulate the issues and facts, the parties may be able to resolve the disputes without arbitration.

The arbitration hearing. The *arbitration hearing,* held on a date convenient to the arbitrator and parties, varies in length from one-half hour to ten or more hours. Variations also occur in the extent to which courtroom procedures and behaviors are used or required during the hearing. Usually, the union and management representatives initiate the proceedings with opening statements which establish their respective issues and contentions on the issues. They attempt to focus the arbitrator's attention on points that will be proved to the satisfaction of the arbitrator in the subsequent discussion.[24]

The *grievance issue* (or submission agreement) to be resolved in the arbitration hearing is often complex, although it may be stated with deceptive simplicity. It is usually a one-sentence question to be answered by the arbitrator's award. Typical examples are:

☐ Did the company violate Section VI, Part 3 of the labor agreement when it transferred S——— S——— from position of leadman to welder III?

☐ Was B——— B——— discharged for just cause? If not, what shall be the remedy?

☐ Did the duties of machinist A's job undergo a significant change, thereby allowing the company to change the wage scale?

☐ Did J——— J———'s off-the-job activities have a significantly adverse effect on the company to justify dismissal?

Unfortunately, the issue is not always agreed upon by union and management representatives. The holiday scheduling grievance example in Chapter 8 can illustrate the problems surrounding issue formulation. Assume, for example, that the labor agreement has two provisions pertaining to arbitration:

Article XX: Arbitration Procedures

Section 1. The arbitrator's authority is solely derived from the clear and unequivocal terms of the labor agreement.

Section 2. The arbitrator may not add to, subtract from, or otherwise modify the express terms of the labor agreement.

In this situation, the union would claim that the issue pertains to the senior janitor's entitlement to holiday pay for the time involved due to the violation of Section 1 on the day in question. Management would contend that the issue of arbitrability is at stake or, more specifically, question whether the arbitrator has the authority to hear the case and fashion a remedy in accordance with the union's desires. The determination of the specific grievance issue could take a lot of time but is important, for the nature of the issue often determines whether the grievance is upheld or denied.

The remainder of the hearing is devoted to the presentation of: (a) the opening statement by each party's spokesperson, in which the major issues are presented to the arbitrator, (b) union and management witnesses for testimony and cross-examination, (c) related evidence to support union and management contentions (such as pictures of a job site, warning letters, performance ratings, and so on), and (d) union or management exhibits and those exhibits jointly recognized (if not entirely accepted) by both parites (such as the collective bargaining agreement and the employee's written grievance). The hearing is concluded with summaries and closing statements made by the union and management representatives, which stress why their respective positions must be accepted by the arbitrator.

The posthearing brief. An option available to the parties after the proceedings have ended is the filing of a written *posthearing brief*. One study found that this option is used in approximately 42 percent of the arbitrated grievances.[25] Some arbitrators believe that posthearing briefs are unnecessary if the parties have prepared and presented their case well during the hearing.[26] The arbitrator's review of the brief also adds time and expense to the grievance resolution decision. However, in a few cases, it becomes necessary. "This could be so, for example, where the evidence has taken many days, or is highly technical or complicated, or includes statistical data of a nature difficult to cover in an oral argument, or is perhaps of exceptional importance."[27]

This summary of arbitration proceedings does not do justice to the dynamics and reality of the hearing. Page limitations of the text do not permit detailing of its drama and the skills demanded of the practitioners. However, for illustrative purposes, assume that you are an industrial relations manager charged with proving an employee deserved discharge for smoking marijuana on company premises. Related concerns are:

☐ How do you prove the employee actually smoked the marijuana, since the evidence was destroyed, and it is the employee's word against supervisory observations?

☐ Will the grievant's testimony be strengthened or broken under cross examination?

☐ How long can the supervisor remain calm under union cross-examination, without losing his temper?

☐ What if the arbitrator gives little weight to the circumstantial evidence presented by the company and a great deal of weight to the grievant's previous long and exemplary work record with the company?

☐ Will the union introduce a surprise contention or witness not previously discussed in the grievance proceedings (for example, that the grievant's discharge was due to the racial bias of the supervisor)?

In the arbitration hearing, management and union officials display skills and reveal emotions and uncertainties in an attempt to prove their respective positions. The arbitrator has the difficult job of keeping an orderly hearing while, at the same time, objectively understanding and recording all of the facts presented by the union and management representatives.

Arbitration and Judicial Proceedings Compared The arbitration proceedings share some similarities with judicial proceedings, but their differences are profound. Many arbitration hearings differ from courtroom proceedings in that testimony of witnesses is not taken under oath and transcripts of the proceedings are also not taken. Except in a few states, arbitrators do not have the power to subpoena witnesses, and arbitrators nearly always have much more latitude than judges in determining admissibility of evidence, including, for example, hearsay testimony.

The most significant difference between the two processes is the arbitrator's reliance on *common law of the shop* principles in the resolution of disputes. Arbitrators, unlike judges, are selected by the parties to the dispute; thus, the arbitrator's major responsibility is to resolve a dispute in a manner that the parties can live with. Unlike judicial decisions in lower courts, the arbitrator's decision is usually final and not subject to further appeals. Consequently, the arbitrator must be concerned with the subsequent effects of his decision on union-management relationships. A judge has no such allegiance to the particular parties, the major responsibility being adherence to the statute in question, to established courtroom and legal procedures, and to precedent resulting from other applicable cases.

The common law of the shop thus often narrows the scope of arbitral decision making to the labor agreement language, intent, and past practices of the union and management officials at a particular industrial facility:

A proper conception of the arbitrator's function is basic. He is not a public tribunal imposed upon the parties by superior authority which the parties are obliged to accept. He has no general charter to administer justice for a community which transcends the parties. He is rather part of a system of self-government created by and confined to the parties. He serves their pleasure only, to administer the rule of law established by their collective agreement. They are entitled to demand that, at least on balance, his performance be satisfactory to them, and they can readily dispense with him if it is not.[28]

But a good arbitrator is more than an "ad hoc judge . . . expert in analyzing issues, in weighing evidence, and in contract interpretation." He must do that in the specialized context of labor relations, in the special community of an industrial plant and a local union. To be meaningful and convincing to the parties, his decisions should impart an understanding and comprehension of that atmosphere and should convey to them the conviction that their controversy is being decided not with reference to abstractions remote from their ken but with reference to the realities which govern their day-to-day in-plant lives.[29]

The distinction between judicial reasoning and common law of the shop principles can be shown through the following example. Assume that an employee has been discharged at Company A for drinking alcohol on the job. After the arbitral decision upholding the discharge has been reached, another employee at Company B is also discharged for drinking alcohol on the job. Strict adherence to judicial principles would uphold the second employee's discharge for drinking on the job. More specifically, the judicial principle of *stare decisis* (letting the decision at Company A stand in Company B's situation) or *res judicata* (refusing to have Company B's situation relitigated since the issue was already heard and resolved for Company A) would suggest the situation at Company B is moot.

However, the common law of the shop principles governing arbitration could lead the arbitrator to render an opposite decision at Company B than that reached at Company A. This decision could be due to the fact that the common law of the shop at Company B is entirely different from that found in other companies, particularly Company A. For example, supervisors at Company B may have been condoning this behavior and other employees at this company may have been caught drinking on the job without being discharged for the infraction. Consequently, the arbitrator recognizes the two companies are independent, with potentially unique circumstances, and therefore deserve mutually exclusive decisions.

It is also important to note that arbitrators are much more liberal than the courts in the types of evidence permitted at the hearing. Rationale for this practice is based on the notion that the parties are seeking a solution to their perceived unique problem. In addition, some arbitrators maintain that arbitration performs a therapeutic function, that the parties are entitled to air their grievances regardless of the eventual decision. Arbitrators may allow aggrieved employees to digress from the pertinent subject or "tell it like it is" in order to serve this therapeutic function.

Occasionally, evidence unknown to the other party is introduced in the arbitration hearing (either or both of the parties may introduce evidence which was not previously introduced in the pre-arbitral grievance steps). The arbitrator may accept or reject this new evidence, depending upon the weight attached to the following sometimes conflicting considerations: (a) the arbitrator's desire to learn of all the pertinent facts surrounding the grievance; (b) the need to protect the integrity of the pre-arbitral grievance machinery; and, (c) general concepts of fairness.[30] Since union and management officials and their designated arbitration panels are entitled to review all evidence presented at the hearing, it may be necessary to allow the opposing party additional time to review and respond to new evidence.

Offers of compromise settlements before the hearing are given virtually no weight by the arbitrator. Management officials, for example, might compromise their third-step discharge decision before arbitration by offering the grievant reinstatement with no back pay. A union could use this evidence to indicate to the arbitrator that management admitted being wrong by revising its original decision. However, arbitrators maintain that the parties should make every effort to resolve their dispute internally instead of going to arbitration. Thus, a compromise settlement between the parties is viewed by the arbitrator as a genuine attempt to accommodate differences, not an admission of guilt.

Other types of evidence are subject to varying arbitral consideration. As previously cited, hearsay testimony is usually admitted; however, it is typically given little or no weight, particularly if it is deduced that the witness has self-serving motives for testifying. Many of the more controversial sources of evidence are presented in discipline cases, which are further discussed in Chapter 11.

The *arbitrator's decision* is a written document submitted to the management and union officials. Its components include:

1. A statement of the issue(s).
2. A statement of the facts surrounding the grievance.
3. A summary of the union and management contentions.
4. A discussion and opinion of the validity and relative weight of the facts and contentions.
5. The arbitrator's award (grievance upheld, grievance denied, or a compromise between union and management contentions).

Few proscriptive guidelines govern the form and content of the arbitrator's decision. However, the arbitrator should demonstrate through the decision a thorough understanding of all the facts and contentions raised in the arbitration hearing. Some arbitrators address the decision to the losing party in the arbitration hearing because the winner does not have to be convinced he is right.

The necessity of the arbitrator's opinion has been subjected to considerable controversy. At least one labor lawyer has suggested that the arbitrator's decision is important, not the opinion explaining the reasoning behind the decision.

I am told by arbitrators that they write opinions because parties want an explanation. As a frequent party, my response is that this is often not true. I can tell you as a practitioner in this field that . . . I turn to the award and find out whether I won or lost. If I won, I really am not concerned with why I won. If I lost, I may read the opinion in order to confirm my conviction created by the award that the arbitrator was, is, and undoubtedly will continue to be as blind as a bat and as ignorant as an ass.[31]

The contrary view maintains that the arbitrator's opinion performs a necessary function for the arbitrator and others who may read his decision.

> Not only is an arbitrator's writing style on display in the usual opinion, but far more important is the exposure given his analytical skills, the fairness he demonstrates in evaluating the arguments of the parties, and his knowledge of the subtleties and unusual equities involved. . . .
> The writing of an opinion is also of tremendous value to the arbitrator. Only too often initial impressions, and even what we would consider well thought-out decisions have been modified or dramatically changed under the potent rigors involved in the discipline of writing an opinion.[32]

Additionally, the reasoning embodied in the arbitrator's opinion can serve as an instructional guideline for labor-management relationships. One arbitrator has stated:

> Parties do not spend many days of preparation, three days of hearings, and thousands of dollars worth of time of important officers and attorneys, for the purpose of finding out whether one girl should or should not have gotten a trivial promotion. They are interested in principles.[33]

To be sure, the arbitrator's opinion can, in some cases, be more important than the award. Assume, for example, the union grieves management's assignment of work normally performed in Job Classification A, loading trucks on Saturday, to an employee in Job Classification B, a laborer. Further, the union seeks a remedy of eight hours at overtime rate of pay for the appropriate employee in Job Classification A, the senior employee in the shipping department, on the reasoning that the company's violation of the contract had deprived a Classification A employee from the overtime opportunity. However, the arbitrator denies the grievance and stresses the following in his opinion: "The various job classifications are for pay purposes only and do not restrict management's prerogative to assign work across different job classifications." This statement significantly harms the union in related matters, particularly if the language was not expressly stated in the labor agreement. Now the union will have a difficult time in grieving any work assignment controversy, though the above decision pertained to one specific situation.

The preceding statement may have been necessary in reaching the grievance decision, but in other situations the arbitrator's gratuitous advice in the opinion may harm one or both of the parties.[34] There is often a thin line between "consulting" management and union practitioners on more effective and humane ways to run the operation and arbitrating the grievance solely on the merits of the case. The latter approach does not advise, merely determines if management's action was justifiable under the terms of the labor agreement and applicable past practice.

Decision-Making Criteria Used by Arbitrators

There are few, if any, consensually defined principles applicable to arbitrators' decisions, and there have been few field research efforts to uncover the arbitrators' decision-making process. One researcher, however, interviewed noted arbitrators and found that they, like others, do not follow precise or identical methods in their decisions.[35] Thus arbitration is considered by most to be a flexible procedure, one which is "continuously tailored to the needs of the particular relationship."[36] Nonetheless, generally accepted guidelines have developed and serve as focal points subject to interpretation, consideration, and application by arbitrators in resolving grievances.

Provisions of the Labor Agreement

The provisions of the labor agreement reflect the collectively bargained rights of union and management officials. Adherence to common law of the shop principles stresses that the major function of the arbitrator is the interpretation of the labor agreement's provisions. Indeed, many arbitrators adhere at least in part to the *parol evidence rule*, which in its classic form holds that evidence, oral or otherwise, cannot be admitted for the purpose of varying or contradicting written language recorded in the labor agreement. Rationale for this rule is that the parties have spent many hours in negotiating standardized employment conditions; thus, disregarding negotiated terms would damage stable labor-management relationships and communicate to the parties that there is little or no point in reducing contract terms to writing.

A problem remains when the labor agreement language is ambiguous. For example, such terms as "reasonable," "make every effort," "minor repairs," and "maintain the work environment as safely as possible" might have resolved negotiation impasses but still pose interpretive problems for the arbitrator. Individual interpretations of the meaning and applicability of these terms to a particular grievance could differ. Arbitrators prefer to approach this problem initially in terms of the labor agreement, and ambiguous language or provisions of the labor agreement would be construed so as to be compatible with the language in other provisions of the agreement. Thus, the contract should be viewed as a whole, not in isolated parts, and any interpretation which would nullify another provision of the contract should be avoided. When ambiguity remains, the arbitrator must seek guidance from sources outside the labor agreement.[37]

Intent of the Parties

Intent of the parties refers to what union and management officials had in mind when they either negotiated the labor agreement or engaged in an action that resulted in a particular grievance. Intent is entirely subjective; however, arbitrators consider observable behavioral manifestations of the intent to determine what a reasonable person would conclude from that behavior.

Assume, for example, that a supervisor believes an employee has stolen some company property. The supervisor approaches the employee stating:

You and I both know you were caught stealing. Therefore, you have two options. You can file a grievance which will be denied in arbitration and the discharge on your record will make it difficult for you to find a job elsewhere. Or you can sign this resignation slip, quit, and we won't tell any other companies about the stealing incident.

The employee hastily signs the slip and leaves the company premises. However, the next day she returns, informing management that she wants to work, since she never really quit. If the company refuses the employee's request and a subsequent grievance is filed, the arbitrator would have to determine the grievant's and management's intent. Observable behaviors of an employee intending to quit are cleaning out the locker, saying good-bye to colleagues, and asking management for the wages earned for that week. An employee usually resigns only after giving the decision careful thought and consideration. Since none of the behaviors were operative in this case, the arbitrator might attempt to determine management's intent in this action. Possibly, the supervisor was simply trying to do the employee a favor by letting her off the hook. However, management may have given the employee the alternative of quitting to avoid subsequent arbitration of the discharge and the risk of their discharge decision being overturned. The latter intent is viewed by arbitrators as being *constructive discharge.*

Under this principle, the arbitrator would view the termination of employment as being subject to the employee discipline provisions of the labor agreement. These provisions usually call for union representation and written explanation at the time of the employee's discharge. Since these procedures were not followed, many arbitrators would reinstate the grievant with full back pay. Sometimes, union and management officials attempt to convince the arbitrator of their specific intent by producing written notes of the contract negotiation discussions so that there will be documentation of their related past behaviors.

Past Practice

Past practice is closely related to the preceding guideline, for it can demonstrate to the arbitrator how the parties intended to carry out the labor agreement. This consideration has been used by both management and the union, depending upon the particular situation. Management is usually more concerned about past practice, since it administers the labor agreement through various supervisory directives to the hourly employees. Since established contractual provisions place restrictions on managerial discretion, management attempts to avoid further reductions on supervisory decision making by pressing for a past practices clause to be included in the labor agreement, similar to the following:

Article XXVIII: Other Agreements

Section 2. The parties do hereby terminate all prior agreements heretofore entered into between representatives of the company and the unions (including all past understandings, practices, and arbitration rulings) pertaining to rates of pay, hours of work, and conditions of employment other than those stipulated in this agreement between the parties.[38]

However, this clause does not guarantee that management does not add to its contractual restrictions by repeatedly handling a situation in a similar manner. For example, one arbitrator agreed with the union that a prevailing practice should be compelling in interpreting the labor agreement's ambiguity or silence on a particular issue.

The repeated execution of collective bargaining agreements which contain exclusive agreement provisions cancelling "all previous agreements" *has no magical dissolving effect* **upon practices or customs which are continued in fact unabated and which** *span successive contract periods*. **Although not verbalized in the current agreement, such practices may nonetheless comprise a part of it** *as any of its written provisions*.[39] **[Emphasis added.]**

Thus, a continued managerial practice of unilaterally giving employees a Christmas bonus might become a binding, implied term of the labor agreement. Further, management might have to negotiate a labor agreement provision to the contrary (even if the current labor agreement is silent on the subject) if they wish to discontinue the Christmas bonus in subsequent years.

In addition to interpreting ambiguous language or resolving problems not covered in the agreement, past practices may even alter clear and convincing contractual provisions. At one company, it had been a practice for many years to require clerks to perform cleanup operations at the end of their work day and to pay them no money for up to ten minutes work, fifteen minutes straight time for eleven to fifteen minutes work, and time and one-half for work of more than fifteen minutes in duration. There was clear contractual language specifying that work in excess of eight hours per day would be computed at time and one-half overtime premium. The union eventually filed a grievance stating that clear contractual language compelled overtime payment for any amount of daily work exceeding eight hours. However, the arbitrator maintained that past practice was more significant than the express terms of the labor agreement.

The written contract is, of course, the strongest kind of evidence of what the parties willed, intended or agreed upon. An arbitrator will not ordinarily look beyond its *unambiguous* **language. Where,** *however*, **as here,**

> the parties have *unmistakably* demonstrated *how they themselves* have read and regarded the meaning and force of the language, and *where the meaning varies* from its normal intendment, the arbitrator *should not,* indeed, *cannot* close his eyes to this demonstration.[40]

Past practice represents a specific and identical action which has been continually employed over a number of years to the recognition and satisfaction of both parties. Moreover, since there are no uniform standards of time, it is very difficult to determine for certain how long or how frequently an action must be continued before it is considered a binding past practice.

De minimis

De minimis refers to a technical but insignificant violation of the labor agreement. Arbitrators using this principle might deny a grievance because of its trivial, inconsequential nature. In one related situation, the union claimed that a contractual provision prohibiting supervisors from performing bargaining unit work was violated. The supervisor in this instance adjusted the prongs of a fork lift mechanism so that it could pick up an object. The supervisory effort took no more than two seconds, as he simply kicked one of the prongs with his foot to make the distance between the prongs wide enough to pick up the object. Therefore, the arbitrator denied the grievance, stating that the union was "scratching with the chickens" on such a small and insignificant issue. To award the union this grievance would be to encourage the filing of more trivial grievances, making a mockery of the labor-management relationship.

As is true with past practice, *de minimis* is not easily defined. This principle would probably be applicable if the supervisor changed one light bulb. The union might have a legitimate grievance, however, if the supervisor changed eight light bulbs (for a time period of fifteen minutes), and if the act deprived a union member of a call-out or overtime opportunity.

Previous Arbitration Awards

Previous arbitration awards are frequently introduced by either party when they have been decided at the same property or at different locations and could bolster either's position in the arbitration case. Similarly, the arbitrator may cite these awards to refute the parties' contentions or to illustrate the divergent arbitral opinion over the issue. However, one study analyzing the role and effectiveness of prior arbitration awards found that arbitrators tend to either ignore or refute them in their decisions.[41] Prior arbitration awards involving other facilities are at best illuminating but not compelling, as one arbitrator has noted:

> Company Counsel, in his post hearing brief, referred the Arbitrator to a number of decisions revolving around this same issue of jury pay. . . .

However, in the final analysis, other arbitrators' decisions, while informative and thought provoking, cannot determine the resolution of this particular issue. Such interpretation must be based on the parties' own contractual wording together with whatever meaning is contributed by customary practice.[42]

Thus, the common law of the shop diminishes the weight of prior arbitration awards from other properties, as arbitrators recognize the uniqueness and autonomy of a particular operation. In fact, arbitrators might negatively regard the introduction of prior arbitration awards into a current arbitration hearing:

Unwillingness to present a case solely on its own merits may come to be interpreted as a sign of weakness. Also it may be considered that citation of prior arbitration awards indicates either a lack of confidence in the judgment of an arbitrator or a belief that he may be swayed by irrelevant considerations. An attempt to induce an arbitrator to follow some alleged precedent may come to be recognized as at least bad etiquette.[43]

Prior arbitration awards presented at the same location carry more weight, particularly if the situation and contractual language are similar. Of course, few prior arbitration awards contain these elements, since the parties would be extremely reluctant to arbitrate the same issue a second time, given the first arbitrator's decision.

In summary, arbitration hearing procedures approximate courtroom behavior but depart from judicial procedures and principles in several ways. As is discussed in the next section, these differences can raise potential jurisdictional problems for various governmental agencies which are also charged with enforcing an employee's job rights.

Current Jurisdictional Issues Involving the Arbitrator

While the current role of labor arbitration has been clarified and enhanced through judicial decisions, jurisdictional problems still remain. Consider a case in which a black union steward, who filed a safety complaint, is discharged for insubordination. A subsequent grievance is filed and proceeds to arbitration under the terms of the labor agreement. However, the employee claims that the discharge was due not only to racial bias but also to the fact that the grievant filed a safety complaint in his capacity as a union steward. Conceivably, the discharge grievance could claim the attention of a number of persons—the arbitrator and representatives from the Equal Employment Opportunity Commission (EEOC), the Occupational Safety and Health Administration (OSHA), and the National Labor Relations Board (NLRB). The problem involves untangling the various jurisdictional squabbles which could arise over this one grievance.

The passage of the 1964 Civil Rights Act (amended by the Equal Employment Opportunity Act of 1972) and subsequent judicial decisions have emphasized that management's well-meant intentions are not sufficient to preclude a possible charge of racial discrimination. Indeed, in administering this aspect of public law, the EEOC holds that employers must actively devise and implement employment procedures which remove present as well as possible residual effects of past discrimination. Hiring and promotion procedures may be carefully scrutinized by the EEOC to protect minority employees from arbitrary and discriminatory practices. In a unionized facility, arbitrators also often assume a related decision-making role, particularly in grievances protesting discipline of a minority employee. This situation poses at least two questions:

1. Should management, the union, and the employee turn to the arbitrator, the EEOC, or both in resolving a minority employee's grievance?
2. How do the courts and the EEOC view the arbitrator's decision in terms of Title VII of the 1964 Civil Rights Act?

The first question was answered by a 1974 Supreme Court decision, *Alexander v. Gardner-Denver Company*. In this case, a discharged minority employee claimed racial discrimination; however, management's action was upheld by the arbitrator. Following the EEOC's subsequent determination that there was not reasonable ground to believe that a violation of Title VII of the 1964 Civil Rights Act had occurred, the employee sought relief from the alleged discriminatory action in the federal district court. This court (subsequently upheld by the court of appeals) dismissed the employee's action since the petitioner, having voluntarily elected to pursue his grievance under the nondiscrimination clause of the collective bargaining agreement, was bound by the arbitral decision and thereby precluded from suing his employer under Title VII. However, the Supreme Court reversed previous judicial decisions, finding that Title VII does not expressly permit deferral and that the arbitrator's major concern is to interpret the labor agreement, not federal law. Additionally, the Court found that the intent of Congress was to have the federal courts exercise final responsibility for the enforcement of Title VII, particularly since the arbitrator's expertise (as outlined in the previously discussed Trilogy) pertains to the interpretation of the labor agreement.

Arbitral procedures, while well suited to the resolution of contractual disputes, make arbitration a comparatively inappropriate forum for the final resolution of rights created by Title VII. This conclusion rests first on the special role of the arbitrator, whose task is to effectuate the intent of the parties rather than the requirements of enacted legislation. Where

> the collective-bargaining agreement conflicts with Title VII, the arbitrator must follow the agreement. To be sure, the tension between contractual and statutory objectives may be mitigated where a collective-bargaining agreement contains provisions facially similar to those of Title VII. But other facts may still render arbitral processes comparatively inferior to judicial processes in the protection of Title VII rights. Among these is the fact that the specialized competence of arbitrators pertains primarily to the law of the shop, not the law of the land. . . .
>
> Moreover, the factfinding process in arbitration usually is not equivalent to judicial factfinding. The record of the arbitration proceedings is not as complete; the usual rules of evidence do not apply; and rights and procedures common to civil trials, such as discovery, compulsory process, cross-examination, and testimony under oath, are often severely limited or unavailable.[44]

Consequently, a minority employee is almost encouraged to pursue the arbitration process as well as appropriate judicial procedures.

> A deferral rule also might adversely affect the arbitration system as well as the enforcement scheme of Title VII. Fearing that the arbitral forum cannot adequately protect their rights under Title VII, some employees may elect to bypass arbitration and institute a lawsuit. The possibility of voluntary compliance or settlement of Title VII claims would thus be reduced, and the result could well be more litigation, not less.
>
> We think, therefore, that the federal policy favoring arbitration of labor disputes and the federal policy against discriminatory employment practices can best be accommodated by permitting an employee to pursue fully both his remedy under the grievance-arbitration clause of a collective-bargaining agreement and his cause of action under Title VII. The federal court should consider the employee's claim *de novo*. The arbitral decision may be admitted as evidence and accorded such weight as the court deems appropriate.[45]

Similar reasoning is prevalent in the Department of Labor, where an Occupational Health and Safety Administration was created to enforce Public Law 91-596, the Occupational Safety and Health Act of 1970. Section 11 (c) of the act indicates that no employer shall discharge or in any manner discriminate against any employee because such employee has either filed a safety complaint or caused a proceeding related to the act. Thus, the secretary of labor is empowered to investigate related disciplinary action, the arbitral decision of the case notwithstanding.

Perhaps the most frequent supplements to arbitral decisions have come from the NLRB, because the grievant could have been discharged for reasons pertaining to provisions of the labor agreement which are similar to laws, such as engaging in union activities on the job or acting overly aggressive in the capacity of a union official. Section 10 (a) of the National

Labor Relations Act provides that the NLRB "is empowered . . . to prevent any person from engaging in any unfair labor practice (listed in Section 8) affecting commerce. This power shall not be affected by any other means of adjustment or prevention that has been or may be established by agreement, law or otherwise."

Although it has the power, the board does not ignore arbitration awards covering unfair labor practice issues. In fact, it often withholds its jurisdictional determination and investigation pending the arbitrator's decision. In 1955, the NLRB's deferral to arbitration policy was formulated in the *Spielberg Manufacturing Company* case. In that case, the board honored an arbitration award that denied reinstatement to certain employees guilty of strike misconduct. Resulting deferral guidelines stressed that the arbitration proceedings must be fair and regular, there must be adequate notice and representation, the arbitrator must approach the issue of the alleged unfair labor practice, and all parties must agree to be bound by the arbitration award.[46] However, the board will disregard the arbitrator's award if it is ambiguous or if the board obtains pertinent evidence not presented in the arbitration proceeding.[47]

The NLRB's deferral to arbitration policy was enhanced in the 1971 *Collyer* case, in which the NLRB trial examiner had found that the company had committed an unfair labor practice when it made certain unilateral changes in wages and working conditions.[48] The company maintained that the issues should be resolved through existing arbitration proceedings instead of the NLRB. The board in essence agreed with the company's position. While reserving the right to investigate the merits of the issue, the board maintained that:

1. Related disputes can be better resolved through the special skills and experiences of the arbitrators.
2. The objectives of the National Labor Relations Act, industrial peace and stability, can be significantly realized through adherence to arbitration procedures established in the labor agreement.

Under *Collyer*, the employee was obligated to use the arbitration procedure before the NLRB would review the merits of the case.

Two current NLRB decisions, however, have modified the broad deferral policy established in *Collyer*.[49] More specifically, the NLRB will defer to arbitration only if the issue does not involve a dispute alleging interference with employees' Section 7 rights. Thus, the NLRB will not currently defer an issue involving discipline for union activity even if the labor agreement specifies discipline for just cause is subject to arbitration. The employee, however, has to elect the remedy, going either to arbitration or to the NLRB for relief. In these cases, unlike racial discrimination cases, the employee forfeits subsequent use of the second option.

In summary, the Supreme Court has recognized the ability of arbitrators to interpret the labor agreement provisions and has even encouraged the parties to arbitrate the issue before proceeding to the NLRB.[50]

However, this encouragement is not given to the same extent in Title VII disputes. Additionally, governmental agencies such as EEOC, OSHA, and NLRB retain jurisdiction of a related issue and can modify an arbitrator's decision if it conflicts with their conception of public policy.

The issue of arbitral consideration of federal policy is still inconclusive. Some arbitrators maintain that their only role is to interpret the labor agreement and that the role of federal law is best left to the courts or to the appropriate administrative agency.[51] Others suggest that the arbitrator has an obligation to consider appropriate judicial decisions in the award.[52]

Appraisal of the Current Arbitration Process

While the Supreme Court Trilogy might typify judicial enthusiasm for arbitration, as noted in the preceding section, some governmental agencies tend to be more qualified in their endorsement. Some critical assessments of arbitration have come from the participants—union and management officials and even some arbitrators. In determining arbitration's various alleged defects, it is also necessary to determine the relative culpability of arbitrators and the other two parties to the arbitration hearing. There appear to be two general areas of criticism: (a) the capability and ethics of the arbitrator, and (b) potential procedural problems in the arbitration process.

The Capability and Ethics of the Arbitrator

As previously discussed, the arbitrators are hired by the parties to resolve disputes in a manner conducive to harmonious subsequent labor-management relationships. However, the arbitrator's devotion to union's and management's needs can be viewed in many different ways. Some critics of arbitration have contended that the arbitrator's decisions are adversely linked with financial dependence on the parties:

A proportion of arbitration awards, no one knows how large a proportion, are decided not on the basis of the evidence or of the contract or other proper considerations, but in a way which in the arbitrator's opinion makes it likely that he will be hired for other arbitration cases. It makes no difference whether or not a large majority of cases is decided in this way. A system of adjudication in which the judge depends for his livelihood, or for a substantial part of his livelihood or even for substantial supplements to his regular income, on whether he pleases those who hire him to judge is per se a thoroughly undesirable system. In no proper system of justice should a judge be submitted to such pressures. . . .

We know that a large proportion of the awards of arbitrators are rendered by incompetents, that another proportion—we do not know how large but are permitted by the circumstances to suspect that it is quite large—is rendered on the basis of what award might be best for the arbitrator's future.[53]

In some instances, union and management practitioners believe that the arbitrator "owes them one" due to their support (financial and otherwise). One arbitrator, who expressed surprise to union and management officials at being selected to replace another prominent arbitrator, was given the following reason why the previous arbitrator was fired:

"I'll tell you why we fired him. The last case he had ended here at about 4:00. Mr. _____ expressed considerable concern since he had to make a plane for New York and was running late. I assured him that he would have no problem. I carried his bags to his car, drove in excess of all the speed limits, went through back roads, even proceeded through changing traffic lights. After a hectic ride and at considerable risk, I got him to the airport just in time to make the plane. I parked my car in a no parking zone. I even carried his bags to the gate. After all this, you know, that son-of-a-bitch ruled against me."[54]

Yet other participants or students of arbitration maintain that the arbitrator's indebtedness to the parties is a necessary ingredient of dispute resolution. They maintain that the arbitrator owes allegiance to both union and management and thus is accountable rather than indebted to the parties:

The arbitrator functions in a glass bowl. The conduct of the hearing is closely observed by sophisticated, knowledgeable advocates. An arbitrator who exhibits a lack of understanding of the process and who fails to conduct a hearing in an orderly fashion will usually find himself unacceptable to the parties for a subsequent hearing. The *ad hoc* arbitrator has no tenure; an umpire has limited tenure, and nothing is so impermanent as the permanent arbitrator. . . . His decisions are read and reread, not only by the parties, but by hundreds of company and union representatives who have access to his awards through their own systems of distribution. Awards that are not based upon logical, sound interpretation of the provisions of the agreement will very quickly make the arbitrator responsible unacceptable to companies and unions alike.[55]

Other criticisms have focused on the quality of the arbitrator's decision. The arbitrator's written opinion and award dissatisfy the parties if they do not reflect the original expectations and understandings of one or both regarding the nature or scope of the grievance. But many arbitral decision problems may be attributed in large part to the union and management officials instead of the arbitrator. For example, some union and management officials ask the arbitrator to isolate and define the issues from the presentations of the case and then resolve the issue on the basis of that haphazard record. Under this situation, the officials must share the greater burden of blame if the arbitrator's decision doesn't directly and concisely resolve the particular problem.

Management and union representatives might also obtain poor arbitration awards under the *garbage in, garbage out theory*. Since the arbitrator's decision is based on the merits of the grievance, a sloppy grievance formulation and presentation might result in a relatively lackluster arbitral decision. Sometimes, union and management officials present the arbitrator with poorly conceived grievances which one of the parties could and should have resolved before going to arbitration. Such grievances are often prompted by political considerations[56]—the union or management officials take the grievance to arbitration to show support for their constituents (union stewards or first-line supervisors) even though they know them to be wrong. Arbitration in this sense serves as a buck-passing device; the errant union steward or supervisor is apparently given support but in reality is provided an education through the arbitrator's decision.

One almost inescapable concern arises from the finality of the arbitrator's award. While the Supreme Court has encouraged single-person resolution of an industrial dispute, opponents of this practice suggest that an arbitrator has more authority than a judge, whose decision may be overturned through judicial appeal. Clearly, a problem can arise from this form of dispute resolution; however, this disadvantage must be compared with the disadvantages associated with a potential appeal of the arbitrator's decision:

Certainly any appeal procedure that might be established would detract from two desirable characteristics of arbitration: speed of reaching a final decision, and economy. But going beyond that, there is no acceptable hierarchy for climbing the judicial pyramid. Even if a David Cole can be found who will differ with, and overturn a decision by a George Taylor, there is no accepted pecking order for appealing a Taylor decision to a Cole or vice versa. Nor is there any accepted body of precedents upon which to make a more objective evaluation. And if such *ad hoc* appeals were permitted, how long should the procedure be allowed to continue? The best two out of three decisions?[57]

Procedural Problems

The second general category of criticisms pertains to procedural problems in the arbitration process. Two interrelated problems pertain to time lag and expense associated with arbitration. One research effort has found that the length of time from request for arbitration to the arbitrator's award averages 168 days.[58] Clearly, this delay affects employees who rightfully maintain that their complaint should be resolved in a prompt and efficient manner. Similarly, management equates the arbitral decision-making delay in many grievance issues, such as discipline and reclassification of a particular job, with unnecessary expense, since adverse awards can also include remedies for back pay retroactive to the date the grievance was filed.

Critics of arbitration claim that there is an inadequate supply of arbitrators. For example, a 1970 survey involving members of the National Academy of Arbitrators found that the average age of arbitrators in 1969 was fifty-seven, compared to the 1962 age average of fifty-three.[59] Clearly, accepted arbitrators tend to belong to a select group, with little opportunity for newcomers to join. If grievance resolution is limited to a relatively small number of arbitrators, then time delays are inevitable. However, the causes for this short supply of arbitrators appear mainly attributable to union and management practitioners, many of whom candidly admit that they will wait months for the "old hands" instead of taking their chances with "newcomers."[60]

Other expenses associated with arbitration include: the arbitrator's daily fee, normally approximately $200 (and in some cases exceeding $500); the arbitrator's travel and study time, normally paid at the daily rate; the fees for the parties' attorneys, which usually exceed the arbitrator's fee; wage payments to plant personnel who take part in the proceedings; and stenographic transcription costs, if a record of the hearing is desired. While most labor agreements provide for sharing of arbitral expenses, excluding the expenses associated with the parties' attorneys and witnesses, the cost of a one-day hearing could run as high as $1,000 for each of the parties.[61]

Whereas arbitral fees have increased over the years, this situation, adjusted for inflation, does not appear unreasonable. In many cases, management and union officials bring added expenses upon themselves when they insist that the arbitrator review unnecessary materials, such as testimony, transcripts, prior arbitration awards, superfluous union and management witnesses, and pre and posthearing briefs. They may also insist on expensive frills, such as the renting of a hotel suite for a neutral arbitration site, which do not materially affect the quality of the decision.[62]

At least one group of union and management officials has attempted to alleviate cost and time problems of the arbitration procedure. In 1971, the ten major steel producers (the Coordinated Steel Companies) and the United Steelworkers of America adopted an expedited arbitration procedure whereby some two hundred relatively inexperienced arbitrators decide routine (non–precedent setting) grievances. This process requires a brief (one- or two-page) decision within two days after the hearing.[63] The success of this experimental approach has not yet been fully resolved. However, its use illustrates two fundamental issues concerning arbitration:

1. This process, while not perfect, appears to offer great advantages over

alternative methods of grievance resolution, such as "pulling the pin" through sudden strike activity.[64]

2. Union and management officials created the arbitration process and are charged with controlling it in accordance with their jointly determined needs. They must monitor the process as well as their actions to insure a relatively inexpensive, efficient, and objective means of dispute resolution.

Summary

The arbitration process was little used during the period from 1865 to World War II; however, during World War II the National War Labor Board encouraged its widespread use. While the increased reliance upon arbitration continued after World War II, a major problem of enforcing the arbitrator's decision remained. Either party could have refused to abide by the arbitrator's decision, with uncertain consequences from the courts. This problem was initially approached by the *Lincoln Mills* decision, which provided a judicial avenue for enforcement, and the Supreme Court Trilogy, three cases which established the superiority of the arbitration process relative to the courts in resolving industrial grievances. Subsequent Supreme Court decisions have indicated that termination of the labor agreement does not eliminate the possibility of arbitration and injunctive relief might be granted when one party refuses to arbitrate according to grievance procedures established in the labor agreement.

Before the arbitration hearing, arbitrators must be selected either on an ad hoc or permanent basis. Each of these selection techniques has unique advantages, depending on the particular circumstances. The same can be said of prehearing and posthearing briefs. Other elements of an arbitration hearing include the grievance issue, presentation of witnesses for testimony and cross-examination, and presentation of separate and joint exhibits.

The hearing scene is a dramatic one; union and management officials display their skills in attempting to convince the arbitrator their positions are correct. The arbitration hearing shares many similarities with a judicial trial but differs in several ways. Perhaps the most significant difference is the arbitrator's reliance on the common law of the shop.

In determining the common law of the shop, arbitrators give particular weight to the provisions of the labor agreement, the intent of the parties, and past practice. Arbitrators may also consider the *de minimis* principle and, to a much lesser extent, prior arbitration awards in arriving at their decisions. Since arbitration procedures differ in some respects from those used in a courtroom, various jurisdictional disputes can occur regarding interpretations of contract provisions by arbitrators and the legal interpretation of federal policy. For example, a discharge case decided by the arbitrator could be subsequently considered by the Equal Employment Opportunity Commission, the Occupational Safety and Health Administration, and the National Labor Relations Board.

Some criticisms directed toward arbitration pertain to the capability of the arbitrator and potential procedural problems in the arbitration process. Certain arbitral problems such as expense, time lag, and excessive formality may be due to labor and management preferences rather than any characteristics inherent in the arbitration process. Yet requests for arbitrators have nearly tripled in the last ten years; arbitration has become an accepted, integral part of labor-management relationships. Arbitration's future as a system of industrial jurisprudence appears equally promising.

Discussion Questions

1. How did World War II and the National War Labor Board greatly expand the use of arbitration?

2. "The Supreme Court Trilogy greatly enhanced the arbitrator's authority when compared to previous years, yet did not give the arbitrator final jurisdiction over certain issues." Thoroughly discuss the preceding statement in terms of the specific features of these judicial decisions; also consider current jurisdictional issues arbitrators face in terms of governmental agencies.

3. Discuss the similarities and differences of arbitration and judicial hearings, with particular emphasis on the common law of the shop, admission of evidence, and the role of the arbitrator versus that of the judge.

4. Why are arbitrators' decisions usually lengthy, since one sentence could indicate who was right and wrong? Your discussion of this question should include the purposes of arbitration and advantages as well as disadvantages of an extensive arbitral decision.

5. Discuss two decision-making criteria used by arbitrators, furnishing rather specific examples (not mentioned in the text) of how these criteria can come into play.

6. Cite and defend three specific methods you would use to make the typical arbitration procedure more effective. Also indicate the advantages and disadvantages of your suggestions.

References

[1]Julius Rezler and Donald Peterson, "Strategies of Arbitrator Selection," *Labor Arbitration Reports 70* (Washington, D.C.: Bureau of National Affairs, 1978), p. 1307. For statistics illustrating the increasing use of arbitration over the years see the Federal Mediation and Conciliation Service, *Thirtieth Annual Report* (Washington, D.C.: Government Printing Office, 1977), p. 43.

[2]R. W. Fleming, *The Labor Arbitration Process* (Urbana: University of Illinois Press, 1965), pp. 9–10.

[3]It should be noted that on October 3, 1942, the board's jurisdiction was extended to all industries and to all employers. Marion Dickerman, "Decisions of the National War Labor Board," *Arbitration Journal* 6 (August 1942), p. 246. Also, Executive Order 9017 was given statutory authority under the 1943 War Labor Disputes Act.

[4]William P. Witherow, "Labor Arbitration in Wartime," *Arbitration Journal* 6 (Spring 1942), pp. 11–12.

[5]Matthew Woll, "Labor Arbitration in Wartime," *Arbitration Journal* 6 (Spring 1942), pp. 94–95.

[6]Brook I. Landis, *Value Judgments in Arbitration: A Case Study of Saul Wallen* (Ithaca, N.Y.: Cornell Studies in Industrial and Labor Relations, Cornell University, 1977), pp. 5–6.

[7]Frank Elkouri and Edna Asper Elkouri, *How Arbitration Works*, 3d. ed. (Washington, D.C.: Bureau of National Affairs, 1973), p. 15.

[8]For an interesting discussion of the intent of this provision see Isadore Katz and David Jaffe, "Enforcing Labor Arbitration Clauses by Section 301, Taft-Hartley Act," *Arbitration Journal* 8 (1953), pp. 80–88.

[9]*Textile Workers Union of America v. Lincoln Mills of Alabama*, 353 U.S. 456 (1957).

[10]*United Steelworkers of America v. American Manufacturing Company*, 363 U.S. 566–567 (1960).

[11]*United Steelworkers of America v. Warrior and Gulf Navigation Company*, 363 U.S. 582 (1960).

[12]Ibid., p. 584.

[13]*United Steelworkers of America v. Enterprise Wheel and Car Corporation*, 363 U.S. 598 (1960).

[14]*Nolde Brothers, Inc. v. Local No. 358, Bakery and Confectionary Workers Union AFL-CIO*, 430 U.S. 254 (1977).

[15]*The Boys Market, Inc. v. Retail Clerk's Union, Local 770*, 398 U.S. 249, 250, 252–253 (1970).

[16]*Buffalo Forge Company v. United Steelworkers of America*, 428 U.S. 397 (1970).

[17]John Hoerr, "Why a Labor Pact Won't End Steel's Problems," *Business Week*, September 26, 1977, p. 56.

[18]Owen Fairweather, *Practice and Procedure in Labor Arbitration* (Washington, D.C.: Bureau of National Affairs, 1973), p. 70.

[19]Bureau of National Affairs, *Basic Patterns in Union Contracts* (Washington, D.C.: Bureau of National Affairs, 1975), p. 39.

[20]Delbert C. Miller and William Form, *Industrial Sociology*, 2d ed. (New York: Harper & Row, 1964), p. 264.

[21]Bureau of National Affairs, *Basic Patterns*, p. 38.

[22]Benjamin C. Roberts and G. Allan Dash, Jr., "How to Get Better Results from Labor-Management Arbitration," *Arbitration Journal* 22 (1967), p. 4.

[23]Samuel H. Jaffee, "It's Your Money! Cutting the Costs of Labor Arbitration," *Arbitration Journal* 26 (1971), p. 170.

[24]For a detailed discussion of the arbitration hearing see Sam Kagel, *Anatomy of a Labor Arbitration* (Washington, D.C.: Bureau of National Affairs, 1961).

[25]Maurice S. Trotta, *Arbitration of Labor-Management Disputes* (New York: American Management Association, 1974), p. 102.

[26]Harold Davey, "Restructuring Grievance Arbitration Procedures," *Iowa Law Review* 54 (February 1969), p. 560.

[27]Jaffee, "It's Your Money! Cutting the Costs," p. 176.

[28]Harry Shulman, "Reason, Contract, and Law in Labor Relations," *Harvard Law Review* 68 (1955), p. 1016.

[29]Byron Yaffe, ed., *The Saul Wallen Papers: A Neutral's Contribution to Industrial Peace* (Ithaca: New York State School of Industrial Relations, Cornell University, 1974), p. 32.

[30]Elkouri and Elkouri, *How Arbitration Works*, p. 258.

[31]Stephen C. Vladek, "Comment: The Use and Abuse of Arbitral Power," in Barbara D. Dennis and Gerald G. Somers, eds., *Labor Arbitration at the Quarter-Century Mark* (Washington, D.C.: Bureau of National Affairs, 1973), p. 84.

[32]Hyman Cohen, "The Search for Innovative Procedures in Labor Arbitration," *Arbitration Journal* 29 (June 1974), pp. 112–113.

[33]Whitley P. McCoy's comments in an arbitration decision (Southern Bell and Telegraph Co., January 29, 1951), cited in Harry J. Dworkin, "How Arbitrators Decide Cases," *Labor Law Journal* 25 (April 1974), p. 208.

[34]See, for example, Anthony V. Sinicropi and Peter A. Veglahn, "Dicta in Arbitration Awards: An Aid or Hindrance?" *Labor Law Journal* 23 (September 1972), pp. 560–566.

[35]Harold Davey, "How Arbitrators Decide Cases," *Arbitration Journal* 27 (December 1972), p. 277.

[36]Roberts and Dash, "How to Get Better Results from Labor-Management Arbitration," p. 1.

[37]Fairweather, *Practice and Procedure*, pp. 166, 167, 169. See also Peter Seitz, "Communications: Value Judgments in the Decisions of Labor Arbitrators," *Industrial and Labor Relations Review* 21 (April 1968), p. 429.

[38]This provision on past practice taken from Walter E. Baer, *Practice and Precedent in Labor Relations* (Lexington, Mass.: Lexington Books, 1972), p. 8.

[39]Ibid., p. 9.

[40]Ibid., p. 38.

[41]Ken Jennings and Cindy Martin, "The Role of Prior Arbitration Awards in Arbitral Decisions," *Labor Law Journal* 29 (February 1978), pp. 95–106.

[42]*FMC Corporation*, 65 LA 266 (M. Warns, 1975).

[43]William H. McPherson, "Should Labor Arbitrators Play Follow the Leader?" *Arbitration Journal* 4 (1949), p. 170.

[44]*Harrel Alexander, Sr., v. Gardner-Denver Company*, 415 U.S. 60 (1974).

[45]Ibid., p. 57. For an analysis of this case's implications for the arbitration process see Sanford Cohen and Christian Eaby, "The Gardner-Denver Decision and Labor Arbitration," *Labor Law Journal* 27 (January 1976), pp. 18–23. It should be noted that the dual options available to the employee are concurrent—the employee is almost obligated to pursue both options at the same time, as the time required for arbitral decisions is credited to the statute of limitations imposed by the EEOC. See Marvin Hill, Jr., "Grievance Procedures and Title VII Limitations," *Labor Law Journal* 28 (June 1977), pp. 339–343.

[46]*Spielberg Manufacturing Company*, 112 NLRB 1080 (1955).

[47]Trotta, *Arbitration of Disputes*, p. 133. For thorough discussions of jurisdictional issues involving the NLRB and arbitration see Edwin R. Teple, "Deferral to Arbitration: Implications of NLRB Policy," *Arbitration Journal* 29 (June 1974), pp. 65–97; Dallas Jones, ed., *The Arbitrator, the NLRB, and the Courts* (Washington, D.C.: Bureau of National Affairs, 1967); and Jay W. Waks, "The 'Dual Jurisdiction' Problem in Labor Arbitration: A Research Report," *Arbitration Journal* 23 (1968), pp. 201–227.

[48]*Collyer Insulated Wire and Local Union 1098, International Brotherhood of Electrical Workers*, 192 NLRB 150 (August 20, 1971).

[49]*Ray Robinson, Inc., and International Association of Machinists and Aerospace Workers, Local Lodge 1224, AFL-CIO*, 228 NLRB (March 20, 1977); and *General American Transportation Corporation and Perry Soape, Jr.*, 228 NLRB No. 102 (March 20, 1977). Both cases cited in Bureau of National Affairs, *Daily Labor Report*, No. 53 (March 18, 1977). It should be noted that these cases reflect the NLRB's split over Collyer's deferral guidelines over the years.

[50]*James B. Carey v. Westinghouse Electric Corporation*, 375 U.S. 261–276 (1964).

[51]For a discussion of this and other related contentions see Michael I. Sovern, "When Should Arbitrators Follow Federal Law?" in Dallas Jones, ed., *Arbitration and the Expanding Role of Neutrals* (Washington, D.C.: Bureau of National Affairs, 1970), pp. 29–47; and Harry T. Edwards, "Arbitration of Employment Discrimination Cases: A Proposal for Employer and Union Representatives," *Labor Law Journal* 27 (May 1976), pp. 265–277.

[52]James A. Gross, "The Labor Arbitrator's Role: Tradition and Change," *Arbitration Journal* 25 (1970), p. 231.

[53]Paul R. Hays, *Labor Arbitration: A Dissenting View* (New Haven, Conn.: Yale University Press), pp. 112–113.

[54]Dworkin, "How Arbitrators Decide Cases," p. 203.

[55]Burt L. Laskin, "Arbitration and Its Critics," in Charles M. Rehmus, ed., *Proceedings of the Twenty-first Annual Meeting, National Academy of Arbitrators* (Washington, D.C.: Bureau of National Affairs, 1968), p. 134. For details concerning legal accountability of arbitrators see Leslie Alan Glick, "Bias, Fraud, Misconduct, and Partiality of the Arbitrator," *Arbitration Journal* 22 (1967), pp. 161–172.

[56]One related empirical study has suggested that almost one out of every four grievances taken by the union to arbitration was for a political goal, not necessarily directly related to the issue or merit of the case. Donald J. Peterson, "Why Unions Go to Arbitration: Politics and Strategy versus Merit," *Personnel* 48 (July–August 1971) pp. 44–49.

[57]Donald B. Straus, "Labor Arbitration and Its Critics," *Arbitration Journal* 20 (1965), p. 201. It should also be known that Messrs. Cole and Taylor have been recognized as eminent arbitrators.

[58]W. J. Ussery, Jr., "Some Attempts to Reduce Arbitration Costs and Delays," *Monthly Labor Review* 95 (November 1972), pp. 3–4. A more recent study has found that the average time from grievance date to the receipt of the arbitration award is over 220 days. Peter A. Veglahn, "Arbitration Costs/Time: Labor and Management Views," *Labor Law Journal* 30 (January 1979), p. 49.

[59]Trotta, *Arbitration of Disputes*, p. 65.

[60]Harold Davey, "What's Right and What's Wrong with Grievance Arbitration: The Practitioners Air Their Views," *Arbitration Journal* 28 (December 1973), p. 220. See also Rezler and Peterson, "Strategies of Arbitrator Selection," p. 1315.

[61]Usery, "Some Attempts to Reduce Arbitration Costs and Delays," p. 3. These expenses pertain to the arbitration hearing. Another potentially significant expense could arise in subsequent litigations of the arbitrator's award.

[62]Jaffee, "It's Your Money! Cutting the Costs," pp. 168, 172. For a thorough discussion of several ways union and management officials can reduce arbitration costs see William B. Werther, Jr., and Harold C. White, "Cost Effective Arbitration," *MSU Business Topics* 26 (Summer 1978), pp. 57–64.

[63]Cohen, "The Search for Innovative Procedures," p. 110. See also B. Fischer, "The Steel Industry's Expedited Arbitration," *Arbitration Journal* 28 (September 1973), pp. 185–189.

[64]This attitude was generally expressed in the following survey of 239 union officials: Harry E. Graham, Brian P. Heshizer, and David B. Johnson, "Grievance Arbitration Labor Officials' Attitudes," *Arbitration Journal* 33 (June 1978), pp. 21–24.

Part 3 examines the variety of work rules which represent the outcome of the labor relations process. Institutional issues pertaining to the rights and responsibilities of the union and management organizations are discussed. Next the significance and elements of effective employee discipline are explored. A discussion of many administrative and economic concerns which are resolved through collective bargaining concludes the section.

Part 3

The Outcome of the Labor Relations Process: Collective Bargaining Issues

Chapter 10

Institutional Issues: Managerial Prerogatives, Union Security, and the Rights of Union Members and Minority Employees

"Today, because of the majoritarian bias inherent in collective bargaining—its commitment to democratic and egalitarian values—there must be some sacrifice of individual freedom. . . . But within the collective framework, the dissenting individual must be protected, and all those represented must be saved from negligent or corrupt representatives."

Harry H. Wellington, Labor and the Legal Process, 1968.

An initial collective bargaining issue pertains to the rights and obligations of the labor and management organizations. Management's major institutional issue concerns its managerial prerogatives, or right to manage. The union has a corresponding institutional concern of union security, or its ability to preserve its organization—mainly by enrolling and retaining employee members. These two concerns are discussed in the chapter, as is the union's institutional obligation to represent its members (fair representation). A concluding section examines the relationship between organized labor and minority (black and female) employees.

Managerial Prerogatives

Chief among management's concerns in the labor relations process is the issue of *managerial prerogatives*—the amount and areas of discretion managers have in operating the facility. The early and, in some cases, current events of collective bargaining are marked by managerial reluctance to recognize the union on the basis that "outsiders" would usurp these inherent rights or prerogatives. Negotiation and administration of the labor agreement are also influenced by the degree that management officials will concede certain issues which they believe are in their exclusive domain. This section illustrates the controversy over the extent of managerial prerogatives and discusses how the collective bargaining agreement and related activities can strengthen or weaken managerial prerogatives.

The Extent of Managerial Prerogatives

Managers have long believed that they have inherent or reserved rights to operate their facilities, and that unions threaten the very existence of management when they attempt to obtain these rights in the collective bargaining process. As indicated by a classic managerial quotation in the early 1900s, unions' "intrusions" were not taken lightly:

Who but a miserable, craven-hearted man would permit himself to be subjected to such rules, extending even to the number of apprentices he may employ, and the manner in which they shall be bound to him; to the kind of work which will be performed in his own office, at particular hours of the day, and to the sex of the persons employed. . . . For ourselves, we never employed a female as compositor, and have no great opinion of apprentices; but sooner than be restricted on these points, or any other, by a self-constituted tribunal outside of the office, we would go back to the employment of our boyhood and dig potatoes. . . . It is marvelous to us how any employer having a soul of a man within him can submit to such degradation.[1]

Controversy over management rights continued, reaching an intense peak immediately following World War II. At that time, President Truman called a joint National Labor Management Conference which, among other items, attempted to establish some guidelines regarding the nature of managerial prerogatives. The conference clearly established one point—labor and management could not agree on what rights, if any, should be reserved for management.[2] This controversy remains today, with many managers concerned about the gradual erosion of their rights in the collective bargaining process. One contemporary management official suggests:

It is not so much what the demand is now, but where does it all end? We can stand the rough seas if we know where we are headed. We have dealt with one union now for 35 years, and 35 years is a long time.

Two questions which help us assess this controversy are:

1. Does management have inherent or reserved rights regarding its employees?
2. To what extent does the union desire to assume managerial discretion?

Under common law, management officials were relatively free to manage their businesses and their employees. In unilaterally running the operation, the employer drew from the concepts of property rights and the laws of agency as well as the legal and social acceptance of "private enterprise," "ingenuity," and the "profit motive."[4] Hence, management assumed the right to manage derived from the property rights of the owners or stockholders. The authority of these owners is delegated to management, which in turn directs the employees in achieving the goals of the company. Following this line of reasoning, management contends it cannot share its prerogatives with employees or any other group, as that would represent a dereliction of legal responsibility to the stockholders.

There is no question that management can organize, arrange, and direct the machinery, materials, and money of the enterprise; however, at least one author contends that managers have no comparable right to direct the employees. Indeed, the employee-employer relationship is similar to a continuing buyer-seller relationship in which the employer purchases the employee's services. In the absence of a written or terminal agreement between the manager and the employee, both parties are free to terminate the relationship if not satisfied with the conditions. Property rights carry no duty on the part of others to be managed—they can quit or be discharged without regard to the employer's property rights. *Thus, management's property rights have never extended over the employees. "What has happened is that, through the union, the employee has acquired sufficient power to exercise the legal right that he has always possessed."*[5]

Unions have typically expressed reluctance to become involved in management's rights pertaining to machinery, materials, and money of the enterprise. For example, two surveys found that most union officials believe management has the right to determine layout of equipment, financial policies and practices, source of materials, and determination of products and services to be rendered.[6] The following comments of a union official place the survey's findings in perspective:

Unions' reluctance to become partners with management is subject to qualification, particularly if managerial actions affect employee job content and opportunities.[8] Generally, the union's interests are restricted to protecting its members' job interests and itself as an institution. The distinction between the employer's property rights and the union's interests is not clear-cut. For example, new machinery or arrangement of production equipment might affect employees' wages and job tenure. Managerial discretion in running operations might be challenged and limited by unions if management's actions affect union members. This lack of clear-cut distinction is further illustrated by related provisions of the labor agreement.

Managerial Prerogatives and the Collective Bargaining Agreement

The labor agreement both restricts and enhances managerial discretion. On the one hand, it restricts managers by telling them what they can't do. But management is free to do as it pleases on issues not in the labor agreement, since the union has either neglected or failed to negotiate related contractual provisions which would restrict management. Following this line of reasoning, a labor agreement maximizing managerial discretion would be only one sentence: "Management has the unilateral right to direct the working force as it sees fit."

It is generally true that, absent contractual language, management assumes a relatively free hand in directing employees. However, this is not an unqualified right, particularly since most labor agreements contain grievance procedures including binding arbitration by a third party neutral.[9] Arbitrators' interpretations of the terms of the labor agreement ultimately affect managerial discretion. For example, labor agreements usually indicate that management has the right to discipline for just cause. Managerial discretion in these activities depends on the arbitrator's interpretation of what constitutes just cause.[10] Also, as we discussed in Chapter 9, past practices might modify or add to the labor agreement. Managerial prerogatives could be further reduced by past practices or implied obligations.

On the other hand, the labor agreement can enhance managerial discretion, since management usually insists on the inclusion of two provisions—the prohibition of a strike during the life of the agreement and the management rights clause. All other provisions typically originate from union desires and concerns.

Management rights clauses can take either the short or the long form. The following management rights provision illustrates the *short form*:

Employer retains all rights to manage, direct and control its business in all particulars, except as such rights are expressly and specifically modified by the terms of this agreement or any subsequent agreement.[11]

Some managers prefer this all-encompassing provision on the assumption that it guarantees management complete discretion in those matters not cited in the labor agreement. Originally, managers felt this provision could justify their refusal in going to arbitration over an issue not specifically stated in the labor agreement. However, as discussed in Chapter 9, the Supreme Court stated that the arbitrator should determine whether an issue is a managerial prerogative if it is not specifically included in the labor agreement.

Many management officials responded to the Supreme Court's decision in *United Steelworkers of America v. Warrior and Gulf Navigation Company* by adopting the *long form* management rights provision—indicating several specific areas where management rights are unqualified (see Exhibit 10–1). Presumably, arbitrators, upon seeing these prerogatives clearly stated in the labor agreement, would rule in management's favor on whether the grievance is subject to arbitration. However, the long form managerial prerogatives clause is not without its problems:

1. It is difficult to list items which clearly specify management's unilateral discretion.
2. Management may overlook an item and fail to include it in the labor agreement. Arbitrators view a detailed management rights provision as expressing managerial intent to define all its prerogatives. Since it is impossible for management to express all of its felt prerogatives, a problem may arise when management omits a particular item from the long form. Most arbitrators reviewing this omission would conclude that management should not view the omitted issue as being within its exclusive domain.

Exhibit 10–1
Example of a Long Form Management Rights Clause

Except as otherwise specifically provided in this Agreement, the Employer has the sole and exclusive right to exercise all the rights or functions of management, and the exercise of any such rights or functions shall not be subject to the grievance or arbitration provisions of this Agreement.

Without limiting the generality of the foregoing, as used herein, the term "Rights of Management" includes:

a. the right to manage the plant;

b. the right to schedule working hours;

c. the right to establish, modify or change work schedules or standards;

d. the right to direct the working forces, including the right to hire, promote, or transfer any employee;

e. the location of the business, including the establishment of new plants or departments, divisions or subdivisions thereof, and the relocation or closing of plants, departments, divisions or subdivisions thereof;

f. the determination of products to be manufactured or sold or service to be rendered or supplied;

g. the determination of the layout and the machinery, equipment or materials to be used in the business;

h. the determination of processes, techniques, methods, and means of manufacture, maintenance or distribution, including any changes or adjustments of any machinery or equipment;

i. the determination of the size and character of inventories;

j. the determination of financial policy, including accounting procedures, prices of goods or services rendered or supplied, and customer relations;

k. the determination of the organization of each production, service maintenance or distribution department, division or subdivision or any other production maintenance, service or distribution unit deemed appropriate by the Employer;

l. the selection, promotion, or transfer of employees to supervisory or other managerial positions or to positions outside of the bargaining unit;

m. the determination of the size of the working force;

n. the allocation and assignment of work to employees;

o. the determination of policy affecting the selection or training of new employees;

p. the establishment of quality and quantity standards and the judgment of the quality and quantity of workmanship required;

q. the control and use of the plant property, material, machinery, or equipment;

r. the scheduling of operations and the determination of the number and duration of shifts;

s. the determination of safety, health, and property protection measures for the plant;

t. the establishment, modification and enforcement of plant rules or regulations, which are not in direct conflict with any of the provisions of this Agreement;

u. the transfer of work from one job to another or from one plant, department, division or other plant unit to another;

v. introduction of new, improved or different production, maintenance, service or distribution methods or facilities or a change in existing methods or facilities;

w. the placing of production, service, maintenance or distribution work with outside contractors or subcontractors;

x. the determination of the amount of supervision necessary;

y. the right to terminate, merge or sell the business or any part thereof; and

z. the transfer of employees from one job to another or from one plant, department, division or other plant unit to another.

It is agreed that the enumeration of management prerogatives above shall not be deemed to exclude other management prerogatives not specifically enumerated above.

Source: Reprinted by permission of the publisher from Walter E. Baer, *Practice and Precedent in Labor Relations* (Lexington, Mass.: D. C. Heath and Company, Copyright 1972 D. C. Heath and Company).

Both long and short forms of management prerogative clauses can cause additional problems. Most of the items cited in these provisions are subject to union involvement. Items in the short form are usually qualified by the terms of the agreement, whereas items in the long form can become eventual collective bargaining topics. By insisting on including the management rights clause in the labor agreement, management runs the risk of stirring up ideological differences with the union. The items in the management rights provision might also influence the union's bargaining goals in subsequent negotiations.

Management apparently believes the advantages of the management rights clause offset potential risks. Approximately 70 percent of the labor agreements contain management rights clauses which help remind arbitrators, union officials, and other managers (particularly first-line supervisors) that management never gives up its administrative initiative to establish the status quo.[12] Reminders notwithstanding, management rights are subject to erosion as the scope of collective bargaining (including worker participation programs discussed in Chapter 12) has expanded over the years. Other factors contributing to the erosion of management rights are the previously mentioned arbitrators' decisions, legislation concerning the subjects of bargaining, NLRB and court decisions, and bad bargaining on the part of management.

In summary, management attempts to strengthen its prerogatives through contractual language and managerial actions. The union likewise seeks contractual language to strengthen its security. This issue is discussed in the following section.

Union Security

Inclusion of a union security clause in the labor agreement makes it easier for the union to enroll and retain members. Unions must be concerned about their security for at least two reasons. First, they are only granted a one-year existence upon NLRB union certification under the National Labor Relations Act. As noted in Chapters 3 and 4, representation or decertification elections may be legally held one year after the union is recognized as the exclusive bargaining agent. Although existing union members are seldom approached ("raided") by other unions for representation purposes, the possibility of a rival union seeking recognition for these employees still exists. A union security provision does not eliminate this possibility but can make it easier for the current union to enroll members, which is an initial step in winning their loyalty.

Second, union security provisions tend to strengthen the union's financial resources by increasing the number of dues-paying members. Unions would like to recoup their initial time and money investments spent on organizing employees at an industrial facility by subsequently obtaining dues from the eligible members. Union leaders also feel they are morally justified in asking employees to pay for services provided by the union, since it is legally obligated to represent all bargaining unit employees regardless of their union membership.

Union security provisions are therefore sought to strengthen the union, a situation which can offer possible benefits to the employer as well as the union. Many might contend that employers prefer dealing with a weak instead of a strong union. Weak unions might aid the employer who wishes to terminate the union-management relationship, but they frustrate an employer who earnestly tries to resolve working condition disputes through an established union-management relationship. It is commonly the union, not the employer, who sells the collective bargaining agreement to the membership. A union has difficulty in accomplishing this objective when there are non–union member factions which vocalize their dissent about the collective bargaining process and the resulting outcomes.

Union officials contend that union security provisions offer other advantages to the employer. They contend that less time will be spent in recruiting new members and collecting dues of existing members during the work day. However, management officials counter that this time saving will not result in more production, since union officials might use the extra time to police the labor agreement and formulate additional grievances. Unions also maintain that morale would be improved if all employees were union members. Tensions arise when some people do not pay for the same services shared by all. However, a counterargument could be made that tensions are not reduced by union security, merely redirected. The possible anger of union members working with nonunion employees is replaced by the anger of forced members who feel they have to pay for unwanted services. [13]

With these potential advantages and disadvantages in mind, union security provisions have taken one or more of the following forms:

Closed shop. In order for an employee to obtain a job in a closed shop, he or she must first become a member of a union. The closed shop was made unlawful by the Taft-Hartley Act of 1947.

Union hiring hall. According to the union hiring hall provision, employers must hire employees referred by the union if the union can supply a sufficient number of qualified applications. [14] This provision is usually found in the construction trades, where a union provides the employer with qualified employees for a relatively short-term project. This provision has been supported by the Supreme Court, with the provision that the union hiring hall does not discriminate between union and nonunion applicants. [15]

Union shop. Under a union shop contract provision, the employee does not have to be a union member in order to be hired by the company. However, he or she must become a union member *after* a probationary period of not less than thirty days in order to remain employed by the company. Under a union shop provision, the company does not always have to discharge an employee who is not a union member if: (a) the employer believes union membership was not offered the employee on the same terms as other employees or (b) membership was denied for reasons other than the failure to tender dues. The union shop provision does not give the union the right to reject certain employees for membership and then seek their discharge for not being union members.[16]

Agency shop. An agency shop provision does not require the employee to join the union; however, in order to remain employed by the company, the employee must pay to the union a sum equal to membership dues. This provision is based on two principles: (a) all employees who are represented by the union should help defray the bargaining and grievance costs, and (b) employees should not be forced to join a union.[17] The Supreme Court has upheld the validity of the agency shop in both the private[18] and public sectors.[19] Under agency shop provisions, nonunion employees may continue to work during a strike and refuse to participate in other strike-related activities without being fired or penalized by the union.

Maintenance of membership. A maintenance of membership provision does not require all employees to become members of a union as a condition of employment. However, an employee who joins the union must remain a member for a specified period of time, such as the duration of the labor agreement. Maintenance of membership provisions also contain an escape period (usually fifteen days) after the subsequent labor agreement becomes effective. Employees who do not leave the union during the escape period must remain members until the next escape period.

"Quasi union shop." It is illegal to require the union shop provision in right-to-work states and areas having similar public sector bargaining statutes. However, union and management officials sometimes get around these legal restrictions by inserting "quasi union shop" provisions in the labor agreement. Usually, the first page of the agreement states that employees will have to join the union as a condition of employment—a union shop provision. The union steward shows the new employee this provision, which usually results in that employee joining the union. A second provision, usually buried in some footnote elsewhere in the labor agreement, states, "Any provision found in this agreement which conflicts with local, state, or federal law is considered null and void." These provisions have the same effect as a union shop (particularly since the new employee will seldom research the labor agreement when confronted by the union steward) and at the same time comply with anti–union shop legislation.

Dues checkoff. A dues checkoff provision can be used in connection with any of the previously cited union security provisions or can stand alone in the labor agreement. It allows the union members to have their dues automatically taken out of their payroll checks (as for any other payroll deduction) and transferred to the union. This provision is most important to the union; indeed, most unions given an either/or choice would prefer dues checkoff over any other union security provision, because it assures the union of an uninterrupted flow of income. Without a systematic dues deduction, union officers would have to spend a great deal of time with recalcitrant members who kept delaying their dues payments. In many cases, the employer automatically agrees to this provision in the first contract negotiation on the assumption that every other labor agreement contains it. Often an administrative fee is charged the union for the collection of dues and other paperwork. In negotiations, astute management officials usually bargain for something in return for this provision, such as flexibility in making work assignments, subcontracting, and writing job descriptions.

Union security provisions are found in over 80 percent of the labor agreements covering 1,000 or more employees. Union shop provisions are by far the most common, followed by agency shops and maintenance of membership provisions. Likewise, over 80 percent of the agreements provide for checkoff procedures for dues, assessments, and initiation fees.[20]

In many cases, however, the parties are not free to negotiate a particular union security provision. Right-to-work laws which restrict this discretion are discussed in the next two sections.

Right-to-Work Laws: Meaning and Controversy

Employers, some employees, and the courts have long been concerned with union security provisions.[21] The *Commonwealth v. Hunt* decision in 1842 indicated that the closed shop agreement was not inherently unlawful. After that decision, individual employers and employer associations began to counter union security provisions. In 1903, the National Association of Manufacturers (NAM) instituted an *open shop* drive which stated that the shop was "open" to all employees—union or nonunion. However, some believe that the open shop was in reality excluding any employee who desired to join a union. For example, the featured speaker at the 1905 NAM convention indicated that union members should be discharged promptly because "it is the common practice of union men in an open shop to harass the upright and capable workmen who may not choose to join a union."[22]

Open shop activities continued, with the Associated Industries of Florida successfully obtaining the first right-to-work amendment to the state constitution in 1943. The Taft-Hartley Act in 1947 gave federal permission to right-to-work laws. More specifically, Section 14 (b) of the act remains in force today and states:

Nothing in this Act shall be construed as authorizing the execution or application of agreements requiring membership in a labor organization

> as a condition of employment in any State or Territory in which such execution or application is prohibited by State or Territorial law.

Under this provision, states may initiate legislation prohibiting union membership as a condition of employment. However, continuing lobbying efforts must be made by individuals or organizations to pass such a state law, a none too simple task since there are corresponding attempts by others to oppose right-to-work legislation. Current efforts are mainly conducted by the National Right to Work Committee founded in 1955. Both employees and individuals have joined this committee,[23] whose stated purpose is to protect the employee's right to determine whether to join unions. The committee does not regard itself as being against unions, merely union security provisions which compel employees to become members. However, it has been alleged that the committee's "pro-union, anti–union security" stance has been modified to a flat "anti-union" approach in recent years.[24] A related but separate organization, the National Right to Work Legal Defense Foundation, provides legal representation in right-to-work cases (see Exhibit 10–2).

The necessity of right-to-work laws and their effectiveness have been subject to much controversy. Supporters of the right-to-work laws base their position on several related arguments:[25]

1. The right-to-work principle affirms the right of every U.S. citizen to work for a living, whether or not he or she belongs to a union. Compulsory unionism in any form (union shop, agency shop, and so on) contradicts a fundamental human right—freedom to join or not to join an organization.

2. No individual should be compelled to join a private organization, particularly if that organization uses the individual's dues to support causes which the individual believes are morally unjust or contrary to his or her religious beliefs. "No other private organization in America insists on having the power to force membership on an unwilling people."[26] The government alone should have the right to tax the citizen or require compliance to its rules.

3. Voluntary union membership insures that unions will be responsible to that membership. With compulsory union membership, the members cannot express their dissent—they must remain "captive passengers" of the union if they wish to keep their jobs. Union leaders can become indifferent or even corrupt, since members have no economic way of voicing their displeasure. Union leaders should have to earn their dues through their responsive, diligent actions. "Good unions don't need compulsory unionism—and bad unions don't deserve it."[27]

4. Right-to-work states benefit the employees from several economic standpoints. First, firms are attracted to these states; indeed, statistics

Join The Union... Or Else.

Sammy Kirkland spends most of his time these days on a hog farm, away from his home in Ft. Myers, Fla. He doesn't answer his mail or the telephone.

He's kept a low profile ever since that terrifying day in May 1971 when a union mob nearly killed him on an excavation job, breaking three of his ribs, putting steel shavings in his eyes and threatening to cut off his arms.

Why were they out to get him? Because he refused to join a local union. Sammy Kirkland's life has been altered, forever, because he refused to abandon his right to work to union goons.

Other lives have been changed too. Four of the union agents responsible for the vicious attack were given five-year jail sentences. Kirkland also filed a damage suit against the local and international unions.

In early 1976, union officials agreed to a $165,000 out-of-court settlement, one of the largest ever obtained in a union violence case. But as Kirkland's attorney provided by the National Right to Work Legal Defense Foundation said, "No amount of money can compensate him for the damage that's been done."

Sammy Kirkland's case, shocking as it is, is not an isolated one. Herbert McGruther of Lake City, Fla., was fired from his construction job in 1975 because he refused to join another local of the same union.

McGruther was subjected to a different kind of intimidation. A union agent prominently displayed a large pistol in his belt while demanding that McGruther pay a union initiation fee and dues.

McGruther, with the support of the National Right to Work Legal Defense Foundation, has filed suit, charging the union with violating his rights and asking for punitive damages.

Sammy Kirkland and Herbert McGruther were fortunate. They found help. But how many other Kirklands and McGruthers in America need similar help?

The National Right to Work Legal Defense Foundation is a publicly supported charitable institution that provides free legal aid to employees whose rights have been violated because of compulsory unionism. The Foundation is currently assisting workers in more than 50 cases across the country.

If you want to help Herbert McGruther, and all the other McGruthers and Kirklands in our society, we'd like to hear from you.

For more information on how you can help workers like Sammy Kirkland and Herbert McGruther, write:

The National Right to Work
Legal Defense Foundation
Suite 610
8316 Arlington Boulevard
Fairfax, Virginia
22038

Source: *Commentary* 64 (August 1977), p. 13. Reprinted by permission of the National Right to Work Legal Defense Foundation.

have shown that right-to-work states have accounted for 60 percent of all new manufacturing jobs for the years 1961 to 1971.[28] Second, in attempting to obtain a union security clause, unions might conduct a strike to pressure the employer. Since there can be no union security clause in right-to-work states, no strike can result over negotiating this issue, and employees do not needlessly lose income.

Opponents of right-to-work legislation counter and extend some of the preceding arguments by contending:

1. "Right-to-work" is a public relations slogan designed for popular appeal. Unions are not denying anyone the fundamental right to seek employment. Yet an employee subjects himself to a number of negotiated working conditions or rules which specify his work schedule, content, and wages. The employee who does not like reporting to work at 8:00 A.M. has the option of going to another firm with a different work schedule. The same option is available if the employee does not wish to be a union member. There is no difference between union security and the other working conditions found in the labor agreement. It is inconsistent to stress employee "freedom" regarding union membership, since the National Labor Relations Act gives the union the authority to negotiate a labor agreement affecting most aspects of the employee's worklife.[29]

2. A moral case can be made in favor of abolishing right-to-work laws. A person is more than an individual; he or she is also a member of society with responsibility for contributing to the common good. Industrial society's common good might demand that individuals conform to norms (for example, a union security provision) for the good of all.[30] An analogy can be found in a recent Supreme Court decision which concluded that an individual employee might have to compromise his or her religious beliefs (for example, work on a day which conflicts with a particular religious principle) if he or she wished to remain in the employment of a company.[31] In essence, the Supreme Court has suggested that the employee has a right to his or her moral objections regarding aspects of the work environment; yet the employer has the right to make work rules which conflict with these objections (for instance, a union security clause) and insist that the employee either follow these rules or seek employment elsewhere.

3. Under the National Labor Relations Act, unions are responsible for representing all bargaining unit employees. Those individuals who do not join the union are regarded by union members as being free riders—ones who never go near the kitchen but always show up for dinner.[32] *Democracy* means abiding by the will of the majority. Employees do have voting rights regarding a representation election and must live with the outcome of the majority vote. Thus, to be fully represented and involved in the democratic processes (voting, attending meetings to formulate bargaining proposals, and so on), em-

ployees should join the union and represent their interests in the processes.

4. An important factor in plant location is the presence of right-to-work laws which offer companies the possibility of a nonunion or weak union environment. But many of these firms are "runaway" firms from the North seeking workers at low wages. Almost all the right-to-work states have a lower per capita income than states that do not have such laws.[33] Also, very few strikes result from union requests for union security provisions in the contract;[34] indeed, some evidence suggests that strike activity in right-to-work states is no different from that in non–right-to-work states.[35]

In summary, the debate over right-to-work laws is crystallized and entrenched—most of the aforementioned reasons have been around since the 14 (b) provision of the Taft-Hartley amendment was passed in 1947. The positions taken by most managers and union officials on this issue are somewhat ironical. On the one hand, union officials pride themselves on leading democratic organizations, yet they seek to compel membership regardless of the employees' preferences. On the other hand, managers have traditionally relied on autocratic rules governing most if not all phases of an employee's work day. Managers who espouse right-to-work laws might be genuinely concerned with the employees' freedom of choice on this related working condition. However, one cannot fail to note that their concern takes a particularly convenient form.[36]

The Experience under Section 14 (b): The Institution and Effects of Right-to-Work Laws

Currently, twenty states have right-to-work laws.[37] Their passage has required procedural and political maneuvering of legislators as well as the skills of labor and business lobbyists and other community interest groups.[38] Some believe that right-to-work laws have had little if any influence on the union's strength and bargaining power. One author contends that this inconclusive relationship might be due to loopholes which negate the impact of right-to-work laws and the fact that right-to-work laws only apply when the union wins a representation election. Regarding the second factor, there is no reason to think that a union will be reluctant to initially organize employees simply because it will be legally unable to require them all to join.[39]

There are also several legal and quasi-legal loopholes which minimize the effects of right-to-work legislation, particularly since these laws seldom have an effective enforcement mechanism to insure that union security provisions do not exist.[40] For example, the Indiana right-to-work provision allowed a grace period for employers and employees to resolve their differences over this issue. Many labor agreements were reopened before their expiration dates and before the effective date of the right-to-work legislation in order to take advantage of this grace period. Union security clauses were extended along with provisions for wage increases in the subsequent years of the "new" contract.[41]

Other legal loopholes depend on court sanctions. In Indiana, for example, agency shop provisions were deemed legally permissible in this state's right-to-work legislation. As stated earlier in the chapter, agency shop provisions do not require union membership; instead, the employee is obligated to pay the equivalent of a service charge to the union. After the Indiana right-to-work law was passed in 1955, an estimated 91 percent of the collective bargaining agreements in the state included an agency shop provision. When Indiana repealed the right-to-work law in 1965, the agency shop provision was dropped from all but 37 percent of the collective bargaining agreements.[42] Union-management cooperation to circumvent right-to-work legislation can result in related contract provisions (such as the "quasi union shop"). In another right-to-work state it was common to include *contingent union shop clauses*—provisions indicating that management and the union would automatically include the union shop arrangement if and when the state's right-to-work law were eliminated.[43] This type of clause performed a psychological function: it told employees that management backed the union's efforts to enroll all employees as members. On some occasions, management gives more direct encouragement to employees to join the union. One union official has commented:

We've found that in the right-to-work states, some of the big nationwide corporations which have the union shop elsewhere, will often cooperate with us in getting new employees to join. The plant supervisor just has a little chat with the man when he's hired and says a few kind words about the union, and the worker usually gets the point.[44]

On the other hand, some evidence exists that right-to-work laws can reduce existing union membership by 6 to 15 percent. Further, this reduction can result in a cutback of union services and staff personnel. The prospect of not obtaining all employees as members might also discourage unions from organizing smaller and automated facilities, particularly since overhead costs for negotiation and contract administration tend to remain the same regardless of the number of dues-paying employees.[45]

Thus, the effects of right-to-work laws on number of union members, union organizing drives, and labor-management relationships are subject to debate. However, related investigations usually agree on one point: it is difficult if not impossible to measure specific impacts of right-to-work laws. States having these laws have a significantly smaller percentage of their work force unionized, but this difference often reflects preferences and attitudes of the affected states' populations instead of the impact of the laws themselves.[46]

Thus far, we have discussed institutional issues that affect the union and management organizations in their relationships with each other.

However, there are also intra-institutional issues. The obligations of the union to represent its members are discussed in the following section.

The Union's Obligation to Its Members: Fair Representation

As mentioned in the previous section, the union is obligated to represent fairly all of the bargaining unit employees, union members and non–union members alike. This section focuses on the extent of the union's obligation, particularly when some of the bargaining unit employees believe the union has acted in an unsatisfactory manner.

The fair representation issue is one of the most difficult to resolve. On the one hand, there must be some sacrifice of individual freedom if the union organization wishes to effectively represent its members. However, the individual member's right to dissent must also be protected, and all employees represented must be safe from negligent or corrupt representatives.[47] The Railway Labor Act and the National Labor Relations Act add to this issue's complexity, since they do not contain any explicit provisions obligating the union to represent fairly all bargaining unit employees.[48]

Fair representation has been subsequently interpreted by the courts.[49] For example, a 1944 Supreme Court decision concerned black railroad firemen, who claimed that they were discriminated against by the labor agreement in matters of seniority and promotion. The union was the exclusive bargaining representative for these employees but excluded black employees from membership. The Supreme Court decided that the Railway Labor Act's ultimate policy goal, industrial peace, would be threatened if minority interest groups' goals could be ignored by the union. If minority groups were ignored by the union, then their only recourse would be to strike, which would run counter to the purpose of the Railway Labor Act.[50] "Since legislation should be read to serve congressional purpose, the statute had to be read as imposing on the majority union a duty of fair representation."[51]

The Supreme Court's interpretation has been applied to both the Railway Labor Act and the National Labor Relations Act. While unions could no longer completely ignore certain bargaining unit employees, the following question remained: How far must the union go in representing employees whose interests or claims could potentially disrupt union goals and policies? The importance of this question is magnified when we consider that there are many decisions which help some members while hurting others. However, if unions were required to process contradictory claims, nothing would be accomplished.

One such double-edged issue is seniority. Union actions pertaining to this issue (such as merging seniority rosters and calculating seniority credits for employees returning from the armed services) will hurt some bargaining unit members while helping others. Not surprisingly, two Supreme Court cases involving fair representation concerned the seniority issue.[52] These decisions indicated that the union must consider all employees and make an honest effort to serve the interests of all members without hostility to any.[53] However, the decisions also realized that unions cannot effectively operate if they must press every unit member's concern to the fullest:

Inevitably, differences arise in the manner and degree to which the terms of any negotiated agreement affect individual employees and classes of employees. The mere existence of such differences does not make them invalid. The complete satisfaction of all who are represented is hardly to be expected. A wide range of reasonableness must be allowed a statutory bargaining representative in serving the unit it represents, subject always to complete good faith and honesty of purpose in the exercise of its discretion.[54]

Thus, the union satisfies its fair representation obligation in collective bargaining and enforcing the labor agreement if it considers all members and takes its ultimate position honestly, in good faith, and without hostility or arbitrary discrimination.

These rather broad guidelines were also applied in another landmark Supreme Court decision, *Vaca v. Sipes*, which considered the union's fair representation obligation in the grievance procedure. A bargaining unit employee claimed that the union "arbitrarily, capriciously and without just or reasonable reason or cause" refused to take his grievance to arbitration. The employee, a long-term high blood pressure patient, returned to work after a sick leave and was judged by the company's doctor as being unfit for reemployment. The employee's personal physician as well as a second doctor indicated that the employee was fit for work; therefore, the employee asked the union to seek his reinstatement through the grievance procedure. The grievance was processed; however, the union, in attempting to strengthen its case before going to arbitration, sent the employee to a third doctor. The third doctor did not support the employee's position; therefore, the union refused to take the employee's case to arbitration.

The Supreme Court indicated that fair representation does not mean that the employee has an absolute right to have his grievance taken to arbitration:

If the individual employee could compel arbitration of his grievance regardless of its merit, the settlement machinery provided by the contract would be substantially undermined, thus destroying the employer's confidence in the union's authority and returning the individual grievant to the vagaries of independent and unsystematic negotiation.[55]

Indeed, taking every case to arbitration could result in an intolerable expense for the union and employer while also clogging up the arbitration process. Also, employees pushing arbitration of every grievance would eliminate the early steps of the grievance procedure, which are designed to have management and the union officials resolve their own disputes. The court also determined that the union in this instance was neither arbitrary nor discriminatory and acted in good faith. The employee has the burden of proof of establishing that the union specifically breached its fair representation obligation.[56]

Currently, fair representation poses two difficult questions to the union and the employee.

1. *What are specific types of conduct that constitute violation of the fair representation duty?* As previously noted, the Supreme Court has given broad bench marks ("arbitrary," "bad faith," "dishonest," and so on); yet, these ambiguous standards are left to the lower courts to resolve. These lower court decisions have resulted in a variety of interpretations of the Supreme Court's reasoning. For example, one circuit court determined that the union's "negligence" in processing a grievance equaled "arbitrary" action, thereby making the union liable for breach of fair representation.[57]

Increased legal complexity regarding this issue will make it most difficult for union officials to administer the agreement on the shop floor. A typical union steward lacks legal training and is a working department member who is usually elected by other departmental employees. In many cases, stewards are elected on their popularity, not on their ability to interpret and process grievances. Any attempt by the union leaders to appoint union stewards on the basis of their competence will probably be strongly resisted by the employees, who maintain that they have the right to select their own work group representatives.[58]

2. *What can the employer do to avoid liability when the union breaches fair representation?* Employees currently can sue the union and the employer for breach of the labor agreement including fair representation under Section 301 of the National Labor Relations Act. Assume, for example, that an employee is discharged, then later establishes that the union breached its duty of fair representation. The employer can also be liable under this suit and might have to reinstate the employee with back pay, even though the union was responsible for bungling the grievance.[59] The courts have contended that the two parties, employer and employee, may be victims innocent of any wrongdoing; however, the employer is sometimes regarded as being in a better financial position than the union to make the employee whole.[60]

Needless to say, employers do not like this situation. To avoid subsequent liability, the employer has to closely monitor the union to make sure that it presents a competent case. Managers believe that they should not be held accountable for the union's errors, particularly since management is legally prohibited from dealing in the internal affairs of the union.[61] The following section discusses the union's institutional relationships to black and female employees, a discussion based on both historical and contemporary perspectives.

Unions and Minority Groups

Unions and Black Employees

Historical Overview There is tremendous variation both historically and currently in the union response toward black employees. A prominent report on this subject has noted that trade union policies regarding black employees have varied from outright exclusion to full acceptance with all privileges of membership.[62] Most of the generalizations in this section focus on the extent to which the union movement has discriminated against black employees. Such discrimination has had two general dimensions: exclusion (through constitutional provisions, initiation rituals, or tacit agreements) and segregation (in either separate locals or separate job classifications).[63]

The Knights of Labor (KOL) actively recruited black members and attempted to treat them in an equalitarian manner.[64] Much of the KOL's enthusiasm was due to its social reform philosophy (discussed in Chapter 2). However, pragmatic reasons also prompted this organization's recruiting efforts because employers during the late 1800s and early 1900s often used black employees as strikebreakers to put pressure on white strikers to resolve their differences. One rather early study of the relationship between black employees and organized labor furnished the following rationale for black strikebreakers:

Strikebreaking has been one method by which thousands of Negro workers have entered industries not previously employing them. In the majority of cases the provocateurs of Negro strikebreakers have been the employers and their representatives rather than the Negro himself. The inducements of higher wages, shorter hours and better work conditions than he previously enjoyed were more powerful arguments than the immorality of preventing the use of labor groups then on strike. . . . Each Negro worker is by most obvious circumstances to seek his immediate advantage.[65]

To be sure, employers actively recruited blacks for strikebreaking purposes. A typical handbill distributed by strikebreaker recruiting agents during an 1896–1897 strike read:

WANTED! COLORED coal miners for Weir City, Kan., district, the paradise for colored people. Ninety-seven cents per ton, September 1 to

---

Racially discriminatory practices have historically excluded blacks from some unions and jobs. Now minority employees have recourse to various legal remedies for such prejudicial practices.
Source: Reproduced from the collection of the Library of Congress.

March 1; 87½ cents per ton, March 1 to September 1 for screened coal over seven-eights opening. Special train will leave Birmingham on the 13th. Transportation advanced. Get ready and go to the land of promise.[66]

Regardless of the initiator of these events, the presence of black employees working while white employees were on strike increased tension and thwarted the KOL's goals of social betterment. One way to stop this disruption was to bring black employees into the union membership.

The American Federation of Labor (AFL) assumed the KOL's equalitarian racial attitude almost from its inception in 1886. The AFL's president, Samuel Gompers, proclaimed a firm antidiscrimination policy regarding black employees. He initially effected this policy by refusing to grant an AFL charter to national unions whose constitutions formally excluded blacks from membership. One such membership qualification clause was found in the Order of Sleeping Car Conductors' Constitution: "The applicant for membership shall be a white male, sober and industrious, and must join of his own free will. He must be sound in mind and body."[67]

Gompers quickly found out that stating a policy is much easier than subsequent enforcement.[68] The first departure from his anti-exclusionary clause stance came in 1884, when he said that unions would be refused a charter if they had an explicit racial exclusion clause in their constitution. In essence, the AFL was unconcerned if national unions resorted to less explicit practices in denying membership to black employees.[69] For example, the International Association of Machinists was granted an AFL charter in 1895 and dropped its constitutional provision prohibiting black members. However, the union excluded blacks from its initiation ritual—in effect, excluding them from membership—until 1948.[70] Indeed, eleven unions affiliated with the AFL had formal race bars as late as the 1930s.[71]

Gompers rationalized accepting unions which discriminated against black employees on the basis that the AFL would have no power to effect change if the unions were outside its jurisdiction. Presumably, once in the AFL, national union leaders would see the errors of their ways and accept black members. This belief was not supported by facts, as a 1902 study found that (a) forty-three international unions did not have any black members and (b) there were only 40,000 black members in the AFL unions, with half of this total belonging to one union, the United Mine Workers.[72] A second strategy to increase black membership while not offending national unions was the AFL's granting of charters to segregated black locals, a policy which continued until 1939.[73]

As early as 1905, the AFL's policy became less enthusiastic and aggressive. Gompers, obviously recalling black strikebreaking activities, expressed only qualified support for racial membership integration:

Tis true that some men have been angered at the introduction of black strike breakers. I have stood as champion of the colored man and have sacrificed self and much of the labor movement that the colored man should get a chance. But the caucasians are not going to let their standard of living be destroyed by negroes, Chinamen, Japs, or any others.[74]

In essence, Gompers informed black employees that they had to earn consideration by the AFL by not engaging in efforts which could hurt their potential union brothers and by obtaining requisite job skills.[75] This self-help emphasis for black employees continued for several decades. In 1941, William Green, Gompers' successor, and two other AFL officials expressed their attitudes toward black membership along the following general lines: "[a] discrimination existed before the AFL was born and human nature cannot be altered . . . [b] the AFL, per se, does not discriminate because it gladly accepts Negro workers into its directly affiliated federal locals . . . and [c] . . . Negroes should be grateful for what the AFL has done for them."[76]

At least two forces have influenced a more progressive union stance for black employees: a prominent black labor leader, A. Philip Randolph, and the emergence of the Congress of Industrial Organizations (CIO). Randolph, president of the Brotherhood of Sleeping Car Porters, became involved in the AFL's racial betterment activities when his union received a national charter from the federation in 1936; his 35,000 members comprised one-half of the total black AFL membership at the time. Randolph's initial skepticism of the AFL's attitude toward minorities did not appreciably change over the years. Indeed, his verbal battles with AFL leadership on civil rights often became quite heated. In 1961 he was censured by the AFL's Executive Committee for getting close to "militant groups," thereby creating a "gap between organized labor and the Negro community."[77] It is difficult to measure the precise success of Randolph's efforts; however, at the least, he continually insured that the AFL's leadership could not forget the black employee.

The independent CIO also pressured the rival AFL to enroll black employees. Unlike the AFL craft unions, the CIO's unions had no control over employment. Therefore, they had to organize all existing employees, black and white, at a facility if they were to be successful.[78]

In some industries such as iron, steel and coal mining, Negroes have long been employed in jobs at relatively skilled levels. In these cases the [CIO] unions accepted and built on the pattern they found, adopting non-racist policies which, whatever their secondary motivation, were calculated to achieve and maintain organizational success.[79]

The CIO also needed broad-based support in pressing its legislative goals of minimum wages, unemployment insurance, and social security. The CIO needed black support to insure representation election victories. The AFL, on the other hand, usually having higher wage earners as members, could not see similarities between their craft jobs and lower wage classifications which were populated largely by black employees.

The Relationship between Unions and Black Employees since the 1964 Civil Rights Act Since the AFL-CIO merger in 1955, unions have attempted to further racial equality in one or more of the following ways:[80]

1. *Avoid expulsion of the national unions where discrimination exists.* As Gompers earlier contended, the AFL can only achieve success if the offending union is within their organization, subject to the federation's sanctions. By retaining these unions, the AFL-CIO, particularly through its Civil Rights Committee and other organizations of black union leaders,[81] can continue to apply pressure for equal opportunity. It should also be noted that the national union can place its local union affiliates under trusteeship if the local union has engaged in discriminatory practices.[82]

2. *Set a favorable example for national and local unions to follow.* The AFL-CIO has on occasion publicly and financially helped civil rights groups such as the NAACP.[83] However, on at least one major occasion—the 1963 civil rights march on Washington—the AFL-CIO was conspicuously absent from the list of sponsors, leaving such preferences, if any, to "individual union determination."[84]

3. *Urge that civil rights legislation be passed at the local, state, and federal levels.* George Meany has gone on record for this alternative on a number of occasions.[85] Bringing unions directly under civil rights legislation gives the union leaders a powerful rationale to bring reluctant union members into line on the civil rights issue.

Unions have also lobbied for another solution to the civil rights issue— more jobs. This position has consistently been taken by union leaders; for example, in 1963 Walter Reuther commented:

Does anybody in his right mind believe we can solve the civil rights social revolution in the framework of mass unemployment? . . . There must be a job for every able bodied worker in America whether he is white or black or brown or yellow.[86]

A recent study has also found that economic gains of black U.S. citizens are tied to full employment problems.[87] Some, however, contend that unions are passing the racial discrimination buck to the employers. Yet, particularly in the nonconstruction sector, there is some merit to the union's notion that they cannot be blamed for something they cannot control—the hiring of additional black employees.

Some evidence suggests that unions have been relatively successful in removing racial discrimination. Studies have found, for example, that: (a) unionized black employees have higher wages than black nonunion employees and (b) the average wage of black workers relative to white workers is consistently higher in unionized than in nonunion labor markets.[88] Yet even these figures suggest two possible areas of discrimination. First, black union workers have lower wages than their white counterparts, an observation possibly stemming from past union policies of segregating black employees in lower wage classifications. Second, unions discriminate against black nonunion employees when they determine they will either organize all-white facilities before organizing all-black facilities[89] or only admit white employees into their membership.

Discrimination also occurs within the union in terms of the day to day attitudes of white union members, the number of black members who are union officers, and the quality of union services given to black employees. The work environment should at least superficially promote positive attitudes between black and white employees, since they are subject to the same labor agreement provisions, working conditions, and supervisory directives. Indeed, both groups should share a common goal of improving their working conditions through collective bargaining.[90]

Yet other factors serve to heighten racial tensions among groups; for example, white employees can feel economically threatened by black employees, with whom they compete for the same jobs, promotions, and job security possibilities. Tension can also be attributed to racism, irrespective of the underlying cause. For example, one report revealed that some white over-the-road truck drivers strongly objected to black Teamster members for the following reasons:

When a man is black I don't care to live cheek-to-cheek with him for a couple of days in the truck. . . .

    I sure would become ill and take sick leave if I was asked to accept two-man truck duty with a nigger and have to alternate sleeping on the same pallet in the back of a truck.[91]

In a number of cases, the racist attitudes of local union members place union leaders in an almost helpless situation—a price of union democracy is the union leader's obligation to abide by the will of the majority. This situation prompts minority union members to solidify their ranks and racial concerns. In some cases, all-black organizations have been formed within the local or national union to monitor or change the union's policies toward minority members. Harvester Revolutionary Union Movement (HRUM) and Dodge Revolutionary Union Movement (DRUM) are two such groups within the United Auto Workers.[92]

White union leaders are also reluctant to press for an increased number of black members because these individuals might vote along racial lines. One study of United Auto Workers local union officers' elections found that the racial composition of the leadership clearly reflects the racial composition of the membership.[93] Consequently, the established white union leaders are fearful that increased numbers of black members would vote them out of office.

The number of black union leaders can be also limited by the reluctance of blacks to seek such positions. Black union leaders usually have a difficult time reconciling union and racial priorities. This difficulty is reflected by one black union leader, who indicates, "If I moved into the White House, I wouldn't paint it, but I also wouldn't forget that I'm black—I can't."[94] The contradictory pressures on black union leaders are increased by age differences.

Usually, black union leaders have had more union experience than their black constituents. They believe they have paid their dues in dealing with union pressures and recoil at the urgings of "young, black upstarts" for "more now." One such black union official has reacted directly to criticisms of "Uncle Tomism" in these terms: "An Uncle Tom is a Negro who has a job that a nigger wants."[95] Perhaps similar pressures have discouraged some blacks from running for office. Regardless of the reason, very few blacks currently hold union leadership positions. (The United Auto Workers, United Steelworkers, and the American Federation of State, County, and Municipal Employees represent notable exceptions.)

The lack of black union leaders coupled with antagonism of white and black members influences the quality of union services provided black members. Much of this potential source of discrimination has been discussed in the section on unions' fair representation obligations to its members. However, there are additional legal possibilities for black employees who charge discrimination.

Legal Considerations Affecting the Rights of Minority Employees at the Local Union Level In Chapter 9 we noted that under the *Gardner-Denver* decision minority employees can file a grievance over alleged discriminatory action while also filing charges with the Equal Employment Opportunity Commission (known as having "two bites at the apple"). Likewise, Chapter 12 will discuss legal remedies for minority employees who successfully contend that seniority systems discriminatorily affect their job progression and retention. The Equal Employment Opportunity Act subjects the union as well as the employer to liability for back pay awards, court costs, and the attorney fees of the plaintiffs.[96]

Minority employees can also seek legal recourse if they believe that the proposed union discriminates racially. A 1973 court of appeals decision, (*NLRB v. Mansion House Center*) upheld the National Labor Relations Board's contention that unions engaging in racial discrimination or sexism should be denied initial certification and that employers could invoke the discriminatory practices of a union as a reason for refusing to bargain with that union. However, the quantity and type of evidence needed for this action has not yet been specifically established by the NLRB.[97]

The extent to which minorities can engage in self-help techniques to prevent discriminatory actions has been before the Supreme Court. The 1975 *Emporium* decision concerned several black employees who believed the grievance procedure in the labor agreement was an inadequate forum to resolve racial discrimination issues. Over the objections of their union officers, these employees picketed the allegedly discriminatory employer instead of processing a related grievance and were eventually discharged for their picketing activities. The Supreme Court addressed itself to the following question: Are such attempts to engage in separate bargaining protected by the National Labor Relations Act? The Supreme Court concluded that the employees' actions were not protected by the act; employees can be discharged for engaging in these unprotected activities. The Court further reasoned:

> The potential for conflict between the minority and other employees in this situation is manifest. With each group able to enforce its conflicting demands—the incumbent employees by resort to contractual processes and the minority employees by economic coercion—the possibility of strife and deadlock is high; the likelihood of making headway against discriminatory practices would be minimized.[98]

Thus, the *Emporium* decision suggests minority employees are on weak ground when they take discrimination issues into their own hands, particularly if the labor agreement has a no-discrimination clause and a grievance procedure which encompasses discrimination issues.

In the construction industry. Concentrated legal and governmental efforts to promote equal employment opportunity have taken place in the construction industry. The Equal Employment Opportunity legislation passed in 1964 did not initially accomplish much in improving the number of black or female union members in the construction industry. For example, three local craft unions in Philadelphia (Sheet Metal Workers, Electricians, and Plumbers) had over 4,000 journeymen members in 1967; of this total, 16 were nonwhite.[99] The lack of minority representation in the construction trades has been in part attributed to one or more of the following union recruiting practices:[100]

☐ Requirements for admission based on endorsement by present members, relationship by blood or marriage to present members, or election by members.

☐ Nonvalidated tests and interview practices containing subjective material. (One union is purported to ask applicants for their views on "law and order".)[101]

☐ Work referral preferences based on a worker's membership in a labor organization, seniority within the union, or length of experience in a trade.

☐ Selections from waiting lists compiled when the union was excluding minority workers.

☐ Word-of-mouth recruiting of members and apprentices.

Most of these practices were not specifically designed to discriminate against minority members, but their application and continuance in an all-white, male union perpetuates discrimination, regardless of intent.

Tangible governmental concern over this issue was first expressed in Executive Order 11246 issued by President Johnson in 1965. It required all contractors, producers, and servicers doing business with the federal government to be equal opportunity employers; firms guilty of discrimination could have their federal projects cancelled and be debarred from future government projects. Affirmative action programs for the construction industry either were imposed by the government (as was the 1967 Philadelphia Plan, revised in 1969)[102] or were voluntary hometown programs (employed in at least seventy geographical areas in the United States).[103]

Success of these affirmative action programs has been qualified. The Philadelphia Plan resulted in a notable increase in the number of hours worked by minority employees, particularly in 1972. However, these plans can also be subjected to one or more of the following problems:

☐ Lack of enforcement by government agencies, such as the Office of Federal Contract Compliance.[104]

☐ The fact that many of the hometown plans are signed by *umbrella organizations* (union building trade councils and contractors' associations) which have little or no authority to force compliance with the plan.[105]

☐ Lack of qualified black employees to assume construction positions.

The government has recognized this last problem and, along with private organizations, has focused much attention on the recruitment of black apprentices. A hopeful note is the upward trend in the number of black and female apprentices.[106]

Unions and Female Employees

Many of the issues confronting female employees are similar to those discussed in the previous section on black employees. This is especially true of legal remedies, since both groups are covered by the Equal Employment Opportunity Act. Yet some differences in relationships of women and unions emerge when the history of female union workers is considered.

Historical Overview One difference is that female employees, unlike their black counterparts, were involved in collective action including strike activities in the early 1800s. The first major strike conducted by females occurred in 1828. The dispute was not over wages; rather, it protested paternalistic work rules prohibiting gambling, drinking, or other "debaucheries" and requiring church attendance.[107] A woman who became known as Mother Jones was one of the more fiery and energetic figures of the U.S. labor movement from the 1880s through the 1920s. Her role in mine workers' strikes and in helping to form the IWW reached legendary proportions. However, female unions during the 1800s were usually short-lived—the organizations were formed prior to a strike and lasted only for its duration.

This characteristic of female labor unions changed somewhat with the Knights of Labor, which welcomed black and white female members. The Knights more aggressively sought female members, who were brought directly into the Knights' mixed assemblies on an equal basis with men.

Mother Jones played an active role in mine workers' strikes and in the formation of the IWW.

Source: Courtesy of the Bettmann Archive.

As many as two hundred local assemblies were comprised entirely of female shoe workers, garment workers, and mill operators. Some female union leaders preferred segregated locals, which gave far more opportunity for female members to become involved and educated in union business and concerns.[108]

From its formation until World War I, the AFL felt that the woman's place was in the home—allowing women to work would be contrary to its public principles supporting motherhood and the family. Some female union leaders at the time believed that women could never physically compete with men in the factories,[109] while one article in the *American Federationist* applauded the federation's efforts in removing females from the factories:

The American Federation of Labor realizes that the normal place for woman is in the home. Much of the most valuable work done by the Federation is in the direction of gaining such conditions for men workers that it will be possible for their wives and daughters to remain at home.[110]

In addition to the lack of tangible support given by the AFL, female union leaders faced many difficulties in organizing female employees into permanent union organizations:

The workers are young and ignorant and therefore they have not learned the necessity for such protection. Their wages are in most cases low, too low for decent self-support. But just because their wages are so inadequate for bare needs it is in many cases all the more difficult to induce them to deduct from such scanty pay the fifty cents a month which is the smallest sum upon which any organization can pay its way and produce tangible benefits for its members.[111]

Other organizational difficulties occurred because of many female workers' view of their work as temporary, strong employer opposition to unions, and the lack of female organizers (only one such organizer was employed by the AFL in 1907).[112]

The AFL increased its attention toward female workers when it appeared likely that the United States would enter World War I. Gompers was initially concerned about women's ability to do work traditionally performed by men.[113] However, some female unionists saw wartime job opportunities as a challenge for the female to rise above the societal view of women as "weaklings" and "cripples".[114]

Gompers was also concerned that women who might be employed during the war could pose a threat to the unionized male employees returning from the war. Trained, experienced female employees who would work for lower wages could place higher salaried male union members at a competitive disadvantage.[115] Hence, the AFL—perhaps out of organizational necessity rather than ideological commitment[116]—became interested in the prospects of enrolling female union members.

The AFL's encouragement of female unionization continued through World War II,[117] although some maintained the AFL was long on words and short on action.[118] The number of female union members increased from 800,000 at the time of Pearl Harbor to 3,000,000 in 1945; however, only one out of five working women belonged to a union. Many male union leaders and members contended that female union members were basically unenthusiastic, even hostile to union principles and efforts following World War II. Some of this hostility was due to the fact that many of the female employees working in the factories during the war were summarily sent home to stay following Armistice Day.[119]

Relationships between Organized Labor and Female Employees after World War II The situation for females in union leadership positions has not been especially promising. In 1966, of about 1,400 members of the executive boards from 65 major AFL-CIO affiliates, only 30 were women. While females constituted 20 percent of the total membership of these organizations, only 2 percent were in leadership positions.[120]

Since 1966, the absolute number of female union members has increased. For example, from 1968 through 1972 female union membership increased by 500,000, equalling the overall gain in union enrollment. This figure is especially significant since females constitute only one-fifth of the total union membership.[121] However, this increase is proportionately less than the increase in number of women who went to work in this period—increase in female union membership lags behind the growth in female employment.

A further concern is that the number of female union officers has not increased since 1966. Undoubtedly some of this lack is due to the attitudes and practices of male union leaders and members. If the following remarks of one male union official are representative, this situation might be changing: "For too long we have looked cynically at the problems of women in industry, only wanting to send them home in order to solve the unemployment problem. But now we realize we can't replace women, and we might as well accept that."[122]

Even if male attitudes toward female union members change, it still appears that many women are reluctant to actively participate in union leadership positions. One female union officer places this possibility in the following perspective:

My own feeling is that there are strong similarities to attitudes that blacks used to have: a fear of losing, or rejection, if a woman does step forward to take an active role; a feeling of "I've never done it before so I might fail"; a feeling that one's husband might object; and always, of course, the problem of time because of domestic responsibilities instead of work.[123]

Female participation in labor unions does appear to be increasing, particularly as women collectively perceive discrimination in working conditions. A potential influence is the effort by various feminist groups to secure passage of the Equal Rights Amendment. However, overtures made by these groups to female union leaders and members have been largely met with mistrust and hostility because of a belief that feminist groups, particularly those involved in the women's liberation movement, do not realistically understand their working problems and prospects.[124]

Yet female union members and leaders are pressing their collective interests over working conditions in a variety of ways. Conventions held by the United Auto Workers, American Federation of Teachers, International Association of Machinists, and American Newspaper Guild in the early 1970s dealt extensively with problems women face in jobs and unions. During this same period, an organization called WAGE (Women's Alliance to Gain Equality) was formed in California. This voluntary organization of female union members is attempting to fight discrimination in the unions and on the job.[125] Perhaps these and other collective efforts among women will improve their relative position in union leadership in the near future.

Summary

Management and union officials want to maintain and strengthen their respective organizations through the collective bargaining process. Management has been long concerned about maintaining its prerogatives to run the organization. While union officials do not appear to be particularly concerned about management's property rights pertaining to the machinery, materials, and money of the enterprise, management's prerogatives regarding its employees have been weakened or eroded through decisions by arbitrators, the NLRB, and the courts as well as collective bargaining. Management prerogatives are usually specified in the labor agreement in either the long or short form.

Unions are also concerned about their organizations when they attempt to negotiate a union security provision (such as union shop, union hiring hall, or agency shop) into the labor agreement. However, certain union security provisions cannot be negotiated in states having right-to-work laws, permitted under Section 14 (b) of the National Labor Relations Act. Arguments for and against these laws have economic and moral dimensions, as do those about whether union security represents an inappropriate working condition.

Unions have an obligation to fairly represent their members. Judicial decisions have not clearly resolved the precise extent of unions' fair representation obligations. However, unions are charged with considering all members and arriving at their ultimate position honestly, in good faith, and without hostility or arbitrary discrimination.

A variety of relationships occurs between unions and minority employees. Although there have been exceptions, blacks have not been well received by organized labor. At least three forces have influenced a more progressive union stance for black employees: a prominent labor leader, the emergence of the CIO, and civil rights legislation. Although female employees became active in labor relations earlier than blacks, women have not been as well integrated into the labor-management relationship. The future for women as leaders in labor relations remains uncertain.

Discussion Questions

1. What are the comparative advantages of the long and short forms of managerial prerogative clauses?

2. Discuss how managerial prerogatives can be eroded, even though most unions have no desire to "run the business."

3. Formulate a one- or two-sentence argument for or against the right-to-work philosophy. Fully defend your statement from arguments which could be made against your position.

4. Briefly discuss the broad judicial guidelines concerning unions' fair representation obligations to members. Also discuss the reasoning behind these guidelines, furnishing some appropriate examples.

5. Discuss the similarities and differences between black and female employees in their experiences with unions.

6. Discuss the various approaches unions have taken toward improving the situation of minority employees, indicating which alternatives have been met with the least resistance from union members.

References

[1]George A. Stevens, *New York Typographical Union No. 6, Annual Report of the Bureau of Labor Statistics* (New York: State Department of Labor, 1911), part 1, pp. 240–241; cited in Neil W. Chamberlain, "The Union Challenge to Management Control," *Industrial and Labor Relations Review* 16 (January 1963), pp. 185–186.

[2]Margaret Chandler, *Management Rights and Union Interests* (New York: McGraw-Hill, 1964), p. 6. For the contents of this conference see *The President's National Labor Management Conference*, November 5 to 30, 1945, vol. III (Washington, D.C.: Bureau of Labor Standards Bulletin No. 77, 1946). For a more complete assessment of management's attitudes during this time period see John G. Turnbull, "The Small Business Enterprise and the Management Prerogative Issue," *Industrial and Labor Relations Review* 2 (October 1948), pp. 33–49.

[3]Gene Huntley, "Diminishing Reality of Management Rights," *Public Personnel Management* 14 (May–June 1976), p. 175.

[4]Samuel Cook, "The Right to Manage," *Labor Law Journal* 9 (March 1958), p. 187; and Turnbull, "Small Business Enterprise," p. 36.

[5]Stanley Young, "The Question of Managerial Prerogatives," *Industrial and Labor Relations Review* 16 (January 1963), p. 243.

[6]Martin M. Perline, "Organized Labor and Managerial Prerogatives: An Empirical Study," *California Management Review* 14 (Winter 1971), pp. 46–50; and Milton Derber, W. E. Chalmers, and Milton T. Edleman, "Union Participation in Plant Decision Making," *Industrial and Labor Relations Review* 15 (October 1961), pp. 83–101.

[7]Neil W. Chamberlain, *The Union Challenge to Management Control* (New York: Harper & Bros., 1948), p. 90.

[8]Derber, Chalmers, and Edleman, "Union Participation," p. 183.

[9]See, for example, Charles C. Killingsworth, "The Presidential Address: Management Rights Revisited," in Gerald G. Somers, ed., *Arbitration and Social Change* (Washington, D.C.: Bureau of National Affairs, 1969), pp. 1–19.

[10]See, for example, Lawrence Stessin, "Management Prerogatives and Plant Rule Violations," *Arbitration Journal* 14 (1959), pp. 3–13.

[11]Huntley, "Diminishing Reality of Management Rights," p. 176.

[12]Paul Prasow, "The Theory of Management Reserved Rights—Revisited," in Gerald G. Somers, ed., *Industrial Relations Research Association Series: Proceedings of the Twenty-sixth Annual Winter Meeting* (Madison, Wis.: Industrial Relations Research Association, 1974), p. 84.

[13]Written correspondence from Dan C. Heldman, Studies Coordinator, the National Right to Work Legal Defense Foundation, Inc., December 28, 1978.

[14]Gerald J. Skibbins and Carolina S. Weymar, "The Right-to-Work Controversy," *Harvard Business Review* 44 (July–August 1966), p. 8.

[15]James N. Wilhoit, III, and Jonathan C. Gibson, "Can a State Right-to-Work Law Prohibit the Union Operated Hiring Hall?" *Labor Law Journal* 26 (May 1975), p. 302.

[16]George W. Cassidy, "Equity Consideration in Public Sector Union Security Arrangements: Should 'Free Riders' Pay?" *Journal of Collective Negotiations in the Public Sector* 5 (1976), p. 37.

[17]Ibid.

[18]*Retail Clerks International Association Local 1625 AFL-CIO v. Schermerhorn et al.*, 373 U.S. 746 (1963). It should be noted that this decision stated that state laws prohibiting compulsory unions (right-to-work states) can also prohibit agency shops.

[19]*D. Louis Abood et al. v. Detroit Board of Education*, 431 U.S. 209 (1977). It should be noted that this decision also called for a rebate of union fees or dues for activities unrelated to collective bargaining.

[20]U.S. Department of Labor, Bureau of Labor Statistics, *Characteristics of Major Collective Bargaining Agreements, July 1, 1974* (Washington, D.C.: Government Printing Office, 1977), pp. 16–19.

[21]For a more detailed account of the history of union security from a union perspective see *Union Security: The Case against the Right-to-Work Laws* (Washington, D.C.: American Federation of Labor and Congress of Industrial Organizations, 1958), pp. 40–53; and "The Employer's Stake in the Open Shop," *American Federationist* 83 (May 1976), pp. 17–24.

[22]Daniel H. Pollitt, "Union Security in America," *American Federationist* 80 (October 1973), p. 19.

[23]Walter Mossberg, "20 Year Fight: Right-to-Work Drive: A Friend to Workers or a Menace to Them?" *Wall Street Journal*, April 22, 1975, pp. 1, 2.

[24]"Labor Letter," *Wall Street Journal*, September 13, 1977, p. 1.

[25]Elements of all the cited arguments favoring right-to-work laws are found in the National Right-to-Work Committee's statement "The Right-to-Work Issue: Questions and Answers," n.p., n.d.

[26]Ibid.

[27]Reed E. Larson, "Are Right-to-Work Laws Desirable? Yes," in Walter Fogel and Archie Kleingartner, eds., *Contemporary Labor Issues* (Belmont, Calif.: Wadsworth Publishing, 1968), p. 272.

[28]For additional statistics supporting this argument see a brochure published by the National Right to Work Committee, "Some Things You Just Can't Ignore! Right-to-Work States Lead Nation in Creating New Jobs," (November 1978).

[29]George Meany, "Are Right-to-Work Laws Desirable? No," in Fogel and Kleingartner, eds., *Contemporary Labor Issues*, p. 270.

[30]Very Rev. Andrew J. McDonald, "The Moral Case against Right-to-Work," *American Federationist* 82 (August 1976), p. 20.

[31]*Trans World Airlines, Inc. v. Larry G. Hardison et al.*, cited in Bureau of National Affairs, *Daily Labor Report*, June 16, 1977, pp. D–1 through D–9. For a further discussion of this decision see John M. Livingood, "The Status of Religious Accommodations after the Hardison Case," *Labor Law Journal* 29 (April 1978), pp. 226–235.

[32]Mike LaVelle, "Half a Loaf Better Than Right-to-Work," *Chicago Tribune*, July 27, 1976, Section 2, p. 4.

[33]Ibid.

[34]AFL-CIO, *Union Security: The Case against the Open Shop* (Washington, D.C.: AFL-CIO), p. 7.

[35]John M. Kuhlman, "Right-to-Work Laws: The Virginia Experience," *Labor Law Journal* 6 (July 1955), p. 460.

[36]James W. Kuhn, "Right-to-Work Laws: Symbols or Substance?" *Industrial and Labor Relations Review* 14 (July 1961), p. 587.

[37]These states include Alabama, Arizona, Arkansas, Florida, Georgia, Iowa, Kansas, Louisiana, Mississippi, Nebraska, Nevada, North Carolina, North Dakota, South Carolina, South Dakota, Tennessee, Texas, Utah, Virginia, and Wyoming. It should be mentioned that this citation applies to private sector employees. The list would be greater if states having similar legislation for the public sector were considered.

[38]For a detailed examination of this particular political process see Fred Witney, "The Indiana Right-to-Work Law," *Industrial and Labor Relations Review* 11 (July 1958), pp. 506, 515; and Glenn W. Miller and Stephen B. Ware, "Organized Labor in the Political Process: A Case Study of the Right-to-Work Campaign in Ohio," *Labor History* 4 (Winter 1965), pp. 51–63. For a study which attempts to quantify the relationship between certain variables (percentage of urbanized population, per capita income, and so on) and the existence of right-to-work legislation see William J. Moore, Robert J. Newman, and R. William Thomas, "Determinants of the Passage of Right-to-Work Laws: An Alternative Interpretation," *Journal of Law and Economics* 17 (April 1974), pp. 197–211.

[39]Frederick Meyers, "Effects of Right-to-Work Laws: A Study of the Texas Act," *Industrial and Labor Relations Review* 9 (October 1955), p. 78.

[40]Ibid., p. 77; and Kuhlman, "Right-to-Work Laws," p. 461.

[41]Witney, "Indiana Right-to-Work Law," p. 516.

[42]Mitchell S. Novit, "Right-to-Work: Before and After," *Business Horizons* 12 (October 1969), p. 64.

[43]Meyers, "Effects of Right-to-Work Laws," p. 82.

[44]"The Right-to-Work Laws," *Fortune* 56 (September 1957), p. 236.

[45]Kuhn, "Right-to-Work Laws," pp. 592–593; see also Skibbins and Weymar, "The Right-to-Work Controversy," p. 10.

[46]Keith Lumsden and Craig Petersen, "The Effect of Right-to-Work Laws on Unionization in the United States," *Journal of Political Economy* 83 (December 1975), p. 1248.

[47]Harry H. Wellington, *Labor and the Legal Process* (New Haven, Conn.: Yale University Press, 1968), p. 129.

[48]Edward H. Nakamura, "The Duty of Fair Representation and the Arbitral Process," in Joyce M. Najita, ed., *Labor Arbitration for Union and Management Representatives* (Honolulu: Industrial Relations Center, University of Hawaii, 1976), p. 87.

[49]For a more detailed account of jurisdictional issues between the NLRB and the courts over fair

representation cases see Benjamin Aaron, "The Duty of Fair Representation: An Overview," in Jean T. McKelvey, ed., *The Duty of Fair Representation* (Ithaca, N.Y.: Cornell University, 1977), pp. 8–16.

[50]*Steele v. Louisville and N.R.R.*, 323 U.S. 200 (1944).

[51]Wellington, *Labor and the Legal Process*, p. 146.

[52]*Ford Motor Co. v. Huffman et al.*, 345 U.S. 320 (1953); and *Humphrey v. Moore*, 375 U.S. 335 (1964).

[53]*Ford Motor Company v. Huffman*, p. 338.

[54]Ibid. See also *Humphrey v. Moore*, p. 349.

[55]*Vaca v. Sipes*, 386 U.S. 191 (1967).

[56]*Amalgamated Association of Street, Electric, Railway and Motor Coach Employees of America v. Wilson P. Lockridge*, 403 U.S. 294 (1971).

[57]Jeffrey A. Swedo, "*Ruzicka v. General Motors Corporation:* Negligence, Exhaustion of Remedies, and Relief in Duty of Fair Representation Cases," *Arbitration Journal* 33 (June 1978), pp. 6–15. For a discussion of varied judicial interpretations of fair representation see Aaron, "Duty of Fair Representation: Overview," pp. 18–21; and Clyde W. Summers, "The Individual Employee's Rights under the Collective Agreement," in McKelvey, ed., *Duty of Fair Representation*, pp. 60–83.

[58]Judith P. Vladeck, "The Conflict between the Duty of Fair Representation and the Limitations on Union Self-Government," in McKelvey, ed., *Duty of Fair Representation*, p. 45.

[59]*Hines v. Anchor Motor Freight*, 424 U.S. 554 (1976), at 556.

[60]Ibid., p. 59.

[61]For a more thorough discussion of employer liability in fair representation cases see C. Paul Barker, "The Employer's Stake in the Union's Duty of Fair Representation: A Form of Liability without Fault—The Employer's Duty to Police the Handling of Employee Grievances," in Martha L. Langwehr, ed., *Labor Law Developments* (New York: Matthew Bender, 1978), pp. 61–87.

[62]Herbert R. Northrup, *Organized Labor and the Negro* (New York: Harper & Bros., 1944), p. 1.

[63]Ray Marshall, *The Negro Worker* (New York: Random House, 1967), p. 57.

[64]For a more detailed account of blacks and the Knights of Labor see Sidney H. Kessler, "The Organization of Negroes in the Knights of Labor," *Journal of Negro History* 37 (July 1952), pp. 248–275.

[65]The Department of Research and Investigations of the National Urban League, *Negro Membership in American Labor Unions* (1930; reprint ed. Westport, Conn.: Negro Universities Press, 1969), p. 165.

[66]Herbert G. Gutman, "The Negro and the United Mine Workers of America," in Julius Jacobson, ed., *The Negro and the American Labor Movement* (Garden City, N.Y.: Doubleday, 1968) p. 99.

[67]Herbert Hill, *Black Labor and the American Legal System*, vol. 1 (Washington, D.C.: Bureau of National Affairs, 1977), p. 20.

[68]Ray Marshall, *The Negro and Organized Labor* (New York: Wiley, 1965), p. 15.

[69]Marc Karson and Ronald Radosh, "The American Federation of Labor and the Negro Worker: 1894–1949," in Jacobson, *Negro and the American Labor Movement*, pp. 155–156.

[70]Marshall, *The Negro and Organized Labor*, p. 16.

[71]Derek C. Bok and John Dunlop, *Labor and the American Community* (New York: Simon and Schuster, 1970), p. 119.

[72]Karson and Radosh, "AFL and the Negro Worker," p. 156. For more details of the role of blacks in the United Mine Workers see Herbert Gutman, *Work, Culture, and Society in Industrializing America* (New York: Alfred A. Knopf, 1976), pp. 121–208.

[73]Bok and Dunlop, *Labor and the American Community*, p. 119.

[74]Samuel Gompers, "Talks on Labor," *American Federationist* 12 (September 1905), p. 636.

[75]For a more detailed account of this shift in philosophy see Bernard Mandel, "Samuel Gompers and the Negro Workers: 1886–1914," *Journal of Negro History* 40 (January 1955), pp. 34–60.

[76]Northrup, *Labor and the Negro*, p. 13.

[77]Herbert Hill, "The Racial Practices of Organized Labor: The Contemporary Record," in Jacobson, ed., *Negro and the American Labor Movement*, p. 288.

[78]Ray Marshall, "Black Workers and the Unions," *Dissent* 19 (Winter 1972), p. 296.

[79]Sumner M. Rosen, "The C.I.O. Era: 1935–1955," in Jacobson, ed., *Negro and the American Labor Movement*, p. 202. For a detailed account of the CIO's efforts to mobilize black employees' support in organizing the steel industry see Horace R. Cayton and George S. Mitchell, *Black Workers and the New Unions* (1939; reprint ed. Westport, Conn.: Negro Universities Press, 1970), pp. 190–224.

[80]These alternatives to further racial equality were formulated by Gus Tyler in "Contemporary Labor's Attitude toward the Negro," in Jacobson, ed., *Negro and the American Labor Movement*, pp. 363–364.

[81]For a discussion of these organizations see Kenneth A. Kovach, "Blacks in the U.S. Labor Movement," *Michigan State University Business Topics* 25 (Autumn 1977), p. 12; and Marshall, "Black Workers and the Unions," p. 300.

[82]For examples of this sanction see Farrell E. Bloch, "Discrimination in Nonreferral Unions," in Leonard J.

Hausman et al., eds., *Equal Rights and Industrial Relations* (Madison, Wis.: Industrial Relations Research Association, 1977), pp. 111–112.

[83]Robert A. Dobkin, "Unions Move to 'Bail Out' NAACP," *Miami Herald*, October 2, 1976.

[84]Julius Jacobson, "Union Conservatism: A Barrier to Racial Equality," in Hausman et al., eds., *Equal Rights*, p. 13.

[85]See, for example, "Equal Rights for All: The AFL-CIO Position," *American Federationist* 71 (March 1964), p. 1.

[86]Walter P. Reuther, *The Values We Cherish* (Washington, D.C.: Industrial Union Department, AFL-CIO, n.d.), p. 15.

[87]Barbara Becnel, "Black Workers: Progress Derailed," *American Federationist* 85 (January 1978), p. 8.

[88]Ibid. See also Orley Ashenfelter, "Racial Discrimination and Trade Unionism," *Journal of Political Economy* 80 (May–June 1972), p. 461.

[89]Bloch, "Discrimination in Nonreferral Unions," p. 105.

[90]Pat Watters, "Workers, White and Black in Mississippi," *Dissent* 19 (Winter 1972), p. 71.

[91]Lee Berton, "Bias in the Cab: Rights Groups Ready Fight on Discrimination in Long-Haul Trucking," *Wall Street Journal*, March 31, 1966, pp. 1, 8. For an additional example of racist attitudes of some union members see Scott Greer, *Last Man In: Racial Access to Union Power* (Glencoe, Ill.: The Free Press, 1959), pp. 149–150. For a more recent discussion of civil rights litigation in the long-haul trucking industry see James C. Hyatt, "Driving Ahead: Accord to Open Long-Haul Trucking Jobs to Minorities Appears to Be Near at Hand," *Wall Street Journal*, October 14, 1976, p. 44.

[92]For additional details of internal black protest organizations see Bernard Rosenberg, "Torn Apart and Driven Together: Portrait of a UAW Local in Chicago," *Dissent* 19 (Winter 1972), pp. 61–69; William B. Gould, *Black Workers in White Unions* (Ithaca, New York: Cornell University Press, 1977), pp. 388–395; and Thomas R. Brooks, "DRUMbeats in Detroit," *Dissent* 17 (January–February 1970), pp. 16–25.

[93]B. J. Widick, "Black City, Black Unions?" *Dissent* 19 (Winter 1972), pp. 138–145.

[94]Roger Lamm, "Black Union Leaders at the Local Level," *Industrial Relations* 14 (May 1975), pp. 228–229.

[95]Rosenberg, "Portrait of a UAW Local," p. 64.

[96]For more discussions of this liability see Robert H. Sand, "Back Pay Liability under Title VII," in James L. Stern and Barbara D. Deniss, eds., *Proceedings of the Twenty-seventh Annual Winter Meeting: Industrial Relations Research Association* (Madison, Wis.: Industrial Relations Research Association, 1975), pp. 225–230; David C. Hershfield, "Labor Relations Pressures for Equal Opportunity," *Conference Board Record* 10 (September 1973), pp. 44–46; and Arthur B. Smith, Jr., "The Impact on Collective Bargaining of Equal Employment Remedies," *Industrial and Labor Relations Review* 28 (April 1975), pp. 376–394.

[97]Hill, *Black Labor*, pp. 159–160.

[98]*Emporium Capwell Co. v. Western Addition Community Org.*, 420 U.S. 68–69 (1975). For additional details regarding the rights of minority employees when they picket over an alleged racial injustice see Kenneth M. Schwartz and Martin Simone, "Civil Rights Picketing," in Walter B. Connolly, Jr., ed., *Strikes, Stoppages and Boycotts: 1978* (New York: Practising Law Institute, 1978), pp. 397–419. The potential for racial discrimination issues being resolved through arbitration is discussed in Lawrence R. Jauch, "The Arbitration of Racial Discrimination Cases as a Result of Employment Practices," *Labor Law Journal* 24 (June 1973), pp. 367–375.

[99]R. L. Rowan, "Discrimination and Apprentice Regulation in the Building Trades," *Journal of Business* 40 (October 1967), pp. 435–447.

[100]Benjamin W. Wolkinson, "The Effectiveness of EEOC Policy in the Construction Industry," in Gerald G. Somers, ed., *Proceedings of the Twenty-fifth Annual Meeting: Industrial Relations Research Association* (Madison, Wis.: Industrial Relations Research Association, 1973), p. 363.

[101]Gould, *Black Workers in White Unions*, p. 285.

[102]For additional details regarding the Philadelphia Plan see Robert W. Glover and Ray Marshall, "The Response of Unions in the Construction Industry to Antidiscrimination Efforts," in Hausman, et al., eds., *Equal Rights and Industrial Relations*, pp. 130–132; and Arthur A. Fletcher, "Whatever Happened to the Philadelphia Plan?" *Business and Society Review/Innovation* 5 (Spring 1978), pp. 24–28.

[103]For a further discussion of voluntary and imposed plans to place minorities in the construction industry see Gould, *Black Workers in White Unions*, pp. 297–315.

[104]For a more detailed discussion of bungling enforcement efforts of the EEOC and OFCC see Arthur Fletcher, *The Silent Sell-Out: Government Betrayal of Blacks to the Craft Unions* (New York: The Third Press, 1974), pp. 47–75; and Benjamin W. Wolkinson, *Blacks, Unions and the EEOC* (Lexington, Mass.: Lexington Books, 1973).

[105]Glover and Marshall, "The Response of Unions," p. 133.

[106]For example, the Department of Labor indicated that in 1975, 18.4 percent of construction apprentices were minority members. Glover and Marshall, "The Response of Unions," p. 124. See also "Unions: Nonwhite Apprentices up 50 Percent," *Chicago Sun Times*, February 14, 1973, p. 48; and Bureau of National Affairs, *Daily Labor Report*, October 27, 1976, p. 2. For a more detailed account of blacks in

apprenticeship programs in various cities see F. Ray Marshall and Vernon M. Briggs, Jr., *The Negro and Apprenticeship* (Baltimore: Johns Hopkins Press, 1967); Richard L. Rowan and Lester Rubin, *Opening the Skilled Construction Trades to Blacks* (Philadelphia: University of Pennsylvania Press, 1972); and Irwin Dubinsky, *Reform in Trade Union Discrimination in the Construction Industry: Operation Dig and Its Legacy* (New York: Praeger Publishers, 1973).

[107]John B. Andrews and W. D. P. Bliss, *History of Women in Trade Unions* (New York: Arno Press, 1974), p. 24.

[108]Alice Henry, *The Trade Union Women* (1915; reprint ed. New York: Burt Franklin, n.d.), p. 152.

[109]Alice Woodbridge, "Woman's Labor," *American Federationist* 1 (June 1894), p. 66.

[110]Eva McDonald Valesh, "Wage Working Women," *American Federationist* 13 (December 1906), p. 965.

[111]Henry, *Trade Union Women*, p. 142.

[112]Agnes Nestor, "The Experiences of a Pioneer Woman Trade Unionist," *American Federationist* 36 (August 1929), p. 928.

[113]Samuel Gompers, "Don't Sacrifice Womanhood," *American Federationist* 24 (August 1917), pp. 640–641.

[114]Florence C. Thorne, "Trend toward Equality," *American Federationist* 24 (February 1917), p. 120; and Gertrude Barnum, "Women in the Labor Movement," *American Federationist* 22 (September 1915), p. 120.

[115]Samuel Gompers, "Women Workers Organize and Win," *American Federationist* 23 (March 1916), p. 201. It should also be noted that the rise of female unionists in the women's and men's garment industries preceded World War I.

[116]It should be noted, however, that the AFL did evidence at least a retrospective concern with the ideological side of women's place in the labor movement during World War I. See "Labor and Woman's Suffrage," *American Federationist* 27 (October 1920), pp. 937–939.

[117]William Green, "Women Wage Earners," *American Federationist* 32 (November 1925), p. 1005; and William Green, "Women Who Work," *American Federationist* 55 (March 1948), p. 19.

[118]Katharine Fisher, "Women Workers and the American Federation of Labor," *New Republic* 27 (August 3, 1921), pp. 265–267.

[119]A. G. Mezerik, "Getting Rid of the Women," *Atlantic Monthly* 175 (June 1945), pp. 79–83.

[120]"Little Room at the Top for Labor's Women," *Business Week*, May 28, 1966, p. 62.

[121]Virginia A. Bergquist, "Women's Participation in Labor Organizations," *Monthly Labor Review* 97 (October 1974). See also Bureau of National Affairs, *Daily Labor Report*, July 13, 1976, p. A–11. For an individual exception of female leadership in the United Farm Workers see Barbara L. Baer and Glenna Matthews, "You Find a Way: The Women of the Boycott," *Nation* 218 (February 23, 1974), pp. 232–238.

[122]Lucretia M. Dewey, "Women in Labor Unions," *Monthly Labor Review* 94 (February 1971), p. 48.

[123]"Women Workers: Gaining Power, Seeking More," *U.S. News & World Report*, November 13, 1972, p. 106. For further potential reasons for lack of participation see pp. 105 and 106 of this article; and Leonard R. Sayles and George Strauss, *The Local Union*, rev. ed., (New York: Harcourt, Brace & World, 1967), pp. 124–126. A more hopeful note for female union officers is reported in Joann S. Lublin, "Getting Organized: More Women Enroll in Unions, Win Office and Push for Changes," *Wall Street Journal*, January 15, 1979, pp. 1, 32.

[124]Edna E. Raphael, "Working Women and Their Membership in Labor Unions," *Monthly Labor Review* 97 (May 1974), p. 32; Bernard Rosenberg and Saul Weinman, "An Interview with Myra Wolfgang: Young Women Who Work," *Dissent* 19 (Winter 1972), p. 32; Alice Cook, "Women and American Trade Unions," *Annals* (January 1968), pp. 124–132; and Studs Terkel, *Working* (New York: Avon Books, 1975), p. 389.

[125]"Women Workers: Gaining Power, Seeking More," p. 104.

Chapter 11

Employee Discipline

"Discipline, in one form or another, is an element of all organized activity. Its function is to maintain order by setting limits to individual behavior which may jeopardize the interests of the group."

Orme Phelps, Discipline and Discharge in the Unionized Firm, 1959.

In many respects, employee discipline represents the most significant labor-management issue after the labor agreement has been negotiated. For example, discipline grievances represent the largest grievance category resolved by arbitrators. Many other issues (such as work assignment or overtime computations) usually are uniquely related to the particular industrial experiences and labor agreement. Since each decision is highly tailored to the particular grievance, space considerations do not permit a close examination of arbitrators' insights on these topics. Disciplinary principles, on the other hand, tend to be more broadly applied across companies, as arbitrators appear to view this topic as having more commonalities than any other grievance topic. Hence, many arbitral reflections on discipline are included so that the reader can apply the general arbitration process (Chapter 9) to a rather specific issue.

Employee discipline can also have implications reaching far beyond the labor-management relationship. Improperly administered discipline can result in a nonunion firm becoming unionized or charged with a discrimination suit.

This chapter initially approaches employee discipline through its changing significance over time. Also discussed are various elements of effective discipline and the role of the supervisor in the disciplinary process.

The Changing Significance of Industrial Discipline

Nature and Significance of Discipline

Employee discipline is a fundamental element of any industrial organization,[1] particularly when viewed as a state of employee commitment, motivation, and self-regulation.[2] In this sense, discipline is both a condition and an attitude—a "disciplined" work group willingly accepts management's directives and behavioral standards.

On the other hand, discipline represents an action taken by management against an employee who has violated organizational rules.[3] This chapter focuses on the action rather than the conditional component of employee discipline by examining situations in which management has either been successful or unsuccessful in disciplining employees. The premise is that, while it cannot solve all industrial problems, discipline is nonetheless a significant option when used with other alternatives or when other approaches have failed.

Management regards the right to discipline its employees as an important element of its broader prerogative to direct its working force. The significance of discipline becomes apparent when it is either neglected or poorly administered. If management does not deal effectively with those who violate organizational rules, then the disrespect for them will spread to other employees. For example, if a few employees are permitted to line up at the time clock before quitting time, then each day the number will grow, until nearly all of the workforce are in line.[4] Management in nonunion firms likewise regards discipline as significant, because any one of these firms could suddenly become unionized if management administered discipline in an arbitrary or capricious manner:

Poorly trained supervisors who have played "favorites" among employees, administered the rules as they saw fit, and failed to do their jobs as communicators and leaders have been the cause of more lost union elections than have complaints about wage and salary and benefit programs or working conditions.[5]

Managers in unionized firms often have belatedly realized the problems arising from incorrect disciplinary action when their decisions have been either reduced or overruled entirely by arbitrators. An early article written by a noted labor arbitrator indicated that management's won-lost record in arbitration appeared to be improving over time.[6] Unfortunately for management, current statistics do not support this trend. A review of published discharge grievances in the Bureau of National Affairs' *Labor Arbitration Reports* (May 1971 through January 1974) reveals that management had its disciplinary action reduced or eliminated in 231 (or 58 percent) of 400 cases.[7] From a statistical perspective, management generally loses in arbitration of discipline grievances, a situation which becomes more apparent when the reinstated employee is brought back to the shop floor. "Nothing is more frustrating—more humbling—for a company than to have its discharge of an employee reduced to a suspension, or even a mere warning, with back pay awarded the offender."[8]

Reinstatement of the employee with back pay represents a financial loss to management (for example, one Playboy Club Bunny received $15,000 for being improperly discharged), and supervisory authority may also be lost, for it is a rare supervisor who, upon experiencing the return of one disciplined employee to his work group with a large back pay check, will pursue subsequent disciplinary action with as much vigor and initiative.

What management loses in arbitration hearings appears to be the union's gain. Most if not all union members believe the union should be responsive to problems arising from their day-to-day working conditions that remain after the formal labor agreement has been negotiated. There is no more dramatic example of union concern for its members than "saving" an employee's job. Almost every union newspaper contains at least one article per issue which describes (along with appropriate pictures of union representatives, the grievant, and the back pay check) how the union successfully defended an employee against an "unjust" act of management. A representative article from one union newspaper proclaimed in bold headlines: "Worker Wins $5,895 in Back Pay When Fired for Opening Beer Can."[9]

Perhaps a disciplinary action carries the most significance for the affected employee. Some writers have contended that discipline is well received by employees, for "it is part of discipline to encourage employees to develop their talents and skills and to acquire attitudes and build patterns of behavior that earn self-respect."[10] On the other hand, discharge, the ultimate disciplinary act, has been viewed by many arbitrators as "economic capital punishment," for it deprives the employee of presently earning a livelihood and at the same time (with the discharge on his or her work record) makes it difficult to find future employment elsewhere. At the least, any form of discipline represents an embarrassment to individuals who do not like being told they are wrong and, in some instances, have to explain a disciplinary layoff or discharge to their friends and family.

Historical Overview of Employer Disciplinary Policies

During the eighteenth and nineteenth centuries, the employer exercised "uncontrolled discretion" in directing the work crew. Discipline during this time period was sometimes harsh—common law considerations allowed the employer to administer severe bodily punishment to employees who refused to follow orders. Hence, employees who were verbally "insolent" to their superiors could expect to have their tongues burned with a hot iron. Public humiliation was another popular form of discipline, with the guilty employee either being whipped in the town square or subjected to wearing a sign indicating that he or she was an unsatisfactory employee.[11]

As society became more humane, the courts frowned on physical punishment. Yet management's right to discharge the employee for any reason was typically upheld until the 1930s, since the employment contract was legally interpreted to mean "freedom for the organization to hire at will, with either party free to terminate the employment relationship at any time, with or without cause."[12] Although the employer was relatively free to discharge or suspend employees, two general movements started during the early 1900s dampened employers' willingness to do so.

A movement toward *psychological reform* had as one of its leaders Whiting Williams, a former business executive, who toured the country viewing work as an hourly employee. His book, *What's on the Worker's Mind*, found a receptive audience among some managers, particularly when they read one of his conclusions, "that everybody wants to be a near normal human being in addition to being a worker."[13] Industrial reformers, psychologists, and management textbooks[14] called attention to the necessity of recognizing employee concerns and attitudes.

Various contributors to the *efficiency movement* gave reasons for this necessity. Some research on employee turnover statistics conducted in the early 1900s concluded that management's whimsical approach to employee discharge resulted in significant costs to the employer.[15] Adherents to the efficiency movement encouraged employers to recognize their employees as an investment in terms of recruiting, development, and training costs. To arbitrarily dismiss an employee without regard to this investment was deemed unwise.

One advocate, Frederick Taylor, shaped modern industrial discipline procedures in two general ways. First, Taylor's *scientific management* approach stressed management's obligation to provide its employees with clear and detailed work rules, along with scientifically designed work equipment and appropriate training. Management, according to Taylor, had obligations to provide clear work rules, train employees to obtain the desired job behavior, and correct (instead of discharge) the employee who deviates from managerial standards. Interestingly, as will be demonstrated later in the chapter, all of these elements help to formulate contemporary discipline administration.

A second change suggested by Taylor was limitation of the foreman's authority to hire and fire employees. Prior to the early 1900s, the foreman operated as an independent contractor, paid partially or completely from the profits of the operation which he directed. The foreman's authority to hire and fire was absolute, conditioned by personal whims (such as eliciting favors from employees in return for job security). Under scientific management, the foreman's responsibility was subjected to many constraints:

The general shop foreman . . . is no longer a "bouncer." . . . He has not the easy device of covering his own incompetence by firing a man. He

> can ask for the transfer of unsatisfactory employees, but if enough of these transfers show that discarded persons are able to make good in another shop where the foremanizing is different, he prepares a prima facie case against himself. [16]

For many companies, the foreman's authority to discharge remained, but major emphasis shifted to coordinating disciplinary efforts through a centralized personnel department which, in a compromise to the foreman's original authority, often transferred the employee to another department where he or she might be more productive.

During the 1930s, legislative influences also affected managerial obligations to administer discipline in a proper manner (see Chapter 3). The philosophy of the 1932 Norris–La Guardia Act became the cornerstone of arbitral concern over employee discharge. More specifically, this act affirmed the relatively helpless nature of the hourly employee, contending that the loss of an employee's job is much more severe to the employee than to the employer. This philosophy is exemplified in a contemporary arbitration case summarized in the *Wall Street Journal*:

> SEMI-CRIME? An arbitrator orders the reinstatement of an Indiana carpenter who was fired after he was caught loading 10 gallons of company-owned paint into a friend's car. The firing was voided because "the conversion of the paint to (his) own use hadn't yet occurred," and the arbitrator concluded the worker might have had a change of heart if he hadn't been caught early in the workday. [17]

One law which did regulate as well as shape management's disciplinary policies was the 1935 Wagner Act. A primary feature of this legislation was the prohibition of discriminatory discipline of employees because of their union preferences or membership. An independent agency, the National Labor Relations Board (NLRB) was created, in part, for enforcement purposes. Management often had to defend disciplinary actions against appeals to this agency, with a potential remedy being reinstatement with back pay. This was the first time that management was legally held accountable for employee discipline, a situation that encouraged further development of corrective disciplinary principles and policies. The NLRB also affected organizational discipline procedures in an indirect fashion when it ruled that discipline and grievance procedures were mandatory issues subject to collective bargaining. As a result of this NLRB decision, over 95 percent of existing collective bargaining agreements now have both a provision regulating discipline and a grievance procedure which enables the submission of discipline issues to arbitration.

From the 1940s to the present, managerial policies regarding employee discipline were greatly influenced by the growth and development of labor arbitration. Currently, arbitrators have three broad powers regarding discipline:

1. To determine what constitutes "just cause" for discipline.
2. To establish "standards of proof and evidence".
3. To review and modify (or eliminate entirely) the penalty imposed by management.[18]

Because the arbitrator has a significant role in formulating principles of contemporary employee discipline, the following section examines arbitral reasoning in discipline cases by indicating those situations and considerations which typically lead arbitrators to either uphold or deny management's disciplinary action.

Principles and Elements of Discipline

Discipline for Just Cause

Most labor agreements contain a statement indicating that management retains the right to discipline employees for *just cause* or simply *cause*; for example, one survey found 79 percent of 400 separate labor agreements contained this provision.[19] Arbitrators consider this concept in any discipline grievance, their rationale being that just cause is an implicit, necessary prerequisite for the collective bargaining relationship.[20] Unfortunately, the arbitrator receives little help from the union and management representatives in defining just cause. Lacking contractual guidelines, the arbitrator must fashion a definition out of his or her own experience and consideration of the individual merits of the case. One arbitrator has suggested, "Whether an employee was discharged for just and proper cause is a matter to be decided from the nature of the employee-employer relationship, from contract provisions, from proper rules of conduct and from established and accepted practices."[21]

There is no uniform, precise definition of just cause which applies to all companies or even all circumstances within one company; instead, what constitutes just cause depends upon the particular combination of circumstances present in each individual case. Arbitrators tend to accept two broad principles of just cause in guiding their consideration of the individual case:

1. There is clear and convincing evidence that a disciplinary offense was committed by the grievant.
2. The disciplinary action taken by management was appropriate for the offense committed.[22]

In following these principles, arbitrators apply several tests or guidelines. Exhibit 11–1 represents a schematic diagram indicating the approximate progression of these considerations. Each consideration will be discussed in terms of its significance for employee discipline.

Exhibit 11-1
Schematic Diagram
Indicating Elements
of Discipline

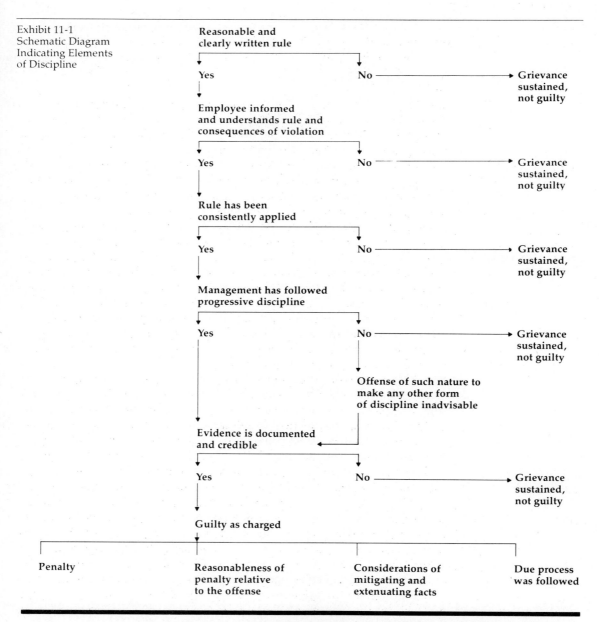

Reasonable and
clearly written rule

Yes   No ————————→ Grievance
sustained,
not guilty

Employee informed
and understands rule and
consequences of violation

Yes   No ————————→ Grievance
sustained,
not guilty

Rule has been
consistently applied

Yes   No ————————→ Grievance
sustained,
not guilty

Management has followed
progressive discipline

Yes   No ————————→ Grievance
sustained,
not guilty

Offense of such nature to
make any other form
of discipline inadvisable

Evidence is documented
and credible

Yes   No ————————→ Grievance
sustained,
not guilty

Guilty as charged

Penalty

Reasonableness of
penalty relative
to the offense

Considerations of
mitigating and
extenuating facts

Due process
was followed

Source: Modified from Floyd S. Brandt and Carroll R. Daugherty, *Instructor's Manual for Conflict and Cooperation: Cases in Labor-Management Behavior* (Homewood, Ill.: Richard D. Irwin, 1967), p. 6. © 1967 by Richard D. Irwin, Inc. Used by permission.

Legitimate Purpose of Employee Discipline

Arbitrators have long held that management has the right to direct the work force and manage its operations efficiently. Indeed, inefficient operations harm both the employer and employees since subsequent reduced profits can result in employee layoffs. Discipline can improve efficiency through the following interrelated purposes:

☐ *Set an example of appropriate behavior.* For example, management impresses upon its employees the seriousness of being tardy by giving one tardy employee a five-day suspension.

☐ *Transmit rules of the organization.* As illustrated in the previous purpose, management has transmitted a rule of the organization—lateness will not be accepted.

☐ *Promote efficient production.* Discipline those employees who either cannot or will not meet production standards.

☐ *Maintain respect for the supervisor.* In a sense, discipline shows the employee who is the boss. A supervisor who does not discipline poor employees weakens managerial authority.

☐ *Correct an employee's behavior.* Indicate what is expected, how he or she can improve, and what negative consequences might result in the future if the behavior does not change. The assumption here is that most employees have good intentions and will improve if management will simply show them the error of their ways.

Discipline can accomplish all these purposes, but labor arbitrators primarily recognize the last purpose, *correction,* as the legitimate disciplinary objective. Arbitrators usually view discipline as corrective rather than punitive in purpose; their corrective emphasis influences the following dimensions of just cause.

Nature of the Work Rules

The right of management to establish (even without initially advising the union) and administer work rules is generally acknowledged as fundamental to efficient plant operations:

> **The rules and regulations of a modern company are designed to promote a constructive working environment, protect the health and welfare of personnel, and assure individual employees full protection from capricious or arbitrary decisions of management. Sensible rules are essential to organizational effectiveness, and if they are understood and accepted by the members of the organization as an intelligent guide to cooperative endeavor, they will be supported.**[23]

Yet managerial administration of work rules also assumes some fundamental responsibilities and obligations which, if not followed, may affect management's disciplinary efforts. A first question that arises is: What happens if management has no rule governing the alleged offense committed by the employee? This situation is not uncommon

---

(1) because the pain of negotiating this would be so great in itself, raising problems of resistance and of trade-off of other needed contract terms, partly because of the understandable fear of union leaders that they may be surrendering in advance some of the industrial civil rights of their members by accepting unchallengeable penalties inexactly labeled as a substitute for a man's right to his day in court, and (2) because of the difficulty (from the employer's point of view) which this again shares with all rule-writing, of the danger that that which is not included may be regarded as unintended. Here the very sanctity presumed by appearance of the rules in the contract might imply an even greater intention of absolution from the offenses omitted or not clearly identified.[24]

In some instances, arbitrators have upheld management's rights to discipline for those offenses which are commonly regarded as unwritten industrial laws (prohibitions against stealing, striking a supervisor, and so on). However, management can be on weak ground when it does not have specific rules and the union contends that this omission results in arbitrary, discriminatory discipline.

A written rule must be clear, be reasonable, and state the consequences of its violation. A reasonable rule is one that is job related and intended to promote safe and efficient work efforts. A no smoking rule instituted because of concern over employees' health would not be reasonable unless management establishes that smoking creates a safety hazard due to flammable materials or processes in the work area. Usually, a rule which subjects an employee to humiliation or personal embarrassment (for example, requesting supervisory permission to go to the washroom) will be labeled unreasonable unless it can be shown that the technology of the workplace necessitates an employee remaining at a work station at all times.[25] For example, an automobile assembly line relies on continual production; therefore, it is normally reasonable to require supervisory permission for lavatory breaks so that a temporary replacement can be found.

Hence, the reasonableness of an industrial work rule can vary according to industrial or company differences. A unilateral ban on *moonlighting* (working a second shift with another employer) is regarded as reasonable in the utility industry, which often needs emergency work performed during off shifts. Other industries not having emergency-related concerns might have a difficult time in establishing the appropriateness of this rule. Rule reasonableness can also vary within an industrial production facility. For example, an employer might reasonably require a long-haired male employee working in the cafeteria to wear a hair net (for sanitary reasons); it would be unreasonable to request the same compliance if he worked in the shipping department.

The clarity of a work rule is also an important issue in corrective discipline, the rationale being that employees cannot adequately perform or correct behavior if they do not know what is expected. Work rules can only serve as guidelines and cannot be applied to every problem. Management officials can, however, create a problem when they discipline employees for infractions of a vague and sometimes confusing work rule. For illustrative purposes, the following examples of work rules are presented:

☐ Horseplay can inflict serious physical harm on other employees and therefore will not be tolerated in any form by the company.

☐ Any individual found guilty of gambling or fighting on company premises will be subject to immediate discharge.

These rules may, at first glance, appear clear and conclusive; however, their vagueness becomes very apparent to the first-line supervisor who tries to enforce them. Horseplay can take place without physical touching. For example, a group of employees puts a dead fish in a "lazy" inspector's testing pan, giving her equipment a lasting smell before she actually performs inspection duties. Yet a question arises as to whether this is actually a form of horseplay. A fine distinction between relatively harmless practical jokes and horseplay may haunt management when it discharges the employees on the rationale that such behavior was indeed horseplay.

A problem also arises with the term *gambling*, particularly when management discharges employees caught at a card game, while at the same time a management representative was sponsoring a World Series pool with hourly employee participants. Also, does gambling occur when employees are playing cards during their lunch break for matches or a numerical score which management (perhaps correctly) assumes will be converted into cash payments once the employees are off the company premises?

The existence of work rules carries the implicit if not explicit obligation for management to inform its employees of the rules as well as the consequences of their violation. In some instances, an employee disciplined for violating a rule contends that he or she was unaware of the directive. In these cases, management usually has to prove that the employee was indeed informed of the rule, a difficult task. Some arbitrators have even suggested that a card signed by an employee indicating he or she has read the rules is insufficient since it is signed in haste as part of the employee's orientation, and the signed card does not indicate that management has actively and patiently explained each rule to the employee, allowing time for questions and explanation.

Little has been written on the managerial obligation to inform the employee of the consequences of rule violation, although many arbitrators appear to give this item serious weight in their decisions. The training or corrective element in discipline should include a discussion of which rules are most important; a related feature of employee orientation would be informing the employee what type of penalty could be expected for violation of a particular work rule. Returning to the work rule examples, it can be easily seen that the admonition "will not be tolerated in any form" fails to inform the employee of the punishment for engaging in horseplay. The employee could interpret the vague penalty to mean a stern, oral reprimand, which he or she would accept in view of successfully completing a practical joke. Knowing in advance that the activity would likely result in a suspension or discharge, the employee would probably think twice before committing the offense.

Management's statement that rule-breakers are "subject to discharge" is qualified. This qualification is necessary in order that the unique, mitigating circumstances of each offense be given consideration, thereby avoiding arbitrary disciplinary measures. Yet management should be advised that arbitrators regard the phrase *subject to discharge* as carrying explicit potential for disciplinary measures other than discharge; the burden of proof is on management to establish why it chose discharge as opposed to the lesser penalty options.

Finally, management must administer the rules consistently for those employees violating the rules under similar circumstances. In assessing the degree of consistency, arbitrators place particular emphasis on past practice, which refers to the "customary way of dealing with given classes of rule violations and covers both methods of handling and the relationship of penalties to offenses."[26]

Some companies seek to impose consistent discipline by including a *price list* in the labor agreement; it cites specific rules and furnishes uniform penalties for single or repeated violations (see Table 11–1). This form of rule making has advantages: (a) the employee is clearly informed of the specific rules and consequences of violations, (b) the standardized penalties suggest consistent disciplinary action is implemented, and (c) if agreed to by the union, the price list assumes more legitimacy than a unilateral work rule posted by management. However, some individuals contend that the price list represents a mechanical imposition of discipline which runs counter to the corrective philosophy, since it does not consider each case on its individual merits. Say, for example, management finds two employees fighting—one a short-term, the other a long-term employee with a fine work record. According to the price list approach, management is obligated to discharge both employees; yet it is likely that the arbitrator will reinstate the senior employee, who, because of his past record, will typically respond to corrective measures in order to retain job seniority investments.

Table 11-1
Example of
Disciplinary
Price List

Type of Offense	First Offense	Second Offense	Third Offense	Fourth Offense	Fifth Offense
1. Abusive language toward a supervisor	3-day suspension	Discharge			
2. Failure to punch in and out on time clock	Oral warning	Written warning	3-day suspension	5-day suspension	Discharge
3. Failure to report an absence	Oral warning	Written warning	3-day suspension	5-day suspension	Discharge
4. Stealing company property	Discharge				
5. Sleeping on the job	Written warning	3-day suspension	5-day suspension	Discharge	
6. Damage of company equipment or property	Written warning	5-day suspension	Discharge		
7. Gambling or engaging in a lottery on company premises	5-day suspension	Discharge			
8. Striking a supervisor	Discharge				

Progressive Discipline

Progressive discipline refers to increasingly severe penalties corresponding with repeated, identical offenses committed by an employee. It relates to correction in at least two ways: (a) by impressing upon the employee the seriousness of repeated rule infractions and (b) by furnishing the employee additional chances to correct his or her behavior before applying the ultimate penalty of discharge. Management typically has to give an oral warning, a written warning, and at least one suspension before it can discharge an employee for repeatedly committing a similar offense, such as failure to wear safety equipment.

An *oral warning* represents an informal effort to correct and improve the employee's work performance. The informality of this reprimand is for corrective training purposes; however, the oral warning can be prejudicial to the employee if it is entered as evidence in arbitration hearings. This disciplinary action, however, is subject to the following employee defenses: (a) the employee might have thought the supervisor's remarks were instructional and been unaware of the disciplinary aspects or consequences of the warning; and (b) an oral warning given in private can lead to conflicting testimony—the employee can state that the supervisor never gave him or her an oral warning. However, because of its relatively harmless nature, the union seldom contests this form of discipline.

A *written warning* is a much more serious matter because it summarizes previous oral attempts to correct the employee's behavior and is entered in the employee's work record file. More official than an oral reprimand, it brings disciplinary actions into focus by warning the employee of future consequences of rule violation.

Suspensions are disciplinary layoffs without pay given by management to impress upon the employee the seriousness of the offense. Oral and written reprimands might also achieve this purpose, but they do not involve a financial sacrifice on the part of the employee. A suspension serves as an example of the economic consequences associated with discharge and at the same time indicates that management is willing to retain the employee who will comply with directives and change errant ways. Management initially imposes a mild (one- to three-day) suspension and will seldom impose a suspension greater than ten days for a repeated offense. Under these circumstances, arbitrators are reluctant to reduce the suspensions, unless it can be shown that other employees were given lesser penalties for identical offenses under similar circumstances:

Unless the employer's actions are such that would "shock" the senses of "an ordinary reasonable man," the arbitrator would do well to avoid interfering with the punishment imposed by a "careful competent management which acts in the full light of all the facts."[27]

Discharge is not a corrective measure, since it means the employee is permanently released from the company. As mentioned earlier, arbitrators have attached tremendous significance to the effects of discharge upon the employee, regarding it as a last resort to be used sparingly when all other corrective attempts have failed and the employee's usefulness to the firm is totally lacking. An exception to this procedure occurs when the nature of the offense is so heinous (stealing, striking a supervisor, setting fire to company property, sexual assault of another employee) as to make other forms of corrective discipline unnecessary.

Progressive discipline also implies a *statute of limitations*. For example, it would be difficult to discharge an employee who has previously received two suspensions for failing to report his or her absence to management if the worker has worked for a fairly long period of time (say, three to five years) before committing a similar, present offense. Management is usually not obligated to return to the first step, that is, an oral warning; however, discharge (the next step after the second suspension) is not warranted—the employee's offense-free performance for the three- to five-year period indicates that corrective measures did have some effect and should be tried again before separating the employee from the firm.

How long a period of offense-free employment should justify an alteration of the progressive discipline procedure? One company has explicitly answered this question with the following labor agreement provision:

With regard to discipline imposed for any cause other than those set forth above, the company will not refer to any disciplinary notices received by an employee more than five years prior to the current situation for which the employee is being disciplined.[28]

This provision is advantageous to management since it furnishes the arbitrator specific guidelines to be applied in progressive discipline. Furthermore, the five-year statute of limitations is longer than that imposed by most arbitrators. One possible disadvantage of this strategy is that its specific inclusion in the labor agreement subjects the time period to collective bargaining—the union will be encouraged to negotiate a reduced statute of limitations, perhaps a time period shorter than most arbitrators would regard as being appropriate.

Finally, it should be noted that a discipline price list does not take statute of limitations into account—its penalties are for repeated infractions regardless of the intervening time period. In these circumstances, should management negate its own price list by returning to a suspension even though discharge is the next step in the procedure? Or proceed with the discharge, knowing that many arbitrators, employing a statute of limitations, would reinstate the employee because of the commendable performance for a period of time between his or her previous and recent offenses? Both courses of action have risks: In the first case, management might establish precedent which can adversely affect other cases; in the second, management might appear arbitrary in its discipline administration.

Degree and Nature of the Evidence

The burden of proof for all disciplinary actions rests with management; however, the degree of proof necessary varies among arbitrators. There are two schools of thought regarding the degree to which a person should be proven deserving of discipline. One arbitral attitude is that an employee must be shown guilty beyond reasonable doubt. This high degree of proof is usually required in discharge cases for criminal offenses (stealing or assault) rather than in discharge cases for noncriminal offenses (absenteeism, sleeping on the job, and so on), because it would be much more difficult for the employee to obtain employment with a work history that includes a discharge for criminal offenses.[29]

The second approach, used by a majority of the arbitrators, is that the preponderance of the evidence must establish the employee's guilt. The testimony and evidence must be adequate to overcome opposing presumptions and evidence; the grievance decision is influenced by who presents the best case instead of an absolute standard. A common problem facing management and union representatives is that neither party knows for sure how much evidence the arbitrator will require to uphold the disciplinary penalty.

Additional problems occur over the type of evidence that is used to support management's contentions and disciplinary action. Management can usually enter the grievant's past work record as evidence that corrective discipline was imposed. This issue becomes more complex when the company offers the employee's past record for the purpose of suggesting the likelihood that the employee has committed the present offense. Assume, for example, a bus driver is disciplined for negligent driving, and he denies the charge. The company then shows the grievant's past record to show that he has had three accidents of a similar nature during the past year and must now be considered "accident prone." Arbitrators do not regard this evidence in a uniform manner; however, "a large majority will admit the evidence and give it weight when the present offense has a functional relationship to the past offense."[30] As can be seen from the following quotation, some arbitrators accept the grievant's past work record as evidence even when it is not functionally related to the present offense:

The existence of "proper cause" for discharge reasonably may be based upon any significant and relevant record of prior disciplinary actions, and it is not necessary that specific prior infractions relied upon involve the same misconduct.[31]

However, in submitting unrelated offenses to the arbitrator, management runs the risk (either through direct challenge by the union or arbitral interpretation) of demonstrating that it is out to get the employee by any means possible.

Another controversial aspect of evidence occurs when management uncovers the evidence while using search and seizure techniques. Few arbitrators deny the employer's right to impose, as a condition of employment, an inspection of the employee's clothes and packages on entering and leaving the plant; however, a problem arises when company officials search an employee's locker or, in some cases, home, with or without the employee's permission. Many arbitrators permit evidence obtained without the employee's knowledge if it is from company property, even if the property (such as locker or tool chest) is momentarily under the control of the employee. On the other hand, few, if any, arbitrators believe evidence should be accepted if management obtained the evidence by forcibly breaking into the employee's personal property, even if the property is located on company premises.[32]

Evidence obtained through alleged entrapment techniques poses an additional problem for the arbitrator. Some arbitrators recognize the legitimacy of evidence obtained by company hired undercover agents, particularly if it is corroborated by other employees and management officials. Problems can arise, however, when a management representative entraps an employee. An illustrative arbitration decision involved a foreman having several discussions regarding marijuana with an hourly employee. On one occasion, the foreman approached several employees standing near the grievant's car, whereupon the foreman said, "I know what you fellows are up to. You better be in shape for work tomorrow." The grievant then asked the foreman if he wanted some and handed the foreman two marijuana cigarettes when the foreman replied, "Yes." After conferring with legal authorities, the foreman was advised to arrange a sale of marijuana. He asked the grievant if he could purchase $5 worth, with the grievant responding in the affirmative. The foreman then notified a representative of the county prosecutor's office, who in turn searched the grievant's automobile at the end of the shift and found a quantity of marijuana. The employee was arrested for possession, pleaded guilty, and received a $25 fine. In discharging the employee, management contended that it could not have an acknowledged pusher on its premises. However, the arbitrator believed that the evidence did not establish the employee as being a pusher and that the foreman provoked the employee to distribute the substance on company premises.

The critical question is whether the record establishes that X acted as a pusher or supplier. There is no proof that he ever sold marijuana. His general statements to Porter [the foreman] that he had done so, in the course of friendly and casual conversation, do not establish that he actually sold the drug on any specific occasion. That he knew the prices of marijuana and was familiar with the language associated with its distribution is also not sufficient to prove that X was a pusher.

While X did give Porter two cigarettes, Porter initiated the conversation and, in earlier talks, had asked for marijuana cigarettes and had just indicated to the employees he suspected they were smoking marijuana and his only concern was that they report to work in good shape the following morning. X's act in giving the foreman two of his cigarettes was not a sale or form of distribution under the circumstances, particularly in view of the foreman's expressed interest in using marijuana and their friendly discussions of the subject.

Quite apart from the foregoing, we are impressed by the union's theory that management has an obligation to deter potential violators. The record is clear that instead of cautioning X during April against engaging in marijuana possession and activity on company property, Porter persisted in approaching him and prodding him on to commit a wrongful act. We do not condone the practice by a supervisor of preying upon an employee's weakness in order to subject him to discipline.[33]

Finally, arbitrators are often faced with the issue of credibility of the witnesses and the accompanying dilemma of how to resolve a grievance when testimony of union and management representatives is completely contradictory. Two general tests appear applicable, the first being an evaluation of the witnesses' behaviors on the stand and their ability to hold up under cross-examination. Arbitrators also attach particular significance to a party's silence in the face of opposing testimony. Arbitrators regard the silence as an implicit acceptance of the other's testimony.

In the second test arbitrators ask themselves what each party stands to gain by lying. The supervisor who does not like the grievant and wants him or her discharged at any cost stands to benefit from lying. Similarly, the foreman does not wish to have the grievant reinstated at the expense of his or her reputation as an efficient management official. However, grievants stand to gain much more by lying—their jobs. Generally, the grievants are in trouble in cases featuring contradictory testimony. This is especially true if the arbitrator is not able to award the first test in his or her favor, because the second test, with rare exceptions, is decided in management's favor.

Nature of the Penalty

In some instances, management establishes that the employee was guilty of the offense but not that the penalty was appropriate. Arbitrators consider the reasonableness of the penalty relative to the offense, particularly if the employee was discharged. Few offenses merit discharge for their single commission, even if management regards the offense as being exceptionally serious. Arbitrators, while reluctant to modify suspensions, have no reservations about reducing a discharge penalty to a suspension. They reason that arbitrary or capricious discharge is a total waste to the employee as well as the firm, which incurs employment costs in hiring a replacement.

In determining whether the penalty is appropriate, arbitrators look to previous practices in the company or, in some instances, rely on precedents established by other arbitrators when management has never encountered the particular disciplinary situation. Arbitrators also scrutinize the disciplinary proceedings to see whether mitigating circumstances were involved and due process was followed.

Mitigating Circumstances If certain mitigating circumstances have influenced the offense, then arbitrators will tend to reduce a disciplinary penalty under one or two assumptions:

1. Management contributed to a problem and must therefore assume part of the responsibility for this wrongdoing.
2. The circumstances of the case were so unusual as to give great doubt that it will occur again, particularly if management uses corrective techniques instead of discharge.

An example of mitigating circumstances under the first arbitral assumption occurs when management has provided the employee with faulty tools and equipment and subsequently disciplines the employee for low production output.

A more common example of mitigating circumstances occurs when a management representative provokes the employee into committing physical or verbal abuse. In a representative discharge grievance, a fellow employee made vulgar and apparently misguided remarks about the fidelity of the grievant's wife. Later in the shift, another employee reported to the grievant that the foreman was asking other employees about the grievant's wife. The grievant thereupon confronted the foreman, who responded by treating the situation as a joke. The arbitrator reinstated the grievant on the basis that the foreman's poor judgment contributed to the grievant's subsequent physical attack on the supervisor.[34] In essence, arbitrators maintain that management must make every effort to avoid continuing an argument with the employee in order that the argument will not turn into a serious breach of industrial discipline.

Management might also contribute to a disciplinary infraction by condoning (either openly or tacitly) similar offenses committed in the shop. This situation is illustrated in a brief summary of an arbitration case from the *Wall Street Journal*:

Humiliating the boss isn't grounds for dismissal, an arbitrator rules.

On the night before his wedding day, a plant supervisor for International Harvester Co. was seized on the factory floor by six male workers. They removed some of his clothes and held him while a female worker put grease on his body. The company fired all seven employees, charging that the pre-wedding prank amounted to "physical abuse of the most degrading and humiliating form."

The union agreed the prank was wrong, but argued that dismissal was an overly severe penalty. Agreeing with the union, arbitrator Louis Crane ordered the workers rehired, reducing the penalty to an unpaid suspension. He reasoned that the workers' "crude joke" wasn't physically harmful and was tacitly condoned by other supervisors who saw it happen.[35]

A thorough discussion of the numerous mitigating circumstances suggested by the second arbitral assumption is beyond the scope of this chapter, but an example is given for illustrative purposes. An employee has been repeatedly warned and suspended for failure to report his absence to management when he is unable to work a production shift; the last suspension informed the grievant that another infraction would result in discharge. One month after suspension, the employee again fails to report his absence to management and is discharged when he reports to work the following morning. The employee contends (and adds evidence in the form of a doctor's slip) that his wife became suddenly, unexpectedly, and seriously ill and that his concern for his wife, coupled with no telephone in the apartment, resulted in his failure to report his absence to management. Here, management has followed all of the principles of progressive discipline; however, the employee's discharge might be set aside if the arbitrator maintains the circumstances were so unusual as to give management no reason to think it will happen again in the future.

Arbitrators often consider the mitigating effects of the grievant's role as a union officer. Compared to other employees, union officials usually have special rights and privileges, particularly when conducting union business. Many arbitrators regard the union steward and foreman as organizational equals in discussion of union matters. Arbitrators therefore give the union steward leeway if harsh words are exchanged in these meetings, while other employees might be successfully charged with insubordination for identical actions.

Union officers also have greater responsibilities that correspond to their rights. For example, arbitrators have upheld more serious disciplinary action for union officers who failed to prevent a wildcat strike than for employees who actually participated in the strike.[36] This differential penalty implies that union stewards should be more knowledgeable about contractual prohibition against a wildcat strike and uphold their contractual obligation to maintain uninterrupted production during the term of the labor agreement.

Due Process *Due process* refers to procedural regularities in the discipline process. Most labor agreements indicate three procedural steps to be followed in discipline:

1. The discipline process will follow certain time limits specified in the labor agreement.
2. The employee will be entitled to union representation when discipline is being administered.
3. The employee will be notified of the specific offense in writing.

The Supreme Court has upheld the employee's right to have union representation in an interview where the employee believes that discipline might result. Rationale for this decision was in part based on the union official's potential contribution to the disciplinary investigation:

A single employee confronted by an employer investigating whether certain conduct deserves discipline may be too fearful or inarticulate to relate accurately the incident being investigated, or too ignorant to raise extenuating factors. A knowledgeable union representative could assist the employer by eliciting favorable facts, and save the employer production time by getting to the bottom of the incident occasioning the interview. Certainly his presence need not transform the interview into an adversary contest.[37]

This decision also refuted the company's contention that union representation is only necessary after the company has made its discipline decision. The Supreme Court contended that this practice would diminish the value of union representation, thereby making it increasingly difficult for the employee to vindicate himself or herself in the subsequent grievance proceedings.

The written notice element of due process has caused some problems for management and is a major reason for the involvement of industrial relations representatives in the discipline process. Say an employee gets into a heated argument with the supervisor, refuses to work the assignment, and shouts an obscenity at the supervisor. The foreman could discipline the employee for "directing obscene and profane language toward a management representative." Once the charges are in writing, management must convince the arbitrator that this charge warrants discipline, a task which is not easy given the usual arbitral recognition that obscene language is regarded as common shop talk in an industrial facility. In this instance, management would have been wiser to have disciplined the employee for a more serious offense: "insubordination: refusal to follow supervisory orders." However, management can seldom change the offense once it is in writing and handed to the grievant. Consequently, a member of the industrial relations department is usually present for consultation (or in some cases direction) before the charges are reduced to writing.

Another related element of due process is *double jeopardy*—assigning an employee a more severe penalty than the one originally given. The rationale against double jeopardy is "since management is held to any decision which purports to be final, it is important that it acts only after ascertaining all relevant facts and determining the magnitude of the offense."[38] Management can avoid the problem of double jeopardy if it makes clear to the grievant that the action taken in the first instance is temporary, pending further investigation by higher company officials. Usually, this takes the form of an indefinite suspension which, pending a subsequent investigation, can be converted to discharge without arbitral disapproval. A final element of due process is the keeping of secret records on the employee, which most arbitrators maintain are worse than no records at all.

One arbitrator notes three alternative positions that the arbitrator can take regarding procedural or due process irregularities:

(1) that unless there is strict compliance with the procedural requirements, the whole action will be nullified; (2) that the requirements are of significance only where the employee can show that he has been prejudiced by failure to comply therewith; or (3) that the requirements are important, and that any failure to comply will be penalized, but that the action taken is not thereby rendered null and void.[39]

Arbitrators tend to favor the third alternative, reasoning that management should suffer the consequences of its errors, but not to the point of exonerating an employee who is guilty of a serious offense (particularly if it has not prejudiced the employee's case). Table 11–2 is intended to bring elements of discipline discussed in this section into perspective by furnishing the relative weights that arbitrators assign them in reinstating discharged employees. Although these data were published ten years ago, they remain excellent indicators of arbitrators' reasoning in reversing management's decisions.

The Importance of the Supervisor in Employee Discipline

While not usually having formal authority to take disciplinary action against any of his or her employees,[40] the supervisor is often the most significant management official in the discipline process. The foreman's importance in administering discipline can be seen from both positive and negative viewpoints.

From a negative view, the foreman may be a major cause of disciplinary problems due to lax enforcement of the rules or to intentional or unintentional encouragement of rule violation. A major reason for apathetic rule enforcement is a supervisory attitude that one should not rock the boat so long as the disciplinary problem doesn't affect the employees or departmental productivity.[41]

Sometimes supervisory apathy is enhanced by a fear that the union will

Table 11–2
Reasons Given
by Arbitrators
for Reversing
Management in 391
Discharge Cases

	Number of Cases
The evidence supported the charge, but there were mitigating circumstances.	77
Evidence did not support the charge of wrongdoing.	52
Inconsistent enforcement of rules.	38
The rule itself was reasonable, but its application in this case was not.	30
The grievant did not know he was risking a penalty by his action.	28
Management was partly at fault in the incident.	27
The penalty was excessive in terms of the company's discipline policy.	25
The grievant was punished under the wrong rule of schedule of penalties.	20
Employees involved in the same incident were dealt with differently without a satisfactory explanation of the difference.	18
Punishment was for a reason the arbitrator thought was beyond management's authority to discipline.	14
Management committed procedural errors prejudicing the grievant's rights.	13
The penalty seemed excessive in terms of customary penalties in industry.	11
Union stewards or officers were disciplined for actions in connection with their official union business.	9
Retroactive application of new rule, or insufficient publicity about a rule.	9
General standards of judicial process were violated.	7
The grievant was substantially guilty, but the arbitrator thought he was entitled to another chance because of special circumstances.	4
The rule which the grievant had violated was inherently unreasonable.	4
The evidence of wrongdoing was held inadmissible by the arbitrator.	3
The company had shown personal bias or discrimination against the grievant.	2

Source: Morris O. Stone, "Why Arbitrators Reinstate Discharged Employees," *Monthly Labor Review* 92 (October 1969), p. 49. Cases reported in American Arbitration Association's "Summary Labor Arbitration Awards," April 1959 through June 1969.

become involved in a subsequent discipline grievance and communicate to other management officials that the foreman is involved in a labor relations "problem." Of course, in many instances, management would favorably regard the foreman's actions as defending management's rights on the shop floor. However, as the following remarks indicate, the supervisor is not always guaranteed this response from management:

I had this one troublemaker. He was a solid goldbricker. He couldn't cut the buck on any job. I tried everything, but he was lazy and he was a loud-mouth. I caught him in the toilet after being away from his machine for over an hour. I told him he was through and to go upstairs and pick up his check. And damn. Do you know what those college boys in personnel did? He gives them some bull about being sick and weakly and the next day he is sitting at a bench in the department next to mine. He says to me, "Well wise guy, you don't count for nothin' around here. Every time I see you, I'm going to call you Mr. Nothin."[42]

Supervisory personnel experiencing similar situations would probably maintain that disciplinary action for future, related offenses isn't worth the time, effort, and aggravation.

As is true of many individuals, supervisors do not like being placed in a confrontation role. One personnel manager has commented:

You hear that the supervisor feels he ought to have disciplinary authority in order to control his department. In our company this right was recently returned to them and you should have heard the howls. They felt we weren't earning our money. Discipline is a dirty business. And they were only too happy to let us do it, as had been done for the past 30 years.[43]

Perhaps the supervisor's reluctance to confront an employee over a disciplinary matter can be best illustrated through an example. A supervisor observes an employee smoking a hand-rolled cigarette in an out-of-the-way location (behind a storage bin). Having a long, good work record with the company, the employee has never received any prior disciplinary action. Before he approaches the employee, several questions will probably run through the supervisor's mind: What do I say to the employee? Do I ask for the cigarette? What if the employee refuses? Could I discipline the employee for not giving the cigarette to me? What if it doesn't turn out to be marijuana? What will this employee and others think if this is the case? What if the employee denies the incident ever took place? Whose version will management believe, the employee's or mine? When faced with all of these questions, a supervisor might avoid the situation by pretending that it did not take place. Yet, in following this course of action, the supervisor has neglected disciplining an employee who may have committed a criminal violation.

The foreman might also contribute to discipline problems by encouraging the employee to commit a wrongdoing. In some cases this encouragement is unintentional (a supervisor who forgets to wear specified safety equipment might encourage his or her employees to do likewise). In some instances the foreman might actually encourage the employee to violate the rules in order to maintain or increase productivity. Perhaps the most vivid documented example of this situation occurred at a New York City airplane manufacturing facility. One of the most serious offenses (resulting in automatic discharge) is the use of a tap to rethread unaligned bolt holes. The use of a tap is strictly prohibited by Air Force regulations; however, the alternative is disassembling and reassembling previous installations to make sure the holes line up for bolt insertion.

In most instances, the supervisor cannot afford to have a large amount of down time recorded for the department. Therefore, many supervisors condoned and encouraged serious rule infractions in the name of efficiency, and the following remarks made to their employees were not uncommon:

Now fellas, there's a big drive on taps. The Air Force just received a special memo. For God's sakes, don't use a tap when I'm around. If somebody sees it while I'm in the area, it'll be my ass. Look around first. Make sure I'm gone.[44]

From the favorable viewpoint, the foreman can be a strong, positive influence in discipline administration and prevention. Almost all of the elements of just cause outlined in Exhibit 11-1 are directly related to the foreman's activities and responsibilities. The supervisor is responsible for furnishing and explaining work rules to the employee and training the employee in desired job performance. More specifically, the supervisor is obligated to give clear, concise directives which indicate (a) what is to be done, (b) how it is to be done, (c) when it is to be done, and, most importantly, (d) that he or she expects it to be done.[45] Also, it is the supervisor who is responsible for treating all employees in a consistent, prompt fashion.

Another key aspect of the supervisor's disciplinary role is the investigation and subsequent interview with the employee to determine whether discipline is appropriate. He or she must uncover all related facts as well as the underlying causes of the alleged offense. In addition, the supervisor must obtain the employee's version of the incident and at the same time restrain any personal emotions or biases which might affect his or her judgment of the employee. Clearly, none of these tasks is easy or pleasant. Supervisors often have to conduct their investigations in an atmosphere stressing production output, quotas, and deadlines, a situation which further taxes and frustrates supervisory discipline.

The supervisor also occupies a prominent role in the arbitration process. Many arbitrators' decisions directly consider the supervisor's involvement in one or more of the following categories: architect of past practice, participant in the events, reporter of the events, and witness. In this latter capacity, arbitrators usually have to assess the supervisor's credibility, testimony, and ability to withstand cross-examination.

Employee discipline will continue to represent a most significant aspect of day-to-day labor relations activities on the shop floor. Union and management officials and the affected employees have rather large investments in the outcome of disciplinary actions. All of the participants need to approach this topic in a rational manner to strengthen labor-management relationships and minimize the possibly far-reaching implications of an arbitrator's award.

Summary

In many respects, employee discipline represents the most significant day-to-day issue in administering the labor agreement. For the union and management organizations, administration of discipline is a key factor related to control and production factors; the supervisor and the affected employee are even more directly and personally affected.

Management had a unilateral right to discharge or discipline employees until the 1930s, although psychological reform and efficiency movements in the early 1900s urged management to critically examine its disciplinary policies. Some managers realized that an employee represented an investment which could be unnecessarily lost due to whimsical disciplinary actions. These individuals realized that they had an obligation to provide employees with clear work rules and proper training, which would minimize the number of discipline problems and lead to increased productivity. The establishment of the NLRB further refined employers' disciplinary policies, as employees discharged for their union activities could be reinstated to their jobs with back pay.

Discipline in unionized settings must be for just cause, a concept consisting of several dimensions. While discipline can accomplish several purposes for the organization, management may have to prove that its actions were taken to *correct* an employee's behavior. Correction suggests that an employee must be aware of work rules which are clear in their content as well as consequences for their infraction. The work rules must also be reasonable—that is, related to the job—and consistently applied to all employees under similar circumstances.

Discipline's corrective emphasis also suggests progressive or more severe penalties given to an employee for repeating a similar offense. Progressive discipline impresses upon the employee the seriousness of repeated rule infractions while giving the employee additional chances to correct work behavior. Usually, management has to give an employee an oral warning for the first offense, then a written warning and suspension for subsequent, similar offenses. Discharge is a last resort—used only when all other attempts at correction have failed or the nature of the offense is so unacceptable as to make corrective efforts unnecessary.

Arbitration of discipline grievances places the burden of proof on management to establish that the employee committed the offense. Arbitrators may require the company to prove the employee guilty "beyond a reasonable doubt" or by establishing a "preponderance of the evidence." Additional dimensions of evidence can occur when the company attempts to enter the employee's work record into the hearing or uses search and seizure techniques, or when contradictory testimony is entered into the hearing. Management must also establish that the penalty fits the crime and that it considered all possible mitigating circumstances before imposing discipline.

Management must also provide the employee with due process in the disciplinary procedure—insure that the appropriate contractual provisions are upheld. The employee usually has the right to union representation and the right to be notified of the offense in writing.

The supervisor is significant to the disciplinary process. Supervisors can exert a tremendous positive or negative influence on the effectiveness of management's disciplinary policies.

Discussion Questions

1. Why is discipline a most significant issue for the union and management organizations? Describe how this significance has shifted over time.

2. One union newspaper indicated how it saved an employee's job. The employee was in the mechanic's classification and was discharged for refusing to comply with management's sudden, unilateral rule that mechanics perform janitorial duties. Given this sketchy situation, discuss the many possible reasons for the disciplinary action, indicating why the arbitrator might not have been convinced that management's discipline was for the "legitimate purpose." (You are free to make assumptions in your answer.)

3. Explain in some detail the difficulties management would have in administering the following work rule in accordance with the disciplinary principles established in the chapter: "Any employee reporting to work under the influence of alcohol will be subject to discharge."

4. Indicate the comparative advantages and disadvantages of the checklist of disciplinary prerogatives in the labor agreement and a one-sentence contractual provision indicating "management has the right to discipline or discharge an employee for cause."

5. While not subject to judicial scrutiny, evidence in an arbitration hearing still has its complexities. Discuss the complexities which could be involved in an arbitration hearing involving an employee who was discharged for smoking marijuana on the job.

6. Assume you are in charge of establishing a training program for supervisors in administering discipline. Based on the supervisor's potential role in the disciplinary process, formulate and discuss three major principles you would stress in this session.

References

[1]The significance of discipline as a labor-management issue is illustrated by the fact that almost one out of every three grievances decided by arbitration pertains to this topic. Federal Mediation and Conciliation Service, *Twenty-ninth Annual Report*, 1976 (Washington, D.C.: Government Printing Office), pp. 55–56.

[2]William P. Anthony and Philip Anthony, "More Discipline, Less Disciplinary Action," *Supervisory Management* 17 (September 1972), p. 18.

[3]Orme Phelps, *Discipline and Discharge in the Unionized Firm* (Berkeley: University of California Press, 1959), p. 1.

[4]Earl R. Bramblett, "Maintenance of Discipline," in Paul Pigors, Charles A. Meyers, and F. T. Malm, eds., *Management of Human Resources*, 3d ed. (New York: McGraw-Hill, 1973), p. 470.

[5]James Menzies Black, *Positive Discipline* (New York: American Management Association, 1970), p. 60.

[6]J. Fred Holly, "The Arbitration of Discharge Cases: A Case Study," in Jean McKelvey, ed., *Critical Issues in Labor Arbitration* (Washington, D.C.: Bureau of National Affairs, 1957), p. 15.

[7]Ken Jennings and Roger Wolters, "Discharge Cases Reconsidered," *Arbitration Journal* 31 (September 1976), pp. 164–180.

[8]Joseph P. Wollenberger, "Acceptable Work Rules and Penalties: A Company Guide," *Personnel* 40 (July–August 1963), p. 23.

[9]*Oil, Chemical and Atomic UNION NEWS*, July 1970, p. 9.

[10]Black, *Positive Discipline*, p. 28.

[11]Lawrence Stessin, *Employee Discipline* (Washington, D.C.: Bureau of National Affairs, 1960), pp. 2–3.

[12]Dallas L. Jones, *Arbitration and Industrial Discipline* (Ann Arbor: Bureau of Industrial Relations, University of Michigan, 1961), p. 5.

[13]Whiting Williams, *What's on the Worker's Mind* (New York: Charles Scribner's Sons, 1921), p. 130.

[14]D. S. Kimball, *Principles of Industrial Organization*, 2d ed. (New York: McGraw-Hill, 1919), p. 53; Charles Gerstenberg, *Principles of Business* (Englewood Cliffs, N.J.: Prentice-Hall, 1918), p. 18; Daniel Bloomfield, *Labor Maintenance* (New York: The Ronald Press, 1920), p. 71; and G. S. Radford, "Handling Men," in Daniel Bloomfield, ed., *Employment Management* (New York: H. W. Wilson, 1919), p. 107.

[15]See, for example, Mangus W. Alexander, "Hiring and Firing: It's Economic Waste," *Annals of the American Academy of Political and Social Science* 45 (May 1916), p. 128.

[16]Edward D. Jones, "Employment Management," in Daniel Bloomfield, ed., *Employment Management*, p. 123; see also Kimball, *Principles of Industrial Organization*, pp. 239–240.

[17]"Labor Letter," *Wall Street Journal*, May 27, 1975, p. 1.

[18]Robert Skilton, *Industrial Discipline and the Arbitration Process* (Philadelphia: University of Pennsylvania Press, 1952), pp. 22–23; Lawrence Stessin, "Is the Arbitrator Management's Friend in Discipline Cases?" *Monthly Labor Review* 72 (April 1959), p. 373.

[19]Bureau of National Affairs, *Basic Patterns in Union Contracts* (Washington, D.C.: Bureau of National Affairs, 1975), p. 9.

[20]Stessin, *Employee Discipline*, p. 36.

[21]*Alden's Inc.*, 61 LA 665 (D. Dolnick, 1973).

[22]*Hoosier Panel Co., Inc.*, 61 LA 983 (M. Volz, 1973).

[23]Black, *Positive Discipline*, p. 52.

[24]Lewis Yagoda, "The Discipline Issue in Arbitration: Employer Rules," *Labor Law Journal* 15 (September 1964), p. 573.

[25]Lawrence Stessin, "Management Prerogatives and Plant Rule Violations," *Arbitration Journal* 14 (1959), p. 9.

[26]Phelps, *Discipline and Discharge*, p. 48.

[27]Roland P. Wilder, "Discharge in the Law of Arbitration," *Vanderbilt Law Review* 20 (December 1966), pp. 124–125.

[28]*Inmot Corporation*, 58 LA 18 (J. Sembower, 1972).

[29]Maurice C. Benewitz, "Discharge Arbitration and the Quantum of Proof," *Arbitration Journal* 28 (June 1973), p. 103.

[30]R. W. Fleming, *The Labor Arbitration Process* (Urbana: University of Illinois Press, 1965), p. 222.

[31]*U.S. Steel Corporation*, 61 LA 1201 (H. Witt, 1973).

[32]Fleming, *Labor Arbitration Process*, p. 189.

[33]*New Jersey Bell Telephone*, 61 LA 255–256 (H. Weston, 1973).

[34]*Gindy Manufacturing Company*, 58 LA 1038–1040 (M. Handsaker, 1972).

[35]"Labor Letter," *Wall Street Journal*, August 30, 1977, p. 1. Reprinted by permission of *The Wall Street Journal*, © Dow Jones & Company, Inc., 1977. All rights reserved.

[36]W. H. Leahy, "Arbitration, Union Stewards, and Wildcat Strikes," *Arbitration Journal* 24 (1969), pp. 50–58. For a discussion of the employee's race as a possible mitigating circumstance see Harry Seligson, "Minority Group Employees, Discipline, and the Arbitrators," *Labor Law Journal* 19 (September 1968), pp. 544–554.

[37]NLRB v. J. Weingarten, Inc., 420 U.S. 262, 1974. It should be noted that this decision recognized several qualifications to the employee's right of union representation. For example, the employee must request the representation; the exercise of the right to representation may not interfere with legitimate employer prerogatives; the employer has no duty to bargain with any union representatives during the meeting. For a discussion of subsequent NLRB cases which appear to expand the principles expressed in *Weingarten* see Bruce Stickler, "Investigating Employee Misconduct: Must the Union Be There?" *Employee Relations Law Journal* 3 (Autumn 1977), pp. 255–265.

[38]Wilder, "Discharge in the Law of Arbitration," p. 96.

[39]Fleming, *Labor Arbitration Process*, p. 139. See also Harry T. Edwards, "Due Process Considerations in Labor Arbitration," *Arbitration Journal* 25 (1970), p. 145.

[40]See, for example, Norman R. F. Maier and Lee E. Danielson, "An Evaluation of Two Approaches to Discipline," *Journal of Applied Psychology* 40 (October 1956), p. 323; Peter B. Schoderbeck, "The Changing Role of the Foreman," *Personnel Journal* 44 (August 1970), pp. 680–687; and David Kipnis and Joseph Cosentino, "Use of Leadership Powers in Industry," *Journal of Applied Psychology* 53 (December 1969), pp. 460–466.

[41]Black, *Positive Discipline,* p. 83. For a discussion of other reasons for supervisory apathy see Wallace Wohlking, "Effective Discipline in Employee Relations," *Personnel Journal* 54 (September 1975), p. 489. For an empirical study examining supervisory apathy in enforcement see William B. Boise, "Supervisors' Attitudes toward Disciplinary Actions," *Personnel Administration* 28 (May–June 1965), pp. 24–27.

[42]D. C. Miller, "Supervisor: Evolution of a Forgotten Role," in Floyd Mann, George Homans, and Delbert Miller, eds., *Supervisory Leadership and Productivity* (San Francisco: Chandler, 1965), p. 113.

[43]Charles Myers and John Turnbill, "Line and Staff in Industrial Relations," in Joseph Litterer, ed., *Organizations: Structure and Behavior* (New York: Wiley, 1966), p. 313.

[44]Joseph Bensman and Israel Gerver, "Crime and Punishment in the Factory: The Function of Deviancy in Maintaining the Social System," *American Sociological Review* (August 1963), p. 593.

[45]R. Dirk Van Horne, "Discipline: Purpose and Effect," *Personnel Journal* 48 (September 1969), pp. 728–731.

Chapter 12

Administrative Issues

"Collective bargaining can help democratize labor-management relations and humanize the workplace and work itself, including the impact of innovation and new technology on workers' jobs and earnings."

Markley Roberts*

Several important administrative issues can cost as much as or more than negotiated wage increases. This chapter focuses on four broad administrative issues: (a) technological change and its impact on labor relations issues; (b) personnel changes and their relationship to make-work practices, subcontracting, work assignments and jurisdiction, job structuring and work scheduling, and the role of seniority; (c) employee and job development, including quality of worklife and job enrichment issues; and (d) safety and health.

Most of these issues involve conflicting priorities. Management wishes to have complete discretion in arranging its work content and schedules in order to maximize efficiency. Unions seek to protect employees' jobs and job rights in cases of new job assignments. The attempts of management and labor to achieve their respective priorities are discussed throughout this chapter.

Technological Change and Job Protection

Technological change refers to changes in the production processes which result in the introduction of labor-saving machinery and changes in material handling and work flow. *Automation*, a type of technological change, goes one step further in that machines perform tasks formerly performed by humans, and the human operator is replaced by automatic controls.[1]

Technological advances have brought about numerous positive effects: more wealth is produced with less effort; machinery that either performs tasks that humans cannot or performs them with more reliability and efficiency has lowered the costs of production and allowed products to be sold at lower prices; better working conditions prevail; back-breaking work assignments are minimized; and skill levels of workers have increased, with consequent increases in pay.[2] While the vast majority of technological changes have had no direct effect on labor relations, some related changes have been most influential: power-driven equipment substituted for hand labor; use of faster, more adaptable equipment, such as the printing press; use of automatic controls; use of conveyors and automatic loading and unloading equipment; use of computers to process, compute, and record data at phenomenal speeds; and substitution of factory production for on-the-job fabrication, such as prefabricated housing units.

Advances in technology have increased the demand for skilled labor and created new occupations, such as computer programming and digital machine operating. Technological advances have also necessitated significant adjustment within industries (increasing opportunities in the automobile and airline industries while lessening opportunities in the railroad industry, for example). They have also caused shifts among industries; for example, growth in the television industry has resulted in a decline in movie production, and development of plastic products for milk bottles and fruit juice and paper products for towels and napkins have adversely affected the glass and textile industries, respectively.[3]

Reactions to Technological Change

Union leaders and members have been far from unanimous in their views on technological change. Some have ranked it as the foremost problem of our age; others welcome advances with open arms as long as the workers share in the rewards and benefits. Union leaders have generally accepted the inevitability of technological change but have wanted to protect their members and negotiate protective clauses to assure job security.

Rank-and-file members' opinions about technological change vary in accordance with the advances made in their particular occupations and industries. For example, in fast-growing industries, such as electronics and paper, union attitudes are quite positive, because the rate of expan-

*Markley Roberts, "Harnessing Technology: The Workers' Stake," *AFL-CIO American Federationist* 86 (April 1979): 20.

sion offsets the unfavorable effects on employment. In those industries that have not been penetrated greatly by automated technology, union members are either indifferent or experience some anxiety (due mostly to unfavorable publicity about automation found in labor publications).[4] Others view management as pressing for labor-saving technological changes to improve production efficiency and lower costs. These changes strike hard at one of the union's primary functions: to protect the jobs of its members. Thus, unions tend to view technological change as they do subcontracting, tough wage negotiations, moving operations away from union influence, and other management actions that cause a reduction in jobs.[5]

Such defensive union responses to technological change seem to evolve in three stages:

1. Unions first attempt to negotiate provisions designed to maintain the existing jobs at existing earnings, such as prohibiting layoffs, seniority preferences in layoffs and job assignments, work sharing, supplemental unemployment benefits, guaranteed hours of work, and retraining for automated jobs.
2. The union recognizes that job and earnings changes cannot be entirely resisted; therefore, its position shifts toward attempts to cushion the problems of worker displacement. The strategy shifts from maintenance of jobs and earnings to moderating the impact of displacement to ease the transition. Unions seek to broaden the use of seniority to interplant, intercompany, and interarea transfers; to negotiate retraining and relocation allowances; to serve in an advisory or joint research capacity in adjustment planning, and so on.
3. The final stage usually indicates the inevitability of technological change and involves the union assertion that any loss of jobs should be compensated in return for employer freedom to maneuver. This strategy assumes that employees have a vested right in their jobs, and any loss of these job rights would justify compensation to the employees via severance pay, dismissal pay, or terminal payments (for accumulated vacations and sick leave) and payment of any accumulated supplemental unemployment benefit accounts.[6]

While union reaction to technological changes ranges from one extreme to another, the majority of cases involve compromise, working together to introduce technological change with a minimum of adverse effect on employees. Both unions and management attempt to soften the impact of automation on workers, but naturally the union's requests are higher than the employer's willingness to consent. For example, the union will frequently request that technological change be scheduled during periods of high employment, that attrition be permitted to reduce the work force, that results of increased productivity be shared, that the workweek be reduced, that seniority be used in decisions, that preferential hiring be considered on other jobs, and so on.[7] Because these union proposals are felt to be either too costly or too restrictive on management's freedom to make changes, they are frequently resisted by management and cause temporary conflicts.

Examples of Various Industries' Reactions One of the most noted examples of willing acceptance of technological change involves the United Mine Workers, led by John L. Lewis, who literally gave employers a free hand to advance technology in the coal mines. This policy was based on two fundamental premises: (a) it is better to have fewer miners engaged in mining at high wages than many at low wages, and (b) high productivity in the coal industry was essential for high wages if coal was to be competitive with oil and gas as a source of energy.[8] On the opposite side, an extreme example of outright resistance occurred in England 160 years ago; Luddite workers, fearing massive unemployment, attempted to prevent the use of any labor-saving machinery by breaking the machines, burning the factories, and resorting to various forms of sabotage and work slowdowns.[9]

Railroads. One classic example of difficulties with technological change occurred in the railroad industry with the elimination of the fireman position in the operation of diesel locomotives. Union and management had argued about its necessity since the introduction of diesel trains. Management believed that the fireman's job of shoveling coal was no longer necessary; however, the union insisted that the fireman still performed tasks essential to train safety. After attempts at mediation and negotiation failed, in 1963 Congress passed the first peacetime compulsory arbitration law to resolve the issue, and an arbitration panel held that 90 percent of the fireman's jobs were unnecessary. Although firemen with less than two years' service were discharged with severance pay, the others remained employed until they were promoted, retired, or resigned. The union never really agreed to the arbitration panel's decision in this case, and it was not until thirteen years later that the carriers and the United Transportation Union finally agreed to the elimination of the fireman position.[10]

In more recent times, other issues related to the change from steam locomotives to diesel engines have caused conflicts; these include the size of the train crew, the elimination of the steam-era wage formula for the train crew's daily pay, and reduction of the number of crew changes required on each train trip.[11] Such issues, long included in labor agreements, have shown that it takes a long time to negotiate change.

Construction. There have been continuing efforts by construction unions and companies to accommodate needed changes in their industry. In 1973, the Building Trade Department and the National Contractors Association negotiated a work rules agreement to achieve increased productivity and labor relations stability. For example, the Sheet Metal International Association negotiated an agreement that provides for a special underemployment benefit for employees who work less than average for their local through no fault of their own. The program was financed through employer contributions of 3 percent of gross earnings to a fund on behalf of each worker in return for the unions' agreement to alter their work rules to insure a fair day's work, no output restrictions, no slow-downs, and no illegal work stoppages.

Many agreements for increased productivity can be traced to the growth of nonunion companies, the wage-price guidelines of the 1962–1966 era, or Phases I to IV of the Nixon administration wage-price program. To protect jobs and obtain wage increases above the guidelines set by the Council of Economic Advisors, productivity improvements were necessary. In the final analysis, construction unions gave up many long-held work restrictions in order to compete with nonunion labor and to obtain higher wages.

Meatpacking. Many national meatpacking firms, confronted with grow-ing competition from small packers who located near the livestock, closed their high-cost urban plants and began constructing smaller, more eco-nomical units closer to their own sources. One company, Armour, closed eleven plants and reduced its production employment from 25,000 to 15,000. Job security emerged immediately as most important in sub-sequent collective bargaining, and Armour offered funds to establish a joint union-management committee to study the problem of moderniza-tion and adjustments to forthcoming changes. The committee recom-mended training or retraining employees for new or changed jobs, al-lowing transfer to other plants, continuing the existing severance pay plan, and providing advance notice of future plant closings. Individual locations went even further to help in the adjustment. For example, in Omaha, where a plant was closing, extensive community resources were obtained by the local union to provide counseling and placement services for the employees who were being laid off.

Longshoring. Longshoremen on both U.S. coasts have adapted to technological change, but they have also benefited at the bargaining table. Traditionally, longshoremen have sought to fix the number of workers on each crew, to resist the introduction of forklifts and load pallets, and to institute work rules covering shipping and loading operations. Today, manual labor in loading and unloading of ships is virtually eliminated; automation and loading onto containers on the docks are accepted; and longshoremen are increasingly required to learn new skills in order to be more flexible in job placement. These adjustments have been accom-plished with guarantees and benefits to the longshoremen. Guaranteed hours of work on the West Coast and guaranteed annual income on the East Coast ports have been provided; early voluntary retirement has been encouraged along with payments of as much as $7,920 to those with twenty-five years service.

Other industries. Other examples of technological change include automated checkout stations, automated warehousing, central meat cutting, and computer scanning of the Universal Product Code on each package in the retail food industry. In the printing industry, technological innovations that continue to affect employee use and productivity include typesetting computers, electronic phototypesetting, new techniques to prepare camera-ready copy, optical character recognition equipment, and the cathode ray tube scanner, which permits bypassing the composing room.[12]

The airline industry and Air Line Pilots Association (ALPA) have long had a running dispute over the cockpit crew sizes on jet airliners, more specifically the Boeing 737. While the airlines contend that the third pilot has no meaningful duties, ALPA claims that weather and terrain factors in some situations require an extra set of eyes. After several arbitration cases and negotiations, the third pilot now remains only with United and Western Airlines. ALPA attention has now been directed toward requiring a third pilot in the Douglas DC-9 Super-80, set for 1980 delivery.[13]

New York newspapers' attempts to revamp their production methods and staffing practices, which would have eventually reduced the number of pressmen positions by 50 percent, forced a three-month strike in 1978. Although the union had been advised one year in advance that the newspapers intended to reduce the man-machine ratio to an amount approximating the average for the country, the union argued that more employees, not fewer, were needed.[14] The final result was a six-year contract that guaranteed jobs for 1,508 pressmen over six years and reduction of the number of pressmen only through attrition.[15]

Job Security and Personnel Changes

A primary concern of unions is insuring that members' jobs are protected from elimination due to technological change or managerial decision making. Unions have been able to protect jobs by negotiating clauses about make-work rules and featherbedding, subcontracting, work assignments and jurisdiction, work scheduling, and the role of seniority in personnel changes.

Make-Work Rules and Featherbedding

Make-work rules require more than the necessary number of workers for a given job or spread the workload in a number of other ways, such as placing limits on the load that can be carried, restricting the duties of employees, limiting the number of machines one operator can tend, mandating work to be performed twice, prohibiting modern tools or equipment, and requiring excessive relief time and unneeded standby crews.[16] Such practices carried to an extreme are known as *featherbedding,* which exhibits "unreasonable limits to the amount of work employees may do in a given period, . . . payment for unneeded workers, unnecessary tasks, work not performed, or jobs duplicating those already done."[17] It is viewed negatively by the public, since it is associated with an economic waste of resources.

Make-work and featherbedding practices have been challenged by management and condemned by labor economists. They associate such practices with the *lump of labor theory,* which assumes that there is only a limited amount of work available and workers therefore must extend the time allowed for this work in order to keep their jobs. While the lump of labor theory has been widely refuted during times of economic growth, union behavior returns to practices of work restrictions in order to preserve jobs during economic slowdown.[18]

Make-work rules, work load restrictions, and featherbedding practices lie at the foundation of many labor relations conflicts. From an overall (macro) viewpoint, union leaders agree that change is necessary for economic progress, but from an individual (micro) view, where significant adjustment would be necessary, change is resisted.[19] Congress attempted to help reduce make-work practices when it amended the National Labor Relations Act in 1947 and included Section 8 (b) (6), which prohibits a labor union from causing or "attempting to cause an employer to pay or deliver or agree to pay or deliver any money or other thing of value, in the nature of an exaction, for services which are *not performed or not to be performed.*"

After two Supreme Court decisions involving newspapers, Section 8 (b) (6) lost much of its potential for restricting featherbedding practices. In one case, the Supreme Court agreed that some of the work practices at issue were wasteful, but the NLRB had found that the work was actually performed and employees had been hired by the employer to perform the work required, some of which was not necessary.[20] The Court concluded:

The Act now limits its condemnation to instances where a labor organization or its agents exact pay from an employer in return for services not performed or not to be performed. Thus, where work is done by an employee, with the employer's consent, a labor organization's demand that the employee be compensated for time spent in doing the disputed work does not become an unfair labor practice. The transaction simply does not fall within the kind of featherbedding defined in the statute. . . . Section 8 (b) (6) leaves to collective bargaining the determination of what, if any, work, including bona fide "make work," shall be included as compensable services and what rate of compensation shall be paid for it.[21]

Thus the courts have given fairly specific direction to unions and management to resolve these make-work practices in collective bargaining. Recognizing that there may be some value to this approach rather than a purely legalistic one, the NLRB and the courts have set ground rules for these issues. The same means by which unions seek to improve wages, hours, and working conditions are available to maintain or establish make-work practices. Employers can resist these union demands, but they may also have to give up or trade something in return.

This trade-off is the essence of collective bargaining. Resolving such employment security issues through collective bargaining enables the parties themselves to deal with the problem in a manner suited to their specific needs and situation (see Chapter 13 on productivity bargaining). Moreover, in some cases, the unions help to minimize the impact on the workers.[22] Abolishing featherbedding and make-work practices in one stroke by legislative decree would abruptly increase the burdens of unemployment dangerously, with serious economic and social consequences.[23]

Subcontracting

Subcontracting occurs when a firm determines that it cannot perform all the tasks that are necessary to operate its business successfully or that another firm can perform the needed tasks (janitorial and cafeteria services, equipment repair, parts production, and so on) at a lower cost. In either case, the firm may contract with others to assume responsibility for certain work requirements. The subcontracting process, apparently a normal economic practice, is a volatile and complicated collective bargaining issue. From management's view, subcontracting raises issues of managerial flexibility, the firm's ability to progress economically, and its right to pursue its economic goals free from union interference. From the union's perspective, subcontracting raises problems of job security, challenges from competing groups of workers, and undermining of contract standards.[24]

Unions have increasingly attempted to influence management's decisions to subcontract. These decisions usually are motivated by the company's need to reduce production costs. Unions generally try to limit management's freedom to subcontract in order to protect and maximize work and economic opportunities for their members, to prevent the firm from escaping from the union, and to protect the members' jobs against competition from nonunion firms.[25]

Since it has been declared a mandatory issue of collective bargaining,[26] unions have made significant inroads on subcontracting in collective bargaining agreements. It is now limited or prohibited in nearly half of the labor agreements, and inclusion of these clauses has increased significantly in the last ten years. Labor agreements seldom strictly prohibit subcontracting, but often limit it in one or more of the following ways: they require advance consultation with the union, prohibit subcontracting if layoffs would occur from such decisions, allow subcontracting only if the necessary skills and equipment are not available, and require use of skilled workers for maintenance and construction jobs within the bargaining unit.[27]

Arbitration likewise has played an increasingly important role in the subcontracting issue. This role has usually involved such aspects as determining whether subcontracting is an arbitrable issue without explicit contractual language on the subject. Arbitrators are commonly asked to interpret the recognition clause and any accompanying bargaining unit work and appraise commonly specified criteria, such as "good faith," proof of "sound business practices," and "no harm to members of the bargaining unit."[28]

Subcontracting has been frequently arbitrated under the management rights clause of the agreements (see Chapter 10). When agreements do not explicitly provide management the right to subcontract, the unions seek to bargain over the subject. When and if management refuses, the union will frequently petition the NLRB, alleging that the employer has committed an unfair labor practice by refusing to bargain in good faith. Where a management rights clause is written in generalities, not specifically alluding to subcontracting, the union challenge will more likely be decided in arbitration.

Work Assignments and Jurisdiction

Management can assign individual duties and tasks to employees on the job more easily than it can assign employees to jobs that have permanent job classifications. While assignments of workers to such jobs are usually limited by contract provisions covering seniority or fitness, labor agreements sometimes contain direct restrictions on the right of management to assign specific duties and tasks to workers. In grievance administration and arbitration, it is usually held that, unless the agreement provides otherwise, employees are not allowed to select only those duties or tasks within their classification which they particularly prefer.[29]

On the other hand, assignment of work to employees often gives rise to union-management confrontation, especially where changes in operations, job descriptions, and technology occur and where more than one union represents employees. While the National Labor Relations Act prohibits unions from engaging in or inducing strike action to force an employer to assign work to a particular union or craft, such strikes do occur.[30] Such disputes occur usually under three types of circumstances:

1. When two or more unions claim jurisdiction over specific work assignments.
2. When bargaining unit employees believe their work is being assigned to other employees outside the bargaining unit, such as supervisors.
3. When disagreement occurs within a union over particular work assignments.

Conflicts between unions over work assignments occur more commonly in industries having craft unions, such as the building and construction industries. Each craft union believes it should have exclusive jurisdiction over some phase of construction work, and the work is performed on job sites for only a short time with frequent movement from place to place. Each craft guards its rights to perform a specific task, and so no intercraft relationship develops between craft unions and their members which could help moderate any disputes over work assignments. To complicate the situation further, the work is characterized by an infinite variety of similar materials and equipment. For example, the plasterers' union will probably claim jurisdiction when carpenters who commonly install accoustical ceilings start using a spray gun to blow materials on a surface that looks like plaster.[31] The disputes can be resolved through procedures established by the NLRB. To avoid going before the NLRB, the Building and Construction Trades Department and several national contractors' associations have agreed to establish a national joint board to consider and decide cases of jurisdictional disputes in the building and construction industry.[32]

Most of the time the work jurisdiction lines are distinct, but in research and technical jobs (such as laboratory heads, engineers, draftsmen, and chemists), work jurisdiction frequently overlaps. For example, if professionally certified engineers are difficult to hire, companies may resort to assigning engineering tasks to draftsmen or technicians. These assignments may be acceptable when jobs for professional engineers are plentiful, but during a recession, when jobs are scarce, these same engineers may resist any assignment of "their" work to others they believe less qualified.

Also, foremen are often asked to perform work assignments that normally go to bargaining unit employees. To prevent such an occurrence, clauses are written in agreements to restrict foremen except in specific exceptional cases: when training new employees, in emergencies, and during experimental projects. Although most companies do not resist these clauses, several interesting issues regarding this matter must be addressed:

☐ Is a clear division between hourly employees and management in the best interest of effective labor relations?

☐ With more college graduates becoming first-line supervisors, how can they realistically get a feel for their subordinates' jobs if they are precluded from working on these jobs?

☐ If challenged over a production standard or promotion, how can management prove that the jobs can be done a certain way and within a certain time?

Intra-union work assignment problems, although not as critical and dramatic as the previous ones, often are very sensitive to local union leaders. Various individual or group interests of members of the same union over work assignments can cause problems, especially in industrial unions having craft and semiskilled employees as members. Whenever production processes are automated, assignment of work from skilled employees to semiskilled production workers causes emotional conflicts within the union. For example, having pipefitters do welding tasks when welding is not included in their job description gives rise to disputes.

To resolve these conflicts, unions favor specific, written job descriptions and would like to refuse to perform work outside their jurisdiction. However, companies prefer general job descriptions, which include phrases such as "perform related duties" and "make minor repairs," in order to provide flexibility in making work assignments.[33] Whether detailed or vague, the particular duties included in a job description often result in disagreements between management and union officials.[34]

Work Scheduling

Collective bargaining agreements frequently deal with *work scheduling*, such as regulating shifts and fixing the workday or workweek. Management also has the right to schedule work unless restricted by the agreement. For example, it usually has the right to suspend operations temporarily, reduce the number of shifts, and change the number of days to be worked. Moreover, it can usually make unscheduled and emergency changes in the work schedule if such changes are made in good faith and for reasonable cause, such as extreme weather conditions, bomb threats, and civil disturbances.[35]

Unions and management continue to negotiate the workday and workweek issues. While the five-day, forty-hour workweek has been standard since 1938 when the Fair Labor Standards Act was passed, unions have continued their attempts to reduce the hours of work. In 1978, a group called the All Unions Committee to Shorten the Work Week, composed of such unions as the United Auto Workers, United Steelworkers, Machinists, Electrical Workers, and Meatcutters, was established. Recognizing that an across-the-board reduction in the forty-hour week is unlikely, their attention has been directed to retirement policies of *thirty and out* (thirty years of work, then retirement with full benefits), longer vacations, sick leaves, and more holidays.[36]

Individual unions continue to attempt to adjust the workweek. The United Auto Workers has inched closer to the four-day workweek with its "paid personal holiday," which allows auto workers with one year's seniority five personal holidays per year (seven in 1980). These personal paid holidays provide more time off for auto workers, while also requiring the company to hire more employee replacements.[37]

Unions in the United States and elsewhere have shown increasing interest in *flexitime programs*, which allow an employee to start and finish work at his or her discretion, as long as the specified total number of hours per week or per day are worked and the employee is present at work during the core-hour period (for example, 9:00 A.M. to 11:00 A.M. and 1:30

P.M. to 3:30 P.M.).[38] These programs are designed to fit together job requirements and personal needs of individual employees. There is proof that flexitime has accommodated such personal needs as avoiding heavy traffic in commuting to work, working during the time of day of peak efficiency, shopping during a two-hour lunch period, and finishing work by the time children are out of school. There is also some evidence that attitudes toward work and production are improved or at least maintained.[39] While flexitime has much potential for meeting employee needs, some operations require all workers on the job at the same time, and work schedules cannot be altered unless the entire group accepts the alternative work schedule.

The Role of Seniority in Personnel Changes

Employers usually have a free hand in selecting those employees who best fit the needs of their organizations and who best meet the prescribed job requirements. However, once any employee has been selected and placed on a job within the bargaining unit, the employer must abide by provisions of the labor agreement regarding personnel decisions such as promotions, transfers, and layoffs. This section highlights issues involving administrative determination and presents the concept of seniority, including its legal complications.

Concept of Seniority *Seniority*, usually measured by the length of an employee's continuous service, is often divided into two categories of employee rights:

1. *Job rights* apply in decisions on promotion, layoff-recall, transfers, work assignments, shift preference, selection of days off, overtime, and vacation date selection. The most senior employee usually will be given preferential treatment—will be laid off last, recalled first, and offered a shift preference and overtime first.
2. *Benefits rights* concern eligibility for certain employee benefits, such as vacations, pensions, severance pay, sick leave, and insurance. These rights are not competitive with those of other employees and begin to accumulate immediately upon employment with the organization.[40]

Seniority provisions, found in nearly 90 percent of all labor agreements,[41] show how seniority accrues over an employee's continuous service and, in some cases, how it can be lost for a variety of reasons (layoff, failure to respond to recall, unauthorized absences, or taking a job elsewhere during leave of absence).[42]

Job seniority may be measured in a number of ways: total length of time with an employer (employment, mill, or plant seniority), length of service in a line of progression (progression line seniority), and length of service in a job classification (job seniority). While the particulars of the seniority system may vary greatly, some type of preference is usually accorded the more senior workers.[43]

Seniority is considered "sacred" by most union members,[44] yet it is doubtful that any other concept of labor relations has been as "influential, persuasive, and troublesome in collective bargaining."[45] Management seldom objects to providing some sense of security to long-service employees,[46] and unions and managements generally agree that senior employees should be entitled to greater security and superior benefits as a matter of equity and fairness. However, for other reasons, seniority has played an increasingly important role in the labor relations environment. For example, it serves as an important objective measure for making personnel decisions—the concept dictates that length of service, not managerial discretion, determines who will be promoted or laid off. In addition, the number and types of employee benefits tied to seniority have increased dramatically.[47]

Seniority can be very costly to the company as well as union members. For example, Lockheed has claimed that it lost $15 million in two years as a result of its complicated seniority system, which allows layoff-threatened employees with more than six years' service to take junior employees' jobs. A study of Lockheed's seniority system, which had been in effect for fifteen years, showed that one layoff caused an average of five job changes—which caused serious problems with employee training.[48] It is difficult to compute the specific costs of other problems caused by seniority systems, such as an aging work force, the possibility of lessening ambition and motivation of younger workers, and the loss of key personnel low in seniority.[49]

Union and management representatives carefully negotiate the seniority provisions of their agreement in anticipation of future negotiations issues and in accordance with rules of clarity, equity, and simplicity. Seniority provisions usually include such items as the seniority unit (company, plant, department, job), how it is used (promotion, transfer, layoff, recall), and how it accumulates (effect of interruptions of service such as military leave or layoff); rules on loss of seniority (voluntary quit, discharge for cause, failure to report from layoff, unexcused absence, and misuse of leave of absence); administration of the seniority list (posting requirements, supplying lists to the union, and keeping lists up to date); special arrangements (mergers, acquisition of firms, and succession); and special exemption for certain employees.[50] In some cases, unions and management include a seniority provision called *superseniority,* which exempts highly skilled technical employees and union officials from layoffs—a move which allows the company to retain essential skills and at the same time promote stable labor relations.

Promotions and Transfers *Promotions* are personnel changes within an organization advancing the employee to a position of more responsibility, usually accompanied by a wage increase. Appearing in the majority of the collective bargaining agreements,[51] promotion provisions usually state that seniority and ability are the deciding factors. While seniority can be easily measured by several indicators, determination of ability is more complex.[52] *Transfer* provisions, appearing in slightly less than the majority of agreements, cover personnel changes from one position to another with relatively equal authority, responsibility, and compensation. Seniority and ability are also usually the determining factors used in making the transfer decision.[53]

Four basic types of seniority clauses are used in promotion and transfer decisions:

1. Seniority as the sole factor.
2. Seniority used after ability to perform the job is demonstrated.
3. Seniority and ability as two determining factors.
4. Relative ability used before seniority.

Straight seniority is the easiest to administer for determining eligibility for promotions and transfers. However, there is a possibility that the eligible senior employee is unfamiliar with the job and will need extensive training for the new assignment.

Seniority with minimum ability simply means that the more senior employee gets the job if minimum qualifications can be demonstrated. Such provision requires that the employer promote or transfer not the most competent candidate nor the most superior one, but the most senior employee among the qualified candidates.

When seniority and ability are given equal weight as determining factors in the agreements, arbitrators have concluded that when seniority is relatively close, it is reasonable to use relative ability, but when seniority differs extensively, ability must be substantially greater to justify equal consideration.[54] Clauses that prescribe the use of relative ability before seniority use seniority as the determining factor only if management determines that all the candidates for a vacancy have approximately the same qualifications for the job.[55]

Ability, the measure usually accompanying seniority, includes "some combination of skill, knowledge, attitudes, behavior, performance, pace, and production and perhaps talent."[56] While the employer has the right to establish any criteria for assessing ability, it must comply with the standards negotiated and written in the collective bargaining agreement[57] and "Uniform Guidelines on Employment Selection Procedures"[58] covering race, sex, national origin, and religious discrimination. These guidelines, used by the Equal Employment Opportunity Commission, Civil Service Commission, and Departments of Labor and Justice, specify requirements covering employment decisions defined broadly as "tests and other selection procedures which are used as a basis for any employment decision. [These] decisions include but are not limited to hiring, promotion, demotion, . . . selection for training, or transfer."[59] Moreover, the provisions of the labor agreement itself must not be discriminatory or perpetuate past discriminatory practices.

Employers may design selection techniques to determine employees' qualifications for promotions and transfers. Techniques most commonly used are tests,[60] experience, education, production records, performance ratings,[61] personality traits, and absence, tardiness, and discipline records. Because each of these criteria may be limited in its specific relationship to the needs of particular jobs, the determination of employee qualifications is usually based on several criteria, not one. Where superior qualifications are identified, the determination may be clearcut. However, where the criteria themselves produce conflicting results, the burden is on the employer to assure accurate determination.[62]

Transfer procedures are basically the same as those for promotion, except that employee requests are used more frequently. An employee dissatisfied in his or her present job and requesting transfer to more pleasant working conditions or work group or to a more favorable line of progression is generally granted the transfer if the employee qualifies and a vacancy occurs.

Other provisions affecting personnel decisions in collective bargaining agreements are included to prevent problems that often emerge. For example, agreements should prescribe whether an employee carries his or her seniority to a new position or whether seniority will be retained only after a predetermined period of time. Other provisions should specify whether an employee who transfers out of the bargaining unit or is promoted to supervision will be allowed to retain seniority or will lose it.[63]

Layoffs and Recall Layoff provisions included in most contracts consider seniority first in retaining employees during layoffs. Increasingly, seniority has become the sole factor in layoff determination; however, some contracts consider seniority as the determining factor only if employees are qualified for available jobs. In others, seniority is given consideration only when factors such as ability and physical fitness are equal.

Of course, there are exceptions to these general rules. For example, union stewards and local union officers might be given superseniority and will be the last ones laid off in their respective departments. Unions sometimes desire this provision to encourage members to run for the many positions available in the union. In some cases, superseniority can be a strong incentive, if not the only one, to become a union steward. To protect the organization from having unqualified employees, some contracts stipulate that the union representatives must be qualified for the jobs available if they are to be exempt from layoff.

Advance notice of impending layoffs to the employees and the union is often required, and some agreements specify one to four days' notice. Frequently, employees scheduled for layoffs are permitted to displace or "bump" less senior employees, although they usually must qualify beforehand for the jobs in order to do so. While nearly a majority of agreements allow companywide or plantwide bumping, others confine bumping to the employee's own classification or work group, to former job classification, or to the department or division. Most agreements provide for recall of employees after layoff. These provisions usually specify that employees be rehired in reverse order of layoff, but only if they show that they are qualified for the open position.[64]

Legal Issues Involving Seniority in Administrative Determinations Job rights guaranteed by the labor agreement may conflict with employee rights guaranteed by the U.S. Constitution and Equal Employment Opportunity Act of 1972. Use of seniority in administrative determinations such as promotions and layoffs has been the focus of much legal attention. In some cases it has been shown that minorities have been locked in departments or jobs with unfavorable lines of progression, and these practices tend to perpetuate past employment discrimination. The following are examples of discriminatory seniority practices:

☐ Separate seniority lists for black and white employees doing the same work.

☐ Black and white employees holding similar jobs, while only whites are eligible for promotion.

☐ Separate seniority lists from which blacks are hired for less desirable jobs and whites for more favorable jobs.

☐ Refusing employment to minorities after the Civil Rights Act went into effect, then, after losing several EEOC cases, starting to hire minorities but maintaining seniority lists that continue to place minorities at the bottom.[65]

In resolving these cases, the courts would probably void the practices of using separate departmental seniority lists or seniority for personnel decisions[66] and might order one or more of the following forms of affirmative action:

☐ Change departmental seniority to plantwide or company seniority, possibly merging seniority lists.

☐ Restore those persons who have suffered under the discriminatory seniority plans to their "rightful place" (a place where they would have been if they had not been discriminated against), thereby awarding retroactive seniority.

☐ Modify seniority rights of the majority and minority, taking into account restored job rights and the merged seniority lists.[67]

☐ Remove any barriers to transferring from previously segregated departments.

☐ Allow a reasonable time for minorities who have been bypassed on promotions because of their seniority status to request consideration—failure to request consideration would constitute a waiver.

☐ Allow minorities who were victims of discriminatory seniority systems to use their plant or employment seniority to bid for vacancies and present their qualifications.

☐ Allow *red-circling* (pay above the rate specified for the particular job) for previous victims of discrimination so that they may move to better lines of progression. Red-circling the wage rate would allow such a move without jeopardizing previously earned seniority credits used in wage determination. [68]

☐ Abolish job residency requirements, except in those jobs where experience is essential to advance up the occupational ladder and equivalent experience cannot be attained by working elsewhere.

☐ Examine the qualifications necessary to perform all jobs, remove all unrelated and artificial promotion prerequisites built into the job structure, develop objective criteria for advancement, and formally spell out these policies and procedures in the labor agreement. [69]

☐ Allow companies and unions to negotiate an affirmative action plan in which a prescribed percentage of the craft trainee openings is reserved for minority applicants until the in-plant percentage of minority craft workers approximates that of the local labor force. [70]

Not only are employers and unions being taken to court over work assignments, promotions, and transfers, but layoff-recall decisions based on seniority have become important issues. Assuming that employers have been hiring minorities recently at a greater rate than in the past, the company seniority list would consist of white males toward the top and minorities toward the bottom. At times when product demand is low, the employer may face the probability of laying off the newly-hired minority employees in accordance with the "last hired, first fired" provision in the labor agreement. [71] In those cases where plant, department, or job seniority is used, the layoffs would erase much of the employer's progress in its affirmative action plan and affect minority employment disproportionately.

Minority groups have attacked these seniority and layoff practices on the basis of two theories:

1. The last hired, first fired layoff practice perpetuates past discrimination, since it takes the minority ratio of the work force back to the days when employment discrimination was practiced.
2. As an employment criterion having a disparate effect on minority employees, the last hired, first fired layoff rule can be justified only on the grounds of its "business necessity" or as a "bona fide occupational qualification" (conditions which minority groups feel are not present). [72]

A few federal district courts at first accepted the position of minority employees and ruled on their behalf. For example, a Louisiana judge voided the last hired, first fired layoff and recall practices, and an Illinois judge ruled that "layoffs should be allocated among minorities and non-minorities in such a way that the minority workers would have the same percentage representation after the reduction in force as they had prior to the layoffs."[73] Although these decisions were overturned on appeal, several issues remained unresolved: What would be the effect after 1964 of continuing discriminatory hiring practices which accompanied last hired, first fired layoff practices? Could not certain individuals be treated discriminatorily even if the seniority list were racially neutral? If there were an act of employment discrimination, what would be the equitable remedy for those who suffered from it?

It was not until 1977 that some of these issues were settled by the Supreme Court. The Court ruled in *International Brotherhood of Teamsters v. U.S.* that unit (company, plant, department, and job) seniority systems are bona fide and protected under the Civil Rights Act under two conditions:

1. If they were instituted prior to enactment of the Civil Rights Act of 1964.
2. If evidence shows that there was no "intent to discriminate" in the genesis or maintenance of the seniority system.[74]

In cases where a company has continued discriminatory acts after enactment of the Civil Rights Act, the seniority system loses its status as a "bona fide" seniority system, and adjustments have to be made. Further, those who suffered must be restored to their rightful place and be eligible for back pay in accordance with the amount to which they are entitled.[75]

Although "intent to discriminate" may seem a vague guideline, the Equal Employment Opportunity Commission (EEOC) has provided employers with its interpretation of the Court decisions. In determining intent to discriminate, it will review all available evidence, such as history of collective bargaining and past and present employment practices. If seniority units had been previously segregated, or if minorities continue to be locked in low-paying jobs or unfavorable lines of progression, discriminatory intent will be inferred. Further, when evidence shows "adverse impact" on minorities regarding work assignments, promotions, transfers, or use of seniority, appropriate relief will be sought by pursuing affirmative action through the courts.[76]

Employee and Job Development

Apprenticeship Programs

Many employees receive on-the-job training from management officials.[77] Unions tend to become much more involved in another training device—*apprenticeship programs*, which refer to formal, supervised programs of training and experience. They are usually supplemented by instruction off the job, and the apprenticeship eventually leads to journeyman status in a skilled craft. Labor and management officials become more deeply involved in the administration of apprenticeship programs than any other method of employee training. There are at least 300,000 individuals involved in such programs in the United States each year, about 60 percent in construction and the remainder in printing, manufacturing, and service.[78] Apprenticeship training can be very complex, and there are countless variations of the types of training available. For example, apprenticeship in construction differs significantly from that in manufacturing; even within manufacturing, apprenticeships vary from employer to employer.

Apprenticeships serve as more than just training experiences; they provide means by which craft unions can protect their wage rates and regulate the supply of union craft workers in a particular labor market. For many years, craft unions have pursued negotiations and legislation to specify the number of apprentices in relation to skilled journeymen, to define the length, content, and administration of the programs, and to select those persons who will become apprentices.[79]

Because craft unions have played a vital role in training and have greatly influenced the labor supply, their *nepotism* (practice of hiring relatives) and discriminatory practices that have prevented minorities from entering skilled occupations have made them prime targets.[80] Since labor unions are now covered under the Civil Rights Act, they too must be conscious of EEOC regulations. Craft unions frequently operate union hiring halls in addition to apprenticeship programs. Because craft unions have an important role in selecting apprentices and assigning union members to jobs through the hiring hall, the EEOC agencies have lately been very interested in their operations.

The equal employment opportunity (EEO) agencies and the courts have significantly affected the internal affairs of craft unions through affirmative action plans, conciliation, consent decrees, and court cases. The following policies are the result of EEO regulations and interventions:

1. Acceptance for apprenticeship training based on valid testing and licensing procedures, legitimate experience requirements, and standard initiation fees.
2. Union advertising of vacancies with the time and place for tests.
3. Policies abolishing nepotism (long a tradition with craft unions).
4. "First-in, first-out" referral procedures continued, but master referral registers, which include names, addresses, sign-in books, and availability sheets, maintained and operated in a nondiscriminatory fashion.
5. Craft unions and construction companies agreeing to an affirmative action plan, including goals, timetables, and specific actions which will increase minority employment in the specific crafts.[81]

Quality of Worklife and Job Enrichment

Quality of worklife and job enrichment issues have been the focus of much national publicity and experiments as well as academic research. The 1973 report *Work in America* alarmed management and unions when it concluded that large numbers of workers found their jobs devoid of meaning, dignity, and prestige and that work-related problems contributed to unstable family and community relations, alcoholism, drug abuse, and delinquent behavior.[82] About the same time, employees at a Lordstown, Ohio, General Motors plant struck over what many described as the dehumanizing work of the assembly line.[83] The prevailing attitudes of employees involved in the strike became known as the Lordstown Syndrome. These events led to significant interest in redesigning jobs to make them more challenging, more responsible, and less monotonous and to provide opportunities for advancement, feedback on performance, and participation in the work process. Programs that have incorporated such job elements have been labeled as quality of worklife or job enrichment programs.

The Reluctance of Unions to Accept Quality of Worklife Programs With few exceptions, successful ventures with such programs have occurred in nonunion companies under very accommodating conditions (for example, in new plants with hand-picked employees). In those few cases where unions and management have cooperated, management has usually been the initiator of the experiments.[84] By and large, labor unions have been either uninterested in or extremely suspicious of job enrichment and quality of worklife programs.[85] Still, with much attention being given to quality of worklife today, unions have found that they either must be involved or must defend themselves from attacks for not being involved. Unions' reluctance about quality of worklife programs is due primarily to the following factors.

Previous experiences with management. Some union leaders recall the era of scientific speed-up schemes and other anti-union devices, some of which date back to the early 1900s. They perceive quality of worklife programs as "ideologically and institutionally unfriendly to trade unions and collective bargaining"[86] and believe such programs are "devices (1) to increase effort norms without compensating increases in effort value, (2) to move workers from job to job without reference to job rights, and (3) to upgrade skill and responsibility without paying for it."[87] Although this belief has not been universally adopted by unions, it does explain in part their reluctance to involve themselves actively in quality of worklife efforts.

Perceptions of the union's role in labor relations. Management has generally considered determination of job content and assignments managerial prerogatives and has been hesitant to enter negotiations with unions over quality of worklife subjects.[88] Furthermore, it is unclear whether management is required by law to negotiate over the content of quality of worklife programs, even if unions press for negotiation of the issues. Labor unions have traditionally left to management the problems of increasing worker satisfaction and have perceived their role as concentrating their efforts on the gut issues such as money and job security.[89]

Interpretations of membership needs by the union leadership. Some union leaders do not believe that there is sufficient support from the rank-and-file union members for negotiating quality of worklife issues. As William W. Winpisinger, president of the Machinist Union and outspoken critic of job enrichment, has said:

In my years as a union representative and officer, I've negotiated for a lot of membership demands. I've been instructed to negotiate on wages . . . noise . . . seniority clauses; health and welfare, . . . and everything else you find in a modern labor-management contract. But never once have I carried into negotiations a membership mandate to seek job enrichment.[90]

For union leaders to insist vigorously on quality of worklife in negotiations with management, they would have to believe that a majority of workers feel that such changes are important, in some cases even worth striking for.[91] Most union leaders and members rank these issues behind the bread-and-butter issues and do not view collective bargaining as a particularly effective method for improving the quality of worklife.[92] To improve worker attitudes and employee motivation, union officials have traditionally placed more emphasis on job security, high wages, and improved working conditions[93] and have given little emphasis to those subjects commonly associated with quality of worklife and job enrichment: opportunities for advancement, more feedback to employees on how well they are doing, more interesting and challenging work, job redesign, enrichment, and enlargement, and more autonomy on the job.[94]

Winpisinger, expressing the views of many unionists, firmly believes that the way to gain job satisfaction is to pay wages commensurate with skill:

If you want to enrich the job, enrich the paycheck. The better the wage, the greater the job satisfaction. There is no better cure for "blue-collar" blues. If you want to enrich the job, begin to decrease the number of hours a worker has to labor in order to earn a decent standard of living. . . . The time has come to translate the increased productivity of automated processes into the kind of enrichment that comes from shorter work weeks, longer vacations, and earlier retirements.[95]

He also believes that employees have a say in their job content through the grievance procedure and the use of seniority, which enables them to transfer to jobs more to their liking.

Other union leaders have not been as harsh in their view; George Nestler of the Amalgamated Meatcutters' International has a somewhat contrasting opinion:

What do workers want? They want to identify with the company, the union, the product, and the group they work with. They want responsibility, they want communication and they want to contribute. They want to participate in their jobs, to have input. These things are meaningful to workers. They want to care about people. They want a share of the aims and goals, and of the financial rewards. Initially, financial rewards are what everyone looks at. This diminishes after a period of time. They are looking for new skills in their work, and for training. They want job security. And they want the right to question what's going on in their environment, in their workplace.[96]

The Potential of Quality of Worklife Programs in a Unionized Environment

The rather dim picture thus far presented for quality of worklife programs appears even worse when (a) union and management officials have had little experience with these programs and (b) administrative issues pertaining to job enrichment, such as specific objectives of the program and payment for training time, have to be negotiated.[97]

Yet, all is not lost for these programs. Contract rejections, employee job dissatisfaction, and prolonged negotiations might stimulate union and management officials to believe "there must be a better way." Thus, out of disenchantment, fatigue, or possibly boredom, both parties might become attracted to an approach that has some potential for providing relief from the adversarial relationship while serving the mutual interests of the respective parties.[98]

Since the release of *Work in America*, the federal government, through the Departments of Labor and Commerce and the National Science Foundation's Research Applied to National Needs Program, has provided funding of quality of worklife projects. The National Center for Productivity and the Quality of Working Life was established to facilitate projects to improve productivity and the quality of worklife; however, most of its functions have been reassigned to other federal agencies. Several unions, such as the United Auto Workers and United Mine Workers, have agreed to joint union-management projects. The United Auto Workers has negotiated a provision in its contracts with the major automobile manufacturers calling for joint union-management quality of working life committees. Universities, led by the Institute of Social Research at the University of Michigan and the Center for Quality of Working Life at the University of California, Los Angeles, have assisted unions and organizations in quality of worklife and job enrichment projects. Two private nonprofit organizations—the National Center for Quality of Work in Washington D.C., and the Work in America Institute in Scarsdale, New York—have been established to facilitate these efforts. Other developments include the growing number of work reforms and quality of worklife research efforts at colleges and universities and an increasing number of job enrichment and quality of worklife courses now offered by colleges and universities.[99]

Safety and Health: The Occupational Safety and Health Act

Safety and health provisions now are quite common in labor agreements;[100] however, these provisions vary considerably from general statements of safety responsibility to specific items,[101] such as:

☐ Guards for machines.

☐ Safety goggles and boots.

☐ Joint union-company investigation of accidents.

☐ Employee obligation to follow safety rules.

☐ Right to refuse hazardous work.

☐ Rules and procedures for joint safety and health committees, such as periodic meetings and inspections, payment for time spent, and authority to resolve safety disputes by use of grievance procedure and arbitration.

Many of these provisions have resulted from governmental legislation,[102] namely, the Occupational Safety and Health Act (OSHA), passed in 1970[103] in an attempt to improve industrial safety statistics.[104]

The employer's overriding duty under OSHA is to furnish each employee with conditions free from recognized hazards that may cause illness, injury, or death and to comply with all occupational safety and health standards adopted by the Department of Labor. Further, employers must permit inspectors to enter their establishments without delay and at reasonable times to conduct inspections. They must place appropriate notices, provide protective equipment when necessary, and maintain designated records of illnesses.

The act has been praised by some and criticized by others. An objective, comprehensive assessment of the entire OSHA program in terms of cost-benefit analysis has yet to be conducted,[105] although preliminary findings indicate a level of effectiveness ranging from limited[106] to pronounced.[107] Hopefully, in the near future a national evaluative research study by impartial analysts will be conducted to determine the benefits and costs of the entire OSHA effort.

Management and union representatives have not been reluctant to criticize the act and its administration. One management official has concluded that

a principal goal of the Act, the protection of worker health, is lost sight of as OSHA presses its regulations upon us, regardless of whether or

Many safety and health hazards, commonplace in the past, have been eliminated through the use of safety equipment. Yet safety remains an issue in current collective bargaining.

Sources: Photo on left reproduced from the collection of the Library of Congress. Photo on right by Bohdan Hrynewych, Stock, Boston.

not those regulations make good sense. Instead of allowing industry flexibility in achieving health protection, the government has attempted to compel industry to do things only one way—the way prescribed by armchair governmental experts and lawyers.[108]

Another, a management official and former president of the Industrial Relations Research Association, Douglas Soutar, has been equally critical:

> The Act [has become] as much a labor-management act as one of safety and health, and this has become excruciatingly the case. Hardly a day goes by, even in my own company, without some disturbance in our labor-management relations because of OSHA. Its abuse has produced bitter confrontations and consequences over such matters as rate retention, walk-arounds, alleged discrimination, refusal to work protected by the "smoke screen" claim of unsafe conditions, "calling in the Feds" (or state agencies) in retaliation against employer's direction of the workforce, and generally obtaining through OSHA and the Act what normally should be subject to collective bargaining. Also, as predicted, the health aspects of the Act are having a far greater impact than the safety side even though the latter produces about 95 percent of the reportable incidents.[109]

Unions also have been critical in their assessment of OSHA. One international union criticized the act primarily because of its lengthy appeals procedure and the time it takes to reach a consensus on various safety standards.[110] Congress was criticized because of budget cuts and underfunding of OSHA functions. Unions have also expressed some concern about discharge of employees who file safety complaints. While the act prohibits such action, unions allege that employers find "other reasons" for these discharges.

The AFL-CIO Executive Council has studied OSHA, and its assessment concludes that "the history of the administration of the Occupational Safety and Health Act is one of missed deadlines, forgotten timetables and endless, needless delay."[111] It cites a number of examples:

☐ Contracting for a study to determine whether state standards were as effective as federal standards, then cancelling the contract and refusing to make the report public.

☐ Consistently missing deadlines, like those for establishing standards and making recommendations to Congress on ways to avoid duplicating services of other federal agencies.

☐ Tolerating continued missing of deadlines for state and regional reports.

☐ Press releases from the Occupational Safety and Health Review Commission emphasizing how many employers have "beat the rap," making it appear that employers had been the innocent victims of overzealous inspectors.[112]

In 1978, after much criticism from others and a self-assessment by OSHA itself, the administration decided to set priorities and focus its attention on major problems. This approach meant "getting serious about serious dangers, . . . helping American businesses save money and lives, and . . . simplifying regulations while eliminating unnecessary rules."[113]

While many "nitpicking" regulations have been eliminated, important regulations concerning possible cancer-causing elements (such as cotton dust, lead, benzene, and acrylnitrate) were issued. Employers were given three to ten years, depending on the industry, to reach new standards. In addition, OSHA issued regulations requiring that workers removed from their jobs because of excessive lead in the body be protected against loss of pay, seniority, and other job rights. The regulations' aim is to encourage workers to take medical exams without the fear of losing their jobs. The Lead Industry Association challenged this regulation and has filed a petition for review of the standard in federal court.[114]

Another OSHA-related controversy has developed in the chemical industry over voluntary sterilization. On certain jobs, female workers are exposed to chemicals which could cause fetal damage. To reduce the risks, companies are restricting certain jobs to men and to women workers who are not capable of having children. Insurance carriers for the companies are worried about potential liability; unions are threatening the companies with sex discrimination suits; OSHA is claiming that they are not controlling and monitoring the conditions under which the women work. To these conflicting concerns is added the inconclusiveness of the existing research on fetal damage caused by the chemicals used in production.[115]

One development which will be interesting to watch unfold is the creation of the AFL-CIO's Department of Occupational Safety and Health. This department will coordinate national unions' efforts to protect workers from job-related injuries and illnesses. Gathering and disseminating data about various OSHA issues, it will employ occupational physicians and specialists and will work with government agencies responsible for administering the laws.[116] In addition, several international unions have already employed their own industrial hygienists and health-engineering technicians to provide educational services to members and to double-check OSHA regulations. Some of the larger unions have already conducted research for presentations before Congress and OSHA regulatory bodies and have sponsored research projects to investigate health-related hazards on the job.[117]

On another front, those hurt on the job are increasingly attempting to pin the blame and monetary damages on the federal government. Their attorneys now are arguing that if government inspectors are "sloppy," they are failing in their responsibility to employees. If their theory is correct, the U.S. Treasury will be obligated to compensate victims of hazards that OSHA inspectors fail to catch.[118]

Finally, another controversial issue involves OSHA's authority to make inspections without notice. The Supreme Court ruled in 1978 that the employer can require OSHA to obtain a search warrant before conducting an inspection but that OSHA does not have to establish "probable cause" for a search in the customary "criminal sense."[119] How the lower courts and OSHA will interpret these rulings will be a source of controversy in the 1980s.

Summary

The four general categories of administrative issues—technological change, personnel changes, employee and job development, and safety and health—each have many important facets which may be negotiated and often end up in labor agreements.

Technological change, an essential ingredient of a dynamic economic system, is broadly defined to include such activities as introduction of labor-saving machines, power-driven tools, and automatic loading equipment. While unions generally accept these changes as inevitable, they attempt to negotiate provisions in labor agreements to protect members' present jobs and establish the means for assuring future protection. Collective bargaining has provided avenues for working together to resolve complicated problems emanating from technological changes; significant examples have occurred in various industries, such as the railroad, construction, meatpacking, and others.

Two interrelated issues, job security and personnel changes, raise questions about employee protection. Often, unions will seek to protect their members by negotiating make-work rules, limiting management's rights to subcontract, demanding specific work assignments and jurisdiction, and structuring jobs and scheduling work to the advantage of the employees. When personnel changes are made, seniority becomes a key issue. Likewise, where firms are growing and opportunities for advancement are present, seniority and merit are key considerations. Employers and unions must consider EEOC regulations and court rulings in addition to labor agreement factors in deciding courses of action on personnel adjustment.

Employee and job development incorporate employee training, emphasis on apprenticeship, and job enrichment programs. Unions and employers alike place great emphasis on and expend much effort in apprenticeship programs. Quality of worklife and job enrichment efforts are often initiated by management, but union cooperation is essential to complete success of such programs. While some unions are reluctant to become involved with them, major breakthroughs have been identified in selected unions, such as the United Auto Workers.

Safety and health issues have become important since the passage of the Occupational Safety and Health Act of 1970. Criticism of the act's administration has led to reevaluation, elimination of nitpicking rules, and a focus on major problems. Much progress has been made in its administration, but vital issues remain: clarification of operations, rules concerning regulation of chemicals which may cause cancer, coverage and obligations of small businesses. On the positive side, considerable progress has been made by employers and unions toward cooperative programs and toward meeting the objectives of the act.

Discussion Questions

1. Why do unions' reactions to technological change vary in accordance with their industry affiliation?

2. Think of an industry or company with which you are familiar and assume that you are the local union president. What types of clauses regarding technological issues would you attempt to negotiate with your employer?

3. Explain why unions place priority on seniority in personnel decisions, while employers seek to identify other determining factors.

4. Compare the legal restrictions that apply in selecting applicants for apprenticeship programs and promoting employees in the bargaining unit.

5. Since many experts in organization behavior and industrial psychology are strong advocates for job enrichment programs, why are some union leaders still reluctant to join the campaign?

6. Why are many unions critical of OSHA, whose purpose is to protect the physical well-being of their members?

References

[1] Julius Rezler, *Automation and Industrial Labor* (New York: Random House, 1969), pp. 5–6.

[2] B. S. Kirsh, *Automation and Collective Bargaining* (New York: Central Book, 1964), pp. 14–15.

[3] Sumner H. Slichter, James J. Healy, and E. Robert Livernash, *The Impact of Collective Bargaining on Management* (Washington, D.C.: Brookings Institute, 1960), pp. 343–345.

[4] Rezler, *Automation and Labor,* pp. 140–141.

[5] It should be noted that only about 17 percent of the collective bargaining agreements restrict technological change, and most of these are job protective clauses, such as guarantees of retraining displaced employees. Editors of Collective Bargaining Negotiations and Contracts, *Basic Patterns in Union Contracts* (Washington, D.C.: Bureau of National Affairs, 1979), p. 64.

[6] Jack Barbash, "Union Response to the Hard Line," *Industrial Relations* 1 (October 1961), pp. 25–29.

[7] Edward B. Shils, *Automation and Industrial Relations* (New York: Holt, Rinehart and Winston, 1963), pp. 130–132.

[8] Slichter, Healy, and Livernash, *Collective Bargaining,* p. 349.

[9] Kirsh, *Automation and Collective Bargaining,* pp. 15–16.

[10] Joseph P. Goldberg, "Bargaining and Productivity in the Private Sector," in Gerald Somers, ed., *Collective Bargaining and Productivity* (Madison, Wis.: Industrial Relations Research Association, 1975), pp. 22–42. Also see U.S. Department of Labor, Bureau of Labor Statistics, *Technological Change and Its Labor Impact in Five Industries* (Washington, D.C.: Government Printing Office, 1977).

[11] "The Railroads' Slowdown with Labor," *Business Week,* January 23, 1978, p. 72.

[12] Goldberg, "Bargaining and Productivity," pp. 34–35.

[13] "A Push to End the Third-Man Dispute," *Business Week,* April 24, 1978, p. 30.

[14] "No Papers for New York," *Time,* August 21, 1978, p. 38.

[15] David McClintock, "New York Times, Daily News Pressmen Tentatively Agree to Six-Year Contract," *Wall Street Journal,* November 2, 1978, p. 10.

[16] Slichter, Healy, and Livernash, *Collective Bargaining,* pp. 317–335.

[17] Robert D. Leiter, *Featherbedding and Job Security* (New York: Twayne Publishers, 1964), pp. 32–33.

[18] Paul A. Weinstein, "Introduction," in *Featherbedding and Technological Change* (Boston: D. C. Heath & Company, 1965), p. v.

[19] William Gomberg, "The Work Rules and Work Practices," *Labor Law Journal* 12 (July 1961), pp. 643–653.

[20] Benjamin Aaron, "Governmental Restraint on Featherbedding," *Stanford Law Review* 5 (July 1953), pp. 687–721.

[21] *American Newspaper Association v. NLRB*, 345 U. S. 110 (1953).

[22] Aaron, "Governmental Restraint."

[23] Kirsh, *Automation and Collective Bargaining,* pp. 16–17.

[24] U.S. Department of Labor, Bureau of Labor Statistics, *Subcontracting* (Washington, D.C.: Government Printing Office, 1969), p. 1.

[25] Slichter, Healy, and Livernash, *Collective Bargaining,* pp. 280–285.

[26]*Fibreboard Paper Products v. NLRB*, 379 U.S. 203 (1964).

[27]Eds. of Collective Bargaining Negotiations and Contracts, *Basic Patterns*, p. 63; U.S. Department of Labor, Bureau of Labor Statistics, *Characteristics of Major Collective Bargaining Agreements July 1, 1976* (Washington, D.C.: Government Printing Office, 1979), p. 75.

[28]Slichter, Healy, and Livernash, *Collective Bargaining*, pp. 309–312.

[29]Frank Elkouri and Edna A. Elkouri, *How Arbitration Works*, 3d. ed. (Washington, D.C.: Bureau of National Affairs, 1973), p. 458.

[30]NLRB, *42d Annual Report of the National Labor Relations Board* (Washington, D.C.: Government Printing Office, 1977), p. 133.

[31]Slichter, Healy, and Livernash, *Collective Bargaining*, pp. 244–266. Also see Robert B. Hoffman, "The Representational Dispute," *Labor Law Journal* 24 (June 1973), pp. 323–339; and Stephen J. Cabot, "How Not to Get Caught in the Middle When Labor Unions Start Squabbling with Each Other," *Labor Law Journal* 24 (September 1973), pp. 626–628.

[32]NLRB, *42d Annual Report*, p. 113. This board uses two procedural rules that are worthy of note:
1. A request for a decision in a specific case does not have to wait until the dispute occurs. Once the contractor makes the initial work assignments, a request for a decision can be made. Thus, time is saved by facilitating the dispute resolution process.
2. Decisions of the board are not precedent setting. This does not mean that similar decisions within an area are not based on patterns; it means that conditions vary from region to region, union to union, even agreement to agreement. Therefore, the board is not bound completely by precedent, but past practice, custom in the industry, and skills, training, and job content are important elements that are considered.

[33]Slichter, Healy, and Livernash, *Collective Bargaining*, pp. 266–276.

[34]Ronald Wiggins, *The Arbitration of Industrial Engineering Disputes* (Washington, D.C.: Bureau of National Affairs, 1970), pp. 2–4.

[35]Elkouri and Elkouri, *How Arbitration Works*, pp. 469–487.

[36]"Unions Campaign to Shrink Work Time," *Business Week*, April 24, 1978, pp. 30–31.

[37]"Detroit Inches Closer to a Four-Day Week," *Business Week*, February 13, 1978, pp. 85–86.

[38]J. Carroll Swart and Robert A. Quakenbush, "Union's Views Concerning Alternative Work Schedules and Proposal to Alter Federal Overtime Pay Legislation," *Proceedings of the 30th Annual Meeting: Industrial Relations Research Association* (Madison, Wis.: Industrial Relations Research Association, 1977), p. 378.

[39]Jeffrey M. Miller, *Innovations in Working Patterns* (Washington, D.C.: Communication Workers of America and German Marshall Fund of the United States, 1978); and W. H. Holley, A. A. Armenakis, and H. S. Feild, "Employee Reactions to a Flexitime Program: A Longitudinal Study," *Human Resource Management* 15 (Winter 1976), pp. 21–23.

[40]George Cooper and Richard B. Sobol, "Seniority and Testing under Fair Employment Laws: A General Approach to Objective Criteria of Hiring and Promotion," *Harvard Law Review* 82 (June 1969), pp. 1601–1602.

[41]Eds. of Collective Bargaining Negotiations and Contracts, *Basic Patterns*, p. 73; and U.S. Department of Labor, Bureau of Labor Statistics, *Characteristics of Collective Bargaining*, p. 69.

[42]Eds. of Collective Bargaining Negotiations and Contracts, *Basic Patterns*, p. 73.

[43]Cooper and Sobol, "Seniority and Testing," p. 1602.

[44]"Why Lockheed's Strike Is a 'Holy War,'" *Business Week*, December 19, 1977, p. 31.

[45]Slichter, Healy, and Livernash, *Collective Bargaining*, p. 104.

[46]C. W. Randle, "The Pros and Cons of Seniority," in E. W. Bakke, C. Kerr, and C. W. Anrod, eds., *Unions, Management, and the Public* (New York: Harcourt, Brace, Jovanovich, 1976), p. 422.

[47]Slichter, Healy, and Livernash, *Collective Bargaining*, pp. 104–105.

[48]"Lockheed's Strike," p. 31.

[49]Randle, "Pros and Cons of Seniority," pp. 423–424.

[50]U.S. Department of Labor, Bureau of Labor Statistics, *Administration of Seniority* (Washington, D.C.: Government Printing Office, 1972).

[51]Eds. of Collective Bargaining Negotiations and Contracts, *Basic Patterns*, p. 74.

[52]Elaine F. Gruenfeld, *Promotion: Practices, Policies, and Affirmative Action* (Ithaca, N.Y.: New York State School of Industrial and Labor Relations, Cornell University, 1975), p. 12.

[53]Eds. of Collective Bargaining Negotiations and Contracts, *Basic Patterns*, p. 75.

[54]Thomas J. McDermott, "Types of Seniority Provisions and the Measurement of Ability," *Arbitration Journal* 25 (1970), pp. 101–105. Also see W. E. Howard, "The Interpretation of Ability by Labor-Management Arbitrators," *Arbitration Journal* 14 (1959), pp. 122-123.

[55]McDermott, "Seniority Provisions," p. 106.

[56]Gruenfeld, *Promotion*, p. 12.

[57]McDermott, "Seniority Provisions," p. 110.

[58]"Uniform Guidelines on Employee Selection Procedures," *Government Employee Relations Reporter*, August 28, 1978.

[59]Ibid., p. 2.

[60]George Hagglund and Duane Thompson, *Psychological Testing and Industrial Relations* (Iowa City: Center for Labor and Management, University of Iowa, 1969); R. E. Biddle and L. M. Jacobs, "Under What Circumstances Can a Unionized Company Use Testing for Promotion?" *Personnel Psychology* 21 (Summer 1968), pp. 149–177; Dale McConkey, "Ability versus Seniority in Promotion and Layoff," *Personnel* 37 (May–June 1960), pp. 51–57.

[61]William H. Holley, Jr., "Performance Ratings in Arbitration," *Arbitration Journal* 32 (March 1977), pp. 8–25.

[62]McDermott, "Seniority Provisions," pp. 110–124.

[63]U.S. Department of Labor, Bureau of Labor Statistics, *Seniority in Promotion and Transfer Provisions* (Washington, D.C.: Government Printing Office, 1970), pp. 15–21, 42.

[64]Eds. of Collective Bargaining Negotiations and Contracts, *Basic Patterns*, p. 53.

[65]Bernard J. Offerman et al., "Legal Update: Seniority and Affirmative Action," working paper, Cleveland State University, Cleveland, Ohio, January 27, 1977. Also see *Quarles v. Phillip Morris Inc.*, 179 F. Supp. 507 (1968); *United Paperworkers v. U.S.*, 416 F.2d. 980 (1969); *U.S. v. Bethlehem Steel Corp.*, 446 F.2d 652 (1971); *Bing v. Roadway*, 485 F.2d 441 (1973); and *Franks v. Bowman Transportation Co.*, 12 FEP 549 (1976).

[66]Cary D. Thorp, Jr., "Racial Discrimination and Seniority," *Labor Law Journal* 23 (July 1972), pp. 401–403.

[67]Bernard J. Offerman, "Legal Update: Seniority and Affirmative Action," *Labor Studies Journal* 2 (1978), pp. 202–214.

[68]Thorp, "Racial Discrimination," pp. 412–413.

[69]Richard D. Sibbernsen, "A Review of Job and Seniority Structures in Light of EEO Liability," *Labor Law Journal* 26 (October 1975), p. 674.

[70]*United Steelworkers of America, AFL-CIO, v. Brian F. Weber et al.*, 47 LW 4851. *U.S. Law Week* (Washington, D.C.: Bureau of National Affairs, June 28, 1979).

[71]William H. Holley, Jr., and Hubert S. Feild, "Equal Employment Opportunity and Its Implications for Personnel Practices," *Labor Law Journal* 27 (May 1976), p. 285.

[72]Barbara Linderman Schlei and Paul Grossman, *Employment Discrimination Law* (Washington, D.C.: Bureau of National Affairs, 1976), pp. 458–459.

[73]Holley and Feild, "Equal Employment Opportunity," p. 285.

[74]*International Brotherhood of Teamsters, et al. v. U.S.*, 45 L.W. 4566 (1977).

[75]*Franks v. Bowman Transportation Company*, 96 S. Ct. 1251 (1976).

[76]EEOC NOTICE, N-915, July 14, 1977, reprinted in Bureau of National Affairs, *EEOC Compliance Manual* (Washington, D.C.: Bureau of National Affairs, August 1977), pp. 480:0001–480:0003. Also see Marvin J. Levine, "The Conflict between Negotiated Seniority Provisions and Title VII of the Civil Rights Act of 1964: Recent Developments," *Labor Law Journal* 29 (June 1978), pp. 352–363.

[77]U.S. Department of Labor, Bureau of Labor Statistics, *Characteristics of Collective Bargaining*, p. 87.

[78]Ray Marshall and Robert W. Glover, *Training and Entry into Union Construction* (Washington, D.C.: Government Printing Office, 1975), p. 7.

[79]Felician F. Foltman, *Apprenticeship Training in the 1970s: Report of a Conference* (Washington, D.C.: Government Printing Office, 1974), p. 4. Skilled workers obtain work in their jurisdiction in four ways: by graduation from an apprenticeship program, by direct admission as a journeyman, by transferring from other local unions of the same international union, and by working on temporary work permits provided nonunion members (college students working in summers). Marshall and Glover, *Training and Entry*, p. 7.

[80]Foltman, *Apprenticeship Training*, p. 4.

[81]Bureau of National Affairs, *EEOC Compliance Manual*, p. 660:0001.

[82]U.S. Department of Health, Education, and Welfare, *Work in America: Report of a Special Task Force to the Secretary of Health, Education, and Welfare* (Cambridge, Mass.: MIT Press, 1973). A 1977 survey by the Survey Research Center, University of Michigan, revealed a decline in job satisfaction from 1969 to 1973 and 1973 to 1977. Graham L. Staines and Robert P. Quinn, "American Workers Evaluate the Quality of Their Jobs," *Monthly Labor Review* 102 (January 1979), p. 4.

[83]Allan Nash, *Quality of Worklife* (Chicago: Roosevelt University, 1977, pp. 3–12.

[84]Mitchell Fein, "Job Enrichment: A Reevaluation," *Sloan Management Review* 15 (Winter 1974), p. 70; Mitchell Fein, "The Myth of Job Enrichment, " in R. P. Fairefield, ed., *Humanizing the Workplace* (Buffalo: Prometheus Books, 1974), pp. 71–78.

[85]Neal Q. Herrick and Michael Maccoby, "Humanizing Work: A Priority Goal of the 1970's," in L. E.

Davis and A. B. Cherns, eds. *The Quality of Working Life* (New York: The Free Press, 1975), p. 71; William Gomberg, "Job Satisfaction: Sorting Out the Nonsense," *American Federationist* 80 (June 1973), pp. 14–20; T. R. Brooks, "Job Satisfaction: An Elusive Goal," *American Federationist* 79 (October 1972), pp. 1–7.

[86]Jack Barbash, "The Union as a Bargaining Organization: Some Implications for Organization Behavior," *Proceedings of the 28th Annual Meeting: Industrial Relations Research Association* (Madison, Wis.: Industrial Relations Research Association, 1975), p. 152.

[87]Ibid.

[88]Sam Zagoria, "Policy Implications and Future Agenda," in Jerome Rosow, ed., *The Worker and the Job* (Englewood Cliffs, N.J.: Prentice Hall, 1974), p. 181.

[89]Albert Blum, "Union Prospects and Programs for the 1970s," *Proceedings of the 22d Annual Winter Meeting: Industrial Relations Research Association* (Madison, Wis.: Industrial Relations Research Association, 1969), pp. 136–141.

[90]Fein, "Job Enrichment," p. 79.

[91]Sar Levitan and William B. Johnston, *Work Is Here to Stay, Alas* (Salt Lake City: Olympus Publishing, 1973), p. 137.

[92]Lee Dyer, D. B. Lipsky, and T. A. Kochan, "Union Attitudes toward Management Cooperation," *Industrial Relations* 16 (May 1977), pp. 163–172.

[93]William F. Giles and William H. Holley, Jr., "The Attractiveness of Job Enrichment versus Traditional Issues at the Bargaining Table: What Union Members Want," *Academy of Management* 21 (December 1978), pp. 225–230; and T. A. Kochan, D. B. Lipsky, and Lee Dyer, "Collective Bargaining and the Quality of Work: The Views of Local Union Activists," *Proceedings of the 27th Annual Meeting: Industrial Relations Research Association* (Madison, Wis.: Industrial Relations Research Association, 1974), pp. 150–162.

[94]Raymond A. Katzell et al., *Work, Productivity and Job Satisfaction* (Chicago: Psychological Corporation, 1976), p. 95.

[95]William W. Winpisinger, "Job Satisfaction: A Union Response," *American Federationist* 80 (February 1973), pp. 8–10. See also *Proceedings of the 25th Annual Meeting: Industrial Relations Research Association* (Madison, Wis.: Industrial Relations Research Association, 1972), pp. 154–159.

[96]Bernard J. White, "Innovations in Job Design: The Union Perspective," *Journal of Contemporary Business* 6 (Spring 1977), pp. 24–25.

[97]Edward E. Lawler, III, and John A. Drexler, Jr., "Dynamics of Establishing Cooperative Quality-of-Worklife Projects," *Monthly Labor Review* 101 (March 1978), pp. 24–26.

[98]Ibid., p. 26; John A. Drexler, Jr., and Edward E. Lawler, III, "A Union-Management Cooperative Project to Improve the Quality of Worklife," *Journal of Applied Behavioral Science* 13 (July–September 1977), p. 386.

[99]Louis E. Davis, "Enhancing the Quality of Working Life: Developments in the United States," *International Labour Review* 116 (July–August 1977), pp. 53–65.

[100]Ninety-four percent of labor agreements include such provisions. U.S. Department of Labor, Bureau of Labor Statistics, *Major Collective Bargaining Agreements: Safety and Health Provisions* (Washington, D.C.: Government Printing Office, 1976), p. 49.

[101]Eds. of Collective Bargaining Negotiations and Contracts, *Basic Patterns*, pp. 109–111.

[102]T. A. Kochan, Lee Dyer, and D. B. Lipsky, *The Effectiveness of Union-Management Safety and Health Committees* (Kalamazoo, Mich.: W. E. Upjohn Institute for Employment Research, 1977), p. 5.

[103]84 Stat. 1590 (1970).

[104]The year that OSHA of 1970 was passed, the following statistics were presented to Congress:
14,500 killed—average of 55 per work week.
2.2 million injured.
390,000 disabling occupational diseases (lung cancer, asbestos, and so on).
250 million man-days lost, ten times that lost from strikes.
$1.5 million lost in wages.
$8 billion lost to GNP.
Benjamin L. Brown, "A Law Is Made: The Legislative Process in the Occupational Safety and Health Act of 1970, " *Labor Law Journal* 25 (October 1974), p. 597.

[105]A study of three industries—aerospace, chemicals, and textiles—was conducted. See Herbert R. Northrup et al., *The Impact of OSHA* (Philadelphia: Industrial Research Unit, University of Pennsylvania, 1978).

[106]Nicholas Ashford, *Crisis in the Workplace* (Cambridge, Mass.: MIT Press, 1976), p. 13.

[107]Lawrence P. Ettkin and J. Brad Chapman, "Is OSHA Effective in Reducing Industrial Injuries?" *Labor Law Journal* 26 (April 1975), p. 242; Wayne Wendling, "Industrial Safety and Collective Bargaining," in B. D. Dennis, ed., *Proceedings of the 30th Annual Winter Meeting: Industrial Relations Research Institute* (Madison, Wis.: Industrial Relations Research Institute, 1978), p. 435.

[108]Kenneth W. Nelson, quoted by Douglas Soutar, "A Management View," in B. D. Dennis, ed., *Proceedings of the 1978 Annual Spring Meeting: Industrial Relations Research Institute* (Madison, Wis.: Industrial Relations Research Institute, 1978), p. 495.

[109]Ibid., p. 493.

[110]*Occupational Safety and Health Act 1970: A Trade Union Review and Analysis* (Kansas City, Kans.: International Brotherhood of Boilermakers, Iron Shipbuilders, Blacksmiths, Forgers, and Helpers, 1978), pp. 19–21. Also see John Zalusky, "The Worker Views the Enforcement of Safety Laws," *Labor Law Journal* 26 (April 1975), p. 235.

[111]"OSHA: Four Years of Frustrations," *American Federationist* 83 (April 1976), p. 11.

[112]Ibid., pp. 11–18.

[113]Eula Bingham, "OSHA: Only Beginning," *Labor Law Journal* 29 (March 1978), p. 131. Also see Robert J. Brown, "Making the Promise of OSHA a Reality," *Labor Law Journal* 29 (February 1978), pp. 66–72.

[114]Leon Bornstein, "Industrial Relations in 1978: Some Bargaining Highlights," *Monthly Labor Review* 102 (January 1979), pp. 63–64.

[115]Gail Bronson, "Issue of Fetal Damage Stirs Women Workers at Chemical Plants," *Wall Street Journal*, February 9, 1979, pp. 1, 33.

[116]OSHA, *Occupational Safety and Health Reporter* 8 (August 10, 1978), p. 339.

[117]"The New Activism on Job Health," *Business Week*, September 18, 1978, pp. 146–149.

[118]"Sticking Uncle Sam for on-the-Job Injuries," *Business Week*, November 6, 1978, p. 182.

[119]*Marshall v. Barlow's Inc.*, 436 U.S. 307 (1978). Also see Tony McAdams and Robert C. Miljus, "OSHA and Warrantless Inspections," *Labor Law Journal* 29 (January 1978), pp. 49–60.

Chapter 13

Economic Issues

A responsible wage policy "provides a modus operandi and keeps the peace, . . . creates a measure of certainty and a basis of planning for a year or two ahead, . . . strengthens the fealty of the union toward the private-ownership system of production."

Arthur M. Ross, "What Is a Responsible Wage Policy?" Southern Economic Journal, 1948.

Wages and other economic benefits are vitally important to everyone in the labor relations picture. They represent income to the employee, cost to the organization, and a basis for taxes to the government. In addition, wages serve important economic functions: they serve as a factor in the allocation of resources; they influence the selection of an individual's occupation and movement from one firm, industry, or location to another; they influence decisions on plant location and investments in machinery and capital equipment and affect employment and unemployment. More importantly, if wages become exorbitantly high, employees may price themselves out of particular labor markets. Thus, wages are both economic indicators and determinants.[1]

Union and management are required by the National Labor Relations Act to bargain in good faith with respect to wages. As a result of NLRB and court decisions, wage-related topics such as pensions, overtime, shift differentials, job evaluation, and incentive systems must be bargained over if either party presents such topics during negotiations.

Scholars have spent much time studying and explaining wage theories and the effects of wages on the economy, and thousands of union and management negotiators spend many hours annually bargaining over wages, wage-related issues, and numerous nonwage items.[2] While both activities are important to an understanding of labor economics as well as labor-management relationships, this chapter does not deal with the theory of wages and the economics of labor markets. Rather it focuses on the methods of wage determination and factors used by negotiators in determining the wage package—wages and other economic benefits.

Wage Determination

Union and management officials have to agree on what the term *wages* means before they can successfully bargain over this issue. For instance, wages may mean the basic wage rate, average gross hourly earnings, average weekly earnings, or incentive pay (payment per product completed). Basic wage rates for each job class are usually listed in the labor agreement; however, other wage payments (overtime, incentive pay, shift differentials, and other compensation earned in the regular work-week) may have to be computed in accordance with provisions in the labor agreement.[3]

After agreeing on the language for the basis of wage negotiations, the parties, together or separately, determine those wage rates and related terms of employment that the employer is willing to make available and at which employees will be willing to work.[4] In this process, the parties will consider various factors and will conclude with numerous wage rates, job classes, and wage ranges. As most readers have already experienced, jobs with varying duties and responsibilities are assigned different wage rates. Besides these occupational differentials within a firm there are regional, industry, and shift differences that cause an employer to pay different combinations of wage rates. Textile workers in the South generally earn less than those in the North; electricians and laborers in the building trades generally have higher wage rates than electricians and laborers in factories.

Wage differentials among jobs, industries, or regions can be explained in a variety of ways. However, any explanation must look at the inter-relationships between labor and capital as factors of production and as contributors to productivity. For example:

It is sometimes said that if productivity rises by "x" percent and the workers receive an "x" percent increase in compensation, then the workers are getting all of the productivity increase, leaving nothing for others. This is incorrect. If productivity rises, say 10 percent, and output increases commensurately, then each factor of production—labor-management, capital—can receive a 10 percent increase. If output does not rise commensurately . . . then total compensation of input factors and rates of return to those factors will depend on the difference between the output increase and the productivity increase, the size of the hourly compensation increase, and the cost of new capital investment.[5]

Industrial Wage Differentials

Industrial wage differentials may be explained in terms of three factors: (a) the degree of competition or monopoly in the product market, (b) the value added by workers in a particular industry, and (c) the percentage of total costs that labor costs represent.

Competition in the product market. First, if a firm has a monopoly or near monopoly (the product is essential, with no available substitute), then increased labor cost can be easily passed on to the consumer. In such cases, the employer will resist higher wages less rigidly in negotiation. For example, if a private or public utility agrees to a 12 percent increase with cost-of-living adjustments, it then can add the increased cost to its customers' bills (unless the utility is heavily regulated). Consumers in this situation frequently have little choice but to pay the higher prices. Thus, in those industries where the firm controls the pricing without competitive threats, wages tend to be proportionately higher.

Value added by employees. *Value added* refers to the contribution of factors of production to the value of the final product. Comparing labor's contribution for different industries helps to explain industrial wage differentials. For example, the value added by labor in sawmills, cotton weaving, clothes manufacturing, and the mobile home industry is significantly lower than corresponding figures in the steel, petrochemical, and tire industries. However, because employees must use machines, which represent capital investments, and because there is such a close interrelationship between labor and capital investments in machinery and equipment, exact determination of labor's contributions has become a complicated process. In unionized settings, negotiations between union and management representatives determine labor's share in the amount of value added.

Labor costs as percent of total costs. The relationship between labor costs and total costs must also be considered in determining the industrial wage rate. Highly interdependent with capital investment per worker and the product market, this relationship is important in wage negotiations. For example, labor intensive organizations, such as health care facilities, textile firms, and city, county, state, or federal governments, have high labor costs in relation to total costs. On the other hand, petroleum and chemical firms, electric-generating plants, and steel mills have relatively low labor costs as a percentage of total costs.

Usually, firms with a high ratio of labor costs to total costs are more likely to resist high wage increases. For example, if a hospital where labor costs are 60 percent of total costs grants a 10 percent wage increase, it must raise prices about 6 percent. A petroleum processing plant where labor cost is 5 percent of total cost would have to raise its price about 0.5 percent to cover a 10 percent increase in wages. We would therefore expect to find workers in the same job classifications receiving higher wages in chemical and petroleum companies than in hospitals or textile firms. Of course, there are many qualifications to this conclusion—for example, consumers may not accept a higher price and a company may choose to cover the wage increase out of its profits. Nonetheless, the relation of labor cost to total cost can be an important factor in industrial wage differentials.

Occupational Wage Differentials and the Role of Job Evaluation and Wage Surveys

Within a company or industry, maintaining a proper and rational wage relationship among various jobs is important. These relationships are often maintained under job evaluation programs but in other cases are determined by individual or collective bargaining.[6] The process of determining the relative importance of each job to the organization helps in understanding occupational wage differentials; therefore, the following steps in a job evaluation program are presented.[7]

How Jobs Are Evaluated within the Organization The first step in *job evaluation* is an organization analysis[8] which appraises and examines the organization's objectives, structure, and authority and responsibility relationships. The findings from this analysis help insure that jobs are properly analyzed and described and that the job content is up-to-date.

The second step is the selection and measurement of job factors which are found at least to some extent in all of the organization's job classifications. Job factors vary substantially depending on the organization, but skill (education and training), effort, responsibility (for people and equipment), and working conditions (hazards, surroundings) are typically selected. Management must consider the minimum amount of each job factor or qualification necessary to adequately perform the particular job. For example, it may be nice to employ a typist who can edit, interpret, and make complex economics subjects understandable, but few organizations can find or are willing to pay wages needed to attract such a qualified person.

Next, an appropriate job evaluation system for appraising jobs according to the established job factors is selected. There are four job evaluation methods available: ranking, classification, factor comparison, and point system. The *ranking* and *factor-comparison* methods compare jobs nonquantitatively in terms of one or more job factors; the *classification* and *point system* methods compare jobs to predetermined numerical rating scales designed to measure one or more job factors about each job. Firms' job evaluation systems may use ten to fifteen different job factors, with these factors often divided into subfactors. For example, effort may be divided into physical and mental effort.[9]

The fourth step involves *job analysis*, a process of systematically securing information and facts about the jobs to be evaluated. (Throughout the job evaluation process, it is the jobs, not employees in the job classification, that are being analyzed.) The job classifications resulting from job analysis will receive the same rating whether the employee holding the job has a master's degree or high school diploma, is lazy or ambitious, or is a high or low performer.

Commonly used methods of job analysis include the method of the U.S. Department of Labor,[10] the critical incident method,[11] and the position analysis questionnaire (PAQ).[12] These techniques use observation, interviews, and questionnaires in gathering data about the jobs which will be used to formulate job descriptions and job specifications. The *job descriptions* include written summations of the duties and responsibilities; the *job specifications* include the personal characteristics a worker must possess to qualify for the job. Both will be used in the job evaluation process. As firms try to relate wages to various degrees of duties and responsibilities, they must also pay more to employ workers who have high qualifications, such as education, training, and skills.

Management often prefers to conduct its job evaluation independent of the union. Management may prefer not to share its weightings of the job factors, particularly when it believes certain factors (such as training, skill, and responsibility for equipment) should receive more compensation than others, such as working conditions. By withholding the weightings, management may avoid confrontations with the union. On the other hand, unions do not want to be totally excluded from the job evaluation process.

Union leaders generally view job evaluation with disfavor, because it tends to limit bargaining and freeze the wage structure.[13] Three surveys of union officials over a ten-year period have revealed that unions prefer to establish wage scales through collective bargaining, although their resistance to job evaluation has declined. While unions reserve the right to file grievances to resist or express dissatisfaction with job evaluation, they seldom show strong opposition unless firms attempt to use job evaluation as the sole criterion for wage determination or try to substitute it for collective bargaining.[14]

Research indicates that if company and union officials communicate their respective positions regarding wage plans in meaningful ways, the benefits can outweigh the deficiencies. Thus, the "need for understanding union compensation policy and attitudes as well as involving union members in updating, improving, and implementing the total compensation program is reinforced."[15] In fact, some unions regard job evaluation techniques not only as useful guides in negotiating wages but as a means by which they can more effectively explain the negotiated wage settlements to their members.[16]

Regardless of the job evaluation method, the objective is to develop a wage structure that prices jobs with less skill, effort, and responsibility at lower wage rates and jobs with greater skill, effort, and responsibility at higher wage rates. Table 13–1 presents an example wage structure for a firm, which includes job titles, labor grades, point ranges, and starting wage rates for each labor grade. Since a numerical score should indicate the relative value of the job, the greater the score, the higher the labor grade and the hourly wage rate. Table 13–2 shows four position classifications and the effective wage rates at different lengths of service and at different dates during the agreement.

Surveys to Compare Firms' Wage Structures *Wage surveys* are conducted to assure that external labor market considerations, such as comparable

Part 3/The Outcome of the Labor Relations Process: Collective Bargaining Issues

Table 13–1
Typical Wage
Structure for a
Manufacturing Firm

Job Titles	Labor Grade	Points	Starting Hourly Wage Rates
Janitor	I	200–249	$4.77
Material Handler	II	250–299	5.04
Shipper	III	300–349	5.30
Tool Room Keeper	IV	350–399	5.57
Machine Operator B	V	400–449	5.82
Machine Operator A	VI	450–499	6.09
Maintenance Man B	VII	500–549	6.33
Tool Grinder B	VIII	550–599	6.59
Maintenance Man A	IX	600–649	6.83
Tool Grinder A	X	650–699	7.10
Electrician A	XI	700–749	7.32
Tool and Die Maker A	XII	750–800	7.65

Source: Adapted from U.S. Department of Labor, Bureau of Labor Statistics, *Major Collective Bargaining Agreements: Wage Administration Provisions* (Washington, D.C.: Government Printing Office, 1978), p. 2.

Table 13–2
Wage Structure for an
Airline Firm with
Incremental
Increases Based on
Experience on the Job

Position Classifications	Effective Wage Rate 1-5-76	Effective Wage Rate 10-4-76	Effective Wage Rate 10-3-77	Effective Wage Rate 6-5-78
Flight Simulator Technician				
First three months	$8.19	$8.68	$9.20	$9.57
Next six months	8.32	8.82	9.35	9.72
Next six months	8.50	9.01	9.55	9.93
Thereafter	8.78	9.31	9.87	10.26
Stock Clerk				
First three months	5.99	6.35	6.73	7.00
Next six months	6.07	6.43	6.82	7.09
Next six months	6.20	6.57	6.92	7.24
Next six months	6.44	6.83	7.24	7.53
Next six months	6.76	7.17	7.60	7.90
Next six months	6.88	7.29	7.73	8.04
Next six months	7.04	7.49	7.91	8.23
Thereafter	7.34	7.78	8.25	8.58
Shop Laborer				
First three months	5.55	5.88	6.23	6.48
Thereafter	5.76	6.11	6.48	6.74
Shop Janitor				
First three months	5.08	5.38	5.70	5.93
Thereafter	5.26	5.58	5.91	6.15

Source: Adapted from labor agreement signed January 14, 1976, between Eastern Air Lines, Inc., and the International Association of Machinists and Aerospace Workers.

wages, are included in the wage structure. While firms attempt to rationalize their wage structure internally through job evaluation, they must also maintain competitive wages externally to insure that the firm can recruit qualified employees and retain productive ones. Usually a wage analyst either visits, sends questionnaires to, or conducts a telephone interview with the wage analysts of similar organizations or comparable firms. The one conducting the survey provides the responding firms with titles, descriptions, and specifications of the jobs in the wage survey. Participating firms will supply the starting wage rate and appropriate economic benefits paid individuals in these job classifications (see Table 13–3). After the wage survey is complete, the firm must determine how the data will be used. For example, does it want to lead the industry, compete with Firm C, or pay the industry average?

These wage surveys may be conducted by the firm, the union, or an employer association or obtained from the Bureau of Labor Statistics, which periodically publishes industry, area, occupational, and national wage survey data.[17] From such abundant data, union and management officials sometimes have difficulty determining which are most appropriate for their particular situation. (This problem is further discussed in the section on wage comparability.)

The wage plan concludes with a certain number of wage classes, wages for each job or job class, wage ranges (starting to top wages) for each class, policies and procedures for wage adjustments (seniority, merit, and so on), procedures for job changes to a different class, temporary job changes, procedures for jobs that pay above or below their wage range (*red-circled* wage rates), and policy on union involvement.

Production Standards and Wage Incentives

Union and management often negotiate provisions in the labor agreement that cover wage-related issues, such as production standards, time studies, and incentive wage payments. *Production standards* refer to the expected employee output which is consistent with workmanship quality, operational efficiency, and reasonable working capacities of normal

Table 13–3 Typical Results from a Wage Survey	Job Title	Firms						Average
		A	B	C	D	E	F	
	Janitor	4.60	4.70	5.20	4.20	4.60	4.70	4.67
	Assembler	5.20	5.10	5.30	6.00	5.40	5.50	5.42
	Shop Clerk	6.10	6.00	6.70	6.10	6.00	5.90	6.15
	Welder	7.00	7.10	7.50	7.00	7.00	7.00	7.10
	Machinist I	6.50	6.40	7.00	6.50	6.60	6.50	6.58
	Machinist II	6.90	6.80	7.40	7.00	6.90	7.00	7.00
	Machinist III	7.40	7.50	8.00	7.50	7.30	7.50	7.53
	Electrician	8.60	8.50	9.20	8.40	8.50	8.60	8.65
	Tool and Die Maker	9.00	9.25	10.30	8.60	9.20	9.50	9.31

operators. These standards are often determined by time studies which involve analyses of time and motions of workers on the job, and the resulting standards are used to assess performance and determine the wage incentives for individual workers or groups of workers.[18]

Where *incentive plans* are negotiated, the structure and design are included in the contract, although specific details may not be included. The role of the union in setting and protesting production standards and rate changes and its right to be consulted on related issues are also usually included. Some contracts include provisions about time studies and the involvement of unions. A small number permit a union observer during the time study, and a few go so far as to provide special training for the union time study representative. Other provisions include procedures used for timing a worker, specification for the meaning of *normal employee*, advance notice to the employee holding the job being studied, and specification for fatigue and personal allowances in setting production standards.[19]

While wage incentive plans vary in structure and specific content, their goals are essentially the same: (a) to increase employee productivity, (b) to attract prospective employees to the company, and (c) to reward employees monetarily for their increased productivity. A typical individual wage incentive plan is one in which workers are paid for the number of pieces or jobs completed. Others pay bonuses or premiums to employees for production above the standard. Many varieties of these incentive plans exist, but, while they are numerous and sometimes confusing to employees, they are similar in concepts.

Group incentive plans are designed so that companies make monetary payments to a specific group or groups of employees for producing more than expected. Incentives include group bonuses, group piece rates, profit sharing, production sharing, and cost sharing. In some cases, the plans are limited to a few employees, to specific departments, or to other organizational divisions; in others, the entire company work force is covered. While group incentives aim to increase production and reduce costs, they are also designed to increase teamwork, provide greater job security, and achieve greater acceptance of new technology.

There are a variety of group incentive plans. One of the most popular is the *Scanlon Plan*, a plan for saving labor costs that was developed by former union leader Joseph Scanlon in the late 1930s. It provides bonus payments based on a computed ratio of total labor costs (TLC) to total production values (TPV), which typically equal monthly sales, plus or minus inventory adjustments. This means that if the TLC/TPV ratio is 50 percent, a reduction in the ratio would be a labor cost savings. For example, if the workers were to reduce costs by working harder, producing more efficiently, and saving on wastes and the TLC/TPV ratio declined to 40 percent, the 10 percent labor savings would be shared with the workers in relation to their basic wages. Discussion of other group and individual plans can be found in most compensation textbooks.[20]

Arguments Used by Management and Union Officials in Wage Determination

Over the years, both labor and management have used one or more of the following wage criteria as justification for wage determination: differential features of the work (usually determined by job evaluation), comparable wages, ability to pay (or financial condition of the organization), productivity, and cost of living.[21] Union and management officials do not always accept the same criteria. Moreover, each might emphasize different criteria at different times. During prosperous times unions tend to emphasize the ability to pay; during recessions management presents its poor financial position. Similarly, during periods of rapid inflation, unions emphasize cost-of-living adjustments; when prices are stable, management places much weight on the lack of necessity for cost-of-living adjustments. Certainly, these criteria cannot be entered into a computer that will yield a precise solution to the wage question, but they do provide a framework within which the parties present their data and arguments in order to resolve their differences over wage issues through collective bargaining.[22]

Differential Features of the Work: Job Evaluation and the Wage Spread

The job evaluation process described in the preceding section can influence the wages assigned to various job classifications in an organization. The relative influence of job evaluation can be seen in *wage spread*, which represents the internal distribution of the proposed or actual negotiated wage increase to the bargaining unit employees (see Table 13–4).

At first glance, the wage spread appears to be a formality, determined after the average hourly rate increase per employee is resolved. Yet the particular wage spread can determine whether the parties ever reach an agreement. For example, the union might refuse the first and second

**Table 13–4
Three Examples of Internal Wage Spreads**

Examples	Number of Employees	Employee Classification	Total of Plant's Employees (in Percent)	Increase (in Cents per Hour)
1	184	A	16	26.0
	197	B	18	25.0
	165	C	15	24.0
	237	D	21	23.0
	149	E	13	22.0
	193	F	17	21.0
	1,125			
2	381	A&B	34	30.0
	402	C&D	36	22.0
	342	E&F	30	17.0
	1,125			
3	1,125	A,B,C,D,E,&F	100	23.6

wage spreads and accept the third wage with no spread (see Table 13–4) even though the total wage costs of the three spreads are nearly identical.

The six employee job classifications in Table 13–4 range in skill and pay from Classification A (highest) to Classification F (lowest). The A through F ranking also conforms to management's job evaluation procedure. Consequently, management prefers the second wage spread, since it gives higher skilled employees higher wages that could maintain or increase their wage differential over unskilled employees. This wage differential is important to management for two reasons:

1. It insures that present skilled employees do not leave because of higher wages offered by other firms.
2. It offers some motivation to employees in lower paid classifications to train for higher level classifications in the company.

Unions are not always concerned with job evaluation as a wage determination factor. The union officer's main concern is to insure that the negotiated wage spread will result in sufficient votes to ratify the agreement. Satisfied union members will also be likely to vote for reelection of union officers. Assume, for example, that Classification C represents a politically influential group of employees. The union officers would not prefer the second wage spread as it stands (22.0 cents per hour increase). Instead, they would prefer the first (24.0 cents per hour increase) or third (23.6 cents per hour increase) wage spread shown in the table. The union might even propose a different wage spread (there are an almost infinite number of possible arrangements) which would give the employees in Classification C a much higher wage increase.

Management is also concerned that employees ratify the agreement. Consequently, it might agree to an across-the-board, cents-per-hour increase (the third in the table) which would give the same cents per hour to all employees regardless of their particular job classification. This wage spread might generate enough votes to ratify the collective bargaining agreement, but it will narrow the wage differential between skilled and unskilled employees. However, over a longer period of time, management cannot continually grant this type of increase if it wishes to attract and retain skilled employees.

Wage Comparability A most frequent argument in wage negotiations is that wage rates in one bargaining unit should be equal to or related to the wage rates in comparable bargaining units.[23] Wage comparisons are given considerable weight in wage determination, although these comparisons can become quite complicated. For example, the job content, method of payment, and regularity of employment vary from job to job. Benefits such as supplemental unemployment benefits, vacations, pensions, and holidays must be considered. Fundamental considerations such as the size of the appropriate labor market and occupational and geographic differentials must be cited. At first glance, it appears that bus drivers in Miami would have duties identical with those of bus drivers in Chicago. However, many differences in these similar jobs can exist: weather conditions, number of scheduled stops, location of scheduled stops, number of passengers, and so on. Further, a major difference could arise in situations where the bus drivers are required to make change. In such cases, the union would claim that this job responsibility creates a safety hazard by increasing the likelihood of robberies. Thus, in negotiations the union would seek adequate compensation for this additional safety hazard.

As with industrial wage differentials, the relative importance of wages to total costs is an important factor in wage comparability. For example, if a modern, highly automated textile mill pays wages that account for 30 percent of total costs, a 10 percent increase in wages would equal a 3 percent change in the sales price. But in an old textile mill with out-of-date machinery, where wages account for 65 percent of total costs, a 10 percent increase in wages would equal a 6.5 percent change in sales price. Although wage data are either largely fragmented[24] or deficient,[25] negotiators still have to rely on wage comparability in arguing for or against certain levels of wages. Therefore, both parties continue to look for commonalities (other companies, local firms, similar jobs) which can provide a base from which to present their proposals.

Ability to Pay The *ability to pay* (or the financial condition of the organization) is a commonly used standard for wage determination. Given much weight by unions during periods of high profitability, it is advanced more frequently by management as the "inability to pay."[26]

Ability to pay has limited usefulness in the wage determination process, for a number of reasons:

1. Wages based solely on ability to pay would create a chaotic wage structure and would cause a change in wage-costs-price-profit relationships that have evolved over time.
2. Unions would not want to apply this criterion uniformly and consistently. To be applicable, it must work both ways, leading to wage reductions when profits are nonexistent or inadequate. Such an approach would be generally unacceptable to unions.
3. It is extremely difficult to determine what part of profits should be used for wage increases. If the profit is distributed to employees in terms of higher wages and none of the profit is shared with stockholders, there will be no incentive for investment, and growth and expansion will be limited.
4. Wages supposedly are paid to workers in accordance with their relative value to the firm, their contribution to its goals, and the relative importance of their services. If ability to pay is the major factor, the

relationships between actual pay and actual value could become disproportionate.

5. Wages are negotiated for future application, and there is no necessary relationship between profits of the past and ability to pay in the future. Profits are the result after costs have been deducted from sales; they are most volatile and fluctuate greatly in good and bad times. If wages are dependent upon profits, they too will fluctuate erratically.[27]

Many companies and government agencies today have modified the ability-to-pay argument. Here the emphasis is not on their financial situation; instead, management pleads inability to pay because of limitations imposed by wage-price guidelines and controls (discussed in Chapter 3). This modified argument is seldom persuasive, as illustrated in the cartoon on the next page, because it is difficult to determine precisely which economic items are subject to coverage and which are excluded.

Productivity While no argument has been advanced with more conviction or sophistication than that wages should vary with changes in productivity, the principle has grave difficulties when applied to specific negotiations. For example, the rate of change in productivity varies widely from industry to industry, firm to firm, even plant to plant. Not only is productivity itself difficult to measure accurately, but any change in productivity (usually measured in output per manhour) results from many causes, only one of which is labor.[28]

Those who study productivity have generally agreed that new capital investment and mechanization have been the primary causes for greater productivity, but there are still important issues to reconcile: Who shall share the results from increased productivity? the workers, stockholders, consumers? What are the relative advantages of higher wages, increased dividends, and lower prices? What is the proper balance among the contributing factors of production—labor and capital investments?[29] Any use of the productivity criterion must be handled carefully because the available data are only approximations. Output per manhour often overstates gains attributed to labor, and hourly earnings data fail to account for the relative contributions of advanced technology, improved methods, better machines, and so on.[30]

Some union and management officials have undertaken cooperative efforts to bring productivity issues directly into collective bargaining. Labeled as *productivity bargaining*, it usually seeks changes in work rules in an effort to achieve greater productivity while insuring that employees receive a comparable share of the resulting savings in the form of higher wages. Traditionally, labor agreements have provided protection to workers who are subject to loss of employment (in such forms as advance notice, use of attrition in work reduction, early retirement, guaranteed wages, and severance pay),[31] and unions have often resisted speed up efforts or productivity improvement campaigns.

President Carter's wage-price guidelines were not strictly adhered to in recent teamster negotiations.

Source: Copyright 1979 by Herblock in the Washington Post.

Originating in Great Britain, a country that continues to have serious labor relations problems, productivity bargaining has become a very important and timely topic in the United States.[32] From a national economic view, productivity gains must be achieved to enable American firms to compete in international markets and to protect the value of the U.S. dollar. From the view of the firm, increased productivity is essential to allow growth, expansion of facilities and employment, greater returns on investments, and higher salaries for management. To the employees, productivity improvement is needed to justify the higher wages sought by nearly all workers.

Productivity bargaining provides a means and opportunity to introduce principles of industrial relations to joint undertakings such as initiatives in the use of labor and greater participation by workers in formulating and applying work-wage rules.[33] Moreover, productivity itself is an area in which labor and management can share their concerns: increased productivity is an obvious concern of management; increased wages and benefits are obvious concerns of labor. Thus, the overriding issues seem to be to identify processes and methods by which each party is able to achieve its own goals while achieving results for mutual benefit.[34]

While the concept seems to offer an innovative approach for mutual gain-sharing and cooperative activity, it, too, has its problems. Foremost is the determination or measurement of productivity, because there are many possible measures. Some jobs just do not lend themselves to measurement of output. It is much easier to measure bricks laid than letters taken by dictation and typed, particularly since letters vary in complexity and length. Many jobs are not routine or repetitive; therefore, exact measures are impossible.

Another problem is locating and organizing productivity data in such a manner that it may be useful to a firm. Serious arguments over the contribution of specific factors to increased productivity can inhibit the success of any productivity bargaining. What is the chief contributor to productivity gains? Is it the skill, efforts, and attitudes of the employees? Or the advanced technology of the machinery and equipment, efficiency of the operations, or scale of operations? Or the interaction between these sets of factors?[35] Since productivity gains will be shared under the productivity bargaining concept, they will certainly give rise to rigorous and complicated negotiations, particularly when bargaining unit employees are accustomed to receiving comparable wages.

One successful experience with productivity bargaining has occurred at the Esso Petroleum Refinery in Fawley, England. The following principles derived from this experience could possibly be applied in other productivity bargaining situations:

1. Management accepted the necessity for change as fundamental and invested time, energy, and patience to make it happen.
2. Involved personnel who were motivated to pursue the issues to a

workable compromise or conclusion—specifically, Esso managers and directors with a drive for recognition and leadership.

3. It assumed that the only way to break the status quo and achieve widespread reforms was to accept full responsibility and initiative itself.

4. It set a course of give-and-take negotiations . . . and responded throughout to ideas, needs, and desires of workingmen, stewards, and union leaders.

5. It offered real incentives to the workers—sharply reduced hours and much higher pay—in exchange for flexibility and elimination of obsolete practices.

6. It met the worker's psychological need for job security.

7. It shared credit for the accomplishments with the trade union leaders who were vital to the agreement and to the application of the written word to actual practice.[36]

Another publicized productivity bargaining situation occurred in New York City. This joint labor-management program stemmed from guidelines set by the State Emergency Financial Control Board and conditions set by former Secretary of the Treasury William Simon. The conditions specified that "no municipality would get cost-of-living adjustments unless matched by productivity savings, which could not be achieved through service reductions or contract items."[37] While much of the stimulus was provided externally, participants were at least committed to short-term results in order to allow payment of cost-of-living adjustments.[38]

Other examples of productivity bargaining have occurred in the private sector. Construction industry negotiations have resulted in understandings to reduce work stoppages and increase productivity. Provisions covering jurisdictional disputes, inefficient work rules, illegal featherbedding, and nonworking stewards have also been negotiated. Interestingly, the stimulus for productivity bargaining in the construction industry was the loss of work that increasingly went to nonunion and open-shop contractors and the desire of union members to protect or expand their employment opportunities, particularly during unfavorable economic conditions.[39]

Labor agreements in the steel industry contain provisions which fit the productivity bargaining model but are not labeled as such. Joint advisory committees have been formed in each plant to deal with problems of imports and promotion of orderly and peaceful labor relations in the plant. The retail food industry has established a joint labor-management committee that aids collective bargaining settlements and technological change. The shipping industry has been involved in joint programs to promote productivity in exchange for improving wages and benefits for longshoremen and their unions. These agreements basically have involved "buy out" of restrictive provisions and practices, which allowed a reduction in the "work gang" size and increased flexibility in manpower use. To obtain these agreements, attractive early retirement provisions and guaranteed work have been included in the labor agreements.[40]

Cost of Living During periods of rising prices, unions support their wage demands by referring to the cost of living. Union negotiations must advance the argument that a rise in the cost of living without a commensurate wage increase is equivalent to a cut in real wages or a drop in purchasing power. Thus, the proposition that wages be raised at least in proportion to the advance in living costs seems quite fair and reasonable. But the complete reliance on use of this criterion needs careful appraisal.[41]

Unions and management must come to an agreement on the meaning of cost of living. *Cost of living* usually refers to the consumer price index (CPI) as determined by the Bureau of Labor Statistics; its computation includes such cost items as housing, food, and automobile which may be out of line with the purchasing patterns of employees in a specific plant or community. The parties must also negotiate the base period, the starting date, and the CPI most appropriate for use (the Bureau of Labor Statistics publishes an all-cities CPI plus CPIs for most major cities).

Automatic increases in general wages present problems in their effect on the cost-price-profit mechanism.[42] In other words, costs of labor which are automatically increased throughout the economy can increase total costs and sales prices unless there is a commensurate productivity increase. The increases in wages are passed on to the consumer; large firms, having some monopolistic control, simply raise their prices. Thus, the market economy is restricted and does not function effectively as a determiner of prices and an allocator of resources—two of its most important functions.

Perhaps management's greatest concern over cost of living is that it receives nothing in return for this wage increase, granted on the basis of factors over which it has no control. The cost-of-living argument seldom if ever considers employees' productivity at a particular facility. Additional considerations of cost of living are discussed in the following section on wage adjustments.

Wage Adjustments during the Life of the Labor Agreement

In addition to wage determination during negotiations, labor and management may agree to provisions that will allow adjustment of wages during the length of the contract—usually cost-of-living adjustments (or COLA, also called escalator clauses), deferred wage increases (also called annual improvement adjustments), and contract reopeners that allow for wages to be negotiated at a predetermined date. While annual wage improvements are specified in nearly 90 percent of the contracts, COLA provisions are included in over half, and reopener clauses are written in less than one-fourth of the agreements covering 1,000 or more employees.[43]

COLA, or escalator, clauses first appeared after World War I in the printing and clothing industries, but they were eliminated during the late 1920s. Immediately after World War II, they were renewed, as employees tried to keep up with rapid inflation.[44] These clauses imposed "a contractual obligation upon an employer to change rates of pay in accordance with a formula embodied in a collective bargaining agreement."[45] Their present popularity (estimates range from 5.6 to 9.0 million employees covered by these clauses)[46] owes much to the long-term contracts pioneered by the United Auto Workers and General Motors in 1948. Since then, not only has the number of agreements having COLA provisions grown, but the average length of contracts has been extended.[47]

Coverage by escalator clauses is concentrated in various industries. Nearly 90 percent of the employees in primary metals, machinery, electrical machinery, and transportation equipment industries have COLA provisions.[48] The majority of the workers under COLA provisions are affiliated with the United Auto Workers, Teamsters, Steelworkers, Communication Workers of America, Retail Clerks, and Machinists.[49]

When negotiating the COLA provisions, union and management representatives usually consider a number of matters:

1. Selection of the particular price index and base point. Usually the all-cities consumer price index (CPI) is selected in nationwide agreements, and the beginning date of the contract is specified.
2. Frequency and timing of the wage adjustment. Half of the agreements call for adjustments every quarter; one-fourth every year; the remainder semi-annually.
3. Formula for adjustment. The most common is cents per hour for each point increase in the CPI; the remainder require a percentage change in wages in accordance with a percentage change in the CPI. The most common arrangement is to have wages adjusted 1 cent for each 0.3 percent change in the CPI.
4. Effect of COLA on other elements of the compensation package. There is little uniformity in this matter. Some agreements adjust the gross hourly earnings after incentives; others adjust only the base wage rate. Still other payments, such as overtime, call-in pay, night work, and differentials, must be considered.
5. Limitations on the adjustment. About one-fourth have formulas with CAPS (limits on the amounts that may be received from cost-of-living provisions within a given period). On the other hand, some agreements specify that wages will not be reduced in the event of a CPI decline.[50]

COLA provisions are becoming more common not only in labor agreements but also outside the collective bargaining arena. For example, 31 million Social Security recipients and 2.5 million military and civil service retirees are now covered. It has been estimated that over 50 million U.S. citizens now have their incomes adjusted by some automatic cost-of-living adjustment.[51]

Wage reopener clauses are usually written in such a way that wages may be renegotiated at a specified time during the length of the agreement or when the CPI has risen by a specified amount. Some of the agreements allow only wages to be renegotiated, whereas others allow nonwage items or do not specify the items. Deferred wage increases, annual improvement factors, and productivity increases enjoy a broad acceptance in most contracts, and many of these are included with cost-of-living adjustments as well as contract reopeners.[52]

Yet cost-of-living adjustments and wage reopeners have their problems. Cost-of-living adjustments are very difficult to negotiate out of a contract, because union officers and members assume the COLA will continue in subsequent contracts. This situation makes it difficult for either union or management to receive credit for the contract. Assume, for example, that management anticipates the COLA will cost 60 cents per employee per year. If the negotiated wage settlement costs 70 cents per employee, then employees will receive only a 10-cent-an-hour increase plus continuation of the COLA. The union officer will have a difficult time selling the labor agreement to the members, particularly since they probably take the established COLA clause for granted. It might be easier to sell the labor agreement if there were not any COLA and the wage package were publicized as an annual improvement increase of 70 cents an hour.

Wage reopeners are also subject to problems, particularly when the union wishes to extend negotiated items to noneconomic items. While this is not allowable in theory, the distinction between economic and noneconomic discussion becomes blurred in practice. Some practitioners have suggested that a wage reopener is similar to an entirely new contract negotiation as the parties bring noneconomic items into the discussion.

Employee Benefits

In 1977, employee benefits payments averaged 36.7 percent of the company's payroll, up from 19.2 percent in 1953. While 8.5 percent of the payments (for example, old age, survivors, disability insurance, unemployment compensation, and workmen's compensation) were legally required, the remainder included a variety of other benefits.[53] To indicate their magnitude, it has been estimated that $150 billion is contributed annually to employee benefits.[54] The following sections present major areas of employee benefits, relying largely on studies of 1,570 agreements by the Department of Labor[55] and 400 agreements by the Bureau of National Affairs.[56]

Insurance

Insurance provisions have been substantially expanded during the 1970s. More than 90 percent of the contracts provide life and hospitalization insurance, while the majority include coverage for major medical expenses, surgery, maternity care, doctor's visits, accidental death and dismemberment, and nonoccupational sickness and accidents. Most contracts continue coverage to employees after retirement but reduce the amount of coverage. Hospitalization and surgical insurance for dependents of employees are covered in over 83 percent of the contracts, and premiums are paid by the company in the majority of cases. The 1970s has also brought increasing numbers of medical-related plans into new areas: prescription drugs (24 percent), dental care (41 percent), optical care (10 percent), and supplements to medicare (21 percent). It is expected that these areas of coverage will show significant growth.

Income Maintenance

Income maintenance provisions that provide income protection for employees are now found in nearly one-half of the labor agreements. Such provisions usually involve work or pay guarantees, severance pay (separation or termination pay), and supplemental unemployment benefits (SUB) plans. Just over 9 percent of the agreements contain work or pay guarantees, with the majority of those providing a weekly guarantee of forty hours of work.

Severance pay plans providing for lump sum payments upon termination are included in 37 percent of the agreements. In most cases, severance pay is extended only to workers whose jobs have been terminated as a result of permanent shutdown, to those whose layoffs continue beyond a minimum length of time, or to those who have no prospect for recall. The amount of severance pay varies with the length of service—each year of service allows for increased benefits. Severance payments are usually restricted for a particular time period or until the worker is reemployed.

Supplemental unemployment benefit plans, included in 16 percent of the agreements, are usually classified as pooled fund systems (benefits are allowed only in the event of lack of work). A few SUB plans provide individual accounts in which the employee has a vested right and from which he or she may withdraw money for reasons other than lack of work. The most common method provides payment of an amount equal to a percentage of the employee's take-home pay. Plans involving the United Auto Workers are the most lucrative for the workers, with SUB payments and unemployment compensation equalling 95 percent of take-home pay minus $7.50 in work-related expenses. Other plans range from $20 per week minimum to 90 percent of take-home pay. Other considerations, such as duration of benefits, eligibility stipulations, employee obligations, and financial requirements, must also be included in the composition of the plan.

Premium Pay—Overtime and Other Supplements

Most labor agreements specify daily or weekly work schedules and provide premium pay for hours worked beyond the normal hours. Most agreements call for eight-hour days and workweeks of forty hours— Monday through Friday. Overtime premiums are usually paid for work over eight hours per day at a time-and-a-half rate, which is more beneficial to the worker than the Fair Labor Standards Act requirement of time-and-a-half payments for work in excess of forty hours in a week. (Workers on a four-day, forty-hour workweek would receive eight hours of overtime pay.) A few agreements provide sixth-day and seventh-day premiums, but the majority of agreements prohibit pyramiding of overtime (combining a number of different premium payments, allowing overtime duplication).

Many labor agreements also contain provisions for overtime administration. For example, overtime assignments may be restricted to employees within a job classification or a given department, to a particular shift, to qualified personnel, and so on. In some cases, where management has had difficulty getting employees to work overtime, provisions that make overtime mandatory have been negotiated. Some agreements have gone so far as imposing penalties for refusing overtime work and specifying a loss of claim to the number of hours reduced. Likewise, unions have sought provisions in the labor agreement which would enable their members to better plan their off-the-job activities: advance notice, relief from mandatory overtime if not notified by a certain time, and others.

Various forms of supplementary pay are included in most contracts. For instance, shift differentials (premium payments for working the night shift, for example) are provided in over 50 percent of the agreements. Other forms, such as reporting pay (employees who report for scheduled work, but find no work, are still paid) and call-back pay (pay to employees who are called back to work at hours other than normal), are also usually included. Reporting pay guarantees range from one hour to eight hours, except with some maritime firms that provide one full week. Call-back or call-in pay guarantees are most frequently for four hours. Other supplements include pay for temporary transfer, hazardous work, travel, work clothes, tools, and bonuses other than production.

Payments for Nonwork—Holidays, Vacations, and Rest Periods

While many agreements provide for such nonwork activities as rest periods, cleanup time, time lost to job-related injury, waiting time, standby time, travel time, and voting time, payments for nonwork involving the most money are holidays and vacations. The median number of holidays provided is 10; the range is from 5 to 15. Nearly all agreements provide holidays for Labor Day, Independence Day, Thanksgiving, Christmas, New Year's Day, and Memorial Day. Good Friday, Christmas

Eve, and the day after Thanksgiving appear in less than 50 percent of the agreements. Most agreements have eligibility requirements, for example, specified length of service (usually four weeks) before being given a paid holiday, or working the day before and after the holiday. More complicated provisions involve issues such as holidays falling on Saturday, Sunday, or a day off or during vacation and premium pay for work on holidays.

Nearly all agreements provide for vacations for covered employees; the latest data show sharp increases in agreements allowing five- and six-week vacations and slight reductions in amount of service to qualify for nearly all types of vacations. Somewhat surprisingly, vacations for one week only are now less frequent than two- and three-week vacations. In most cases, vacation entitlement is linked to length of service.[57]

Nearly all agreements have provisions that pertain to the administration of vacations. The majority contain specific work requirements, such as a minimum number of hours, days, weeks, or years necessary to qualify for various lengths of vacation. Vacation scheduling provisions appear in 88 percent of all agreements; they cover such items as annual plant shutdowns and consideration of employee seniority and employee preference. These provisions are essential in organizations employing large numbers of employees, not only to reduce friction between employees but to allow management to properly plan its production schedules.

Pensions

Nearly all labor agreements make some reference to pension plans, whether in the form of a general statement mentioning the plan or a fully detailed provision. Items usually mentioned include age for retirement (normal and early), disability retirement, benefits available and requirements for qualifying, vesting provisions, administration procedures, and financial arrangements. Most plans have stipulated 65 as the retirement age,[58] but this limitation will be modified by the 1978 amendment to the Age Discrimination in Employment Act, which prevents mandatory retirement before age 70.[59]

Most plans guarantee the retired employee a flat monthly dollar amount for each year of service ($10.50 is the median) or a percent of earnings times years of service. Special provisions are usually included for employees forced to retire due to total or permanent disability. In addition, voluntary early retirement is allowed in 97 percent of the plans.

Frequently, early retirement plans offer several options to the employee. For example, the United Auto Workers' agreements provide three options: retirement at age 60 after ten years of service; retirement at age 55, but before age 60 only when the combined age and service years equal eighty-five; and retirement after thirty years of service, without regard to age. The financial arrangements in 92 percent of the agreements show that the employer finances the pension plan entirely (that is, it is noncontributory); where plans are contributory, labor agreements include very specific provisions about the amounts that the employer and the employees contribute.

Although 89 percent of the contracts contain *vesting* provisions (an employee whose service is terminated continues to be entitled to earned benefits), the Employer Retirement Income Security Act of 1974 (also known as either ERISA or the Pension Reform Act) has very specific regulations governing vesting requirements of pension plans. Although management and labor may negotiate provisions covering pensions which are more favorable than the law requires, most agreements for the time being will no doubt closely correspond to the legal minimum.[60]

Under ERISA, employees eligible for participation in a pension plan earn credits toward their pension. After they have worked a specified period of time with the employer, they have the right to prescribed earned pension benefits that they will receive on retirement, even though their employment may be terminated. ERISA requires provisions for minimum vesting under one of three schedules (shown in Exhibit 13–1). Under any

---

| Exhibit 13–1
Minimum Pension
Vesting Schedules
under ERISA | Five-to-fifteen year rule: **Employees must be at least 25 percent vested in accrued benefits derived from employer contributions after five years of covered service. Vested benefits will increase until 100 percent of the employer contribution is vested after fifteen years.** |

Ten-year rule: **Employee's accrued benefits from employer contributions is 100 percent vested after ten years.**

Rule of 45: **An employee with five or more years must be at least 50 percent vested when the sum of his or her age and years of covered service totals 45. After this sum of 45 is reached, the percentage of the employee's vested pension will be adjusted in accordance with the following schedule:**

If years of service equal or exceed	And the sum of age and service equals or exceeds	Then, the nonforfeiture percentage is
5	45	50
6	47	60
7	49	70
8	51	80
9	53	90
10	55	100

However, regardless of the above rules, the benefits of each employee with ten years of service must be at least 50 percent vested and 10 percent must be vested for each year thereafter until 100 percent is reached.

Source: Based on information from Commerce Clearing House, *Pension Reform Act of 1974: Law and Explanation* (Chicago: Commerce Clearing House, 1974), pp. 22–23.

of these options, an employee must be at least 50 percent vested after ten years of service and 100 percent vested after fifteen years of service, regardless of age.[61]

In addition to the vesting obligations and provisions, other ERISA provisions protect the interests of workers and their beneficiaries covered under employee pension and welfare plans. The employer is responsible for reporting to the U.S. Department of Labor, the Pension Benefit Guaranty Corporation, and the Internal Revenue Service. Employers have responsibilities of providing certain information to those covered, such as a summary of the plan in understandable language, a summary of any change in plan, updates every five years, an annual report summary, and a statement of total accrued benefits and the amount vested. Specific rules are established for funding, protection of pension benefits, and joint-survivor annuity. To assure that these responsibilities are fulfilled, the Department of Labor has been assigned both investigative and enforcement powers. These include the authority to inspect books and records which must be submitted for inspection and the right to impose fines for violations and interference with employee rights.[62]

Prepaid Legal Services

Only ten years ago, prepaid legal services did not exist. In fact, any attorney who contracted with a group to provide legal services for a predetermined fee would have been disbarred.[63] Now legal assistance is available to organized group members who have pooled prepaid amounts. By January 1978, 3,500 prepaid plans covering 2 million families had been filed under ERISA.[64]

These group plans began after a 1971 Supreme Court decision that declared that a United Transportation Union's legal service plan was an exercise of First Amendment rights. One year later, a highly publicized experiment involving the Laborers' International in Shreveport, Louisiana, and the American Bar Association was established. Two other actions have helped in the growth of these plans: (a) legal services were recognized as a valid subject for collective bargaining in which unions and employers negotiated the financial arrangements for the plans,[65] and (b) the Tax Reform Act of 1976 clarified the tax status of prepaid plans (neither employer contributions nor employee benefits were taxable).[66]

Existing plans vary in terms of whether the parties will set up open panels (the client chooses the attorney) or closed panels (legal services are provided by a law firm retained under the plan or by an attorney staff).[67] Some plans offer a full array of services, ranging from counsel for criminal offenses to routine matters (such as wills, divorces, house closings, and landlord-tenant problems). Most believe prepaid legal services will become more common; these projections are supported by a recent American Bar Association study that predicts that prepaid legal service plans will be as common in ten to fifteen years as medical insurance is today.[68]

Summary

Economic issues pertain to wages and the variety of economic benefits which make up what is commonly called the wage package. The discussions focused on reasons for wage differentials—industrial, occupational, and regional. A more specific presentation on job evaluation began with an organizational analysis and concluded with a wage structure which includes job classes, wage rates, and wage ranges.

In addition to the basic wage structure, some firms provide either individual or group wage incentives. Negotiators use certain wage-determining criteria in arriving at an acceptable wage structure; commonly accepted criteria include: differential features of jobs, comparable wages, ability to pay, productivity, and cost of living.

Since labor agreements usually are negotiated for periods greater than one year, provisions are commonly negotiated to adjust wages during the life of the contract. A common form of wage adjustment is the cost-of-living adjustment (COLA), or escalator clause, which adjusts wages in accordance with the consumer price index or cost of living. Another form of wage adjustment less frequently included in agreements is the wage reopener clause, providing that wages be renegotiated at a predetermined time during the life of the agreement.

Employee benefits have now increased to consume 36.7 percent of the company's total payroll. Numerous types of benefits exist. The major ones include: insurance, income maintenance, premium pay, payments for nonwork, and pensions. One type of benefit, prepaid legal services, has recently come into existence and has growth potential and interest among employees.

Discussion Questions

1. List the main factors that help explain the wage differentials for five jobs in an organization with which you are familiar.

2. Explain why job evaluation plans must take into consideration not only internal factors but also external factors if they are to be successful.

3. Assume that labor and management are negotiating a labor agreement and the wage spread becomes an issue of disagreement—management wants a wider wage spread, and the union wants a smaller wage spread. Why should management be cautious about the union's proposal, even though the total costs may be the same?

4. For each of the wage criteria given in the chapter, state the union's expected arguments and management's expected counterarguments, given the following conditions:
   a. High profits, a growing firm, a healthy economy, and the cost of living rising at 8 percent per year.
   b. Low profit, no anticipation of growth, questionable economic conditions, and the cost of living adjusting upward but by wide variations each month.

5. Assuming that a firm's costs of employee benefits are 36.7 percent of payroll, why doesn't the firm just let the union determine the manner in which the amounts are apportioned to the variety of benefits, such as insurance, holidays, and vacations, without negotiating each specific clause, especially since the overall costs probably would be the same?

6. Of the employee benefits explained in this chapter, which do you expect to grow in the future? Which do you expect to decline? Why?

References

[1]Jules Bachman, *Wage Determination: An Analysis of Wage Criteria* (Princeton, N.J.: D. Van Nostrand, 1959), pp. 1–7.

[2]Ibid., p. 14.

[3]Ibid., pp. 20–21.

[4]George W. Taylor, "Wage Determination Process," in George W. Taylor and Frank C. Person, eds., *New Concepts in Wage Determination* (New York: McGraw-Hill, 1957), p. 84.

[5]Leon Greenberg, "Definitions and Concepts," in Gerald Somers, ed., *Collective Bargaining and Productivity* (Madison, Wis.: Industrial Relations Research Association, 1975), p. 12.

[6]Bachman, *Wage Determination*, p. 58.

[7]For further reference see David W. Belcher, *Compensation Administration* (Englewood Cliffs, N.J.: Prentice-Hall, 1974); J. O. Dunn and F. M. Rachel, *Wage and Salary Administration: Total Compensation Systems* (New York: McGraw-Hill, 1971); Richard Henderson, *Compensation Management* (Boston, Va.: Reston Publishing, 1976); Allan N. Nash and Stephen J. Carroll, Jr., *The Management of Compensation* (Monterey, Calif.: Brocks/Cole Publishing, 1975); M. L. Rock, *Handbook of Wage and Salary Administration* (New York: McGraw-Hill, 1972); Robert E. Sibson, *Compensation* (New York: American Management Association, AMACOM, 1975); T. A. Mahoney, *Compensation and Reward Perspectives* (Homewood, Ill.: Irwin, 1979).

[8]Approach developed and advocated by L. T. Hawley and H. D. Janes.

[9]David W. Belcher, "Wage and Salary Administration," in Dale Yoder and H. G. Heneman, Jr., eds., *Motivation and Commitment* (Washington, D.C.: Bureau of National Affairs, 1975), p. 6–95.

[10]U.S. Department of Labor, *Handbook of Analyzing Jobs* (Washington, D.C.: Government Printing Office, 1972).

[11]W. K. Kirchner and M. D. Dunnette, "Identifying the Critical Factors in Successful Salesmanship," *Personnel* 34 (September–October 1957), pp. 54–59; and M. D. Dunnette, *Personnel Selection and Placement* (Belmont, Calif.: Wadsworth Publishing, 1966).

[12]E. J. McCormick, D. R. Jeanneret, and R. C. Mecham, "A Study of Job Characteristics and Job Dimensions as Based on the Position Analysis Questionnaire (PAQ)," *Journal of Applied Psychology* 56 (April 1972), pp. 347–368.

[13]Harold D. Janes, "Issues in Job Evaluation: The Union View," *Personnel Journal* 51 (September 1972), p. 675; also see Research Department, International Association of Machinists, *What's Wrong with Job Evaluation?* (Washington, D.C.: International Association of Machinists, 1954).

[14]Harold D. Janes, "Comparative Issues in Job Evaluation: The Union View, 1971–1978," *Personnel Journal* 58 (February 1979), pp. 80–85.

[15]Ibid.

[16]Sibson, *Compensation*, p. 120.

[17]Belcher, *Compensation Administration*, pp. 6–98 to 6–103. Also see footnote 7.

[18]Herbert G. Zollitsch, "Productivity, Time Studies, and Incentive-Pay Plans," in Dale Yoder and H. G. Heneman, Jr., eds., *Motivation and Commitment* (Washington, D.C.: Bureau of National Affairs, 1975), pp. 6–61.

[19]Editors of Collective Bargaining Negotiations and Contracts, *Patterns in Union Contracts* (Washington, D.C.: Bureau of National Affairs, 1979), pp. 103–105. Of 1,570 agreements, 378 covered production standards, 314 included time studies, and 455 required incentive wage payments. U.S. Department of Labor, Bureau of Labor Statistics, *Characteristics of Major Collective Bargaining Agreements, July 1, 1976* (Washington, D.C.: Government Printing Office, 1979), pp. 28–30.

[20]Zollitsch, "Productivity," pp. 6–66. Also see references in footnote 7 and J. Kenneth White, "The Scanlon Plan: Causes and Correlates of Success," *Academy of Management Journal* 22 (June 1979), pp. 292–312.

[21]Irving Bernstein, *Arbitration of Wages* (Berkeley: University of California, 1954), pp. 26–27; Craig Overton, "Criteria in Grievance and Interest Arbitration in the Public Sector," *Arbitration Journal* 28 (1973), pp. 159–166; Howard S. Block, "Criteria in Public Sector Interest Disputes," in G. G. Somers and B. D. Dennis, eds., *Arbitration and the Public Interest* (Washington, D.C.: Bureau of National Affairs, 1971), pp. 161–193.

[22]Bachman, *Wage Determination*, pp. 14–15.

[23]John Dunlop, "The Economics of Wage-Dispute Settlements," *Law and Contemporary Problems* 12 (Spring 1947), p. 282; and Bernstein, *Arbitration of Wages*, pp. 26–27.

[24]Bachman, *Wage Determination*, pp. 18–32.

[25]J. Fred Holly and Gary A. Hall, "Dispelling the Myths of Wage Arbitration," *Labor Law Journal* 28 (June 1977), p. 346.

[26]Sumner Slichter, *Basic Criteria Used in Wage Negotiation* (Chicago: Chicago Association of Commerce and Industry, January 30, 1947), p. 25.

[27]Bachman, *Wage Determination*, pp. 251–258.

[28]Dunlop, "Wage-Dispute Settlements," pp. 286–289.

[29]Bachman, *Wage Determination*, p. 174.

[30]Ibid., pp. 202–203.

[31]Greenberg, "Definitions and Concepts," p. 2.

[32]R. B. McKersie and L. C. Hunter, *Pay, Productivity, and Collective Bargaining* (London: Macmillan Press Ltd., 1973), pp. 1–4.

[33]Ibid., p. 4.

[34]Jerome Rosow, "Productivity and the Blue-Collar Blues," *Personnel* 48 (March–April 1971), pp. 8–10.

[35]Greenberg, "Definitions and Concepts," pp. 2–4.

[36]Jerome M. Rosow, "Now Is the Time for Productivity Bargaining," *Harvard Business Review* 50 (January–February 1972), p. 85.

[37]Anna C. Goldoff, "The Perceptions of Participants in a Joint Productivity Program," *Monthly Labor Review* 101 (July 1978), p. 33.

[38]Ibid., p. 34.

[39]William F. Maloney, "Productivity Bargaining in Contract Construction," *Proceedings of the 1977 Annual Spring Meeting: Industrial Relations Research Association* (Madison, Wis.: Industrial Relations Research Association, 1977), pp. 533–534.

[40]Joseph P. Goldberg, "Bargaining and Productivity in the Private Sector," in Gerald Somers et al., eds., *Collective Bargaining and Productivity* (Madison, Wis.: Industrial Relations Research Association, 1975), p. 28–42.

[41]Slichter, *Basic Criteria*, pp. 14–15.

[42]Dunlop, "Wage-Dispute Settlements," pp. 289–290.

[43]U.S. Department of Labor, Bureau of Labor Statistics, *Characteristics of Major Collective Bargaining Agreements*, p. 40.

[44]John Zalusky, "Cost of Living Clauses: Inflation Fighters," *American Federationist* 83 (March 1976), p. 1.

[45]H. L. Douty, "Escalator Clauses and Inflation," *Collective Bargaining Negotiations and Contracts* (Washington, D.C.: Bureau of National Affairs, December 1975), p. 16:1.

[46]Douglas R. LeRoy, "Scheduled Wage Increases and Escalator Provisions in 1978," *Monthly Labor Review* 101 (January 1978), pp. 3–8; Beth A. Levin, "Scheduled Wage Increases and Escalator Provisions in 1979," *Monthly Labor Review* 102 (January 1979), pp. 20–27; Victor Sheifer, "Cost-of-Living Adjustments Keeping Up with Inflation?" *Monthly Labor Review* 102 (June 1979), p. 14.

[47]The average length increased from 26 months in 1972 to 32.5 months in 1977. Those with COLA averaged 36.1 months; without COLA, 27.4 months. Janice D. Murphy, "Wage Developments during 1977," *Monthly Labor Review* 101 (April 1978), p. 5.

[48]U.S. Department of Labor, Bureau of Labor Statistics, *Characteristics of Major Collective Bargaining Agreements*, p. 39.

[49]LeRoy, "Scheduled Wage Increases," pp. 5–6.

[50]Audrey Freedman, "Cost-of-Living Clauses in Collective Bargaining," *Compensation Review* 6 (third quarter 1974), pp. 11–19; Robert H. Ferguson, *Cost-of-Living Adjustments in Union Management Agreements* (Ithaca, N.Y.: Cornell University, 1976), pp. 15–27; and LeRoy, "Scheduled Wage Increases," pp. 7–8.

[51]Robert J. Thornton, "A Problem with the COLA Craze," *Compensation Review* 9 (second quarter 1977), pp. 42–44.

[52]U.S. Department of Labor, Bureau of Labor Statistics, *Measures of Compensation* (Washington, D.C.: Government Printing Office, 1977), pp. 46–47.

[53]*Employee Benefits, 1977* (Washington, D.C.: Chamber of Commerce of the U.S.A., 1978), pp. 5–8.

[54]Colman S. Ives, "Benefits and Services—Private," in Yoder and Heneman, eds., *Motivation and Commitment*, p. 6–186.

[55]U.S. Department of Labor, Bureau of Labor Statistics, *Characteristics of Major Collective Bargaining Agreements*.

[56]Eds. of Collective Bargaining Negotiations and Contracts, *Basic Patterns*.

[57]Ibid., pp. 18–40, 88–96. For example, the medial length-of-service requirement for one week's vacation is one year, two weeks after two years, three weeks after ten years, four weeks after seventeen years, five weeks after twenty-four years, and six weeks after thirty years. Some of the United Steelworkers' agreements allow extended vacations up to thirteen weeks; however, these vacations are provided only in intervals of five years to senior employees.

[58]Ibid., p. 68.

[59]Age Discrimination in Employment Act, as amended in 1978 by Public Law 95–256.

[60]Eds. of Collective Bargaining Negotiations and Contracts, *Basic Patterns*, pp. 70–71.

[61]U.S. Department of Labor, Office of Employee Benefits Security, *Often-Asked Questions about the Employee Retirement Income Security Act of 1974* (Washington, D.C.: Government Printing Office, 1976), pp. 16–17. Also see Ian D. Lanoff, "Civil Enforcement and Criminal Penalties under the Employee Retirement Income Security Act of 1974," in Virginia S. Cameron, ed., *Labor Law Developments* (New York: Matthew Bender, 1976), pp. 1–31.

[62]U.S. Department of Labor, Office of Employee Benefits Security, *Often-Asked Questions*, pp. 26–27.

[63]Sandy DeMent, "A New Bargaining Focus on Legal Services," *American Federationist* 85 (May 1978), pp. 7–10.

[64]"Pay Now, Sue Later," *Time*, September 4, 1978, p. 71.

[65]T. J. St. Antoine, "Growth Patterns in Legal Services," *American Federationist* 83 (February 1976), pp. 19–21.

[66]DeMent, "New Bargaining Focus," p. 7.

[67]Ibid.

[68]"Pay Now, Sue Later," p. 71.

Part 4 gives the reader an opportunity to apply the previous chapters' discussions of the labor relations process to emerging labor relations sectors. Collective bargaining in the public sector at all governmental levels is discussed, and a discussion of foreign labor relations processes is presented for comparative purposes. A concluding chapter describes labor relations activities in the professional sports, health care, and agricultural industries.

Part 4

Emerging Labor
Relations Processes

Chapter 14

Labor Relations in State and Local Government

"Collective bargaining in the public sector is . . . still developing. It is, therefore, much too soon to pronounce it a success or a failure."

**Benjamin Aaron
U.C.L.A.**

The public sector has grown to become an important factor in the U.S. labor scene. As the number of public employees has increased, so has the number of these employees joining unions. This chapter presents an overview of labor relations in the public sector and provides a brief summary of the similarities and differences found in public and private sector labor relations. It also examines public sector bargaining at the state and local levels and concludes with a discussion of one of the affected groups—educators.

Currently, the public sector witnesses the most dynamic, diverse, and possibly crisis-laden aspects of labor relations in the United States.[1] With many state legislatures becoming interested in Proposition 13–like legislation to cut taxes, these actions have caused public employees to become more concerned about their job security and welfare. Thus, union leaders are showing increased attention to public sector employees, hoping that gains in membership in this area will offset the lack of membership gains in the private sector.[2] Although unions received a setback in a 1976 Supreme Court decision which led many to believe that a national public sector labor relations law would be declared unconstitutional, their optimism was furthered by passage of state and local legislation and positive (if qualified) public opinion favoring public sector bargaining.[3] Table 14–1 illustrates the large success that various unions have had in organizing public sector employees.

The tremendous growth in government employment at all government levels (see Table 14-2) affects not only government agencies but the organized labor community (AFL-CIO) as well. The precise strength of this influence on AFL-CIO policies is currently undetermined. However, at least some public employee union officials maintain that their unions are not given enough consideration in the AFL-CIO; they charge that the AFL-CIO is dragging its feet regarding unionized public employees' concerns and the desires of other public employees to form unions. Some of this dissension has prompted Jerry Wurf, president of the American Federation of State, County and Municipal Employees (AFSCME), to consider pulling his organization out of the AFL-CIO.[4] Perhaps AFSCME's stance has been modified with the recently developed Public Employee Department of the AFL-CIO. The relative degree of influence exerted by public employee unions on the AFL-CIO's structure and

Table 14–1 Unions in the Public Sector That Have Gained 100,000 or More Members, 1966-1976[a]	Employee Classifications of Unions in the Public Sector[b]	Membership (in Thousands)			Increase 1966–1976	
		1966	1974	1976	Number (in Thousands)	Percent
	State and county employees	281	648	750	469	166.9
	Teachers	125	444	446	321	256.8
	Service employees	349	500	575	226	64.8
	Laborers	475	650	627	152	32.0

[a]Includes several unions in which a portion of the membership gain was due to a merger with one or more other unions. Excludes merged unions where the membership of the smaller organization represented a significant proportion of the total and the combined membership did not increase 100,000.

[b]Includes more than one union in each category.

Source: Bureau of National Affairs, *Government Employee Relations Reporter*, September 19, 1977, p. 726:27.

Table 14–2 Governmental Employment by Levels of Government, 1967–1974	Numbers of Employees (in Thousands)				
Year	Total	Federal (Civilian)	Total State and Local	State	Local
1967	11,867	2,993	8,874	2,334	6,539
1968	12,342	2,984	9,358	2,495	6,864
1969	12,685	2,969	9,716	2,614	7,102
1970	13,028	2,881	10,147	2,755	7,392
1971	13,316	2,872	10,444	2,832	7,612
1972	13,759	2,795	10,964	2,955	8,002
1973	14,139	2,786	11,353	3,013	8,339
1974	14,628	2,874	11,754	3,155	8,599
1975	14,986	2,890	12,097	3,268	8,826

Source: U.S. Department of Labor, Bureau of Labor Statistics, *Handbook of Labor Statistics*, (Washington, D.C.: Government Printing Office, 1977), p. 96.

policies in the near future remains an interesting and speculative topic for labor relations students.

Private and Public Sector Labor Relations Compared

Differences in Private and Public Sector Bargaining

Although labor relations in the private and public sectors have much in common, there are at least five general differences that aid in obtaining a full appreciation of the public sector's labor relations process.

1. The nature of the public service. One difference between the public and private sectors can be explained in terms of the economic system and the market economy. Unlike the private sector situation, many of the services in the public sector (such as public education and police and fire protection) are supplied to the citizens at little or no additional cost. The market economy therefore does not operate in the public sector and cannot act as a constraint on the labor union and management negotiators.

Moreover, monopolistic conditions often exist in the public sector, and public organizations often control the services rendered or the products offered. For example, the police and fire departments are the primary organizations that provide certain types of security protection. Public education has very little real competition from the private sector, and even that is usually among only the more affluent families. Thus, products and services provided by the government cannot be readily substituted if they become more costly.[5]

The lack of substitute goods or services distinguishes public sector collective bargaining from related activities in the private sector and adds to the critical nature of public services. For example, citizens usually take garbage collection services for granted; yet a strike by city garbage collectors would be regarded by the public as a crisis, since there is no immediate alternative means for garbage disposal. The lack of substitute services also eliminates one of management's strike costs: loss of business to a competitor. In fact, some union leaders contend that municipal leaders use a strike to their advantage—the payroll savings during a strike are transferred to other governmental budgetary accounts.

Finally, the relatively vague aspects of the particular public service institutions make productivity bargaining difficult. Clear and precise productivity measures are a necessary first step in productivity bargaining (although many private sector companies have these figures and do not engage in productivity bargaining). Most public sector bargaining parties do not have specific productivity measures at their disposal and could not engage in productivity bargaining even if they desired this approach. Many public services are provided regardless of customer use. Policemen and bus drivers can legitimately contend that they should not be financially punished for nonuse of their services—their salaries should not be a direct function of the number of crimes detected and punished or riders served if the service is available to all. Hence, much of the public sector wage determination process is based on comparisons with similar jobs in the public and private sectors rather than on employee performance records.[6] Because the market does not act as a moderator in the public sector, budgetary limitation, public attitudes, and administrative discretion must operate to successfully maintain order, equity, and balance in collective bargaining relationships.[7]

2. The relationship between the budget and public sector bargaining processes. The budget usually tends to have a more conspicuous if not significant role in public sector collective bargaining. Most municipal budgets are posted in advance before public hearings and subsequent adoption. Although many citizens ignore public hearings, key taxpayers such as local companies give close attention to the budget in terms of its implications for increased property taxes. The anticipated salaries for public employees are recorded as separate line items on the budget, something not done in the private sector. Thus, the opportunity exists for concerned taxpayers to pressure city officials in the hopes of keeping the budget and subsequent taxes at a minimum.

The specific influence of the budget on the public sector collective bargaining process remains uncertain. Some suggest that there is a great deal of flexibility in the budget-bargaining relationship in terms of budget padding, transfer of funds among line items, and supplemental or amended budgets that can often be filed after the final approval date.[8] In these cases, the governmental officer in charge of labor relations may have little concern with the agency's financial activities. The following related comments were expressed by a former director of the budget for New York City:

> The director of the budget is less a part of a unified management team than a part of the problem, an adversary not unlike the union leaders themselves. . . . Underlying the situation is the belief held by most labor negotiators that they know "what it takes" to effect a settlement and that, in the large complex public body, alleged or actual limits on available resources have no effect upon the ultimate settlement. And they are, in fact, largely correct.[9]

Similarly, as illustrated by one union official's comment, public sector unions seldom allow the budget to influence their collective bargaining strategies and settlements:

> The budget does not mean too much to me—if we based our bargaining demands on the budget, we would never get any money. The union is never cognizant as to the amount [in the budget] because there never is enough money. We are aware of the dire need for money and campaign politically [to obtain additional funds], but when we go into negotiations we don't discuss the budgetary problems.[10]

Their major concern pertains to securing benefits for their members; it is up to management to find sufficient funds for an equitably negotiated settlement. Thus, there is little union-management agreement over the budget's significance in contract negotiations; few if any public sector collective bargaining agreements have provisions specifying the role the budget will assume in the collective bargaining process.

This situation poses a dilemma. On the one hand, if the budget were a controlling factor in contract negotiations, unilateral managerial decision making would render collective bargaining a farce. On the other hand, if collective bargaining were entirely removed from budgetary constraints, fiscal responsibilities would be abated at taxpayer expense. Some degree of union involvement in the budget-making process might be needed in instances of severe fiscal constraints. A hopeful note is reflected in the observations of a New York City Emergency Financial Control Board member: "I have found the municipal labor unions to be the most practical people in this [financial] crisis. They understood the problem more quickly than the city administration."[11]

3. Collective bargaining structures and decision-making processes. It is more difficult to define the appropriate bargaining unit in the public sector than in the private sector.[12] Private sector legislation and related administrative enforcement agencies provide direction for determining the appropriate bargaining unit. For example, plant guards in the private sector are required to be in separate bargaining units, and supervisors are not eligible for membership in the bargaining unit. The public sector, especially at the state and local levels, experiences many different combinations of appropriate bargaining units. Depending on the particular applicable state law or administrative determination, public sector supervisors can be prohibited from joining unions, they can be in the same bargaining units as other employees, or they can join unions in separate bargaining units. All these combinations can be found in states having no statutory regulations. [13]

Another organizational difference applies to the chief negotiator in the public sector, who often lacks authority to reach a final and binding agreement with the union on behalf of the public organization. The doctrine of sovereignty makes it difficult to delegate decision-making authority to specific administrative officials. Many elected officials still refuse to give up their legislative authority to make final decisions on matters that they believe are important to effective governmental operations, since they feel responsible directly to the electorate. They do not want appointed negotiators to bind them to wage settlements and other provisions of collective bargaining agreements which they believe are unworkable. [14] For example, unionized school teachers might encounter a variety of managers in collective negotiations—the school principal, the superintendent of schools, the school board, and possibly state education officials. The problem of determining "who is management?" can negatively affect the negotiations process in two ways.

a. Management can pass the buck to other management officials in the bargaining process. Union officers are often shuffled off to a variety of governmental officials in collective bargaining on the premise that another individual has specific authority for a particular issue or a portion of available funds. Often, political rivalries prompt certain government officials to either intervene or pass the buck in the hopes of looking good at another official's expense. [15] This situation can result in a more confusing collective bargaining relationship than is typically found in the private sector. In some cases, it can almost entirely prevent serious collective bargaining efforts between management and the union. [16]

b. The unwillingness of some government agencies to give sufficient labor relations authority to a government official can result in a lack of labor relations expertise on management's side of the negotiation table. In some cases, taxpayers are affected if unions take advantage of the inexperienced management negotiators. Perhaps in other cases a public strike could have been avoided if the parties had had a more realistic understanding of the collective bargaining process.

4. Negotiable issues and bargaining tactics. Exemption by statute of many of the traditional collective bargaining subjects from negotiations is another difference between private and public sector labor relations. Under the Civil Service Reform Act of 1978, wages and position classifications of federal employees cannot be negotiated. (The postal service is covered under another law.) In many states operating under merit system rules and regulations, related subjects such as promotion, pension plans, and layoff procedures cannot be negotiated.[17]

A problem arises if public sector negotiation topics are restricted to those found in the labor agreement, particularly since one study found that some public sector labor agreement provisions are not actually negotiated between the parties, while other decisions are jointly determined but not included in the formal labor agreement.[18] Thus, relatively few generalizations can be made regarding collectively bargained items in the public sector.

Sometimes the public sector's bargaining tactics differ from those in the private sector. Certain bargaining practices allowed in the public sector would probably be considered unfair labor practices in the private sector. Negotiations in the private sector stem from a bilateral relationship—management and union representatives negotiate the terms of the labor agreement with little involvement from outside groups. Public sector bargaining, particularly at the state and local levels, is multilateral, involving various groups of community citizens and government officials as well as the formally designated negotiators. Thus, it often becomes an exercise in politics—who you know and what you can do to help or hurt the government official's political career can play a decisive role. Public sector unions therefore often have opportunities to *end-run* the negotiations before, during, or after their occurrence; that is, they make a direct appeal to the legislative body that will make final decisions on the agreement in the hope that they will gain a more favorable agreement. For example, in 1970 Boston Mayor Kevin White made concessions to the Boston Police Patrolmen's Association in return for its endorsement in the gubernatorial primary. He changed the regular police work schedule from five days on and two off to four days on and two off (increasing annual days off by 17), guaranteed two patrolmen in all cars, and agreed that 50 percent plus one of the patrol cars in each police district would be on the street during night hours.[19] Because public labor unions in many settings are politically potent, elective officials are generally more receptive to this end-run process than a corporation president, members of the board of directors, or majority stockholders of a corporation would ever be in the private sector.[20] In fact, such attempts by the union to bypass the management negotiators of a private sector organization would probably result in an adverse NLRB determination of refusal to bargain in good faith.

Occasionally, the media aid the end-run tactic—management and the union present their positions to the press rather than to the other party at the bargaining table. Public sector bargaining is usually given more press coverage than similar activities in the private sector since more related information is typically furnished to the press and the eventual settlement will have a more direct impact on the government's constituents. The end-run to the news media can harm the collective bargaining approach, as evidenced by a union leader's account of the 1970–1971 negotiations between New York City and the uniformed forces:

All of this [bargaining issues] should have been brought to the bargaining table. It would have given both labor and management a chance to work out of these very difficult trouble spots. . . . But, almost nothing was done at the table; instead both sides took to the television, advertising, and the loud and dramatic press releases. . . .

Experts . . . know the best way to insure trouble is to bring collective bargaining into the public arena. Instead of labor and management representatives talking to each other, they will talk to the public and to their principals only. Invariably, the wrong things will be said.

Management will talk of the "irresponsibly high demands" of the workers, and about how services will have to be cut back or taxes raised. . . .

The labor leader now has to talk tough. The strike threat becomes almost obligatory, because he is now put in an impossible squeeze. When the union leader goes public he first must talk to the people he represents, and retain their confidence. Understandably, the public responds not to the facts of the situation but to the militant rhetoric. Everybody loses in the process, a process that has little or nothing to do with collective bargaining.[21]

A related distinction in public sector bargaining is that many of the negotiations are now open to the public under the so-called "sunshine laws,"[22] the rationale being that the citizens are the owners of the public service and are entitled to observe and offer input into the collective bargaining process. However, this "fishbowl" approach to public sector bargaining differs widely from the private sector, as a private enterprise's owners (stockholders) are excluded from collective bargaining sessions. Also, flexibility and honesty are necessary prerequisites of successful labor-management relationships, and these qualities are often lost if union and management negotiators have to posture their efforts before a public audience.

5. The right-to-strike controversy. The right to strike, considered by many a vital instrument for successful collective bargaining, is usually prohibited by statute in the public sector. The federal government and most state governments prohibit strikes. The basic argument given for legislative prohibition of strikes is that the services provided by public organizations are essential to the general welfare of the citizens, and work stoppages or refusals to work would adversely affect the delivery of these vital services and create disorder in the community. As is true with many industrial relations concepts, the words *essential services* are subject to many diverse interpretations. Some maintain that all public services are essential, while others suggest that many public employee classifications (such as clerks, mechanics, and motor pool personnel) are no more essential than their counterparts in private industry. Police and firefighters are almost always viewed as crucial for public safety; however, at least one police strike saw no increase in the area's crime rate. One police official, believing that criminals fear irate citizens more than they fear the police, commented, "Hoods have no rights without police protection. Shop owners will use their shotguns."[23]

The right to strike in the public sector has other debatable dimensions. Some would prohibit public sector strikes because they would place too much power in the hands of the unions relative to the taxpayers. Also, unions would unnecessarily benefit at the expense of other groups that are dependent on government revenues but that do not strike or participate in power ploys with public officials.[24]

George Taylor further elaborates on the effect of the right to strike on political processes:

It is ultimately the legislative and the political processes which have to balance the interests of public employees with the rest of the community. The balancing involves considering the relation of the compensation of public employees to tax rates, an appraisal of the extent and quality of public service desired by the taxpayer, and an evaluation of the efficiency of the performance of public employees as related to the performance. Methods of persuasion and political activity, rather than the strike, comply with our traditions and with the forms of representative government to which we are dedicated as the appropriate means for resolving conflicts of interests in this area. . . . Strikes are not the answer, new procedures are.[25]

One research project found that successful bargaining gains in the public sector occur when unions either use the threat of a strike despite its illegality or intertwine themselves closely with their employers through patronage–political support arrangements. If this assessment is correct, prohibiting strikes would lead to changes in patterns of political decision making which would subvert the "normal" political processes.[26]

Some contend that prohibiting public sector strikes distorts the collective bargaining process:

The conclusion is inescapable that collective bargaining cannot exist if employees may not withdraw their services or employers discontinue them. This is not a statement of preference, but a statement of fact. But it is now also evident that collective bargaining is the best way of composing differences between workers and their employers in a democratic society even though there is much room for improvement in the process. So, if we believe public employees should have bargaining rights, we must accept the possibility of a strike and consider how best to guard against it. If we believe the case against strikes by public employees is so overwhelming that all such strikes must be prohibited, let us then say frankly that public employees cannot be given bargaining rights and that the use of such euphemisms as collective negotiations cannot alter the basic structural differences the strike ban entails.[27]

Yet others believe that the right to strike in the public sector is not essential to collective bargaining, since public sector unions are already influential interest groups and effectively use their lobbying and political support techniques to obtain collective bargaining goals.[28]

Regardless of the arguments for or against the right to strike or statutory penalties assigned to strikers, significant strikes have occurred in the public sector in the last few years, involving teachers, firefighters, police, and sanitation workers in many large cities and postal employees in the federal sector. In fact, since 1960 there has been a considerable increase in public employee strikes, not only in number but in the number of employees involved and in man-days lost as a result of the strikes. In 1960, there were only 36 public sector strikes, causing 58,400 lost man-days, but in 1974 there were 378 strikes involving 180,700 workers and causing 1,690,700 man-days lost.[29] Moreover, strikes are often prolonged until all strikers or discharged employees have been granted amnesty or reinstatement to former positions. Thus, laws have not prevented strikes: they have not been invoked against all employees who have participated in strikes, and, when invoked, the law has not been applied with like effect to all strikers. Some believe that laws prohibiting strikes may have deterred some strikes and injunctions may have had a sobering effect on some strikers, but prohibiting strikes by passing a law has not realized a great degree of success.[30]

Similarities in Private and Public Sector Bargaining

One major similarity shared by public and private sector negotiations is that the collective bargaining settlement will often be influenced by the personalities of the union and management negotiators and their respective abilities to increase their bargaining power relative to the other party (the bargaining power model has been discussed in Chapter 6). To reiterate briefly, each party increases bargaining power over the opponent by either increasing the cost to the opponent of disagreeing or reducing the cost to the opponent of agreeing.

Public opinion represents a most significant cost item in public sector labor relations—both union and government officials often structure their tactics in a manner that gains public support for their position, which places pressure on their opponent to concede a negotiation item.

The president of a major public employee union has frequently appealed to public opinion (see Exhibit 14–1), contending that public opinion often translates into election votes—government officials approach

"One of these could educate every kid in Cincinnati."

"One brand-new B-1 bomber costs $87 million.

Enough to wipe out the cost of public education in Cincinnati. With enough left over to fund the libraries in the District of Columbia.

A single B-1 could pay for fire protection in Los Angeles for one year. Or finance the entire budget for the city of Atlanta.

Or pay all yearly expenses for streets, parks, and sanitation for Indianapolis, St. Louis, Pittsburgh, Hartford, and Milwaukee. *Combined.*

But what about the military benefits of the B-1?

According to a host of experts, there aren't any.

A Brookings Institution study found: 'No significant military advantages [are] to be gained by deploying a new penetrating bomber such as the B-1.'

Yet, two weeks ago, Congress voted full speed ahead on the most expensive weapon in U.S. history — a 244-plane system that could cost $100 billion.

Our union wants to stop the B-1 funding.

And we urge the Democratic Convention to join us.

We support a military strong enough to deter any aggressor foolish or venal enough to attack us.

But what good is it to be able to destroy Moscow ten times over if our own cities die in the meantime?"

—**Jerry Wurf,** President
American Federation of State,
County and Municipal Employees

AFSCME
the union that cares

American Federation of State, County, and Municipal Employees, 1625 L Street, N.W., Washington, D.C. 20036   Jerry Wurf, President   William Lucy, Secretary-Treasurer.
In New York City, AFSCME Is The Parent Organization of The 105,000 Municipal Employees Who Belong To District Council 37, AFSCME: And 10,000 Members of District Council 1707, The Community And Social Agency Employee Union.

Source: *Columbia Journalism Review* 15 (November–December 1976), p. 41. Courtesy of the AFSCME.

labor relations with their political careers uppermost in mind.[31] He further believes that public opinion usually prompts government officials to take a hard-line approach regarding union proposals and strategies:

[I]f we're [public unions] so powerful, why does every mayor and governor try to make his political reputation by fighting our union? If you sat in this office all day, you'd get the impression that every public official in the United States thinks he can win his epaulets by declaring war on our members.[32]

To be sure, some municipal and state officials have taken a stern approach toward public union strikers. For example, government officials in West Virginia and Atlanta, Georgia, discharged striking state and municipal employees and started hiring their replacements.

However, public opinion and political support can be a double-edged sword in the bargaining power model. Public unions can use at least three general strategies to increase management's cost of disagreeing with the union's position.[33] The first technique is the union's threat to "blow the whistle" on a questionable practice unless the government agency agrees with the desired negotiated settlement. Examples of such strategy include an announcement by union officials releasing information on the unpublicized practice of dumping raw sewage in a river or on the dollar amount of government officials' liquor bills, which are paid by the taxpayers. Of course, the union is hoping that government officials will capitulate rather than risk potential vote loss in subsequent elections due to the public revelation of a particular incident. Management's cost of disagreeing can be more directly increased by the union's threat of withdrawing political support.[34] The success of this tactic depends on the number of union members and the ability of the union to mobilize a cohesive voting bloc.

Finally, the union can use various job action techniques to raise management's cost of disagreeing. As mentioned earlier in the chapter, a complete withdrawal of service is usually prohibited by statute, but strikes by public employees have occurred frequently in spite of these legal sanctions. Perhaps these actions are taken under the assumption that most public sector strikes have been eventually resolved without fines or other sanctions, even though their activity runs counter to the established laws. However, some other job actions that have been used are outside the law or proscribed by the job requirements (for example, government employees in New York raising the toll bridges at rush hour when walking off the job), while others are marginally outside the law or job requirements (for example, all public employees calling in too sick to work).[35]

From the union standpoint, a most promising job action is working within the law while at the same time placing pressure on management to resolve the dispute. Job slowdowns fall into this category marginally, since most public sector labor agreements give management the right to discipline employees for poor production performance. Yet there is a thin line between a job slowdown and *malicious obedience,* by which the employees follow the agency's rules to the letter. For example, a fingerprint technician is charged with verifying an individual's address during his criminal booking. This can be done by simply telephoning the individual's purported residence. However, fingerprint technicians desiring to follow the malicious obedience technique might personally visit the individual's residence for a more accurate verification. Needless to say, this approach creates an assignment backlog. Other public employees can also use bureaucratic rules to their advantage. For example, toll booth employees could check paper currency serial numbers against a list of counterfeited bills, and postal workers could check each item to insure a proper zip code. Malicious obedience has the tactical advantage of cutting back services. More importantly, employees continue to receive wages under this tactic while being relatively immune from disciplinary actions.

The variety of job action techniques depends on the creativity and resourcefulness of the union leaders. In 1975, New York City's police and firefighters announced that off-duty personnel would distribute a pamphlet at the city's airports, railroad stations, bus terminals, and hotels. The cover of the pamphlet featured a human skull in a shroud with the caption, "WELCOME TO FEAR CITY." Union officials contended that this pamphlet represented an educational "survival guide" for tourists, since the city was contemplating police and firefighter layoffs. Included in the pamphlet were the following helpful hints:

☐ Stay off the streets after 6 P.M.

☐ Avoid public transportation.

☐ Do not walk.

☐ Beware of fire hazards.

Job actions of this nature, although not initially illegal, run the risk of an eventual restraining order. This occurred in the aforementioned New York City pamphlet example when the New York supreme court at least in part accepted the city's contention that such conduct endangers the citizens' lives and threatens the economic well-being of the city.

Public sector unions can also reduce management's cost of agreeing with the union by campaigning for referendums to fund the negotiated labor settlement or eliminating some of their initial proposals. They can also push for certain issues that contribute significantly to their economic well-being at little cost to the political incumbents. Employee pensions usually fall into this category since they can be increased without immediate cost implications; indeed, the bulk of pension costs will be incurred by some unhappy politician in the distant future.

Management can reduce its political cost of agreeing on wages by publicizing a rather low across-the-board settlement along with general improvements in the pay step plan. This plan usually gives progressive salary increases to each job classification. For example, an employee in one particular classification might receive a 5 percent wage increase after three years' service in that classification. Management can improve the employee's situation by either raising the percentage increase or reducing the number of service years needed for a step wage increase. However, it is difficult to determine and report the precise cost of these changes. Most news media presentations are limited to specific reports on the average wage gain of public employees and ignore the more detailed cost implications of the modified pay plan.

In summary, the form of public sector collective bargaining is generally similar to that found in the private sector. In both situations, the parties are trying to increase their bargaining power relative to their opponent's by increasing the cost to the opponent of disagreeing with the party's position or by reducing the cost to the opponent of agreeing with the party's position. This section also highlighted some differences in public and private sector bargaining processes. Once these differences are acknowledged and understood, one can better appreciate the public sector as it fits into the overall framework of labor-management relations in the United States.

Development of Labor Relations in State and Local Governments

Historical Developments

The first municipal employees to join unions were skilled laborers—members of craft unions that recruited both private and public employees. Later, other public employees (sanitation workers, firefighters, teachers, and police, for example) organized into separate unions. There were a number of real successes in the early days of municipal collective bargaining. The Chicago Teachers' Federation won salary increases in 1902, street cleaners in Providence won a Saturday half-holiday in 1907, and New York Patrolmen's Benevolent Association won several salary increases and a three-platoon system between 1890 and 1907. There were also failures—most notably, the Boston police strike (1919) which helped launch the successful presidential campaign of Calvin Coolidge. The Boston police commissioner refused to recognize an agreement that had been negotiated with the mayor, and 1,100 men struck. After minor violence and looting, Governor Coolidge called out the state guard to control what he portrayed in the press as a major insurrection. The strikers were dismissed and replaced, and Coolidge became a national hero.[36] More importantly, the notoriety gained by the Boston strike dampened development of unionization in the public sector for some time, especially in the twenties and early thirties.

Struggling against unfavorable publicity and adverse state laws, local ordinances, and departmental regulations, the unions' activities during the 1920s were devoted primarily to their own survival. During the 1930s, public employees strengthened their membership totals and organizations. The American Federation of State, County and Municipal Employees (AFSCME) was organized in 1935, and other public employee unions such as the American Federation of Teachers and the International Association of Firefighters regained their pre-1920s strength.[37] Steady progress continued until the 1950s, but substantial growth began in the late fifties and early sixties. Reasons for this growth include:

1. The AFL-CIO merger in 1955, which allowed a more unified labor effort.
2. More favorable legislation, local ordinances, and public attitudes.
3. Favorable legislation permitting federal sector collective bargaining (discussed in Chapter 15), which encouraged state and local employees to pursue their own collective bargaining interests.

Although the states of New York and Wisconsin showed the most activity in the legislative area in the early sixties, most states today and many of the larger cities have now passed legislation that sets up a legal framework for labor relations in their state or city, even though many do not have applicable statewide legislation. Employees in states having no legislation setting up a labor relations framework still have the legal right to be members of unions or employee associations as a result of the *AFSCME, AFL-CIO v. Woodward* (406 F.2d 137 [1969]) decision, which stated that the right of employees to join unions is protected by the First and Fourteenth Amendments and public administrators who deny these rights are subject to court action for damages under the Civil Rights Act of 1871.[38]

Current Membership Status in State and Local Government Employee Unions and Organizations

State and local governments had 4,702,228 full-time employees who were members of labor unions or employee organizations in 1975, a decrease of 0.5 percent from 1974. There were 11,895 state and local governments that either engaged in collective negotiations or participated in meet-and-confer discussions with representatives of the employees. School districts are the most organized, followed by municipalities and state governments.[39] Table 14–3 demonstrates that the percentage of union membership is higher in local governments than in state governments, with the exception of employees in highway departments and hospitals. Overall, in both state and local government, the highest percentage of membership is in education, fire protection, and police protection. Yet, collective bargaining in state and local governments is far from universal; only 15.2 percent of the 78,268 state and local units engage in collective negotiations and hold meet-and-confer sessions with employee representatives.[40]

Table 14–3
Percent of Full-Time Employees Organized by Function and Level of Government, 1975

Function	State and Local Governments	State Governments	Local Governments
Total	49.9	39.6	53.9
Education	58.0	28.6	64.7
Highways	46.3	59.0	34.4
Public welfare	39.0	37.5	40.2
Hospitals	42.1	50.2	33.1
Police protection	54.0	47.4	55.0
Local fire protection	72.4	—	72.4
Sanitation other than sewerage	48.1	—	48.1
All other functions	36.9	37.5	36.6

Source: U.S. Department of Commerce, Bureau of the Census, *Labor-Management Relations in State and Local Governments: 1975* (Washington, D.C.: Government Printing Office, 1977), p. 1.

State and Local Government Labor Relations Policies, Statutes, Executive Orders, and Ordinances

State and local government units and labor unions may establish their labor relations framework in several ways: by policy, statute, executive order, or ordinance. By 1975, 15 percent of the local governments had labor relations policies or related guidelines, whereas 88 percent of the state governments and 48 percent of the nation's school districts had policies.

An analysis of the existing laws and policies suggests that favorable legislation is concentrated in the states located in the Northeast, North, Midwest, West Coast, Alaska, and Hawaii. The so-called sunbelt states, located in the lower Atlantic Coast, Southeast (except the state of Florida), Southwest, and lower Rocky Mountains, generally do not have labor relations legislation that comprehensively covers the public sector (that is, covering administrative agency, bargaining rights, scope of bargaining, impasse provisions, unfair labor practices, and strike provisions).[41] By 1977, most states (thirty-seven) prescribed bargaining over wages, hours, terms of employment, and working conditions for some or all public employees. In fact, a majority of the states now have statutory limitations, such as management rights, on the scope of collective bargaining.[42]

Another important element of labor legislation is unfair labor practices. Although these vary somewhat from state to state, most states (thirty-five) have legislation defining unfair labor practices for some or all public employees. The existing legislation typically prohibits strikes. Exceptions to outright prohibition are twofold: either they are not mentioned in the statute, or the states (Alaska, Hawaii, Minnesota, Montana, Oregon, Pennsylvania, Vermont, and Wisconsin) allow strikes only under specific circumstances.

Municipal and county policies tend to have similar provisions and coverage. The bargaining obligation is enforced by an administrative agency and includes either the duty to bargain or to meet and confer over such topics as wages, hours, and terms of employment. Strikes are usually prohibited, and procedures have been established in the event an impasse occurs.

Provisions in Collective Bargaining Agreements —State, County, and Municipal Employees

Unions representing state, county, and municipal employees generally negotiate collective bargaining agreements similar to those negotiated in the private sector. These agreements in the public sector fall into two categories: (a) contractual agreements and (b) memoranda of understanding. A Census Bureau study reported 25,770 agreements in effect between state and local governments and their respective employee organizations in 1975.[43] Although specific bargaining items, such as merit system subjects, are often excluded by statute, most issues are quite similar to those negotiated in the private sector.[44]

Many bargaining issues cut across public employee job classifications. Wages, for example, are a concern of state, local, and county employees regardless of their particular job duties. However, as indicated in Chapter 1, the technological features of the workplace can generate certain unique work rules and concerns. For example, firefighters and police are often more concerned than other public employees about safety provisions. In 1975, nearly 50 percent of all firefighters were injured on the job.[45] Labor and management officials have explored technological advances (improved fire hose nozzles, fire coats, chemicals, and so on); however, many of these improvements require rather large expenditures. For example, one company has introduced "Rapid Water," a chemical additive that reduces friction in the fire hoses, resulting in 50 percent more flow with the same pump pressure. Yet in 1975, only 20 of the nation's approximately 25,000 fire departments spent funds to obtain this system.[46]

Police are also concerned about safety problems; a recent demand by a Washington, D.C., policemen's union sought two related proposals: (a) better marksmanship training and (b) deadlier, "all-lead semi-wadcutter" bullets, which are used in other cities.[47] In some cases, safety issues can involve broader issues of management's right to schedule and direct the working force. One of the more emotional issues in police negotiations concerns one-person versus two-person squad cars. Management wants the freedom to assign one-person cars on the basis of crime data reported for various areas and shifts. The unions want two-person cars to maximize patrolman safety under unsafe street conditions.[48] Police are also concerned about other job-related issues, for example, the benefit of "false-arrest" insurance.[49]

Types of Impasse Procedures: Description and Effectiveness

Although statutes usually prohibit public employee strikes, policy makers recognize that neither no-strike legislation nor related penalties for striking are sufficient for obtaining labor peace. Consequently, impasse procedures are established in many states and localities as a substitute for the strike alternative.[50] These procedures normally involve a third party, who assists the parties in reaching an agreement without interrupting services or endangering the public interest.

Public sector impasse procedures are controversial and have received considerable attention; they have been instituted in thirty-eight states. The most popular impasse procedure combines mediation, fact-finding, and arbitration (available in twenty states); a variety of other forms also exist: arbitration only (eight states), fact-finding only (seven states), mediation and fact-finding (nine states).[51]

Mediation The oldest and most common public sector impasse procedure, *mediation* works much like the process in the private sector in that a neutral attempts to persuade the parties to a labor dispute to settle their own differences. In these efforts, the mediator keeps the talks going, translates and analyzes positions and proposals, helps identify what is important and what is expendable, assists each party's evaluation of a particular issue, influences the bargaining climate, makes suggestions, exerts pressure where and when necessary, and remains even-handed and neutral.[52]

The advantages of public sector mediation are also similar to those found in the private sector[53] (discussed in Chapter 7). Mediation has worked well in those disputes where the parties were inexperienced in labor relations and unsure of themselves, lacked knowledge of contract language, and were susceptible to personality conflicts. It has been less successful where strong pressures from constituents were present, resources were scarce, and sophisticated negotiators who could manipulate the procedures to their own tactical advantage were involved. This can be especially true when mediation is followed by another impasse procedure, such as by fact-finding or arbitration.[54] In comparison, mediation works better when followed by arbitration than by fact-finding, especially when the type of arbitration is final offer selection.[55]

Mediation has been used quite often in local and state government negotiations. For example, the Federal Mediation and Conciliation Service (FMCS) has reported dramatic increases in numbers of cases closed. Because the FMCS will generally defer to state and local agencies if they are available, the largest percentage of cases for this agency have occurred in states having either new public collective bargaining laws or active unions but no applicable laws.[56] However, there are other indications of the success of mediation as a process of dispute resolution. In New York, 30 percent of all negotiations eventually resulted in an impasse, and half of these (or 15 percent of the total) were settled by mediation. This percentage does not include all those disputes settled prior to impasse with the assistance of mediators.[57]

Fact-Finding and Arbitration Fact-finding and arbitration are separate impasse resolution procedures; however, they are discussed and assessed jointly because of their many similarities. *Fact-finding*, the second most popular type of impasse procedure, is a process in which a neutral (a fact finder) conducts a hearing where management and the union define the issues in dispute and each party proposes its own resolutions supported with evidence and justifications. The fact finder then studies the materials provided and in many cases structures a position on the basis of what management and union will accept.[58] However, these recommendations are not binding, and the parties may accept them or not.[59]

This procedure is similar in many respects to arbitration: both procedures are quasi-judicial in that both management and the union have similar obligations in preparing and proving their respective cases, and both parties are bound by similar concepts of conduct and evidence in defending their positions. Also, the neutrals have similar roles in that they must objectively assess the evidence and in many cases develop rationales for their eventual decisions. The fundamental difference between the two processes is that arbitration is final and binding and by definition terminates the impasse, whereas fact-finding is terminal only if both parties agree to conform to the fact finder's report and recommendation.[60]

Arbitration of negotiation impasses (interest arbitration) can be classified as voluntary or compulsory and as conventional or final offer selection.[61] In *voluntary arbitration,* the parties voluntarily agree to submit issues to a third party neutral for dispute resolution, whereas in *compulsory arbitration* the parties are required by statute, city ordinance, or court decree to submit unresolved issues to arbitration. *Conventional interest arbitration* involves submitting the issues in dispute to the arbitrator, who will make a settlement, based on the proposals presented by the parties, within the extremes of the public employer's and the union's last offers. Often, interest arbitrators have been accused of compromising or splitting the difference between these offers in an attempt to please everybody.

Final offer selection (FOS) arbitration is a relatively new procedure in which the union submits its final demand for settlement and management submits its final offer to the arbitrator, who selects the most reasonable final offer without modifications.[62] It attempts to make the failure to agree more expensive by eliminating the arbitrator's discretion and avoiding any arbitral compromise whatsoever. The theory on which this type of arbitration is based is that each party will develop a more realistic final position, hoping that it will be accepted by the arbitrator. Both parties bargain in earnest up to the point of arbitration, increasing the chances that they will resolve or at least reduce their differences.[63]

Fact-finding and arbitration share several basic advantages that help to show why they have gained acceptance in the public sector:

1. Both help to conclude the negotiations process, which could otherwise drag on indefinitely, since they give the parties deadlines for resolving their differences.
2. The neutrals in both processes provide fresh viewpoints and ap-

proaches to the unresolved issues. Because of their experience in similar situations, many are able to provide insights to the issues not available from the parties themselves.

3. These processes can offer the parties political advantages in resolving their impasse. Both the public employer and the union can use the neutral as a buck-passing device for the eventual settlement—they can blame the fact finder or the arbitrator instead of themselves if they don't receive a completely desirable settlement. In some cases, the union and management negotiators are in close agreement; however, they need to persuade their constituents that the settlement is equitable. Fact-finding can help structure public opinion and prepare the public for the negotiated settlements.

4. The mere possibility of these procedures may encourage the parties to resolve the dispute on their own. This would particularly be the case if one or both of the parties feared the neutral outsider would not understand its position. Thus, fact-finding or arbitration may serve to keep the parties "honest" in attempting to resolve their differences.[64]

Fact-finding and arbitration also have their disadvantages. Although they may resolve issues for the short run, both procedures have been accused of leaving the two parties in disharmony.

1. If either party is not receptive to the fact finder's report or the arbitrator's decision, the basic causes of their differences have not been resolved—much negotiation remains to settle the real differences. A related concern is that neither process can guarantee that there will be no strike, slow-down, sick-in, blue flu, or similar tactic. Fact finders have no binding authority over the parties, and arbitrators usually do not have access to information that accurately sets priorities for the true interests and preferences of the parties.

2. Fact-finding and arbitration tend to cement positions, because the parties believe that there is a possibility of getting a better deal from the arbitrator or a more favorable report from the fact finder.[65] Instead of earnestly attempting to resolve their differences in the final negotiations, the representatives focus their time and thoughts on preparing for the fact finder or arbitrator.

3. The role of the fact finder or arbitrator has often been challenged, since these individuals are not held accountable for their decisions. Neither is elected by the taxpayers, and often the official comes from a different town or state. Many politicians have claimed that they do not want to give the keys to the government's treasury to an "outsider" or a "limousine liberal," who makes the decision and then leaves town.[66]

Describing impasse procedures is much simpler than assessing their effectiveness for two main reasons: (1) there are problems in obtaining relevant operational data, and (2) it is difficult to control for the many variables that influence the bargaining process and outcomes.[67] The following section summarizes findings and opinions of noted experts who have examined the effectiveness of fact-finding and arbitration at the state and local levels.

Effectiveness of fact-finding and arbitration. Assessing fact-finding is particularly difficult. Its effectiveness does not hinge on the fact finder's ability; this individual is presented facts by the parties in hopes that he or she will agree with their respective positions. The success of such a procedure is based on the assumption that the fact finder's report will structure public opinion, which will in turn place pressure on the parties to resolve their differences in accord with published recommendations. Thus far, there is no concrete evidence to show that public pressure has noticeably affected public sector management and union officials. Indeed, one experienced fact finder has observed:

I do not view fact-finding as being quite the exact science your administrative agency believes (or hopes) it to be. For these [*sic*] of you who have visions of becoming cultural heroes as a result of your peacemaking efforts, you are probably in for a disappointment. In most instances such status will be rudely denied you—by the parties, by the public, and most grievously, by your fellow fact finders. Fact-finding, in short, is not an endeavor that flatters the ego. As for the distinctive contribution of your carefully wrought analysis, most of you, I suspect, will eventually come around to the view, as I have, that aside from poison [pen] letters and ransom notes, there is probably no literary form in which there is less pride of authorship than a fact-finding report.[68]

Studies conducted in two states (New York and Wisconsin) found that both labor and management officials have rejected relatively high proportions of fact finders' recommendations (39 percent and 51 percent respectively).[69] A similar, more recent observation of Florida's experience found an even higher rate of fact finder rejections.[70] Over the years, acceptance of fact-finding as a dispute resolution procedure dwindles, especially when there is a high percentage of rejection and where parties incorporate fact-finding into their bargaining tactics (primarily to postpone a settlement).[71]

Overall, interest arbitration in the public sector seems to have passed the test, at least in the short run; most of the participants as well as the analysts have been satisfied with the process. It has not substantially lessened serious negotiations despite its availability. Also, the number of strikes has been reduced substantially in cases where employees have been covered by compulsory arbitration legislation. Even though some management officials feared arbitration, arbitrators have not stripped them of their rights and authority. The settlements have not been significantly greater than the parties would have reached themselves in similar circumstances, and the public in general has not openly indicated displeasure with the process. Most significantly, arbitration has been increasingly adopted as an impasse resolution procedure in the public sector, and the parties express satisfaction with the initial experience.[72]

One of the bigger concerns about public sector interest arbitration is its *chilling effect* on the parties' incentives to reach their own agreement. If either believed that it could get a better settlement from an arbitrator than from negotiation, there would be an incentive to maintain excessive demands in hopes that the arbitrator would "split the difference" and make a favorable award. When one side acts in such a manner, the other side has no realistic choice but to respond similarly, widening the gap between the parties.[73]

Research into this arbitral aspect has produced mixed results. An analysis of arbitral decisions regarding police impasses found that some management officials are reluctant to negotiate their best offer before arbitration on the assumption that the arbitrators will use management's final offer as a starting point in their decisions.[74] Yet this concern is somewhat dampened by a study of several arbitration awards of fire-fighter interest disputes, which revealed that a large majority of arbitrators take an intermediate or compromise stance between the union's and management's stance on a few negotiation issues, such as wages and clothing allowances. However, arbitration settlements did not compromise the other issues; they either supported management's or the union's final position. It seems that there is no guarantee that arbitrators will compromise any or all of the issues presented for their decisions.[75]

Another concern about public sector interest arbitration is that the mere existence of impasse procedures could create a *narcotic effect*. That is, once the parties start using the procedures, they become increasingly reliant upon them in subsequent negotiations. In New York, the impasse procedure covering police and firefighters changed from fact-finding with recommendations followed by hearings to fact-finding terminating in conventional compulsory arbitration. This switch to arbitration in the first year resulted in an increased probability of going to impasse and to the final step of the procedure by approximately 16 percent. Research revealed a definite narcotic effect pattern of reusage of impasse procedure.[76] However, researchers found no more of a chilling effect under arbitration than under fact-finding in New York.[77]

Several states (Iowa, Massachusetts, Michigan, Minnesota, and Wisconsin) and at least two municipalities (Indianapolis and Eugene, Oregon) have had experience with final offer selection arbitration. Experiences in these settings as compared to conventional interest arbitration have been analyzed closely by Peter Feuille, who concluded:

Final offer arbitration does a reasonably good job of protecting the parties' incentives to negotiate but . . . it does not operate as effectively as its theoretical rationale suggests it could. . . .

However, over time there seems to be a general tendency for the parties to increase their reliance upon the final-offer procedures either as a forum for continued negotiations or as a source of an imposed settlement. This increased usage may be related to the lack of costs attached to declaring impasse and using the early steps of the impasse procedure.[78]

After examining data from the city of Eugene, Oregon, and the states of Wisconsin and Massachusetts, Feuille and Dworkin found little support for the criticism that final offer arbitrators tend to balance the winners and losers over a longer period of time.[79]

Arbitrator Witney concluded from his experiences in Indianapolis, Indiana, that final offer arbitration is successful in that it has been accepted by the parties, prevented strikes, and resulted in no subsequent work slowdowns or interruptions of services. Yet he also felt that arbitration would be more effective if arbitrators were given more flexibility in which to rule on the merits of the multitude of issues to be decided.[80]

Flexibility, however, is relative, and arbitrator Theodore Kheel believes at least some guidance is needed to insure that the arbitration award is realistic and appropriate. He found when he served as the first arbitrator to be appointed under the applicable 1968 statute in Pennsylvania that there were no guidelines regarding wage determination. The union contended that the arbitrator should determine what a policeman is worth in today's society. Management, on the other hand, argued that the arbitrator should be guided by the fiscal responsibilities and limitations of the deficit-ridden municipal government. Without guidelines, the arbitrator's award could have been grossly out of line with either management's or the union's legitimate concerns.[81] The degree of arbitral flexibility should possibly depend on the nature of the issues to be resolved. For example, a study in Eugene, Oregon, found that certain "yes-no" positions, such as the union's insistence on agency shop (a worker does not join the union but pays a service fee equal to dues) versus the city's proposal for maintenance of membership shop (once joining the union, a member must continue membership for the duration of the contract), are difficult to resolve through final offer selection arbitration.[82]

Referendum Another impasse resolution procedure places the unresolved issues on a taxpayer referendum or vote. The following item, for example, might be placed on a ballot: "Do you approve of granting a wage increase of 'X' cents per hour to our police officers at an estimated additional annual cost to property taxpayers of 'Y' millions?"[83]

This procedure would avoid the problems of an outsider (fact finder or arbitrator) determining the cost of a negotiated settlement. Citizens could not complain if the union's settlement was achieved in a democratic manner. Similarly, the union's integrity would be at stake if it refused to abide by the "will of the public." Yet, this procedure could turn collective bargaining into a public relations campaign directed at a body of individuals (citizens) largely unfamiliar with labor relations' complexities. Further, the procedure has no precedent in private sector labor relations, since no company submits labor agreement proposals to a stockholder vote.

Additional Options While mediation, arbitration, and fact-finding remain the most commonly used procedures, various states have started to experiment with various forms of impasse procedures. For example, Massachusetts provides mediation followed by final offer selection arbitration. Hawaii and other states allow some strikes after mediation and/or fact-finding have been tried. The New Jersey law that covers police and firefighters allows the parties to choose from a variety of options: final offer package, final offer issue by issue, final offer on some issues, conventional arbitration, and so on. Iowa allows parties to negotiate their own impasse procedures for local use. While there are many options, there is no single best way to resolve labor disputes. However, the multiple objectives remain the same: to avoid strikes, to minimize dependence on outsiders, to maximize "good faith" bargaining between parties, to protect the public interest, and to build a commitment to accountability and mutual problem solving.[84]

This section on labor relations in state and local governments included a brief description of historical development; status of union membership; labor relations policies, statutes, executive orders, and ordinances; the subjects in collective bargaining; and the variety of impasse procedures. While labor relations in state and local governments is rapidly developing and offers unique complexities for students to consider, the following section provides specific application to a sector of society with which students should immediately identify—the academic community.

Labor Relations Application to the Academic Community: Teachers and Professors

In this labor relations application, teachers at the elementary and high school levels and professors at the college level are treated as one occupational group, because they share many common working conditions. However, some characteristics and working conditions unique to different educational levels will be cited when appropriate. Collective bargaining has also involved students, research and graduate student assistants, and college administrators at some campuses, but space limitations do not allow discussion in this section.[85]

Development and Growth of Unions in the Teaching Profession

While teachers' unions date back to the late nineteenth century, it was not until the 1960s that many teachers turned to collective bargaining to resolve issues in education. One of the early attempts for union recognition and negotiation involved the Norwalk, Connecticut, teachers in 1946. The school board refused to recognize and negotiate with the teacher organization, which in turn appealed to the state supreme court. The court decided that the board could negotiate if it so desired but the teachers could not force the board to negotiate. Furthermore, it ruled that the board had full authority to make decisions concerning school matters and this authority could not be delegated. The court agreed that the board could bargain collectively over wages, hours, and employment conditions but only the school board had authority to make decisions.[86] However, teachers through collective bargaining could provide useful inputs for these decisions.

The Norwalk decision publicized teacher unionization, but the major breakthrough occurred in New York City in 1961. After considerable negotiations and a strike, the board of education accepted collective bargaining and agreed to an election for choosing a bargaining agent. The United Federation of Teachers—a local of the American Federation of Teachers (AFT)—won an overwhelming victory for its members, representing over 30,000 teachers.

The increasing acceptability of collective bargaining resulted in professional teacher associations changing their emphasis to traditional union concerns. A rival of the AFT, the National Education Association (NEA) decided to become more aggressive in collective bargaining and union activities, especially after losing major elections to the AFT in several major metropolitan centers in the Northeast.[87] By 1977, the two major teacher organizations, AFT and NEA, had grown to be among the largest employee organizations in the United States, with 441,000 and 1,679,689 members, respectively.[88]

The secondary and elementary school teachers prompted college and university faculty members to become more interested in engaging in collective bargaining activities. By 1977, almost 25 percent of the full-time faculty members were covered by collective bargaining agreements.[89] In 1978, unions had been chosen to represent the faculty on 600 campuses; on only 77 had they been rejected.[90] The biggest successes have been at two-year community colleges, but key victories have also occurred at some of the largest and most respected schools in the country (State University of New York, University of Hawaii, Temple University, Rutgers University, State University System of Florida, University of Massachusetts, and University of Illinois). In several states (Massachusetts, New Jersey, Connecticut, Rhode Island, New York, Delaware, and Hawaii) nearly every public institution of higher education is organized. Similarly, with the exception of large research-oriented universities, nearly all institutions in Michigan, Pennsylvania, and Minnesota are organized.[91] But generally, unionism in higher education has remained mostly in public institutions where state laws permit collective bargaining.

While education unions have developed in private institutions, they remain primarily a public sector phenomenon. Whether they will continue to grow as in the past few years will depend on the following factors:

□ Salary levels keeping up with prices.

□ Success in organizing areas that have been difficult to organize, for example, the South and Southwest.[92]

□ Increases in the number of states having public employee bargaining laws, since collective bargaining tactics depend on having established and recognized unions.[93]

□ Improvements in union organizing efforts, such as more funds, reduction in union rivalry, and possible merging of efforts.

□ Continuing reductions in educators' positions and relative salaries caused by falling student population and shifting public interests and attitudes.

□ Continuing attacks on tenure and other forms of job security and protective policies by administrators.[94]

□ Whether the NLRB continues jurisdiction over private colleges and universities.

Bargaining Units

The NLRB decided in 1970 to assert jurisdiction over private, nonprofit colleges and universities, admitting openly that it was venturing into uncharted areas.[95] The same could have been said about public education institutions in various states with no statutory guidance or with state laws widely varied in content.[96]

Deciding the appropriate bargaining unit in elementary and secondary schools has not been as complex as in higher education, but it has been complicated by the ambiguous role of the principal. The principal represents the board of education and school superintendents in many situations and then joins the teachers in other situations. Principals' status is further complicated by the failure of most state laws to prescribe whether they should be included with the teachers, organize a union of their own, or remain separate from the teachers and represent the board and superintendents. Whatever the situation, they have a key role in any negotiations that affect the policies, programs, and working climate of their schools.[97]

Defining the appropriate bargaining unit in higher education is often a complex task given the collegial decision-making process and relatively active role played by faculty members in the governance of the institution. Some more complex cases have involved such issues as: (a) multicampus, multidepartmental universities in one or more units and (b) the exemption or inclusion of department chairpersons, principal investigators on research units, visiting lecturers, adjunct professors, librarians, administrative support personnel, and graduate teaching/research assistants.[98] In some cases, certain academic departments can be exempted from the major bargaining unit. Certain disciplines, such as medicine and law, may claim a community of interest different enough to warrant their exclusion from the major bargaining unit.

The provisions of labor agreements in education are similar to those in other occupations in many ways; nonetheless, some provisions (for instance, those on faculty governance, types and duties of committees, selection and duties of administrators, content and access to personnel files, faculty reduction, overload, compensation for extra courses, academic freedom, office space, and professional development[99]) are unique to educators. In elementary and secondary schools, additional issues may include definition of the school day and year, number and duration of after-school meetings, nonteaching duties such as bus duty and selling tickets at athletic events, competency testing, rotation of classes, selection of textbooks, class size and teaching loads, curriculum development, student discipline, preparation time, use of free time, use of automated teaching methodologies, access to personnel files, and teacher evaluation.[100]

Discipline One of the more significant employment concerns of elementary teachers relates to student discipline and violence. Senator Birch Bayh, chairman of the Senate Subcommittee to Investigate Juvenile Delinquency, has noted that school violence and vandalism have increased in frequency and intensity, making the already difficult tasks of education nearly impossible. Indeed, the estimated 1974 expenditures to repair school vandalism ($590 million) exceeded the total amount spent on textbooks in 1972.[101]

Student violence and vandalism might reflect more permissive parental and administrative attitudes that in turn can make it more difficult for teachers to adequately perform their administrative duties. Comments from teachers tend to reflect this frustration:

Once you are in that classroom you're all alone. Lots of discipline problems go unreported: verbal assaults, a teacher gets shoved. Sometimes it's just easier to forget it all. If you complain or report it, there's always the implication that maybe you're incapable of handling your own problems. . . .

I taught one high school reading class where I could look out my window and watch kids getting high behind the trunk of one of the pine trees. When I complained about it, I was told that the kids hadn't been caught smoking marijuana and so nothing could be done. But all the principal had to do was come up to my classroom and look out the window; the principal couldn't be bothered to do that.[102]

Job Security Another issue confronting educators at all levels is job security. Academicians in higher education who are renowned consider job security irrelevant, since they are eagerly sought by many colleges and universities.[103] But most faculty members are not in this position, particularly those in disciplines supplying more applicants than available jobs. Recently, for example, there have been over 400 applications for one college-level English professorship, and some prestigious schools have received 5,000 applications for a similar position. [104]

As the school population has declined and the labor market changed, job security has been affected in other ways. First, institutions have rapidly increased use of part-time or adjunct instructors, who usually receive less money and need few if any supporting services such as office space or student assistants. Part-time instructors also contribute to administrative flexibility because they can be hired for specific courses and dismissed after the course is completed. [105]

Second, more schools appear to be restricting new faculty positions and the number of instructors who can receive tenure. [106] Tenure has been labeled by some as a device that locks an inept professor into a job for life with no possibility of removal. Actually, tenured faculty members can be removed but only for just cause and only after going through appropriate procedures. [107] As is true in other industries, tenure places the burden of proof on academic administrators to justify their discharge decisions.

The tenure and just cause concepts have long been challenged in the courts by both tenured and nontenured teachers (for example, single, female teachers who were discharged because they were pregnant) who believe they have inherent rights to their jobs. [108] Judicial decisions on such cases appear to be contradictory; however, teachers continue to seek due process redress in the courts. Unions continue to approach the tenure issue in collective bargaining by seeking formal justification in cases where tenure is denied[109] and by clarifying the peer review process. [110]

Negotiations

Although the inclusion of these issues in a labor agreement formalizes the policies and procedures, many teachers and administrators have found lately that collective bargaining is time-consuming and costly, particularly in terms of negotiators' preparation. Some factors influencing the length of negotiations are the scope of prior agreement, the degree of impasse, the bargaining itself, team changes during negotiations, and the extent to which professionals are used in the bargaining process. [111] Negotiations might be prolonged over issues such as compensation for extra duty, teacher work loads, length of the school day, association and union rights, grievance procedures, salary, fringe benefits, paid leaves, and roll-back of previous rights. [112]

Collective bargaining might also be delayed when unions are unable to locate the appropriate managerial decision maker—as frequently happens in the bargaining process. In some cases, the union negotiates with administrators who do not have authority to sign a bargaining agreement; in others, it is prohibited from negotiating with officials who do have the authority to approve the agreement. A recent Supreme Court decision has given teachers some flexibility in this area. [113] In essence, the decision holds that a school board meeting open to the public cannot exclude teachers from presenting their opinions on the collective bargaining sessions and agreement.

Strikes and Teacher Militancy

Strikes are infrequent in education, though the ones that occur receive much publicity. For example, the 152 strikes in 1977–1978 represented less than 1 percent of the total teacher bargaining relationships.[114] There have been a number of attempts to identify predictors and causes of strikes and teacher militancy. Research suggests that the propensity to strike is influenced by personal characteristics of the strikers. For example, support for strikes has been greatest among male teachers, younger teachers, teachers with advanced degrees, and junior and senior high school teachers.[115] Other studies, however, question whether the teacher's personal characteristics explain strike activity.[116] This research suggests that more general environmental factors (such as general labor market conditions, consumer prices, and a permissive bargaining climate[117]) help explain the frequency of teacher strikes.

The relatively few strikes in higher education have involved mostly the two-year community colleges represented by the American Federation of Teachers. Generally, the difficulties in reaching agreement can be traced to either the lack of experience of the negotiators on the first contract or the wage issue. Most of these strikes have been brief and have caused little loss in enrollment or faculty salary; they have occurred mostly at the beginning of the fall term, some causing a postponement of fall opening, temporary closing of college dormitories and food services, and rescheduling of classes to compensate for lost time; but thus far no fall sessions have been cancelled by strikes.[118]

This new militancy and aggressive behavior in negotiations and organizing efforts have generally resulted from a number of factors. One significant factor is the attitude of university administrators toward faculty unions. Some evidence suggests that administrators tend to view them in negative terms, although a more positive administrator response tends to be found at universities with collective bargaining experience.[119]

In many cases, initial labor-management relationships in this occupation do not differ from similar relationships in the private sector. Administrators become upset when employees express dissatisfaction by joining a union, and union leaders have to take a strong antimanagement stance to prove their mettle. Thus, the initial negotiations are often conducted in an atmosphere of bitterness. For example, in one such incident, the union leader called the university president the "Idi Amin of Higher Education." The university president responded by asking the professors, "Do you want to be guided by degenerate fools?"[120]

Militancy and hostile collective bargaining attitudes among teachers may also be affected by one or more of the following interrelated factors:

☐ Teachers' beliefs that unions will help them achieve better salaries and economic benefits.

□ Demographic changes among teachers; for example, more males, lower turnover.

□ Teachers' desire to have a stronger voice in formulating rules and policies that control their work lives.

□ More favorable legislation concerning collective bargaining.

□ Better training and educational preparation and increased emphasis on professionalism among teachers.

□ AFT-NEA rivalry, causing each organization to become more aggressive and militant.

□ Defensive reaction by teachers to the continuing and widespread criticism of public education at all levels.

□ Changes in the climate of and attitudes toward collective actions and political activism, which have become both effective and fashionable.[121]

□ Teacher reaction to Proposition 13–like legislation and other tax-cutting measures.[122]

Effects of Collective Bargaining

Two areas of teacher collective bargaining that have had pronounced impact are wages and collegiality (shared administrative activities).

Wages Unions have had mixed success in increasing wages in education. In some instances, academic unions have had little[123] or no[124] success in increasing wages, while other situations have reflected a markedly positive union influence on higher wages.[125] Realistically speaking, it is difficult, if not impossible, to isolate the single causal factor of higher teacher salaries. Yet collective bargaining has notably affected the wage structure, if not total wages.[126] In some cases, proportionately higher wage increases have gone to the higher ranked and more senior faculty members.[127] In other cases, negotiated wage settlements have emphasized across-the-board increases that tended to deemphasize differences in teacher competency, experience, and academic discipline.

Union emphasis on across-the-board increases may pose problems for managements and unions, particularly in higher education. For example, some higher educational disciplines, such as medicine, law, and accounting, have relatively few available applicants, particularly since academicians in these areas could command much higher salaries in related private sector endeavors. While across-the-board increases may benefit the greatest number of union members, academic unions' long-term success will depend on the degree of membership consensus. Thus, the extent to which the market-privileged groups can influence the unions' egalitarian wage policies is still subject to speculation. There is a strong possibility that these groups will feel their wages proportionately lessened by across-the-board wage settlements, and their dissatisfaction may lead to internal union squabbles that could in turn undermine the success and existence of academic unions.

Collegiality Collective bargaining has also altered traditional forms of faculty governance. Many schools, particularly at the university level, have emphasized *collegiality*—an attitude that faculty should have input into administrative decisions (for instance, those involving course content, graduation requirements, and promotion of faculty members) because they have professional expertise and concerns. Collegiality has been traditionally fostered through two mechanisms: (a) faculty senates and (b) faculty committees (for example, the promotion and tenure committee).

Some maintain that collegiality is more symbol than substance,[128] since most if not all faculty recommendations can be vetoed by an administrative official such as the university president. Following this line of reasoning, administrators can use collegiality to their own benefit. Assume, for example, that the faculty promotion and tenure committee recommends that a particular faculty member not be promoted. The administrative official who has the final say on the matter can either overturn or support the committee's position. In either instance, the administrator's task is made easier. In overturning the committee's recommendation, the administrator will be a "good guy" in the eyes of the faculty member. The administrator can also absolve himself or herself of blame if he or she supports the committee's position by informing the faculty member that the decision to deny promotion was made by fellow faculty members.

Regardless of its actual usefulness, collegiality affects unions and vice versa. It can be contended that unions enhance collegiality, particularly if a grievance is subject to a neutral arbitrator (not the university administrator) for a final decision. Yet faculty unions, accepting the traditional union model, also realize that administrators are managers and the faculty members are employees. A strong union needs to present a unified protest of a particular administrative decision or action. Returning to our promotion example, assume the union grieves the promotion denial of the particular member. Its case is weakened or ruined if fellow union members on the promotion and tenure committee recommended that promotion be denied. Also, internal union dissension is increased when some members aid in an adverse managerial action taken against other union members.

Thus, unions may need to virtually eliminate the use of collegiality if they are to be successful.[129] If collegiality remains, then members can continually be played off against each other. A major problem arises when faculty members place a higher value on their continued collegial roles as quasi-administrators than on potential gains offered by the union. Apparently, this situation has occurred at the State University of New York (SUNY) system, where fewer than 4,500 people of some 15,000 in the bargaining unit are dues-paying members.[130] The success of university unions will largely depend on their ability to resolve the collegiality issue in a manner satisfactory to most members and traditional union principles.

While it seems clear that the economic, political, and demographic conditions within a given state have more effect on the quality of education than does collective bargaining,[131] there are reasons for caution in pursuing negotiations. Collective bargaining, which is usually conducted in closed meetings, may raise the level of suspicion among students, parents, and the public and cause problems to all concerned with education. Furthermore, it could create an adversarial relationship between the administration and faculty, one unsuitable for dealing with complex and delicate education matters such as curriculum design, credits required for graduation, professional conduct, and grade inflation.[132]

The complexities of labor relations, requiring procedures and policies that must be administered accurately and carefully, could also lead to an increase in administrative bureaucracy. Because all personnel decisions must be fully documented and justified, labor agreements will become larger over time and the red tape will grow in length, breadth, and width. The burgeoning bureaucracy means additional costs, such as more time in preparation and negotiations, attorney fees, and training costs,[133] none of which are particularly attractive to an increasingly cost-conscious institution.

Summary

This chapter presented an overview of public sector labor relations and collective bargaining at the local and state levels, as well as specific coverage of a public sector segment with which college students can identify—educator unions.

Public and private sector labor relations differ in numerous ways: (a) in its very nature, public service differs economically and demand-wise; (b) the effect of the budget on bargaining processes differs; (c) the bargaining structure differs, affecting decision-making processes; (d) negotiable issues and bargaining tactics tend to be less predictable; and (e) the right to strike is usually prohibited by law. Public and private sector similarities include areas like the role of personalities and skills of negotiators and the interplay of bargaining power model variables such as public opinion, political support, and various forms of job actions.

Developing first in the major metropolitan areas in the Northeast and North, unionization in state and local governments spread throughout the country. While unions struggled against unfavorable public opinion and publicity and adverse state legislation in the early days, the early sixties brought permissive legislation, favorable judicial interpretations of constitutional rights, and an increasing interest among public employees in joining unions. Such events coupled with union efforts culminated in organizational representation for a majority of employees in education, police protection, and fire protection in state and local governments.

Permissive state labor relations legislation or policy generally developed according to geography. Alaska and Hawaii passed favorable legislation as did states located on the West Coast and in the Northeast, North, and Midwest. Most of the lower Atlantic Coast, Southeast (except Florida and Tennessee), Southwest, and lower Rocky Mountain states have no permissive legislation. In states having laws, the legislation typically specifies the administrative set-up, bargaining rights, impasse procedures, unfair labor practices, and strike provisions. Within this framework, the parties attempt to negotiate labor agreements covering permissible subjects.

The impasse procedures often established as the substitute for the strike alternative include mediation, fact-finding, arbitration, and various combinations of these; the latter seem to be most popular. Such terms as *splitting the difference, chilling effect,* and *narcotic effect* have become common in assessing effectiveness of these procedures. Definitive conclusions about impasse procedures have not been made, and further research into their effectiveness is needed. However, some promising results, such as serious negotiations and low evidence of strikes, have been identified in many states. In some states, chilling effects and narcotic effects have been identified.

As an example of application, the chapter concluded with coverage of the academic community. Teachers in elementary and secondary education and professors in higher education share many common employment concerns, but different salient concerns exist at the two levels: shared governance and collegiality in higher education and student discipline in elementary and secondary schools. Future developments and problems may well stem from the decline in enrollments, scarcity of jobs, and increasing numbers of qualified graduates.

Discussion Questions

1. Think of a public organization with which you are familiar. Explain how it differs from a private company in terms of the following:
   a. nature of its service
   b. relation between its budget and collective bargaining processes
   c. bargaining structure and decision-making processes
   d. negotiable issues and bargaining tactics
   e. its right to strike

2. Using the same public organization (as in 1 above), discuss the similarities between collective bargaining in this organization and a typical negotiation between a private company and its union.

3. Give reasons why unions developed later in the public sector than in the private sector, especially at the local level.

4. Public sector labor relations legislation differs on a geographic basis. Explain why this might have occurred.

5. Describe the different types of impasse procedures used in the public sector and discuss the relative effectiveness of each.

6. Compare the chilling effect and the narcotic effect as they pertain to negotiations and impasse procedures in the public sector.

7. How does shared governance or collegiality affect collective bargaining in higher education? For what reasons do administrative officials in higher education prefer shared governance over collective bargaining?

8. Considering the predicted decline in school enrollment, a growing scarcity of faculty positions, and an increasing number of available instructors, what are the prospects for increased unionization and collective bargaining in public educational institutions? Explain.

9. At the school that you attend, are faculty members "managerial employees" as described by the circuit court of appeals in the Yeshavia University case (see footnote 95)?

References

[1]Robert E. Walsh, ed., *Sorry . . . No Government Today: Unions vs. City Hall* (Boston: Beacon Press, 1969); and A. Lawrence Chickering, ed., *Public Employee Unions: A Study of the Crisis in Public Sector Labor Relations* (San Francisco: Institute of Contemporary Studies, 1976).

[2]Bureau of National Affairs, *Government Employee Relations Reporter,* September 19, 1977, p. 726:24. Government employee membership in unions is 20.1 percent of the total government employment and 39.2 percent if employee organizations are counted. See John F. Burton, Jr., "The Extent of Collective Bargaining in Public Sector," in Benjamin Aaron, Joseph R. Grodin, and James L. Stern, eds., *Public Sector Bargaining* (Washington, D.C.: Bureau of National Affairs, 1979), p. 3.

[3]B. V. H. Schneider, "Public-Sector Labor Legislation—An Evolutionary Analysis," in Aaron, Grodin, and Stern, *Public Sector Bargaining,* p. 222. See also *National League of Cities, et al. v. Usery et al.,* 426 U.S. 833 (1976).

[4]Walter Mossberg, "The Labor Movement's Maverick," *Wall Street Journal,* October 14, 1974, p. 14.

[5]Harry H. Wellington and Ralph K. Winter, Jr., *The Unions and the Cities* (Washington, D.C.: Brookings Institution, 1971), pp. 10–17.

[6]Walter Fogel and David Lewin, "Wage Determination in the Public Sector," *Industrial and Labor Relations Review* 27 (April 1974), pp. 410–431. It should be mentioned that productivity bargaining has been approached in some public sector collective bargaining situations. For a discussion of productivity considerations in public sector negotiations see Rudy Oswald, "Public Productivity Tied to Bargaining," *American Federationist* 85 (March 1976), pp. 20–21; Walter L. Balk, "Why Don't Public Administrators Take Productivity More Seriously?" *Public Personnel Management* 3 (July–August 1974), pp. 318–324; Paul D. Staudohar, "An Experiment in Increasing Productivity of Police Service Employees," *Public Administration Review* 35 (September–October 1975), pp. 518–522; and Marvin Friedman, *The Use of Economic Data in Collective Bargaining* (Washington, D.C.: Government Printing Office, 1978), pp. 53–56.

[7]Michael Moskow, J. J. Loewenberg, and E. C. Koziara, *Collective Bargaining in Public Employment* (New York: Random House, 1970), pp. 14–18; and H. H. Wellington and R. K. Winter, Jr., "Structuring Collective Bargaining in Public Employment," *Yale Law Journal* 79 (April 1970), pp. 806–822.

[8]Milton Derber et al., "Bargaining and Budget-Making in Illinois Public Institutions," *Industrial and Labor Relations Review* 27 (October 1973), pp. 49–62; and Kenneth M. Jennings, J. A. Smith, and Earle C. Traynham, Jr., "Budgetary Influences on Bargaining in Mass Transit," *Journal of Collective Negotiations in the Public Sector* 6, no. 4 (1977), pp. 333–339.

[9]Frederick O'R. Hayes, "Collective Bargaining and the Budget Director," in Sam Zagoria, ed., *Public Workers and Public Unions* (Englewood Cliffs, N.J.: Prentice-Hall, 1972), p. 91.

[10]Derber et al., "Bargaining and Budget-Making," p. 58.

[11]Arvid Anderson, "Local Government-Bargaining and the Fiscal Crisis: Money, Unions, Politics,

and the Public Interest," in James L. Stern and Barbara Dennis, eds., *Proceedings of the 1976 Annual Spring Meeting: Industrial Relations Research Association* (Chicago: Commerce Clearing House, 1976), p. 518. It should be mentioned that this board was formed to alleviate the recent fiscal crisis in New York City.

[12]William H. Holley, Jr., "Unique Complexities of Public Sector Labor Relations," *Personnel Journal* 55 (February 1976), p. 75.

[13]Stephen L. Hayford, "An Empirical Investigation of the Public Sector Supervisory Bargaining Rights Issue," *Labor Law Journal* 26 (October 1975), pp. 641–652; Alan Balfour, "Rights of Collective Representation for Public Sector Supervisors," *Journal of Collective Negotiations in the Public Sector* 4, no. 3 (1975), pp. 257–265; and William H. Holley, Jr., J. Boyd Scebra, and William Rector, "Perceptions of the Role of the Principal in Professional Negotiations," *Journal of Collective Negotiations in the Public Sector* 5, no. 4 (1976), pp. 361–369.

[14]George Hildebrand, "The Public Sector," in John T. Dunlop and Neil Chamberlain, eds., *Frontiers in Collective Bargaining* (New York: Harper & Row, 1967), pp. 126–127; Louis V. Imundo, Jr., "The Federal Government Sovereignty and Its Effect on Labor-Management Relations," *Labor Law Journal* 26 (March 1975), pp. 145–152; Louis V. Imundo, Jr., "Some Comparisons between Public Sector and Private Sector Collective Bargaining," *Labor Law Journal* 24 (December 1973), pp. 810–817. For an excellent discussion on the issue of "who is management?" in the public sector, see Milton Derber, "Management Organization for Collective Bargaining in the Public Sector," in Aaron, Grodin, and Stern, *Public Sector Bargaining*, pp. 80–117.

[15]For a vivid example of political considerations affecting collective bargaining, see A. H. Raskin, "Politics Up-ends the Bargaining Table," in Zagoria, *Public Workers*, pp. 122–146; and A. H. Raskin, "Mayor and Governor: Knee-Deep in Trouble," in Robert T. Woodworth and Richard B. Peterson, eds., *Collective Negotiation for Public and Professional Employees* (Glenview, Ill.: Scott, Foresman, 1969), pp. 288–292.

[16]For a case study example of this situation see Arnold R. Weber, "Paradise Lost: Or Whatever Happened to the Chicago Social Workers?" *Industrial and Labor Relations Review* 22 (April 1969), pp. 323–338.

[17]I. B. Helburn and N. B. Bennett, "Public Employee Bargaining and the Merit Principle," *Labor Law Journal* 23 (October 1972), p. 619; and I. B. Helburn, "The Scope of Bargaining in Public Sector Negotiations: Sovereignty Reviewed," *Journal of Collective Negotiations in the Public Sector* 3 (Spring 1974), pp. 147–166.

[18]Paul F. Gerhart, "The Scope of Bargaining in Local Government Negotiations," *Labor Law Journal* 20 (August 1969), pp. 545–552.

[19]Peter Feuille, "Police Labor Relations and Multilateralism," *Journal of Collective Negotiations in the Public Sector* 3 (Summer 1974), p. 216.

[20]Lee C. Shaw and R. Theodore Clark, Jr., "The Practical Difference between Public and Private Sector Collective Bargaining," *UCLA Law Review* 19 (August 1972), p. 885.

[21]Victor Gotbaum, "Collective Bargaining and the Union Leader," in Zagoria, *Public Workers*, pp. 83–84.

[22]Hugh Jascourt, "What Is the Effect of a 'Sunshine Law' on Public Sector Collective Bargaining: An Introduction," *Journal of Law and Education* 5 (October 1976), pp. 479–480; and Harry H. Rains, "Industrial Relations in the Public Sector," *Employee Relations Law Journal* 3 (Summer 1977), pp. 139–144.

[23]"Crime Rate Is Same Despite Police Strike," *Miami Herald*, July 20, 1975, p. 15-A.

[24]Wellington and Winter, "Structuring Collective Bargaining," pp. 822–851.

[25]George W. Taylor, "Public Employment: Strikes or Procedures?" *Industrial and Labor Relations Review* 20 (July 1967), p. 636.

[26]John F. Burton and Charles Krider, "The Role and Consequences of Strikes by Public Employees," *Yale Law Journal* 79 (January 1970), pp. 418–440.

[27]Theodore Kheel, "Resolving Deadlocks without Banning Strikes," *Monthly Labor Review* 91 (July 1969), pp. 62–63.

[28]Wellington and Winter, "Structuring Collective Bargaining," pp. 822–825.

[29]U.S. Department of Labor, Bureau of Labor Statistics, *Analysis of Work Stoppages, 1976* (Washington, D.C.: Government Printing Office, 1978), p. 17.

[30]Bonnie G. Cebulski, "Analysis of Twenty-two Illegal Strikes and California Law," *California Public Employee Relations* 18 (August 1973), pp. 2–17.

[31]Henry B. Burnett, Jr., "Interview with Jerry Wurf," *Skeptic*, May–June 1976, p. 13.

[32]Ibid., p. 54.

[33]These techniques were formulated in various discussions with Paul Gerhart of Case Western Reserve University.

[34]See, for example, Raymond D. Horton, *Municipal Labor Relations in New York City: Lessons of the Lindsay-Wagner Years* (New York: Praeger Publishers, 1973), p. 134; Michael Marmo, "Public Employee

Unions: The Political Imperative," *Journal of Collective Negotiations in the Public Sector* 4, no. 4 (1975), p. 371; and Jay F. Atwood, "Collective Bargaining's Challenge: Five Imperatives for Public Managers," *Public Personnel Management* 5 (January–February 1976), p. 29.

[35]For a discussion of the variety and legal interpretations of these strikes, see Paul D. Staudohar, "Quasi-Strikes by Public Employees," *Journal of Collective Negotiations in the Public Sector* 3 (Fall 1974), pp. 363–371.

[36]For a more detailed history of this strike as well as the history of the police labor movement see John H. Burpo, *The Police Labor Movement: Problems and Perspectives* (Springfield, Ill.: Charles C. Thomas, 1971), pp. 3–19.

[37]Hugh O'Neil, "The Growth of Municipal Employee Unions," in R. H. Convey and W. V. Farr, eds., *Unionization of Municipal Employees* (New York: Academy of Political Science, 1971), pp. 1–7.

[38]Benjamin J. Taylor and Fred Witney, *Labor Relations Law*, 2d ed. (Englewood Cliffs, N.J.: Prentice-Hall, 1975), pp. 557–570.

[39]U.S. Department of Commerce, Bureau of the Census, *Labor-Management Relations in State and Local Governments, 1975* (Washington, D.C.: Government Printing Office, 1977), p. 1.

[40]Ibid., p. 2.

[41]For analysis of public collective bargaining situations in southern states, see John R. Stepp, "The Determinants of Southern Public Employee Recognition," *Public Personnel Management* 3 (January–February 1974), pp. 59–69.

[42]Schneider, "Public-Sector Labor Legislation," pp. 192–212.

[43]U.S. Department of Commerce, Bureau of the Census, *Labor-Management Relations*, p. 4.

[44]U.S. Department of Labor, Bureau of Labor Statistics, *Municipal Collective Bargaining Agreements in Large Cities* (Washington, D.C.: Government Printing Office, 1972); and U.S. Department of Labor, Bureau of Labor Statistics, *Collective Bargaining Agreements for State or County Government Employees* (Washington, D.C.: Government Printing Office, 1976).

[45]"Labor Letter," *Wall Street Journal*, December 7, 1976, p. 1.

[46]Jeffrey A. Tannenbaum, "Frustrated Firemen: Fire Fighting Gear Improves, but Cities Can't Afford to Buy It," *Wall Street Journal*, January 30, 1975, pp. 1, 21.

[47]"Labor Letter," *Wall Street Journal*, April 8, 1975, p. 1.

[48]Hervey A. Juris and Peter Feuille, *Police Unionism* (Lexington, Mass.: Lexington Books, 1973).

[49]Thomas J. Hilligan, "Police Employee Organizations: Past Developments and Present Problems," *Labor Law Journal* 24 (May 1973), p. 298.

[50]David Lewin, Peter Feuille, and Thomas Kochan, *Public Sector Labor Relations: An Analysis and Readings* (Glen Ridge, N.J.: Thomas Horton & Daughters, 1977), p. 222.

[51]U.S. Department of Labor, Labor-Management Services Administration, *Summary of Public Sector Labor Relations Policies, 1976* (Washington, D.C.: Government Printing Office, 1976), pp. 1–126. Totals are greater than 38 because some states have different impasse procedures for different types of employees; for example, Connecticut has mediation, fact-finding, and arbitration for state employees; fact-finding and arbitration for municipal employees; and mediation and fact-finding for teachers.

[52]Eva Robbins and Tia S. Denenberg, *A Guide for Labor Mediators* (Honolulu: Industrial Relations Center, University of Hawaii, 1976), pp. 3–4; and Paul D. Staudohar, *Public Employment Disputes and Disputes Settlement* (Honolulu: Industrial Relations Center, University of Hawaii, 1972), p. 41.

[53]Thomas P. Gilroy and Anthony Sinicropi, "Impasse Resolution in Public Employment: A Current Assessment," *Industrial and Labor Relations Review* 25 (July 1972), pp. 500–501.

[54]Ibid., p. 499.

[55]James L. Stern et al., *Final Offer Arbitration* (Lexington, Mass.: D. C. Heath, 1975), p. 175.

[56]Federal Mediation and Conciliation Service, *Twenty-ninth Annual Report* (Washington, D.C.: Government Printing Office, 1977), pp. 18–20.

[57]Lewin, Feuille, and Kochan, *Public Sector Labor Relations*, p. 225.

[58]Robert E. Doherty, "Fact-Finding: A One-Eyed Man Lost among the Eagles," *Public Personnel Management* 5 (September–October 1976), p. 366.

[59]Arnold Zack, *Understanding Fact-Finding and Arbitration in the Public Sector* (Washington, D.C.: Government Printing Office, 1974), p. 1.

[60]Ibid., p. 3.

[61]Also called final-offer arbitration, last-offer arbitration, and last best-offer arbitration.

[62]Nels E. Nelson, "Final Offer Arbitration: Same Problems," *Arbitration Journal* 30 (March 1975), p. 51.

[63]Lewin, Feuille, and Kochan, *Public Sector Labor Relations*, p. 230.

[64]Zack, *Understanding Fact-Finding and Arbitration*, p. 4.

[65]Ibid., p. 5.

66For a further discussion of related concerns and possible remedial alternatives see Joseph R. Grodin, "Political Aspects of Public Sector Interest Arbitration," *California Law Review* 64 (May 1976), pp. 678–701.

67Lewin, Feuille, and Kochan, *Public Sector Labor Relations*, p. 223.

68Doherty, "Fact-Finding," p. 367.

69William R. Word, "Fact-Finding in Public Employee Negotiations," *Monthly Labor Review* 95 (February 1972), pp. 60–64. Also see James L. Stern, "The Wisconsin Public Employee Fact-Finding Procedure," *Industrial and Labor Relations Review* 19 (July 1966), p. 8.

70William McHugh, Seminar for Special Masters, Tallahassee, Florida, Spring 1978.

71Lucian B. Gatewood, "Fact-Finding in Teacher Disputes: The Wisconsin Experience," *Monthly Labor Review* 97 (October 1974), pp. 47–51. For earlier and somewhat more optimistic assessments of fact-finding see Robert G. Howlett, "Comment," in G. S. Somers and B. D. Dennis, eds., *Arbitration and the Expanding Role of Neutrals* (Washington, D.C.: Bureau of National Affairs, 1970), pp. 181–182; and Byron Yaffe and Howard Goldblatt, *Fact-Finding in Public Employment Disputes in New York State: More Promise than Illusion* (Ithaca, N.Y.: Cornell University, 1971), p. 62.

72J. Joseph Loewenberg, "Compulsory Arbitration in the United States," in J. J. Loewenberg et al., eds., *Compulsory Arbitration* (Lexington, Mass.: D. C. Heath, 1976), p. 166. Also see Hoyt N. Wheeler, "An Analysis of Fire Fighter Strikes," *Labor Law Journal* 26 (January 1975), pp. 17–20; and Charles M. Rehmus, "Legislated Interest Arbitration," *Proceedings of the Annual Meeting: Industrial Relations Research Association, 1974* (Madison, Wis.: Industrial Relations Research Association, 1975), pp. 307–312.

73Lewin, Feuille, and Kochan, *Public Sector Labor Relations*, p. 229; and Charles M. Rehmus, "Public Employees: A Survey of Some Critical Problems on the Frontier of Collective Bargaining," *Labor Law Journal* 27 (September 1976), pp. 588–599.

74Craig E. Overton and Max S. Wortman, "Compulsory Arbitration: A Strike Alternative for Police?" *Arbitration Journal* 28 (March 1974), p. 40.

75Hoyt N. Wheeler, "Is Compromise the Rule in Fire Fighter Arbitration?" *Arbitration Journal* 29 (September 1974), pp. 176–185.

76Thomas A. Kochan and Jean Baderschneider, "Dependence on Impasse Procedures: Police and Fire Fighters in New York State," *Industrial and Labor Relations Review* 31 (July 1978), pp. 431, 447.

77Thomas A. Kochan et al., *Dispute Resolution under Fact-Finding and Arbitration: An Empirical Evaluation* (New York: American Arbitration Association, 1979), p. 158.

78Peter Feuille, "Final-Offer Arbitration and Negotiating Incentives," *Arbitration Journal* 32 (September 1977), pp. 203, 220.

There is an increasing use of arbitration in most states permitting this legislation (Wisconsin, Massachusetts, and Michigan), with Iowa being an exception to this trend. For additional details regarding this situation see Stern et al., *Final Offer Arbitration*; Paul C. Somers, *An Evaluation of Final Offer in Massachusetts* (Boston: Massachusetts League of Cities and Towns, 1976); Laurence T. Holden, Jr., "Final Offer Arbitration in Massachusetts: One Year Later," *Arbitration Journal* 31 (March 1976), pp. 26–35; Charles M. Rehmus, "Legislated Interest Arbitration," *Proceedings of the Twenty-seventh Annual Winter Meeting: Industrial Relations Research Association* (Madison, Wis.: Industrial Relations Research Association, 1975), pp. 310–313.

79Peter Feuille and James B. Dworkin, "Final-Offer Arbitration and Intertemporal Compromise, or It's My Turn to Win," *Proceedings of the Thirty-first Annual Meeting: Industrial Relations Research Association* (Madison, Wis.: Industrial Relations Research Association, 1979), pp. 87–95.

80Fred Witney, "Final-Offer Arbitration: The Indianapolis Experience," *Monthly Labor Review* 96 (May 1973), pp. 20–25. It should be noted that Witney, unlike Feuille (footnote 79), found no substantial evidence to conclude that final offer arbitration either encouraged or discouraged the parties from resolving their differences on their own.

81Theodore W. Kheel, "Strikes and Public Employment," *Michigan Law Review* 67 (March 1969), pp. 939–940. It should also be noted that vague guidelines, such as "public interest," have often plagued at least one fact-finder; see Doherty, "Fact-Finding," p. 366.

82Gary Long and Peter Feuille, "Final-Offer Arbitration: Sudden Death in Eugene," *Industrial and Labor Relations Review* 27 (January 1974), p. 203.

83J. H. Foegen, "Public Sector Strike-Prevention: Let the Taxpayer Decide," *Journal of Collective Negotiations in the Public Sector* 3 (Summer 1974), p. 223.

84Thomas Kochan, "Dynamics of Dispute Resolution in the Public Sector," in Aaron, Grodin, and Stern, *Public-Sector Bargaining*, pp. 155–189.

85For information involving student activity see Mario F. Bognanno and Edward L. Suntrip, "Graduate Assistants' Response to Unionization: The Minnesota Experience," *Labor Law Journal* 27 (January 1976), pp. 32–37; John Forsythe, "Collective Bargaining with Graduate Student Employees: The University of Michigan Experience," in T. N. Rice, ed., *Campus Employment Relations* (Ann Arbor, Mich.: Institute of Continuing Legal Education, 1976), pp. 299–315; William H. Holley, Jr. and Pleas

Davis, "Attitudes toward Joining Unions and the Educational Environment: A Study of College Students," *Journal of Collective Negotiations in the Public Sector* 7, no. 2 (1978), p. 135; H. B. Means and P. W. Semans, eds., *Faculty Collective Bargaining*, 2d ed. (Washington, D.C.: Editorial Projects for Education, 1976), pp. 107–111; and Melvin Aussieker, "Students and Bargaining at Public and Private Colleges," *Monthly Labor Review* 99 (April 1976), pp. 31–33. Also see A. R. Shark, K. Brouder, and Associates, *Students and Collective Bargaining* (Washington, D.C.: National Student Educational Fund, 1976); W. F. McHugh, "Collective Bargaining and the College Student," *Journal of Higher Education* 42 (March 1971), pp. 175–185; Alan Shark, *Current Status of College Students in Academic Collective Bargaining* (Washington, D.C.: Academic Service, 1975); Neil S. Bucklew, *Students and Unions* (University Park: Pennsylvania State University, 1973); and Raymond L. Hagler, "Collective Bargaining in Education and the Student," *Labor Law Journal* 27 (November 1976), pp. 712–720.

[86]Robert L. Walter, *The Teacher and Collective Bargaining* (Lincoln, Nebr.: Professional Educators Publications, 1975), pp. 14–15.

[87]Ibid. The National Education Association is now listed by the Department of Labor as a labor union for reporting purposes.

[88]Bureau of National Affairs, *Government Employee Relations Reporter*, August 29, 1977, p. 723:17.

[89]National Education Association, *1977–1978 NEA Handbook* (Washington, D.C.: National Education Association, 1978), p. 143.

[90]"Faculty Bargaining Agents at 600 Campuses," *Chronicle of Higher Education*, June 26, 1978, p. 8. The American Association of University Professors has organized 55 campuses; the AFT, 213; the NEA, 244; AAUP-NEA, 11; others were independent.

[91]Joseph Garbarino and John Lawler, "Faculty Union Activity in Higher Education, 1977," *Industrial Relations* 17 (February 1978), pp. 117–118.

[92]William J. Moore, "An Analysis of Teacher Union Growth," *Industrial Relations* 17 (May 1978), pp. 204–214.

[93]Robert J. Thornton and Andrew R. Weintraub, "Public Employee Bargaining Laws and the Propensity to Strike: The Case of Public School Teachers," *Journal of Collective Negotiations in the Public Sector* 3 (Winter 1974), p. 35. As of April 1978, thirty-two states had collective bargaining legislation for teachers allowing negotiations on pay and other working conditions.

[94]Joseph W. Garbarino and Melvin W. Aussieker, "Faculty Unionization in Institutions of Higher Education," *Monthly Labor Review* 97 (April 1974), pp. 48–51.

[95]Ralph E. Kennedy, "NLRB and Faculty Bargaining Units: The Charting of an Uncharted Area," in Thomas M. Mannix, ed., *Collective Bargaining in Higher Education* (New York: National Center for the Study of Collective Bargaining in Higher Education, City University of New York, 1975), pp. 35–50. U.S. Court of Appeals, 2nd Circuit, overruled the NLRB in the Yeshavia University case, where the NLRB had held that faculty members were employees entitled to collective bargaining rights; however, the court ruled that they were "managerial employees." This case was appealed to the Supreme Court in 1979.

[96]For an illustration of divergent state statutes regarding a most significant academic working condition, tenure, see L. H. Schramm, "Is Teacher Tenure Negotiable? A Review of Court Decisions," *Journal of Collective Negotiations in the Public Sector* 6, no. 3 (1977), pp. 245–257.

[97]Holley, Scebra, and Rector, "Perceptions of the Role," pp. 361–369; Charles T. Schmidt, Jr., "The Question of the Recognition of Principal and Other Supervisory Units in Public Education Collective Bargaining," *Labor Law Journal* 19 (July 1968), pp. 283–291.

[98]Peter D. Walther, "The NLRB in Higher Education," *Labor Law Journal* 29 (April 1978), pp. 209–218; and David Feller and Matthew W. Finkin, "Legislative Issues in Faculty College Bargaining," in *Faculty Bargaining in Public Higher Education* (San Francisco: Jossey-Bass Publishers, 1977), pp. 82–111.

[99]Means and Semans, *Faculty Collective Bargaining*, pp. 11–20.

[100]Charles R. Perry and Wesley A. Wildman, *The Impact of Negotiations in Public Education* (Worthington, Ohio: Charles A. Jones Publishing, 1970), pp. 137–214.

[101]Birch Bayh, "School Violence and Vandalism: Problems and Solutions," *American Educator*, Summer 1978, p. 5; and David L. Manning, "Discontent in Teaching Ranks," *Wall Street Journal*, January 9, 1978, p. 12.

[102]"Teacher to Teacher: Interviews on Discipline Policy and School Violence," *American Educator*, Summer 1978, p. 10.

[103]Rich Jaroslovey, "Bidding for Brains: Despite Glut of Teaching Applicants, Colleges Raid Other Schools for Distinguished Faculty," *Wall Street Journal*, June 28, 1976, p. 24.

[104]Miami Herald, *Tropic Magazine*, August 7, 1977.

[105]"Labor Letter," *Wall Street Journal*, March 7, 1978, p. 1.

[106]"Labor Letter," *Wall Street Journal*, January 24, 1978, p. 1.

[107]Walter S. Griggs and Harvey W. Rubin, "Legal Ramifications of the Tenure Cases," *Journal of Collective Negotiations in the Public Sector* 6, no. 2 (1977), p. 123.

[108]Jim Montgomery, "Breaking the Mold: Teachers Fight Effort to Remove Them for Personal Conduct," *Wall Street Journal*, January 28, 1978, pp. 1, 24.

[109]Paul D. Staudohar, "Negotiation and Grievance Arbitration of Teacher Tenure Issues," *Labor Law Journal* 29 (July 1978), pp. 413–419.

[110]Joseph W. Garbarino and Melvin Aussieker, *Faculty Bargaining* (New York: McGraw-Hill, 1975), pp. 257–258; and A. W. J. Thomson, *An Introduction to Collective Bargaining in Higher Education* (Ithaca, N.Y.: Cornell University, 1974).

[111]Robert F. Cook and Barbara W. Doering, "Negotiating a Teachers' Contract," *Arbitration Journal* 32 (September 1977), pp. 145–179.

[112]Barbara Doering, "Impasse Issues in Teacher Dispute Submitted to Fact-Finding in New York," *Arbitration Journal* 27 (March 1972), pp. 1–17; Willis J. Nordlund, "A Critique of Teacher Negotiations in 1974–1975," *Labor Law Journal* 26 (February 1975), pp. 119–124; and Bureau of National Affairs, *Government Employee Relations Reporter*, July 17, 1978, p. 768:14.

[113]*City of Madison Joint School District 8 v. Wisconsin Employment Relations Commission*, 97 Supreme Court Reporter, December 12, 1977, pp. 421–429.

[114]Bureau of National Affairs, *Government Employee Relations Reporter*, July 17, 1978, p. 768:14.

[115]Charles Winick, "When Teachers Strike," *Teachers College Record* 64 (April 1963), pp. 563–604; Don Hellriegel, Wendell French, and Richard B. Peterson, "Collective Negotiations and Teachers: A Behavioral Analysis," *Industrial and Labor Relations Review* 23 (April 1970), pp. 380–396; and William S. Fox and Michael H. Wince, "The Structure and Determinants of Occupational Militancy among Public School Teachers," *Industrial and Labor Relations Review* 30 (October 1976), p. 50.

[116]Roy R. Nasstrom and Robert L. Belsford, "Some Characteristics of Militant Teachers: A Reassessment Based on an Indiana Study," *Journal of Collective Negotiations in the Public Sector* 5, no. 3 (1976), pp. 247–256; J. A. Alutto and J. A. Belasco, "Determinants of Attitudinal Militancy among Nurses and Teachers," *Industrial and Labor Relations Review* 27 (July 1974), pp. 216–227; and C. Mushel, "Teacher and Administrator Attitudes toward Collective Negotiation Issues," *Education and Urban Society* 1 (May 1974), pp. 216–227.

[117]Andrew R. Weintraub and Robert J. Thornton, "Why Teachers Strike: The Economic and Legal Determinants," *Journal of Collective Negotiations in the Public Sector* 5, no. 3 (1976), p. 205.

[118]Melvin Aussieker, "The Incidence and Impact of Faculty Union Strikes," *Labor Law Journal* 28 (December 1977), pp. 777–784.

[119]Charles A. Odewahn and Allan Spritzer, "Administrators' Attitudes toward Faculty Unionism," *Industrial Relations* 15 (May 1976), pp. 206–215.

[120]Lynn Langway, "Union Problems," *Newsweek*, June 12, 1978, p. 73. Also see John E. Cooney, "Stevens Tech Professors' Strike Disturbs Campus Tranquility; Outcome Watched," *Wall Street Journal*, February 11, 1977, p. 10.

[121]Perry and Wildman, *Impact of Negotiations*, pp. 13–14; and Marshall J. Donley, Jr., *Power to the Teacher* (Bloomington: Indiana University Press, 1976), pp. 193–202.

[122]"Proposition 13's Impact on Collective Bargaining," *PERS Information Bulletin* 1 (June–July 1978), pp. 1–2; and Beverly T. Watkins, "The Budget Cutting Begins in California Community Colleges," *Chronicle of Higher Education*, June 26, 1978, p. 5.

[123]Hirshel Kasper, "Reply," *Industrial and Labor Relations Review* 25 (April 1972), pp. 417–423. Also see Robert H. Baird and John H. Landon, "Comment: The Effects of Collective Bargaining on Public School Teachers' Salaries," *Industrial and Labor Relations Review* 25 (April 1972), pp. 410–416; Robert J. Thornton, "The Effects of Collective Negotiations on Relative Teachers' Salaries," *Quarterly Review of Economics and Business* 11 (Winter 1971), pp. 37–47; Hirshel Kasper, "The Effects of Collective Bargaining on Public School Teachers' Salaries," *Industrial and Labor Relations Review* 24 (October 1970), pp. 57–72; and W. Clayton and Norman Carroll, "The Effects of Teachers' Organizations on Salaries and Class Size," *Industrial and Labor Relations Review* 26 (January 1973), pp. 834–841.

[124]David B. Lipsky and John E. Drotning, "The Influence of Collective Bargaining on Teachers' Salaries in New York State," *Industrial and Labor Relations Review* 27 (October 1973), pp. 18–24; and G. A. Balfour, "More Evidence That Unions Do Not Achieve Higher Salaries for Teachers," *Journal of Collective Negotiations in the Public Sector* 3 (Fall 1974), pp. 289–303.

[125]Charles Rehmus and Evan Wilner, *The Economic Results of Teacher Bargaining: Michigan's First Two Years* (Ann Arbor: University of Michigan and Wayne State University Research Papers, No. 6, 1968).

[126]Trevor Bain, "Collective Bargaining and Wages in Public Higher Education: The Case of CUNY (New York City)," *Journal of Collective Negotiations in the Public Sector* 5, no. 3 (1976), pp. 207–214; Bureau of National Affairs, "PSRC Finds Bargaining Laws Limit Teachers Pay Gains, Foster Strikes," *Government Employee Relations Reporter*, September 25, 1978, pp. 778:11–778:12, 778:33–778:35.

[127]*Salaries under Unions* (Washington, D.C.: Academic Collective Bargaining Information Service, March 1978), p. 1. For an excellent discussion see F. R. Kemerer and J. V. Baldridge, *Unions on Campus* (San Francisco: Jossey-Bass Publishers, 1975).

[128]Alfred Loewenthal and Robert Nielsen, "Unions in Academia: A Bargaining Frontier," *American Federationist* 80 (April 1977), pp. 18–23.

[129]John E. Dougherty, "Collegiality, Governance, and Collective Bargaining in the Multi-Campus State University of New York," *Labor Law Journal* 28 (October 1977), pp. 645–650; Donald H. Wollett, "Historical Development of Faculty Collective Bargaining and Current Extent," *Proceedings: First Annual Conference, National Center for the Study of Collective Bargaining in Higher Education* (New York: City University of New York, 1973), p. 29; Donald Wollett, "Self-Governance and Collective Bargaining for Higher Education Faculty: Can the Two Systems Coexist?" in J. P. Vladeck and S. C. Vladeck, eds., *Collective Bargaining in Higher Education—The Developing Law* (New York: Practising Law Institute, 1975), pp. 33–51. For an opposite viewpoint see Caesar Naples, "Collegiality and Collective Bargaining: They Belong Together," in Mannix, *Collective Bargaining and Higher Education*, pp. 51–57; and James P. Begin, "Grievance Mechanism and Faculty Collegiality: The Rutgers Case," *Industrial and Labor Relations Review* 31 (April 1978), pp. 308–309.

[130]Dougherty, "Collegiality, Governance, and Collective Bargaining," p. 646.

[131]Victor E. Flango, "The Impact of Collective Negotiations in Educational Policies," *Journal of Collective Negotiations in the Public Sector* 5, no. 2 (1976), pp. 133–155.

[132]George LaNoue and Marvin R. Pilo, "Teacher Unions and Educational Accountability," in Robert H. Connery and William V. Farr, eds., *Unionization of Municipal Employees* (New York: Academy of Political Science, 1970), p. 157.

[133]Kemerer and Baldridge, *Unions on Campus*, pp. 166–195.

Chapter 15

Collective Bargaining in the Federal Government

"There are many questions to be answered and procedures to be worked out and this will require a joint effort, and the best efforts, of all involved an federal sector labor-management relations. We have a big challenge before us."

Henry B. Frazier, III, Member of the Federal Labor Relations Authority

The preceding chapter presented an overview of labor relations in the public sector, highlighting comparisons and contrasts with corresponding activities in the private sector and focusing on state and local governments. While many similarities can be found within public sector bargaining units, there are differences across the governmental levels. The purpose of this chapter is to examine labor-management relationships at the federal government level, concentrating on federal executive orders and the 1978 Civil Service Reform Act. Two particular areas of the federal government not covered under the Civil Service Reform Act, the postal service and the military, are also presented.

Federal Sector Labor Relations

Historical Developments

The historical development of unions in the federal government can generally be considered in four phases: (1) the 1830s to the passage of the Lloyd–La Follette Act in 1912, during which time unions were actively discouraged by the administration but were formed despite this discouragement; (2) 1912 to the 1950s, a period in which federal employees' and unions' rights began to be recognized; (3) 1961 to the 1970s, when a series of presidential executive orders established an operational framework for labor relations in the federal sector and formalized unions' rights; and (4) the current period, during which statutory rights were provided to federal employee unions, starting with the Postal Reform Act of 1970 and continuing with the Carter/Congress Civil Service Reform Act of 1978.

The postal service was part of the Civil Service system until 1970, and its employees were intricately involved in the development of unions in the federal government. Up to 1970 all laws and executive orders covering federal employees also applied to the postal service. Thus, the following section on the development of federal employee unions will include the role of postal unions until 1970.

Early union activity in the federal government appeared first in 1835 and 1836, when work stoppages occurred at the Washington and Philadelphia navy yards. Workers at these sites sought a ten-hour workday and general redress of their grievances. Union members at this time were primarily laborers and mechanics who belonged to the same unions as private employees; therefore, the federal government did not resist their efforts to unionize. In fact, it was not until the postal employees began to organize in the 1860s that the federal government showed any marked resistance to union organizational efforts. President Theodore Roosevelt followed his predecessor's (President Cleveland's) policy of opposing union activity of federal employees and proclaimed that the federal government had special status as an employer and union actions would interfere with his presidential authority to manage the government.

These earlier unions did not negotiate labor agreements; but, led by the postal unions, they did become vigorously involved in lobbying and petitioning members of Congress for better wages, job security, and improved working conditions. It was these activities that led to a series of gag orders from Presidents Roosevelt and Taft and orders from the postmaster general that prohibited federal employees from visiting Congress in efforts to influence favorable legislation.

This authoritarian position of the administration resulted in low employee morale, work interruptions, defiance of orders, and threats of formal strikes. Congress reacted to this strained situation by passing the Lloyd–La Follette Act of 1912, which guaranteed employees the right to join unions, secure a trial for suspension or discharge, and communicate directly with Congress without interference. In addition, Congress attempted to eliminate anti-union activities of federal government officials.

The Lloyd–La Follette Act produced limited results, but the 1930s administration of President Franklin Roosevelt brought a rapid expansion of government programs to improve economic and social conditions. These expansions increased federal government employment. Although there was tremendous union growth in the federal sector during the thirties and forties, Roosevelt resisted any extension of full collective bargaining rights to federal employees. Unions therefore continued to rely on Congress for any improvement in their employment conditions.

The 1950s and early 1960s brought new interest in labor relations in federal government. Subsequent support from the National Civil Service League, the Committee on Labor Relations in Government of the American Bar Association, the second Hoover Commission report, and the election of President Kennedy (a Democrat who was heavily supported by organized labor) generated legislative and administrative interest in changing the rules of federal sector labor relations.

In the Eighty-Seventh Congress, the Rhodes-Johnston Bill, strongly supported by the unions, was favorably reported out of committees in both the House and the Senate but never reached the floor for a vote. The bill would have recognized the right of union officers to present grievances on behalf of their members, required conferences on personnel matters and related policies on union request, and provided for discipline of any administrative official who denied these rights.

When Congress adjourned in 1961 without passing this legislation, President Kennedy appointed a Task Force on Employment-Management Cooperation to review the status of labor relations in the federal sector and to make any appropriate recommendations. On the basis of the task force report and its recommendations and influenced heavily by Secretary of Labor Arthur Goldberg, President Kennedy on January 17, 1962, signed two executive orders: (a) Executive Order 10987, which set up federal agency appeal systems for appeals of adverse action and (b) Executive Order 10988, which set up the framework for labor-management relations in the federal government.[1]

Executive Order 10987 required each federal agency to establish a procedure for the appeal of administrative decisions that adversely affect employees and to communicate these procedures to the employees. The Civil Service Commission was given the authority to issue appropriate regulations for these appeal procedures.[2] Executive Order 10988 gave significant impetus to unionization in many federal agencies. For the first time, employees were given the protected right to join or refrain from joining labor organizations.

Employee organizations were given the opportunity to gain three types of recognition: (a) informal, (b) formal, or (c) exclusive. *Informal recognition* was given an employee organization when it did not qualify for formal or exclusive recognition. *Formal recognition* was awarded when (1) there was no exclusive bargaining representative, (2) the organization had at least 10 percent of employees in the unit, and (3) the organization had submitted a roster of officers and representatives, a copy of the constitution and by-laws, and a statement of objectives. *Exclusive recognition* was granted to employee organizations that were eligible for formal recognition and were designated by a majority vote (secret ballot) of the employees in the bargaining unit as representative of such employees. After an employee organization received designation by the Assistant Secretary for Labor-Management Relations as an exclusive bargaining unit, it was required to represent all employees in the unit without discrimination and without regard to their union membership. The levels of recognition combined with the emphasis on employee-management cooperation enabled unions to obtain greater recognition, to grow numerically, and to gain influence with management.

Although the executive order exempted certain decision-making areas from negotiations, such as selecting employees and directing employee activities, it allowed negotiation of policy subjects to be used in promotion procedures. However, management retained the right to decide which employee would be promoted. It further stated that the agency must confer with representatives of the employees regarding negotiable issues. Any negotiated agreement *could* contain a grievance procedure, but arbitration was only allowed for the interpretation or application of the agreement. Another provision, disliked by unions, allowed federal agencies themselves to determine whether a labor organization was to be granted exclusive recognition.[3]

Executive Order 10988 did not offer many substantive benefits to organized labor, and the three types of recognition actually generated much confusion, since an agency could conceivably deal with two unions representing the same employee classifications. Additionally, the management rights section gave public administrators considerable discretion in labor relations activities. This order can be compared with the Norris–La Guardia Act in the private sector in that it recognized employees' right to form and join unions but offered little in the way of procedural enforcement.

Regardless of its specific impact, Executive Order 10988 provided the framework for labor relations in the federal government for eight years before it was amended by Executive Order 11491 in 1970, the same year in which the Postal Reorganization Act was passed (its contents will be covered later in this chapter). Executive Order 11491 was amended three times, by Executive Orders 11616, 11636, and 11838.[4] Then, the Civil Service Reform Act (CSRA) was passed in 1978, making major changes in labor relations in the federal government.

Current Federal Labor-Management Relations under the Civil Service Reform Act of 1978

While the CSRA has retained many provisions of previous executive orders, the following discussion centers on the provisions of the CSRA as they currently exist. The act's ramifications extend beyond the labor relations function—it deals with other functions, such as merit system principles, civil service functions, performance appraisal, adverse actions, staffing, merit pay, and senior executive service. Its Title VII, the primary focus here, covers labor relations.

The CSRA establishes a new Federal Labor Relations Authority (FLRA),[5] an independent, neutral agency that administers the federal labor relations program and investigates unfair labor practices. The FLRA oversees the creation of bargaining units, supervises elections, and assists federal agencies in dealing with labor relations issues. It is headed by a chairperson and two members, appointed on a bipartisan basis for five-year terms. Its structure provides for a General Counsel, who prosecutes unfair labor practices and incorporates the existing Federal Service Impasse Panel (FSIP), which will continue to provide assistance in resolving negotiation impasses.[6]

The FLRA's leadership responsibilities include determining appropriate bargaining units, supervising and conducting elections, prescribing criteria for determining national consultation rights, conducting hearings and resolving complaints on unfair labor practices, and resolving exceptions to arbitrator awards.[7] The General Counsel investigates any alleged unfair labor practices, prosecutes complaints under the act, and exercises such powers as the FLRA may prescribe.[8]

The *Federal Service Impasse Panel* within the FLRA structure consists of at least six president-appointed members and one chairperson. It investigates any negotiation impasse presented to it and is authorized to take any action that it considers necessary to settle the dispute. Although the Federal Mediation and Conciliation Service (FMCS), the federal agency established in 1947 by the Taft-Hartley Act, is required to assist the parties in resolving negotiation impasses, either party may request that the FSIP consider the matter or pursue binding arbitration. The panel must investigate the impasse and recommend a procedure for resolution or assist the parties through whatever means is necessary, including fact-finding and recommendations. If these actions fail, it may conduct a formal hearing and take whatever action is necessary and legal to settle the dispute.[9]

Of the thousands of negotiations that took place in the federal government between 1970 and 1976, only 240 cases were sent to the FSIP; therefore, it can be reasonably concluded that the parties have negotiated their own contracts successfully in the vast majority of cases. In fact, in the entire history of the executive orders, the panel has issued recommendations that later formed the basis for settlement in only twenty-eight cases and has issued a binding decision and order in only four cases. Thus, the system set up by executive orders seems to have met all the criteria necessary for achieving an effective and credible system for impasse resolution—timeliness, awareness, acceptability, and finality[10]—which are important ingredients retained in the CSRA.

The FMCS was able to assist the parties in settling impasses in 362 cases in 1975,[11] involving such issues as union security, seniority, grievance procedures, arbitration, guarantees, hours (overtime), management prerogatives, duration of the contract, job classification, and working conditions.[12]

Appropriate Bargaining Units and Union Recognition in the Federal Sector The appropriate bargaining units for exclusive recognition may be established on an agency, plant, installation, functional, or other basis in order to assure a clear and identifiable community of interest among employees and to promote effective dealings and efficiency of the agency operations. The criteria used for determining community of interests are similar to those which have been used by the National Labor Relations Board in the private sector. These include common duties and skills, similar working conditions, and common supervisor and work site. Similarly, certain positions are generally excluded from the bargaining unit, such as confidential employees, management and supervisory personnel, personnel employees, and professionals from the nonprofessional unions unless they vote in favor of inclusion.[13]

Under CSRA, federal agencies may give either exclusive recognition or national consultation rights to unions that meet the appropriate requirements. The granting of *national consultation rights* indicates that the union is the representative of a substantial number (10 percent or 5,000) of the civilian employees in the specified federal agency. This recognition only allows the union to be notified of proposed substantive changes in conditions of employment and provides a reasonable opportunity for the union to present its views and recommendations on any proposed changes.[14]

A federal agency accords *exclusive recognition* to a labor union if the union has been selected as the employee representative in a secret ballot election by a majority of the employees in the appropriate unit who cast valid ballots.[15] The current popularity of exclusive recognition in the federal government is demonstrated by the fact that the majority (60 percent or 1,228,136) of federal civilian (nonmilitary) employees are currently in bargaining units bearing this designation. Table 15–1 indicates the number of exclusive recognitions, agreements, and employees under agreement for the twelve largest federal agencies. Federal employees are reported to be members of a number of different international unions, although the American Federation of Government Employees AFL-CIO leads by far, with 1,723 exclusive recognitions and 687,965 employees.[16]

Negotiable Subjects in the Federal Sector As in the private sector, the federal agency and the exclusively recognized union must meet at reasonable times and confer in good faith with respect to *mandatory* subjects of collective bargaining, such as certain personnel policies and practices and working conditions, to the extent that appropriate laws and regulations allow such negotiations. The parties are allowed to bargain over subjects that are *permissible*, but the CSRA does not require negotiation over permissible subjects—one party can legally refuse to negotiate

Agency	Recognitions	Number of Agreements	Employees under Agreements	Percent of Employees under Agreement
Treasury	144	36	92,482	75
Army (nonmilitary)	573	350	166,709	50
Navy (nonmilitary)	568	432	170,867	58
Air Force (nonmilitary)	251	171	151,250	64
Defense Logistics Agency	76	54	33,429	70
National Guard Bureau	124	101	33,300	65
Interior	220	171	21,980	28
Agriculture	148	121	317	20
HEW	376	218	90,496	58
Transportation	131	79	16,176	22
General Services Administration	156	74	19,565	53
Veterans Administration	376	303	145,921	65

Table 15–1
Exclusive Recognitions and Agreements by Agency, 1977 (Twelve Largest Federal Agencies in Terms of Number of Exclusive Unions)

Source: Advance sheets from U.S. Civil Service Commission, Office of Labor-Management Relations, *Union Recognition in the Federal Government 1978* (Washington, D.C.: Office of Personnel Management, 1979), Table A.

these issues. Permissible subjects include numbers, types, and grades of positions assigned to any organizational unit, work project, or tour of duty; technology of the workplace; and methods and means of performing the work. Subjects *prohibited* from negotiations pertain to various management rights:

☐ To determine the mission, budget, organization, number of employees, and internal security practices.

☐ To hire, assign, direct, lay off, and retain employees in accordance with applicable law.

☐ To suspend, remove, reduce in grade or pay, or take other disciplinary action.

☐ To assign work, subcontract, and select personnel for promotion from properly ranked and certified candidates and other appropriate sources.

☐ To take whatever actions may be necessary to carry out the agency mission during emergencies.[17]

Although the CSRA limits the negotiable subjects, the parties have ample opportunity to negotiate many issues,[18] as illustrated in Table 15–2. However, it should be noted that federal unions and management representatives do not have a totally free hand in negotiating these items and

Table 15–2 Potential Negotiation Issues in the Federal Sector	Issue Category	Potential Issue Dimension
	Implementation of pay rates and scales	Procedures for assigning overtime, call-in and call-back pay, pay scheduling, etc.
	Personnel policies	Promotion methods, consultation on reduction-in-force, use of seniority, job posting, etc.
	Working conditions	Safety, health, special clothing, light and heat, and ventilation
	Design and scheduling of work	Work schedules, rotation, holiday and vacation schedules
	Grievances	Grievance procedures, number of steps, time limits, arbitration, time off for handling grievances
	Leave	Annual leave formulas, automatic approval, burden of proving sick leave abuse, etc.
	Meeting with union representatives	Agenda, time limits, facilities, frequency, purposes, number of representatives
	Employee benefits and services	Lunch rooms, coffee breaks, recreation, parking
	Services to the union	Use of bulletin boards, meeting places, use of intra-office mail
	Contract terms	Expiration date, duration of agreement

Source: Adapted from Bob F. Repas, *Collective Bargaining in the Federal Employment*, 2d. ed. (Honolulu: Industrial Relations Center, University of Hawaii, 1973), pp. 54–64. Used by permission.

either party may run the risk of committing an unfair labor practice by refusing to negotiate their mutual working conditions concerns in good faith.

Unfair Labor Practices in the Federal Sector The Civil Service Reform Act specifies unfair labor practices in order to protect the rights of individual employees, labor organizations, and federal agencies. The General Counsel investigates charges of unfair labor practices and prosecutes them before the three-member FLRA. Employee grievances over matters concerning adverse action, position classification, and equal employment opportunity are issues covered by other laws and cannot be raised in the forum of an unfair labor practice hearing.

Unfair labor practices under the act are very similar to those covered under previous executive orders, the National Labor Relations Act, and the Labor Management Relations Act. For example, prohibited management activities include restraining and coercing employees in the exercise of their rights; encouraging or discouraging union membership; sponsoring, controlling, or assisting the labor organization; disciplining union members who file complaints; and refusing to recognize or negotiate with a designated labor organization. The labor organization is prohibited from interfering with, restraining, or coercing employees in the exercise of their rights; attempting to induce agency management to coerce employees; impeding or hindering an employee's work performance; calling or engaging in job action; and discriminating against employees or refusing to consult, confer, or negotiate with the appropriate federal agency. In such cases, the FLRA can issue cease-and-desist orders and/or require reinstatement with back pay.

The CSRA makes it an unfair labor practice to refuse or fail to cooperate in impasse procedures and decisions. Moreover, an agency cannot enforce regulations that conflict with a negotiated agreement, and the union cannot picket if it interferes with the agency's operation.

The FLRA has authority to withdraw recognition of a union which commits an unfair labor practice or encourages a strike or slowdown. It can also require the parties to renegotiate a labor agreement in accordance with an FLRA decision and seek temporary restraining orders in unfair labor practice cases.[19]

Grievance and Arbitration Procedures in the Federal Sector Executive Order 10988 permitted negotiation of grievance procedures that conformed to Civil Service Commission standards and did not diminish or impair any existing employee rights. Advisory (non-binding) arbitration provisions could be negotiated, but these only dealt with interpretation or application of the agreement. After five years under Executive Order 10988, only 19 percent of the federal employees were covered under negotiated grievance procedures. Since separate appeal procedures were available, grievance resolution was a confusing process.

In 1969, President Nixon issued Executive Order 11491, which introduced binding arbitration as an option in the negotiated grievance procedures and permitted it to be the exclusive procedure available to employees if the bargaining agreement so specified. Subsequent executive orders were issued to minimize conflicts between employee rights created by negotiations and rights established by law or regulation. More specifically, negotiated grievance and arbitration procedures could cover only interpretation or application of the negotiated agreement and could not cover matters outside the agreement, such as those for which statutory appeals already existed.[20]

The CSRA requires that all negotiated agreements in the federal sector include a grievance procedure with binding arbitration as its final step. A grievance now is broadly defined to include *any* complaint by any employee or labor organization relating to employment with an agency and any claimed violation, misinterpretation, or misapplication of any law, rule, or regulation affecting conditions of employment. Certain issues are exempt from the grievance procedure, such as employee appointment, certification, job classification, removal for national security reasons or political activities, issues concerning retirement, and life and health insurance.[21] However, the scope of grievance procedure coverage has been extended considerably. In fact, *all* matters within the allowable limits of the CSRA shall be *within* the scope of any grievance procedure negotiated by the parties, unless the parties have specifically agreed to exclude certain matters from coverage. Thus, departing from previous practices and private sector practices, the parties will *not* be negotiating matters into coverage; they will, however, be negotiating them out of coverage.[22]

Negotiated grievance procedures now serve as the exclusive forum for bargaining unit employees in most cases; however, in cases of adverse action and removals and demotions for poor performance, the employee may choose *either* the negotiated procedure or the statutory procedure, but not both. Moreover, in discrimination cases, the grievant may proceed to arbitration and then appeal to the EEOC or the Merit System Protection Board, an independent agency established to hear federal employee grievances under CSRA.

Arbitration awards may be reviewed by the FLRA, but judicial review is available only for adverse action and equal employment opportunity cases. Conflict over whether a grievance is arbitrable can be decided by arbitration and then reviewed by the FLRA. Remedial action can include back pay and attorney fees in discrimination and adverse actions cases where the federal agency's action is clearly without merit.[23]

In 1977, 87 percent of the 3,032 federal sector labor agreements reported by the Civil Service Commission provided for grievance arbitration, with 81 percent of the arbitration clauses containing a binding decision. The annual number of arbitration cases has continually increased in the federal sector since 1970, and most of these cases now result in a binding rather than an advisory decision.[24]

Concluding Comments The Civil Service Reform Act, although new and with many labor relations issues still to be determined, is a major achievement. First, it is consistent with one of President Carter's campaign pledges to the voters to attempt to improve the quality of government services and be more responsive to the needs of the public. Second, it replaces Executive Order 11491 with a law that stabilizes labor relations in the federal government—major changes will now have to be legislated by Congress, and federal unions and agencies will not be faced with recurring changes in executive orders when a different president is elected.[25] Third, enactment of the CSRA demonstrates Congress's belief that federal labor relations has matured enough that many activities currently taking place in the private sector can be made available to federal employees. While there will be many problems and obstacles with the act, there are an equal number of challenging opportunities.

The remainder of this chapter looks specifically at the federal labor relations process in the postal and military areas of employment.

**Application:
The Postal
Unions**

The U.S. Postal Service was covered under executive orders until 1970, when separate legislation was enacted to govern labor relations in this important service area. While there are a number of reasons for the passage of the Postal Reorganization Act of 1970, a major impetus came from the 1970 postal strike.

**The Postal Strike
of 1970**

Even before the 1970 negotiations, postal employees, who were heavily unionized, believed they were grossly underpaid, especially those in the large metropolitan, high-cost areas. For example, members of the National Association of Letter Carriers (NALC) received a 1970 starting annual salary of $6,176; employees with twenty-one years' service earned $8,442.[26] The mass media recognized the discrepancies, and President Nixon agreed there were wage disparities and inequities. At the same time, postal employees were aware that far higher salaries had been achieved by sanitation workers and others at local levels through illegal strikes.

The economic considerations were reinforced by rather outdated working conditions; for example, restroom facilities were often shared by female and male employees. The assistant postmaster general reflected on working conditions at the time of the strike:

For years, the government has been telling the private sector how to treat its personnel, how to run a safety program, how to do everything better. When I came down here, I thought I was coming straight to the Messiah. I found just the opposite. I found an operation that's back in the 19th century. The Post Office doesn't begin to approach the progressive practices industry found pay off long ago.[27]

Accidents in this occupation were above the nation's average due to the working conditions in the facility and on deliveries. In heavy crime areas, postmen secretly packed pistols to ward off muggers.[28]

Starting in New York City and spreading quickly to cities in New Jersey and Connecticut, then to Philadelphia, Cleveland, Chicago, Milwaukee, and San Francisco, a large portion of the postal service virtually came to a halt as an estimated 200,000 postal employees went on strike.[29] Although the Post Office Department secured an injunction, strikers did not return to work, and much of the mail service was paralyzed. Administration officers, Postmaster General Winton Blount, Assistant Secretary W. J. Ussery, and Secretary of Labor George Shultz negotiated vigorously with AFL-CIO President George Meany and postal union leaders to end the strike. Twenty-five thousand U.S. Army soldiers were called out to perform the tasks of the striking postal employees in the New York City area; however, 90 percent of the strikers returned to work fairly soon, and serious collective bargaining began (a historic event in the federal sector). The negotiations resulted in a memorandum of agreement, a general

The postal strike of 1970 virtually paralyzed the mail service, despite the efforts of armed forces personnel to keep the mail moving. This strike, though illegal, did lead to negotiations and to the Postal Reorganization Act of 1970.

Source: Courtesy of UPI.

wage increase, a change in the wage schedule, a joint commitment to postal reform, establishment of a system of collective bargaining similar to the private sector's, and, most importantly, amnesty for postal strikers. For the first time, leaders of federal employee unions sat with administration officials and negotiated a collective bargaining agreement.[30] While the strike was declared illegal,[31] its effect had been legitimized by the passage of the Postal Reorganization Act of 1970.

The Postal Reorganization Act of 1970

The Postal Reorganization Act (PRA), signed by President Nixon on August 12, 1970, fulfilled the desires of the postal unions to have their labor-management relations programs established by statute. Under Kennedy's executive orders, the Post Office Department never fully accepted collective bargaining, even though it was the largest single employer in the United States and had the largest proportion of employees belonging to unions.

The act created the U.S. Postal Service (USPS) as an independent establishment within the executive branch of the federal government. The office of postmaster general, previously a position in the cabinet, was made independent of Congress and the president. The postmaster general was to be selected by an eleven-member board of governors. Further, under the PRA many new policies of vital importance to the postal unions, such as an 8 percent retroactive pay increase, attainment of the highest wage rate in job classifications in eight years instead of twenty-one, acceptance of the concept of federal-civilian pay comparability, and establishment of self-supporting postal service by 1984, were adopted.

Under the PRA, the national labor rules that have evolved over the years under the Wagner, Taft-Hartley, and Landrum-Griffin Acts apply to the USPS. Wages, hours, benefits, and terms and conditions of employment are to be determined through collective bargaining. Grievances, adverse actions, and arbitration procedures are subject to negotiations. The NLRB supervises representation elections and prosecutes unfair labor practices. Although the right to strike was prohibited, a fact-finding–arbitration procedure was made available if a bargaining impasse persisted longer than 180 days after bargaining began.

Since the PRA was passed, contracts have been negotiated in 1971, 1973, 1975, and 1978 without major disruptions of postal services. Each negotiation, however, has been accompanied by serious threats; and a few minor work stoppages by urban postal employees, who believed that their wages did not compare with other urban wage earners of similar skills and responsibilities, have occurred.[32]

The 1978 agreement, which reflected the postal employees' major concerns, was successfully negotiated with only minor walkouts but was rejected by the membership. Both parties had made extensive preparations for a possible national strike, and after seventeen weeks of negotiations, a tentative agreement was reached on the last day before the old contract expired. The rejected agreement included a 19.5 percent wage and cost-of-living increase over three years (average annual salary would be about $19,000 by 1981) and a no-layoff clause. Although the agreement was deemed noninflationary, it pushed the average pay of postal employees to $7.58 per hour as compared to $5.62 for private nonfarm workers,[33] a wage differential that researchers have been taking to task.[34]

After the contract was rejected and under the threat of a national mail strike, the postal union leaders insisted upon further negotiations; however, Postmaster General William Bolger would accept no alternative except arbitration, as outlined by law.[35] Then, under an unusual agreement worked out by the FMCS, Harvard Professor James Healy was asked to serve as mediator while the negotiations were resumed for fifteen days. If no agreement was reached by negotiation, Mr. Healy would impose an arbitrated settlement that would be final and binding on both parties.[36]

Because the parties were unable to reach a settlement on the issues themselves, Healy issued an arbitration award. The wage and cost-of-living payments over three years were projected at 21.3 percent (based on estimated 6.5 percent inflation rate); however, the *cap* (ceiling on the cost-of-living adjustments) was removed. The no-layoff provision included in the rejected contract, which would have expired in three years and would have reemerged as a critical issue in future negotiations, was also changed. Healy's award protected current postal employees from layoffs for the rest of their working lives; however, the no-layoff provision does not apply to new postal employees until they have worked for the postal service for six years. After that, they too will have the same protection from layoffs.[37]

Thus, the 1978 negotiations introduced a new era for collective bargaining in the federal government. While the arbitrated settlement was unusual, it demonstrated that the impasse procedure can be applied peacefully and the settlement can be rendered with considerations given to future problems, such as inflation and layoff caused by technological change.

Contemporary Issues and Problems

Postal employees will continue to face such crucial issues in negotiation as automation, work jurisdiction, and attitudes of some management officials and the public that wages are too high. The postal service has introduced new labor-saving machines and operational methods in an attempt to increase employee efficiency. Such changes have caused jurisdictional disputes between the clerks' and the mail handlers' unions.

Critical problems occur over mail distribution and handling. Previously, mail clerks handled mail, processing it by the piece, while the mail handler's job required manual strength and dexterity for conveying heavy sacks of mail. Modern innovations include ZIP codes and mail processing machinery, such as optical character readers that can sort mail at the rate of 42,000 pieces per hour; thus the mail handlers' tasks have increased while the clerks' have decreased. These technological advances have blurred the distinction between the traditional sorting and mail handling functions, causing a rift between clerks and mail handlers. One step toward resolving these disputes has been the creation of the Committee on Jurisdiction, which is composed of members from postal unions and postal service management. It plans frequent meetings to resolve jurisdictional disputes between the represented unions.[38]

Postal unions have negotiated provisions for grievance arbitration in USPS, which has led to some managerial dissatisfaction. Under the executive orders, management was free to act unilaterally in disciplining employees and setting work standards; under the PRA and a national labor agreement, management's flexibility in these matters has been limited. Thus far, management has fared poorly in cases going to arbitration, due mostly to its failure to provide specific justification for its actions. Both parties are currently increasing their efforts toward better training and preparations for grievance administration and arbitration.[39]

Another concern of the postal unions is that the USPS is still an agency of the federal government and not a separate corporation, as was proposed at one time. Although the eleven-member board of governors is responsible for policy formation, its members can be paid for no more than thirty days in any year for their services, a factor which makes continued involvement in the management of the postal service unattractive. The board is empowered to select and remove the postmaster general and approve expenditures,[40] but the 1978 negotiations showed again that the president and his staff, not the board of governors, have the greatest influence within the USPS. Reacting to presidential involvement, Mr. LaPenta, a negotiator on the union side, explained: "Unless they [the White House] butt out of our collective bargaining—we're not bargaining." In fact, he alleged that any interference in the negotiations by the executive branch was a violation of the Postal Reorganization Act of 1970.[41]

Postal unions are also concerned about continuing technological advances that could affect employment opportunities of their members. For example, many firms now make deposits in banks electronically rather than mailing them, pay bills by telephone, and use payments electronically deducted from customer accounts—all without checks or postage. The effect of such moves can be substantial; the U.S. Treasury Department plans to move the bulk of its checks out of the mails and into electronic deposits, causing a loss of 400 to 500 million pieces of mail per year, approximately 1 percent of the total volume of first-class mail. Since these reductions are readily converted to losses of jobs and layoff of employees, the postal unions will continue to make job security and technological change important issues in negotiations.[42]

Concluding Comments

Both the postal unions and management of the USPS have many issues to face and resolve. While technological change, work jurisdiction, employee compensation, presidential intervention, and arbitration problems will have to be resolved by the parties, the past few years have shown that collective bargaining works. These experiences have also demonstrated that new skills and talents must be developed by both parties and cooperative efforts and attitudes are essential to successful labor relations.

Application: Potentials of Military Unionization

While military personnel have been concerned over their wages, benefits, and other working conditions, the prospect of military unions remains remote. This conclusion is based on a 1978 law which prohibits military personnel from joining unions (and unions from soliciting military personnel)[43] and on an overwhelming majority of the public (74 percent) opposing military unions.[44]

Nonetheless, the prospect of military unionization deserves some consideration, since the statutory prohibition could be protested on constitutional grounds. Also, insights into this category are necessary for a fuller appreciation of labor relations' problems and prospects in the public sector.

Goals of Affected Employees and Union Leaders

Collective action by military employees is not new. In 1946, an estimated 140,000 service personnel engaged in a collective effort to speed up their discharge. In 1971, twenty servicemen formed a union at Fort Sill, Oklahoma, but were rebuffed by the AFL-CIO, which maintained that no employer-employee relationship existed.[45]

Some evidence of dissatisfaction currently exists among military personnel. In 1976, over 300,000 Article 15 (nonjudicial punishment) proceedings were required, and the proportion of less than fully honorable discharges (14 percent) was the highest rate ever recorded.[46] Also, one survey has found that a majority of commissioned and noncommissioned officers concerned over their employment situation believe that a union could help preserve their retirement, medical, and other benefits.[47] There is no reason to think that employee discontent would automatically result in a union; yet concerns over various employment policies and working conditions might encourage military personnel to at least consider the union alternative.

There has been serious concern over possible reductions in the rate of wage increases and benefits or both. Such reductions could lower the military employees' standard of living below that of their civilian counterparts,[48] making it more difficult to attract and retain capable personnel.[49]

Other general concerns are job security and advancement opportunity, which have been threatened by proposals for personnel reductions. Further, since Vietnam it has been more difficult to advance in rank, and careers are jeopardized when promotion does not occur within certain time intervals.[50]

Finally, military employees have become more interested in protection from arbitrary decisions made by military officials. Although appeal procedures are available and the right to legal representation exists, some maintain that military due process has many "in-house" or "partial" characteristics. "In many cases it is like taking a family fight to your mother-in-law. You are taking it to the same people who started the problem."[51]

Although military employees have many working concerns similar to those of their private sector counterparts, the question remains whether labor organizations will be eager to represent them. In fact, some union leaders have been unenthusiastic about organizing the military. For example, George Meany, president of the AFL-CIO, has long been skeptical of the unionized army concept.[52] Members of the American Federation of Government Employees (AFGE), the labor organization most identified with organizing military employees, voted against efforts to attempt organizing the military by a four-to-one margin.[53]

Legal Considerations

While there is statutory prohibition against military unionization, there are still constitutional issues that must be answered. The First Amendment to the Constitution states that: "Congress shall make no law . . . abridging . . . the right of people peaceably to assemble, and to petition the government for a redress of grievances." Thus, it appears that military personnel should have the right to join a labor organization for the purpose of discussing and resolving labor grievances.

However, Article I, Section 8 of the Constitution also states that "Congress shall have the power . . . to make rules for the government and regulation of the land and naval forces." Consideration of the current prohibition against military unions raises a fundamental question: Which provision of the Constitution is paramount—the First Amendment rights of military personnel or Congress's powers to regulate the military?[54]

It is difficult to predict union and judicial action, but the involvement of the Supreme Court in these matters is certainly possible. If the Supreme Court decides this issue, it will probably be guided by its previous reasoning.

One military case involved an army captain and physician who was convicted by a general court martial for inappropriate remarks made to other military personnel.[55] His court martial was in part based on violations of Articles 133 and 134 of the *Uniform Code of Military Justice,* which refer to "conduct unbecoming an officer and a gentleman" and "all disorders and neglects to the prejudice of good order and discipline in the armed forces." More specifically, his remarks to special forces and enlisted personnel were described as "intemperate, defamatory, provoking, disloyal, contemptuous, and disrespectful to Special Forces personnel and to enlisted personnel who were patients or under his supervision."[56] In essence, he informed enlisted personnel that "colored soldiers" should not go to Vietnam if ordered since (a) they are "given all the hazardous duty," and (b) "Special Forces personnel are liars and thieves and killers of peasants and murderers of women and children."[57]

The captain claimed Articles 133 and 134 were vague—in essence, could be applied to any infraction, with the military being the ultimate interpreter of the remarks. The Supreme Court disagreed, upholding the court martial while at the same time recognizing the unique disciplinary prerogatives of the military:

This Court has long recognized that the military is, by necessity, a specialized society separate from civilian society. . . . The differences between the military and civilian communities result from the fact that "it is the primary business of armies and navies to fight or be ready to fight wars should the occasion arise."

. . . While the members of the military are not excluded from the protection granted by the First Amendment, the different character of the military community and of the military mission requires a different application of those protections. The fundamental necessity for obedience, and the consequent necessity for imposition of discipline, may render permissible within the military that which would be constitutionally impermissible outside it.[58]

Thus, the Supreme Court could conceivably rule that thwarting union organizing by legal enactment would not conflict with the First Amendment rights,[59] particularly because of the military's unique purpose and characteristics. The following section illustrates the controversy over this reasoning.

Controversial Issues Concerning Military Unions

Arguments for and against military unions are grouped into the following categories: characteristics of the job, the potential consequences of military unionization, and the experience of military unions in other countries.

Characteristics of the Job Some believe the "separate society" aspect of the military ended in 1973, when the Congress established the all-volunteer army. This action is tantamount to a government admission that the military is no different from any other employer. The recruiting slogans emphasize training in a career skill and economic benefits instead of a patriotic obligation; union supporters have also pointed out that civilian and military personnel in the volunteer army perform similar tasks. More specifically, the military has "created an integrated work situation where the uniformed military work side by side with the civilian workers performing the same tasks, many of which are not combat-readiness related, but they work under different rules and receive different benefits and privileges."[60]

More sensitive is the issue of military personnel, who cannot legally consider union membership, working side by side with many civilian personnel who are members of unions (see Table 15–1). Union advocates emphasize that discipline, adherence to command, and life and death situations associated with military positions exist also for police and firefighters, who have been allowed to unionize.

Consequences of Military Unionization Another controversial issue pertains to consequences of military unionization. Some contend that unions could mount an organized opposition to various aspects of United States foreign policy. This opposition could, at the least, embarrass the president and also possibly rupture delicate negotiations between the United States and foreign countries. Yet at least one individual suggests that this potential difference of opinion might cause the United States to seriously examine national priorities:

Do we as a nation really subscribe to the three fundamental democratic ideals of individual liberty, limited government, and majority rule? Or is it really a welfare state for the masses managed by a benevolent elite that we seek? The more democratic way necessarily involves more risks, but that does not mean that the democratic way should be rejected.[61]

Many individuals believe military unions would result in lax and unruly behavior that could culminate in strikes or related job action at times of critical emergencies. The strike potential of military unions cannot be easily dismissed. As Senator Strom Thurmond has noted on several occasions, police and firefighter unions have conducted strikes in defiance of anti-strike laws.[62] Even an official of the AFGE has admitted that union officials would have limited capabilities in preventing unauthorized or unlawful strikes:

There isn't any way to stop those things. They don't ask me to go on strike. They don't ask their national vice president to go on strike. . . . But the thing about it is that you cannot control individual elements of an organization whether it happens to be the United States Army, as has been demonstrated a couple of times in the last three or four years, or the Navy or the Air Force or the AFGE. People take into their own hands what they think they have to.[63]

Even if strikes are not conducted, there is a possibility that members of military unions would honor picket lines of other union members.[64]

Experiences of Military Unions in Other Countries Related experiences with foreign military unions are cited by both advocates and opponents of military unions. Six Western European nations (Austria, Denmark, the

Netherlands, Norway, West Germany, and Sweden) have military unions.[65] Some contend that these armed services offer concrete proof of deteriorating morale and respect for authority, while others claim the opposite.

One objective measure of foreign military unions' success is the occurrence of strikes, which are prohibited by all affected countries except Sweden. Two countries, the Netherlands and Sweden, have had military strikes. Military personnel in the Netherlands conducted an illegal and unsuccessful strike in 1971; some attribute the rather dramatic reduction in military union membership to this strike.[66] Sweden's 1971 military strike was very brief, and the union has agreed to bar strikes among higher officers and to submit any proposed action to a government labor board that can rule on any national security impact of a possible strike.[67]

Concluding Comments

While some believe that military unionization is a moot issue, a review of labor history, an analysis of public sector labor relations in recent years, and a study of constitutional rights may leave the issue open for serious discussion and future consideration. Although a 1978 law prohibits military unions, many important questions must be resolved before the issue of military unions in the United States is dead.

Summary

This chapter presented the historical development of unionism in the federal government and the effect of the executive orders of the president and the Civil Service Reform Act of 1978. While legislation and executive permission to allow federal employee unions was absent for many years, unions still developed, even under adverse conditions. Executive Order 10988 did not offer many substantive benefits to federal employee unions but provided the framework for a labor relations system in the federal government and gave tremendous impetus to union organization and growth. Each subsequent executive order added new features, and federal employees were eventually given many rights similar to those of employees under many state statutes and the National Labor Relations Act.

The administrative agencies under the Civil Service Reform Act include the Federal Labor Relations Authority, the General Counsel, and the Federal Service Impasse Panel. Also available for assistance are the Federal Mediation and Conciliation Service, labor arbitrators, and fact finders, who provide important services for the parties. Since the CSRA has only been in effect since early 1979, directions and many interpretations remain for the future.

Two important segments of the federal government not covered by the CSRA are the postal service and the military. The postal unions have a critical effect on the effective operations of the postal service. Although no major strike has occurred since the enactment of the Postal Reorganization Act of 1970, such a strike could drastically affect commerce and create emergency conditions in many sectors of our economy. Thus, continuing efforts by the postal unions and the U.S. Postal Service are essential to assure successful labor relations. Views on the very controversial subject of military unions provide insights into the constitutional issues and commonalities of military personnel with civilian employees in the Department of Defense and raise questions concerning the feasibility of unionization of an organization so vital to U.S. security.

Discussion Questions

1. Do you see any similarities between the development of labor unions in the federal sector and those in the private sector (outlined in Chapter 2)? Describe these.

2. What were weaknesses in the three types of union recognition allowed under Executive Order 10988?

3. What are the administrative agencies under the Civil Service Reform Act? What are their responsibilities?

4. Considering the multitude of subjects that are bargainable in the federal sector, list some of the more important ones that are not.

5. Compare and contrast the negotiated grievance procedures under the CSRA with most found in the private sector.

6. What type of impasse resolution procedure was used in the 1978 postal negotiations? Why do you think this procedure was used? (See Chapter 7.) How effective was it?

7. If a majority of employees in other segments of the federal government are already members of unions, why is it so critical that a law be passed to forbid military personnel from organizing unions?

8. If the law prohibiting unions in the military were declared unconstitutional, what would be the likely consequences?

References

[1]Murray B. Nesbitt, *Labor Relations in the Federal Government Service* (Washington, D.C.: Bureau of National Affairs, 1976), pp. 6–17; and Richard J. Murphy, "The Federal Experience in Employee Relations," in Richard J. Murphy and Morris Sackman, eds., *The Crisis in Public Employee Relations in the Decade of the Seventies* (Washington, D.C.: Bureau of National Affairs, 1970), pp. 1–2.

[2]K. L. Hanslowe, *The Emerging Law of Labor Relations in Public Employment* (Ithaca, N.Y.: Cornell University, 1967), p. 40.

[3]Ibid., pp. 41–43.

[4]United States Federal Labor Relations Council, *Labor-Management Relations in the Federal Service* (Washington, D.C.: Government Printing Office, 1975), p. 28.

[5]This agency assumes many of the responsibilities of the Federal Labor Council and Assistant Secretary of Labor for Labor-Management Relations.

[6]U.S. Civil Service Commission, Office of Labor-Management Relations, *Introducing the Civil Service Reform Act* (Washington, D.C.: Government Printing Office, 1978), pp. 1–4.

[7]92 Stat. 1212–1213 (1978).

[8]92 Stat. 1196–1197 (1978).

[9]92 Stat. 1208–1209 (1978).

[10]Testimony by Anthony F. Ingrassia, Briefing before the U.S. House Subcommittee on Civil Service of the Committee on Post Office and Civil Service, Federal Labor Relations Program, Serial no. 95-3, March 15, 1977, p. 1.

[11]Ibid., p. 10.

[12]Federal Mediation and Conciliation Service, *Twenty-ninth Annual Report: 1976* (Washington, D.C.: Government Printing Office, 1977), p. 20.

[13]United States Federal Labor Relations Council, *Labor-Management Relations,* p. 11.

[14]92 Stat. 1201 (1978).

[15]92 Stat. 1199 (1978).

[16]Office of Personnel Management, *OPM News,* April 3, 1979, p. 1–6. The AFGE is followed by National Federation of Federal Employees, 641 units and 138,672; National Treasury Employees Union, 16 units and 98,989; National Association of Government Employees, 254 units and 78,421; and Metal Trades Council, 52 units and 65,088.

[17]92 Stat. 1198 (1978).

[18]92 Stat. 1194 (1978). Section 7103 (a) (14) states that "conditions of employment means personnel policies, practices, and matters, whether established by rule, regulation, or otherwise, affecting working conditions, except that such term does not include policies, practices, and matters—(A) relating to political activities . . . ; (B) relating to the classification of any position; or (C) to the extent such matters are specifically provided for by Federal statute."

[19]92 Stat. 1204–1205 (1978).

[20]W. J. Kilberg, T. Angelo, and L. Lorber, "Grievances and Arbitration Patterns in the Federal Service," *Monthly Labor Review* 95 (November 1972), pp. 23–24. For an excellent review, see Henry B. Frazier, III, "Labor Arbitration in the Federal Service," *George Washington Law Review* 45 (May 1977), pp. 712–756.

[21]92 Stat. 1204–1206 (1978).

[22]Henry B. Frazier, III, "Labor-Management Relations in the Federal Government," *Labor Law Journal* 30 (March-1979), p. 136.

[23]92 Stat. 1211–1214, 1216 (1978).

[24]U.S. Civil Service Commission, Office of Labor-Management Relations, *Grievances Arbitration in the Federal Service* (Springfield, Va.: National Technical Information Service, 1977), p. iii. For example, in 1976, 96 percent of the total federal sector arbitration cases (254) featured a binding decision compared with only 4.7 percent of the *total cases* (121) heard by arbitrators in 1970.

[25]Frazier, "Labor-Management Relations," pp. 131–133.

[26]"The Strike That Stunned the Country," *Time,* March 3, 1970, p. 11.

[27]"Federal Workers March to a New Drummer," *Business Week,* March 28, 1970, p. 91. For a visual and descriptive depiction of working conditions, the reader is also referred to pp. 86–87 and pp. 90–92.

[28]Ibid., p. 91.

[29]S. C. Shannon, "Work Stoppage in Government: The Postal Strike of 1970," *Monthly Labor Review* 101 (July 1978), pp. 15–17.

[30]Nesbitt, *Labor Relations in the Government,* pp. 8–90.

[31]*United Federation of Postal Clerks v. Blount,* 325 F. Supp. 879 (1971); 404 U.S. 802 (1971).

[32]Nesbitt, *Labor Relations in the Government,* pp. 316–347.

[33]"A Stop-the-Clock Postal Pay Deal Aids the Battle against Inflation," *Time,* July 31, 1978, p. 50.

[34]Sharon Smith, "Are Postal Workers Overpaid or Underpaid?" *Industrial Relations* 15 (May 1976), pp. 168–176.

[35]"Postal Strike Threat Apparently Averted as Two Sides Agree to Resume Talks," *Wall Street Journal,* August 29, 1978, p. 2.

[36]"Postal Labor Uncertainty Will Linger Despite Arbitrated Settlement of Dispute," *Wall Street Journal,* September 18, 1978, p. 7.

[37]Ibid. Also see Leon Bornstein, "Postal Accord Retains 'No Layoffs' Clause," *Monthly Labor Review* 101 (September 1978), p. 13; and Leon Bornstein, "Arbitration Awards Higher Pay to Postal Employees," *Monthly Labor Review* 101 (November 1978), p. 44.

[38]Harriet Berger and Edward A. Bloustedt, "Clerk versus Mail Handler: Jurisdictional Disputes in the Postal Service," *Labor Law Journal* 27 (October 1976), p. 641. The unions included United Federation of Postal Clerks, National Association of Special Delivery Messengers, and National Association of Post Office and General Maintenance Employees.

[39]David M. Cohen, "Grievance Arbitration in the United States Postal Service," *Arbitration Journal* 28 (December 1973), pp. 258–262.

[40]Stuart R. Wolk, "Postal Reform: Fact or Fiction?" *Labor Law Journal* 22 (June 1971), pp. 365–374.

[41]Bureau of National Affairs, *Government Employee Relations Reporter,* July 3, 1978, p. 766:3. Also see

Urban C. Lehner, "Odds Don't Favor an All-Out Postal Strike, but Mail Users Prepare for One Anyway," *Wall Street Journal*, July 7, 1978, p. 8.

[42]"Postal Crisis: Preserving a Public Service," *American Federationist* 84 (May 1977), pp. 12–13.

[43]In November 1978, President Carter signed a law that forbade unionization of the armed forces. This law provides a penalty of a fine of up to $10,000 and five years in prison for military personnel who knowingly join a military union or who solicit membership in a military union. To keep unions from developing an interest in any union organizing campaign, the law provides that unions enrolling military personnel for purposes of collective bargaining could be fined as much as $250,000. See 47 USLW 2315, November 14, 1978.

[44]"Huge Majority Opposes Unionized Armed Forces," *Gallup Opinion Index: Report No. 146* (Princeton, N.J.: American Institute of Public Opinion, September 1977), pp. 1–4.

[45]Norma Meacham Crotty, "Unionization of the United States Military: Prospects and Pitfalls," *Industrial and Labor Relations Forum* 12 (1977), pp. 3–4.

[46]David Cortright, "Unions and Democracy," *AEI Defense Review*, no. 1, 1977, p. 3.

[47]James K. McCollum and Jerald F. Robinson, "The Law and Current Status of Unions in the Military Establishment," *Labor Law Journal* 28 (July 1977), pp. 421–430. It should also be noted that the same survey found only 32 percent of the respondents would join a union if they were legally allowed to do so. For a related empirical study of U.S. Army Reservists, see Patrick W. Carlton and Maxine A. Enderlein, "Attitudes of U.S. Army Reservists toward Military Unions," *Journal of Collective Negotiations in the Public Sector* 7, no. 2 (1978), pp. 111–127.

[48]See, for example, "Military Pay: What the Furor Is All About," *U.S. News & World Report*, August 22, 1977, pp. 28–30.

[49]"Why Discriminate against Military People?" *U.S. News & World Report*, August 22, 1977, p. 31.

[50]Paul D. Staudohar, "An Assessment of Unionization in the Armed Services," *Journal of Collective Negotiations in the Public Sector* 6, no. 1 (1977), pp. 4–5.

[51]U.S. Senate, Committee on Armed Services, *Unionization of the Armed Forces* (hearings before the committee), S.274 and S.997, 95th Cong., 1st sess., 1977, p. 285.

[52]Walter J. Mossberg and Richard J. Levine, "Union Plans '76 Drive to Represent Servicemen: Legalities Are Explored, and Pentagon Shudders," *Wall Street Journal*, June 27, 1975, p. 30. President Carter has noted apathy of various unions toward organizing the military. *Army Times*, April 14, 1977, pp. 8, 12.

[53]"AFGE's Blaylock Will Keep Eye on Military Problems," *Navy Times*, October 10, 1977, p. 4.

[54]Charles D. Phillips and Judith A. Crosby, "Public Sector Unionization and the U.S. Military: A First Amendment Issue," in Alan Ned Sabrosky, ed., *Blue-Collar Soldiers?* (Boulder, Colo.: Westview Press, 1977), p. 89. For another discussion of related private and public sector cases which might guide the Supreme Court's reasoning if a constitutional conflict should arise, see Paul D. Staudohar, "Legal and Constitutional Issues Raised by Organization of the Military," *Labor Law Journal* 28 (March 1977), pp. 182–186.

[55]*Parker v. Levy*, 417 U.S. 733 (1974).

[56]Ibid.

[57]Ibid., p. 739.

[58]Ibid., pp. 743–758. For a similar application of this reasoning on Article 134, see *Secretary of the Navy v. Mark Avrech*, 418 U.S. 676 (1974).

[59]Even if unions were granted constitutional protection, their efforts to organize the military could be thwarted by another Supreme Court decision. *Greer v. Spock*, 424 U.S. 828 (1976).

[60]U.S. Senate, Committee on Armed Services, *Unionization of Armed Forces*, p. 273.

[61]W. Gene Phillips, "For a Brotherhood of Men-at-Arms: The Case for Military Unionization," in Sabrosky, *Blue-Collar Soldiers?* p. 58.

[62]U.S. Senate, Committee on Armed Services, *Unionization of Armed Forces*, p. 9.

[63]*New York Times Magazine*, September 24, 1975, p. 53.

[64]Strom Thurmond, "Military Unions: No," *AEI Defense Review*, no. 1, 1977, p. 19.

[65]For a thoroughly researched discussion of foreign military unions see Ezra S. Krendel, "European Military Unions," in Ezra S. Krendel and Bernard Samoff, eds., *Unionizing the Armed Forces* (Philadelphia: University of Pennsylvania Press, 1977), pp. 179–195; see also William Gomberg, "Unionization of the U.S. Armed Military Forces—Its Development, Status, and Future," in Barbara D. Dennis, ed., *Proceedings of the Thirtieth Annual Winter Meeting: Industrial Relations Research Association* (Madison, Wis.: Industrial Relations Research Association, 1978), pp. 51–54.

[66]Crotty, "Unionization of the Military," p. 10.

[67]Cortright, "Unions and Democracy," p. 8.

Chapter 16

Foreign Labor Movements and Transnational Collective Bargaining

"We began wondering whether we really understood the American system of industrial relations and particularly its uniqueness. Why was it so different from others elsewhere . . . ?"

Clark Kerr
John T. Dunlop
Frederick H. Harbison
Charles A. Myers

Growing interdependency among nations, major improvements in communication and travel between countries, and the increasing role of multinational corporations (MNC) have all led to the need to learn more about labor relations systems in other parts of the world. Books have been written about many of the specific topics in this chapter, and no attempt will be made to present detailed descriptions or analysis of labor relations systems in the countries mentioned. The chapter presents a number of unique and interesting features of a variety of countries with the hope of encouraging the readers to pursue more serious investigations in the future. Its coverage ranges from the developing countries of South America, Asia, and Africa to the countries nearest our borders—Mexico and Canada—to those with which the United States does the largest volume of trade—Japan and the Western European countries. From these discussions, specific attention is directed toward multinational corporations and transnational collective bargaining.

Unions in Other Countries

Many U.S. residents tend to view the rest of the world in terms of their own patterns of living. The fact is that virtually no country has labor relations like ours; even the most similar country, Canada, has several major departures from typical U.S. labor relations practices. Unions of Eastern and Western Europe have much closer ties to political parties; Japanese unions are organized on the enterprise level; Latin American unions are split along ideological lines. By contrast, the United States' industrial relations system is based on majority rule, exclusive representation for bargaining agents, and political independence.[1]

Canada

Canada's labor relations system is affected by a number of variables: foreign influences, climate, natural resources, and two major linguistic and cultural groups. Its economy is subject to cyclical fluctuations resulting from harsh winters, seasonality of its industries, and foreign influences (mostly the U.S.). In addition, Canada's geographical spread and regional concentration of resources and production have led to decentralized and fragmented collective bargaining. The penetration of United States corporations into Canada has had a significant effect on Canadian labor relations due to the fact that many major decisions still are made in the United States. The French- and English-speaking division of Canada has produced two distinct labor movements; further, relationships between management, which is primarily unilingually English-speaking, and the predominantly French-speaking work force have not been ideal.[2]

In Canada, governments within the provinces (similar to the various states in the U.S.), not the federal government, have established the legal framework for 90 percent of the collective bargaining.[3] These laws are similar to the United States' in many ways and include such components as appropriate bargaining unit, prohibition of work stoppages during the tenure of agreements, and guidelines for workers voting for representation rights.[4] On the other hand, the emphasis on provincial determination has resulted in many different legal frameworks for Canadian collective bargaining (much the way it has in the public sector in the United States).

More recently, because there has been significant union activity in the public sector (for example, postal and teacher strikes), the Canadian federal government has been asserting itself more and accumulating more centralized authority to produce a stronger national government with respect to labor relations and standards. In response, the Canadian Labour Council (CLC), a labor federation similar to the AFL-CIO in the U.S., has more and more become the central voice for organized labor. As the federal government continues to gather more power over collective bargaining, the provincial governments will lose control, and the CLC will gain power in its role.[5]

Probably the most controversial issue in Canadian labor relations grows out of the alleged domination by U.S. unions and corporations. Over 35 percent of Canada's industry is foreign owned, but this segment accounts for 70 percent of the business activity.[6] Of the twelve largest labor unions (representing over 50,000 members), eight are affiliated with major U.S. labor unions, such as the United Auto Workers and Teamsters, and the remaining ones are AFL-CIO affiliates.[7] This means there is a potential for undermining Canadian sovereignty if foreign-based unions and companies are not sensitive to Canada's needs. For instance, Canadians have serious concerns over decisions which are made by U.S.-based unions and corporations but implemented in Canada.

A typical example is the wage parity for Canadian workers that resulted from the recent U.S. automobile negotiations; this parity led to wage scales that were not consistent with the Canadian government's interest in fighting inflation through moderate wage increases.[8] As a rule, U.S. union leaders do not involve themselves in Canadian negotiations; however, they will intervene when they believe labor relations are being mishandled or where there is a crisis.[9]

Latin America

Collective bargaining in Latin America is far less extensive and sophisticated than corresponding activities in the United States. While the percentage of workers covered by labor agreements is greater in Mexico, Venezuela, and Argentina than in the United States, this amount reflects more a government extension of contract terms than actual industry-wide bargaining patterns. The extent of development of collective bargaining may be illustrated in three categories:

1. The advanced group, as exemplified by Mexico and Argentina.
2. A much larger middle group in which bargaining ranges from advanced collective bargaining with larger firms to very simple or no bargaining in smaller firms, as in Chile and Brazil.
3. A large third group in which collective bargaining is virtually unknown, as in Colombia, Ecuador, and Uruguay.[10]

In the more industrialized countries of the world, people interpret labor-management relations activities to mean the wide nature of the relationships between employers and employees. However, people of Latin American countries tend to define labor relations in terms of the voluminous labor codes and governmental regulations.[11]

Labor relations vary widely among the countries in Latin America, but one common thrust is present: the close connection between trade unions and political parties. For example, in Mexico unions constitute a large section of the ruling political party and therefore are assigned a quota of candidates on the party's ticket for office. Thus, unions have some assurance of having a voice in the party's program and on its council.[12] Some unions have been very effective in gaining relatively high wages for members. For example, the electrical workers in Mexico earn two to three times more than the urban working class.[13] Likewise, unions have been criticized because they have made gains for their own members while neglecting the interests of the great mass of people, including the peasants, who are terribly poor.[14]

Labor agreements vary in content both within countries and among countries. In Argentina, labor agreements include provisions that set forth in some detail the employment conditions and establish a highly developed shop steward system to administer grievances and assure that employers abide by the agreements. In Chile, labor agreements are more general, but they do establish certain minimum rules and include a grievance machinery to enforce the agreement. In Brazil, where unions have struggled since 1945 to have a greater say in determining employment rules and conditions for their members, they have achieved more through labor legislation than by engaging in collective bargaining.

In these countries, political parties maintain close ties with unions for their support, votes, and influence. Likewise, trade unions depend on the politicians for laws to protect their members, to legalize their organizations, and to regulate their relations with employers.[15] On the other hand, political parties have appealed to organized labor to favor their own policies, and in some cases, they have assimilated these organizations in hopes that they will remain temporarily satisfied and continue to support the existing economic and political system.[16]

Western Europe and Great Britain

Unionization in Western Europe is significantly greater than in the United States, with the exception of France and Italy. The range is from 38 percent in Germany to 80 percent in Sweden. Unions have been able to use this membership strength to accumulate political influence at the national level. Further, they have been able to coordinate their efforts with large, well-established labor parties in government to achieve their goals. Unions have achieved significantly greater worker participation in the operation of the firm—many times through legislative mandate and sometimes through management reaction to wildcat strikes and worker dissatisfaction.[17] In addition, public opinion in these countries strongly supports the idea that worker participation enhances production, fosters harmony, and enriches the worker's personality.[18]

The labor relations system in Western Europe can be contrasted with that of the United States in a number of ways:

1. In the United States, unions are selected by the majority of the appropriate bargaining unit, whereas in Western Europe exclusive representation is an unknown concept.
2. In the United States, the exclusive bargaining representative has a monopoly over all employee bargaining, and the employer is required to bargain only with the legally certified union. In Western Europe, the employer often bargains with a number of unions in addition to councils elected by the workers.
3. In Western Europe, negotiations take place between representatives of

employer associations and those representing a confederation of unions; in the United States, this bargaining arrangement is adopted only in a few industries.

4. In the United States, the collective bargaining agreement supersedes the individual contract; in Western Europe, the individual contract is still used within the general framework of collective bargaining, and the individual worker can still separately negotiate employment conditions within the collective bargaining guidelines.

5. The number of fringe benefits established by law is greater in Europe; therefore, trade unions have found that they can obtain benefits more quickly through the political area and have tied themselves more closely with political parties.[19]

The traditional system in Great Britain is characterized by voluntary collective bargaining, implemented without legal compulsion through unenforceable labor agreements that have been negotiated by a large number of multi-union–multi-employer negotiating committees.[20] There are nearly 600 labor unions in the United Kingdom, over three times the number in the United States, and a manufacturing firm typically negotiates with about seven unions. Because there is little labor relations law, there is a wide diversity in the collective bargaining arrangements. One of the most important negotiations involves the Engineering Employers' Federation, representing 4,500 plants, and the Confederation of Shipbuilding and Engineering Unions, representing 34 unions and over 2 million employees. This agreement sets forth general guidelines that establish the floor for additional bargaining at the plant. Labor agreements are administered at the plant level; however, they are not enforceable by law and grievances are not privately arbitrated.

Although coordinated at the national level, each union negotiates its own agreements at the plant level. Shop stewards, unlike their U.S. counterparts, are volunteers serving without pay and cannot be removed by union executives. Often, they accumulate authority and influence at the plant and have more control over local union affairs than any national union official. Steward councils composed of union stewards from various unions and works councils representing members of the various departments are important in the labor relations system.

Labor agreements at the plant level are often negotiated by representatives of the national union, steward councils, and works councils. These agreements usually have no fixed term and include letters of understanding, minutes of meetings, and oral understandings. While there is no legal obligation to negotiate, unions have gained extensive power and control over jobs, refusing to work with any employee whom they find in bad standing and maintaining strict membership discipline.[21]

Co-determination Policies One unique feature of Western European labor relations is the interest in and wide implementation of co-determination concepts. These concepts include the policies of shared authority on personnel matters, protected employee rights, guarantees of worker participation, and appeal of alleged unfair personnel decisions. West Germany has moved further in co-determination than other European countries, but Luxembourg, France, Austria, Norway, and Sweden all have some sort of legal requirements for worker representation on company boards—generally in the form of works councils that vary greatly in authority. Other countries (for example, Belgium, England, Italy, and Switzerland) have no laws requiring worker participation on boards, but forms of worker participation are present in various stages of development.[22]

A look at West Germany's co-determination system. West Germany's highly developed system of co-determination is highlighted here in order to give readers a definitive idea of its operation. Co-determination in West Germany can be traced back to 1920, but formulated principles were not legally established until the Co-determination Law of 1952, applicable to the iron, coal, and steel industries. This law provided for a labor director on the executive committee and a parity agreement in the supervisory board (half representing the owners and shareholders, half representing employees, plus a neutral chairperson).

Formalized co-determination after World War II can be attributed to some degree to union reactions to the Nazi era, during which unions were dissolved and industrialists amassed tremendous power. Co-determination developed at least in part to allow worker involvement at a level in organizations where any possible extremism among industrialists and government officials could be monitored.[23]

Enacted in 1972, the Labor-Management Relations Act (of West Germany) redefined the functions of the works councils and specified rights of the individual worker. The council functions were oriented toward increased worker participation in the immediate labor environment. Workers' rights include the right to be informed about matters pertaining to their jobs, to make suggestions about their jobs, to see all of their work-related files, and to appeal management decisions that are considered unfair. Works councils were established at the plant level in such a way that they could guard and monitor these rights. They also serve as useful instruments of conflict resolution and a means of communication between management and the worker.

Co-determination expands the voice of labor in the two governing boards of large corporations: the supervisory board and board of executive directors.[24] While the supervisory board concerns itself with overall strategic business issues, the board of executive directors runs the daily business operation. The Co-determination Act of 1976 extended co-determination coverage to all companies, except the already covered coal and steel industries, which employ more than 2,000 workers (smaller companies remain under the 1952 law). The supervisory boards continued to have equal representation between capital and labor; however, the labor side was divided into three distinct groups: (a) union representatives, (b) white- and blue-collar employees, and (c) executives (see Exhibit 16–1).

Employee members of the supervisory boards are elected by a direct vote by employees or by a vote of electors who themselves have been elected to represent the employees. Employees in the firms decide by direct vote which election approach they will use, even though the law suggests that direct vote be used in small firms and election by employee representatives in larger ones. Union leaders tend to favor the indirect approach, and conservatives prefer the direct. The chairperson and vice chairperson are elected by two-thirds vote; if this two-thirds vote is not obtainable, the shareholders elect the chairperson and labor the vice-chairperson. The chairperson's position is important because he or she casts the deciding vote on all issues that the supervisory board cannot resolve in the first round.[25]

Since the 1952 act, the works councils have been involved in regulating personnel and industrial relations practices and policies. These include: daily hours, breaks, remuneration, leave schedules, discipline, welfare

Exhibit 16–1
Selection Model of
Co-determination
Membership for
Large Corporations

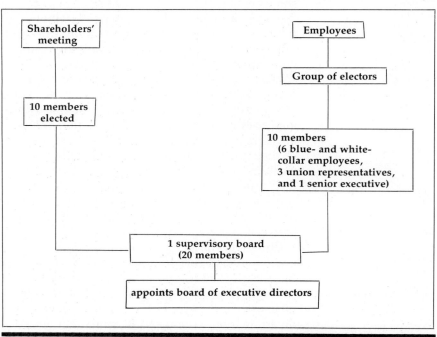

Source: Adapted from David T. Fisher, "Worker Participation in West German Industry," *Monthly Labor Review* 101 (May 1978), p. 61.

services, job and piece rates, new methods of compensation, vocational training, and review of major alterations that could involve substantial disadvantages for the company employees. Then, in 1972, the powers of the works councils were increased. They now also police union contracts, handle employee grievances, and co-determine personnel forms, wage plans, training, and related programs.[26]

Co-determination has had both advocates and critics. It has been labeled a "social partnership" that has brought about "social harmony" between unions and employers.[27] It has been credited as the main reason for relative labor peace in West Germany for the last twenty years, when compared to nearby countries like England, France, and Italy.[28] West German Chancellor Helmut Schmidt acclaimed it as the key to his country's postwar economic recovery and the competitive economic advantage which West Germany has held internationally.[29]

Critics have enumerated several deficiencies in this worker participation system. Chief among these are: the limited involvement and consequent alienation of the rank-and-file employees, the lack of final control over major decisions, the potential for co-opting union delegates (making private deals) by the employer,[30] the likelihood of elected representatives becoming nearly permanent fixtures of power, and workers' feeling of detachment from their representatives on the board.[31]

Japanese Industrial Relations

Japan's industrial relations system has three special characteristics: lifetime employment, a unique wage system, and the enterprise or "company" union. *Lifetime employment* simply means that an employee, after joining the company, will remain employed until retirement (usually at 55 years of age, although 20 percent of the Japanese firms have extended the age to 60). Only in extreme circumstances will a company discharge an employee.

The *wage system* in Japan has several distinguishing characteristics:

1. Salaries paid monthly, even though the employee may be absent (with justification) from work.
2. Small wage differentials between regular line employees and staff personnel, all of whom are members of the same union.
3. Wage distinctions between amounts earned for one's work (for example, efficiency output) and amounts earned for just being an employee (such as allowances for housing, transportation, and dependents).
4. Wages accepted as permanent and lasting for the employee's entire career, including a minimum annual increase and lump sum at retirement.

The *enterprise union* is composed of employees working for a single employer at a single location. These unions comprise nearly 90 percent of all union organizations in Japan and include all categories of skills among employees of a company. The development of the enterprise union has been aided substantially by the system of lifetime employment and a heavy reliance on seniority. Thus, the individual employee identifies more closely with the company than the typical employee in many Western countries.

Although labor unions for the textile, electricity, shipbuilding, automobile, steel, appliance, and chemical industries hold conferences to discuss industrial policies, they do *not* consider such topics as wages, working conditions, and other employment policies. These topics are covered by direct negotiations involving the enterprise union. Instead, they discuss industrial problems in a more general context (for example, economic growth, employment forecasts, retirement ages, and improved communications).[32]

As a result of higher oil prices, rising protectionism abroad, revaluation of the yen (Japanese currency), lowering trade barriers, and slower economic growth (down from 10 percent to 6 percent per annum), several Japanese firms have recently been considering abandoning their policies of lifetime job security. Compounding these economic problems have been the gradual aging of the work force, automatic wage increases based on seniority, and higher labor costs. Some firms have offered "sayonara" (the Japanese word for goodbye) premiums to encourage early retirement; some have set up in-house plant maintenance units for workers over 48 years old at a 20 percent reduction in pay; others have taken a harsher approach of laying off the older workers.[33]

Since 1973, one of Japan's largest unions, Japanese Federation of Synthetic Chemical Workers' Union, has lost 8 percent of its members through firings and layoffs. Some have concluded that lifetime employment as a policy has begun to expire and that Japanese employers will begin laying off workers during recessions and linking pay raises more closely to skill than seniority. If employers abandon the security of a lifetime employment system, they will have to adjust to job-hopping by employees and to a more adversarial type of labor relations system.[34] Moreover, the government will probably become more involved with problems of unemployment and industrial conflicts. For example, almost 700 man-days per 1,000 workers were lost in larger establishments due to strikes in 1974, and the strike participation rate of employees was a rather high 10 percent—both figures exceeding U.S. statistics for most years since 1950.[35]

Some Japanese union leaders believe that many social and economic problems cannot be solved by collective bargaining alone. In fact, Sohyo, Japan's large labor union federation, has not only proposed wage demands but has also submitted demands to government officials for public housing, a national minimum wage, and better living standards in its annual *shunto* or people's spring offensive.[36]

In the final analysis, Japanese employers and unions eventually will have to face a number of critical issues that may cause a break with the traditional system: early retirement, higher unemployment, elimination of automatic pay increases and promotions, introduction of labor-saving devices, union emphasis on job security rather than wage hikes, decline of worker loyalty to the firm, and declining competitiveness with countries that are developing rapidly, such as Brazil, South Korea, Singapore, and Taiwan.[37]

Australia and New Zealand

Australia has developed a compulsory arbitration system at the federal level and in four of its six states,[38] and while the system relies mostly on negotiation and conciliation, it is very legalistic.[39] Two of the states have established wage boards that are quasi-legislative, tripartite bodies for the direct regulation of wages and conditions. For labor agreements to be legal under Australian law, unions must register them with the appropriate arbitration tribunal. This form of compulsory arbitration is designed to restrict the number of strikes and lockouts, although these activities do occur at a moderate rate after the rather complicated arbitration procedures are followed.[40]

As is true with other of the world's more advanced economies, industrial democracy has become a subject of widespread interest in Australia, and the state Labor Party has adopted a platform that encourages joint consultation, worker directors, job enrichment, and worker control. Several large employers have already begun experimenting with a variety of these approaches, for example, semi-autonomous work groups, joint consultation, and work redesign.[41]

New Zealand's system of industrial relations is based on conciliation and arbitration quite similar to Australia's. Even though arbitration is not compulsory, the parties are usually pressured to arbitrate when they have labor disputes. Still, the greatest percentage settle their disputes through collective bargaining, and no dispute is referred to arbitration until after the parties have negotiated and referred their cases to conciliation.[42] Where there are disputes, the unions and employers are required to follow precise procedures for resolving them. Conciliators who have legal authority to make recommendations for settlement merely suggest formulas for settlement. If both parties accept, the formulas will be incorporated into their agreement. If not, the unsettled dispute must be submitted to the court of arbitration, whose decision is final and cannot be appealed. Since strikes are illegal, there are a number of legal sanctions (such as fines) available. But in reality, these penalties are rarely invoked, and strikes have been on the increase.[43] Because of this high incidence of strikes, mediation has been recently introduced as another means for resolving labor disputes without strikes.[44]

Eastern Europe — Soviet Bloc Countries

After World War II, Communists took power in most of the East European countries and began transforming their political, economic, social, and cultural systems to the Soviet model—formalizing and bureaucratizing institutions and social systems that are primarily authoritarian and controlled and directed by the Communist Party. The result has been increased similarities in the industrial relations systems among the various countries, although Yugoslavia launched a rival model in 1950.[45]

In these countries, trade unions represent all employed persons, white- and blue-collar alike, and are authorized to represent both their members and nonmembers. Thus, trade unions represent nearly 90 percent of the occupied populations. Theoretically, they are independent organizations, and nobody can interfere with their internal affairs. Realistically, they recognize the influence of the party, their autonomy is low, and they are subordinate to the party. Unions are governed in accordance with principles of democratic centralism, where each member may vote in a democratic manner; however, the organization structure entails centralized authority at the top. The union members have only meager rights and very extensive duties, and they can be punished for failing to perform their duties according to union statutes.[46] Under the Soviet-type system, the party "elite" will not allow trade union members to associate and dissociate at will. If such freedom were allowed, party officials believe that articulation of group interest would increase, unity of the official trade unions would be endangered, and the party "elite" would lose control over them.

In Eastern Europe, trade unions have two major functions:

1. Production promotion, which includes promoting the state plan, strengthening work discipline, and raising productivity.
2. Political indoctrination, which includes fostering the political consciousness, dedication to the public interest, and education of trade unionists on party matters.

Other proclaimed functions include defending the workers' interests, complying with labor legislation, administering social insurance, and promoting opportunities for physical training, sport, and recreation. Unions have attempted to perform these functions through only a small number of trade unions. For example, there were nineteen in Hungary in 1966, thirty in Czechoslovakia in 1969, twenty-five in the Soviet Union in 1970, and twenty-three in Poland in 1976.

To accomplish these functions, workers have been granted rights ranging from the right to make suggestions to the right to make decisions. These include the right to consummate a collective bargaining agreement that enumerates the rights and obligations of employees. But the agreements are not the result of collective bargaining as in the United States; their content is more the result of legal and political directives. Therefore, the labor agreements differ greatly in content, character, and role when compared to those in the West even though they may be labeled identically.[47]

The Soviet labor system has many critics, one of whom, Vladimir Bukovsky, appeared before the AFL-CIO Executive Council with its president, George Meany, and met at the White House with President Carter and Vice-President Mondale. Mr. Bukovsky alleges:

> Soviet trade unions do not protect the workers against hunger, persecution or exploitation. Labor unions in the USSR are part of the party-government machine, which addresses itself not to defense of the interests of working people, but only to the implementation of party-government projects. Even the Soviet Supreme Court, having looked into the practice of court cases involving illegal firings, was forced to point out that the labor union organizations are not observing labor legislation and do not defend the workers actively enough. Workers' complaints to labor union organizations are handed over to the KGB [Soviet secret police].[48]

Further, Bukovsky contends that Soviet union members are prevented from using instruments of industrial conflict which many countries have accepted. He states:

> The rare, desperate strikes in the Soviet Union do not occur in the demand of better working conditions or a raise in pay—but only when the workers and their families literally have nothing to eat.
>
> The weavers in Ivanovo struck in 1970 when food ceased to be supplied to the city. As the USSR Helsinki Accords Monitoring Group informs us, four port workers in Riga were arrested in May 1976 and in August sentenced to 1½ to 3 years deprivation of freedom after a strike which took place because of the absence of meat in the food stores.
>
> The Soviet Union has signed various international conventions recognizing the right of workers to strike. But it has not bothered to formulate this right in its own legislation. Moreover, strikes are regarded as a "rude, group violation of social order," for which one can be deprived of freedom for up to three years. This is for a completely peaceful strike—merely a refusal to work. When it comes to other forms of struggle—such as sit-down or picketing—these are punishable under the article entitled "mass disorders," by deprivation of freedom, up to 15 years in jail or by the death penalty.
>
> In the West, the decision to strike is usually taken for granted by the labor union. In the Soviet Union, this is beyond imagination. Soviet trade unions do not protect the workers against hunger, persecution or exploitation.[49]

Hungarian Labor Relations The Hungarian trade unions have been an exception to the Soviet model in that their freedom of action was legally expanded in the late 1960s. At the enterprise level, the local unions have been granted the right of veto to suspend action on certain issues. Theoretically, workers could strike at the local level if decisions were made without their participation, applicable laws were violated, or policies of the party were distorted. In practice, trade unions have not used their full potential but have continued to act reluctantly in their role as a protector of the workers' interests. The union committees have actually been ineffectual, and negotiated labor agreements have often been adopted without any real participation. In addition, the content of the agreements has reflected a controlled environment because some of the more important economic issues have been omitted and excessive detail and trivia have been included.[50]

Yugoslavia: An Alternative System Unlike other East European countries under Communist control, Yugoslavia has a socio-political system of self-management and a market-oriented economy. Its constitution of 1974 promotes development of the self-management system, self-managed labor associations, and self-governed communes. These communes are based on self-management by workers through their various labor organizations and local communities; workers make decisions that affect their common interests—economic, social, and political.

All means of production and natural resources are socially owned; thus, all enterprises are the property of society. Income is generated by the operation of the market and by selling to other economic units (communes). In their respective organizations, workers manage their own business and productive resources, regulate their mutual labor relationships, and decide the income various forms of labor will earn. Further, each operational working unit is integrated with other units until the entire system is fully integrated.[51]

This system stands as a clear alternative to the centralized system of Soviet Russia because the Yugoslav system has a worker council which serves as the major policy- and decision-making body. It elects the chief operating officer, the executive board, and the professional staff, which submits reports of economic activity periodically to the worker council. If the year-end economic report is rejected, it is equivalent to a vote of no confidence, and the executive board resigns. If it is accepted, the board proceeds to propose its plan for the next period.[52]

Developing Nations in Asia and Africa

Many of the labor relations systems in the developing countries are in their embryonic stages when measured by Western World standards. One exception to this generalization is India, where collective bargaining over wages, employment conditions, and other subjects has been fairly widespread in manufacturing, mining, trade and commerce, transport, and service industries.[53] Although strikes have been problems in India (3,270,000 worker-days lost in 1974), a system for dispute settlement (including conciliation and voluntary arbitration) has been established.[54]

On the other hand, other countries are considerably further behind in labor union development. In Korea, for example, it was not until the 1960s that efforts to implement modern labor relations activities were seriously made.[55] In Malaysia, there was no legal provision in the statutes that would allow trade unions to claim recognition until 1967.[56] To understand and appreciate the special qualities of unionism in these developing nations, one must review the evolution of unions in the Western Hemisphere in the eighteenth, nineteenth, and twentieth centuries. As in the Western World, as more workers in the less developed nations became wage earners and discovered that they were likely to remain wage earners for the remainder of their lives, they became more interested in forming unions.

In Africa, many unions were formed to resist unfair treatment and exploitation by firms located in other countries (mostly Europe and the U.S.) that have difficulty communicating with local workers, especially since many of the managers only speak English, French, or Dutch. In these African countries, trade unions have aligned themselves with political parties, but they seldom have been successful in eliciting broad support, even from the workers. In some cases, the governing political parties have gone so far as to establish party branches at workplaces, but even these do not seem to have aroused much enthusiasm among the workers.[57] In Ghana, Tanganyika, and Kenya, unions have been reorganized, reduced in number, and placed under state control. When Algeria became independent, organized labor was included in the governing party's inner circle, but the government then decided to change the union's leadership when it became too independent and demanding.

Several other factors have limited African labor union growth and development:

1. A relatively low percentage of its work force is composed of wage earners (workers employed by others).[58]
2. The range of different unions in African countries has been a limiting, almost overwhelming, factor. For example, there are "tribal" unions, which serve mostly social welfare functions; "craft" unions organized by occupation or skill; "house" unions organized within the particular company or firm; "industrial" unions established for a particular industry; and "general" unions, which cover a substantial portion of a country's work force. For instance, in one country, Nigeria, there are 873 unions (mostly "house" unions); in Tanzania, there is only one official union.
3. Divisiveness within many African unions has meant a lack of coordination among unions. The higher union officials are usually from the technical and clerical occupations, while the ordinary members are largely manual workers; thus a lack of unity results from occupational differences. In addition, suspicion and mistrust grow out of ethnic differences. That is, one group of workers and its leaders may view

another ethnic group as seeking to monopolize jobs and power at its expense. This tribal heterogeneity in union membership seldom builds employee solidarity.[59]

In parts of Asia (India and Ceylon, for example) where the caste system plays a dominant role in the social system, workers often turn to higher caste members instead of unions in presenting their cases to management. As in parts of Africa, the less developed economic systems have made it difficult for either industrial or craft unions to develop. Because there were never enough printers, machinists, mill workers, etc., on which to form a base for "true" trade unions, unions developed on geographic and political bases rather than on industrial or craft bases. But more than likely, as these nations develop, leaders will emerge from the ranks and the likelihood of union growth and development will increase.[60]

Efforts at Cooperation among Unions across National Boundaries

Any discussion of foreign labor movements would be incomplete without mentioning efforts made by unions in different countries to develop some type of cooperative activities. One of the earliest efforts in this regard was the creation of the International Labor Organization (ILO). Founded in 1919 by a small group of social innovators, among whom was Samuel Gompers, president of the American Federation of Labor, the ILO was established to help raise the standards of life and work around the world by adopting uniform standards. In its early years, the organization established such norms as the eight-hour day, limits on child labor, freedom to form unions and strike, and a score of others.

In 1954, the Soviet Union rejoined the ILO after twenty years of absence, and by 1976 the ILO's membership had doubled. Gradually, it became more political, taking such stances as condemning Israel in 1974 for discriminating against Arab workers and seating the Palestine Liberation Organization (PLO) as one of its members. Such actions provoked the United States to withdraw its membership and support (25 percent of the organization's operational budget) from the ILO.[61]

Other efforts have been made more along the lines of the international trade secretariats, which are union coordinating bodies on an international scale designed to counteract the multinational firms. While these organizations have achieved only limited success in fostering collective bargaining, coordinating strikes and boycott activities, and enacting laws regulating companies' activities, they have been successful in exchanging data and providing information useful to their memberships. Although these international trade secretariats vary in size, a 1975 Conference Board report found nine of the international organizations with affiliated memberships ranging from 3 million to more than 11 million and representing unions in thirty-two to eighty-two countries.[62] The role of these organizations will be discussed further in the next section.

Part 4/Emerging Labor Relations Processes

Multinational Corporations and Transnational Collective Bargaining

The growing interdependency among nations and the activities of multinational corporations (MNCs)[63] have become important facets of economic life in the 1970s. Although multinational firms have existed for more than 150 years, their numbers and share of world output have expanded their importance and visibility. In addition, they have expanded consideration of the production phase of business to include marketing and distribution activities which cut across countries' borders.[64] MNCs are now developing production facilities and marketing their products in other countries instead of producing only at the home base and selling abroad, and they are doing so with increasing impact. For example, $36.8 billion were planned to be invested in foreign production facilities by U.S. firms in 1979, an increase of 16 percent over 1978, and sales of U.S. companies operating in foreign countries reached $514.7 billion in 1976.[65] Interestingly, foreign direct investment in the United States reached $34.1 billion in 1977, an increase of 11 percent, following an 11-percent rise in 1976.[66] More startling is the fact that fifty of the world's hundred largest economic units are MNCs; the other fifty are countries.[67] While U.S.-based multinationals still dominate the world economy, increasing numbers are operating from Western Europe and Japan.

Some union leaders view multinational firms as the root cause of American economic troubles. They contend that unemployment has resulted from the exportation of U.S. jobs to foreign countries and that the balance of payment deficits stem from the increase in the dollar outflow caused by U.S. investments abroad.[68] They further believe that the MNC "owes its allegiance to no one and has no interests above its goals of maximizing profits."[69] Therefore, the MNCs will move to those countries "where overhead and labor costs are lowest, where tax advantages are highest and where transportation facilities can be made available to transport goods and equipment."[70] One union leader believes that the MNC has "power to influence, if not dictate, national policies . . . [because of] . . . its readiness to locate capital, technology, administration, manufacture, merchandising, and other vital business operations wherever it pleases and to remove these resources from lands where it is displeased."[71]

Union Approaches to Multinational Bargaining and Employer Reactions

To combat the power of the MNCs and to seek objectives that are mutually beneficial to the unions and their members, union leaders have tried two main approaches: (a) collective bargaining and (b) legislative enactment. Through collective bargaining, unions have either attempted to directly bargain with the MNCs or coordinate their bargaining activities with unions in other countries by sharing information and supporting each other's activities. Legislative approaches typically have involved protective national legislation: regulations on foreign investments; international codes of conduct (fair labor standards) for the MNCs, such as minimum wages and full employment;[72] tax measures and regulatory schemes to limit outflow of capital and technology; and reporting requirements that provide unions information on MNCs.[73]

In addition to these two main approaches, unions have proposed *Guidelines on Multinational Companies* to regulate their modes of operations. Thus far, through the Organization for Economic Cooperation and Development, a Paris-based clearinghouse for economic policy makers in twenty-four industrial democratic countries, unions in most countries have adopted the guidelines. These guidelines include certain rights: the right to organize and bargain collectively, to have access to data for negotiations, to be trained as a member of the work force, and to be given advance notice for changes in operations. Further, subsidiaries of MNCs are expected to observe employment standards comparable to those in the host countries; MNCs are expected not to threaten to shift production to other countries to influence negotiations or to prevent unionization; and local management representatives should be authorized to negotiate on behalf of the MNCs.[74]

Although there have been efforts toward developing multinational union activities in the chemical,[75] food,[76] flat glass,[77] metal working,[78] and other industries,[79] MNCs have not accepted the unions' preferences for realistic transnational collective bargaining. Extension of collective bargaining from a national scale to an international scale would require a major change in the present attitudes of corporation management. Although some form of transnational industrial relations seems to be inevitable, most MNCs generally consider it a distant project and one which will not be lightly entertained by management.[80]

Part of management's opposition stems from the unions' potential for shutting down production on an international basis. Further, multinational bargaining would introduce a trilevel structure of bargaining which would include multinational negotiations, followed by national ones, then local. This additional level would increase the complexity of negotiations as well as companies' vulnerability to strikes at the international level without a comparable reduction in vulnerability at the national and local levels.[81]

In some cases, countries themselves are not encouraging investments by MNCs; taxation policies, building limitations, requirements for local partners, the possibility of nationalization and expropriation of facilities, and the risks of political uncertainties are factors deterring MNC investment.[82] Less developed countries seek additional investments by MNCs for economic stimulus to the countries' development, income, employment programs, and so on, and MNCs find these countries atttractive because of the low wage structures, tax incentives, and political guarantees. Such advantages are particularly appealing to the MNC, which must operate in a very competitive product market.[83] But when unions press via transnational bargaining for improved wages, benefits, and working conditions—all socially desirable goals for the populace—they become a force running counter to the short-run national economic goals of the country.[84] The economic boost MNCs can give a developing nation will not occur if firms fail to locate there; MNCs might well decide to avoid countries with the high wages and benefits that transnational bargaining has instituted.

Obstacles for Unions in Bargaining with MNCs

Unions face formidable tasks in their efforts to arrange transnational bargaining because they must be successful in mediating and balancing the conflicting interests of different groups encompassed by the MNC's employees, labor leaders, companies, and governments.[85] In fact, unions themselves provide some of the more important obstacles to transnational bargaining, and only when these are overcome can their attention be turned to external factors.

Absence of a central authority. Unions lack a strong, centralized decision-making authority regarding transnational affairs, and most national union leaders are reluctant to allow an international council to make decisions that affect their unions and members.

Cultural differences. Another complicating factor is the differences in ideological and religious beliefs among, for example, free trade unions and socialist- or communist-linked unions. Such differences have made it almost impossible for joint undertaking between unions in the free world and elsewhere.[86]

Lack of coordination of activities. Unions have not been very successful in coordinating their international bargaining, boycott, and strike activities. An excellent example occurred in the 1976 rubber strike of Goodyear, Uniroyal, B. F. Goodrich, and Firestone. (Each has extensive overseas operations; for example, Goodyear has thirty and Firestone has twenty-five non-U.S. operations.) Support for the U.S. strikes was to come from a multinational union, the International Federation of Chemical and General Workers Unions (ICF), which has affiliates in Europe, North America, and Japan. The ICF Rubber Division approved a ban on overtime by employees of nonstrike companies and a system of monitoring and preventing shipments to the United States. At the end of the strike— the longest rubber strike in U.S. history—the ICF claimed that its efforts had had a significant effect on the bargaining outcome; however, the facts seemed to contradict this claim. A study by Northrup and Rowan of the 1976 strike did not reveal a single instance of interference with tire shipments from Europe, Japan, or North America; in fact, they found that imports jumped substantially in anticipation of the strike and never fell below the prestrike level. Furthermore, even Canadian imports were significantly increased during the strike, reversing what had occurred several years before, when U.S. rubber workers refused to support a strike by Canadian rubber workers.[87]

Differing national priorities. The existing economic, social, legal, and political differences between countries serve as yet another obstacle to transnational bargaining. Few if any countries would subvert their national needs on behalf of and in the interests of developing an international system of industrial relations.

Employer resistance. Employer resistance is less obvious than other obstacles at this particular time, mostly because of the inability of the unions to overcome the other hurdles that they face.[88] No doubt once the initial hurdles are overcome, employers' true opinions and attitudes concerning transnational collective bargaining will emerge, but in the meantime MNCs may sit idly by until the unions get their own house in order.

Activities of Multinational Unions

Although much of what unions have accomplished in achieving international cooperation and coordination is considered by some a "public relations coup,"[89] there have been some tangible activities among unions. The International Conference of Free Trade Unions and international trade secretariats have proposed that the United Nations adopt charters for MNCs, specifying their obligation to recognize trade unions, observe fair labor standards, observe prevailing wage rates, attempt betterment of social conditions, reinvest profits made from less developed countries in those countries, establish works councils worldwide, and use labor-intensive technology when possible. In Western Europe, unions have backed the European company statutes that require worker participation and works councils' agreement on such issues as rules for recruitment, career advancement, dismissal, training, health and safety, welfare and social programs, pay methods, and holidays.

In addition, four multinational labor organizations have been quite active in international activities: International Federation of Chemical and General Workers' Unions (ICF), International Metalworkers Federation (IMF), International Federation of Petroleum and Chemical Workers (IFPCW), and International Federation of Air Line Pilots' Associations (IFALPA). Their activities thus far have essentially included gathering information about MNCs, providing education programs, and coordinating collective bargaining activities (although the federations themselves do no actual collective bargaining).[90] Each of these organizations believes that it must establish a firm foundation upon which to develop more penetrating actions in the future.

Effects of Unions on MNCs

Research conducted mostly in European countries has indicated that unions have had little direct effect on investment and production allocation policies of MNCs. However, they have had considerable effect indirectly because union relations with employers help shape the investment climate of a country.

Thus far, MNCs rarely have been able to afford to switch production to other countries as a bargaining or union intimidation tactic because of the costs involved. They no doubt would shift production to another country in cases where a labor dispute stops production and the move is economically and practically possible. However, such decisions are considerably limited because companies must have the necessary excess production capacity available and management must expect the labor dispute to last sufficiently long to justify any shift in production before it would be feasible.

Overall, there is little evidence of substantial negative effects of MNCs on industrial relations in countries in which they operate. They usually offer prevailing or superior wage standards and provide comparable working conditions for several reasons. The strengths of unions in the respective countries, the highly integrated and institutionalized nature of industrial relations systems, and the socioeconomic-political climate of the countries have clearly constrained the potential for direct adverse effect.[91]

Conclusions and Predictions on Transnational Bargaining

Systematic investigations of transnational collective bargaining reveal that it does not yet exist in any realistic form and will not likely occur in the near future. MNCs are generally opposed to it, and trade unions are not of a single mind regarding its desirability. While there have been several cases of information exchange between multinational unions and MNCs and a few instances of union-management consultation, only one trade union secretariat—the International Transport Workers' Federation (ITF)—has actually negotiated an agreement with shipping companies. Further, only in the unique U.S.-Canadian environment does much transnational bargaining occur.[92]

There has been no identifiable trend toward transnational collective bargaining by companies and unions in the U.S., Europe, or Japan.[93] Some believe that there will be no effective transnational collective bargaining in the near future.[94] However, others believe that such collective bargaining is inevitable.[95] It will probably develop first in either North America, the European community, or Central America and deal initially with general topics, such as employment protection, investment policies, and codes of fair practices, before broadening into other bargaining topics.[96]

Summary

This chapter first presented the substantive elements of labor unions in other countries and then discussed the multinational corporation (MNC) and union activities related to transnational collective bargaining. The extensiveness of discussion of each country's labor relations system was determined by its proximity to the United States; its trade, economic, and political relationships with the United States; and its uniqueness among the world's labor relations systems.

Discussion of the labor relations system of Canada revealed concern over the United States' economically dominant role in North America and its influence in the internal affairs of that country. Western Europe coverage focused on co-determination and worker participation. West Germany's system of co-determination was described in some detail.

A view of the labor movements in some East European, Soviet bloc countries revealed the major influence of the Communist Party on the labor unions of these countries. In fact, their trade unions seemed to serve as tools of the party, unlike those in most of the free world. Special attention was given to the Hungarian and Yugoslavian systems because each has developed some independence from the dominant Soviet model.

Unique features of the Japanese system include a lifetime employment policy, a unique wage system, and the enterprise union. However, international money exchange rate fluctuations, trade agreements, rising oil prices, and slower economic growth could quickly alter these special union-management relationships of the Japanese system. The Australian and New Zealand systems, which involve mediation, conciliation, and arbitration procedures, were also briefly presented. Labor relations in the developing countries of the world have not reached the level of sophistication observed in more developed nations, but in view of these countries' large contributions of vital natural resources and supplies, an overview of their labor movements' rudiments was attempted.

Brief mention was made of the international labor organizations which have been established across national boundaries to represent the interests of their constituents. While none of these plays a major role in collective bargaining, their informational assistance to their members is important.

Multinational corporations and transnational collective bargaining are becoming increasingly important topics of labor relations. While multinational corporations continue to grow in sales volume, capital investments, and economic influence, they have also aroused trade unions in various countries to combine their energies, skills, and power in an effort to negotiate on an equal footing. Thus far, little success has been achieved, because of legal, political, social, economic, and organizational obstacles. However, one must clearly appreciate the fact that transnational collective bargaining could have a tremendous impact on the world's economy if the obstacles can be eliminated.

Discussion Questions

1. While we share a common border with Canada, its labor relations system is affected by a number of variables that do not greatly affect the United States. Enumerate and explain these variables.

2. Explain why labor unions in many of the Latin American countries have developed more slowly than those in the United States.

3. Western Europe seems to be uniquely involved with various forms of worker participation. What are some reasons that these worker participation systems have developed so fully there instead of elsewhere?

4. What are the three special features of the Japanese system? Why haven't they been adopted in the United States?

5. How does the Yugoslavian labor relations system differ from that found in Soviet Russia?

6. How can unions play a greater role in the economic development and growth of developing nations?

7. While multinational corporations seem to be growing in size and influence, what must occur before transnational collective bargaining can be effectively carried out?

References

[1] David C. Hershfield, *The Multinational Union Challenges the Multinational Company* (New York: Conference Board, 1975), pp. 4–5.

[2] "Report of the Task Force of Labour Relations," *Canadian Industrial Relations* (Ottawa: Information Canada, 1968), pp. 14–16.

[3] John Crispo, "Multinational Corporations and International Unions: Their Impact on Canadian Industrial Relations," in Robert J. Flanagan and Arnold R. Weber, eds., *Bargaining without Boundaries* (Chicago: University of Chicago Press, 1974), p. 106.

[4] Arthur Kruger, "The Direction of Unionism in Canada," in R. U. Miller and Fraser Isbester, eds., *Canadian Labor in Transition* (Ontario: Prentice-Hall, 1970), pp. 88–90.

[5] Ronald Lang, "Labour's Manifesto for Canada: A New Independence?" in J. L. Stern and B. D. Dennis, eds., *Proceedings of the Twenty-ninth Annual Winter Meeting: Industrial Relations Research Association* (Madison, Wis.: Industrial Relations Research Association, 1977), pp. 91–99.

[6] Crispo, "Multinational Corporations and International Unions," pp. 103–104. It should be noted that 15 to 20 percent of foreign ownership is outside the United States.

[7] "Unions Grow," *Labor Gazette*, October 1974, pp. 687–688.

[8] I. A. Litvak and C. J. Maule, "U.S. Union Domination of Canadian Labor," *Columbia Journal of World Business* 7 (May–June 1972), pp. 57–63.

[9] Crispo, "Multinational Corporations and International Unions," p. 109.

[10] James O. Morris, "Latin American Collective Bargaining Agreement: An Illustration," in Stanley M. Davis and Louis W. Goodman, eds., *Workers and Managers in Latin America* (Lexington, Mass.: D.C. Heath, 1972), p. 209.

[11] International Labour Office, "Labor Legislation and Collective Bargaining," in Davis and Goodman, eds., *Workers and Managers in Latin America*, pp. 217–229.

[12] Everett M. Kassalow, *Trade Unions and Industrial Relations: An International Comparison* (New York: Random House, 1969), pp. 302–303.

[13] Howard Handelson, "Oligarchy and Democracy in Two Mexican Labor Unions: A Test of Representation Theory," *Industrial and Labor Relations Review* 30 (January 1977), pp. 205–218.

[14] Kassalow, *Trade Unions*, p. 303. For a current discussion see James L. Schlagheck and Nancy R. Johnson, *The Political, Economic, and Labor Climate in Mexico* (Philadelphia: Industrial Research Unit, University of Pennsylvania, 1977).

[15] Robert J. Alexander, *Labor Relations in Argentina, Brazil, and Chile* (New York: McGraw-Hill, 1962), pp. 11–13. For a specific discussion of Brazilian labor relations see James L. Schlagheck, *The Political, Economic, and Labor Relations Climate in Brazil* (Philadelphia: Industrial Research Unit, University of Pennsylvania, 1977).

[16] Hobart A. Spaulding, Jr., *Organized Labor in Latin America* (New York: Harper & Row, 1977), p. x. For excellent discussions on Peru and Venezuela see Nancy R. Johnson, *The Political, Economic, and Labor Climate in Peru* (Philadelphia: Industrial Research Unit, University of Pennsylvania, 1978); and Cecilia

M. Valente, *The Political, Economic, and Labor Climate in Venezuela* (Philadelphia: Industrial Research Unit, University of Pennsylvania, 1979).

[17]Everett M. Kassalow, "Conflict and Cooperation in Europe's Industrial Relations," *Industrial Relations* 13 (May 1974), pp. 156–163.

[18]Milton Derber, "Cross Currents in Workers' Participation," *Industrial Relations* 9 (February 1970), p. 123.

[19]Owen Fairweather, "Western European Labor Movements and Collective Bargaining: An Industrial Framework," in Alfred Kanan, ed., *Western European Labor and the American Corporation* (Washington, D.C.: Bureau of National Affairs, 1970), pp. 69–72.

[20]John F. B. Goodman, "Great Britain: Toward the Social Contract," in Solomon Balkin, ed., *Worker Militancy and Its Consequences, 1965–75* (New York: Praeger Publishers, 1975), pp. 39–81.

[21]Fairweather, "Western European Labor Movements," pp. 71–74. Also see "Britain's Renegade Stewards," *Business Week*, February 19, 1979, pp. 92–95.

[22]Robert Ball, "The Hard Hats in Europe's Boardrooms," *Fortune* 93 (June 1976), p. 189; and Robert J. Kuhne, "Co-determination: A Statutory Restructuring of the Organization," *Columbia Journal of World Business* 11 (March–April, 1976), pp. 17–25.

[23]Heinz Hartman, "Co-Determination Today and Tomorrow," *British Journal of Industrial Relations* 13 (March 1975), p. 54. Also see Wolfgang Heintzler, *The Codetermination Problem in Western Germany* (London: Aims of Industry Publications, 1974).

[24]David T. Fisher, "Worker Participation in West German Industry," *Monthly Labor Review* 101 (May 1978), pp. 59–63; and Kuhne, "Co-determination," pp. 17–25.

[25]Kuhne, "Co-determination," pp. 18–19.

[26]G. David Gaison, "The Codetermination Model of Workers' Participation: Where Is It Leading?" *Sloan Management Review* 18 (Spring 1977), pp. 63–78.

[27]B. C. Roberts, "Industrial Relations and the European Economic Community," *Labor Law Journal* 24 (August 1973), pp. 484–490.

[28]Neil Ulman, "The Workers' Voice: Giving Employees a Say in Firm's Management Seen Gaining in Europe," *Wall Street Journal*, February 23, 1973, p. 21.

[29]Gaison, "Codetermination Model," p. 63.

[30]Ibid.

[31]Hartman, "Co-Determination Today and Tomorrow," pp. 58–59.

[32]Katsumi Yakabe, *Labor Relations in Japan* (Tokyo: International Society for Educational Information, 1974), pp. 1–14; Hisashi Kawada and Ryuji Komatsu, "Post-War Labor Movements in Japan," in Adolph Strumthal and James G. Scoville, *The International Labor Movement in Transition* (Urbana: University of Illinois Press, 1973), pp. 122–148; and Tadashi A. Hanami, "The Multinational Corporation and Japanese Industrial Relations," in Duane Kujawa, ed., *International Labor and Multinational Enterprise* (New York: Praeger Publishers, 1975), pp. 183–185.

[33]Masayoshi Kanabayaski, "Economic Woes Spur Firms in Japan to Alter Life-time Job Security," *Wall Street Journal*, December 21, 1976, pp. 1, 23.

[34]"Japan: The End of Lifetime Jobs," *Business Week*, July 17, 1978, pp. 82–83.

[35]Solomon B. Levine and Kaji Taira, "Japanese Industrial Relations—Is One Economic Miracle Enough?" *Monthly Labor Review* 101 (March 1978), pp. 31–33.

[36]H. Taskahaski, "Japan Industrial Relations—Retrospect and Prospect," *Industrial Relations in Asia* (Geneva, Switzerland: International Labour Organisation, 1976), pp. 110–113.

[37]"Japan: End of Lifetime Jobs," pp. 82–83.

[38]R. C. Simpson, "The Significance of Legal Status of Trade Unions in Britain and Australia," *Journal of Industrial Relations* 18 (September 1976), pp. 229–242.

[39]J. W. Mohony, "Decisions Affecting Industrial Relations in 1977," *Journal of Industrial Relations* 20 (March 1978), p. 72.

[40]Kenneth F. Walker, *Australian Industrial Relations System* (Cambridge, Mass.: Harvard University Press, 1970), pp. 13–14.

[41]Milton Derber, "Advancing Australian Industrial Democracy," *Industrial Relations* 17 (February 1978), pp. 112–116.

[42]Alan J. Geare, "The Right to Strike under New Zealand's Industrial Relations Legislation," *Labor Law Journal* 27 (April 1976), pp. 217–219.

[43]John M. Howells, "Causes and Frequency of Strikes in New Zealand," *Industrial and Labor Relations Review* 25 (January 1972), pp. 524–532.

[44]John M. Howells, "Successful Mediation: A New Zealand Case Study," *International Labour Review* 115 (March–April 1977), pp. 225–238.

[45]J. L. Porket, "Industrial Relations and Participation in Management in the Soviet-Type Communist System," *British Journal of Industrial Relations* 16 (March 1978), pp. 70–71.

[46]Ibid., pp. 72–73.

[47]Ibid., pp. 73–74.

[48]Vladimir Bukovsky, "We Have Looked with Hope at the West," *American Federationist* 84 (March 1977), pp. 20–21.

[49]Ibid.

[50]Porket, "Industrial Relations," p. 75.

[51]Janko Kralj, "Yugoslav System of Self-management in Associated Labor," *Atlanta Economic Review* 25 (July–August 1975), pp. 39–41.

[52]S. Benjamin Prasad, "The Growth of Co-Determination," *Business Horizons* 20 (April 1977), p. 26.

[53]T. S. Sankaran, "India Industrial Relations—Retrospect and Prospect," *Industrial Relations in Asia*, pp. 72–76.

[54]C. S. Krishnaswami, "India Industrial Relations—Retrospect and Prospect," *Industrial Relations in Asia*, pp. 77–84.

[55]Yun-Il Ma, "Korea Industrial Relations—Retrospect and Prospect," pp. 127–131.

[56]Teoh Kong San, "Malaysia Industrial Relations—Retrospect and Prospect," *Industrial Relations in Asia*, pp. 132–135.

[57]Richard Sandbrook and Robin Cohen, *The Development of an African Working Class* (Toronto: University of Toronto Press, 1976), pp. 130–136.

[58]Ibid. The Republic of South Africa leads with 67 percent; Zambia, Kenya, and Ghana have about 20 percent; Nigeria, 5 percent. With the exception of South Africa, only a small percent of the wage earners are employed in manufacturing.

[59]Ibid.

[60]Kassalow, *Trade Unions*, pp. 292–318.

[61]Lane Kirkland, "A Time for Testing at the ILO," *American Federationist* 83 (August 1976), pp. 11–15.

[62]Hershfield, *Multinational Union Challenges Multinational Company*, p. 4.

[63]"There is no agreed definition of the multinational enterprise. Some find its determining characteristics in the organization of its activities; that is, the extent to which its operations in different countries are actually co-ordinated by a corporate centre, or the degree of 'global outlook' to be found in the enterprise's decision making. Others use as criteria the number and types of its subsidiaries, the number of countries in which these subsidiaries operate, and the proportion of foreign sales, assets, and employment in the enterprise's total sales, assets, and employment. Still others look to the nationality mix of its management or to its ownership characteristics." International Labour Office, *Multinational Enterprises and Social Policy* (Geneva, Switzerland: International Labour Office, 1973), p. 3.

[64]Robert F. Banks and Jack Stieber, "Introduction," *Multinationals, Unions, and Labor Relations in Industrial Countries* (Ithaca: New York State School of Industrial and Labor Relations, 1977), p. 1.

[65]L. A. Lupo, "Capital Expenditures by Majority-Owned Foreign Affiliates of U.S. Companies, 1978 and 1979," *Survey of Business* 58 (October 1978), pp. 42–45.

[66]William K. Chung and Gregory G. Fouch, "Foreign Direct Investment in the United States, 1977," *Survey of Business* 58 (August 1978), p. 39.

[67]International Labour Office, *Multinational Enterprises*, p. 4.

[68]William J. Curtin, "Multi-National Corporate Bargaining," *Collective Bargaining: Negotiations and Contracts* (Washington, D.C.: Bureau of National Affairs, 1972), p. J-2. Little mention is made by union leaders of the relatively high wage rates in the United States and other foreign nations.

[69]Andrew C. McLellan and Michael D. Baggs, "Multinationals: How Quick They Jump," *American Federationist* 80 (September 1973), pp. 22–24.

[70]Ibid., p. 22.

[71]Gus Tyler, "Multinationals: A Global Menace," *American Federationist* 79 (July 1972), pp. 1–7.

[72]Banks and Stieber, *Multinationals, Unions, and Labor Relations*, p. 11.

[73]Curtin, "Multi-National Corporate Bargaining," p. J-2.

[74]Hermian Rebhan, "Building a Counterforce to Multinational Corporations," *Monthly Labor Review* 100 (March 1977), pp. 46–47.

[75]Herbert R. Northrup and Richard L. Rowan, "Multinational Union Activities and Plan Closings: The Case of Akzo," *Industrial Relations Journal* 9 (Spring 1978), pp. 27–36.

[76]Herbert R. Northrup and Richard L. Rowan, "Multinational Bargaining in Food and Allied Industries: Approaches and Prospects," *Wharton Quarterly* 7 (Spring 1974), pp. 32–40.

[77]Herbert R. Northrup and Richard L. Rowan, "Multinational Bargaining Approaches in the Western European Flat Glass Industry," *Industrial and Labor Relations Review* 30 (October 1976), pp. 32–46.

[78]Herbert R. Northrup and Richard L. Rowan, "Multinational Union-Management Consultation: The European Experience," *International Labour Review* 116 (September–October 1977), pp. 153–170.

[79]Herbert R. Northrup and Richard L. Rowan, "Multinational Collective Bargaining Activity: The Factual Record in the Chemicals, Glass, and Rubber Tires, I, *"Columbia Journal of World Business* 9 (Spring 1974), pp. 112–124; and "Multinational Collective Bargaining Activity: The Factual Record in the Chemicals, Glass, and Rubber Tires, II," *Columbia Journal of World Business* 9 (Summer 1974), pp. 49–63.

[80]B. C. Roberts and Jonathan May, "The Response of Multinational Enterprises to International Trade Union Pressures," *British Journal of Industrial Relations* 12 (November 1974), pp. 403–416.

[81]Northrup and Rowan, "Multinational Bargaining Approaches in the Western European Flat Glass Industry," pp. 32–46.

[82]George B. McCulloch, "Transnational Bargaining—Problems and Prospects," *Monthly Labor Review* 101 (March 1978), pp. 33–34.

[83]Arnold R. Weber, "Bargaining without Boundaries: Industrial Relations and the Multinational Firm," in Flanagan and Weber, eds., *Bargaining without Boundaries,* pp. 233–249.

[84]McCulloch, "Transnational Bargaining—Problems and Prospects," p. 33.

[85]Weber, "Bargaining without Boundaries," pp. 233–249.

[86]Banks and Stieber, *Multinationals, Unions, and Labor Relations,* pp. 11–12.

[87]Herbert R. Northrup and Richard L. Rowan, "Multinational Union Activity in the 1976 U.S. Rubber Tire Strike," *Sloan Management Review* 18 (Spring 1977), pp. 17–28.

[88]G. B. J. Bomers, *Multinational Corporations and Industrial Relations* (Amsterdam, Netherlands: Van Gorcum, Assen, 1976), pp. 179–195.

[89]Richard L. Rowan and Herbert R. Northrup, "Multinational Bargaining in Metals and Electrical Industries: Approaches and Prospects," *Journal of Industrial Relations* 17 (March 1975), pp. 1–29.

[90]Hershfield, *Multinational Union Challenges Multinational Company,* pp. 4–5.

[91]Banks and Stieber, *Multinationals, Unions, and Labor Relations,* pp. 15–16; and Bomers, *Multinational Corporations and Industrial Relations,* pp. 179–185.

[92]Herbert R. Northrup, "Why Multinationals Bargaining Neither Exists Nor Is Desirable," *Labor Law Journal* 29 (June 1978), pp. 330–331.

[93]Owen Fairweather, "Trends in International Collective Bargaining with Multinationals and the Respective Strategies," *Proceedings of the Twenty-sixth Annual Winter Meeting: Industrial Relations Research Association* (Madison, Wis.: Industrial Relations Research Association, 1973), pp. 145–154.

[94]McCulloch, "Transnational Bargaining—Problems and Prospects," p. 34.

[95]Paul A. Heise, "The Multinational Corporation and Industrial Relations," *Labor Law Journal* 24 (August 1973), pp. 480–483; Betty S. Murphy, "Multinational Corporations and Free Coordinated Transnational Bargaining: An Alternative to Protectionism?" *Labor Law Journal* 28 (October 1977), pp. 619–632.

[96]Hershfield, *Multinational Union Challenges Multinational Company,* pp. 4–5.

Chapter 17

Emerging Labor
Relations
Sectors:
Professional
Sports, Health
Care, and
Agriculture

"The opera ain't over
til the fat lady sings."

Anonymous[*]

This chapter is intended to pose the
reader with a very real challenge—the application of the previous material to three discrete,
emerging, and interesting areas of
labor-management relationships:
professional sports, health care, and
agriculture. While the three sections
in this chapter are independent, they
should be read with two issues in
mind: (a) the extent to which these
areas share similarities and differences, and (b) their respective applications to the elements in the
labor relations process portrayed in
Exhibit 1–1 of Chapter 1.

Collective Bargaining in Professional Sports

The total number of unionized athletes in professional baseball, basketball, hockey, and football is less than the number of unionized employees at one medium-sized manufacturing facility. Although there are few participants, professional sports generate a tremendous interest among the American public. Anyone who has been to a professional baseball stadium has experienced the excitement of the game:

> **The lack of violence but the sense of menace in the thrown ball, the slashing spikes, the swing of the bat; the sudden splendid bursts of action—a runner going from first to third, or even home, on a single, sliding in inches ahead of or behind a perfect peg; the suspense of pitcher vs. hitter in a late-inning rally, with the winning runs on base; . . . the power and the glory of an overwhelming pitcher in his prime; the art and cunning of an experienced pitcher past his prime; the swagger of a big hitter at the plate.**[1]

Behind the scenes union-management relationships seldom are as exciting as on-field action; yet a consideration of these unique activities adds to our understanding of the game as well as the labor relations process.

Presenting a detailed discussion of collective bargaining in each of the professional sports would result in a confusing array of issues, personalities, and negotiation settlements. Therefore, professional baseball is discussed in some detail, because its collective bargaining activities have had a longer and possibly more successful tradition than corresponding activities in other sports. However, concluding observations in this section furnish several examples taken from three professional team sports (hockey, football, and basketball) in addition to baseball.

The Experience in Baseball

The Early Years Collective bargaining in baseball has had a long, if not always successful, tradition. The Brotherhood of Professional Baseball Players, formed in 1885, attempted to resolve several problems, including the owners' elimination of wage increases, poor conditions of playing fields, and owners' insistence that substitute players also work at the turnstiles.[2] The unsuccessful efforts in resolving these problems were in part responsible for the formation of the Brotherhood League in 1889; outside investors built the facilities, and the players were to be paid 50 percent of the profits. Many players jumped from the established National League to the new Brotherhood League, signing three-year contracts which represented the minimum of their 1889 salaries.

Early efforts at collective bargaining were relatively unsuccessful due to the poor financial condition of the baseball clubs.[3] Subsequent collective action among ballplayers was almost nonexistent until the winter of 1913, when a second player organization, Ball Players' Fraternity, was formed.

*Attributed to a nineteenth century ranch foreman who was explaining what signals the end of an opera.

The formation of this organization was no doubt motivated by participation of some players in the "Ty Cobb strike" during the prior season. This strike was touched off by an incident involving Claude Lueker, a New York pressman who continuously heckled Cobb, a player for the visiting Detroit Tigers. Cobb, sitting on the bench during the Detroit half of the inning, heard still another tirade from Lueker, "Hey Cobb, you're nothin but a yellow-bellied bastard!"

When the Detroit side was retired and Cobb started back out toward his position, manager Jennings, glancing at him, could tell what was going to happen. "I knew he was going to do it," Hughie said later. "Once I saw the look in his eyes, I was sure of it. But there was no way of stopping him."

Ty trotted down the left-field line. As he turned to go out into center field, Lueker cut loose with another stream of blue sparks. Cobb suddenly swung around and charged. He advanced on the bleachers in the direction of the voice, vaulted over the rail, and shoved his way through the mass of spectators until he reached Lueker. Then he began punching the daylights out of him.

"He hit me in the face with his fists, knocked me down, jumped on me and kicked me in the ear," Lueker told police later.

The New York fans were so amazed and startled that nobody moved a muscle until Cobb had finished with Lueker. Nobody could believe what they had just seen. No ballplayer had ever dared hop into the stands that way. As Cobb finished, they began to rise in rage. Ty had to fight his way back down to the playing field. All his teammates, led by Wahoo Sam Crawford, stood along the field brandishing bats. They were certain the fans would storm on the field and mob Cobb. They almost did.[4]

Cobb was indefinitely suspended for his actions, and the entire Detroit team voted to strike until he was reinstated. This action was not taken out of affection for Cobb; rather, the players realized that his .400 batting average was necessary for team success. Management somewhat frantically responded by hiring replacements off the street, or "any ballplayer who could stop a grapefruit from rolling uphill." The first game played with replacements resulted in a 24–2 defeat for the Tigers. The second game was cancelled, with the striking players given a $100 fine and threatened with permanent removal from baseball. Cobb encouraged the players to return for the next game. Cobb eventually received a $50 fine plus a ten-day suspension for his actions.[5]

The Ball Players' Fraternity was successful in obtaining one reform from managers—the *waiver rule*, which stated that no player could be sent to a club of lower classification until clubs similar to his old team were given an opportunity to obtain the player's services.[6] After this accomplishment, the fraternity vanished, largely because of membership apathy. No subsequent collective activities occurred until 1946. Much of this inactivity was due to the rather imposing and fair nature of the commissioner of baseball, Keenshaw Mountain Landis.

In the spring of 1946, Robert Murphy, a Boston lawyer, attempted to organize all professional baseball players in the American Baseball Guild. Some of the organization's requests included:

1. Freedom of contract, so that a player would not be forced to join a particular team against his will.
2. Arbitration for salary and other player-owner disputes. [7]

The issues were important for the ballplayers; however, management did not agree to these terms. In fact, these issues remained unsettled for nearly thirty years after Murphy's initial proposal.

In June 1946, the players informed the owners of the Pittsburgh Pirates that they would strike if they could not obtain a representation election for the American Baseball Guild. The National Labor Relations Board refused to order an election, on the grounds that baseball wasn't equivalent to "commerce." However, a subsequent vote conducted by the Pennsylvania Labor Board resulted in only three affirmative player votes for the guild.

Some of the guild's failure to win player support was due to the joint determination of club owners to unilaterally improve the uniform player's contract. In essence, management preempted the union's ability to claim success in improving working conditions by voluntary improvements. Also, Mr. Murphy was viewed as an outsider to baseball and the guild as a one-man union with no official participation by players and no bylaws or constitution. [8]

Yet the owners were at least somewhat influenced by the guild's efforts, for they allowed the new commissioner of baseball, A. B. Chandler, to pick player representatives to jointly discuss working conditions with the owners. In a July 1946 meeting, the player representatives from each of the sixteen clubs presented the owners with several proposals and eventually received a few concessions from management, including a pension plan, minimum salary, and miscellaneous expense money. [9]

In spite of these gains, the late 1940s and early 1950s saw little advancement of the collective bargaining relationship in the true sense of the term. The player "negotiation" minutes during this period reveal that players would sit next to the owners of their teams and discuss issues. High turnover among player representatives was a major problem. Agreed-upon issues were not always remembered over the years. Indeed, some time was spent in renegotiating issues which had been previously resolved. [10]

In 1953, controversy arose over the allocation of revenues obtained mainly from the All Star Game and the World Series. Additional efforts to obtain pension plan alterations culminated in the formation of the Major League Baseball Players' Association (MLBPA) in 1954. The MLBPA did have some definite ideas regarding wage determination. Whereas players' salaries equalled 67 percent of gross revenues in 1880, this proportion was continually reduced over the years, until in 1956 the players' salaries equalled only 13 percent of the gross revenues.[11] Management responded to the players' attempts to negotiate by stating that they preferred to deal with player salaries on an individual rather than a budgetary basis, a preference still characteristic of collective bargaining in sports.

Although the MLBPA remained intact, few serious attempts were made at collective bargaining during the late 1950s and mid 1960s. Perhaps this inactivity was due to the belief of many baseball player representatives that they had already achieved sufficient gains and unions were detrimental to the game. Bob Feller, an official of the MLBPA, denied the organization was a union, commenting "You cannot carry collective bargaining into baseball. . . . Our aim is to promote baseball, not hurt it."[12]

Serious Collective Bargaining Efforts Including Strike Activities In 1966, Marvin Miller was appointed executive director of the MLBPA, an event which significantly altered the form and content of collective bargaining in professional baseball. Mr. Miller's previous negotiation experience with the Steelworkers Union proved beneficial to the baseball players. In less than two years after Mr. Miller's appointment, baseball players received substantial increases in pension and disability benefits, life and health insurance, and minimum salary requirements.[13] The latter issue added symbolic as well as pragmatic significance to the MLBPA's efforts. The minimum salary for players, $6,000, had been in effect for eleven years until 1968, when it was raised to $10,000.[14]

Still unresolved were pension plan issues and the reserve clause (discussed later in the chapter). The players wanted the pension plan related to broadcast rights revenues for the All Star Game and World Series. To enforce their demands, the player representatives urged that the players not sign their 1969 contracts. This strategy prompted the vice-president of the Altanta Braves to remark, "Miller speaks mainly for a few rabble-rousers and greedy ballplayers. As for the players who want to leave [not sign a 1969 contract], we could cover them with triple-A minor leaguers and keep all the TV money and be better off."[15] Mr. Miller, aware that the National Broadcasting Corporation had agreed to a $50 million, three-year contract with the owners, replied, "If Richards thinks the networks will pay that kind of money for minor leaguers, he has another think coming."[16]

Bargaining continued over the pension plan, with owners eventually offering an annual contribution of $5,100,000 with no reference to television rights receipts. The owners' proposal was defeated by an employee vote of 491–7.[17] A three-year pension agreement was reached in February 1969, with the owners' annual contribution equalling $5,450,000. After the agreement, players who deferred signing their contracts until the pension settlement started negotiating their salaries with the owners.

Negotiations on the basic labor agreements began in late 1969 and continued into mid-May 1970. The three-year labor agreement ratified in June 1970 raised the minimum salary ($12,000 in 1970; $12,750 in 1971; and $13,000 in 1972), increased expense allowances, and established arbitration of issues not involving the "integrity of the game."[18] The latter issue represented a significant gain for the players because previously the commissioner of baseball had been the last resort on almost all baseball disputes. Indeed, the first grievance arbitrated under the new rules resulted in a reversal of management's unilateral decision to change World Series pool allocations.[19] Agreement was also reached on deferring the reserve clause issue until judicial resolution of the Curt Flood case (discussed later in the chapter).[20]

The 1968–1969 collective job action regarding employment contract deferrals appears minor in view of subsequent collective bargaining efforts. The 1972 season spring training had begun when the MLBPA announced the nearly unanimous strike vote taken among the players. A second strike vote was taken at the end of spring training with similar results. Management officials reacted to the first general players' strike in this sport's history with a mixture of anger and surprise. The following reactions were made by management representatives of the Chicago White Sox, Cleveland Indians, and Pittsburgh Pirates:

I thought we had a better rapport with our players than this, but I guess that just doesn't matter now. They have a lawyer [Marvin Miller] working for them, and they just follow whatever he tells them to do.

They've made their decision and that's it as far as I'm concerned. All expenses will stop and the players will stop and the players will be given a ticket home, if that's what they request. When the strike is over, they'll be expected to pay their way back.

I doubt very much that the owners will back down from their present stand. . . . Never in my years in baseball have I seen the owners so solidified on any issue.[21]

The "issue" mentioned in the preceding quotation concerned determination of the type and amount of pensions—the previous pension contract had expired in March 1972. Management eventually proposed an increase of $300,000 to the health benefit part of the plan, to be spread over a four-year contract. The MLBPA sought an increase of approximately $1,000,000, contending that this increase represented a cost of living adjustment since the 1970 negotiations. The players' association also contended that each club would only have an increased annual cost of $11,000, as there was an $817,000 "surplus" in the present plan.[22]

From the union standpoint, the 1972 strike could have been ended in one of two ways: (a) by managerial agreement to the union's proposal or (b) by submitting the issue to binding arbitration. Management officials strongly opposed arbitration of the pension issue. Some of the management representatives initially considered the strategy of opening the season with minor league players; however, this alternative was never implemented. Management also rejected an MLBPA counteroffer—increasing the pension plan with the $817,000 surplus without the additional $11,000 club contribution. Mr. Miller's response to these managerial actions suggested a long, bitter strike:

The owners were and are intent on making the players eat dirt. . . . I will let the players know that the owners are insistent that the players bend down and kiss the shoes of the owners. The owners have now taken on the full responsibility for prolonging the strike right into the season. I think the owners have miscalculated grievously.[23]

A second major issue arose during the progression of the 1972 strike, namely, compensation for time lost during the strike. This issue was settled on the basis that lost games would not be made up and the players would not receive payment for them. Settlement of the strike was reached on April 13, 1972. The pension plan was increased $500,000 on a one-year contract, and players were docked nine days' pay for the missed portion of the regular season. Players at the $13,500 minimum lost $675; players making more than the minimum lost more money (for example, Henry Aaron lost $9,880).[24]

Perhaps the 1972 strike had a sobering effect on the 1973 contract negotiations, which started in September 1972. The commissioner of baseball, Bowie Kuhn, labeled the previous strike as a "bitter lesson," and observed, "sometimes you have to walk through fire to find out how hot it is."[25] Also, some of the players may have echoed player Pete Rose's remarks: "If there's another strike . . . the players' association will not get my support. . . . Last year's strike cost me $7,500 and a chance for 200 hits."[26]

Many additional issues were introduced into the 1973 negotiations. Commissioner Kuhn felt that management might make some concessions on the reserve clause. However, he also indicated that the owners would never agree to binding arbitration of salary disputes because this working condition, not subject to binding arbitration in the previous labor agreements, involved the "integrity of the game."[27]

A three-year agreement was reached before spring training began. As was true with the 1972 contract, the 1973 settlement represented a compromise. Management's positions regarding the reserve clause and trades were accepted by the union, and baseball players received a minimum wage guarantee of $15,000 during the 1973 and 1974 seasons, with a raise to $16,000 in 1975.[28]

Clearly, the major gain for the players, contrary to the predictions of Commissioner Kuhn, was submission of salary disputes to binding arbitration. Any player having at least two years of major league service in at least three championship seasons[29] could submit the salary dispute to final and binding arbitration. In essence, this meant use of the final offer arbitration technique (discussed in Chapter 14), for the arbitrator must choose either the player's or management's offer.

The 1976 negotiations eventually resulted in a four-year labor agreement. Players received a 29 percent increase in owner pension plan contributions and the following increases in minimum salary: $19,000 during the 1976 and 1977 seasons and $21,000 during the 1978 and 1979 seasons. Management, on the other hand, won the right to reduce their twenty-five-man active roster to twenty-four players. However, the prominent and most complex issue in these negotiations was the reserve clause. The details of this issue are discussed in the following section.

<table>
<tr><td>

**Issues
Continually
Affecting Labor-
Management
Relationships
in Baseball**

</td><td>

Three of the more dominant and interrelated issues in collective bargaining and day-to-day administration of the labor agreement for baseball are: (a) player mobility, (b) the relationship between player salary and player performance, and (c) player-management relationships.

Player Mobility The first issue concerns the right of players to select their particular team. As previously discussed, players have expressed major concern over the *reserve rule* throughout the history of collective bargaining. In essence, this rule or clause, found in the player's individual contract, gives the hiring baseball club a *continuing and exclusive right to the player's services.*[30]

Baseball owners have traditionally contended that the reserve clause is essential to the well-being of the game and players. Revenues depend solely on competition among the teams and fan identity with a particular baseball team. If the reserve clause were lifted, many of the best players would jump to the "richer" teams or to locations which are more attractive financially (offer players endorsements or business contracts, for example) or aesthetically (climate, region of the country, or winning tradition, for example). Consequently, the sport would have only a few dominant teams, competition would be drastically reduced, and fan interest would rapidly deteriorate, particularly if local favorite players jumped to other teams. The resulting drop in broadcasting and admission revenues would reduce salaries. In some cases, a few teams might have to fold their operations, thereby eliminating players' jobs. Finally, much of the owner expense is incurred in player development (training camps, scouting, coaching, and the minor leagues); therefore, owners should have the right to protect their financial investments.[31]

</td></tr>
</table>

On the other hand, players maintain that they have only a few years to compete in their sport professionally. The relatively limited opportunity for financial rewards is further reduced when one team controls the player's financial destiny. Some players and sports writers are openly cynical about owner concern for their fans. For example, in the winter of 1976, eighty-nine players were traded away by the owners, including several individuals who were considered local favorites among the fans.[32] As for reduced revenues resulting from lessened competitiveness, opponents of the reserve clause might cite the experience of the Toronto Blue Jays, an expansion team having one of the worst won-lost records (54–107) in 1977. This team's owners estimated a $2 million profit for this season, in part derived from $1.7 million paid admissions and $10 million in concession sales.[33]

Players are most concerned with the restraint-of-trade aspect of the reserve clause because, unlike other employees, baseball players are not free to choose their employer. In 1969, Curt Flood refused to be traded to another team, protesting the legality of this action before the Supreme Court:

A salesman reluctant to transfer from one office to another may choose to seek employment on the sales force of a different firm. A plumber can reject the dictates of his boss without relinquishing his right to plumb elsewhere. At the expiration of one contract, an actor shops among producers for the best arrangement he can find. But the baseball monopoly offers no such option to the athlete. If he elects not to work for the corporation that "owns" his services, baseball forbids him to ply his trade at all. In the hierarchy of living things, he ranks with poultry.[34]

Flood contended that the trade was made without his knowledge or consent, in violation of the federal antitrust laws and civil rights statutes. The Supreme Court, noting two previous decisions (*Federal Baseball*, 1922 and *Toolson v. New York Yankees*, 1953), ruled against Flood, maintaining Congress has intended that professional baseball represent a unique exception to coverage under federal antitrust laws.[35]

The reserve clause therefore represented a moot issue before the Supreme Court. Yet players seeking a change in the reserve clause still had three avenues: Congress, the arbitrator's decision of a related grievance, and collective bargaining. A landmark arbitration decision in 1975 motivated more union and management bargaining attention on this issue. The details of this published decision are beyond the scope of this section. Readers are encouraged to examine it,[36] for it clearly indicates how at least one party's (in this case, management's) perception of negotiation results can be modified by subsequent arbitral interpretation of the labor agreement.

This decision, subsequently upheld by the courts, prompted union and management officials to resolve their differences at the bargaining table. The July 1976 labor agreement settlement included many modifications in the original, vaguely defined reserve clause. Individuals playing without a signed contract would become free agents at the end of the 1976 season. A signed player had to play out the renewal year in the contract before becoming a free agent. Under future contracts, a player with six years of service who had not executed a contract for the next succeeding season could become a free agent by notifying the club of his intention. Finally, a player with five years' major league service had a right to demand a trade at the end of a season, listing a maximum of six clubs to which he did not want to be traded. The player then would become a free agent if he had not been traded by the following March 15. A negotiation rights draft was also established for the free agents.

These changes in the reserve clause had been sought since the beginning of professional baseball. Mr. Miller termed the 1976 reserve provisions "the greatest improvement made to date by the Players' Association and its members."[37] While the 1976 provisions represent a significant departure from the original reserve clause, it appears that this new system will continuously be subject to collective bargaining modification in subsequent labor agreement negotiations. It will also be interesting to see if free agent procedures reduce the number of players who are traded to other teams. Owners might be reluctant to acquire a player who could become a free agent in the next season.[38] A parallel development might be an increase in multi-year contracts signed by the individual player and owner.

The Relationship between Player Salary and Performance Many of baseball's fans and participants predicted the free agent draft would sharply escalate player salaries. They were right. The 1976 free agent draft resulted in twenty-four players being signed for an estimated $25 million; one pitcher in the draft increased his previous season's salary of $20,000 to a $1,075,000 five-year contract.[39] Many baseball observers predicted that this "inflated" bidding would not be repeated in subsequent free agent drafts, particularly since the 1976 bidding did not automatically improve the performance of the affected teams. It was predicted that the owners would see the error of their ways—one high-priced free agent cannot lead the team to a championship season. Of course, additional experience is needed to fully test the salary prediction.

Experience with the 1976 free agents produced mixed results. Some consider at least three free agent hitters to be a bit expensive based on their 1976 performance. Management paid these individuals $7,045, $6,531, and $3,867 for each hit they made during the 1976 season. Similarly, two free agent pitchers were paid $22,619 and $16,808 for every 1976 victory.[40] Yet at least two teams, the Baltimore Orioles and the Chicago

White Sox, made unexpected pennant challenges largely due to the efforts of relatively inexpensive free agents.

Player salary increases have not gone unnoticed by the public. Some fans believed there was a direct relationship between increased player salaries and increased ticket prices in 1977, although this relationship cannot be factually proven for all clubs over time. Others contended that nobody should be paid that much for a part-time job (six months a year) which amounts to no more than recreational exercise. Players have had to address this argument continually. One contemporary baseball player contends his salary motives are no different from any other wage earner or, for that matter, union officer:

People talk like they wouldn't take the money players are signing for, like they'd turn most of it back in so the government could put up housing projects or something. But if the average guy was a player, he wouldn't be giving any of that back. He'd be out there scratching for every penny he could get.[41]

Babe Ruth used to take a somewhat different approach in justifying his salary. He argued that no owner would pay a player more than he was worth.[42] Ruth's argument has been reiterated some fifty years later by one baseball arbitrator who claims the owners are not "economic innocents."[43] However, Reggie Jackson, a 1976 free agent who signed an estimated $3 million contract, has somewhat modified the preceding pay-performance arguments: "Everybody thinks I'm going to electrify New York. . . . So I hit 35 home runs. How do I turn that city on?"[44] Ironically, Jackson managed to "turn that city on" with just three home runs occurring in the sixth game of the 1977 World Series.

Yet aspects of his question still remain. More specifically, how do fans, players, and owners determine whether a player is overpaid? Possible insights come from empirical research efforts and the arbitration experiences of player salary disputes.

Arbitration experience and related empirical research. There have been several rigorous attempts to specify the relationship between player performance measures and team performance (athletic and financial) records.[45] These efforts are hindered by the inability to determine the individual player's impact on team attendance.[46]

Also, bargaining over player salaries always involves a complex set of factors not easily measured and plugged into an equation. The personalities and desires of the parties play a major role in this one-on-one wage bargaining effort. For example, managerial egos are often involved in the bidding war over a particular player. One owner has commented, "Much of last year's bidding was created by the impression that if you didn't bid, you were a cheap bum."[47] Bargaining also includes a variety of tactics which can distort the desired positive relationship between player performance and salary. At least one team has gone public in a player salary dispute, using half-page newspaper advertisements to explain their position to the local fans.[48] On at least one occasion, management has informed the player it would inform his wife of his sexual promiscuity in an attempt to reduce the player's bargaining power.[49]

Empirical research also flounders in attempts to isolate the unique effects of performance variables on either management revenue or player salary. This problem is echoed by at least one arbitrator of baseball salary disputes, who asserts that, while there are statistics summarizing every baseball performance measure, a problem remains in determining the relative significance of various offsetting statistics. For example, management could present data showing a pitcher had a poor won-lost record. The pitcher, however, might present additional data indicating that he gave up few runs in those lost games but the team hit for a lower percentage in those games than for the entire season. The arbitrator must then determine the relatively vague contribution of team performance to the pitcher's success. Similarly, a hitter could explain his relatively low runs batted in (RBI) total with the fact that he was assigned to a lower position in the batting order, for which fewer runners were on base to score with a hit. In short, the arbitrator maintains that, while statistics are helpful, the salary decisions are also affected by imponderables less objective and susceptible to measurement than traditional statistical categories.[50]

Arbitration is a relatively new avenue for baseball salary determination. During the first year of this practice, fifty-four of the 500 players invoked the final offer arbitration provisions, with twenty-five of these individuals eventually settling their disputes before the arbitrator's award. Related research suggests that arbitration has remained a viable salary determination alternative but has not replaced traditional salary bargaining techniques between player and owner.[51] While arbitration might not be used by many of the players, it still appears necessary to establish some sort of common definition regarding significant performance criteria. Article V of the 1976–1979 labor agreement specifies some criteria to be excluded from arbitral consideration. However, it also expressly gives the arbitrator authority to determine the weight assigned to the evidence presented in the hearing.

Related empirical research can offer appropriate insights into a common wage determination definition, although it will be difficult for owners and players to accept all of the findings. For example, research has found that the team's revenue is positively associated with population size and negatively associated with the percentage of black baseball players on the team, the latter appearing to be a result of fan racial discrimination in baseball.[52] Players will not agree to be judged on factors beyond their control, particularly if the factor runs counter to legal proscriptions in the Equal Employment Opportunity Act of 1972.

Player-Management Relationships A major league baseball manager has to represent one of the most perplexing occupations in the United States. The manager's success or failure is often due to factors beyond his control (player injuries, the relative success of other teams in the division, and so on). This individual is also charged with maintaining harmony among twenty-four players having different backgrounds and aspirations. In many situations, young rookies are on the same team with players old enough to be their fathers. It is difficult to imagine this as a harmonious situation, particularly since the rookie is competing for the older player's job. Some players also resent the large salaries given to other players on the team. A player earning $30,000 a year might acknowledge that another player earning $300,000 is a better performer. Yet few if any players aware of the salary differences and comparative hitting, pitching, or fielding statistics would believe another player is ten times better. In some cases, tension is created between racial or ethnic factions on the team. Finally, the manager must be able to motivate the nonplayer, who sits in the dugout believing he is as good as the starting player on the field.

Discipline problems. The preceding situations coupled with relatively high player salaries can pose disciplinary problems which represent perhaps the most significant aspect of player-management relationships. One former manager somewhat bitterly comments:

It isn't the game I used to know. In the first place there are the players. They're a different breed. . . . You can't tell them what to do. They have to be consulted; they want to know why. Not *how* but *why*. The battle cry to today's player is: *I don't have to.*

And do you know something? He doesn't. What are you going to do with a guy making $60,000, fine him? He'll laugh at you. . . .

The other slogan of the day is *I'll do it my way.* The prevailing attitude is that they've got everything coming to them. Not by accomplishment but just cause they're alive.[53]

Discipline has always been an issue in professional sports, with baseball being no exception. One of the earlier, somewhat consistent "disciplinary problems" was Babe Ruth. On one occasion his response to his manager's disciplinary action was so obscene and threatening it would make many people blanch.[54] Recently, disciplinary fines and suspensions have resulted from one player fracturing his manager's cheek in a fight, another player refusing to play a game, and a third player leaving the playing field without permission to take a shower.[55]

There appear to be many explanations for disciplinary problems. Some players have suggested much of the blame rests with managerial inabilities, contending that some managers have been hired by the front office to serve as organizational "yes men" with possibly little understanding of either the game or player concerns.[56] Even experienced managers might be a bit confused about the successful managerial style to be applied to a particular group of players. There is no universal approach to managing a baseball team. In recent seasons, both hard-line and soft-shoe approaches have been successful.[57]

Additional disciplinary problems occur when the manager has not been given sufficient authority to resolve disputes. Professional baseball, like other sports, has a variety of management officials (owners, presidents, general managers, managers, coaches, and so on) who can potentially direct a player's activities. Problems arise when players either receive conflicting directives or go over the manager's head to other officials. Conflict can become more acute when the other management officials usurp the manager's authority in front of the players.[58]

Some management officials suggest that disciplinary problems are a result of player unionization—labor agreements restrict managerial discretion and authority, while at the same time subjecting discipline issues to the grievance procedure. The existence of the union might make it more difficult to discipline baseball players, yet its presence does not eliminate the employer's disciplinary alternative. The 1976–1979 labor agreement actually appears to give management more disciplinary latitude than is found in most industrial situations. Action taken by the commissioner against a player to preserve the "integrity" of or "public confidence" in baseball is not subject to arbitration. Disciplinary fines or suspensions imposed upon a player by a league or commissioner follow a similar procedure (Article 10–C of the labor agreement). Finally, the Uniform Player's Contract (3–a) included in the 1976–1979 labor agreement contains a broad player commitment to keep in "first-class physical condition" and "conform to high standards of personal conduct, fair play, and good sportsmanship." Consequently, most if not all of the disciplinary actions mentioned in the media are allowed to stand. Management can also unilaterally establish work rules to preserve discipline. For example, the New York Yankees have recently established a rule prohibiting commercials filmed by players on the day a game is scheduled to insure that the player is mentally and physically fresh for the day's activities.

As is true in the industrial situation, union officers can sometimes help prevent a disciplinary situation from occurring. In 1976, Marvin Miller helped dissuade the Oakland Athletic players from taking a wildcat strike against their owner. In summary, it is uncertain whether contemporary players pose more disciplinary problems than their predecessors. Yet management officials still have the authority (spelled out in the labor agreement) if not always the ability to resolve the problems.

Collective Bargaining Problems and Prospects in Professional Sports

Collective bargaining in baseball shares many similarities with that occurring in three other professional sports: hockey (the National Hockey League or NHL, whose players are organized by the National Hockey

League Players Association or NHLPA), football (the National Football League or NFL, whose players are organized by the National Football League Players Association or NFLPA), and basketball (the National Basketball Association or NBA, whose players are organized into the National Basketball Players Association or NBPA). Therefore, collective bargaining's problems and prospects for all sports are briefly summarized and integrated. The labor relations processes occurring in professional sports can be compared to similar activities in other industries in terms of (a) characteristics of the job, (b) characteristics of union and management officials, and (c) unique aspects of the collective bargaining relationship.

Job Characteristics Like other employees, professional athletes are interested in material benefits. Therefore the union's success in representing these employees can in part be measured in terms of gains in type and amount of benefits. Professional baseball has made significant advances in salaries, expense allowances, and severance pay over a twelve-year period in addition to obtaining arbitration of salary disputes and provisions pertaining to "free agents."[59] Other professional sports unions have succeeded in obtaining and increasing benefits in minimum salaries, pensions, and increased compensation for postseason games, such as the Stanley Cup Playoffs, the Super Bowl, and so on.[60]

Salaries. One key material benefit in each sport is player salaries. The average professional athlete earns a comparatively good wage. In the 1977 season, football players averaged $55,288; baseball players, $76,349; and hockey players, $90,000; in the 1975–1976 season, basketball players averaged $109,000.[61] Of course, averages distort the applicability of these figures. One superstar's salary can add $40,000 a year to ten other athletes' salaries.[62]

Yet the relatively high salaries could have three adverse effects on professional sports, none of which have been verified through empirical research. High salaries have been alleged to negatively affect a player's performance. A highly paid player might either become apathetic about the game or concerned with protecting his own interest at the expense of teamwork.[63] Yet one owner of a professional football team contends there are not many differences between yesterday's and today's players in spite of salary increases.[64] As mentioned earlier, higher salaried players might also pose more discipline problems since they are relatively unaffected by fines. However, a quick review of related cases shows that disciplinary fines or suspensions are upheld in hockey, football, and basketball as well as in baseball.[65]

High salaries might also raise the operating cost of a professional team. There are numerous accounts of baseball, basketball, hockey, and football teams currently in financial trouble.[66] Management on occasion has blamed at least part of the financial plight on "exorbitant" player salaries, contending that something has to give, since "the amount of money in the pay pot is finite. . . . You can't keep raising the seat price to the fans or squeezing more cash out of television."[67] Yet, in some cases, a high salaried athlete can draw enough increased fan attendance to pay his salary.[68]

Length of career. Professional athletes do share one rather unique job characteristic—a short tenure. For example, in 1971, the average career for professional athletes was 7.5 years in hockey, 7 years in basketball, 4.5 years in football, and 4 years in baseball.[69] Player unions therefore focus on the access of players into the league and the ability of a player to move from one team to another to maximize income and playing potential during a relatively short tenure.

Baseball players' concern with the reserve clause and the ability of a player to move to another team has been discussed earlier. Professional football players would contend they were at least as restricted since they could only be drafted by one professional club when they graduated from college. Further, if a football player for Team A subsequently played out his option and agreed to play for Team B, the commissioner of football could determine whom Team B should give to Team A for appropriate compensation. This rule (called the *Rozelle Rule*) was put into effect to insure that the football teams would be balanced. If compensation were not ordered, then the wealthiest teams would dominate the sport since they could pay for the superstars; fan interest (gate and television revenues) would drop off, and everyone would suffer.[70] Opponents of the Rozelle Rule claim that a football player, unlike any other employee, cannot freely choose his employer and thus his career opportunities are unjustly restricted.[71]

Currently, all major professional team sports have resolved through various procedures the key issue of player mobility.[72] It is difficult to determine the precise union emphasis regarding this issue; there is a thin line between maximizing existing members' material benefits and preserving the job security of the membership. Consider, for example, the draft of professional football players from collegiate ranks by a single employer. The union could disapprove of this action on the basis that potential union members are being deprived of maximizing their initial employment income since they cannot bargain with more than one club. However, union concern over the draft might also be based on the needs of existing players (current dues-paying members).

For example, one veteran NFL player contends that the lack of a draft of new players might prolong veterans' careers—clubs would think twice before engaging in a bidding war over an untested rookie. Instead, they might tend to rely on a veteran who has demonstrated his ability in the professional ranks.[73] Similarly, the NFLPA's cooperation in reducing the number of exhibition games from the regular season might have been motivated out of job protection concerns. The smaller number of exhibition games translates into fewer opportunities for rookies to prove they should displace veteran performers.[74]

Characteristics of Management and Union Officials In each of the professional sports, owners of all the affected teams or their designated representatives negotiate with the exclusive bargaining representatives for the players. In many cases, the owners have not presented a unified front in collective bargaining. Owners can be differentiated along several dimensions: experience with and knowledge of the professional sport, extent that the sport represents their entire financial investments, financial wealth, and conservative vs. liberal philosophies regarding game rules and player involvement in managerial decisions.[75] Many of these differences have resulted in public name-calling among owners.[76] More important are the publicized owner differences regarding the players' collective bargaining rights.[77]

These differences can be compounded when each of the owners or their designated management officials interpret and administer the negotiated labor agreement. Each team can have a different labor relations climate, with some players not being able to appreciate administrative problems occurring on another team. For example, the NFL players' strike in 1974 met with some player resistance. One player representative for the Los Angeles Rams stated, "It's difficult to resist an [adverse managerial] attitude when you haven't been affected by it."[78]

It is therefore difficult to speak of *the* management side in professional sports' collective bargaining activities. This situation is further complicated by the presence of another individual in each sport, the commissioner. Ed Garvey, executive director of the NFLPA, admits confusion in his dealings with the commissioner of football (Pete Rozelle):

Who *is* Pete Rozelle? Is he the Neutral Guardian of the Sport, as the public thinks, and as the owners would be pleased to have us think? Or, is he, as the players think, a man with quasi-governmental power who is the primary spokesman for the owners in their effort to preserve the current system?[79]

Sports commissioners have often been involved in administrative decisions affecting the players—those on player mobility (Rozelle Rule) and disciplinary penalties for various infractions, for instance. These actions might cause dissatisfaction within the managerial ranks as well as within organized labor's. For example, one of the more recent significant acts of the commissioner of baseball was his voiding of one owner's sale of three baseball players to other baseball teams.[80]

The current, prominent union officials in each of the four professional team sports have not come up through the ranks of the sports. They initially approached their positions as "outsiders," not having performed in professional sports. As previously suggested, superstar athletes might not tend to push for collective bargaining goals since they are unaffected by concerns such as minimum salary and possibly even pensions. An individual who has had previous labor relations experience might be better qualified to formulate and guide an athletes' union.

However, a union leader has to convince the membership that strong player commitment is needed for collective bargaining. Marvin Miller of the MLBPA has observed, "I am neither the smartest, most skilled, nor ablest person alive, but if I were, it would cut no ice if I had no support from the players. The owners would pay no attention unless they were convinced there was a unified group."[81] This is not an easy task for any union leader, particularly an "outsider" who cannot state to the members, "I have been in your shoes, and this is what we must do to get what you need." The 1972 baseball strike appears to have been almost mandated by the players;[82] therefore player commitment was very high. The 1970 and 1974 football strikes, however, did not generate as much commitment from the players, and some subsequently expressed discontent over the union's role and philosophy.[83] The executive director of the NFLPA suggests that a union leader in professional sports might have a unique problem regarding membership: "Football players are young, but they have limited careers. It's harder to get them to fight for causes that may not bring them immediate benefits. They're playing now; what do they care about the rights of players in the future?"[84]

Another factor complicating the union's organization is the significant presence of nonunion individuals who perform a traditional union function—agents, who help negotiate compensation for various athletes. Unlike in other industries, the union only negotiates the salary minimum. It is up to each "employee" to negotiate the best salary possible with management.[85] In short, the collective bargaining relationship is somewhat more complex in professional sports, an observation which is further illustrated in the following section.

Unique Aspects of Collective Bargaining Activities in Professional Sports

Collective bargaining in professional sports has been relatively uneven, usually gaining impetus from sources other than the labor and management officials. The previous discussion of collective bargaining in baseball indicated how an arbitrator's decision motivated serious collective bargaining over a key issue, the reserve clause. Also, unlike other sports, baseball has been accorded an exemption from antitrust considerations.

Unions representing hockey, football, and basketball players were formed in the late 1950s,[86] but collective bargaining gains for these sports were sporadic. For example, hockey players achieved early collective bargaining gains only after agreeing that they would drop litigation against management for refusing to recognize the union's existence.[87] In essence, the hockey players "won" when they agreed that management did not have to recognize their union.[88]

The NFLPA's early bargaining gains were also relatively uneven, with improvement possibly coming from the involvement of "outside" sources. The 1977 collective bargaining agreement was undoubtedly affected by a favorable NLRB ruling against management's action of removing players who were active union representatives from their teams.[89] Perhaps more significant were judicial decisions which supported players' concerns regarding mobility to other teams. In essence, the Rozelle Rule governing compensation for traded players as well as the arbitrary assignment of a player to only one team in the entry draft were found to be illustrative of a "group boycott," or a per se violation of the antitrust laws.[90] Ed Garvey of the NFLPA believed that "the court decisions, plus the fact that the union was obviously increasing in strength, made these people [management officials] sit down and think it would be a lot cheaper to negotiate than go on spending $5 or $6 million every year in legal fees."[91]

From time to time, Congress has become involved in the unionization of professional sports. While congressional involvement in this subject may have prompted managerial recognition of the NFLPA,[92] there is little reason to think that this source is effective in resolving collective bargaining impasses since "congressional committees have been poking and prodding the NFL for years and have hardly left a bruise."[93] For example, some members of Congress urged the parties, particularly management, to negotiate a settlement to the 1974 football dispute or else be subject to appropriate legislation.[94] Yet this did not appreciably affect management since the players worked without an agreement for the next two years and eleven months.

Thus, it appears that collective bargaining in professional sports can be more strongly affected by judicial decisions than by congressional pronouncements. For example, the NBA recently signed a ten-year labor relations agreement which precluded costly appeal litigation of basketball players' mobility rights.[95]

The use of a key collective bargaining tactic, the strike, has had limited use in professional sports; strikes have occurred only three times—in baseball in 1972 and in football in 1970 and 1974. Several factors suggest that the strike will continue to be used infrequently in the future:

1. As previously mentioned, it is difficult to rally a group of relatively young athletes who are reluctant to sacrifice their immediate financial gains for long-term goals applicable to future players. Yet the owners are aware that most of the players are union members and in at least some cases have demonstrated their commitment to collective action.

2. To some extent, athletes have proven that they cannot be replaced during a strike. For example, the 1974 football players' strike resulted

Disputes over working conditions in professional sports have in some instances extended beyond the athletes to the officials—in this case, baseball umpires.

Source: Courtesy of Wide World Photos.

in mass substitution of rookies in exhibition games. Many fans reacted to this situation by staying home in droves.

3. Both management and the union realized that games, indeed the season, could be lost forever due to a strike. Games cannot be stockpiled like inventory before a strike is taken. Similarly, a strike which lasts for a month might make it impossible to extend the season to make up the games because of weather conditions and conflicting television rights to show another sport at that time.

Collective bargaining in professional sports can be more dependent on an external constraint discussed in Chapter 1, public (or fan) opinion, which can become pronounced if higher player salaries are followed by higher admission prices.[96] The mass media (particularly television) can also exert a strong influence on the collective bargaining outcome.[97] Television appears to have much influence in the scheduling of athletic events in order to attract a sizable media audience. One television commentator of baseball games suggested, "If television wanted a game played in six inches of snow it just might be aired."[98] It was disclosed that a television station, mindful of increased ratings and revenues, made it financially possible for the Philadelphia Phillies to obtain Pete Rose from the Cincinnati Reds.[99] The increased role of the mass media on subsequent labor-management activities is just one of several future uncertainties facing professional sports.

Health-Care Employees

The hospital as a social institution affects many lives. For example, nearly 1.3 million Americans are hospitalized in a given year.[100] In order to better communicate the impact of labor-management activities on health-care practices, this section is divided into two general areas. First, legislative coverage of hospital employees is discussed, including the pros and cons of unions in hospitals and a perspective for analyzing the collective bargaining activities of affected employees. Second, the collective bargaining history and goals of affected employees—nurses and physicians and/or house staff—are described.

Legislative Influences on Health Care Bargaining

Prior to 1935, the health-care industry was relatively unaffected by labor legislation. The Wagner Act of 1935 did not specifically exempt hospital organizations; thus the NLRB and the courts determined whether certain hospitals came under its coverage.[101] In 1947, Section 2 (2) of the Taft-Hartley Act exempted voluntary, nonprofit hospitals from federal labor relations laws.[102] Employees working in veterans' hospitals of the federal government were eventually granted organizational and collective bargaining rights under the 1962 Executive Order 10988 (now covered under the Civil Service Reform Act of 1978). Employees working in state administered hospitals (for example, mental institutions) usually had to rely upon applicable state statutes in attempting to engage in collective bargaining activities.

Because voluntary, nonprofit hospitals constitute the largest single sector of the health-care industry in terms of number of hospitals, admissions, payroll expenses, and union activity,[103] their omission from federal labor legislation coverage greatly blunted collective bargaining prospects in the industry for many years. Unions seeking to organize these hospitals could not rely on procedures found in the National Labor Relations Act due to the industry's exemption. Therefore, rights to form unions would have to be found in state statutes, which in 1974 were grouped into the following three categories:

1. States which had collective bargaining laws governing hospitals (twelve).
2. States which had no laws governing collective bargaining in hospitals (thirty-one).
3. States which had laws prohibiting collective bargaining in hospitals (seven).[104]

Unions were free to bargain with hospitals in Category 1. They could also establish a collective bargaining relationship with those in Category 2, although hospital management officials in these states could refuse to recognize the union.

This situation changed in 1974 with the Taft-Hartley amendments extending federal labor relations coverage to all private sector hospitals, including convalescent hospitals, health maintenance organizations, health clinics, and nursing homes. These amendments were controversial; opponents considered their impact on various aspects of the health care organization negative. Some maintained that the critical services supplied by voluntary nonprofit hospitals would be hindered by unions and collective actions:

What is so magic about the National Labor Relations Act in this regard? Are we to assume that this be the panacea? Are we to assume the broad right to strike is fair and just? Are we to assume that the right to strike over an economic demand to force its acceptance is of greater value to the overall interest of a community than the continued availability of health care? Are we to assume that the private sector balance of economic power of a union against economic power of an industrial complex is similarly appropriate where human life is in the balance instead of money?

If the answers to the above questions are "yes," then we had better check our sense of values. I wonder whether the answers would be different if there were close personal involvements where seriously ill family members or friends were languishing, or even dying, in a strikebound hospital.[105]

Proponents of the 1974 amendments contended that the service provided by voluntary hospitals is no more critical than that performed by proprietary or profit-making hospitals included under Taft-Hartley, that in fact

there have . . . been instances of proprietary hospitals becoming nonprofit hospitals. This can happen without any visible signs. The employees may not even be aware of this change in status. The patients in the beds would not be aware. There would be no change in any function, service, or cost to the patients. The only difference would be a nondiscernible change in the type of ownership. Certainly this is ridiculous.

Nonprofit hospitals are not only a giant part of the health industry, they are "big business." In their business and labor relations, they should be treated the same as other industries—all of which employ the sophisticated labor relations methods available from the NLRB.[106]

There was also disagreement over the effects of these amendments on increased strike activity. Union officials have repeatedly maintained that most strikes have been over union recognition, a situation which would be eliminated by the orderly election procedures established and monitored by the NLRB. Yet other individuals anticipated that these amendments would eliminate the previously established strike prohibitions in many state labor relations laws and lead to an increase in the number of strikes.[107]

Controversy notwithstanding, the 1974 Taft-Hartley amendments brought nearly 4,000 nonprofit private hospitals and 1.6 million employees under the jurisdiction of the NLRB. Although the impact of these amendments on health-care bargaining is not conclusive, in the first three months in which they were in effect, approximately 300 election petitions were filed with the NLRB—a substantial increase in activity over previous NLRB elections in health-care institutions.[108]

One recent study examining the impact of these amendments in a three-state area (Wisconsin, Minnesota, and Illinois) concluded that the predicted wave of unionization after the amendments went into effect has not occurred. Also, even after unionization, changes in labor costs and management discretion have been quite limited and possibly offset by reduced employee turnover costs. However, the authors also cautioned against generalizing to other geographical locations, particularly the San Francisco Bay area and the Northeast (discussed later in the section).[109]

Roughly speaking, the NLRB believes the following classifications are appropriate units or groupings of hospital employees for union representation elections:

1. A unit of professional employees.
2. A separate unit for registered nurses.
3. A separate unit for office and clerical employees (for example, switchboard operators and employees in the billing and credit departments).
4. A separate unit for technical employees (for example, licensed practical nurses and X-ray and lab technicians).
5. A unit of service and maintenance employees.[110]

A current problem concerns areas in the hospitals where unions may solicit employees. One court of appeals has decided that employers have a legitimate interest in barring union solicitation of employees in areas accessible to patients.[111] Another has contended that unions are "common entities" on the American scene and that only an "extraordinary patient" would be so dismayed at witnessing a solicitation effort that his or her health would be impaired.[112] The Supreme Court partially resolved some of the controversy in a case where solicitation was prohibited in areas accessible to patients (such as the cafeteria). Its decision in effect indicated that the NLRB has the proper expertise to determine appropriate places for union solicitation. The Court also reasoned that there was no congressional intent in the 1974 amendments to restrict solicitation. Indeed, Congress determined that improvements in health care might result from unions and possibly even from strike activity.[113]

Collective bargaining in the health-care industry first started in the San Francisco Bay area in 1919, although it did not spread to many hospitals in that area until the middle 1930s. During World War II, the few advances in collective bargaining were primarily limited to San Francisco, Seattle, and Minnesota.[114] Active unionization of health care personnel occurred during the period of 1959–1972, particularly in New York City.

The activity of Local 1199 in New York City encouraged similar organizing efforts throughout the country. Although Local 1199 was originally formed by Jewish drug clerks in Harlem and the Bronx in 1932, it began considering hospital employee members in 1958. One reason for this union's success was its ability to mobilize various minority and ethnic groups under a common group identity to collective action. For example, Martin Luther King, Jr., used to call Local 1199 his favorite union.[115]

Local 1199 quickly recognized the ethnic backgrounds of hospital service employees and found it advantageous to link its union organizing efforts with civil rights groups. Appeals to racial pride motivated some employees to take necessary job action, as illustrated by the reaction of an active strike participant, who was surprised that Local 1199 and the Southern Christian Leadership Conference

---

would risk jail, time, money and their very lives to help hundreds of poor people like me, whom a lot of other people may think wasn't important enough even to consider.

It helped me to realize how important I am as a person, which I'm afraid I didn't quite realize before. . . . I further realized that the power structure isn't all-powerful, but that they are to do the bidding of the people, and the people can make them do it.[116]

This union also effectively used other labor organizations in the bitter strikes of 1959 and 1962 in New York. An illustration of this assistance was the 113-day recognition strike in Charleston, South Carolina (1969):

George Meany took the lead in raising $100,000 from the A.F.L.-C.I.O. and its affiliates. The rival Alliance for Labor Action, headed by Walter P. Reuther, contributed $35,000. Perhaps the most potent assistance of all came from Thomas W. (Teddy) Gleason, tough-talking head of the International Longshoremen's Association, whose threat to shut down the port got a lot of Charleston businessmen interested in a settlement.[117]

Hospital unions such as Local 1199 needed more than organizational skills—they also needed at least a potentially responsive group of employees. There is no denying that hospital employees have traditionally been at the bottom of the economic ladder—underpaid for their work efforts.[118] When Local 1199 started organizing in 1959, income ranged from $26 to $28 per forty-four-hour week. Between 1959 and 1975, wage levels at these hospitals increased almost 800 percent ($181 per thirty-seven-hour week).[119]

However, in their detailed analysis of a union organizing drive and strike at a Chicago hospital, McKersie and Brown found that wages appeared to be a secondary influence on employees' union preferences and that the four-month strike was unsuccessful, since it did not result in the union's recognition. One factor which hindered the strike's effectiveness was the relatively high unemployment rate in the area, which made it easy for management to hire strike replacements. Another fact was that the "high rewards" employees (those receiving greater wages) had different union preferences according to their investments. Employees with greater investments (older, more seniority, high school education, and so on) were more likely to refrain from union organizational activity than similarly paid hospital employees with lower investments.[120]

Many collective bargaining agreements have been negotiated in the health-care industry.[121] While these efforts have resulted in some strikes, the Federal Mediation and Conciliation Service stated in its 1977 study that hospitals had a lower strike incidence than is found in the rest of the private sector.[122] This study, of course, does not mean a complete absence of labor unrest among health-care employees. One example is the 1976 New York area hospital employees' strike (involving 40,000 at forty-eight institutions), which became the largest hospital labor dispute in American history.[123]

Nurses The American Nurses Association (ANA), while having less than 30 percent of all employed nurses as members, is the major organization representing nurses.[124] Since its inception in 1897, the ANA has been concerned with economic protection of its members. The organization avoided direct involvement with collective bargaining; however, in 1946 it encouraged state nurses' associations to actively implement collective bargaining programs aimed at economic benefits and participation of nurses in the planning and administration of nursing services. Under this arrangement, the state nurses' associations negotiate with employers when authorized to do so by the membership. The ANA believes that its state affiliates have more direct knowledge about actual and desired working conditions, and it will not become involved in a dispute from a financial or advisory standpoint unless requested to do so by the appropriate association.

This program has continued, although it was modified in 1950 when the ANA adopted a no-strike policy and formulated a *nurses in dispute policy*, which contended that because nurses have direct legal and ethical obligations to patients they should take a neutral position if their facility is involved in a labor-management dispute.[125] Hence, the ANA emphasized that nurses were not to strike; instead, they should tend to their patients during employee-employer negotiations.

Throughout the 1950s the ANA economic program had limited application, with very few job actions or strikes. As was true in other health-care occupations, union activity of nurses increased dramatically in the 1960s and 1970s. In spite of ANA's no-strike and nurses in dispute policies, several strikes have taken place since 1965 (1966 and 1974 San Francisco strikes, the 1975 Ohio Nurses' Association strike, and others). Other state nurses' associations (in Connecticut, Iowa, Massachusetts, and so on) have had active collective bargaining roles in recent years.[126]

Nurses have received a surprising amount of public support during their strike activities. Few people directly blame them for dislocations during a strike.[127] In most strike situations, ample time has been given to transfer already admitted patients or to stop accepting patients for elective surgery.[128] Also, the public has begun to view hospitals as big business concerns rather than charitable institutions.[129]

As is true with other employee classifications, nurses have varying attitudes toward collective bargaining.[130] Differences of opinion can be due to relative emphasis given to two bargaining objectives: professional nursing standards and economic gains.[131] For example, "the Ohio Nurses' Association insisted that the ANA Code of Ethics for nurses be incorporated into the collective bargaining agreement, thus ensuring from their point of view that management will adhere to the highest standards for nursing care given to patients."[132] Factions within the ANA could develop when one bargaining objective is stressed over the other.

Other attitudinal differences may cause divisiveness among nurses—the degree of career satisfaction found with their present positions, for example. One study found that nurses who are dissatisfied with their careers view themselves as having few professional advancement opportunities; there are few if any organizational promotions available in a hospital. Furthermore, career dissatisfaction has been one of the major contributors to militancy—belief in collective bargaining and strikes. Another factor contributing to attitudinal differences among nurses has been age. Younger nurses tend to view strikes and unions more favorably than do their older colleagues.[133]

House Staff Graduates from medical schools have not been immune to collective concerns and actions. House staffs consist of hospital-based interns, residents, and fellows in training programs. These individuals, in many cases, have to participate in hospital training programs, since nearly all medical practices are specialties which require hospital training for certification.

Labor relations concerns arise over the various working conditions that house-staff personnel face—for example, low wages and extensive working hours, averaging in some cases a hundred hours a week, often for consecutive periods ranging from thirty-six to seventy-two hours.[134] Additionally, training necessary for certification makes house-staff officers particularly vulnerable; they are subject to arbitrary actions by medical supervisors. In some cases, the training program is designed to eliminate a specified number of personnel before completion. Those completing the program still have to depend on the good will of their supervisors and other hospital administrators for future hospital privileges and recommendations for other positions.[135]

Currently, two organizations represent the house staff: (a) New York City Committee of Interns and Residents (CIR) and (b) the Physicians' National Housestaff Association (PNHA). Both pursue collective bargaining activities, yet neither is chartered by a national union, and both are headed by house staff officers actively engaged in a training program. Although strikes occur very infrequently, in 1975 the CIR organized the first major strike by interns and residents in the United States. Three thousand doctors struck twenty-one voluntary and municipal hospitals in New York City. Being mainly concerned about work schedules, the CIR requested that its members be required to work no more than eighty hours a week and no more than fifteen hours consecutively in one twenty-four-hour period. The strike lasted four days and resulted in some concessions in the work schedules. In essence, a joint house-staff and hospital management committee was formed at each hospital. These committees were charged with formulating work schedules which would be compatible with patient care and the interns' education and well being.[136]

As was true of many other strikes in the health-care industry, the New York strike did not arouse a great amount of adverse public opinion. Perhaps this was due to its short duration and mandated advance notices by the CIR which minimized the patients' inconveniences. The public may have also sympathized with the employees' stated goal of improving patient services. This goal had previously been demonstrated in a 1975 strike in Los Angeles, where half of the wage increase funds for interns and residents was made available for patient care projects.[137]

In their effort to gain new members, house-staff officials and their organizations maintained that the 1974 Taft-Hartley amendments brought them under coverage of the National Labor Relations Act and the NLRB. However, in 1976, the NLRB decided in the *Cedars-Sinai Medical Center* case that hospital interns and residents are students, not employees; therefore, they are exempt from the National Labor Relations Act.[138] Yet a U.S. court of appeals has subsequently overturned the NLRB's decision, thereby making it easier for house-staff employees to participate in union organizing drives and representation elections.[139]

Physicians Apart from house-staff personnel, there are some 16,000 physicians belonging to twenty-six organizations committed to some form of collective bargaining. It should be noted that only four of fourteen of these organizations responding to a survey had negotiated labor agreements. [140] Some of this inactivity is no doubt due to the rather strong anti-union positions taken by the American Medical Association and American Dental Association. While the American Medical Association gave some support to the concerns of house-staff personnel involved in the 1975 New York strike, [141] the organization has long maintained that unions would harm the physician-patient relationship.

However, physicians have become more militant, particularly in their response to increases in malpractice insurance. A slowdown of physicians in northern California occurred in 1975 when Argonaut Insurance Company increased malpractice insurance from $5,377 to $18,184 a year for anesthesiologists, gynecologists, and orthopedic surgeons. This slowdown was not taken against patients or hospitals but as a protest against the insurance company's move. As indicated by one official of the San Francisco Medical Society:

It would be very easy . . . if the doctors could pay the higher premium rates and pass along the added costs to the consumer, but they are convinced the increase is not justified. All they have to do is look at the insurance companies and see that they lost more than 6 billion dollars last year on the stock market. They are convinced the increased rates aren't coming because of malpractice suits. [142]

Similar collective protests have occurred in Los Angeles, New York, Seattle, and Washington, D.C. Additional efforts at collective action and the possibility of altered attitudes by the American Medical Association remain interesting, speculative topics of labor relations.

Farm Workers

Instead of describing agriculture labor relations activities across the nation, this section focuses on union efforts in California, a state which has experienced significant union activity and has farm working conditions similar to those throughout the United States. California labor relations activities have been pronounced, directly involving more employees and related research efforts than those of any other state. This state has also witnessed a comprehensive labor relations law as well as the emergence of a charismatic union leader, Cesar Chavez. Finally, Chavez's union, the United Farm Workers, provides vivid examples of problems and prospects that all farm worker unions face.

Overview of Farm Laborer Working Conditions and the Rise of Cesar Chavez

Statistics on the number of farm workers often vary because of the rapid mobility of migrants. There are an estimated 3 million farm workers in the United States; almost 200,000 are seasonal migrant laborers. Migrant working and living conditions have often been described as brutal. [143] For example, in 1973, a typical agricultural laborer had eight and one-half

Cesar Chavez, the powerfully charismatic leader of the United Farm Workers, has successfully organized migrant workers to gain wage increases and contracts. His nonviolent approach, based on worker loyalty to "La Causa," usually relies on boycotts of products.

Source: Photo by Paul Fusco, Magnum.

years of education and worked an average of eighty-eight days a year at $13.20 per day, for an annual wage of $1,160. Further, these individuals are employed in the third most dangerous occupation in the United States. In 1967, there were more fatal accidents in agriculture than in any other industry.[144]

Four unique working conditions further illustrate the migrant worker's plight.

1. *"El Cortito."* The dreaded, common piece of equipment, "El Cortito," or "the short hoe" used in crop tending, has a handle less than three feet long. The migrants have to stoop in the fields to use it, so that their backs are practically parallel to the ground. Governor Jerry Brown outlawed the use of this equipment in California; however, "El Cortito" still remains in other states.[145]

2. *Transitory nature.* Another unpleasant aspect of this job is its transitory nature, necessitating frequent relocations to find work. Cesar Chavez's recollection of his typical work year is presented in Exhibit 17–1 to illustrate a representative work schedule.

3. *Employer attitudes.* It is, of course, impossible to identify the growers as having a common attitude regarding their employees. Yet the following

Exhibit 17–1
Cesar Chavez's
Recollections
Regarding His Work
Year

We did not pick the same crops every year, but there was a pattern. Most winters we spent in Brawley where there were carrots, mustard, and peas. I did cabbage and lettuce in January, picking or working it, tying or loading it on a trailer. Then a little later we capped cantaloupe and watermelon, putting a wax paper over the plant to keep it from freezing and to keep the ground warm, just like an individual hothouse for every plant. When it got warmer, we came back, took the cap off, worked the ground around the plants, and thinned them, using a short-handle hoe. Probably one of the worst jobs was the broccoli. We were in water and mud up to our necks and our hands got frozen. We had to cut it and throw it on a trailer, cut and throw, cut and throw. We slipped around in the mud, and we were wet. I didn't have any boots, just shoes on. Those crops were in December through March. In January to March there also were the cauliflower, mustard greens, onions, carrots, cabbage, and lettuce.

Then we worked in the watermelon, just picking up the vines which grew in the irrigation ditches and training them away from the ditches. The melons started in May, and I would work in the sheds for a labor contractor who was related to us.

In late May we had two or three options, Oxnard for beans, Beaumont for cherries, or the Hemet area for apricots, places that no longer have much or any of those crops. I think we did all at one time or other. Most of the time my dad would leave it up to us. "Do you think you'll like it?" he would ask.

We started making the apricots in Moorepark where they pick them up from the ground, just like prunes. In San Jose, on the other hand, we had to climb a ladder.

That would be the early part of summer. From there we had all kinds of options. We never did asparagus, and we only did figs once. The milk of the fig eats through your skin like acid. Some people put grease on their hands, but we couldn't do that. It was just awful.

We worked in lima beans, corn, and chili peppers, picked fresh lima beans for fifty cents a basket. Then in August we had grapes, prunes, cucumbers, and tomatoes. Those go into September and part of October. We would go before those crops started and wait in a camp until they were ready. For example there were raisin grapes about ten miles beyond Fresno. We had to be there at least a week in advance, or we couldn't get a job. That was a week of lost time, sometimes more, with no pay whatsoever.

Then we did cotton from October through Christmas. I just hated it. It was very hard work, but there was nothing else. After the cotton, just like ducks, we usually went back to Brawley to start with the crops in January.

So we traveled from the Imperial Valley in the south as far north as Sacramento and San Jose.

Source: Selection is reprinted from *Cesar Chavez, Autobiography of La Causa,* by Jacques E. Levy, with the permission of W. W. Norton & Company, Inc. Copyright © 1975 by Jacques E. Levy.

quotations from growers illustrate employment philosophies ranging from indifference to paternalism to racism:

The class of labor we want is the kind we can send home when we are through with them.[146]

> It wasn't fair for Chavez to strike my ranch. . . . My workers were sim-
> ple people, good people, and I liked them and took good care of them.
> If a man and his family worked hard, I gave them a low-rent room and
> sold them groceries at only slight markups. Once, I even paid for the
> funeral of the daughter of one of my workers.

> Those people were made to suffer; some of them even enjoy the work.
> God made the Mexicans with stubby legs and greasy hair. So, you see,
> they can lean low and tolerate the sun in the fields. Chavez made those
> people think they're something better.[147]

---

4. *Exemption from labor relations laws.* Finally, agricultural employees continue to be specifically exempted from federal labor relations laws, and
this lack of federal labor relations coverage has made it most difficult for
farm workers to organize.[148] Without federal legislation, legal emphasis
shifts to appropriate state laws and judicial interpretations of legal organizing and collective bargaining tactics (for example, picketing and
boycotts of farm products).[149] Only six states (Arizona, Idaho, Kansas,
California, Wisconsin, and Hawaii) currently have laws covering farm
workers.[150]

It should be noted that at least one farm workers' union has reservations about being included under the National Labor Relations Act.
Under this act, most migrant workers could be denied voting rights in
union elections since employers could request elections during the off-
season, when a handful of steady, company-dominated workers would
decide the representation issue for the majority of seasonal workers.
"Only the California Agricultural Labor Relations Act guarantees peak
season elections."[151]

Early Organizational Attempts In 1905, the Industrial Workers of the
World (IWW) made the first efforts to organize farm workers, meeting
with some success by 1922. But the organizational problems of the farm
workers were quite similar to others faced by the IWW (discussed in more
detail in Chapter 2)—loose, ineffective organizational structure and an
emphasis on widening class conflict instead of settling disputes.[152] Labor
relations activities remained sporadic for the next forty years due to the
lack of membership base and labor legislation.[153]

Another major obstacle to union organization has been the *bracero
program,* which allowed importation of Mexican farm workers *(braceros)*
under war emergency agreements between the United States and Mexico
during World War II. Almost overnight, the haphazard system of recruiting farm labor was replaced by a highly organized recruiting process.
This method insured growers a plentiful supply of cheap labor, while
allowing Mexico to send its restless unemployed to another country. The
two countries continued this program after World War II until Congress
officially terminated it in 1964.[154]

The bracero program presented a major obstacle to union organizing drives. Indeed, Cesar Chavez began confronting this problem in 1958, four years before he formed a union of agricultural workers. While registering voters and signing up people for citizenship classes in Oxnard, California, Chavez was repeatedly questioned by unemployed farm workers about the 28,000 braceros working in this area. Chavez assessed the situation in the following terms:

> The jobs belonged to local workers. The braceros were brought only for exploitation. They were just instruments for the growers. Braceros didn't make any money, and they were exploited viciously, forced to work under conditions the local people wouldn't tolerate. If the braceros spoke up, if they made the minimal complaints, they'd be shipped back to Mexico. We always felt that ending the program would be the best thing we could do for them and for everybody.[155]

Later modifications in the bracero program did not allow use of braceros if local workers were available and registered for employment. Then Chavez conducted extensive registration drives which resulted in employment of local farm workers. This victory was short-lived, however, since these employees were subsequently replaced by braceros.

Chavez's Formation of a Union Forming a union in 1962 enabled Chavez to approach the farm worker's employment conditions more directly. Using the approaches proposed by Ghandi, Chavez relied on nonviolence in union activities. He viewed nonviolence as necessary to obtain favorable public opinion; the concept also had pragmatic value—a nonviolent act (a boycott, for example) on a supermarket hurts the employer economically, while a violent act (such as arson) enables the employer to collect insurance and receive a refund on taxes.[156] Chavez was also influenced by another aspect of Ghandi's movement, the loyalty of followers which allows an insistence that many rules be obeyed.[157] As will be discussed later in this section, Chavez's reliance on loyalty might blunt his union's collective bargaining effectiveness.

The first strike conducted by Chavez occurred in the rose fields in the spring of 1965. This dispute lasted four days, with employees receiving a wage increase but no labor agreement. The growers were eager to resolve the dispute since skilled rose grafters were in short supply.

The most publicized activities of this union were the 1965 Delano strike and the grape boycott. These efforts were initially successful in that longshoremen refused to load "scab" grapes on ships. However, the boycott became somewhat difficult when the growers increased the number of different labels from 6 to 100, thereby confusing the pickets. Thus, the boycott was enlarged to include all California-grown grapes.[158]

The grape boycott received national attention, particularly in the 1968 presidential campaign, during which it was endorsed by candidates Kennedy, McCarthy, McGovern, and Humphrey. On the other hand, Nixon denounced the boycott while eating grapes at a press conference in Fresno, California.[159] The Nixon administration later gave more tangible support to the grape growers during the Vietnam War. The Defense Department countered reduced consumer interest in grapes by increasing 1968–1969 grape shipments to the troops some 350 percent (2.5 million pounds) over the previous year.[160]

Two major companies recognized the union in the relatively early stages of the grape boycott: Schenley, which experienced Teamster refusal to deliver its products from a major warehouse, and the DiGorgio Corporation. The later agreement included several important provisions, such as an employer-financed health and welfare fund, layoffs and promotions based on seniority, holiday pay, and vacation benefits. By mid-July 1970, five years after the initial dispute, the Delano growers agreed to the principle of collective bargaining and signed labor agreements which raised economic benefits and established grievance procedures. Delano could be termed a success for the farm workers, yet the labor settlement increased jurisdictional battles among unions for the right to represent farm workers.

Jurisdictional Problems among Farm Worker Unions and Current Issues Facing Farm Labor Organizations

The union formed by Cesar Chavez was originally independent from the AFL-CIO, which had been conducting its own organizational drives with farm workers. After extensive negotiations, Chavez merged his union with the related AFL-CIO organizing committee during the grape boycott. This merger culminated in an AFL-CIO charter in 1972. The union, after numerous name changes, became the United Farm Workers (UFW).

Teamster-UFW Conflict While jurisdictional problems were somewhat peacefully worked out with the AFL-CIO, serious problems remained with an independent union, the Teamsters. A discussion of these disputes helps explain the internal problems of the UFW and the emergence of related labor legislation and also enables an examination of a rather rare impediment to the contemporary labor relations process—intense union rivalry for the same employees.

Although at least one Teamster local provided assistance to the UFW during the grape boycott, cooperation between the two unions was the exception rather than the rule.[161] The 1970 UFW victory in Delano heightened jurisdiction problems, for it prompted other growers to resolve labor relations in an expedient manner. In fact, 170 labor agreements were signed with Salinas and Santa Maria growers one day before Chavez announced the Delano settlement.

The UFW intended to switch its attention to the lettuce and vegetable fields of the Salinas and Santa Maria valleys after the Delano settlement. Growers in these valleys realized that unions were inevitable, and their concern shifted to minimizing their losses. They had previously approached the Teamsters, who were initially reluctant to break a 1966–1967 jurisdictional treaty with the UFW. Yet a Teamster-grower settlement was reached when Teamster drivers, who were on a brief strike, agreed to return to work only if their jobs were not disrupted by field hand strikes. This rationale prompted the Teamsters to push for (and quickly receive from the growers) extension of truck driver agreements to include the farm workers.

The UFW was predictably outraged by this turn of events, charging that the Teamsters had "sweetheart contracts" with the growers and the agreements were secured without asking the employees to vote for their union preference. The UFW countered with a strike (involving some 10,000 employees) to put pressure on the growers; violence often occurred between UFW and Teamster employees. Although this effort and the related lettuce boycott hurt the growers, problems continued to exist between the Teamsters and the UFW.

Teamsters made huge inroads into the UFW's bargaining victories. In 1973, the UFW held agreements with approximately 300 growers, involving some 60,000 employees. In 1974, this number was reduced to 12 agreements covering only 5,000 employees, while the Teamsters held some 350 collective bargaining agreements with the growers.[162] A large part of this turnaround was due to the eager reception given to the Teamsters by the growers. To be sure, employees under these sweetheart arrangements were not able to vote their particular union preference (Teamsters or UFW). When this situation changed in California, many of the farm workers indicated their preference for the UFW.

Yet there might be other reasons for the Teamsters' success, as illustrated by the following remarks of a farm worker on Chavez's "La Causa."

La Causa is good, and its time will come again. When I hear the cry of 'Huelga' I want to, you know, walk out of the fields, to screw the grower right at Harvest time, to help Cesar in this hard time he has. But look around you at all these open mouths to feed. We will keep thinning the lettuce because we need the dollars. I like the Chavez union most, but they made some mistakes. The Teamsters are not as bad as he says. They helped me get food stamps in January when there was no work.[163]

The Teamsters' traditional approach to collective bargaining clashed with the UFW's broader social goals. The Teamsters' use of much greater financial resources and of skilled staff personnel in their collective bargaining efforts may have raised doubts among some farm workers as to the appropriate method of union representation and the most efficient method of attaining these goals.[164] As suggested by the preceding quotation, many farm workers still revere Chavez as a hero; however, their concerns are shifting to bread and butter issues.

Part of the tactical difference between the unions is due to Chavez's formulation of the UFW as a social movement:

I once said you couldn't organize farm workers in conventional ways. . . . It has to be a movement. . . . What happens is the people get to feel that the idea, the movement, belongs to them. It's theirs, not ours. No force on earth, including the Teamsters and the growers can take that away from them. The more the people get beaten, the more they'll fight. The more persecution, the more strength they have. . . . When you learn about your movement, . . . you get to love it.[165]

Viva la huelga! can be roughly translated as meaning strike; yet its Spanish meaning carries a much more social connotation, particularly when associated with the UFW flags symbolizing hope, aspiration, and sacrifice.[166] The movement for which the cry is the catchword has also had strong religious overtones since its inception—religious officials of many denominations have historically lent their efforts to farm workers in general.[167]

As previously noted, Chavez has always considered loyalty to the movement a prerequisite for participation. Most of the UFW's staff have been volunteers, paid $5 a week.[168] The lack of full-time, experienced personnel placed the UFW at a disadvantage to the Teamsters. The administration of the UFW became somewhat haphazard—terms and records of negotiations were either slipshod or nonexistent. Also, with few exceptions, negotiators could not make binding agreements with the growers on even routine matters without Chavez's personal approval. Turnover among volunteers further added to haphazard administration.[169]

Chavez countered the Teamster invasion with at least two approaches. First, he promoted a boycott of all crops, especially lettuce and grapes, grown by nonunion growers and growers who had signed agreements with the Teamsters. He repeatedly attempted to persuade George Meany to endorse a secondary boycott of all the products at stores selling affected produce. Mr. Meany, however, cognizant of the implied illegality of this boycott as well as the concerns of an AFL-CIO affiliate (Retail Clerks), refused. While Mr. Meany eventually endorsed a product boycott,[170] public support of these boycotts was considerable but not complete. For example, a 1975 nationwide Harris Survey found that 12 percent (17 million adults) had stopped buying grapes and 11 percent (14 million) had stopped buying lettuce.[171]

The California Agricultural Labor Relations Act In addition to continuing organizing activities and administering the UFW, Chavez also pressed for farm labor legislation. After years of lobbying efforts and negotiations with various legislative officials, the California Agricultural Labor Relations Act (CALRA) went into effect on August 28, 1975.[172] This act has several provisions which strengthen farm worker unions in general and the UFW's position relative to the Teamsters in particular. Two major provisions of CALRA require secret ballot elections before union certification at times when the employer's payroll reflects at least 50 percent of the peak agricultural employment. Also, elections are to be held within seven days after the receipt of the election petition. "Under the law, a union may not conduct a secondary boycott against an employer that handles the products of a company where the union has lost an election conducted under the Act."[173] However, consumer boycotts of a particular struck product remain legal.[174] Recently, CALRA has adopted a make-whole remedy for employees when the employer has been found not to have bargained in good faith.[175] The AFL-CIO has long desired that this remedy for bad faith bargaining be included in the National Labor Relations Act; however, they have to date been unsuccessful.

In the first five months after the act was passed, over 32,000 farm workers voted in 429 elections. The pro-union sentiment of these elections was evident (84 percent of the workers voted for union representation), as was the pro-UFW sentiment. The UFW once again became the major bargaining representative, winning 198 elections during this five-month period.[176]

The implementation of the CALRA and the voting results prompted the UFW and the Teamsters to resolve their jurisdictional differences. On March 10, 1977, the unions signed a pact. The UFW would organize all employees in elections conducted by CALRA's Agricultural Labor Relations Board, and the Teamsters would organize all employees in NLRB elections. In essence, the UFW will represent the field workers, and the Teamsters will represent cannery workers and most agricultural truck drivers.[177]

The Future The future of the farm workers and particularly of the UFW seems to be subject to at least two crucial issues:

1. The extent to which the UFW will modify its current goals and administrative procedures to reflect those found in more traditional unions. Chavez has taken steps in that direction, noting, "Now we have to get the workers, especially the younger ones, to learn the mechanics of operating the union. . . . We want to train them to be professionals, to negotiate and administer the contracts we've already won."[178] Mexican farm laborers comprise the largest employee category, yet their numbers still represent an ethnic minority of farm laborers in California. The UFW, on the other hand, is dominantly Mexican in both leadership and ethos. Ethnic pride and heritage have been successful building blocks of the UFW; however, this organization will need to rely on traditional union goals to attract non-Mexican laborers.[179]

2. The potentially devastating impact of mechanization on the number of farm workers. For example, Libby, McNeil and Libby countered a successful union organizing drive of Wisconsin cucumber workers by mechanization. Within one year of the union's *(Obreros Unidos')* successful election, harvesting machines rendered the bargaining unit nonexistent.[180] In view of mechanization advances, farm worker unions will face a difficult dilemma: do they fight mechanization as a job destroyer, or do they attempt to win higher wages for a smaller number of workers?[181]

Recently, the UFW has used the first approach—confronting the University of California Board of Regents regarding university research projects aimed at agricultural mechanization. It has been estimated that machines developed from University of California research projects will result in the loss of 120,000 jobs in the harvesting of thirteen crops. The UFW desires that the university develop complementary programs for the displaced workers on the assumption that research should benefit everyone, workers as well as growers.[182] The UFW also contends:

The taxpayer pays twice for state-supported farm research. He pays, first, when public funds are used to develop the machines with no thought for the men and women whose jobs are wiped out; he pays again when these once gainfully employed workers turn to the state for support and the public is forced to absorb the social costs of mechanization.[183]

As of this writing, little concern over the effects of this research has been expressed at the university level, and the mechanization issue still poses a challenge to the agricultural labor movement.

Summary

Serious collective bargaining in professional baseball did not take place until 1966, when Marvin Miller was appointed executive director of the Major League Baseball Players' Association. In 1972 a strike occurred, with pension funding representing a major issue. Current and continuing issues in professional baseball include player mobility, the relationship between player salary and player performance, and player-management relations. The experiences in some other unionized professional sports (football, basketball, and hockey) were also discussed to illustrate how their job characteristics and relationships between union and management officials differentiate these labor relations activities from those found in most other occupations.

Until recently, collective bargaining in health-care organizations has been hindered by a lack of labor legislation. This situation changed in 1974 with the Taft-Hartley amendments that extended federal labor relations coverage to all private-sector hospitals. Yet subsequent labor relations activities (such as union organizing and strikes) are differentiated from other occupations because of the critical nature of work in the health-care fields. Similarly, nurses, house staff, and physicians often modify their collective bargaining concerns with the concept of "professionalism."

While many of the conditions found in the agricultural industry are described as "brutal," collective bargaining in this sector was virtually nonexistent until 1962, when Cesar Chavez founded a union (subsequently called the United Farm Workers). This union faced several obstacles, such as rival union activity, opposition from the growers, and absence of federal labor legislation. One of its major concerns is the effect mechanization can have in reducing the agricultural work force.

Discussion Questions

1. Considering the variables shown in Exhibit 1–1 (elements in the labor relations process), discuss two differences each emerging sector (professional sports, health care, and agriculture) has when compared to the others. Also indicate two general similarities of all three sectors, qualifying your answer when appropriate.

2. Select one emerging sector and present a detailed discussion of how this sector relates to all of the variables in Exhibit 1–1. You might have to engage in some speculation and outside research to complete this question.

References

[1]Tom Wicker, "Baseball," *Esquire*, December 1975, p. 135.

[2]Lee Allen, *100 Years of Baseball* (New York: Bartholomew House, 1950), pp. 94–96. The authors are indebted to Ken Walker, whose unpublished monograph, "The History of Collective Bargaining by Athletes Engaged in Professional Team Sports," represents a most definitive analysis of the history of collective bargaining in professional sports. Most of the references cited before 1970 were originally obtained from this manuscript.

[3]Ibid., p. 110.

[4]John D. McCallum, *Ty Cobb* (New York: Praeger Publishers, 1975), p. 83.

[5]Ibid., p. 86.

[6]Jay Topkis, "Monopsony in Manpower: Organized Baseball Meets the Anti-trust Laws," *Yale Law Journal* 62 (1952–1953), p. 587.

[7]"Minimum of $7,500 in Majors Sought," *New York Times*, May 3, 1946, p. 16.

[8]Erwin G. Kransnow and Herman M. Levy, "Unionization and Professional Sports," *Georgetown Law Review* 51 (1963), pp. 762–764. For a more detailed description of early baseball associations see Mark L. Goldstein, "Arbitration of Grievance and Salary Disputes in Professional Baseball: Evolution of a System of Private Law," *Cornell Law Review* 60 (August 1975), pp. 1051–1053.

[9]For details of these concessions see Louis Effrat, "Minimum Salaries, Other Reforms Gained by Major League Players," *New York Times*, September 17, 1946, p. 4; and John Drebinger, "Pension Reform for Players Voted by Major Leagues," *New York Times*, February 2, 1947, sec. 5, p. 1.

[10]Telephone conversation with Marvin Miller, Executive Director of the Major League Baseball Players' Association, MLBPA, November 8, 1978.

[11]John Drebinger, "Plan Ties Majors' Pay to Receipts," *New York Times*, December 3, 1958, p. 48.

[12]"Players Ask Joint Meeting," *New York Times*, December 11, 1956, p. 52; see also Dave Brady, "Player Rep Friend Raps Proposal That Athletes Form Labor Union," *Sporting News*, August 3, 1963, p. 4.

[13]*Major League Baseball Players Benefit Plan*, April 1, 1967, pp. 14–15, 23.

[14]"Ballplayers' Raise Is Unconditional," *New York Times*, January 27, 1968, p. 20.

[15]Leonard Koppett, "Baseball Club Owners' $5.1 Million Pension Offer Is Assailed as Inadequate," *New York Times*, December 18, 1968, p. 58.

[16]Ibid.

[17]Leonard Koppett, "Players Seek Owners' Compromise on Baseball Pension," *New York Times*, February 7, 1969, p. 41.

[18]Leonard Koppett, "Baseball's Pact Put at 4 Million," *New York Times*, May 26, 1970, p. 47.

[19]"Runners-Up Get More Series Cash," *New York Times*, June 23, 1970, p. 51.

[20]*Basic Agreement between the American and National Leagues of Professional Baseball Clubs and the Major League Baseball Players Association*, January 1, 1970, p. 16.

[21]"Officials React Firmly to Strike News," *New York Times*, April 1, 1972, p. 16; see also Arthur Daley, "The Players Vote to Strike," *New York Times*, April 2, 1972, sec. 5, p. 2.

[22]This "surplus" resulted from increased interest rates on loans, overfunding, and overestimated payments for permanently disabled players. Murray Chass, "No Progress Reported in Baseball Strike Talks," *New York Times*, April 2, 1972, sec. 5, p. 3. For a detailed discussion of the pension plan's funding and administration see Leonard Koppett, "Pension Money Surplus: What Makes It the Issue," *New York Times*, April 9, 1972, sec. 5, p. 3.

[23]Murray Chass, "Players' Offer Is Rejected; Long Strike Seems Likely," *New York Times*, April 2, 1972, pp. 49–50.

[24]Joseph Durso, "Baseball Strike Is Settled; Season to Open Tomorrow," *New York Times*, April 14, 1972, p. 1.

[25]Joseph Durso, "Owners Wait as Players Study Peace Pitch," *New York Times*, February 10, 1973, p. 25.

[26]Ibid. For a related concern see Cleon Jones and Ed Hershey, *Cleon* (New York: Coward-McCann, 1970), pp. 89–90.

[27]"Kuhn Calls Owners Firm on 2 Points," *New York Times*, December 12, 1972, p. 66.

[28]For more details of this settlement see "Player-Owner Issues," *New York Times*, December 8, 1972, p. 58.

[29]A "championship season" equals 172 days on the active player roster.

[30]Additional details of the reserve clause are found in the following Supreme Court decision: *Toolson v. New York Yankees, Inc.*, 346 U.S. 356 (1953).

[31]Ford C. Frick, *Games, Asterisks, and People* (New York: Crown Publishers, 1973), p. 193. See also Sparky Anderson and Si Burick, *The Main Spark* (Garden City, N.Y.: Doubleday and Company, 1978), p. 210.

[32]Red Smith, "In the Spring an Owner's Fancy," *New York Times*, March 19, 1976, p. 41. It should also be noted that the manner in which trades are conducted can also rankle with the players, particularly for trades in which management shows little regard for the traded players' concerns. See, for example, "Brewers' Thomas Has Some Security," *Miami Herald*, March 18, 1979; and Sparky Lyle and Peter Golenbock, *The Bronx Zoo* (New York: Crown Publishers, 1979), pp. 127–128.

[33]"Toronto's Profitable New Passion," *Business Week*, October 24, 1977, p. 37.

[34]Curt Flood, *The Way It Is* (New York: Trident Press, 1970), pp. 14–15.

[35]*Curtis C. Flood v. Bowie Kuhn et al.*, 407 U.S. 258 (1972). For additional details regarding this decision see Phillip L. Martin, "The Labor Controversy in Professional Baseball: The Flood Case," *Labor Law Journal* 23 (September 1972), pp. 567–571.

[36]Professional Baseball Clubs 66 LA 110 (P. Seitz, 1975).

[37]Murray Chass, "Terms of Baseball's Four-Year Accord Explained," *New York Times*, July 25, 1976, sec. 5, p. 8.

[38]For some evidence of this situation see Melissa Ludtke Lincoln, "The Deal Is No Deals," *Sports Illustrated*, February 19, 1979, pp. 48, 50.

[39]Peter Gammons, "Cashing in Their Tickets," *Sports Illustrated*, November 22, 1976, p. 82.

[40]Larry Keith, "Is It Daft—or Deft—to Draft?" *Sports Illustrated*, November 7, 1977, p. 32. It should be noted that these figures are oversimplified and dramatic—they are not used by the players, the MLBPA, and management in negotiations. However the figures do become significant if and when they are accepted by the public reading these articles. As of April 1979, more than 100 players have changed teams through free agency. For a brief examination of free agency see Frederick C. Klein, "Shuffled Lineups: Baseball Is Prospering Despite Shifts Caused by New 'Free Agents,'" *Wall Street Journal*, April 4, 1979, pp. 1, 31. For specific contractual terms of the players who went through the November 1978 free agent draft see Murray Chass, "110 Aging Free Agents Hit $15 Million Jackpot," *Sporting News*, March 3, 1979, p. 13.

[41]Bill Lyon, "Big Salary Means Extra Incentive Says Ozark," *Sporting News*, May 28, 1977, p. 14.

[42]Robert Creamer, *Babe: The Legend Comes to Life* (New York: Simon and Schuster, 1974), p. 291.

[43]Peter Seitz, "Are Professional Sports Sports or Business? or How Much Would You Pay for Catfish Hunter?" in James L. Stern and Barbara D. Dennis, eds., *Proceedings of the Twenty-ninth Annual Winter Meeting: Industrial Relations Research Association* (Madison, Wis.: Industrial Relations Research Association, 1977), p. 326. A specific application of this concept pertains to the Philadelphia Phillies, who signed Pete Rose to a contract that pays him $3.2 million over four years. It has been estimated that an

increased television contract to cover the Phillies and increasing attendance because of Pete Rose means that Philadelphia will take in $2 million in 1979 before he picks up a bat, ball, or glove. "Pete Rose," *60 Minutes* 11, no. 24 (as broadcast over the CBS Television Network, February 25, 1979) transcript, p. 15. Marvin Miller contends that teams paid out just 27.6 percent of their revenues in player salaries in 1978, a figure similar to those of past years; see Klein, "Shuffled Lineups," p. 31.

[44]Steve Jacobsen, "Amid the Wealth of Former Free Agents, a Season of Agony for Reggie Jackson?" *Miami Herald,* April 3, 1977.

[45]See, for example, Marshall H. Medoff, "On Monopolistic Exploitation in Baseball," *Quarterly Review of Economics and Business* 16 (Summer 1976), pp. 113–121. For an approach to this problem and discussion of related research see Gerald V. Scully, "Pay and Performance in Major League Baseball," *American Economic Review* 64 (December 1974), pp. 915–931. For an earlier conceptual approach to wage determination see Simon Rottenberg, "The Baseball Players' Labor Market," *Journal of Political Economy* 64 (June 1956), pp. 242–258.

[46]Scully, "Pay and Performance," p. 918.

[47]Keith, "Is It Daft?" p. 36.

[48]"Reds' Ad Hits Rose Demands," *Chicago Tribune,* April 3, 1977.

[49]Roy Blount, Jr., "Let's Hear It for the Best Kept Secret in Sports," *Esquire,* August 1976, p. 68. For a different managerial strategy see Hal Butler, *Al Kaline and the Detroit Tigers* (Chicago: Henry Regnery, 1973), pp. 57–58. For an analysis of applicable wage negotiation strategies found in other professional sports see Sheldon M. Gallner, *Pro Sports: The Contract Game* (New York: Charles Scribner's Sons, 1974), pp. 34–49.

[50]Peter Seitz, "Footnotes to Baseball Salary Arbitration," *Arbitration Journal* 29 (June 1974), pp. 100–101.

[51]James B. Dworkin, "The Impact of Final-Offer Interest Arbitration on Bargaining: The Case for Major League Baseball," in Stern and Dennis, eds., *Proceedings of the Twenty-ninth Annual Winter Meeting: Industrial Relations Research Association,* pp. 161–169.

[52]Scully, "Pay and Performánce," p. 920. For a discussion of this reason as it applies to another sport, basketball, see John Papanek, "There's an Ill Wind Blowing for the NBA," *Sports Illustrated,* February 25, 1979, pp. 22, 27.

[53]Leo Durocher, *Nice Guys Finish Last* (New York: Simon and Schuster, 1975), pp. 410–411.

[54]Ruth's exchange with his manager is quoted in Creamer, *Babe,* pp. 291–292.

[55]"Mets Jones in Trouble after Refusing to Play," *Miami Herald,* July 20, 1975; and "Dick Allen Gets Suspended for Early Shower," *Los Angeles Times,* June 21, 1977, part III, p. 1.

[56]Flood, *The Way It Is,* pp. 58–59.

[57]Edwin Pope, "Daddies and Despots Heating Up Baseball," *Miami Herald,* May 29, 1977.

[58]See, for example, Milton Richman, "Martin Gets Reprieve from Steinbrenner, but He's Not Safe Yet," *Los Angeles Times,* June 21, 1977, part III, p. 1; Reggie Jackson, *Reggie: A Season with a Superstar* (Chicago: Playboy Press, 1975), pp. 66, 68–69; Larry Keith, "A Bunt That Went Boom," *Sports Illustrated,* July 31, 1978, pp. 14–19; and Ed Linn, *Inside the Yankees: The Championship Year* (New York: Random House, 1978). One of the more publicized situations involving owner-manager frictions occurred when Billy Martin left the New York Yankees in 1978 only to return in 1979. The following articles describe events leading to Martin's departure and subsequent return: Murray Chass, "Martin Resigns; Bob Lemmon to Manage Yankees," *New York Times,* July 25, 1978, pp. A-1, B-11; and Pete Axthelm, "Stars in Their Eyes," *Newsweek,* July 2, 1979, p. 55.

[59]Comparisons of these benefit gains can be made from two sources: Leonard Koppett, "6-Year-Old Union Keeps Players' Benefits in Step," *New York Times,* February 26, 1973, p. 39; and the 1976–1979 *Basic Agreement between the American League of Professional Baseball Clubs, and the National League of Professional Baseball Clubs, and Major League Baseball Players Association.* It should be further noted that at least one researcher has cautioned that increases in the consumer price index offset some of the player gains in salaries. James G. Scoville, "Wage Determination and the Development of Collective Bargaining in Baseball," in Stern and Dennis, eds., *Proceedings of the Twenty-ninth Annual Winter Meeting: Industrial Relations Research Association,* pp. 317–333.

[60]"National Football League Accedes to Demands of Players," *New York Times,* December 3, 1957, p. 47; Sam Goldaper, "N.F.L. Club Owners and Player Group Reach Agreement," *New York Times,* July 15, 1968, p. 38; "N.B.A. to Increase Rookies' Salaries," *New York Times,* August 9, 1968, p. 55; "N.B.A. Minimums to Reach $17,500," *New York Times,* October 9, 1970, p. 27; "National Hockey League Players Organize; Name Lindsay Head of Association," *New York Times,* February 12, 1957, p. 34; Leonard Koppett, "N.B.A. Players Threaten Strike in Dispute over Pension Plan," *New York Times,* January 15, 1964, p. 34.

[61]*Florida Times Union,* January 26, 1978.

[62]For a case study of one of the comparatively "poorer athletes" and the applicability of this situation to the union's concerns see Bill Braucher, "Hill's Wanderings Leave a Man Wondering," *Miami Herald,* November 21, 1976.

[63]John Devaney (interview with Wayne Embry), "The Owners Are Destroying the Game," *Sport* 64 (June 1977), p. 31.

[64]"Dan Rooney Keeps Faith with Pros," *Miami Herald,* November 13, 1977.

[65]"Tomjanovich Looking to Next Year," *Florida Times Union and Jacksonville Journal,* January 7, 1978. See also "Scorecard," *Sports Illustrated,* August 7, 1978, p. 7, where the president of the National Hockey League suspended a player for the upcoming season for possession of cocaine.

[66]For an analysis of financial problems facing the four team sports in Detroit see Terry P. Brown, "Ultimate Defeat, Many Pro Sports Clubs Lose Crucial Contest: Their Fight to Survive," *Wall Street Journal,* May 14, 1975, pp. 1, 22.

[67]A. H. Raskin, "Crowd of 150 at Seminar on Labor Relations in Sports Sees a Scoreless Tie," *New York Times,* December 12, 1976, p. 6. One owner of a baseball team has commented, "Fans are just starting to realize that players are not entitled to what they are getting. They don't like the fact that some players are getting more money for playing one year than they can expect to make in a lifetime. I've had more people side with me than against me." He also suggests another possibly detrimental aspect of high salaries. "Do you realize major league baseball owes $250 million in deferred payments? . . . It's hard to sell a club with all those liabilities. I owe a little, but not near what most others do." Greg Larson, "Twins' Calvin Griffith Defends Frugal Dealings," *Florida Times Union,* April 4, 1979.

[68]"Scorecard," *Sports Illustrated,* May 22, 1978, p. 10. For another quick estimate of the financial stability of the NFL regardless of player salaries see "Scorecard," *Sports Illustrated,* May 22, 1978, pp. 13, 14. Also see information on Pete Rose, footnote 43.

[69]*Face Off,* September 1971, p. 2.

[70]William N. Wallace, "Rozelle Rule Found in Antitrust Violation," *New York Times,* December 31, 1975, p. 27. It should be noted that this article stressed the labor relations phenomenon that principle might be more important than practice, since the Rozelle Rule was only implemented 5 times out of a possible 176 cases in the last twelve years. See also statement of Pete Rozelle, Commissioner of National Football League, U.S. Congress, House, Hearing before the Subcommittee on Monopolies and Commercial Law of the Committee on the Judiciary, House of Representatives, 94th Cong., 1st sess., 1977, p. 49.

[71]Statement of Edward R. Garvey, Executive Director, NFL Players Association, U.S. Congress, House, Hearing before the Subcommittee, pp. 18, 19. See also Bill Paul, "Now the Buccaneers Pick Up Their Prize for Losing 14 Games," *Wall Street Journal,* May 3, 1977, pp. 1, 18; and Michael Roberts, "Athletes as Chattel," *New Republic,* August 10 and August 17, 1974, pp. 14–16.

[72]For a thorough discussion of how this issue applies to professional sports see James B. Dworkin and Thomas J. Bergmann, "Collective Bargaining and the Player Reservation/Compensation System in Professional Sports," *Employee Relations Law Journal* 4 (Autumn 1978), pp. 241–256.

[73]"A Bidding-War Product, Neely Advocates the Draft," *Miami Herald,* January 23, 1977.

[74]"Scorecard," *Sports Illustrated,* June 19, 1978, p. 13; "New Ball Game," *Newsweek,* December 30, 1974, p. 46.

[75]Arthur A. Sloane, "Collective Bargaining in Major League Baseball: A New Ball Game and Its Genesis," *Labor Law Journal* 28 (April 1977), pp. 205–206. For additional insights into the background of some owners see Don Kowet, *The Rich Who Own Sports* (New York: Random House, 1977); Devaney, "Owners Are Destroying the Game," p. 31; CBS Reports, "The Baseball Business" (as broadcast over the CBS television network, Tuesday, April 26, 1977), transcript, p. 4; Philip Taubman, "Caroll Rosenbloom's Obsession," *Esquire,* January 21, 1978, p. 112; Geoffrey Norman, "The Dallas Cowboys' Art of Hiring Winners," *Esquire,* September 12, 1978, pp. 69–72, 74–75; Hal Lancaster, "Baseball's Big Hit: Los Angeles Dodgers, Again Seeking Pennant, Keep On Winning Fans," *Wall Street Journal,* October 5, 1978, pp. 1, 35; and William Oscar Johnson, "Jerry Is Never behind the Eight Ball," *Sports Illustrated,* June 18, 1979, pp. 22–24, 29.

[76]See, for example, Douglas S. Looney, "OK, What's the Pitch?" *Sports Illustrated,* March 8, 1976, p. 46; and "Name Tiff Leads to Name-Calling," *Miami Herald,* February 16, 1978.

[77]Leonard Koppett, "Baseball Owners Vote to Make No New Offer," *New York Times,* April 5, 1972, p. 53.

[78]Ron Reid, "It's One Big Happy Family, But," *Sports Illustrated,* August 26, 1974, p. 20.

[79]Gwilym S. Brown, "The Battle Is Joined," *Sports Illustrated,* March 18, 1974, p. 62.

[80]Pete Axthelm, "Baseball's Money Madness," *Newsweek,* June 28, 1976, pp. 62–66; Ron Fimrite, "Bowie Stops Charlie's Checks," *Sports Illustrated,* June 28, 1976, pp. 22–25.

[81]Robert H. Boyle, "This Man Miller Admits He's a Grind," *Sports Illustrated,* March 11, 1974, p. 21. For an account of the early days of the MLBPA under Miller see Flood, *The Way It Is,* pp. 156–170.

[82]"Going to Bat," *Wall Street Journal,* February 22, 1974, p. 1.

[83]For example, 427 of the 1,300 members of the NFLPA crossed picket lines in 1974. "Owners, 7; Players, 0," *Newsweek,* August 26, 1974, p. 77. See also "Striking Players Fear Reprisals," *New York Times,* August 1, 1970, p. 17; Dave Anderson, "N.F.L. Owners Open Camps Tonight to Seasoned

Players," *New York Times,* July 30, 1970, p. 27; "Griese: Get Garvey Out," *Florida Times Union,* January 29, 1976, p. A–20; and "Scorecard," *Sports Illustrated,* September 13, 1976, p. 13. For a somewhat earlier account of internal problems and prospects in the NFLPA see Bernie Parrish, *They Call It a Game* (New York: Dial Press, 1971), pp. 237–288.

[84]Bob Rubin, "Dolphin's Disinterest? Maybe It Was the Sun?" *Miami Herald,* June 5, 1977.

[85]For a discussion of the role of player agents see "The Fearsome Onesome," *New Times,* December 9, 1977, pp. 69–74; and Allen S. Keller, "Pinch-Hitting at the Bargaining Table," *Wharton Account* 18 (Winter 1978), pp. 14–18.

[86]"Football Players Form Pro Bargaining Group," *New York Times,* November 29, 1956, p. 45; "National Hockey Players Organize, Name Lindsay Head of Association," *New York Times,* February 12, 1957, p. 34; "Cousy to Discuss Union with Labor Executives," *New York Times,* January 13, 1957, sec. 5, p. 9.

[87]"Hockey Players Win Concessions," *New York Times,* February 6, 1958, p. 35. For background information see "Hockey Clubs Hit in Antitrust Suit," *New York Times,* October 11, 1957, p. 38.

[88]For a discussion of the reorganization of the hockey players' union see "Hockey League Players Look to Teamwork, Union Style," *IUE News,* July 20, 1967, p. 10.

[89]"NFL, Team Owners Told to Bargain on Rules That Involve Safety," *Wall Street Journal,* July 12, 1976, p. 11. See also Thomas P. Gilroy and Patrick J. Madden, "Labor Relations in Professional Sports," *Labor Law Journal* 28 (December 1977), p. 773; and Cym H. Lowell, "Collective Bargaining and the Professional Team Sport Industry," *Law and Contemporary Problems* 38 (Winter–Spring 1973), pp. 3–41.

[90]"NFL Owners Get Tackled," *Business Week,* October 11, 1976, p. 36. For a historical development of the Rozelle Rule's judicial implications see Leonard Koppett, "Development of Rozelle Rule Is Traced from Owen's Case," *New York Times,* December 31, 1975, p. C–28.

[91]Bob Rubin, "Ed Garvey Enjoys R & R," *Miami Herald,* June 5, 1977.

[92]"Bell Recognizes Football Union," *New York Times,* August 2, 1957, p. 7; and "Bell Will See Lawyers on Written Union Pact," *New York Times,* August 11, 1957, sec. 5, p. 4.

[93]Mitchell C. Lynch, "Tackling the Pros," *Wall Street Journal,* December 15, 1975, p. 1.

[94]*The National Football League Player's Audible* 6 (August 24, 1974), pp. 2, 7.

[95]Raskin, "Crowd of 150 at Seminar," p. 6.

[96]It should be noted, however, that the average 1977 attendance for all major professional sports (football, baseball, basketball, and hockey) increased over comparable 1967 figures, even though players' salaries rose during this period. Ray Kennedy and Nancy Williamson, "The Fans: Are They Up in Arms?" *Sports Illustrated,* July 31, 1978, p. 39. See also "Behind Baseball's Comeback: It's an Island of Stability," *U.S. News & World Report,* September 17, 1977, pp. 56–57. Recently, however, the commissioner of the NBA has expressed the concern that there will be "a real crunch" for fan attendance. "NBA's O'Brien 'Not Satisfied' with Attendance," *Miami Herald,* February 21, 1979.

[97]Glenn Dickey, "The T.V. Tail Wags the Dog," *San Francisco Chronicle,* June 24, 1977.

[98]Richard O'Connor, "Will Free Agents Kill Baseball?" *Sport,* April 1978, p. 42.

[99]William Oscar Johnson, "The Greenbacking of Pete Rose," *Sports Illustrated,* January 22, 1979, p. 38.

[100]Norman Metzger and Dennis D. Pointer, *Labor-Management Relations in the Health Services Industry* (Washington, D.C.: Science and Health Publications, 1972), p. 3.

[101]For a discussion of some of these cases see Dennis D. Pointer, "The Federal Labor Law Status of the Health Care Delivery Industry," *Labor Law Journal* 22 (May 1971), pp. 279–280.

[102]The application of Taft-Hartley to profit-making hospitals and nursing homes remained uncertain until 1969, when the NLRB indicated it would retain jurisdiction if the hospitals and nursing homes exceeded $250,000 and $100,000 gross annual revenues, respectively. Emil C. Farkas, "The National Labor Relations Act: The Health Care Amendments," *Labor Law Journal* 25 (May 1978), p. 259; Harry E. Graham, "Effects of NLRB Jurisdictional Change on Union Organizing Activity in the Proprietary Health Care Sector," in Gerald G. Somers, ed., *Proceedings of the Twenty-fourth Annual Winter Meeting: Industrial Relations Research Association* (Madison, Wis.: Industrial Relations Research Association, 1972), pp. 273–283.

[103]Dennis D. Pointer, "Toward a National Hospital Labor Relations Policy: An Examination of Legislative Exemption," *Labor Law Journal* 23 (April 1972), pp. 239–240.

[104]Richard L. Epstein, "Labor Relations in Hospitals and Health Care Facilities before the National Labor Relations Act Amendments: Proprietary versus Nonprofit Hospitals," in A. Eliot Berkeley, ed., *Labor Relations in Hospitals and Health Care Facilities* (Washington, D.C.: Bureau of National Affairs, 1975), pp. 9–10.

[105]U.S., Congress, Senate, Committee on Labor and Public Welfare, *Coverage of Nonprofit Hospitals under National Labor Relations Act, 1973,* hearings before the Subcommittee on Labor, S.794 and S.2292, 93rd Cong., 1st sess. 1973, pp. 479–480.

[106]Ibid., p. 5.

[107]It should be noted that the 1974 amendments do place unique reporting and fact-finding requirements on health-care facilities, which must be followed before they strike in order that patients might be moved to another location. For a discussion of these procedures and their use see James F. Scearce and Lucretia Dewey Tanner, "Health Care Bargaining: The FMCS Experience," *Labor Law Journal* 27 (July 1976), pp. 387–398.

[108]Rudy Oswald, "A Voice for Hospital Workers," *American Federationist* 82 (January 1975), pp. 15, 16.

[109]Richard U. Miller, Brian B. Becker, and Edward B. Krinsky, "Union Effects on Hospital Administration: Preliminary Results from a Three-State Study," in James L. Stern, ed., *Proceedings of the 1977 Annual Spring Meeting: Industrial Relations Research Association* (Madison, Wis.: Industrial Relations Research Association, 1977), pp. 518–519.

[110]Peter Nash, "Impact of the Amendments on the Law—NLRA and NLRB Changes," in Berkeley, ed., *Labor Relations in Hospitals*, p. 27.

[111]Bureau of National Affairs, *Daily Labor Report*, July 21, 1977, pp. 2, 3.

[112]Bureau of National Affairs, *Daily Labor Report*, October 14, 1977, p. 2.

[113]*Beth Israel Hospital v. National Labor Relations Board*, 98 S.C. 2468 (1978).

[114]Metzger and Pointer, *Labor-Management Relations*, pp. 22, 23.

[115]A. H. Raskin, "A Union with 'Soul,'" *New York Times Magazine*, March 22, 1970, p. 24. For a research effort which examines the racial impact on collective bargaining issues see Ken Demarko, James W. Robinson, and Ernest C. Houck, "A Pilot Study of the Initial Bargaining Demands by Newly-Organized Employees of Health Care Institutions," *Labor Law Journal* 29 (May 1978), pp. 275–291.

[116]Raskin, "A Union with 'Soul,'" p. 38.

[117]Ibid., p. 39.

[118]William B. Werther, Jr., and Carol Ann Lockhart, *Labor Relations in the Health Profession* (Boston: Little, Brown, 1976), p. 4.

[119]Harry Weinstock, "The Organized Hospital Worker's View," in Berkeley, *Labor Relations in Hospitals*, p. 55. It should also be noted that one empirical study has found that unions have had a statistically significant impact on wages, although the difference is not particularly high in dollar terms. Myron Fottler, "The Union Impact on Hospital Wages," *Industrial and Labor Relations Review* 30 (April 1977), pp. 342–355. For another study of hospital unions' relatively moderate effect on wages, see Miller, Becker, and Krinsky, "Union Effects on Hospital Administration," p. 516.

[120]Robert B. McKersie and Montague Brown, "Nonprofessional Hospital Workers and a Union Organizing Drive," *Quarterly Journal of Economics* 77 (August 1973), p. 395.

[121]For a detailed examination of labor agreements in the health-care industry see Hervey A. Juris, "Labor Agreements in the Hospital Industry: A Study of Collective Bargaining Outputs," in James L. Stern, ed., *Proceedings of the Annual 1977 Spring Meeting: Industrial Relations Research Association*, pp. 504–511.

[122]Bureau of National Affairs, *Daily Labor Report*, August 25, 1977, p. A–6.

[123]"New York Hospital Strike Spreads; 40,000 Idled," *Miami Herald*, July 11, 1976. For a discussion of reasons leading up to this strike see "New York Hospital Workers Plan Strike; More City Budget Cuts, Controls Sought," *Wall Street Journal*, June 3, 1976, p. 8.

[124]Archie Kleingartner, "Nurses, Collective Bargaining, and Labor Legislation," *Labor Law Journal* 18 (April 1967), p. 237.

[125]Daniel H. Kruger, "Bargaining and the Nursing Profession," *Monthly Labor Review* 84 (July 1961), p. 702.

[126]John M. Boyer, Carl L. Westerhaus, and John H. Coggeshall, *Employee Relations and Collective Bargaining in Health Care Facilities*, 2d. ed. (St. Louis: C. V. Mosby Company, 1975), p. 240.

[127]Kleingartner, "Nurses, Collective Bargaining, and Labor Legislation," p. 243.

[128]Martha Belote, "Nurses Are Making It Happen," *American Journal of Nursing* 67 (February 1967), p. 287.

[129]Philip D. Rutsohn and Richard M. Grimes, "Nightingalism and Negotiations—New Attitudes of Health Professionals," *Personnel Journal* 56 (August 1977), p. 399.

[130]See, for example, Anne B. Mahoney, "Bargaining Rights: Convincing the Membership," *American Journal of Nursing* 66 (March 1966), pp. 544–548.

[131]William G. Scott, Elizabeth K. Porter, and Donald K. Smith, "The Long Shadow," *American Journal of Nursing* 66 (March 1966), p. 539.

[132]Sally T. Holloway, "Health Professionals and Collective Action," *Employee Relations Law Journal* 1 (Winter 1976), p. 414.

[133]Joseph A. Alutto and James A. Belasco, "Determinants of Attitudinal Militancy among Nurses and Teachers," *Industrial and Labor Relations Review* 27 (January 1974), pp. 212–217.

[134]Murray A. Gordon, "Hospital Housestaff Collective Bargaining," *Employee Relations Law Journal* 1

(Winter 1976), p. 419. For a detailed analysis of one intern's working conditions see Barry Newman, "Calling Dr. . . . For an Intern, the Life Is Intense, and a 'Day' Can Last for 36 Hours," *Wall Street Journal*, April 17, 1975, pp. 1, 75. For a different viewpoint of house staff officials' economic conditions see "Socialized Medicine Still Means a Lot of Friendly Doctors at a Party," *New Times*, February 20, 1978, p. 23.

[135]Gordon, "Hospital Housestaff Collective Bargaining," p. 420.

[136]Peter Kihss, "Pact Ends Doctor Strike; Staffs Return to Hospitals," *New York Times*, March 21, 1975, p. 42.

[137]Murray Gordon, "The Organized Physician's View," in Berkeley, ed., *Labor Relations in Hospitals*, p. 39.

[138]Bureau of National Affairs, *Daily Labor Report*, January 26, 1978, p. 1.

[139]"Court Overturns NLRB's Interns, Residents Ruling," Bureau of National Affairs, *Daily Labor Report*, April 3, 1979, p. 1.

[140]Mario F. Bognanno, James B. Dworkin, and Omotayo Fashoyin, "Physicians' and Dentists' Bargaining Organizations: A Preliminary Look," *Monthly Labor Review* 98 (June 1975), p. 34.

[141]"Doctors Hit the Streets with a New Strike Law," *Business Week*, March 31, 1975, p. 19; and "A.M.A.'s Militancy," *New York Times*, March 22, 1975, p. 30.

[142]"When Doctors Went Out on Strike," *U.S. News & World Report*, May 26, 1975, p. 34.

[143]For a detailed analysis of social and economic conditions confronting migrant labor in the Northeast see William H. Friedland and Dorothy Nelkin, *Migrant* (New York: Holt, Rinehart and Winston, 1971).

[144]Stephen D. Jacobson, "Labor Legislation and the Agricultural Laborer," *Industrial and Labor Relations Forum* 11 (Summer 1975), p. 135.

[145]Personal correspondence from Marc Grossman, assistant to the president of the United Farm Workers of America, November 13, 1978.

[146]Sam Kushner, *Long Road to Delano* (New York: International Publishers, 1975), p. 95.

[147]Winthrop Griffith, "Is Chavez Beaten?" *New York Times Magazine*, September 15, 1974, p. 24. © 1974 by The New York Times Company. Reprinted by permission.

[148]Pros and cons of this exemption can be found in Jacobson, "Labor Legislation and the Agricultural Laborer," p. 135; Karen S. Koziara, "Collective Bargaining in Agriculture: The Policy Alternatives," *Labor Law Journal* 24 (July 1973), pp. 424–435; and Sylvester Petro, "Agriculture and Labor Policy," *Labor Law Journal* 24 (July 1973), pp. 24–51.

[149]For a detailed review of these tactics see Harriet E. Cooperman and Marc P. Gabor, "Legal Implications of the Farmworker Exemption," *Industrial and Labor Relations Forum* 11 (Summer 1975), pp. 154–184.

[150]For a comparative analysis of some of these laws see Karen S. Koziara, "Agricultural Labor Relations Laws in Four States—A Comparison," *Monthly Labor Review* 100 (May 1977), pp. 14–18.

[151]Grossman, personal correspondence, November 13, 1978.

[152]Alexander Morin, *The Organizability of Farm Labor in the United States* (Cambridge, Mass.: Harvard University Press, 1952), p. 13.

[153]For a detailed history of labor relations activities during this period see S. M. Jamieson, *Labor Unionism in American Agriculture* (Washington, D.C.: Government Printing Office, 1946); and Ernesto Galarza, *Farm Workers and Agri-business in California, 1947–1960* (Notre Dame, Ind.: University of Notre Dame Press, 1977).

[154]Kushner, *Long Road to Delano*, p. 96.

[155]Jacques E. Levy, *Cesar Chavez: Autobiography of La Causa* (New York: W. W. Norton, 1975), p. 129. Reprinted with the permission of W. W. Norton & Company, Inc. Copyright © 1975 by Jacques E. Levy.

[156]Ibid., p. 93. For a behavioral analysis of nonviolence as it applied to one of Cesar Chavez's speeches see Winthrop Yinger, *Cesar Chavez: The Rhetoric of Nonviolence* (Hicksville, N.Y.: Exposition Press, 1975).

[157]Ibid., p. 92.

[158]Ibid., p. 267.

[159]Mark Day, *Forty Acres* (New York: Praeger Publishers, 1971), p. 89.

[160]Dick Meister and Anne Loftis, *A Long Time Coming* (New York: Macmillan, 1977), p. 157.

[161]See, for example, "The Rape of the Farm Workers," *Steel Labor*, September 1973, pp. 8–9.

[162]Griffith, "Is Chavez Beaten?" p. 18.

[163]Ibid., p. 24.

[164]For an example of this consideration see Joel Solkoff, "Can Cesar Chavez Cope with Success?" *New Republic*, May 22, 1976, p. 14.

[165]Griffith, "Is Chavez Beaten?" p. 18.

[166]Levy, *Autobiography of La Causa*, p. 175.

[167]See, for example, Joan London and Henry Anderson, *So Shall Ye Reap* (New York: Thomas Y. Crowell, 1970), pp. 79–98; and Day, *Forty Acres*, pp. 53–60.

[168]Griffith, "Is Chavez Beaten?" p. 30.

[169]Michael Yates, "The Trouble with Chavez: A Union Is Not a Movement," *Nation*, November 19, 1977, p. 520.

[170]Griffith, "Is Chavez Beaten?" p. 35.

[171]Harry Bernstein, "UFW Leads in Farm Balloting and Opinion Poll," *Los Angeles Times*, October 30, 1975, part 2, pp. 1–2.

[172]For details of the early implementation of CALRA and voting procedures (for example, bargaining unit determination and voter eligibility) see Joseph R. Grodin, "California Agricultural Labor Act: Early Experience," *Industrial Relations* 15 (October 1976), pp. 275–294. See also William Wong, "California Votes Farm-Labor Election Bill, Presaging a New Unionizing Drive in the Fall," *Wall Street Journal*, May 30, 1975, p. 30; and "Farm Turmoil from a Model Labor Law," *Business Week*, October 13, 1975, p. 88. For a more current assessment of California's Agricultural Labor Relations Board see Bureau of National Affairs, *Daily Labor Report*, May 2, 1978, pp. 1–2.

[173]Grossman, personal correspondence, November 13, 1978.

[174]Refugio I. Rochin, "New Perspectives on Agricultural Labor Relations in California," *Labor Law Journal* 28 (July 1977), p. 398.

[175]Bureau of National Affairs, *Daily Labor Report*, May 19, 1978, pp. 1–2. See also "ALRB Make Whole Remedy," *National Farm Worker Ministry Newsletter* 7 (September 1978), p. 5.

[176]W. H. Segur and Varden Fuller, "California's Farm Labor Elections: An Analysis of the Initial Results," *Monthly Labor Review* 99 (December 1976), p. 29. See also "Chavez versus the Teamsters: Farm Workers' Historic Vote," *U.S.News & World Report*, September 22, 1975, pp. 82–83.

[177]Rochin, "New Perspectives," p. 400. For additional details of this pact see "Questions and Answers about Teamster-UFW Agreement," *National Farm Worker Ministry Newsletter* 6 (Spring 1977), p. 2.

[178]William P. Coleman, "Chavez, UFW in the Midst of Changes," *Oakland Tribune*, March 27, 1978.

[179]Varden Fuller and John W. Mamer, "Constraints on California Farm Worker Unionization," *Industrial Relations* 17 (May 1978), p. 51.

[180]Phillip L. Martin, "Harvest Mechanization and Agricultural Trade Unionism: *Obreros Unidos* in Wisconsin," *Labor Law Journal* 28 (March 1977), pp. 166–173.

[181]"The Latest Threat to Chavez: Mechanization," *Business Week*, January 30, 1969, p. 69.

[182]Cesar Chavez, "The Farm Workers' Next Battle," *Nation*, March 25, 1978, p. 330.

[183]Ibid., p. 331.

Cases

Montgomery Ward & Co., Inc., and Teamsters, Local 348

Composition of bargaining unit.

Montgomery Ward contends in this bargaining unit case that the warehouse and retail bargain store employees at the Gilroy Road warehouse and repair facility share a community of interest with all employees at the facility. In addition, because of the high degree of functional integration of the operations, it contends that a single facility-wide unit is appropriate. On the other hand, the Teamsters contend that the warehouse employees, including retail bargain store employees and furniture refinishers, should not compose a single bargaining unit.

The Gilroy Road facility serves the employer's five retail stores in the vicinity of Akron and Canton, Ohio, and handles mainly big ticket merchandise, such as furniture, lawn and garden equipment, campers, and major appliances. This facility is functionally divided into three principal departments: (1) the warehouse operations, (2) the central repair service, and (3) the drapery workroom. Each has its own manager, who reports directly to the district manager, as well as its own budget. Department managers have final authority over hiring for their departments.

The facility is divided into two sections by a fire wall running east and west: the north section, much the larger of the two, houses the warehouse storage area, shipping and receiving docks, and delivery office; the south section contains the warehouse office, repair service areas,[1] service parts department, service office, furniture refinishing room, drapery workroom, retail bargain store, restrooms, and employees' lunchroom.

The warehouse, under the supervision of warehouse manager Clark, has approximately nineteen employees classified as warehousemen, order pickers, dockmen, delivery clerks, in-stock control clerks, invoice records clerks, and furniture refinishers. It performs such general warehouse functions as ordering, receiving, and shipping merchandise and processing the accompanying paperwork. Various clerical functions, such as inventory control and bookkeeping, are performed in the warehouse office, adjacent to the repair service area. Furniture refinishing is performed by two employees working in a room which is also adjacent to the repair service area. This work involves repairing scratched merchandise such as TV and stereo equipment having wood cabinets, attaching hardware, and polishing furniture prior to delivery.

This case is taken from 230 NLRB 33 (1977). The names of the people involved have been changed.
[1]There are separate shops for refrigeration, TV, laundry and range, and lawn mower repairs.

The retail bargain store, located in the southwest corner of the facility, is administratively part of the warehouse operation under Clark's supervision. Damaged and overstocked items, drapery remnants, and rejected custom-made draperies are sold there.

The repair service department employees prepare certain types of merchandise sold by the five area retail stores. Repair work is performed both in the warehouse and in customers' homes. The field crew, comprising approximately half of the fifty-four repair service employees, spend about half of their working time visiting customers' homes to effect repairs. The other repair service employees work at the facility. Some make shop repairs on merchandise which is returned for service both by customers[2] and by the retail stores; those in the parts department provide parts to the service employees and make parts sales to customers; some perform service clerical functions; and a few part-time employees sell service contracts to customers by telephone. The repair service department employees punch a separate time clock and are paid under a wage plan and method of wage computation different from those of other employees at the facility.

The drapery workroom is situated adjacent to the retail bargain store and service department office. Its nine employees are engaged primarily in making draperies to the specifications of customers as given to the employer's interior decorators at the retail stores. Drapery workroom employees also perform some upholstery work, such as making throw pillows and similar items. An installer, part of the drapery workroom operation staff, delivers and hangs the finished draperies in customers' homes.

The respective work stations of repair service department employees and drapery workroom employees are physically separate from the warehouse operation, and these employees perform distinctly different job functions and use different skills from those of employees engaged in warehousing tasks. The contact between the warehouse and store employees on the one hand and repair service and drapery employees on the other is limited primarily to the routing movement of merchandise between the various departments within the facility. The degree of interchange between the departments is minimal; there have been at most three permanent transfers between the repair service department and the warehouse operation, one of which involved a supervisory promotion. There have been no permanent transfers into or out of the drapery workroom.[3]

---

[2]The field crew also brings to the shops those items which cannot be repaired in customers' homes.

[3]The only instance of temporary transfer at the facility involved the drapery installer, who apparently works in the warehouse for one to three weeks during the Christmas season and briefly at other times when the warehouse workload is high.

1. Do you agree with the company that the warehouse and retail bargain store employees share a community of interest? Explain.
2. What factors should you consider in determining the appropriate bargaining unit?
3. How should the board rule on the composition of the appropriate bargaining unit? Why?

Case 2

Greenpark Care Center and Local 144, Service Employees, AFL-CIO, and District 1199, Retail, Wholesale, and Department Store Union, AFL-CIO

Issue

Did the employer interfere with the election and violate Section 8 (a) (1) of LMRA?

Facts and Background

In early 1978, the company comptroller, Victor Feildson, asked William Williamson how he was planning to vote in the upcoming union election. When Williamson told him that he did not know, Feildson told Williamson that he would discharge him unless he voted for District 1199. Right before the election, when it looked as though Local 144 would win, Feildson ordered Williamson to "get on the ball" and "urge others to vote for 1199."

In addition, the chief administrator of Greenpark, Simon Pell, called a meeting of all employees and explained his position regarding the upcoming election. He said that he would rather deal directly with employees, not through a union, and urged them to vote no in the election. Further, he promised all bargaining unit employees new Blue Cross and Blue Shield benefits if they rejected the union.

The election took place on March 31, 1977, and 104 ballots were cast (11 for Local 144, 20 for an independent sales service union, 72 for District 1199, and 1 for no union). Upon the count of the election ballots, the officials of the independent sales service union filed objections to the election.

Questions

1. Have the election results been affected by either Feildson or Pell?
2. What should be the remedy if the company is found to have committed an unfair labor practice?

This case is taken from 236 NLRB No. 68 (1978). The names of the people involved have been changed.

3. What arguments could District 1199 offer against the NLRB setting aside the election results?

Case 3	Winn-Dixie Stores, Inc., Hialeah, Florida, and Meat Cutters, District No. 657, AFL-CIO
Subject	Discrimination against former union employee.
Facts and Background	Robert Alderman, a former international union representative with the Meat Cutters, decided that he wanted to seek employment which would not include the usual travel requirements of an international union representative. Having had experience as a meat cutter several years before, he applied for a job at a Winn-Dixie store in Hialeah, Florida. Knowing that the store manager had made statements that he would rather close than "have anything to do with unions" and was reputed to have a hostile attitude toward unions, Alderman did not disclose his former employment with the union when he completed the application form.

Alderman was hired as a meat cutter, but when the store manager found out that Alderman had falsified his application concerning his previous employment with the union, he was discharged. When Alderman was gathering his belongings after the discharge, his immediate supervisor stopped by and told him the company would never have hired him if the store manager had known about his union employment.

Alderman petitioned the NLRB, alleging discrimination due to previous union activities, and the NLRB investigated his case. The company argued that it had validly discharged Alderman under its policy of terminating employees for falsifying applications. It presented records of eighteen employees who had previously been discharged for misrepresentation on the application form, for example, for falsified educational background, criminal records, and workmen's compensation claims. The company contended that the information on the application form was one of the primary considerations in making any employment decision. Prior union employment was not the reason; discharge was for application falsification. However, Alderman continually insisted that the discharge was the direct result of the company finding out that he once worked for the Meat Cutters.

This case is taken from 236 NLRB 204 (1978). The names of the people involved have been changed.

1. Is it illegal for a company to have a policy in which employees are discharged for falsifying the application?
2. Who is to determine whether a company has a reputation for being hostile to the union?
3. If an employer has been known to make statements against unions, is this employer more likely to incur charges of unfair labor practices?
4. How should the NLRB rule in this case? Why?

Case 4

Schwenk, Incorporated, Kansas City, Kansas, and Sheet Metal Workers, Local 2

Subject

Company interference in internal union affairs.

Facts and Background

Schwenk, Incorporated, has been a member of the Sheet Metal and Air Conditioning Contractors National Association, Kansas City chapter. The association is a multi-employer bargaining group which is a party to a collective bargaining agreement with the union. Schwenk is a family-owned business, and all executive positions are filled by family members. The company employs sixty employees, two of whom are Wesley Freely, plant manager since 1968, and Jim Shyfill, project manager since 1967. Both are supervisors as defined under Section 2 (11) of the NLRA.

Freely supervises seventeen employees (on average) who produce the materials that are fabricated for installation. Shyfill schedules work to be done in the plant and coordinates the workers' activities. Both are skilled tradesmen and work with the tools of the sheet metal trade. When a particular job requires a foreman under the terms of the collective bargaining agreement, Shyfill designates which employee will be foreman on the job.

Because the current contract expires in two months, the union is demanding that work performed by Freely and Shyfill be done by regular members of the union, not supervisors, and that such clause be written in the new agreement. Presently, Freely and Shyfill are members of the union, having participated in a three-month strike eight years ago. Neither has participated in negotiations for either side, nor does either have financial interest in the company. However, from June 1970 to February 1976,

This case is taken from 228 NLRB No. 94 (1977). The names of the people involved have been changed.

Freely was vice-president of the union and served as president for four months. Shyfill was the recording secretary of the union from June 1970 to June 1976. While occupying these positions, both voted in internal union elections to determine who would administer the affairs of the union.

The General Counsel of the NLRB contended that both Freely and Shyfill were high-level supervisors and that the company, by permitting them to participate in internal union affairs by holding union offices and voting in union elections, was interfering with the administration of a labor organization in violation of Section (a) (2) of the NLRA.

The company contended that Freely's and Shyfill's status was identical to that of master mechanic.[1] The company listed other arguments to support its position:

1. Neither is an executive or officer in the firm.
2. Neither has ever participated in collective bargaining negotiations.
3. Neither helped form the union.
4. The company never acted in a way that led other employees to believe that either of them acts on behalf of the employer.
5. The collective bargaining agreement requires that they be members of the union.
6. Both are rank-and-file union members who have worked their way up in the company while remaining active and concerned with their union. To strip them of a voice and a right of participation in their union would in effect strip them of their job security.

Questions

1. Can supervisors be members of a union? What are the legal requirements?
2. What is the legal definition of a supervisor?
3. In reference to the bargaining unit, what is the status of supervisors?
4. How should the board rule in this case? Why?

---

[1]See Nassau and Suffolk Contractors' Association, Inc., 118 NLRB 174, 40 LRRM 1146 (1957).

International Longshoremen's Association, AFL-CIO, Local No. 1911 *and* Cargo Handlers, Inc., and Zapata-Haynie Corporation

Subject

Jurisdictional dispute.

Facts and Background

The employer, Cargo Handlers, performs its stevedoring services at a dock facility in Cambridge, Maryland, called the "main dock," which is owned by the city of Cambridge, county of Dorchester, Maryland, and the Maryland Port Authority and leased to the employer. The employees of Cargo Handlers are covered by a collective bargaining contract between the employer and the union.

Zapata-Haynie, a second employer, is engaged in the distribution of fish and fish products at a dock situated approximately three hundred yards upstream from the "main dock"; it leases this dock from a real estate corporation known as Cam-Storage, Inc., some of whose stockholders are also stockholders of the Cargo Handlers. Zapata-Haynie is under no collective bargaining agreement.

On Tuesday, May 31, 1977, a Norwegian vessel, the steamship *MS Eva,* docked at the main dock and the Cargo Handlers' employees began to unload 2,500 tons of fishmeal, using a crane or "crab bucket," from the *MS Eva.* On June 1, 1977, the *Marylander,* a smaller vessel which habitually operates on the Chesapeake Bay and not on the ocean, docked at the Zapata-Haynie dock with a cargo of approximately 300 tons of fishmeal. The following morning, employees of Zapata-Haynie and the two-man crew of the *Marylander* began unloading the fishmeal from the *Marylander* using a vacuum-operated evacuator.

The union president informed Cargo Handlers' officials that Local No. 1911 was claiming the work of unloading the *Marylander* and its members would not continue to unload the *MS Eva* unless and until Local No. 1911 members were used to unload the *Marylander.* Cargo Handlers' representatives responded that they had no authority to assign the work of unloading the *Marylander.* On that same day, Local No. 1911's president demanded of the captain of the *Marylander* that the work of unloading the vessel be assigned to its members, but this demand was refused. On June 2 employees of the Cargo Handlers ceased unloading the *MS Eva.*

The employers contended that there was no contractual relationship between Local No. 1911 and either Zapata-Haynie or the *Marylander.* The union has a contract only with the Cargo Hand-

This case is taken from 236 NLRB 191 (1978). The names of the people involved have been changed.

lers, and this contract covers only its employees. They also maintained that the unloading method used by the *Marylander* (vacuum evacuator) was more efficient and less expensive than using the work crew of Local No. 1911, particularly in view of the small size of the *Marylander*. Finally, no evidence was presented that the parties involved had established any voluntary means for settling the dispute.

Questions

1. Is this case a jurisdictional dispute or a secondary strike?
2. What authority does the Cargo Handlers have over the employees of Zapata-Haynie Corporation?
3. What authority does the NLRB have in cases like this?
4. What should be the appropriate decision in this case?

Case 6

Nathan Littaver Hospital Association and Gloversville Extended Care and Nursing Home Company and New York State Nurses Association

Subject

Refusal to bargain.

Facts and Background

The New York State Nurses Association (NYSNA) represents units of full-time and part-time registered nurses at the hospital and nursing home. Until the employer installed its time clocks, its registered nurses did not have to record their time except when claiming overtime compensation. However, the employer had recently installed time clocks as a replacement for the previously required sign-in and sign-out procedure without any discussion of the change with the full-time or part-time nurses. Further, the employer implemented new work rules and disciplinary procedures designed to enforce this new requirement without negotiation with the union.

Contending that the employer's conduct amounted to refusal to bargain about material, substantial, and significant changes in employment conditions, work rules and practices, and employee tenure, the union filed a charge with the NLRB.

Questions

1. Is the requirement to have employees use time clocks a mandatory subject of collective bargaining?

This case is taken from 229 NLRB No. 166 (1977). The names of the people involved have been changed.

2. Are the rules and disciplinary procedures concerning the new reporting procedures mandatory subjects?
3. What are possible objectives of the NYSNA in filing an unfair labor practice charge?
4. If the company does negotiate, must the company agree to take the time clocks out?

Case 7

Jerr-Dan Corp. and Local 72, Meat Cutters, AFL-CIO

Issue

Did the company violate Section 8 (a) (5) of the Labor Management Relations Act (refusal to bargain) when it withdrew recognition from the union that it voluntarily had recognized on the basis of signed authorization cards?

Facts and Background

The union conducted an employee-initiated organizational drive among production and maintenance employees on February 28 and March 2, 1977. By March 3, 1977, the union had secured thirty-three authorization cards out of a bargaining unit of forty-five employees. On March 3, the union representative, Nancy Gant, visited the company and requested union recognition from the company president, Mr. Pauley. As support, she presented the thirty-three signed authorization cards. Mr. Pauley examined the cards and replied "You got them all." In response, Ms. Gant said that the company should grant recognition and negotiate a contract. Mr. Pauley asked whether the union expected him to sign a contract at that time, and Ms. Gant replied that it did not but that collective bargaining would commence at a later date.

The parties agreed to meet on March 7, 1977, for the purpose of engaging in collective bargaining. However, before the March 7 meeting, Mr. Pauley retained legal counsel and sent a telegram to Ms. Gant cancelling the meeting. In his telegram, he also indicated that:

1. He doubted the union majority status.
2. He doubted the appropriateness of the unit.
3. He refused to recognize the union, absent an NLRB election.

On March 7, 1977, when the company president, Mr. Pauley, did not meet with the union, the thirty-three employees went out on strike in protest of Mr. Pauley's action in repudiating his March 3 agreement. The strike lasted until April 19, 1977. Upon the com-

This case is taken from 237 NLRB No. 49 (1978). The names of the people involved have been changed.

mencement of the strike, the union also petitioned the NLRB for an unfair labor practice charge against the company for refusal to bargain.

Questions

1. Can collective bargaining take place without an NLRB election?
2. What are the conditions under which a union can be recognized without an election?
3. If you had been Mr. Pauley, on March 3 what would you have done?
4. What do you believe was the NLRB decision and order? Why?

Case 8

Ford Motor Company and Automobile Workers, Local 588

Issue

Did the company commit the unfair labor practice of refusing to bargain when it refused to provide information about or discuss cafeteria and vending prices?

Facts and Background

The management at the Chicago Stamping Plant, Ford Motor Company refused to bargain and supply information to the United Auto Workers, Local 588 in regard to the plant's vending machine and cafeteria prices and services.

The company provides its employees with two air-conditioned cafeterias and five air-conditioned vending areas. These are serviced by ARA Services, pursuant to a 1972 agreement. Under the agreement, ARA furnishes food and machines and is reimbursed for all direct costs of food and vending machine operations, plus a general administrative cost of 4 percent net receipts and a service fee of 5 percent net receipts. Should the net receipts exceed costs plus the 9 percent surcharge, the excess funds are returned to the company. If revenues are less than costs plus the 9 percent surcharge, the company makes up the difference, a situation which the company has faced in recent years.

The company has in the past at all times refused to bargain over prices set by ARA but has bargained over the quality of the service provided. Since 1967, the local contract has included provisions dealing with vending and cafeteria services such as service lines, machine repairs, and menu variety.

The employees have a thirty-minute lunch break and two

This case is taken from 230 NLRB No. 101 (1977).

twenty-two-minute rest breaks. They are not allowed to leave the plant during the rest breaks, and it is not feasible to leave during the lunch breaks. Employees are permitted to bring their own food into the plant, and lockers are furnished. Usually only a small number ever leave the plant during lunch.

On February 6, 1976, the company reviewed its financial situation concerning cafeteria and vending machine prices and, hoping to break even, decided to raise prices on items from 5 to 10 cents per item. The union responded by letter a week later, asking to meet with the company in order to bargain over the prices and services. The company refused to bargain, and the union began a boycott of the food service operations (over half of the bargaining unit employees participated). On March 23, 1976, the union requested information concerning the company's role in cafeteria and vending operations in order to administer the present agreement and to prepare for the upcoming negotiations. The company refused to provide the information. The case was sent to the NLRB for a determination.

Questions

1. Should cafeteria and vending prices be considered "wages, hours, and other terms of employment"?
2. What are the consequences of the company's refusal to bargain?
3. If the company should lose, what alternatives are available to it?

Case 9

Playboy Club of Central City

Subject

Discharge for theft.

Issue

1. Was Laura Kuller (called Bunny Mary) discharged for just cause?
2. If not, what should the remedy be?

The grievant, Laura Kuller, was employed under the name of Bunny Mary at the Central City Playboy Club for four years. No disciplinary action had been taken against her prior to her discharge on August 2, 1977. Then she was terminated for allegedly changing the server's name on a customer's check on July 19,

This case has been adapted with the permission of the Bureau of National Affairs from its publication *Labor Arbitration Reports*. 70 LA 304 (Stuart P. Herman), 1977. The names of the people involved have been changed. The name of the particular Playboy Club has also been changed.

Cases

1977, so that she could obtain the $7.64 tip rather than the employee who provided the service. The following paragraphs present the key events that transpired on that evening.

On July 19, 1977, the grievant was one of four Bunnies working the evening shift in the Living Room section of the Central City Playboy Club. Her station was located in the club's disco dancing area. At approximately 10:00 P.M., one of the Bunnies, Terri James, who was working in the same room away from the dance floor, wanted to leave early for the night, a practice allowed when business was slow. She obtained permission from management to leave after her customers moved forward to tables closer to the disco dancing area, which left her without anyone to serve. Among the customers moving on the night in question was a party of three women who moved to a table in the grievant's area.

Customers at the Central City Playboy Club are charged a 17.5 percent serving charge. This money is given to the Bunny whose name appears on the check, and it is her primary source of earnings. When the party in question moved forward, Ms. James closed out the check with her name on it (included on the check were the cover charge and the cost of dinner and a round of drinks prior to and after dinner). It was undisputed she had served these items, for which her tip was $7.64. She then opened a new check with the grievant's name on it, got the guests another round of drinks, and left. A second cover charge was not imposed, and the grievant continued to serve drinks to the party as requested between 10:00 and 12:00; her total service charge was $2.27.

Feeling that Ms. James had "skimmed the cream" by serving the customers dinner and including the cover charge on her bill, the grievant expressed unhappiness with her leaving early, causing the grievant to have to provide the customers the less lucrative part of their service. There was no dispute that the grievant informed the other Bunnies and the assistant Bunny trainer of the actual facts and what she intended to do. It was not disputed that before closing that night she retrieved the first check with Ms. James's name on it and crossed it out, inserting her own name. The grievant made no attempt to hide what she had done, made the changes in front of other employees, and told several other Bunnies what she had done. While the grievant never informed Ms. James about what she did, the other Bunnies did tell her. Although there was disagreement as to whether any conversation took place between the grievant and Ms. James later that night or within a few days thereafter, there was agreement that Ms. James was informed within a week of the incident. She chose not to discuss it with the grievant but instead reported it to the union shop steward, who informed management of the situation.

No written policy was presented by the employer concerning the changing of a server's name on checks or the signing of someone else's name on them, but shortly after the termination of the grievant, the employer posted a written memo informing the Bunnies such practices were prohibited.

On August 2, 1977, the club supervisor, Janet Thomas, upon being informed of the incident of July 19, 1977, called a meeting with the grievant and her union representative. At that meeting, the grievant admitted changing the check to get the tip for herself and that she had never subsequently discussed the matter with Ms. James. Upon conclusion of the meeting, the decision was made to terminate the grievant.

Pertinent Contract Provisions

Article VII (q) (1):
No Bunny will be discharged, suspended or otherwise disciplined without just cause.

Article VII(x):
Pertaining to Bunnies: **Except as limited and restricted by this Agreement, PCI has and shall retain the right of management and the direction of the Clubs, as it pertains to Bunnies. Such rights of management include, among other things, but are not limited to: the right of PCI to plan, direct, control, increase, decrease or diminish operations in whole or in part; to remove any Club or any portion thereof to another location; to hire, suspend, discharge or discipline employees for just cause or lack of Bunny image, subject to grievance and arbitration procedures as herein provided; and to determine the number of employees that it shall employ at any time and the qualifications necessary to any of the jobs, provided it is not inconsistent with this Agreement; to adopt and from time to time modify, rescind or change reasonable safety and work rules and regulations so long as such rules are not inconsistent with a provision of this Agreement and to enforce such rules; and to select and assign such work and duties not covered by this Agreement as it deems appropriate to supervisory and other categories of employees excluded from this Agreement, as specified in this Agreement.**

Article IX(g):
The arbitrator shall have no authority to alter or amend the terms of this Agreement.

Positions of the Parties

Company The employer argued that it is undisputed that the grievant altered a check in order to get a tip belonging rightfully to another Bunny. The employer further contended that it was undisputed that the policy among the Bunnies, through custom and practice, if not formally reduced to specific writing, that checks should not be altered without the knowledge and consent of another Bunny entitled to receive a tip based on a portion of that check.

Based on the above, the employer contended in its presentation that what the grievant did actually constituted theft from another employee. It presented supporting cases that theft was an adequate ground for discharge, regardless of the value of the item or the employee's work record. (S.A. Shenk, 26 LA 395; Franz Food Products, 28 LA 543; Plough, Inc., 57 LA 369; Borg-Warner, 47 LA 903; United Hosiery Mills, 22 LA 573; Hawaiian Telephone Co., 43 LA 1218.) Therefore, the employer contended that the discharge of Laura Kuller (Bunny Mary) was with just cause pursuant to the provisions of the current collective bargaining agreement.

Union It was the position of the union that the conduct of Laura Kuller (Bunny Mary) did not constitute just cause for discharge within the meaning of Article VII (q) (1) of the current collective bargaining agreement, and that she should be reinstated to her former position with full back pay. The union further argued that the supporting cases named by the employer were unlike the present case in both facts and issues.

Questions

1. Assume you are the union representative. Formulate the best, most thorough case that you could present before the arbitrator. Repeat the process, assuming that you are a management representative. On the basis of both sets of formulated contentions, how would you decide the issue as an arbitrator? Why?
2. Who has the burden of proof in this case?
3. To what extent should the arbitrator consider and use the supporting cases referenced by the employer in making the decision?
4. Should the grievant, Laura Kuller, be reinstated? If so, what should be the remedy? What is your reasoning?
5. Where did the employer fail in its managerial practices in this case?

WNAA and Radio Employees Union

Subject   Discharge.

Issue   Was Mr. Raymond Crandall discharged for just cause? If not,
                     what should the remedy be?

Facts and   Mr. Raymond Crandall had been a salesperson with WNAA for
Background   seventeen years when he was discharged on November 4,
                     1977. His notice of discharge alleged that his continued failure to
                     perform his job within the intent and purpose of the agreement
                     and his poor record keeping following four warnings to change
                     his behavior prompted the company's action.

                     To protest this discipline, Crandall filed a grievance on November
                     7, 1977. However, the agreement covering this grievance expired
                     on November 15, 1977, and a new agreement was not signed until
                     December 15, 1977, but was retroactive to December 1. Crandall's
                     problem arose when the new agreement specifically excluded the
                     sales unit (it was bargained out of the agreement).

                     Still, Crandall's grievance was appealed to arbitration and was
                     properly before the arbitrator.

Pertinent   *Article I Intent and Purpose*
Contract
Provisions   **1.1 It is the intent and the purpose of the parties to this Agreement to
                     set forth herein the provisions . . . in order to secure closer and har-
                     monious relations between the parties.**

                     **1.2 It is further the purpose of the parties to this Agreement to prevent
                     interruption of work and to promote the efficient operation of the busi-
                     ness through increased productivity with maximum quality. . . .**

                     **1.8 Management—The Company, except as clearly and explicitly
                     abridged by any provision of this Agreement, reserves and retains ex-
                     clusively all of its normal and inherent rights with respect to the man-
                     agement of the business, whether exercised or not . . . to introduce new
                     and improved methods; . . . to select and direct the working forces in
                     accordance with the requirements determined by management to be
                     necessary to the orderly, efficient and economical operation of the busi-
                     ness, such measures to be administered without discrimination against
                     any employee; management reserves the right to maintain and require
                     methods of record-keeping.**

Special appreciation to Dr. Donald Crane, professor and arbitrator, Georgia State University, for providing this case. All names have been changed to prevent identification.

Article II Grievance, Arbitration, Inspection

2.3 Arbitration

When the services of an impartial arbitrator are required, the parties will meet in an effort to agree on a person to fill that position. If an agreement on this point is not reached within five days after the meeting, the arbitrator shall be chosen from a list or lists to be submitted by the American Arbitration Association. The decision of the arbitrator so chosen shall be final and binding on the Employer, the Union, and the Employees covered by this Agreement, and he shall have no right to add to, subtract from, alter, or in any way modify the terms and conditions of this Agreement.

2.4 Discharge and Suspension

(a) The Company shall not discharge, suspend or otherwise discipline any employee without just cause but in respect to such discharge, suspension or other disciplinary action shall give at least two (2) warning notices of the complaint against such employee to the employee with a copy of same to the Union. . . .

(b) Warning letters and discharge notices—Discharge must be by proper written notice to the employee and the Union. Warning notice shall have no force or effect after nine months from the date thereof.

Position of the Company

The company's position is that Crandall was discharged for just cause because of his refusal to perform his duties accurately and completely, blatant disregard for record keeping requirements, constant challenge of management authority, rebellious attitude, deportment unbecoming a professional salesperson, and "self assumed direction" in setting rates with accounts. These acts affect customers, the company's sales revenues, and the morale of other salespeople. He made no effort to be responsive to repeated counseling by his manager, and no employee, regardless of seniority, has the right to disregard rules, procedures, and authority.

The company pointed out that it gave Crandall more than the required number of written warnings within the contractual nine-month period: the first on April 5, 1977, for posting on the employee bulletin board information derogatory to the station; the second on April 11, 1977, for failure to present a special program series to accounts; the third on September 29, 1977, for refusal to abide by established procedures in servicing an account; and the fourth on October 25, 1977, for failure to comply with management's request for information on delinquent accounts. In addition to these formal warnings, the company pointed out, Crandall was cautioned orally and in writing on many occasions to improve his performance. The final incident that led to his discharge was his report to a key account on times available for program sponsorships which contained thirty errors, or a 21 percent error rate.

The company emphasized that it would discharge Crandall again were he to be reinstated because: (1) the sales unit had been bargained out of the agreement soon after he was discharged, so that he was no longer protected by it, and (2) testimony of a union witness revealed that Crandall had taken kickbacks for referring clients to a customer, an act of dishonesty that would be a basis for immediate dismissal.

A final argument was that any liability to back pay was limited to the eleven days from the date of discharge to the signing of the new agreement, which excluded the sales unit.

Position of the Union

Counsel for the union cited as the cause of the problem in this case a conflict between an employee with seventeen years of experience with his employer and a sales manager who was insecure in his position and felt threatened by a veteran employee.

The union argued that the memos issued by the company to Crandall did not qualify as warning letters as far as the agreement is concerned. It emphasized that the "warnings" failed to delineate the consequences of Crandall's alleged delinquencies and were based on unsubstantiated claims.

Further, the union contended that Crandall was a competent employee according to the testimony of several major clients. Negotiating prices for advertising is a common practice in the industry, and Crandall negotiated substantially higher rates than other salesmen. In response to the charge that Crandall failed to promote a special program ("The Fight against Inflation"), it was pointed out that he appropriately used his discretion on how strong a pitch to make and called the program to the attention of a major account's buyer.

Regarding the September 29 warning about the failure to follow established procedures, Crandall explained that he solicited the account (Mirror City) with the approval of the salesperson involved and their sales manager. Crandall and the other salesperson had planned to exchange accounts, but the final resolution of the matter was unfair to him. Concerning the delinquent account charge, Crandall did substantially comply with the manager's request in that the information was received by the deadline.

Crandall was characterized as an experienced salesperson who consistently gave a 110 percent effort. The union cited Crandall's sales record, including top earnings for seventeen years and sales production that consistently exceeded quota. Moreover, he was featured by the company in a national magazine as one of the "professionals who care about their jobs and their community."

The union argued that the arbitrator has the authority to award reinstatement with back pay beyond the expiration of the contract and insisted that it is generally accepted by the courts and arbitrators that seniority rights extend beyond the contract.

Questions

1. Do employee rights in grievances extend beyond the contract expiration date?
2. How can the company and union legally agree to exclude certain employees (such as the sales unit) from the bargaining unit?
3. Has the company complied with the rules of corrective discipline?
4. If the arbitrator rules that Crandall is not covered by the agreement, will the arbitrator automatically deny the grievance?
5. How much consideration should Crandall's seventeen years of experience be given in this case?
6. If you were the arbitrator, how would you decide this case? Why?

Case 11

Celluloid Corporation and Local 123, International Woodspersons Union of America

Subject

Overtime assignment.

Issue

Did the company improperly seek to correct an erroneous overtime assignment by offering the grievant a makeup overtime day rather than paying for the mistaken assignment?

Statement of Grievance

The grievant was scheduled to work Saturday, July 9, 1978, and Sunday, July 10, 1978, but on Saturday, July 9, she was replaced

Special appreciation is extended to A. Dale Allen, professor of behavioral management and labor relations, Baylor University, Hankamer School of Business, for providing this case. All names have been changed to prevent identification.

by a probationary employee. Remedy sought—eight hours pay at time and a half.

Pertinent Contract Provisions	*Article II Recognition*

Article II Recognition

Section 1. The Company recognizes the Union as the sole and exclusive representative bargaining agent for all production, maintenance and laboratory employees, including production department inspectors, at the Detroit, Michigan, plant for the purpose of collective bargaining with respect to wages, hours of work, and other conditions of employment, subject to and in accordance with the provision of the National Labor Relations Act. . . .

Article V Management Rights

Section 1. Any and all management rights are fully and exclusively retained, and may be exercised by the Employer, except to the extent specifically modified by the provisions of this Labor Agreement, with respect to wages, hours of work, and other working conditions. . . .

Article VII Working Hours

Section 7. Employee regular work schedules will be posted no later than 3:00 P.M. on Thursday preceding the scheduled work week. Wherever possible, overtime work schedules will be posted at the same time. . . .

Article XVII Procedure for Handling Disputes

Section 2. Grievances shall be settled in accordance with the following grievance procedure:

(A) The aggrieved employee or employees shall within 5 work days of the event giving rise to the grievance, and at a time that does not interfere with production, take the matter up with his immediate supervisor. The Department Steward shall be notified of the grievance and the employee may request the Department Steward to be present at this step of the grievance.

Provisions of Company Notice (February 27, 1975)

Probationary employees *will not* be scheduled to work if work is low. Nonprobationary Production & Maintenance employees must notify their foreman prior to scheduling day if they desire to have a probationary man replace them on the schedule for the weekend. A scheduling discrepancy brought to the foreman's attention prior to the weekend can be corrected. The following Monday is too late to make any changes, and the balancing of the days off would average out within the following weeks.

Facts and Background

On Thursday, July 7, 1978, the company posted the weekend work assignments. The grievant, Jan Mitchell, appeared on the

Saturday and Sunday overtime schedule. At some time the next day, a company official altered the schedule and, by error, removed her name and replaced her with a probationary employee. The company admitted that the grievant was not notified of this change, nor did she become aware of this mistake until she was punching out at 3:00 P.M. that same Friday afternoon. According to past practice and Article VII, Section 7, discrepancies in the overtime schedule are altered before 3:00 P.M. on Friday because it would be difficult to contact workers who have punched out for the weekend.

Upon reporting for work on Sunday, the grievant discovered that a probationary employee had indeed worked in her position. Paragraph six of a company notice of February 27, 1975, had stated that probationary employees are not to work overtime unless management is unable to obtain enough regular, non-probationary workers.

On Monday, July 11, Jan Mitchell contacted the scheduling foreman, Dan Hotson, to inquire about the change. Hotson offered to the grievant a makeup overtime day at some future date to rectify the acknowledged scheduling error. The grievant agreed "if it would not take someone else's overtime." The union contended that such an agreement between Hotson and any employee would not be valid in any case, since no union representative was present and this "side agreement" would violate overtime payment practices and provisions.

The union steward, Joe Olson, later informed the company that the union could not accept a makeup day on Sunday, August 14, 1978, and Mitchell refused to accept this assignment as settlement of her grievance. The foreman later asked Mitchell if she would work anyway and she agreed, again commenting, "But not in settlement of the grievance." Thus, although she worked on Sunday, August 14, 1978, she did not accept the time as a makeup day, nor did the union.

Position of the Union

The union contended that the company attempted to "cook up" a settlement directly with Mitchell in violation of the recognition clause and contrary to past practice for handling such errors. On several occasions in the past, lost overtime simply had been paid by the company. In only one instance, the Lanton case, had a makeup been allowed. This was agreed to by the union because it was believed that Lanton knew about the error soon enough to get it changed before the 3:00 P.M. Friday deadline. Moreover, Lanton sat in the guard shack on his makeup day to assure that he confiscated no one else's overtime hours. Further, Lanton's case did not involve a probationary employee.

The union maintained that overtime hours cannot be made up, especially hours worked by a probationary employee, since these employees are not eligible for overtime in competition with regular employees. The company simply made an error on the overtime schedule which Jan Mitchell did not discover until she was punching out at 3:00 P.M. on Friday, too late to seek a correction. To allow Mitchell to make up overtime hours worked by a probationary worker would only create another overtime grievance for some other regular employee. Hence, the only proper remedy is to order the company to pay the grievant for the lost overtime hours.

Position of the Company

The company acknowledged that the grievant's name was erroneously removed from the weekend overtime roster and replaced with that of a probationary employee. However, the company maintained that it was legitimate to offer Jan Mitchell a makeup overtime day without consulting the union. The grievant did work a makeup day on Sunday, August 14, at double-time rates. She was the fifth person on what is normally a four-person crew. Thus, she did not usurp some other worker's overtime hours.

The labor agreement does not specify any penalty or method to be invoked when management errs in assigning overtime. The February 27 notice states that "a scheduling discrepancy brought to the foreman's attention prior to the weekend can be corrected. The following Monday is too late to make any changes, and the balancing of the days off would average out within the following weeks." Even though schedules normally are not changed after Friday at 3:00 P.M., had Mitchell notified supervision of the error at that time, a remedy might have been discovered. Nonetheless, the notice language permits "lost overtime" to be "balanced out" in future weeks, which is precisely what the company did with Mitchell on Sunday, August 14. The Lanton incident is one historical example of this solution.

In summary, the union has not adequately demonstrated that the grievant or any other employee has lost overtime earnings because of management's solution to the clerical error. Mitchell was given a makeup overtime day on Sunday, August 14, and no other employee was deprived of overtime hours because of it. Thus, the grievance should be denied.

1. How much bearing does the Lanton case have on the arbitrator's decision in the present case?
2. Could the company be committing an unfair labor practice by making a "side agreement" with an employee without the union's consent?
3. Should the company have to pay for time not worked because of a clerical error?
4. If you were the arbitrator, what would be your ruling?

Case 12

Portland Community Schools (School Board) and Local 555, International Union of Bus Drivers

Subject

Date for bidding on bus routes.

Issue

Did the board improperly post bus routes for bidding in June 1978 instead of posting them after commencement of school in the fall of 1978? Moreover, should special education bus routes have been posted along with the regular runs?

Provisions of the Contract

Article 31 Bus Drivers

Section 1 *Vacancies*

(a) **On or before November 15th of each year all bus routes will be open for bids on the basis of seniority. All bidding shall be completed within four (4) work days.**

(b) **The following procedure shall be used:**
   1. **The bus drivers shall be divided into three groups, by seniority, as equal in number as possible and routes posted on the first day.**
   2. **The upper third will, on the second day, be given first opportunity to bid and their bidding will be frozen at the end of that day.**
   3. **The second third will, on the third day, be given the opportunity to bid and their bidding will be frozen at the end of that day.**
   4. **The remaining third will, on the fourth day, be given the opportunity to bid and their bidding will be frozen at the end of that day.**
   5. **Thereafter any routes unbid may be assigned by the District to drivers without routes.**

Special appreciation is extended to A. Dale Allen, professor of behavioral management and labor relations, Baylor University, Hankamer School of Business, for providing this case.

(c) No seniority shall be given for substitute or probationary employees.

Section 2 *Work Year*

Bus drivers' schedules will be set each year according to the needs of the children. The statements in this Article shall not be considered as a guarantee of hours per day or week.

Statement of Grievance

On June 6, 1978, the employer posted all bus runs for bidding except Special Education runs. This is a direct violation of the contract, Article 31, Section 1, (a) and (b). The intent of the language at the negotiating table was that the runs would be bid after the start of each school year on or before November 15. The drivers were not given ample time to review the runs and the runs were not complete as to the changes when the drivers went in to bid on them.

The Union requests that all runs including the Special Education runs for the 78–79 school year be reposted and be rebid after September, 1978, prior to November 15, 1978.

Position of the Union

The union contended that the board violated Article 31, Section 1 (a) when bus routes were posted for bids on two occasions within one school or fiscal year—in November 1977 and again in June 1978. The disputed article states that "on or before November 15th *of each year all* bus routes will be open for bids on the basis of seniority." (Emphasis added.) Regardless of whether one uses a fiscal year or a school year, the language clearly states that bids are made only once each year.

The union presented testimony that the board had no unilateral right to move the bidding period to June, some three to four months prior to the opening of the school year. Requiring drivers to bid on bus routes in accordance with seniority this early forces them to request runs which may change considerably before they finally go into effect by the next fall. Thus, senior drivers may end up with less desirable routes than they might have been entitled to.

The union pointed out that the words "on or before November 15th" were placed in the contract to indicate that route bidding would take place sometime after the commencement of a new school year but not later than November 15. Veteran drivers wanted to start the routes because they would be familiar with the old stops, children, and directions, thereby avoiding a lot of confusion created by having a new driver and bus number. Once the veteran drivers had worked out any changes in the route, then they could record these alterations on the route sheet and more efficiently pass this information on to new drivers. In contrast, if new drivers started at the beginning of the year, it would be very confusing for drivers and children alike. When, several years ago, it was decided to bid the routes before school started, chaos was the result. For example, one driver picked up the wrong load of children and took them to the wrong school district. Thus, that idea was dropped; it was revived again this year by the board, however, in spite of contract language and established past practice.

The union also noted that the board could have requested a change in language of Article 31 in the last negotiations if it had wanted to move the bidding to June. However, no such demand was made by the board. Therefore the board cannot after the fact unilaterally alter the contract's intent and a past practice of ten years or more without consulting with the union.

The union also contended that *all* bus routes were supposed to be posted for bid per Article 31, including special education runs. These latter routes had not been posted along with regular ones. Since the language does not exempt special education routes, they must also be posted each year.

The board charged that only a few bus drivers were interested in the present grievance; the union countered this notion by submitting a list of names of twenty-five drivers who were present when this complaint was presented orally to Mr. Morehouse, Director of Transportation. Hence a majority of the drivers in the bargaining unit were upset with the change in bidding procedure.

For these reasons, the union requested that the grievance be upheld.

Position of the School Board

The board maintained that Article 31, Section 1 (a) merely required that route bids be posted "on or before November 15th." Hence this language does not preclude the possibility of bidding in June. The board further contended that Article 31 does not state that posting must occur after school has commenced nor is that the intent of the provision. The posting of November 1977 was for school year 1977–1978 and the June 1978 posting was for school year 1978–1979. Since the two postings were for different school years, they were not violations of Article 31, Section 1 (a).

The board chose to move the bidding period to June because of several resulting advantages. First, drivers would begin with a given route and stay with it throughout the year, avoiding the confusion of mixing drivers about after school had been in session several weeks. Second, there would be less uncertainty among the students and school administrators. Third, the board pointed out that with the stabilizing school enrollment more accurate predictions concerning school bus routes could be made at an earlier time than in previous years, when enrollments fluctuated. Thus the board contended that there was merit to altering the past practice.

The board maintained that the desire to retain posting of bids in the fall had been the wish of only a few in the bargaining unit, that the majority of the drivers were not concerned one way or another. Thus, the board should not be constrained from moving to an earlier posting time simply because a few stubborn members were opposed. No drivers lost any wages as a result of this change.

Finally, the board noted that the issue regarding posting of special education runs had been the subject of another grievance already presented under arbitration, but that no decision had been rendered.

Questions

1. Of what relevance is the intent of the parties when they negotiated the labor agreement in this arbitration case?
2. Discuss the political implications or internal union rivalries which could possibly underlie the grievance.
3. What should be the arbitrator's decisions after thoroughly considering union and management contentions, the facts, and the evidence?
4. What are the possible effects of your decision in Question 3 on the following:
   a. internal union affairs
   b. political maneuvering by officers
   c. future negotiations

Case 13

Rehmus Manufacturing Company, Springfield, Massachusetts, and Local 484, United Machine Operators

Subject

Reporting pay.

Issue

Does the company owe James Manley four hours' pay at time and one-half for reporting between shifts to the personnel department on December 5, 1977, for a disciplinary investigation?

Much appreciation is extended to Dr. Mathew W. Jewett, professor and arbitrator, Memphis State University, for use of this case. Names of persons and places have been changed.

At the time the grievance was filed, James Manley was employed as a systems cleaner in the plant department. The following grievance, number 132, dated December 6, 1977, was filed: "The Company refused to pay me for time which was other than my regularly scheduled shift but for which I was ordered to report to Personnel." The grievant sought a remedy of payment for four hours at the rate of one and one-half times the rate of the job to which he was assigned.

The events which led to the grievance had their beginning on the third shift, Sunday evening, December 4, 1977. At approximately 9:30 P.M., John Harrison, the general foreman, had been told by another employee in the paint department that the grievant was sleeping instead of working. The shift actually runs from 10:30 P.M. until 7:00 the next morning, but the company encourages its employees to come in at approximately 8:00 P.M. and thereby obtain approximately two hours overtime.

The grievant had clocked in at about 8:00 P.M. and was on the clock when Mr. Harrison went looking for him. Mr. Harrison, accompanied by two other supervisors, Mr. Jones and Mr. Trapp, found the grievant hidden in a box, with a piece of cardboard covering him, lying down, and appearing to be asleep. The grievant was thereupon suspended by Mr. Harrison for sleeping on the job.

The usual penalty for sleeping on the job in this company was discharge. In the instant case and in another one which occurred in 1976, in which the grievant was found apparently asleep on the job, the company imposed only a three-day suspension because the supervisors who found the grievant each time could not be certain that his eyes were closed. In each case, the employee was found in a prone position.

On the night of December 4, 1977, the grievant was suspended and paid four hours' pay for the period of time that he was in the plant that night. Manley filed a grievance, number 131, dated December 6, 1977, which stated: "Unjust suspension on 12-4-77 for sleeping during working hours." The remedy sought was eight hours' pay. The grievance was processed to the fourth step, denied by the company, and dropped by the union.

When he was suspended on December 4, 1977, the grievant was told to report to the personnel department at 10:00 P.M. on Monday, December 5, 1977, for further investigation of his case. He did report with Mr. Joe Joyce, the grievance committeeman. Upon reporting, both men clocked in and put their time cards in their pockets. After waiting for approximately two and one-half hours to see the industrial relations representative, Mr. Ivey, Manley learned that he would be suspended for three days. Since there had been a similar incident in 1976, the four hours' suspension on December 4th, the previous night, was considered by the company to be part of the disciplinary action it assessed against the grievant. The company did pay the grievance committeeman four hours' pay at one and one-half times his hourly rate of pay for the time he spent in the investigation, but the grievant was not paid for his time in the investigation.

<table>
<tr><td>**Pertinent Contract Provisions**</td><td>

Our plant provides you and others with employment and a means of livelihood. It represents a substantial investment on the Part of the Company. To protect the safety and welfare of all employees and to provide for the efficient operation of the plant, it is necessary for all employees to comply with reasonable rules of conduct.

Employees committing any of the following acts will be subject to disciplinary action, including discharge:

11. Leaving your job without permission, wandering through the plant, washing up or otherwise making preparations to quit work before quitting time, or leaving the plant without permission during working hours. . . .

19. Carelessness, failure to meet standards of workmanship or production, or other neglect of duties.

The above list is not intended to be complete, and appropriate action will be taken with reference to other forms of misconduct. This list may be revised from time to time.
</td></tr>
</table>

These rules were introduced as evidence. They were issued to each employee and a copy was posted on the employees' bulletin board.

Position of the Company

1. The company is not required by the agreement to pay call-back pay to an employee who is justly suspended for a violation of a company rule and required to be in the personnel office during the investigation of the incident.

2. The seriousness of the offense in the instant case, along with the fact that the grievant had been guilty of a similar offense in 1976, validates the company's decision to withhold, as part of the disciplinary action, call-back pay for the time he spent in the personnel office on December 5, 1977.

3. The decision to pay or not pay an offender for investigation time is based on the seriousness of the offense and whether or not the employee is guilty of the alleged violation. The grievant

had been treated fairly in this matter, and because he had been involved in a similar violation the year before, it was decided not to pay him call-back pay this time.

4. Based on past practice which denied call-back pay to employees guilty of serious offenses, the grievant should not be paid for investigative time.

Position of the Union

1. The purpose of reporting and call-back pay in labor agreements is to provide for the payment of an inconvenience.

2. The company admitted to paying other employees under the same circumstances as those involving the grievant, but it contended the seriousness of the offense was the determining factor.

3. Although the company classified sleeping on the job as a serious offense, it had paid employees who were sent home for safety violations when they reported the following day to learn the extent of their penalty. The circumstances involving this grievant were identical to those in past incidents.

4. The grievant was sent home for sleeping on the job. He was instructed to report the following day between shifts. After deliberations of nearly three hours, the company decided that the grievant was not sleeping on the job, and he was given a written warning.

5. The grievant should receive four hours' pay at one and one-half times his regular rate for reporting under instructions of the company on December 5, 1977, as prescribed in the agreement.

Questions

1. Has this employee been penalized twice, and is this unfair?

2. Should an employee have the right to grieve while on disciplinary suspension?

3. What effect would the arbitration decision in this case have on future cases with this company and union?

4. You be the arbitrator. What would you decide? Why?

Case 14	Reliable Trucking Service and International Truckers of America, Local 112

Subject   Discharge, insubordination, safety.

Issue   Did the company violate the contract by the discharges of the grievants, Fred James and Bill Wood? If so, what should the remedy be?

Facts and Background   Reliable Trucking Service, located in Minneapolis, provides hauling services for building contractors or other companies. The drivers are represented for collective bargaining purposes by the International Truckers of America, Local 112.

On September 9, 1978, the date on which the incident leading to arbitration occurred, the company was hauling base materials from Spellings Construction Company in Minneapolis to Excelsior, Minnesota. The round trip distance was 52 miles by state highway and took approximately one and a half hours. Thirty drivers were assigned exclusively to the Spellings Construction project; work began at 6:30 A.M. Drivers reported to the site for their first load, traveled to Excelsior, unloaded their trucks, and returned to Spellings for other loads. Because Spellings was experiencing plant difficulties, drivers had some waiting time in Minneapolis. By afternoon, only fifteen drivers (including the two grievants) were still on the job, and no drivers were available for call-in. The grievants, James and Wood, had hauled four loads each during the day before the incidents that led to their discharge.

About 4:45 P.M. on the date in question, James called the dispatcher, Marie Grace, and told her that he was tired and didn't feel like working any more. Grace told him to finish the job before coming in, and James hung up. According to James's testimony, he then went to the Spellings's restroom, washed his face, went to the truck, and sat for ten minutes. The foreman asked him if he was going to load his truck, and he answered that he needed a little rest so he could make another load. After sitting there and thinking about it, he decided to take the truck in and drove into the company yard about 5:15 P.M.

About 5:00 P.M. on the same day, Wood, a cousin of James, called the dispatcher and said that he "was tired," "didn't feel like working," and "didn't feel like it was safe for him to drive any more." Grace told him that he would have to stay and finish the job. Instead of

The authors thank Alex J. Simon, professor emeritus, consultant, arbitrator principal—A. J. Simon & Associates, Port Arthur, Texas—for providing this case. The names of people and places have been changed.

Cases

remaining on the job, Wood, too, drove his truck to the company yard.

After talking with the grievants over the phone, Grace called Ben Frank, vice-president of Reliable, and was advised to give the grievants another opportunity to return to work. When the grievants went to the dispatcher's window, Grace asked each of them individually to return; but they refused, and Grace "let them go." When asked in the arbitration hearing whether she terminated them then, Grace said she told them that if they didn't go back to work, they left her no other choice. After work, both grievants drove their cars to their separate homes, and no evidence indicated they saw each other until Monday morning, when they reported to work.

On the following Monday morning, the two grievants reported to work at 6:30 A.M., but neither went to work. When the payroll clerk came to work about 8:00 A.M., their checks were processed. Thereupon, the grievants filed two separate grievances with the following identical statement:

I (the grievant's name), am filing this grievance against Reliable because I was discharged Saturday, September 9, 1978, because I had worked 11 hours and I was tired and was not able to drive or be safe any longer with this truck. I was driving 26 miles one way on the highway and I refused to drive this truck any longer because we have a safety program and we are taught safety every first Monday in the month. Any time that you are not capable of handling this truck you are to stop this truck. I did not want to tear up the company truck neither did I want to hurt anybody or maybe kill someone. So therefore, I refused on this ground. I am asking for my job back and all lost earnings.

Being unable to resolve this grievance through the negotiated grievance procedure, the parties appealed to arbitration.

Pertinent Contract Provisions

Article 5   Grievance Procedure
The job steward or business representative of the Union shall act for the Union in all matters of difference that may arise respecting the interpretation and application of the Agreement and all grievances relating thereto. . . . The arbitrator shall not be permitted to vary the terms of this Agreement or add or take anything away from the same. . . . If the parties are unable to agree on an arbitrator, then they shall by joint request obtain the appointment of such by the Federal Mediation & Conciliation Service. . . .

Article 7   Management Rights
Except where specifically otherwise provided in this contract management's right to manage and operate this business, to impose such disci-

pline, including discharge, as it may determine and to direct the working force is hereby recognized. Without limiting the generality of the foregoing, management shall have the right to introduce new or changed methods, procedures or equipment, to assign jobs and equipment, and to make such changes, including increases or reductions, in its operation as it shall deem to be desirable.

Article 11   Discharge
No employee shall be discharged without cause. Where discharge is for any matter relating to the manner in which an employee performs his job (but not including fighting, dishonesty, drunkenness, the carrying of prohibited items such as firearms, other weapons or the bringing of any narcotics, alcohol or other such items on the job or any act of recklessness resulting in serious accident involving injuries to person or property, the refusal to carry out a bona fide direct order of a supervisor or the hauling of unauthorized passengers while on the job, for any of which no warning is required), the employee shall have a warning notice in writing which shall be placed in the employee's personnel file. . . . Any employee may request an investigation as to his discharge. If following investigation the Employer and the Union are in disagreement as to whether the employee has been wrongfully discharged, the matter may be taken to arbitration as hereinabove provided.

Position of the Company

The company argued that the contract provisions gave it the right to discharge employees for "the refusal to carry out a bona fide direct order of a supervisor" and that no warning was needed to discharge employees for insubordination. In fact, the supervisor had given the grievants an opportunity to go back to the job. Since the company was anxious to get all the materials hauled to Excelsior and no other drivers were available, it was important that the grievants remain on the job to help complete the hauling.

The company also contended that the employees were not extraordinarily tired because the Spellings Construction Company's plant was shut down part of the day and the drivers sat around much of the time. Saturday was only the fifth day of working that week, and the grievants had done no more than the other drivers. Drivers usually worked ten to twelve hours a day during the busy season, and neither of the grievants had been on medication on the day in question. Furthermore, five drivers had made more loads than the grievants on that day, worked longer hours, and voiced no complaints.

James had driven his car home by himself and had not gone to bed immediately. Rather, he cleaned up, ate, then retired. Wood also drove his car home by himself but did not remember what he had done that evening.

Last, the company claimed that the complaints were pretextual or feigned and that the grievants obviously had an opportunity during the day to discuss their situation and their desire to quit work at 5:00 P.M. The company further contended that it was not accidental that the phone calls came fifteen minutes apart; nor was it coincidental that both grievants used the same excuse and drove in one right after the other.

The union argued that it did not take issue with management's authority under the contract provisions to discharge employees for cause, but it strongly contended that the grievants did not conspire to leave work around 5:00 P.M. on September 9, 1978. Their decisions for needing to leave work were independent and necessary for their own personal safety and the safety of others.

The union challenged the company's contention of urgency because the job had been easily finished on time by the remaining truck drivers. Since Grace, the dispatcher, had let other drivers off earlier that day—one for dizziness from medication and others for truck problems—urgency was not indicated. In addition, drivers with truck problems usually could radio in their trucks' conditions, and in such cases company cannot determine specific problems with each truck or specific reasons for letting each driver off early. The grievants also could have called in and lied about their trucks or their health, and the supervisor could have excused them for the rest of the shift.

The major union argument was that all drivers, including the grievants, had been trained to be extremely conscious of safety rules and violations. For example, Frank had recently issued a warning letter to James about the violation of a safety rule concerning abuse of equipment. These safety rules and regulations were attached to the contract; the company held monthly safety meetings on company time, with union representatives in attendance on occasion. Four deaths of drivers had occurred in recent times, and their names had been frequently brought up in these safety meetings. The company has a safety bonus system in which $10 is deposited each month in the name of a driver-employee for every full month of employment. At the end of four months, provided an employee has not received any warning letters or had any chargeable accidents, the remaining money is divided among eligible employees after $50 has been deducted for each chargeable accident. However, each driver having an accident or receiving a warning letter is disqualified from receiving a safety bonus.

The union further contended that both grievants had good performance records—James for two years and Wood for four to five months. Both liked their jobs and wanted to work. Both said they would refuse to drive if they were unable to handle the vehicle. James stated on his last trip that he was sleepy and thought someone would call the police about his unsafe driving. In fact, he told Grace that his truck had left the road and had almost hit another car. When told that he would be discharged, James replied, "I'd rather get discharged than kill myself or kill somebody else." Wood also said that he had had difficulty on his last trip to Excelsior. His truck was weaving across the white line on the highway, and instead of damaging the truck or hurting someone, he brought the truck in.

Questions

1. What are examples of occasions when an employee can refuse a supervisor's order?
2. Should these employees and their union have taken their cases to OSHA rather than to arbitration? What would be the advantages and disadvantages?
3. Which party has the burden to prove that the employees were or were not too tired to work?
4. Could the company have placed too much emphasis on safety?
5. What would happen to industrial discipline on the job if employees stopped work when they felt tired or thought the conditions were not safe?
6. You be the arbitrator. What is your decision? Why?

Case 15

Roller Ball and Bearing Company and Ball-Bearing Workers of America

Subject

Bumping during layoff.

Issue

Did the company violate the agreement and the rights of P. Mann and A. Roberts by the manner in which it allowed them to exercise their bumping rights in accordance with the provisions of Article VI of the agreement? If so, what should the remedy be?

Facts and Background

Roller Ball and Bearing Company operates the Wingfield Products Division Plant in Denver, Colorado. The bargaining unit employees

The authors thank Alex J. Simon, professor emeritus, consultant, arbitrator principal—A. J. Simon & Associates, Port Arthur, Texas—for providing this case. The names of people and places have been changed.

are represented by Local 610 of the Ball-Bearing Workers of America. Plant operation involves a manufacturing process without a finished goods inventory; as a result, staffing changes occur at this installation frequently. The change in the level of operations is rather extensive at times, as is indicated by the fact that in April 1974 the company had employed two hundred fifty employees, but the number had fluctuated from only twenty-two in April 1975 to approximately one hundred employees in January 1976.

As a result of reduced customer demands in January 1976, the company was required to lay off a number of employees. Five employees classified as brass die cast operators were displaced on a permanent basis, and they had bumping rights in accordance with Article VI, Section 8, of the agreement between the parties. The manner in which these five displaced employees were allowed to exercise their rights is the issue in this case.

The grievance, filed on February 2, 1976, alleged that "Company violated the contract by laying off employees P. Mann, A. Roberts, M. Jones, H. Norris, and T. Rickson out of line of their seniority in Dept. 12 on January 30, 1976." The grievance was processed through the negotiated grievance procedure and appealed to arbitration.

There was no disagreement between the parties that Mann, Roberts, Jones, Norris, and Rickson were the junior employees who were to be displaced from the brass die cast machine operator classification. The union did not challenge the fact that the company had the right to place these employees on a layoff status; furthermore, the company and the union were in complete agreement that there were only four remaining junior noninterchangeable employees that the five grievants could have bumped. These four employees, their classification, seniority date, and rate of pay are listed below in order of their seniority.

Employee	Seniority Date	Rate of Pay
J. Septine, aluminum die cast machine operator	1-17-74	$4.51
J. Kenton, furnace tender brass	4-1-74	$5.21
J. Murphy, aluminum die cast machine operator	5-10-75	$4.51
W. Rouse, furnace tender aluminum	11-10-75	$5.11

The question to be resolved was whether the company offered the appropriate remaining job(s) to each of the five brass die cast machine operators when it was determined they were to be displaced and/or laid off from that classification. Both the company and union agreed that these five grievants had bumping rights. The disagreement was over whether only four of the five could, in effect, bump the four junior noninterchangeable employees remaining in the appropriate job families who had less seniority. The union, basically, challenged the order in which the company offered the four existing job openings. The five displaced noninterchangeable brass die cast operators and their seniority dates were as follows: P. Mann, July 25, 1972; A. Roberts, November 21, 1972; M. Jones, February 12, 1973; H. Norris, March 20, 1973; and P. Rickson, May 31, 1973.

The company explained the nature of its operation and the accompanying problems caused by being required to have a rapid layoff and/or recall system. It presented the method used in determining how many employees would be laid off and how many would be retained. It then proceeded to effect the layoff provisions as follows:

1. P. Mann, with a seniority date of July 25, 1972, was offered the job of furnace tender aluminum held by the junior employee to be displaced, W. Rouse, at the maximum base rate of $5.11 per hour. Mann refused that job and signed an employee refusal form entitled "notification of job offer." It was stipulated that Mann had the right to do so in accordance with Article VI of the agreement between the parties. In other words, Mann could accept a reduction in force and retain his seniority, and, according to the agreement, this would not affect his right to draw unemployment compensation as far as the company was concerned.

2. The company then proceeded to offer that position to Roberts, the next senior displaced noninterchangeable employee. He accepted the furnace tender aluminum classification in department 10, on the second shift, starting the following Monday, February 2, 1976.

3. Then, in line of seniority, the company offered Jones the job of aluminum die cast machine operator held by J. Murphy at the rate of $4.51 per hour. He accepted that position.

4. The next senior employee, H. Norris, accepted the job of furnace tender brass held by J. Kenton, with a pay rate of $5.21 per hour.

5. P. Rickson, the junior displaced employee, then accepted the job held by J. Septine (classified as aluminum die cast machine operator), with a base rate of $4.51 per hour.

These transactions are exhibited in the chart below along with the seniority date of the employees and the base rate of the laid-off employees as follows:

Displaced Employees in Order of Seniority		Junior Bumpable Employees in Reverse Order of Seniority	
P. Mann	7-25-72 refused ⌐		
A. Roberts	11-21-72 accepted →	W. Rouse	11-10-75 @ $5.11
M. Jones	2-12-73 accepted →	J. Murphy	5-10-74 @ $4.51
H. Norris	3-20-73 accepted →	J. Kenton	4-1-74 @ $5.21
P. Rickson	5-31-73 accepted →	J. Septine	1-17-74 @ $4.51

Close examination of this information shows that one of the least senior employees, H. Norris, with a seniority date of March 20, 1973, actually bumped the highest paid man of the four remaining employees, with a pay rate of $5.21 per hour. This upset Mann and Roberts and resulted in the filing of the aforementioned grievance.

Pertinent Contract Provisions

Article VI   Seniority

Section 8. Reduction, Layoff and Recall Procedure. When it is necessary to reduce the number of employees in a job classification or to reduce the number of employees in the plant, the following procedure shall be used:

(a) Temporary Layoff. Temporary layoff, not to exceed two (2) consecutive working days, shall be made by canvassing the employees by seniority in the classification(s) and shift to be laid off to determine if any such employees desire to be sent home. In the event an insufficient number of employees decline to be temporarily laid off, the lowest seniority employees in the selected classifications shall be laid off.

(1) Members of the Shop Committee shall head the plant-wide seniority list and shall not be laid off during said two (2) day period while any work is available which they are capable of performing.

(b) Permanent Layoff. At the expiration of the temporary layoff period as set forth in subsection (a) above, or immediately if the temporary layoff provisions of subsection (a) are not used, reduction in a job classification in the plant shall be in accordance with the following procedure:

(1) If the job classification to be reduced is a non-interchangeable job classification, the employee with the least seniority shall be removed from such job classification and he shall, seniority permitting, replace the most junior employee then working, irrespective of shift, in all of the other non-interchangeable job classifications that he is capable of filling, subject to the provisions of subsection (e) hereof. . . .

(f) When a permanent layoff becomes effective in the manner provided above, employees affected shall be informed in writing by the Company as to the job classification he may have, and such employee shall at that time agree to accept the job or, if it is a different classification from his own, he may refuse to accept the job in writing by signing an "Employee Refusal Form."

> An employee who signs the Employee's Refusal Form shall not be recalled until there is a vacancy in his own classification, but he shall not thereby lose his seniority and this procedure shall not affect his right to draw unemployment compensation so far as the Company is concerned.

(h) Exceptions to the reduction, layoff and recall procedure as set forth above may be made by mutual agreement of the Company and the Shop Committee.

Position of the Union

The union contended that the order in which the jobs were offered to the employees was in violation of Article VI, Section 8 (b) (1). The company should have determined specifically how many of the nine employees would be needed to keep the plant operating according to its anticipated needs. Having determined that only four would be needed, the company then should have gone first to the fourth junior employee in the brass die cast machine operation, Norris, and offered him the job held by Rouse, who was the junior of the noninterchangeable bumpable employees. That job should not have been offered to Mann. In fact, Mann was not the one who should have been offered the first opening. Then, the union contended that Jones should have been offered the job held by Murphy at $4.51 per hour, Roberts should have been entitled to the job held by Kenton, and Mann should have been entitled to the job held by Septine. These personnel transactions can be reflected as follows:

Brass Die Cast Machine Operators		Junior Noninterchangeable Employees		Base Pay Rate
P. Mann	7-25-72	J. Septine	1-17-74	$4.51
A. Roberts	11-21-72	J. Kenton	4-1-74	$5.21
M. Jones	2-12-73	J. Murphy	5-10-74	$4.51
H. Norris	3-20-73	W. Rouse	11-10-75	$5.11

Of course, any of the four employees—Norris, Jones, Roberts, or Mann—could have exercised his contractual rights by refusing to bump any of those employees, and then Rickson would have been able to bump into the available job.

Following this line of thinking, Mann knew he was being offered the improper job. Instead of being entitled to Rouse's job, he was actually entitled to the job held by Septine, thus, he turned it down and filed a grievance requesting to be paid at the rate of pay he was entitled to for the time that he was on layoff.

Because of this order of job offers, Roberts was required to take the furnace tender aluminum position at $5.11 per hour; but, according to the union, he should have received the job held by Kenton, blast furnace tender, at $5.21 per hour. Therefore, he should receive through this award an extra ten cents per hour for every hour he worked in the improper classification.

Position of the Company

The company took the position that with the refusal system negotiated by the parties in Article VI, Section 8(f), it was necessary to offer the most senior displaced employee first opportunity of the junior noninterchangeable position. If the job was refused, it could then be offered to the next senior employee, and so on down the line.

The company then presented exhibits to document the use of the system as an established practice prior to the date of the grievance and explained its uniform application to both the interchangeable and the noninterchangeable groups of job classifications. Furthermore, the company contended that no language existed in the current agreement to cover what company officials called "multiple employee displacements." Thus, the agreement did not provide for any specific order of job offer in the present case, and since there were no applicable provisions in the current agreement, the order of offer continued to be the exclusive responsibility of the company as specified in Article I, Section 4, of the agreement. The language in Article VI, Section 8(a) was presented to support the company's argument that the order of offer the company used in this layoff was consistent with the canvassing by seniority required in the case of a *temporary* layoff—that is, giving the senior displaced employee first choice of either accepting a layoff or the opportunity to bump the junior employee in another classification.

The bargaining unit employees at the Wingfield plant currently exercise great latitude when they are displaced from their job classification. They may accept an offer for another position and exercise their shift preference or refuse the offered job, go on layoff, and draw their unemployment benefits. Therefore, the current system does not infringe on any of these rights; this system has been in use over a period of time and has proved to meet the unique staffing requirements of the company.

Since no language existed in the agreement to cover multiple employee displacements or any specific order of offer as in this case, the "residual rights rule" has definite application—that is, the order of offer continues to be the exclusive responsibility of the company as specified in Article I, Section 4.

Furthermore, the company argued that the union's suggested remedy for the alleged violations would not provide a remedy but would perpetuate the same violations. It can be seen by examining the language of the agreement that Rickson was the junior employee to be displaced from the brass die cast machine operator's classification and not Norris. Thus, if the union's argument is maintained, Rickson should have first chance at any job. But if the four junior employees accepted the positions, this would leave the senior employee, Mann, with no job. He would then be forced to take a layoff. It would prove disruptive to the work force if the company were required to notify the junior noninterchangeable employee of his layoff on one day and, if another displaced employee refused a specific job, to renotify the original employee at a later date to continue to work in another classification.

Finally, the company pointed out that the arbitrator must review the union's prior acceptance of the company's established past practice in light of the principle of waiver and estoppel. The union, having failed to show any challenge of the company's established practice in the past, must be barred from achieving unilateral change of this position through arbitration in the absence of clear and explicit language to the contrary.

In conclusion, the company argued that the arbitrator must sustain the company's position because to sustain the union's position would require the arbitrator to well exceed the scope of his authority. The company closed by asking: How could an impartial arbitrator, who is limited to matters involving the application or interpretation of the agreement (he does not have the right to add to, subtract from, or modify the terms of the agreement), effect the sweeping change of unknown consequence inherent in the union's position?

Questions

1. Does this unusual situation allow the company to resort to its management's rights position?

2. If the union's proposal is accepted and Rickson is laid off, will he have a grievance?

3. What is the principle of waiver and estoppel that was used in the company's arguments?

4. If the arbitrator ruled in favor of the union, would the arbitrator's authority be exceeded?

5. You be the arbitrator. What is your decision?

Rockhard International and International Metal Workers of America, Local 125

Subject

Work assignments, subcontracting.

Issue

Is the company in violation of the agreement between the parties by utilizing contractor employees to perform much of its trash hauling operations?

Facts and Background

Rockhard International in 1974 purchased a facility constructed in 1970 by the Bathware Company, originally a highly automated grayiron bathtub foundry. After investing several months and $7 million to convert the facility to a gray and ductile iron automotive castings foundry, production started on a limited basis in October 1974 in order to supply many of the castings required by the company's automotive operation. At the time of the hearing, the plant operated two shifts with maintenance and cleanup work being done on the third shift. Many of the employees (approximately 80) who had originally worked for Bathware became Rockhard International employees. These employees came to Rockhard with all seniority rights when the company assumed the agreement then in existence.

On February 6, 1978, a situation existed that caused Otto H. Dollar to file grievance no. 26–78 on behalf of the employees, contending the following:

The company has recently bought a new truck, and contracted the operation of this vehicle to an outsider. He also operates front end loader and other equipment belonging to the company at the rate of $25 an hour. This job is classified under the yard dept. which at the present has men laid off—@ hourly rate of $4.52. [See Exhibit 1.]

Honor existing contract—Post job now being done by outsider Mr. Jim Atkinson.

On February 14, 1978, the company responded to the grievance with the following memorandum, signed by Tim P. Lyman:

The Company does not intend to fill the truck operator classification at this time. As you know, this classification has never been in use since January,

---

The authors thank Alex J. Simon, professor emeritus, consultant, arbitrator principal—A. J. Simon & Associates, Port Arthur, Texas—for providing this case. The names of people and places have been changed.

Exhibit 1
Hourly Rate Range[a]

Yard Department	Hourly Rate Range			
	Starting Minimum	After 60 Days	Maximum	Time Limit, Hours
Unloader	$4.24	$4.29	$4.48	12
Truck operator	4.24	4.29	4.52	24
Tractor operator	4.24	4.29	4.52	24
Painter	5.11	5.16	5.66	18
Janitor	4.19	4.22	4.48	12

[a]Effective May 16, 1977.

1974. **The recently purchased truck is being used by outside contractor J. Atkinson to remove waste materials for the plant and haul them to the dump. The Company sees no contract violation in this situation. However, his operation of the payloader in performing duties unrelated to his contract is improper, and will cease.**

Being unable to resolve the dispute through the negotiated grievance procedure, the parties appealed the case to arbitration. Both parties were allowed to present any evidence and/or exhibit they believed pertinent through witnesses, who testified under oath, and posthearing briefs in accordance with their understanding at the conclusion of the hearing.

Pertinent Contract Provisions

Article 2   Purpose
Section 1. **It is the general purpose of this Agreement to assure the continuous, efficient, economical, and profitable operation of the plant, enabling the Company to provide, so far as economic conditions may permit, security and continuity of employment; prevent strikes, slowdowns, and other disturbances which interfere with production; and set forth the basic agreements covering wages, hours of work, and conditions of employment to be observed by the parties.**

Article 3   Management
Section 1. **The Company has the right to manage the plant and to direct the working forces, except where such rights have been specifically waived in this Agreement. The Company will not exercise such rights in derogation of the rights of the Union or of the employees as those rights are set forth in this Agreement.**

Position of the Union

The union contended that its bargaining unit members had either loaded the truck for the previous contractors or at times actually operated the truck carrying trash to the dump. This practice had been going on since the company took over operations from the Bathware Company. While Sanitation, Inc. was the outside contractor hired to haul trash to the dumps, it used its own equipment and worked both inside and outside the plant. Rockhard employees working in the yard department drove the equipment at times, helped load trash, and performed all the related miscellaneous duties. When Sanitation's contract with the company expired, the company then signed a contract with Jim Atkinson to move the materials from the plant site to the dump. In this case, however, the company had purchased a new truck, and Atkinson had used the new truck and the payloader to remove slag and trash from around the cupola and to haul trash to the dump. During this time, four employees had been laid off from the yard department—employees who had normally performed this work.

It was the union's contention that the company was in error in contracting out work that was specified in the collective bargaining agreement. Since there were employees presently laid off, this was a violation of the agreement. The company should have posted this job for bids, allowed a bargaining employee to bid on such a job, and promoted an employee to the position of truck operator as designated in the agreement. Thus, the union believed the company had gone out of its way to erode the job presently held by employees of Rockhard by subcontracting this work. It requested that the grievance be deemed meritorious and that they be granted the relief sought.

Position of the Company

The company took the position that no violation of the agreement had taken place. Utilization of outside contractors had been an integral and important part of the operation since 1974 and a positive past practice had been established. While the union accused the employer of acting in bad faith, it presented no evidence to substantiate this charge.

The company had utilized contractor employees to perform a variety of duties since it began operations in 1974. Furthermore, there was no contract language that controlled, restricted, or prohibited this practice. The company denied that any of the existing employees had lost earnings as a result of the protested work arrangement, nor had any employee been displaced or laid off.

A decision in favor of the grievants based on the fact that there was a truck driver classification in the agreement was definitely not warranted. Mary Joseph, the payroll supervisor for the company, testified that no bargaining unit employee had filled the truck operator position since January 1974, when Rockhard took over the facilities. Furthermore, company testimony indicated that the time Atkinson spent in the company truck on a daily basis never exceeded two hours in any one day. While the union alleged that four employees had been laid off when Atkinson assumed the duties of subcontractor, a company witness, Jack Layford, testified that the reduction in force in the yard department was completely unrelated to the subcontracting of work.

In addition, the company contended that the union in this instance was asking the arbitrator to require the company to fill a position it had never filled before in order to perform duties that on the average required only two hours per day at the most. The fact that two previous cases had gone to arbitration on this subcontracting issue and that both arbitrators had ruled in favor of the company firmly upheld the company's position that a past practice had been established. Finally, there existed no mutual agreement, understanding, or practice that had precluded the company from using contractor employees.

Finally, the company pointed out that Article 3 of the agreement actually spelled out the right of the company to manage the plant and to direct the work forces—except where such rights have been previously and specifically waived in the agreement. Since the right to use contract workers had not been waived by the company and the evidence proved conclusively that the company had done so consistently since it started operating the facility, the practice in the present case did not violate the agreement, and, accordingly, the grievance should be denied.

Questions

1. On what basis do seniority rights transfer from Bathware to Rockhard?
2. What are the factors to consider in establishing past practice in subcontracting cases?
3. Of what value are the two previous arbitration awards favoring the company position?
4. How would you categorize the management rights clause in reference to Chapter 9?
5. What should be the arbitrator's decision? Give a justification for the decision.

Case 17

James Hope versus East Side Medical Clinic

Subject

Promotion and due process.

Issue

Did the employer follow its own personnel handbook rules? If not, did any deviation from such rules materially affect the promotion deliberations or the due process procedures in the present situation?

Facts and Background

This case arises under a provision in the personnel handbook of the East Side Medical Clinic. The grievant, James Hope, was employed on June 14, 1976, at the clinic in Fairfax, Virginia, as a food service worker I. The initial appointment was as a temporary replacement, full time, for another employee who was on leave. Hope was terminated on September 10, 1976, when the regular employee returned. On September 22, 1976, he returned to work on a part-time basis as a regular employee; on November 1 he was given full-time regular employee status.

During late February 1977, Hope ascertained that an employee in the department, Cathy Gant, would soon be taking a maternity leave. Discussion with the present supervisor, Allen Jackson, was held. On or about April 7, 1977, Gant resigned effective April 29, 1977. Hope and one other employee in the department applied for the higher level position of food preparation worker. The other employee, Renee Fulgham, was promoted on May 1, 1977, by the new supervisor, Daisy Pitts.

Hope filed his grievance under Section 16 (complaint and grievance procedure) of the East Side Clinic's current personnel handbook. The grievance was initiated on or about May 6, 1977, and was denied by the employer at each of the four steps in the established procedure.

Under the rules outlined in the handbook, the employee filed a demand for arbitration dated August 8, 1977, seeking employment as a food preparation worker retroactive to May 1, 1977, alleging that the rules of the personnel procedures were violated in his promotion case. On August 30, 1977, the employer answered the demand by denying that the rules of the personnel handbook procedures had been violated and that the grievant had not been wrongly denied an advancement.

The authors express appreciation to Jerald Robinson, Virginia Polytechnic and State University, for providing this unpublished case. The names of people and places have been changed.

Relevant Provisions of the Personnel Handbook

Section 13 Promotion and Transfer

The Personnel Office will make a continuing effort to assure that the filling of vacant or new positions by current employees shall take account of ability, skills, ingenuity, industry, seniority, and those other intangible factors which determine an employee's contribution to the Authority.

The Personnel Office shall *post open positions* and opportunities for promotion each week in conspicuous places for a period of one week. The posted positions shall contain the following information: Title of Job, Department, Schedule of Weekly Hours; Pay Grade; Minimum Qualifications; Date of Posting.

An employee who meets the minimum qualifications may apply for a position. The Personnel Office will interview all employee applicants who qualify.

Section II Confidentiality of and Access to Personnel Files

Letters of caution, consultation, warning, and reprimand shall be considered temporary contents of the personnel records and shall be removed and destroyed no later than two years after they have been placed in the records.

Position of the Employee

The employee, through his legal counsel, alleged that the employer's own rules of personnel procedure were violated by the employer's representatives and others so that he was improperly denied the promotion to food preparation worker. The rules violated included the rule on posting of open positions as well as the criteria for the filling of vacant positions. Both of these policies are found in Section 13 of the personnel handbook. Further provisions of the same section, relating to the interviewing process and the notification of applicants after the selection has been made, were also violated.

Hope also charged that Pitts attempted to intimidate him and did, in fact, threaten to harm him if he discussed the promotion denial further. He further claimed that during the early stages of the grievance procedure, he was offered a raise if he did not pursue the remaining steps of the procedure. Finally, the grievant alleged that the failure of the clinic president to hear and respond personally to the step 4 grievance substantially violated his due process rights.

Specifically, the employee suggested that several categories of handbook rule violations damaged his promotion chances:

1. Procedural errors in the process
   a. The supervisor, Pitts, changed the job content and the hours of work. This should have been noted on the posting. However, no posting was made—a violation of handbook rules. If

the posting had been made as required, the employee would have had the opportunity to respond in a more informed manner in the interview with the supervisor.

b. The supervisor chose Fulgham for the position prior to gaining access to the personnel records that would have shown Hope to be the more senior employee.

c. When the supervisor discussed the promotion question with the personnel director, James Lowrey, after she had conducted the interviews, the letter of "reprimand" or of "poor performance" or both (dated September 30, 1976) was used to damage the promotion chances of the grievant; the letter should have been disallowed as a promotion variable.

d. The president's failure to hear the grievance as required by the handbook damaged the employee's due process rights.

e. The personnel office is required to interview all applicants; it did not. This failure to follow the rules allowed the supervisor to show bias in her choice rather than being assured that all criteria were properly weighted.

2. Supervisor's selection criteria

a. The job was being restructured by the supervisor without clearance from the personnel office, and such actions are not permitted by supervisors acting alone.

b. The restructuring may actually have been a preselection technique.

3. Role of seniority

The grievant has been employed longer than the promoted worker and meets the minimum job requirements. His seniority was overlooked by the supervisor in the selection.

4. Intimidation and promises

When the supervisor advised Hope that the promotion had been given Fulgham, he was naturally disappointed. However, Pitts told him not to discuss the promotion further and that if he did, he "would be out the door." The grievant was offered a twenty cent hourly increase on his present job if the other applicant were to be selected; after her selection, he was again offered the raise if he would stop the grievance.

Position of the Employer

The employer, through its legal counsel, argued that the mandates of the personnel handbook were followed to the extent that any minor technical violation did not prejudice Hope, the grievant, in any fashion.

According to the personnel director, Lowrey, it is the practice of the employer to post all open positions unless it is evident that a promotion will be made from within that particular department. Since the job in question was other than an entry level position within the dietary department, he did not feel that persons outside the department would be both qualified and interested. Thus, it was not unusual in his view for there to have been no formal job posting in this present situation. Most employees knew before the new supervisor, Pitts, that Cathy Gant was planning to resign and not merely take maternity leave. The fact that both Hope and Fulgham did apply for the job indicates that the grievant's position was not endangered due to the absence of formal posting; the vacancy was openly discussed in the department. Hope did not even raise this issue until an intermediate step of the procedure.

The testimony of the new supervisor, Pitts, indicates that she discussed the promotion at least two times with the personnel director. Lowrey discussed the personnel files of both applicants with her on the phone due to the different physical locations of their offices and the centralized nature of the personnel files. The September 30th letter of reprimand to the grievant from Allen Jackson is significant, shows the employee's work problems with his supervisor, is relevant to the case, and should not be disallowed by the arbitrator.

The employer contended that the procedural matter of who hears the grievance is really immaterial to the case. Although the procedure does designate the president as the management representative in step 4, the employer's efforts to respond as quickly as possible and not delay the process was proper. The vice president for administration acted in the president's absence, and that was proper delegation. This was hardly a violation of the grievant's due process; if so, why then this arbitration hearing?

On the matter of the personnel office interviewing all applicants, the employee misread the policy statement. The requirement holds only in the case of transfers between departments. Otherwise, it would be impossible to talk with all applicants for promotion due to the personnel department's small staff size. The director of personnel indicated that he allows department heads to make the selection, as was done in this case. This is the practice within all parts of the employer's organization.

In regard to the selection criteria, Section 13 of the handbook lists seniority as only one of several factors to consider, certainly not the sole or dominant one. There is no policy or past practice that requires seniority to be the determining factor in promotions. In the interview, Pitts explained to each applicant that the job would be changed somewhat; Fulgham responded with enthusiasm and excitement to the challenge of the job, and the grievant showed no reaction and had few comments.

The employer argued that the role of the arbitrator, if he should decide that the procedures were not followed, would only be to require the employer to vacate the position and go through with the proper procedure. The arbitrator should not substitute his judgment of the relative merits of the two applicants for promotion for that of the employer.

Questions

1. Since there is no union, under what legal authority is this arbitration taking place?
2. Does this employee have the right to sue the employer because of alleged lack of due process?
3. Could the grievant pursue his grievance to the EEOC? Explain.
4. Should the grievance be upheld by the arbitrator? Why or why not?
5. How do the parties share the expenses of arbitration if there is no labor agreement specifying the rules?

Case 18

The Organizing Campaign at Hartsville University

Crunch

Joe Laurens, the election observer for the National Professors Association (NPA) union, listened as Hartsville University's tower clock struck 4:00. He saw the NLRB agent move to the door of the room in which the voting had taken place and turn the lock. The second day of voting by the faculty had ended; the election was over. Had the union won the right to represent Hartsville's faculty? The answer would come soon.

Joe looked down the list of eligible voters. Every name was initialed. All 117 members of the bargaining unit had voted! Was that good? Only time would tell.

The local chapter of the NPA had petitioned the NLRB for certification as the faculty's representative on November 20, 1979, and had accompanied the petition with seventy-two cards, signed by members of the faculty, requesting that the chapter be designated their bargaining agent. Now it was February 1, 1980. Like the rest of the organizing committee, Laurens knew that there had been some loss of zeal during the intervening time. Instead of the election being held before the Christmas break, as the NPA chapter had hoped, the university's attorney had successfully maneuvered to delay the balloting. Not only had he claimed that the NPA was not a union

The authors thank Asa Gardiner for providing this case. The names of people and places have been changed.

within the meaning of the Taft-Hartley Act (as amended), but he simultaneously had challenged the appropriateness of the bargaining unit as defined in the union's petition. Both motions were subsequently denied by the NLRB local examiner, and that decision was confirmed by the region; however, it resulted in the Direction of Election not being issued by the NLRB until January 2, 1980, and the voting dates being set for January 31 and February 1. "Contracts for the next academic year are due to be tendered next week, too," thought Laurens. "That isn't a plus for the union."

Frank Jeffries, the NLRB agent, took out the box in which the previous day's ballots had been sealed and began to cut away the tape that the administration's observer, Roger Beatty, and Laurens had carefully signed the previous day. He opened the box and began to tally the votes under the watchful eyes of both observers. "Union, no union, union, union, no union, no union," Jeffries intoned aloud. Laurens realized that the vote was going to be very, very close. The organizing committee had felt that it had at least 60 percent of the vote when the balloting started. Had something gone wrong? As the counting proceeded, Laurens' mind raced back over the events that had led to the organizing campaign.

Background

Hartsville University, a private university located in a suburb of a growing, busy product distribution center, is one of a number of small liberal arts colleges that dot the country. Attractively situated on a multi-acre wooded site with a lake view, the campus is a special point of interest to Hartsville visitors. HU's enrollment is larger than that of most "small" institutions. At the time of the organizing campaign, there were about 2,400 students, down from an all-time high of nearly 3,200 two years earlier.

HU was born during the Great Depression. Jules Perrot, one of the community's leading citizens, and some of his business friends started it as a two-year night college. It gradually increased in size but remained relatively undistinguished until the 1950s, when the purchase of a large tract of land by the trustees and generous financing from a local industrialist enabled it to move to the present site and to expand into a full four-year accredited institution. The addition of a master of arts in teaching degree provided the basis for the university designation.

Programs of study leading to the bachelor's degree are offered in some thirty areas of the liberal arts, the fine arts, the sciences, premedicine, predentistry, prelaw, physical education, business administration, and education. Of the students receiving degrees, however, more than half come from the combined areas of business and education.

The student body is composed of two groups, about equally divided in number: Day students from the community are in the slight majority; the remainder are resident students drawn from some thirty states and a few foreign countries.

Administratively, HU is governed by a large board of trustees, the president, the vice-presidents of academic affairs and of financial affairs, the deans of the college of fine arts and of arts and sciences, and seven division chairpersons appointed by the president.

The faculty, including librarians, physical education instructors, and the seven division chairpersons (who teach only a half load) number 126. However, when administrators who hold faculty status are added, the number swells to 164. More than 60 percent of the faculty holds earned doctorates, a fact stressed frequently by the administration. It is essentially a faculty of teachers. Course loads are a minimum of twelve semester hours, with three class preparations being the norm. Some professors teach fifteen semester hours in fields where they feel that small class size is important to the learning process. The HU catalog emphasizes the faculty's concern with classroom teaching. In point of fact, there is virtually no time for research and publication. Only a very few of the faculty have produced any work of note. Salary levels, as reported by the NPA annually, are consistently in the lower quartile, and the university has not attracted any outstanding scholars. HU depends on student tuition and fees for about two-thirds of its income, and increases in faculty salaries are customarily coupled with higher tuition. HU's endowment is small; donors give buildings but not the funds to staff and maintain them.

The management style of the administration has tended strongly toward the autocratic. Tight control rests in the trustees and the president. University governance is nonparticipative. There existed at the time of the case a nineteen-member Faculty Administration Council on which six elected representatives of the faculty served. But the FAC's role is strictly advisory. It makes no decisions. In any case, the seven division chairpersons who serve automatically on the FAC weight the balance whenever issues about which the administration holds strong views arise.

Development of the Issues

HU's enrollment for the fall semester of 1979 was down about 15 percent from the previous year's. Administrative response was quick and sharp. Without prior consultation with the general faculty, but with the assistance of the seven division chairpersons, the number of teaching faculty for the next academic year was immediately reduced so as to bring the budget into balance. Several young, able faculty members who had been hired in 1977 were notified by the third week in September that their contracts would not be renewed. The administration announced that several existing vacancies would not be filled and that retirees would not be replaced. It became apparent that there would not be a proportionate cut in administrative staff.

Not only was the faculty aroused, but there was spontaneous student reaction. Resident students held mass meetings and demanded an evaluation of possible alternative courses of action. Concurrently, at a stormy faculty meeting, ten representatives were elected for a similar purpose. The groups then combined at a formal meeting on October 9, elected cochairpersons as their only officers, adopted the name "Student-Faculty Committee on Alternatives," and proceeded to establish fact-finding subcommittees: alternatives in budget, new sources of funds, student recruitment, student retention, and faculty workload.

These subcommittees worked diligently but unfruitfully. The trustees refused to provide any financial information, even after a two-hour meeting with representatives of the Committee on Alternatives. The committee's final report on October 27 was largely an exercise in futility. About the only tangible result was prompt administrative action to remove the garbage collecting bin from under the students' dormitory windows!

Many of the young faculty members whose contracts were not being renewed were active members of the NPA chapter, which now became the only organized change agent possible. For several years, the chapter had been urging the HU administration to enlarge the role of the faculty in university governance in accordance with long-standing principles of the national association. A faculty-administration-trustee committee had been named in 1975, had met spasmodically, and had been quietly placed in limbo by the administration in early 1977. Faculty representation on the FAC was increased from three to six members as a result of chapter pressure, and a committee was appointed in 1979 to revise the faculty bylaws, which were badly outdated. There was no other action.

Collective bargaining had been endorsed by the NPA national as an additional way of realizing the association's goals in higher education. It became a more and more appealing avenue of action as the days dragged on and the administration continued to ignore requests for a detailed explanation of the rationale for its action in reducing faculty size.

A meeting of all teaching and research faculty called by the leadership of the NPA chapter on November 1 provided a forum for discussion of the issues. The faculty members at a chapter meeting held the same day decided to test the will of the entire HU faculty in regard to collective bargaining. A broad-based organizing committee was quickly formed; representation authorization cards were obtained, and instructions for organizers (Exhibit 1) were prepared and distributed with the cards.

Exhibit 1
Instructions for
Organizers

```
                        Instructions for Organizers


    1.  Here are ten (10) representation cards and envelopes.  There are more
        where these came from, so don't hold back in your efforts.

    2.  The faculty member should make out his or her own card, place it in the
        envelope, and seal it.  The envelope can then be opened only by an
        NLRB examiner.

    3.  Write the name of the faculty member very lightly in pencil in the upper
        right-hand corner of the envelope.  It will be erased later so that
        the signer will remain anonymous.

    4.  DO NOT LET THE CARDS OUT OF YOUR HANDS EXCEPT FOR SIGNING.

    5.  Return the sealed envelopes to the organizer in your division who
        enlisted you.

    6.  It is necessary to obtain signatures from at least 50 percent (50%)
        of the faculty right now, so be your most persuasive.

    7.  Here are some arguments you may want to use if you encounter resistance:

        a.  After the cards have been signed and an agreement has been reached,
            the faculty will be able to run its own affairs.  Hence, organizing
            assures faculty freedom and participation in governance.

        b.  Two styles of management are available to administrators:

            1.  autocratic/dictatorial
            2.  democratic/participative

            If the faculty member recognizes our type of administration as
            being autocratic, then the only protection he or she has as an
            individual is to organize.

        c.  Faculty on tenure have much greater security than other faculty,
            but will they deny the benefits of solidarity to others by not signing?

    8.  Remember that any discussion initiated by any administrative personnel
        regarding the signing of representation authorization cards is an unfair
        labor practice under the Labor Management Relations (Taft-Hartley) Act.
        If anyone asks, "Are you planning to sign?" or "Have you signed?"
        or makes any similar inquiry, be sure to keep a record of the exact
        words used, the time and place they were used, and the name of the
        person making the inquiry.

    9.  Ask that your division meeting be terminated a few minutes early so you
        will be free to discuss the possibility of organizing.  If the division
        chairperson refuses to leave the room, or if you move to another room
        and he or she follows you, this also is an unfair labor practice.

   10.  GO TO IT!
```

By November 4, more than half the faculty in the prospective bargaining unit had signed, 20 percent more than the minimum required by the Labor Management Relations (Taft-Hartley) Act (as amended). A special meeting of the chapter was therefore called for November 9, at which time the chapter would vote to offer itself to the teaching and research faculty as their collective bargaining representative.

More than two-thirds of the active members of the chapter attended the meeting. The vote was almost unanimous for the chapter to proceed with a collective bargaining effort. The organizing committee was officially named, and approval was given for it to contact the president of HU to inform him of the chapter's action.

The Campaign

The committee met with the president on November 10. It informed him about the chapter's action and told him that more than half the faculty had requested it to represent them. The president was polite but said he could make no reply until he had consulted with the trustees.

An official reply (Exhibit 2) was received on November 17. It dashed any hope of a consent election. Its phrasing, according to a professor who taught labor management relations, indicated that it had been dictated by an attorney specializing in labor law. The chapter accordingly filed a "Petition for Certification of Representative" with the local office of the NLRB on November 20. The definition of the proposed bargaining unit purposely excluded the seven appointed division chairpersons. Six members of the library staff were also left out of the unit, with the idea that they would be included if the administration challenged the appropriateness of the unit. On the same day, the chapter organizing committee distributed a memorandum (Exhibit 3) to each member of the faculty; it gave the expected chronology of the collective bargaining election process.

A series of letters now flowed from the president of HU to each member of the faculty. The letters began on December 1 and continued through January 29. The December 1 letter explained the recognition process. It associated collective bargaining with "blue collar" activities and urged faculty members to learn all they could about the unionization of faculties. It suggested that any problems existing at HU could best be solved "without interjecting a union between the faculty and the administration."

A longer letter, dated December 5, stressed the loss of the faculty member's individual rights should the NPA chapter become the bargaining representative. It stated that terms of faculty contracts could no longer reflect the individual professors' abilities and per-

Exhibit 2
President's Official
Reply

17 November 1979

Dr. Duncan Black, President
Hartsville University Chapter
National Professors Association
Hartsville University

Dear Dr. Black:

The purpose of this letter is to respond to the comments you made to me during our meeting on November 10, 1979, in which you stated that on November 9, 1979, the Hartsville University chapter of the National Professors Association had taken action to form a collective bargaining unit, that 50 percent of the full-time teaching faculty had indicated their desire to form such a unit, and that the NPA wished to engage in collective bargaining.

We do not believe that you represent the faculty of Hartsville University, and thus we are unwilling to recognize you as their bargaining representative until your status is resolved by an election conducted by the National Labor Relations Board.

Whether or not it is ultimately determined that you are the representative of the faculty members of Hartsville University, we will, of course, respect our faculty members' rights under the National Labor Relations Act.

Very truly yours,

Thomas A. Daniels
President

TAD: B

formance. Individual complaints, it said, might be compromised by the union grievance process no matter how meritorious they were. It claimed that collective bargaining would introduce "an adversary process which is wholly incompatible with the traditional university ideal of a community of scholars." Furthermore, it noted, the presence of a union on the campus would have an adverse effect on donations, contributions, and grants. The letter closed by asking each faculty member to give careful consideration to the question of whether a union would be in his or her best interest.

The chapter countered these two letters with a memorandum rebutting each point raised. It made frequent reference to the official publications of the NPA and to chapter statements on policy. The memo touched on two matters not covered in the president's letters: the adoption of new faculty bylaws as an alternative to collective

Exhibit 3
Expected Chronology
of the Election
Process

DATE: November 20, 1979

TO: The Faculty of Hartsville University

FROM: HU Chapter NPA

SUBJECT: Chronology of Collective Bargaining Election

In accordance with an earlier memorandum, the NPA chapter now estimates that the collective bargaining election process will follow the approximate pattern shown below. Unopposed recognition of the chapter as bargaining agent will shorten the process, whereas determined opposition will stretch it out.

10 November: NPA organizing committee asked President Daniels to recognize the chapter as the collective bargaining agent. No official reply was given.

17 November: President Daniels refused to recognize the chapter as agent.

20 November: Petition for Certification of Representative has been filed with the National Labor Relations Board (NLRB). The NLRB examiner privately checked the representation authorization cards signed by members of the faculty and submitted with the petition to make sure that more than 30 percent of the members of the prospective bargaining unit want the NPA chapter to represent them.

December: The NLRB will investigate the chapter's definition of the bargaining unit ("full-time teachers/researchers").

The NLRB will decide on the bargaining unit and eligibility of voters.

The NLRB will set an election date, ballot, and place.

January: A secret ballot election by members of the bargaining unit, as defined by the NLRB, will be held. The NLRB will conduct the election on campus in accordance with prior notice. A ballot booth will be set up, and balloting will be Secret. Ballots will be placed in a locked box and will remain in the possession of the NLRB. Only the voter will know how he or she votes. Results will be announced after the ballots have been counted by the NLRB.

You will be kept informed about the progress.

THE ORGANIZING COMMITTEE

Duncan Black
Eugene Grady
Samuel Jacobs
Joseph Laurens
Arthur McDearmon

bargaining and the decertification of the union if the faculty became disenchanted with collective bargaining.

During the next few weeks, there was a lull in the flow of written material. The administration's motion to dismiss the chapter's petition on the ground that the NPA was not a union and its challenge as to the appropriateness of the bargaining unit as defined by the union led to a day-long hearing before the local NLRB examiner. The motion to dismiss was denied. The chapter agreed to include the six librarians and succeeded in excluding the seven administration appointed division chairpersons, holding that they were in fact supervisors under the terms of the Labor Management Relations Act. NPA national provided skilled legal assistance for the hearing and for the subsequent preparation of briefs to be submitted to the regional director for review. The examiner's decision, confirmed by the region, was announced January 2, 1980, three weeks after the hearing.

In a letter dated January 3, the president responded to the basic questions raised at the hearing. He pointed out that whereas the NPA had long been a professional association, it was now a labor union, regardless of what the chapter might say. The letter reemphasized the question of the adversary relationship and deplored the fact that four administrative officers and five faculty members had been tied up for a whole day, noting that they could have made "much better use of their time by performing their normal duties." It stated again that collective bargaining simply did not fit the economic conditions existing at HU and invited faculty cooperation in overcoming the current problems.

This letter drew a sharply worded, one-page response from the chapter (Exhibit 4). It said that it was the administration which was to blame for having created an adversary relationship and for having wasted time at the hearing. The administration had failed to plan properly for declining enrollment. Collective bargaining was necessary to check the downward spiral.

The chapter also put out a question-answer type memorandum on the same day, January 10, dealing mostly with the issues raised by the president's letter of December 5. It contained facts and made reference to a publication of the NLRB, *A Layman's Guide to Basic Law under the National Labor Relations Act*, published in 1976. It also quoted from the collective bargaining agreement which the faculty of St. Johns University, New York, had reached with its administration, copies of which had been distributed to each faculty member at HU.

Exhibit 4
NPA Response to
January 3 Letter

HARTSVILLE UNIVERSITY

TO: The Faculty   January 10, 1979

    With reference to the president's letter to you of January 3, you
may be interested in the following facts:

    1. The regional director of the National Labor Relations Board
on January 2, 1979, issued a decision denying the administration's contentions regarding the composition of the voting unit for collective bargaining at HU.

    2. The "adversary" nature of the NLRB hearing was entirely the
result of the administration's determination not to yield on any points
at issue. Specifically, the administration insisted on trying to pack
the voting unit with the division Chairpersons, although the NLRB position on
division chairpersons voting in a faculty election had been clearly and repeatedly stated in a series of landmark decisions: Where the division
Chairpersons "make recommendations on hiring and change of status" of faculty
members, they are excluded from the voting unit. The NLRB decision to exclude such people from our voting unit was cut and dried. It merely recited
the obvious fact that our division Chairpersons had made recommendations
regarding termination of faculty and cited landmark cases. It was indeed a
waste of time and money for the administration to argue the point. We could
not agree more! Let us all hope that the administration will approach its
obligations under the forthcoming election and ensuing events with greater
concern for university resources and without further futile adversary action.

    3. With respect to the statement, "Collective bargaining cannot
make more funds available to the University," nothing is further from the
truth. Many students have already left because of the administration's
failure both to plan properly for declining enrollment and to permit full
student and faculty participation in exploring and passing judgment on
alternative solutions to the problems which continue to plague us. More
students will leave unless full and genuine participation is implemented
before the end of this term and unless better solutions than the simplistic
ones of cutting off personnel and raising tuition are found. The Committee
on Alternatives was a step in the right direction, but it was completely
frustrated by the refusal of the administration and the trustees to cooperate.
Short of collective bargaining, any further efforts to secure full faculty and
student participation in university affairs which affect them will surely fail
and will make bad matters worse. Only collective bargaining can bring about
the balance between the administration on the one hand and students and faculty
on the other which is absolutely necessary to check the downward spiral in
enrollment.

                                        THE ORGANIZING COMMITTEE

                                        HU Chapter NPA

A chapter memorandum of January 12 continued the question-answer response to the administration's statements. However, it went beyond response in two areas. It brought up the possibility of meaningful faculty bylaws as a substitute for collective bargaining, pointing out that they could be made part of the collective bargaining agreement. It also raised the question of voting at faculty meetings by thirty-two administrators who had no teaching, research, or library responsibilities.

The next letter from the president was dated January 18. It gave the administration's view of the December 11 NLRB hearing in response to the chapter's sharp criticism of January 10. "Any attempt on this campus to draw a rigid distinction between 'administration' and 'faculty' is artificial," the letter stated. The distinction, it claimed, was indicative of the harmful effects of possible faculty unionization. The letter expressed a desire for faculty participation in university problem solving and mentioned that the draft of new faculty bylaws was currently being discussed by the Faculty Administration Council. A union could well decrease the opportunity for meaningful faculty participation in governance, it added.

On January 19, the chapter answered questions about collective bargaining which had been asked during the intervening week—questions about the equality of women faculty, the recovery of "banked" teaching credit hours lost when HU had shifted from a teaching load of fifteen semester hours to that of twelve, and the possible future participation of division chairpersons in the bargaining unit.

The president's letter of January 26 seemed to take advantage of any derogatory information about the union which has been revealed in investigation or publicity. It gave excerpts from the speech of the outgoing NPA president, made at the 1979 annual meeting, in which he expressed serious reservations about the association's endorsement of collective bargaining. The letter also talked about the damage a faculty strike might cause to HU as well as about the divisive nature of the collective bargaining process itself. It closed with the hope that the faculty members would vote "no union" at the election on January 31 and February 1.

The union's response came on January 29. It quoted NPA official policy relative to strikes. It focused attention on the administration's use of excerpts out of context, noting that, after debate, the NPA annual meeting had endorsed collective bargaining by a vote of 373 to 54. The letter stated that while collective bargaining could not have prevented the drop in enrollment, it could have prevented the administration's unilateral action in reducing faculty size. It asked the faculty to give serious consideration to how it would vote.

The last word came from the president. In a letter dated January 29 but distributed January 30, he repeated each of the major points made in the earlier communications. He pointed to the progress that was being made in increasing faculty participation in the governance of the university. He said that that goal could best be achieved by the adoption of reasonable bylaws. He explained that the presence of a union would reduce the responsiveness of the community to appeals for much needed gifts and bequests. "A vote for unionization will seriously impair our unity and weaken our financial base," the letter continued. "The decision is now yours. I know that you will consider it carefully and will vote your honest conviction about what is best for you and the university."

The Tally

Now they had cast their votes! Joe Laurens felt uneasy as Frank Jeffries opened the box in which today's ballots had been placed and continued to count. The numbers swung inexorably toward "no union"; when the last vote was tallied, it stood union 52, no union 65. The campaign was over. Twenty faculty members who had signed representation authorization cards had voted against the chapter!

Questions

1. What caused the faculty to initiate actions that eventually led to an NLRB election?
2. Under what authority does the NLRB have jurisdiction for accepting a petition for an election from faculty members?
3. Examine the administration's reaction to the campaign. Compare it to behavior at a local manufacturing plant.
4. Why was the union's organizing campaign a failure?

Exercise

Collective Bargaining Negotiations Exercise: QFM Company and IWU

Learning Objectives

1. To gain an understanding of negotiation preparations, actual negotiations, and assessment of negotiations outcomes.
2. To develop an appreciation for the psychological influences and the realism of contract negotiations.
3. To learn the mechanics of give-and-take, compromise, and trading issues and to practice the art of negotiations.
4. To familiarize the participants with the issues in collective bargaining and the difficulty of writing provisions to the satisfaction of both parties.
5. To realize the importance of and problems associated with teamwork in a bargaining situation.

Exercise

Rules of the Negotiations Exercise

1. Participants must not discuss the exercise with anyone except team members.
2. Each participant will be assigned a role (organization position) by the instructor.
3. The negotiations must take place within the framework of the present company and union. Creativity is encouraged, but a realistic and pragmatic approach is recommended.
4. Data, materials, and information used for each position or argument on behalf of a proposal should not be falsified.
5. Each team may have as many meetings outside of class as are needed and desirable.
6. Team members must follow the instructions of their respective team leaders.
7. All activities of team members should be directed toward negotiating an agreement that is mutually acceptable and that the parties can live with for the next period.

Instructions to the Participant

1. Each participant will be assigned to either the management or the union team. An organization position will be assigned to each person.
2. The team leaders—the president of the Industrial Workers United (IWU) of the AFL-CIO and the industrial relations director of Quality Manufacturing Company—will call separate meetings to discuss and prepare for the upcoming negotiations and anticipate each other's proposals.

   Major issues for negotiations should include:
   a. Union security, checkoff, union shop
   b. Wages, classes, premiums
   c. Management's rights
   d. Promotions and layoffs (use of seniority)
   e. Grievance procedure and arbitration
   f. Affirmative action plans
   g. Pension plans
   h. Supplemental unemployment benefits
   i. Vacations
   j. Holidays
   k. Sick leave
   l. Other issues allowed by instructor
3. In the preparatory meeting, each team will study the present agreement, identify its problems, and gather materials, data, and information to justify the team's proposals and positions.
4. Based on study, analysis, strategy, and plans, each team will complete Form I and give it to the instructor. (The form is not to be shown to anyone else.)

Form I

Bargaining Priority (1 = Most Important, 2 = Second Most Important, and so on)	Subject Area for Negotiations (Brief Description)	Proposals to Other Party (First Day)	Realistic Objective for Negotiations	Actual Accomplishment (to Be Completed after Negotiations)

5. The union president and the industrial relations director and their respective teams will meet at a time specified by the instructor for the purpose of negotiating a new agreement. Union will present its proposals first. Then management will present its proposals and/or counterproposals.
6. Actual negotiations will begin after the proposals are exchanged and will continue until a new agreement is negotiated and signed or the present contract expires. (The instructor will specify time periods.)
7. Upon completion of the negotiations, each team will determine the annual total costs (anticipated) of the new agreement.
8. Additional instructions will be given the participants by the instructor.

Government publications: U.S. Department of Labor, Bureau of Labor Statistics. *Area Wage Surveys, Employment and Earnings, Handbook of Labor Statistics,* and *Characteristics of Major Collective Bargaining Agreements.* Washington, D.C.: Government Printing Office.

Binder services of Bureau of National Affairs, Commerce Clearing House, and Prentice-Hall. Especially helpful are the BNA *Collective Bargaining Negotiations and Contracts.*

Business Publications: *Business Week* and *Wall Street Journal.*

Professional industrial relations journals: *American Federationist, Arbitration Journal, Employee Relations Law Journal, Industrial and Labor Relations Review, Industrial Relations, Industrial Relations Law Journal, Journal of Collective Negotiations in the Public Sector, Labor Law Journal,* and *Monthly Labor Review.*

Proceedings: Industrial Relations Research Association, Labor Law Developments, National Academy of Arbitrators, and NYU Conference on Labor.

Labor agreements between companies and labor unions (as available).

**Furniture
Manufacturing
Industry**

The furniture industry can be characterized as a "highly competitive, nonintegrative industry composed largely of small and medium-sized, family controlled business."[1] Net profits in 1979 were $328 million, or 4 percent of the $8.8 billion in total sales. While the industry in 1979 consisted of 1,200 companies, only 50 were publicly held, and most of the others were family operated. The latter showed little inclination to adopt efficiencies already common in other manufacturing industries. Furniture manufacturers still operate only one shift and remain highly labor-intensive. Quality of workmanship and craftsmanship have been their goal, and much of the work is still done by hand to give the products their distinctiveness.[2] The industry is intensely competitive.

While plants are scattered throughout the United States, two thirds are located in the Southeast, the Middle Atlantic, and the Great Lakes regions. Since the Pacific Coast has an ample supply of

[1]Wickham Skinner and David C. D. Rogers, *Manufacturing Policy in the Furniture Industry,* 3rd. ed. (Homewood, Ill.: Richard D. Irwin, 1968), p. 1.
[2]"Why Furniture Makers Feel So Comfortable," *Business Week,* July 30, 1979, p. 76.

softwood and hardwood, more plants are currently locating there. Manufacturers using plastics and metals (rather than wood) in their furniture are able to locate more closely to their markets and have therefore spread throughout the country.

Products are distributed over fairly wide geographic areas, and 70 percent of the output is sold directly to retailers. Brand names and product line identity are important to some of the larger manufacturers, but there are problems of design copying and enormous pressures for frequent restyling.[3]

Even though sales are very sensitive to economic conditions, the U.S. furniture manufacturers have several reasons to be optimistic about the 1980s. First, the thirty to thirty-nine age group, which spends more money per capita on furniture than any other group, will increase by 26.2 percent during the 1980s. Second, the uncertainty of gasoline availability and its soaring prices will cause many consumers to redirect their leisuretime recreation to home-related activities. Also, since the automobile may not be a prestige possession in the 1980s, household items may be substituted as status symbols. Third, the continuing trend toward two-income families will enable families to make more expensive purchases. If consumer and population age shift predictions are accurate, not only more but more expensive furniture will be bought.[4]

The QFM Company and the Union

QFM Company began in 1820 in Laconia, New Hampshire, as a family-owned and operated furniture manufacturer. It was headed by Herman Sweeny, one of the early settlers in Laconia. The company grew to 30 employees by 1920, but at that time B. F. Sweeny, Herman's son, decided to move the firm to St. Louis, Missouri—a location more central to the firm's market. Barely surviving the 1930s depression, QFM was one of the first companies to convert its manufacturing processes to the production of war materials. The company prospered during the war, and afterwards Sweeny decided to expand, sell stock publicly, and focus on producing metal and plastic-laminated furniture. With the production experience it had gained during the war and with its location some distance from the predominantly wood furniture manufacturers, QFM Company launched a new era for itself in 1946.

[3]Skinner and Rogers, *Manufacturing Policy*, pp. 2–12.
[4]"Why Furniture Makers Feel So Comfortable," pp. 75–76.

Exercise

By 1970, the St. Louis plant had 1,300 employees and was producing 450 dinette sets, 200 sets of lawn tables and chairs, and 300 bar stools and miscellaneous furniture daily. Then came the 1971–1973 furniture boom, with its expectations of continuous growth. QFM's new president, Gerald Brooks, decided that a new, modern plant and more diversity in the product line were necessary to meet the expected demand. Taking into consideration location, material supply, transportation, markets, labor situations, and other factors, Brooks decided to build the new plant in Dallas, Texas. This plant was to specialize in the new product lines, and the St. Louis plant was to concentrate only on dinette sets. In 1972, 200 employees were transferred from St. Louis, and another 200 were hired from the Dallas–Fort Worth area. The Dallas plant started with no union and 400 employees. By 1979, it had grown to an 800-employee work force, still with no union. It pays its Dallas employees at least $1 less per hour than it pays the St. Louis workers in comparable jobs. The St. Louis plant continues to produce 450 dinette sets per day, mostly for chain retailers, and employs about 1,100 workers. No new product lines have been added at the St. Louis plant, and its employment level is only slightly more than the level in pre-1970 days. The Dallas plant has started producing a new product line—dinette sets under the Eagle brand name. Consumer response has been positive, and the Dallas plant's future looks very promising.

Throughout its history, QFM Company has prided itself on being a progressive employer; however, recent events—building the Dallas plant, increasing employment in Dallas while lowering it in St. Louis, paying QFM workers in St. Louis less than comparable area wages (Dallas workers were paid $1 less than St. Louis workers)—resulted in an NLRB representation election for the Industrial Workers United Union in 1975. After a heated campaign by both management and the union, NLRB investigations of unfair labor practices, and challenged ballots, the union lost the election by a vote of 497 to 481. Two years later, the union returned and won the election by a vote of 611 to 375. The election campaign was bitter, and the negotiations that followed were even bitterer. After a six-week strike, the following labor agreement was signed. Although the company officials now express a commitment to return to the era where management and labor trusted each other, worked cooperatively, and shared mutual goals and benefits, the union leaders are reacting by waiting to see their deeds. The upcoming negotiations will determine the company's commitment.

	Assets	
Exhibit 1	Current assets:	
QFM Company Balance	Cash	$ 1,073,600
Sheet, 1979	Notes and accounts receivable	24,824,800
	Inventories	31,365,600
	Prepaid expenses	411,200
	Total current assets	$57,675,200
	Fixed assets:	
	Land	5,000,000
	Buildings	12,500,000
	Machinery and equipment	9,819,600
	Total fixed assets	$27,319,600
	Total assets	$84,994,800
	Liabilities and Stockholders' Investment	
	Current liabilities:	
	Notes and accounts payable	$ 8,254,400
	Accrued payroll	3,300,000
	Taxes (local, state, federal)	26,500,000
	Total current liabilities	$38,054,400
	Stockholders' investment:	
	Common stock (common @ $20 per share)	$20,000,000
	Earned surplus	26,940,400
	Total stockholders' investment and earned surplus	$46,940,400
	Total liabilities and stockholders' investment	$84,994,800

		1978	1979
Exhibit 2	Net sales	$96,006,956	$105,607,750
QFM Company	Cost of goods sold:		
Income Statement	Production (labor, materials, overhead, etc.)	77,400,125	80,859,270
	Administrative	6,500,200	7,010,400
	Sales	3,200,000	4,200,000
	Other	812,213	921,400
	Total cost of goods sold	$87,912,538	$ 92,991,070
	Income before taxes	$ 8,094,418	$ 12,616,688
	Taxes (local, state, federal)	−2,334,000	−3,112,000
	Net income	$ 5,760,418	$ 9,504,688

		Net Sales	Net Earnings
Exhibit 3	1977	$ 90,572,600	$7,245,808
QFM Company Net	1978	96,006,956	5,760,418
Sales and Earnings	1979	105,607,750	9,504,688
	1980 (estimated)	109,775,978	3,263,276

Exhibit 4
Number of QFM
Production and
Maintenance
Employees by
Seniority in St. Louis
and Dallas Plants

Years	St. Louis	Dallas
0–1	55	120
1–2	35	90
2–3	60	130
3–4	55	135
4–5	45	148
5–10	205	110
10–15	200	25
15–20	105	20
20–25	120	10
25–30	152	10
30 or more	68	2
	1,100	800[a]

[a]Includes those transferring from St. Louis.

Exhibit 5
Number of QFM
Employees in Each
Job Title, by Wage
Grade

Wage Grade	Job Title	St. Louis	Dallas
1	Janitor	12	8
2	General laborer	34	30
3	Materials handler	52	42
4	Packer	40	32
	Machine operator–B	128	110
	Utility worker	42	20
	Interplant truck driver	18	16
	Sander	46	38
	Assembler	320	302
5	Welder	18	6
	Machine operator–A	122	62
	Electrician–B	6	6
	Maintenance worker–B	12	6
	Gluer	62	31
6	Mechanic	12	6
	Spray painter	48	32
	Cutoff saw operator	29	16
7	Electrician–A	16	6
	Maintenance worker–A	12	6
	Inspector	28	16
8	Tool grinder–A	5	3
9	Tool and die maker–A	12	6
10	Leadman	26	0
		1,100	800

Exhibit 6 Average Hourly Earnings, Excluding Overtime, for All Manufacturing Employees		1978	1979
	Total	$5.75	$6.28
	Durable goods	6.12	6.67
	Lumber and wood products	5.17	5.57
	Furniture and fixtures	4.41	4.81
	Stone, clay, and glass products	5.77	6.27
	Primary metal industries	7.59	8.32
	Fabricated metal products	5.93	6.44
	Machinery, except electrical	6.29	6.82
	Electric and electronic equipment	5.50	5.96
	Transportation equipment	7.29	7.94
	Instruments and related products	5.43	5.83
	Miscellaneous manufacturing industries	4.47	4.82
	Nondurable goods	5.19	5.63
	Food and kindred products	5.43	5.85
	Tobacco manufacturers	6.10	6.68
	Textile mill products	3.99	4.33
	Apparel and other textile products	3.82	4.13
	Paper and allied products	5.97	6.51
	Printing and publishing	6.11	6.49
	Chemicals and allied products	6.56	7.05
	Petroleum and coal products	8.14	8.87
	Rubber and miscellaneous plastic products	5.11	5.58
	Leather and leather products	3.76	4.10

Figures are for March of each year.

Source: U.S. Department of Labor, Bureau of Labor Statistics, *Employment and Earnings, May 1979* (Washington, D.C.: Government Printing Office, June 1979), p. 100.

Exhibit 7 Average Earnings for Selected Occupations in St. Louis, Missouri, and Dallas, Texas	Occupation	St. Louis (March 1978)	Dallas (October 1978)
	Automotive mechanics	$8.25	$7.59
	Carpenters	7.81	7.66
	Electricians	8.69	7.98
	Helpers, trades	7.62	6.24
	Machine-tool operators (toolroom)	7.85	7.31
	Machinists	8.53	7.57
	Painters	8.09	7.85
	Forklift operators	7.11	6.48
	Janitors	6.31	5.07
	Tool and die makers	8.86	8.60

Sources: The St. Louis data are from U.S. Department of Labor, Bureau of Labor Statistics, *Area Wage Survey, St. Louis, Missouri–Illinois Metropolitan Area, March 1978* (Washington, D.C.: Government Printing Office, 1978), pp. 16–25. The Dallas data are from U.S. Department of Labor, Bureau of Labor Statistics, *Area Wage Survey, Dallas–Fort Worth, Texas, Metropolitan Area, October 1978* (Washington, D.C.: Government Printing Office, 1979), pp. 20–24.

Exercise

Exhibit 8 Average Gross Hours and Earnings of Production Workers on Manufacturing Payrolls, 1976–1979	St. Louis			Dallas		
	Weekly Earnings	Weekly Hours	Hourly Earnings	Weekly Earnings	Weekly Hours	Hourly Earnings
1976	$243.05	40.4	$6.01	$189.60	40.6	$4.67
1977	268.79	41.1	6.54	205.44	40.6	5.06
1978 (March)	283.46	41.2	6.89	218.65	41.1	5.32
1979 (March)	303.97	40.7	7.36	236.96	40.3	5.88

U.S. Department of Labor, Bureau of Labor Statistics, *Employment and Earnings, May 1979* (Washington, D.C.: Government Printing Office, June 1979), p. 111.

Exhibit 9 Consumer Price Index for Urban Wage Earners and Clerical Workers and Percent Changes, 1967–1979	Year	Index	Percent Change
	1967	100	—
	1968	104.2	4.2
	1969	109.8	5.4
	1970	116.3	5.9
	1971	121.3	4.3
	1972	125.3	3.3
	1973	133.1	6.2
	1974	147.7	11.0
	1975	161.2	9.1
	1976	170.5	5.8
	1977	181.5	6.5
	1978	195.3	7.6
	1979 Jan.	204.7	
	Feb.	207.1	
	Mar.	209.1	

Source: U.S. Department of Labor, Bureau of Labor Statistics, *Monthly Labor Review* 102 (June 1979), p. 77.

Exhibit 10 Average Gross Hours and Earnings of Manufacturing Production Workers and Furniture Production Workers, 1976–1979	Manufacturing			Furniture		
	Weekly Earnings	Weekly Hours	Hourly Earnings	Weekly Earnings	Weekly Hours	Hourly Earnings
1976	$209.32	40.1	$5.02	—[a]	—	—
1977	228.90	40.3	5.44	—	—	—
1978 (April)	243.61	40.4	5.79	$167.91	38.7	$4.35
1979 (April)	254.02	38.9	6.32	184.70	38.4	4.81

[a]The dashes indicate that figures are not available.

Source: U.S. Department of Labor, Bureau of Labor Statistics, *Employment and Earnings, May 1979* (Washington, D.C.: Government Printing Office, June 1979), pp. 83–84.

Exercise

Exhibit 11
Average Hourly and
Weekly Earnings for
All Private Workers
and for
Manufacturing
Workers

Hourly Earnings	1978 (April)	1979 (April)
Total private	$5.61	$6.04
Manufacturing	6.05	6.55
Average Weekly Earnings		
Total private:		
Current dollars	$202.52	$213.82
1967 dollars	105.59	103.48 (March)

Source: U.S. Department of Labor, Bureau of Labor Statistics, *Employment and Earnings, May 1979* (Washington, D.C.: Government Printing Office, June 1979), p. 106.

**The Labor Agreement between
Quality Furniture Manufacturing Company (QFM)
and Industrial Workers United (IWU),
AFL-CIO**

This agreement is entered into on ——————— by the Quality Furniture Manufacturing Company (QFM), located in St. Louis, Missouri, and Industrial Workers United (IWU), whose principal office is located in Washington, D.C.

QFM and IWU have agreed to the following provisions.

Article I
Recognition   The Company recognizes the IWU as the sole and exclusive collective bargaining agent in all matters pertaining to rates of pay, wages, hours of employment, and other conditions of employment for all production and maintenance employees, excluding professional employees, storeroom employees, office clerical employees, guards, and supervisors, as defined in the National Labor Relations Act.

Article II
Union Security   The company agrees not to interfere with the right of employees to join the Union and will not discriminate against employees who are Union members. Employees in the bargaining unit are completely free to participate in the affairs of the Union, provided that such activities do not interfere with their work duties and responsibilities.

While no employee will be required to join the Union as a condition of employment, union dues will be deducted from any bargaining unit employee's pay check, provided proper written notification is given to the Company. At the end of each pay period, the Company will forward the collected dues, minus a 5 percent administrative fee, to the Union.

Article III
Management Rights   All management functions of the enterprise that are not specifically limited by the express language of this agreement are retained by the Company. The functions and rights listed here are exam-

ples of the exclusive responsibilities retained by the Company and are not intended as an all-inclusive list: to manage the manufacturing operations and methods of production; to direct the work force; to decide what work shall be performed in the plant by subcontractors or by employees; to schedule working hours (including overtime work); to hire, promote, demote, and transfer; to suspend, discipline, and discharge for cause; to relieve employees due to lack of work or for other legitimate reasons; to create and enforce reasonable shop rules and regulations; to establish production standards and rates for new or changed jobs; to introduce new and improved methods, materials, equipment, and facilities; to change or eliminate existing methods, materials, equipment, and facilities.

Article IV
No Strike and No Lockout   The Company agrees that during the life of this agreement there shall be no lockout of bargaining unit employees.

The Union agrees that during the life of this agreement there shall be no strike, work stoppage, slowdown, work refusal, delay of work, refusal to report for work, or boycott.

Article V
Hours of Work   The normal workweek shall consist of eight (8) hours per day, forty (40) hours per week, for a five (5) day week, from Monday to Friday. The starting time shall be made by the Company, and it can be changed by the Company to suit varying conditions of the business. Such changes in working schedules shall be made known to the Union representative in the plant as far in advance as possible. Employees shall be notified by a written bulletin or other communications medium.

Article VI
Grievances and Arbitration Procedures   Grievances arising out of the operation and interpretation of this agreement shall be handled and settled in the following manner:

☐ *Step 1.* The aggrieved employee and/or shop steward shall discuss the grievance with his or her supervisor.

☐ *Step 2.* Should the answer provided by the supervisor not produce a satisfactory solution to the grievance, the grievance shall be reduced to writing and shall state the provision of the agreement which has been violated. The department head shall arrange for a meeting of the aggrieved employee, the shop steward, the supervisor, the employee relations supervisor, and himself or herself for the purpose of discussing the grievance. The department head shall provide a written answer to the grievance after the close of the meeting.

☐ *Step 3.* If a satisfactory conclusion is not reached, the grievance can be referred to the plant manager by the Union. The plant manager shall schedule a meeting to discuss the grievance with the Union. The local Union can bring in a representative of the international Union at this step, and the plant manager can bring in anyone who he or she feels may aid in the resolution of the grievance.

☐ *Step 4.* If a grievance is appealed to arbitration, the Company and the Union shall attempt to select an arbitrator. If this attempt fails, the

Company and/or Union shall ask the Federal Mediation and Conciliation Service to submit a list of seven (7) arbitrators. Each party shall eliminate three (3) names from the list by alternately striking one name at a time, and the person whose name remains shall serve as the arbitrator.

The arbitrator shall render a decision in writing that shall be final and binding upon the parties.

The arbitrator to whom any grievance is submitted shall have the authority to interpret and apply the provisions of this agreement, and the arbitrator's decision must be in accordance with and based upon the terms of this agreement or of any written amendment thereto. But the arbitrator shall have no jurisdiction or authority to add to, take from, or modify any of the terms of this agreement.

The Company and local Union shall each pay its own expenses incurred in connection with the arbitration and one-half of the expenses and fees of the arbitrator and the facilities used in the arbitration hearing.

Article VII
Seniority   "Seniority" as used in this agreement shall be the period of continuous service in the job or plant from the date of the employee's appointment.

"Probationary employment" consists of a period of one hundred twenty (120) days of employment.

Layoffs shall be made in the following order:

a. Probationary employees
b. Other employees in order of job seniority

Recall shall be made in the following order:

a. Employees in order of job seniority, given equal job ability
b. Probationary employees

Promotions shall be made on the basis of qualifications, merit, and seniority. Promotions out of the bargaining unit remain management's prerogative.

An employee who quits or is discharged for cause shall lose all seniority rights.

If the Company decides to terminate any operation or job and the employees remain on layoff for a period of twelve (12) months, the employees shall be considered to have been discharged for cause at the expiration of said twelve (12) month period.

Article VIII
Wages and Classifications   Job classifications and a wage schedule setting forth the rates of pay of the various classifications are included in Schedule A and are hereby made part of this agreement.

If and when the Company creates a new job classification or modifies, alters, amends, or combines existing jobs, or revises the skills and responsibilities of a job, job descriptions will be drawn and a wage rate assigned. The Union shall have a maximum of five (5) working days to examine the job description to determine whether it accurately describes the principal

Exercise

functions and whether the pay range is consistent with established job classification pay ranges.

If the Union takes exception, it can review both factors with the Company. If the issue cannot be resolved, the Union can take the issue through the grievance procedure.

Job classifications are for pay purposes only and do not pertain to whoever might perform the work in that classification—unless modified by the terms of the agreement.

Article IX

Insurance   An employee who has completed ninety (90) days of employment is eligible for enrollment in the company group insurance programs on the monthly premium date for each particular insurance coverage that next follows the completion of ninety (90) days of employment.

1. *Group life insurance.*

Group Life Insurance	Accidental Death and Dismemberment
$3,500	$3,500

2. *Accident and health insurance.* One-half of the employee's weekly pay up to a maximum of $65. It is understood and agreed that the cost of the hospitalization, medical and health insurance, major medical insurance, accident and health and life insurance will be borne 50 percent (50%) by the Company and 50 percent (50%) by the employee, when subscribed to by the employee. It is understood and agreed that in the event that the Company wishes to change carriers, there is no obligation to negotiate with the Union prior to instituting the change.

Employees on medical leave for a period in excess of ninety (90) consecutive days may continue to be covered under the group insurance program after the first ninety (90) days, providing the employee pays the total insurance premium.

Article X

Pension Plan   A pension plan for bargaining unit employees of the Company is hereby incorporated as a part of this agreement.

As of October 6, 1977, the normal retirement benefit for all years of service continues to be $3 per month per year of service.

Effective January 1, 1978, the normal retirement benefit for all years of service will be $3.25 per month per year of service.

Article XI

Holidays   All employees, after completing six (6) months of service with the Company, shall be paid seven (7) hours' pay for the following holidays:

☐ New Year's Day
☐ Independence Day
☐ Labor Day
☐ Thanksgiving Day
☐ Day after Thanksgiving Day
☐ Christmas Eve Day
☐ Christmas Day

To be eligible for holiday pay, the employee must have worked the days immediately preceding and following the holiday. Legitimate excuses for absences will be considered.

Article XII

Vacation Employees shall qualify for vacation with pay in accordance with the following (determined June 1 of each year):

Continuous Service	Vacation with Pay
More than 1 but less than 5 years	1 week
More than 5 but less than 10 years	2 weeks
More than 10 but less than 20 years	3 weeks
More than 20 years	4 weeks

Vacation pay shall be computed on the basis of each employee's average weekly earnings from June to June. Payment will be made on the work day prior to the vacation period.

Article XIII

Sick Leave A full-time employee is eligible for sick leave after completing six (6) months' service with the Company. An eligible employee will accumulate sick leave at the rate of one-half day per month of service from date of hire. Sick leave will not be carried over from one year (January 1 to December 31) to the next, and it can be used only for personal illness not covered by workmen's compensation. The Company retains the right to require a doctor's certificate as proof that absence was due to a legitimate injury or illness.

Schedule A Wages and Classifications	Wage Grade	Job Title	Wage Rates
	1	Janitor	$4.50
	2	General laborer	5.00
	3	Materials handler	5.50
	4	Packer	6.00
		Machine operator–B	6.00
		Utility worker	6.00
		Interplant truck driver	6.00
		Sander	6.00
		Assembler	6.00
	5	Welder	6.50
		Machine operator–A	6.50
		Electrician–B	6.50
		Maintenance worker–B	6.50
		Gluer	6.50
	6	Mechanic	7.00
		Spray painter	7.00
		Cutoff saw operator	7.00
	7	Electrician–A	7.50
		Maintenance worker–A	7.50
		Inspector	7.50
	8	Tool grinder–A	8.00
	9	Tool and die maker–A	8.50
	10	Leadman	9.00

Article XIV

Duration of Agreement   This agreement shall become effective as of
_____ , 1977, and shall continue in effect until 11:59 P.M.,
_____ . Thereafter, it shall renew itself for yearly periods unless
written notice of termination is given by one party to the other not less than
sixty (60) nor more than ninety (90) days prior to the expiration date.

Zack, Arnold, 465
Zagoria, Sam, 398, 463, 464

Zalusky, John, 399, 425
Zartman, I. William, 199

Zimny, Max, 137
Zollitsch, Herbert G., 424

Subject Index

bargaining, 177
Informational picketing, 212
Injunctions, 81–83
Integrative bargaining, 173–174
Intent of parties, as guideline for
  arbitrator decision, 286–287
Interest arbitration, 207–210
  in public sector, 448, 450–452
  types of, 208–210
International Brotherhood of Teamsters.
  See Teamsters Union
International Conference of Free Trade
  Unions, 512
International Federation of Air Line Pilots
  Associations, 512
International Federation of Chemical and
  General Workers Unions, 511, 512
International Federation of Petroleum
  and Chemical Workers, 512
International forces, influencing labor
  relations process, 12
International Labor Organization, 508
International Metalworkers Federation,
  512
International trade secretariats, 508, 512
International Transport Workers
  Federation, 513
Intra-organizational bargaining, 174

Jamestown plan, 233
Job action techniques, to raise
  disagreement costs, 441–442
Job analysis, 403–404
Job classification, as end product of job
  analysis, 403
Job description, 378, 404
Job development 385–390
Job enrichment, 386–390
Job enrichment program. *See* Quality of
  worklife programs
Job evaluation, 403–404
  influence on wage spread, 408
  methods, 403
  union attitudes, 404
  and wage structure, 404, 406
Job factors, selection and measurement
  for job evaluation, 403
Job security,
  enhanced by union membership, 21
  as issue for teachers' unions, 456–457
  need for, 20–21
  threatened by technological change,
    62–63, 369–370, 484, 556
Job security issues, resolved by collective
  bargaining, 374–375
Job security protection tactics, 373–385
  featherbedding, 373–375
  make-work rules, 21, 373–375
  seniority provisions, 379–385
  subcontracting, 375–376
  work jurisdiction, 376–378
  work load restrictions, 374
  work scheduling, 378–379
Job slowdowns, 442
Job specifications, as part of job
  evaluation, 404
Journeyman Bootmakers Society, 79
J. P. Stevens Company, anti-union
  activities, 131–132
Judicial branch, role in labor relations

activities, 77, 91–92
Judicial proceedings, compared with
  arbitration proceedings, 281–285
Jurisdictional disputes,
  in construction industry, 377
  farm workers, 551–554, 555
  of postal unions, 483–484
Jurisdictional standards, of NLRB,
  108–110
Jurisdictional strike, 212
Just cause, 345

Knights of Labor, 33–42
  affected by Haymarket riot, 41–42
  attitude to female members, 330–331
  goals, 34–35
  organizational structure, 35
  racial policy, 322–323
  reasons for failure, 39–40
  strategies, 35, 38–39

Labor agreement, 6, 286
Labor arbitration, 269–298. *See also*
  Arbitration
  development, 269–277
  jurisdictional problems, 290–294
  popularized by War Labor Board
    activities, 271
Labor arbitrator. *See* Arbitrator
Laboratory conditions doctrine, 126
Labor costs as percent of total costs, 402
Labor law reform, 85
Labor-Management Committee of
  Jamestown, 233
Labor-management cooperation,
  Experimental Negotiating Agreement,
    235–236
  in impasse resolution, 232–236
  Jamestown plan, 233
  Relations by Objectives, 233–235
Labor-management negotiations. *See*
  Negotiations
Labor Management Relations Act, 84, 86
  loopholes on secondary boycotts, 228
  national emergency procedures,
    229–230
Labor-management relationships. *See also*
  Federal sector labor relations; Labor
  relations; Public sector labor relations
  early legal, 78–81
  legal influences on , 77–104
  in professional sports, 521–540
  types, 16
Labor-Management Reporting and
  Disclosure Act, 84, 156
Labor market, as factor in labor relations
  process, 14–15
Labor relations. *See also* Federal sector
  labor relations; Labor-management
  relationships; Public sector labor
  relations
  in academic community, 453–461
  in state and local government, 443–453
  Western Europe compared with United
    States, 497–498
Labor relations in other countries,
  495–508
  in Africa, 507–508
  in Asia, 506–507, 508
  in Australia, 503

  in Canada, 495–496, 594
  in developing nations, 506–508
  in Eastern Europe, 503–506
  in Great Britain, 498, 499, 501
  in Japan, 501–503
  in Latin America, 496–497
  in New Zealand, 503
  in the Soviet Union, 504, 505
    contrasted with the Yugoslav system,
      506
  in Western Europe, 497–501
    co-determination in West Germany,
      499–501
    co-determination policies, 498–501
    contrasted with the United States,
      497–498
    political influence of unions, 497
    public opinion, 497
    worker participation in operating
      firms, 497
Labor relations law, 77, 78
Labor relations process,
  elements, 5–15
  influences, 8–15
  participants, 8–11
  steps, 15–17
Labor unions. *See* Organized labor;
  Unions
Landrum-Griffin Act, 84, 146, 156
  closing loopholes on secondary
    boycotts, 228
  impact, 156–157
Layoff, 382–383
  protection for postal workers, 482, 483
Layoff practices, attacked by minority
  groups, 383–385
Legal assistance, group plans, 422
Legislative branch, role in labor relations
  activities, 77
Licensed trades, 32
Lifetime employment, in Japan, 501, 502
Lloyd-LaFollette Act, 471
Lobbying, to strengthen job security, 21
Local central bodies, of AFL-CIO, 154
Local department councils, of AFL-CIO,
  154
Local unions,
  assistance and services from national
    unions, 147–148
  control by national unions, 147–148
  craft versus industrial, 141–143
  duties of president, 143
  functions of meeting, 144–145
  government and operation, 143–145
  joint councils, 151
  participation in meetings, 143–144
Lockheed Aircraft Company, 380
Lock-in agreement, 180
Lockout, 211, 224
Longshoring, 371–372
Lordstown Syndrome, 387
Lump of labor theory, 374

Maintenance of membership, 312
Major League Baseball Players
  Association, 523–525
Make-work problems, 374
Make-work rules, 373–375
Malicious obedience, 442

Management,
identifying, in public sector, 435, 457
involvement in decertification
procedure, 123–124
obligation to provide work rules, 343
reaction to union organizing campaigns,
117
Management officials, in labor relations
process, 8–9
Managerial rights (prerogatives), 305–310
affected by arbitrator decision, 307
and collective bargaining agreement,
307–310
controversy over, 305–306
eroded in collective bargaining process,
305–306, 310
extent, 305–307
subcontracting, 376
work assignment, 376–378
Managerial rights clauses, 307–310
Managerial unions, 25
Mass production, effect on growth of
organized labor, 32, 34
Meatpacking industry, responses to
technological change, 372
Mechanization, impact on farm workers,
556
Mediation, 205–207
as face-saving device, 206
factors leading to negotiation of
settlement, 206
in public sector, 447
in railroad labor disputes, 95, 97
Mediation-arbitration, 208–209
Mediator, 205–207
Mergers, between unions, 63–64,
149–150
Merit System Protection Board, 479
Military, as employer, 487
Military employees,
collective action, 485
and unionization, 485–486, 488
legal considerations, 486–489
working with civilian employees, 488
Military Selective Service Act, 104
Military strikes, 488, 489
Military unionization, 485–489
Military unions, 487–488
experiences in other countries, 488–489
Minority employees, legal protection of,
291–292. *See also* Black employees
Minority groups,
attacks on seniority practices, 384–385
and construction industry, 329–330
and unions, 322–334
Modified union shop, 22
Mohawk Valley Formula, 55
Molly Maguires, 32–33
Monitoring of wage-price guidelines, 101
Moonlighting, 348
Multi-employer bargaining, 178, 179–180
Multinational corporations, 509–513
and collective bargaining, 509, 510
effects of unions on, 512–513
legislative approaches by unions,
509–510
management opposition to unions,
510–511
obstacles to transnational bargaining,
511–512

power, 509
regulation proposed by unions, 510
union response to, 509–511
as viewed by union leaders, 509
Multinational unions, 510, 511, 512
Mutual aid pacts, 217–218

Naroctic effect of impasse procedures, in
public sector, 451
National Association of Letter Carriers,
480
National Association of Manufacturers,
313
National consultation rights, of federal
employee unions, 475
National Education Association, 454
National emergency strikes,
congressional intervention, 229
criticism of procedures, 231–232
resolution procedures, 228–232
National Football League Players
Association, 534, 535, 538
National Industrial Recovery Act, 83, 84
National Labor Board, 83
National Labor Relations Act (Wagner
Act), 83–90, 344
amendments, 84, 86, 89, 374
enforcement, 90–94
fair representation obligations, 319, 321
passage, 61, 62
requiring good faith negotiation, 191
rights and restrictions on employees,
223, 224
National Labor Relations Board, 78
actions reviewed by the courts, 91–93
ally doctrine, 227–228
assessment of administration, 93–94
decision on interns and residents, 546
deferral to arbitration policy, 292–294
enforcement problems, 93–94
establishment, 60, 83
functions, 90–93
invalidated by Supreme Court, 83
involvement with bargaining issues,
191–196
jurisdictional standards, 108–110
limits on effectiveness, 93–94
position on discrimination, 328
position on enmeshing employees of
neutral employer, 227
procedure in unfair labor practice cases,
91–92
responsibilities under Postal
Reorganization Act, 482
responsibility to health care employees,
542
role in decertification procedure,
123–128
role in enforcement of National Labor
Relations Act, 90–91
role in representation elections,
115–122, 523
role in union organizing, 115–122
ruling on discipline and grievance
procedures, 344
ruling on secondary picketing, 227–228
structure, 90
National Mediation Board, 78, 97, 98, 99,
229
mediation of national emergency

disputes, 229
National Railroad Adjustment Board, 78,
97–98, 99
National Recovery Administration, 83
National Right to Work Legal Defense
Foundation, 314–315
National unions,
administration, 146–147
authority of president, 145
constitution, 145
convention, 145–146
influence, 145
intermediate organizational units,
150–151
leadership, 146–147
and local unions, 147–148
mergers, 149–150
operational departments, 147
opportunities for misuse of power, 146
revenues, 148
sources and uses of funds, 148–149
Negotiated security and layoff
provisions, 21
Negotiation. *See also* Collective
bargaining; Labor management
negotiation
of agreements, 15–17
in federal sector,
mandatory subjects, 475
permissible subjects, 475–476, 477
prohibited subjects, 476
versus games, 172–173
with teachers' unions, 457–458
Negotiation team, selecting, 184
Negotiation unit, 178–180
Nepotism, 386
Neutrality pact, 134
Newlands Act, 95
Newspaper industry, union reaction to
technological change, 373
Nonunion firms, 128–134
Nonunion status,
company efforts to maintain, 129–133
union reaction to, 128, 133–134
Norris–La Guardia Act, 81–83, 276, 344,
473
Nurses, and unions, 544–545

Occupational Health and Safety
Administration, 292
Occupational Safety and Health Act, 104,
292
controversy over voluntary sterilization,
393
criticisms, 390–393
employers' duty under, 390
Occupational wage differentials, 403–404
Open shop, 55, 313
Organization analysis, as part of job
evaluation, 403
Organized labor. *See also* Craft union;
Industrial union; Local union;
National union; Union
anti-union sentiment of potential
members, 56–57
challenges for future, 160–161
characteristics since World War II, 63–68
concerns since World War II, 62
developments since World War II, 62–64
employee attitudes, 60

bargaining, 437
Superseniority, 380, 382
Supplemental unemployment benefit
plans, 418
Supplementary pay, 419
Supreme Court,
decisions affecting labor relations, 49,
80, 81, 82, 83, 84, 93, 95, 96, 97, 115,
132, 195, 196, 225, 226, 227, 271–277,
291, 293, 308, 311, 312, 319, 320, 328,
359, 374, 385, 422, 431, 444, 457, 528,
542
position on military unions, 487
recognition of Wagner Act, 84
ruling on Occupational Safety and
Health Act inspections, 393
Supreme Court Trilogy, 272–275, 294
Suspension, 352
Sweetheart contracts, between growers
and Teamsters Union, 553
Sympathetic relationship,
between management and union
officials, 16
between participants in grievance
procedure, 256–258
Sympathy strike, 212

Taft-Hartley Act, 84, 86, 271–272, 311,
313, 317–319, 541–542
Task Force on Employment-Management
Cooperation, 472
Teacher collective bargaining,
ambiguous role of principal, 455
affected by collegiality, 460–461
attitudes of university administrators,
458
effect on wages, 459–460
issues, 456–458
problems, 461
Teacher militancy and strikes, 458–459
Teachers' unions,
effect on negotiated wage settlements,
459–460
emphasis on across-the-board wage
increases, 459–460
growth and development, 453–455
attitude of university administrators,
458
Teachers' wages, 459–460
Teamsters Union, 84, 385
conflict with United Farm Workers,
552–554, 555
expulsion from AFL-CIO, 66
lockout against, 224
sweetheart contracts with growers, 553
use of Relations by Objectives program,
234–235
Technological advance,
affecting farm workers, 556
affecting job security, 62–63, 369–370,
484, 556
in the post office, 483, 484
Technological change, 369–373
accepted by United Mine Workers, 371
adaptation to by longshoremen, 371–372
causing increased demand for skilled
labor, 369
construction industry efforts to
accommodate, 371–372
creating new occupations, 369

eliminating farm jobs, 556
examples of industry reaction, 371–373
meatpacking industry response, 372
in newspaper industry, 373
positive effects, 369
problems in airline industry, 373
railroad industry response, 371
stages in union response, 370
threatening job security, 62–63,
369–370, 484
union reactions, 369–371
Technology of the workplace, as factor in
negotiating work rules, 11–12
Tenure, 456
Texas Instruments, position on unions,
129
Textile Workers Union of America, 132
Third party neutral. *See also* Arbitrator
in public sector, 446–447, 448
role in grievance procedure, 251
role in impasse resolution, 205–211
Thirty and out, 378
Time studies, 407
Totality of conduct doctrine, 126
Trade and industrial departments of
AFL-CIO, 154
Trade conferences, 150
Transfer, 381, 382
Transnational bargaining, 510, 511–512,
513
obstacles to, 511, 512
Transportation Act, 95
Twenty-four Hour Rule, 127
Ty Cobb strike, 522

Unfair labor practices,
control, 88–93
economic returns, 131
in federal sector, 477–478
legal constraints on employers, 88–89
legal constraints on unions, 89–90
by management, 88–89, 477–478
National Labor Relations Board
procedure, 91, 92
per se violations by management, 192
per se violations by union, 192–193
by unions, 89–90, 478
Unfair labor practice strike, 212
Union(s). *See also* Craft unions; Industrial
unions; Local unions; National
unions; Organized labor
and black employees, 322–330
district offices, 150
duties as bargaining agents, 122
fair representation obligation, 319–322
and female employees, 330–334
functions in Eastern Europe, 504, 505
historical counterparts, 32
international cooperation, 508
methods for establishing, 115–122
and minority groups, 322–334
multinational, 510, 511, 512
noninvolvement in quality of worklife
programs, 387–389
organization, 113–134
organizational levels, 141–157
regional offices, 150
trade conferences, 150
Union corruption, 156–157
Union dues, 148, 154

Union hiring hall, 142–143, 311
Union leaders, in professional sports,
536–537
Union literature, distribution on
company property, 127–128
Union members, characteristics of, 144
Union membership,
apathy, 147
decline, 157, 158–160
forced, 21–22
for managers, 25
opposition from employers, 55–56
as percentage of total labor force,
157–159
for public employees, 444–445
perceptions affecting, 22–24
for professionals, 25–26
of public employees, 443–445
reasons for, 17–26
reasons for growth in 1930s and 1940s,
59
required, 21–22
social influences, 22
white-collar, 24–26
Union mergers, 63–64, 149–150
Union officials, in labor relations process,
8–9
Union organizers' activities, 113–115
Union organizing, 113–134
activities prior to election, 117–121
barriers to elections, 120
conduct of election campaign, 124–128
composition of bargaining units,
118–120
consent election, 118
counteractions by employers in 1920s
and 1930s, 55–56
decertification procedure, 123–128
determination of appropriate bargaining
unit, 118–120, 434–435, 455, 475
election campaign initiation, 117
election investigation and hearing, 118
of farm workers, 550–556
in federal sector, 471–479
filing of election petition, 117–118
first national labor organizations, 33–53
of health care workers, 540–544
history, 32–68
of hospital employees, 543–544
industrial unionism issue, 57–58
management obligations, 118, 120, 122
management reaction, 117, 131–132
of military personnel, 485–489
names and addresses rule for elections,
120–121
of postal workers, 480–485
problems of anti-union sentiment,
56–57
in public sector, 431
representation election procedures,
117–122
role of NLRB, 115–122
among teachers, 453–455
voter eligibility, 120
after World War I, 54–61
Union raiding, 63–64
Union security, 22, 310–319
Union security clauses, 310–311
Union security provisions,
counter measures, 313

Union security provisions,
  forms of,
    agency shop, 312
    closed shop, 311
    dues checkoff, 312–313
    maintenance of membership, 312
    quasi-union shop, 312, 318
    union hiring hall, 311
    union shop, 311–312
    restricted by right-to-work laws,
      313–319
Union shop, 22
  to provide union security, 311–312
Union structure, 141–146, 150–151,
  153–154
United Auto Workers, 13, 134
  agreement with General Motors, 63
  leaving AFL-CIO, 66
  supplemental unemployment benefit
    plans, 418
  union-management quality-of-
    working-life committees, 389
United Farm Workers,
  conflict with Teamsters Union, 552–554,
    555
  modification of goals, 555
  social movement as well as union,
    553–554
United Federation of Teachers, 454
United Hatters of America, 80
United Mine Workers Union, 58
  acceptance of technological change, 371
  problems with grievance procedures,
    262
  requirement for fully ratified agreement,
    214
  strikes during World War II, 61
United Rubber Workers Union, 134
  actions against primary employers, 223
  strike benefit plans, 216
United Steelworkers of America,
  expedited arbitration procedures,
    297–298
  use of Experimental Negotiating
    Agreement, 235–236, 276
Unit of direct impact, in collective
  bargaining, 177

Vacation, 419–420
Value added by employees, as factor
  influencing wage differentials, 402
Vesting provisions, 421–422
Vietnam Era Veterans Readjustment
  Assistance Act, 104
Violations of labor agreement, 243
Vocational Rehabilitation Act, 103
Voluntary arbitration,

  in public sector, 448
  under Railway Labor Act, 99
Voluntary collective bargaining, in Great
  Britain, 498

Wage adjustments, 415–417
Wage comparability, 409–410
Wage comparisons, in wage
  determination, 409–410
Wage determination, 401–415
  ability to pay as consideration, 410–411
  adjustments during life of labor
    agreement, 415–417
  cost of living as factor, 415
  criteria used by management, 408
  criteria used by unions, 408
  factors considered, 401
  influence of wage comparison, 409–410
  relationship with productivity, 411,
    413–415
Wage differentials,
  industrial, 401–402
  occupational, 403–404
Wage guidelines, 101
  as source of conflict, 103
Wage incentive plans, 407
Wage legislation, 100–101
Wage-price guidelines, 101–103
Wage-related issues,
  group incentive plans, 407
  incentive plans, 407
  negotiated in labor agreements, 406–407
  production standards, 406–407
  time studies, 407
Wage reopener clause, 417
Wages,
  call-back pay, 419
  defined, 401
  incentive pay, 407
  overtime premiums, 419
  reporting pay, 419
  shift differential, 419
  supplementary pay, 419
Wage spread,
  influenced by job evaluation, 408
  management preference, 409
  union position on, 408–409
Wage structure, 404–406
  examples, 405
  in teaching profession, 459
  use of wage surveys to compare,
    404–406
Wage surveys, 404–406
Wagner Act. *See* National Labor Relations
  Act
Waiver rule, 522
Walsh-Healy Public Contract Act, 100

War Labor Board, 12, 54
  definition of grievance arbitration as
    judicial process, 271
  dispute resolution powers, 270
War Production Board, 61
White-collar employees, organization, 63
White-collar unions, 24–26
Wildcat strike, 212, 224–225
Work assignment, 376–378
  causing conflicts between unions,
    376–377
  causing conflicts within unions, 377–378
  problems caused by job descriptions,
    378
  resulting in union-management
    confrontation, 376
Work attitudes, 18
Work councils, in Western Europe, 499,
  500–501
Work environment, 11–12
Work Hours Act, 101
Working conditions, 17–22
  of farm workers, 547–550
  of postal workers, 480
  of residents and interns, 545–546
Work jurisdiction, 376–378
Work load restrictions, 374
Work rules, 5–15
  accommodating technological change in
    construction industry, 371–372
  categories, 5
  consequences of violating, 350
  examples, 5, 7
  factors influencing administration,
    11–15
  factors influencing negotiation, 11–15
  as focal point of labor relations, 5–8
  need for clarity, 349
  need for consistent administration, 350
  need for reasonableness, 348–349
  obligation of management to provide,
    343
  participants in negotiations, 8
  price list for violations, 350–351, 353
  in professional baseball, 533
  to promote union membership, 21–22
  relationship to discipline problems,
    347–351
Work schedules, 378–379, 419
  flexitime programs, 378–379
  for interns and residents, 546
  negotiated by collective bargaining, 378
Work stoppages, 211–232

Yellow-dog contract, 79, 82